- Historical interpretations

Skills in historical interpretation at GCSE are also developed in Sixth Form History. The ability to put forward different historical interpretations is important. Students will also be expected to explain why different historical interpretations have occurred.

Extended writing: the structured question and the essay

When faced with extended writing in Sixth Form History students can improve their performance by following a simple routine that attempts to ensure they achieve their best performance.

Answering the question

What are the command instructions?
Different questions require different types of response. For instance, 'In what ways' requires students to point out the various ways something took place in History; 'Why' questions expect students to deal with the causes or consequences of an historical question.

Are there key words or phrases that require definition or explanation?
It is important for students to show that they understand the meaning of the question. To do this, certain historical terms or words require explanation. For instance, if a question asked 'how far' a king or politician was an 'innovator', an explanation of the word 'innovator' would be required.

Does the question have specific dates or issues that require coverage?
If a question mentions specific dates, these must be adhered to. For instance, if you are asked to answer a question on the foreign policy of Russia it may state clear date limits such as 1881 to 1914. Also questions may mention a specific aspect such as 'domestic', 'religious', 'social' or 'economic'.

Planning your answer

Once you have decided on what the question requires, write a brief plan. For structured questions this may be brief. This is a useful procedure to make sure that you have ordered the information you require for your answer in the most effective way. For instance, in a balanced, analytical answer this may take the form of jotting down the main points for and against an historical issue raised in the question.

Writing the answer

Communication skills
The quality of written English is important in Sixth Form History. The way you present your ideas on paper can affect the quality of your answer. Since 1996 the Government (through QCA) have placed emphasis on the quality of written English in the Sixth Form. Therefore, punctuation, spelling and grammar, which were awarded marks at GCSE, require close attention. Use a dictionary if you are unsure of a word's meaning or spelling. Use the glossary of terms you will find in this book to help you.

The introduction
For structured questions you may wish to dispense with an introduction altogether and begin writing reasons to support an answer straight away. However, essay answers should begin with an introduction. These should be both concise and precise. Introductions help 'concentrate the mind' on

the question you are about to answer. Remember, do not try to write a conclusion as your opening sentence. Instead, outline briefly the areas you intend to discuss in your answer.

Balancing analysis with factual evidence

It is important to remember that factual knowledge should be used to support analysis. Merely 'telling the story' of an historical event is not enough. A structured question or essay should contain separate paragraphs, each addressing an analytical point that helps to answer the question. If, for example, the question asks for reasons why the First World War began, each paragraph should provide a reason for the outbreak of war.

Seeing connections between reasons

In dealing with 'why'-type questions it is important to remember that the reasons for an historical event might be interconnected. Therefore, it is important to mention the connection between reasons. Also, it might be important to identify a hierarchy of reasons – that is, are some reasons more important than others in explaining an historical event?

Using quotations and statistical data

One aspect of supporting evidence that sustains analysis is the use of quotations. These can either be from an historian or a contemporary. However, unless these quotations are linked with analysis and supporting evidence, they tend to be of little value.

It can also be useful to support analysis with statistical data. In questions that deal with social and economic change, precise statistics which support your argument can be very persuasive.

Source analysis

Source analysis forms an integral part of the study of History. In Sixth Form History source analysis is identified as an important skill in Assessment Objective 3.

In dealing with sources you should be aware that historical sources must be used 'in historical context' in Sixth Form History. Therefore, in this book sources are used with the factual information in each chapter. Also, a specific source analysis question is included.

Assessment Objectives

1 knowledge and understanding of history

2 evaluation and analysis skills

3 a) source analysis in historical context

   b) historical interpretation

How to handle sources in Sixth Form History

In dealing with sources a number of basic hints will allow you to deal effectively with source-based questions and to build on your knowledge and skill in using sources at GCSE.

Written sources

Attribution and date
It is important to identify who has written the source and when it was written. This information can be very important. If, for instance, a source was written by Trotsky, whilst in exile in Mexico, to a member of the Commission of Enquiry investigating charges made against Trotsky in the Moscow show trials (see Chapter 7), this information will be of considerable importance if you are asked about the usefulness or reliability of the source as evidence of Trotsky's behaviour during the Kronstadt rebellion of 1921.

It is important to note that just because a source is a primary source does not mean it is more useful or less reliable than a secondary source. Both primary and secondary sources need to be analysed to decide how useful and reliable they are. This can be determined by studying other issues.

Is the content factual or opinionated?
Once you have identified the author and date of the source it is important to study its content. The content may be factual, stating what has happened or what may happen. On the other hand, it may contain opinions that should be handled with caution. These may contain bias. Even if a source is mainly factual, there might be important and deliberate gaps in factual evidence that can make a source biased and unreliable. Usually, written sources contain elements of both opinion and factual evidence. It is important to judge the balance between these two parts.

Has the source been written for a particular audience?
To determine the reliability of a source it is important to identify to whom it is directed. For instance, a public speech may be made to achieve a particular purpose and may not contain the author's true beliefs or feelings. In contrast, a private diary entry may be much more reliable in this respect.

Corroborative evidence
To test whether or not a source is reliable, the use of other evidence to support or corroborate the information it contains is important. Cross-referencing with other sources is a way of achieving this; so is cross-referencing with historical information contained within a chapter.

Visual sources

Maps
Maps which appear in Sixth Form History are either contemporary or secondary sources. These are used to support factual coverage in the text by providing information in a different medium. Therefore, to assess whether or not information contained in maps is accurate or useful, reference should be made to other information. It is also important with written sources to check the attribution and date. These could be significant.

Statistical data and graphs
It is important when dealing with this type of source to check carefully the nature of the information contained in a date or in a graph. It might state the information in old forms of measurement such as pre-decimal currency: pounds, shillings and pence. One pound equalled 20 shillings, or 240 pence. It might also be stated in foreign currency, such as Reichsmarks in Wilhelm II's Germany. Be careful to check if the information is in **index numbers**. These are a statistical device where a base year is chosen and

given the figure 100. All other figures are based on a percentage difference from that base year. For instance, if 1900 is taken as base year for coal output it is given a figure of 100. If the index number for 1905 is 117 it means that coal output has risen 17% since 1900.

An important point to remember when dealing with data and graphs over a period of time is to identify trends and patterns in the information. Merely describing the information in written form is not enough.

Historical interpretation

An important feature of both GCSE and Sixth Form History is the issue of historical interpretation. In Sixth Form History it is important for students to be able to explain why historians differ, or have differed in their interpretations of the past.

Availability of evidence

An important reason is the availability of evidence on which to base historical judgements. As new evidence comes to light, and historian today may have more information on which to base their judgements than historians in the past. For instance, sources for late 19th and 20th-century Europe include the state papers, including government papers on meetings and policies on individual issues. Occasionally new evidence comes to light which may influence judgements about modern European history (e.g. the War Cabinet meeting in Germany on 8 December 1912).

Archaeological evidence is also important. The archaeological study of ships such as the 'Lusitania', 'Titanic' and 'Bismarck' can provide historical evidence of why those ships sank.

'A philosophy of history?'

Many historians have a specific view of history that will affect the way they make their historical judgements. For instance, Marxist historians – who take the view from the writings of Karl Marx, the founder of modern socialism – believe that society has been made up of competing economic and social classes. They also place considerable importance on economic reasons in human decision making.

The role of the individual

Some historians have seen past history as being moulded by the acts of specific individuals who have changed history. Vladimir Lenin, Josef Stalin and Adolf Hitler are seen as individuals whose personality and beliefs changed the course of 20th-century European history. Other historians have tended to 'downplay' the role of individuals; instead, they highlight the importance of more general social, economic and political change. Rather than seeing Otto von Bismarck, Tsar Nicholas II or Gustav Stresemann as individuals who changed the course of history, these historians tend to see them as representing the views of wider social, religious or economic groups.

Placing different emphasis on the same historical evidence

Even if historians do not possess different philosophies of history or place different emphasis on the role of the individual, it is still possible for them to disagree because they place different emphases on aspects of the same factual evidence. As a result, Sixth Form History should be seen as a subject that encourages debate about the past based on historical evidence.

Progression in Sixth Form History

The ability to achieve high standards in Sixth Form History involves the acquisition of a number of skills:

- Good written communication skills

- Acquiring a sound factual knowledge

- Evaluating factual evidence and making historical conclusions based on that evidence

- Source analysis

- Understanding the nature of historical interpretation

- Understanding the causes and consequences of historical events

- Understanding the themes in history which will involve a study of a specific topic over a long period of time

- Understanding the ideas of change and continuity associated with themes.

Students should be aware that the acquisition of these skills will take place gradually over the time spent in the Sixth Form. At the beginning of the course the main emphasis may be on the acquisition of factual knowledge, particularly when the body of knowledge studied at GCSE was different.

When dealing with causation students will have to build on their skills from GCSE. They will not only be expected to identify reasons for an historical event but also to provide a hierarchy of causes. They should identify the main causes and less important causes. They may also identify that causes may be interconnected and linked. Progression in Sixth Form History will come with answering the questions at the end of each sub-section in this book and practising the skills outlined through the use of the factual knowledge contained in the book.

Examination techniques

The ultimate challenge for any Sixth Form historian is the ability to produce quality work under examination conditions. Examinations will take the form of either modular examinations taken in January and June or in an 'end of course' set of examinations.

Here is some advice on how to improve your performance in an examination.

● *Read the whole examination paper thoroughly*
Make sure that the questions you choose are those for which you can produce a good answer. Don't rush – allow time to decide which questions to choose. It is probably too late to change your mind half way through answering a question.

● *Read the question very carefully*
Once you have made the decision to answer a specific question, read it very carefully. Make sure you understand the precise demands of the question. Think about what is required in your answer. It is much better to think about this before you start writing, rather than trying to steer your essay in a different direction half way through.

● *Make a brief plan*
Sketch out what you intend to include in your answer. Order the points you want to make. Examiners are not impressed with additional information included at the end of the essay, with indicators such as arrows or asterisks.

● *Pace yourself as you write*

Success in examinations has a lot to do with successful time management. If, for instance, you have to answer an essay question in approximately 45 minutes then you should be one-third of the way through after 15 minutes. With 30 minutes gone you should start writing the last third of your answer.

Where a question is divided into sub-questions make sure you look at the mark tariff for each question. If in a 20-mark question a sub-question is worth a maximum of 5 marks then you should spend approximately one-quarter of the time allocated for the whole question on this sub-question.

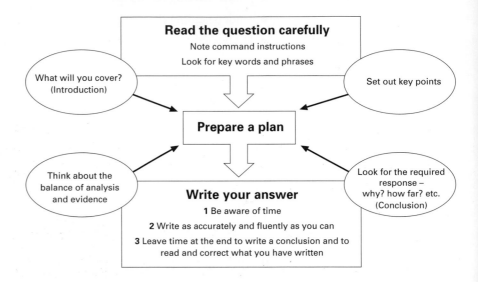

Europe 1870–1991: a synoptic assessment

Key Issues

● *How did European society and the European economy change during this period?*

● *In what ways did the political map and the political balance of power in Europe change during this period?*

● *What political ideas had the greatest influence upon Europe during this period?*

1.1 What were the main economic and social developments in Europe during this period?

1.2 How did the political map of Europe change during this period?

1.3 How were European states governed during this period?

1.4 What political ideas had the greatest influence upon Europe during this period?

1.5 How did the role played in international relations by military strength and by warfare change during this period?

Overview

Two decades before the end of the 20th century, historians of different political persuasions might have felt that it was possible to detect a degree of continuity in the European history of this period (see panel on page 13). Liberal historians in the democracies of western Europe could point to the advance of parliamentary government. They could trace its triumph, first over the great aristocratic empires of central and eastern Europe, and then over the extreme right-wing regimes that grew up in Germany and in Italy. Socialist historians, at the same time, could point to the establishment of a workers' democracy in the Soviet Union, and to the growth of communism in eastern Europe. Their case appeared to be strengthened by the establishment of communist governments in many parts of the world beyond Europe. The division of Europe between the two great ideologies of the modern world – capitalism and communism – appeared to be the clearly defined outcome of a century of history.

The sudden collapse of the Soviet Union in 1991, however, disrupted this tidy picture and forced many historians to take a more fragmented view of the years between 1870 and 1991. To make sense of this period, we could view it in three sections.

1 1870–1918
2 The period between the two world wars
3 The period from 1945 to 1991.

1 Between 1870 and 1914 a collection of powerful social and economic forces pressed upon governments that were still largely dominated by traditional

ruling classes, and established a gradual process of modernisation. Social reforms, such as those that Bismarck brought about in Germany (see Chapter 3), helped to mould societies that we can recognise as the forerunners of our own. In some states, major political measures dismantled large elements of the regimes' medieval structures. The abolition of serfdom was the most striking and far-reaching of these reforms, but the steady erosion of the political influence of the Catholic Church in France, Italy and Germany also did a great deal to alter traditional social mentalities. Above all, the traditional structures of Europe were eroded by industrialisation. The growth of manufacturing industry on a very large scale had an impact upon every area of society. It created enormous economic wealth for a new economic élite group, the owners of the mines and the factories, and these groups quickly sought to acquire enough political authority to protect and consolidate their interests. The process also created a huge class of industrial workers, concentrated in cities of great size, whose economic and social demands could not logically be resisted. If they remained poor and downtrodden, industry lost a very high proportion of its market.

Even the traditional élites could not ignore the benefits of industrialisation. Landowners quickly appreciated the usefulness of railways in delivering their produce to distant markets, and army commanders came to realise (perhaps a little more slowly) the advantages of modern artillery, and of moving their troops by rail. By 1900, although some states were more advanced in the process than others, no major European state ignored the importance of a strong industrial base.

The First World War (1914–18) consolidated some of these elements, but destroyed others. It confirmed beyond doubt that power lay with those states that possessed the strongest industrial bases, yet it undermined the leadership of the traditional élites. The traditional rulers of Germany, Russia and Austria-Hungary were unable to survive their military defeat, and their collapse created terrifying political vacuums in those states.

2   The period between the two world wars (1919–39) appears now to have been chaotic. Some contemporaries, however, saw logic in the situation at the time. Nationalists in many countries saw the collapse of traditional governments as the natural prelude to the self-determination for which they had struggled (see Chapter 3). Marxists considered it to be a logical stage in the development of socialist societies, in which workers, rather than bosses, would reap the rewards of industrialisation. For many, the establishment of such a regime in Russia indicated the desirable shape of things to come. In some respects, the feeling that Europe was on the brink of a 'brave new world' made the 1920s and the 1930s an exciting and innovative period. On the other hand, fundamental disagreement as to the form that this new world should take ensured that these years would be dangerous and unstable. Many in Europe were not ready for Marxist revolution. Industrialists, tradesmen, surviving aristocrats, peasant landowners and churchmen, all retained the appetite to defend their vested interests and their traditional values. Without the conservative monarchies to which they had traditionally turned, many of these were attracted to the dynamic, but often confused and incoherent, conservative movements cobbled together by extremists. In many European states, these movements lacked the

'Liberal' historians

Working predominantly in the parliamentary democracies of the western world, such writers are likely to explain historical changes primarily in terms of the development of individual freedoms. In particular, they will regard the development of free capitalism and parliamentary representation as the major products of recent history. Such interpretations have gained considerable strength since the end of the 'Cold War' (see page 14) and the collapse of the communist regimes in the Soviet Union and eastern Europe.

'Marxist' historians

Such historians have based their study of the subject upon the teaching of Karl Marx (see page 34) that 'the history of all society is the history of class struggle'. All historical events must be seen, therefore, in the context of the economic struggle between the governing classes, with their desire to exploit and to control the working classes, and the working classes with their corresponding desire to achieve their freedom through class struggle. All other issues of causation will be regarded as secondary, or as attempts by the governing classes to disguise the reality of class struggle.

'Socialist' historians

Although sharing some common ground with Marxist historians, 'socialist' historians are less likely to be directly attached to the teaching of Karl Marx. They are less likely than 'liberal' historians to view the development of capitalism as a natural and desirable product of history, and are more likely to stress the importance of studying 'history from below'. They are less likely to be concerned with major political developments at governmental levels, than to study the processes whereby these have been channelled towards social and economic reform.

leadership to fill the political vacuum effectively. In Germany and in Italy, however, charismatic leaders, with considerable political ability, were able to mobilise this conservative support in ways that made it appear that a radical, classless ideology had emerged to confront communism. Adolf Hitler's movement, with its control of Germany's vast economic resources, was capable of making a particularly strong impact upon Europe.

3   In the years immediately after 1945, the terrible cost that Europe paid to defeat Nazism and Fascism in the Second World War created general agreement that European governments should work for security and for prosperity (see Chapter 13). On the other hand, there was little agreement about the best means to these ends. With American funding, the states of western Europe opted for the development of their capitalist, consumer economies, stimulated by the opening of a **free market**. States such as Britain, Spain and Portugal were drawn towards this 'common market'. In eastern Europe, the Soviet Union adopted a different approach, staking both its security and its prosperity upon the maintenance of rigid political control over those eastern European

Free market: Access by buyers and sellers is unrestricted by government or by any arrangements between buyers and sellers (e.g. retailing, manufacturing, industries except where nationalised).

'Cold War': Hostilities short of armed conflict, consisting of threats, violent propaganda, spying etc. Specific application of the term came to be used with reference to the state of affairs between the USSR and the western powers after the Second World War. It lasted until the Communist regimes in eastern Europe collapsed in the late 1980s.

'Eastern bloc': The countries in the east of Europe and the Soviet Union which had Communist regimes in the post-war period.

countries that the Soviet army had 'liberated' in 1944–45. For 40 years these two strategies confronted each other as key components in the '**Cold War**'.

By the end of the 1980s, however, the Soviet strategy was no longer viable. Several contributory factors can be identified:

● the repressive nature of some of the eastern European regimes;

● the continuing importance of national identity among the eastern European peoples;

● the difficulty encountered by many of the states within the '**Eastern bloc**' in satisfying consumer demands while maintaining a high level of military expenditure.

At the end of the 20th century, although many problems remained to be solved regarding the relationship of eastern European states to their more prosperous western neighbours, the broad tendency in the east to regard the west as an economic role model was unmistakeable.

Do the years between 1870 and 1991 constitute a period of continuity or of confusion? The answer probably depends upon whether you concentrate upon political movements or upon economic forces operating within European societies. The rapid advance of industrialisation and technology provides the period with its greatest element of continuity. Political responses to this advance, on the other hand, have varied greatly. At the end of the 20th century, it appeared that none had succeeded, and that industry and technology had shaped politics, rather than the other way around. It remains to be seen whether this will be the dominant theme of the 21st century.

1.1 What were the main economic and social developments in Europe during this period?

What was the size of Europe's population?

One of the most striking features of European history throughout the period covered by this book is the dramatic increase in the continent's population. If we include the Russian Empire in the calculations, the population of Europe rose by about 150 million in the years between 1870 and the outbreak of the First World War (1914). This represented an increase of about 50%, and left the continent with a total population of about 450 million. Despite the impact of two world wars, the increase in Europe's population in the first 50 years of the 20th century was also in the region of 150 million.

As the table opposite illustrates, this rate of increase varied considerably from state to state, from region to region, and from period to period. European Russia had by far the largest rate of increase. In the last 30 years of the 19th century it stood at the remarkably high level of 1.5% per year, at least 50% greater than the increase in any other state. Even in the first half of the 20th century, a period of terrible hardships for Russia, the increase (0.9% per year) was among the highest in Europe, and the trend has been maintained in the post-war years. At the other end of the scale, the population of France remained almost static. It increased by a bare 500,000 in the last 30 years of the 19th century, and increased by less than four million in the 80 years between 1870 and 1951.

Population in Europe, 1870–1988 (figures in millions)

	1870	1900	1950	1971	1988
Russia/USSR	63.9	98.4	208.8	241.7	283.7
Austria-Hungary	35.8	45.5	16.1*	17.7*	18.2*
Germany	43.4	59.3	69.1†	74.5†	77.9†
France	38.4	38.9	42.8	50.9	55.9
Britain	31.2	37.0	49.0	54.0	57.8
Spain	17.0	18.6	28.0	33.8	39.1
Italy	25.7	32.5	46.7	54.4	57.4

* Combined populations of the modern states of Austria and Hungary.
† Combined populations of the West German and East German states.

Demographers: People who study population trends.

Birth rates/death rates: These are usually measured by recording the number of births or deaths that occur among every thousand of the population.

Social historians and **demographers** have found it hard to agree on the exact reasons for this population growth. They have put it down to a combination of three main factors.

1   The **birth rate** alone does not explain the rise in population, although it does help to explain the different population trends between one state and another. The birth rate in European Russia in 1870, for instance, has been calculated at nearly 50 per thousand, while that in France was only 24.5 per thousand. Indeed, rates in eastern Europe were generally much higher than in the west. Demographers have suggested earlier marriage, involving longer periods of reproduction, and less widespread use of birth control as the major reasons for this. By 1951, European birth rates had fallen dramatically. Russia, whose population continued to grow at a rapid rate, now produced only 20 babies per thousand of the population, a figure very close to that recorded in France (19.5).

2   There was an even steeper decline in the **death rate** in most European countries. Great advances in medicine had already ensured by the end of the 19th century that far fewer people in western Europe would die of infectious diseases. These medical advances spread widely in the course of the early 20th century. Overall, for instance, the decline in the death rate in France between 1870 and 1951 (from 27 per thousand to 13 per thousand) was less than that in Russia (35 per thousand to 10 per thousand) or in Italy (30 per thousand to 10 per thousand). By contrast, the population of Africa (where medical improvements were not so widely available), remained roughly stationary, while that of China probably declined slightly. Of particular importance was the decline in Europe of **infant mortality**. The number of infant deaths declined steadily in the course of the 20th century, but went into a spectacular decline in the decades after the Second World War. The rate was halved between 1950 and 1970 in West Germany (40.6 per thousand to 20.2), in Italy (56.6 per thousand to 25.8), and in France (34.2 per thousand to 12.7). By the early 1990s, no state in western Europe had a higher rate of infant mortality than 7.9 per thousand.

Infant mortality: The rate at which children die from infection or insufficient care in the early stages of life.

3   The last major factor governing European population figures is **migration**. In the years between 1870 and the outbreak of the First World War much of this movement was away from Europe, particularly to the USA. During this period, an estimated 37 million Europeans emigrated to the USA alone – about one-third of them from Great Britain and Ireland, and about a fifth from Italy. France and Germany had the lowest rates of emigration. This pattern changed

Migration: The movement of population from one place to another.

Immigration: The movement of foreign nationals, mainly into western Europe, attracted by the prosperity and stability of the region.

What factors have

(a) contributed most to the growth of Europe's population since 1900?

(b) caused the migration of European populations during this period?

dramatically after the First World War. With the economic depression of the early 1930s many states, and most notably the USA themselves, placed strict limits upon the **immigration** of foreigners, to safeguard the interests of their own citizens. A high degree of migration still occurred, as it had done for centuries, within states or regions; most notably the rural population moved to towns in search of work.

The Second World War stimulated migration between European states on an unprecedented scale. During the war itself, Germany imported large numbers of foreign workers, many of them as forced labour, to serve German war industries. The total had reached about seven million by 1944. At the end of the war a different form of international migration took place, not only because foreign workers returned home, but also because large German minorities in eastern Europe, perhaps ten million in all, were expelled by the liberating armies and driven into Germany. At the same time, other significant migrations took place, such as the movement of 2.5 million Russians into the Baltic territories that had recently been absorbed into the Soviet Union.

Since the war, the most striking form of population movement has been immigration. Most commonly such immigration originated from southern Europe, from Turkey and North Africa. Sometimes it was triggered by specific historical events – as when the independence of Algeria stimulated the migration of large numbers to take up residence in France. The foreign resident population in West Germany increased from 568,000 in 1950 to 6.8 million in 1991, while that of France in the same period rose from 1.7 million to 3.6 million.

What economic developments took place in Europe during this time?

By 1870 most of western Europe had undergone an 'industrial revolution'. The importance of coal deposits, of modern processes for iron production, and of railway construction, was clearly understood. Henry Bessemer's revolutionary method for the production of steel had been unveiled in 1856, and by 1870 its application had already reduced the cost of production by two-thirds.

Many historians consider that the last years of the 19th century and the opening years of the 20th century witnessed a 'second industrial revolution' in parts of Europe. One of the radical features of these years was the emergence of a new, dominant industrial economy in Europe, that of the united German Reich (Empire). Unification provided the new state with resources (including valuable iron ore in Alsace-Lorraine) and with increased domestic markets to stimulate industrial growth. New industrial techniques also contributed to a spectacular development which saw German steel production grow from 0.7 million tons in 1880 to 13.7 million in 1910, twice that of Great Britain.

This 'second revolution' can also be defined by the development of new products. The most influential of these was the motor car, which quickly became an important factor in the industrial economies of Germany, France and Italy. By 1913, there were already 100,000 cars on the roads of France. Although the manufacture of aircraft began during this period, it was less successful industrially. Aircraft remained a mere curiosity until the experience of the First World War demonstrated their military applications, and transformed them into another major element of industrial production. The spectacular pace of technological change during this period is illustrated by the fact that only 66 years – less than a single human lifetime – separated the first flight of the Wright brothers from the first landing upon the moon.

Chemical developments and the extended use of electricity were also important features of this 'second revolution'. Artificial fertilisers were increasingly used in European agriculture, and manufacturing industry benefited in a variety of ways from the cheaper production of chemical dyes and alkalis. The development of electricity as a source of power had an enormous impact upon both the industry and the society of Europe. Commercially available from the late 1870s, it brought about such changes and benefits that, in the early 1920s, Lenin could regard electrification as one of the primary aims of the Russian Revolution. The discovery that electricity could be generated by the power of fast-flowing water was of enormous benefit to the economies of countries such as France and Italy, where hydro-electric power compensated for shortages in such traditional power sources as coal. By-products of this 'age of electricity', such as the telephone (1876) and the radio (1895), help further to underline the crucial importance of this resource.

In the years before the First World War this industrial growth was reflected by an enormous increase in the population of Europe's great industrial cities. Between 1880 and 1914 the population of Greater London rose by 40% to 7 million. Paris increased its population by 50% over the same period (2 million to 3 million), while the population of Berlin doubled, reaching 2 million. Smaller towns might expect similar increases, especially if they were centres of heavy industry. Thus the towns of northern France and of the Ruhr region in Germany developed into huge industrial complexes in this period. Russia, which had only three towns in 1863 with a population of over 100,000, could boast 15 by the end of the century. Overcrowding and slum housing, combined with poor working conditions, provided the circumstances in which socialist politics thrived. In that respect, economic and political developments were inextricably connected.

How did the position of agriculture in the European economy change during this period?

By way of contrast with this industrial expansion, the major agricultural developments of the 1870s and 1880s tended to make life more difficult for Europe's farmers. In some respects agriculture benefited from technological advances.

- Chemical fertilisers had a considerable impact, in areas where farmers could afford them.

- The science of cross-breeding plants advanced rapidly.

- The development of the motor tractor was important enough to play a central role in Stalin's agricultural revolution of the 1930s (see Chapter 8).

In general, however, the greatest impact upon European agriculture was that made by the opening up of vast new food sources in other parts of the world. As the USA recovered from the Civil War of the 1860s, enormous areas were turned over to corn production. Although Russian agriculture was never so productive, the development of railways made it quicker and easier for cheap Russian produce to reach European markets. Production of meat and wool increased rapidly in Australia, New Zealand and in parts of South America, and the development of canning techniques and of refrigerated shipping made such goods more easily available in Europe.

The impact upon the European economy was striking. On the one hand, food prices fell by an estimated 40% in the last 25 years of the 19th century. On the other hand, in many parts of Europe, local farmers found it hard to compete, and agriculture ceased to be the major economic activity. It has been estimated that the number of sheep bred in Germany and in France fell by 50% in that same period. Nearly 70% of the German workforce at the time of unification was employed in agriculture, yet this figure had been halved by 1907. Politicians in many countries were confronted with difficult decisions in order to balance the interests of industrialists, landlords and workers. In general, however, the agricultural history of the period confirms the advance of manufacturing industry as the dominant economic force within Europe.

What factors influenced the trading policies of European states?

By the middle of the 19th century, it was already well established that a state might conduct its trading policies in one of two main fashions. It might pursue a 'protectionist' policy – placing taxes and tariffs upon foreign goods to make them more expensive, and thus to make it more likely that the population would buy domestically produced goods. Alternatively, if domestic industries were strong and able to produce cheaper goods than their rivals, the state might decide to pursue a free-trade policy. This was normally founded upon treaties with trading partners by which each state accepted the products of the other without taxing them, confident that both would benefit from the arrangement. The benefits of free trade were felt to be considerable: wider markets for domestic products, cheaper goods from abroad for the country's consumers, and perhaps stimulation of domestic industries through competition with strong foreign industries.

These two approaches to international trade alternated according to economic circumstances. In 1870, in the midst of 'boom' conditions, the leading economies of Europe were mainly committed to free-trade policies. The late 1870s and the 1880s witnessed widespread depression, with financial confidence at a low ebb, and with a steady rise in unemployment. Agricultural producers in particular suffered from the vast amount of cheap corn that the USA could now put on the European market. The response in many countries was to return to protectionism. The introduction of new tariffs in Germany in 1879 was of particular political importance (see Chapter 3), and France and a number of other states quickly followed suit. Sometimes states waged 'trade wars' with their rivals. Such competition badly undermined relations between France and Italy in the 1880s.

The First World War and its consequences upset the normal shape of European trade in a number of ways. Russia, for instance, was taken out of the trading equation altogether, partly by the terrible economic damage caused by war and revolution, and partly by the establishment of a Communist regime, hostile to capitalist commerce. Other states, and Germany provided the best example, chose a policy of '**autarky**'. Many of the new states of eastern Europe, formed from the ruins of the Austro-Hungarian Empire, opted for protectionist policies to stimulate weak economies. Matters became even more complicated in 1929, when the **collapse of the Wall Street stock market** contributed directly to a mentality of 'every man for himself'. Each state sought its own best route to survival in a decade of unparalleled economic depression.

At the end of the Second World War it was evident to most political and economic thinkers that it was as important to restore international trade and prosperity as it was to secure international security. It was equally evident that the two tasks were closely linked to one another. The USA now lavished enormous sums of money, through the channels of the Marshall Plan (see Chapter 13), in order to revive economic life in Europe.

Autarky (or autarchy): Economic policy aiming at national self-sufficiency in terms of raw materials and other essential economic resources. Such a policy obviously disrupted the normal channels of international trade.

Wall Street stock market collapse, 1929: On 24 October 1929 nearly 13 million shares changed hands on the New York Stock Exchange as share values fell and confidence in shares collapsed. Shock waves from the 'Crash' were felt all around the world. Many people lost a lot of money.

Where France had built elaborate defences in the 1920s to keep Germany at bay, it sought economic co-operation with West Germany in the 1950s as a better way to avoid future confrontation. This was the mentality that led to the creation of free-trade areas, first in the Benelux countries (see Chapter 14), and then over much of western Europe in the form of the European Economic Community (EEC). Even those states that did not seek, or could not achieve, membership of the EEC recognised the benefits of free trade, and formed free trade organisations of their own, such as the European Free Trade Association (EFTA). In the long term, it was always intended that the EEC should be more than just a free-trade area. From the doctrine of free trade was to grow a wider concept of economic liberalism, comprising such ideas as the single market and monetary union. In the latter stages of the 20th century movement towards such ideals was slow and difficult. Periods of depression, such as that caused by the rise in oil prices in the 1970s, still caused states to concentrate upon the protection of their own economic interests. In general, however, the free-trade principles that developed in the 19th century have emerged since 1945 as the dominant forces in western European economics.

In eastern Europe a different kind of economic integration took place under the leadership of the Soviet Union. The creation of *Comecon* (see Chapter 13) in 1949, in response to the Marshall Plan, created the illusion of economic co-operation. In reality, *Comecon* was primarily an instrument for the control and exploitation of eastern European economies in the Soviet interest. It is true that from the late 1960s the organisation concentrated to a greater extent upon the co-ordination of trade within the Soviet bloc, but it was unable to rival its western European equivalent in this respect. In the last decades of the 20th century, it was the higher standards of living in the consumer societies of western Europe that undermined the economic credibility of the Soviet bloc, and of the Soviet Union itself.

> **?**
>
> *1. What grounds are there for claiming that parts of Europe experienced a 'second industrial revolution' in the three decades before the First World War?*
>
> *2. Explain why European states pursued free trade policies at some points during this period, but favoured the use of protective tariffs at other times.*

1.2 How did the political map of Europe change during this period?

The European state system in and after 1870

The years 1870–1991 form a period of remarkable instability in the political map of Europe. It began and ended with important sequences of events, which brought about significant changes in Europe. The most important of the forces driving such changes at the start of our period was nationalism, and the political unit most vulnerable to that force was the Austro-Hungarian Empire. In the middle of the 19th century this Empire was the dominant political feature in central Europe, its direct or indirect influence extending from the southern border of Denmark to the Balkans, and embracing a wide range of national groups (see map on page 21). The Austro-Hungarian Empire came into contact with two other great empires whose populations embraced a complex mixture of different ethnic groups. The political control of the Romanov dynasty (see Chapter 2) over the Russian Empire still appeared to be secure in 1870, although the challenges mounted by Poles, Ukrainians and others were troublesome. The Turkish Empire, on the other hand, had already experienced the impact of nationalism and its disintegration was well advanced. Greece had broken free in the 1820s, Serbia had effectively thrown off Turkish control, and Bulgaria was similarly in revolt in the course of the 1870s.

By 1870 the breaking down of the Austro-Hungarian Empire into its ethnic parts was well advanced. In several cases nationalism had expressed itself in the formation of independent states. The Kingdom of Italy first emerged from the Austrian defeat in the war of 1859, and steadily extended its authority over the whole of modern Italy in the course of the 1860s. Similarly, Austria's defeat at the hands of Prussia in 1866 was the prelude to the creation of an independent and unified Germany, which occupied the central position in European politics for the next 80 years. Evidence that this might not be the final extent of Austria's instability was provided by the establishment of a semi-independent Hungarian state in 1867. It was administratively separate from Austria, but linked to it through Franz Josef, simultaneously King of Hungary and Emperor of Austria.

The next 40 years provided a period of relative stability in the political map of Europe. During this time, the continent was dominated by four major power blocs. Germany's vast industrial potential advanced its status as the most powerful state in continental Europe. The sheer size of the Russian Empire, and of the armed forces that it could mobilise, guaranteed it a considerable degree of influence, despite its economic backwardness. France enjoyed a high degree of economic and social stability, which limited the political impact of its defeat in 1870–71. Austria was still a significant influence in eastern Europe, despite its expulsion from Germany and from Italy.

What was the impact of two world wars upon the European state system?

In negative terms, the First World War was undoubtedly the most influential European event during this period. It had a powerful effect upon every aspect of contemporary European history, and naturally its impact upon the European state system was considerable. In western Europe, the war's impact upon the political map was relatively minor, amounting to the transfer of some border territories, such as Alsace, Lorraine, Eupen, Malmedy and the South Tyrol, in accordance with the fortunes of war. The map of eastern Europe, on the other hand, was transformed. Most notably, the war completed the destruction of the Austro-Hungarian Empire. A new group of **'successor' states** appeared in eastern Europe, including Czechoslovakia and Hungary. Another group of 'successor' states emerged from the wreck of the Russian Empire: Finland, Poland, Estonia, Latvia and Lithuania. In part, this transformation was brought about by nationalism. However, the new states owed their existence to the war, and to the role that it played in destroying the ability of the great empires to hold national demands in check. In many cases, events were to prove that this was not a sufficiently firm foundation for the survival of these states in the long term.

Few of these 'successor' states survived the 1930s in their original form. By the beginning of 1940 the Baltic states and half of Poland had been swallowed up by the Soviet Union, while Austria, Czechoslovakia and the western part of Poland had all come under the direct rule of Nazi Germany. This period witnessed a brief, but radical, redrawing of the map of Europe in which most of the continent lost its individual, political identity under the impact of German invasion (see map on page 371). Whether as **'puppet' governments**, **protectorates**, regions under military rule, or territories annexed to the Reich, most of Europe was for three or four years effectively governed from Berlin, with 260 million Europeans, twice the population of the USA, living briefly under German rule.

To all outward appearances, the destruction of Germany in the Second World War led to the restoration of much of the pre-war state system. Estonia, Latvia and Lithuania remained within the Soviet Union, the German Reich was partitioned, and a number of frontiers were adjusted,

'Successor' states: Term used to describe those states which emerge from the collapse or defeat of a larger state.

'Puppet' governments: Term used to describe governments which appear to be independent, but which in fact have been set up to serve the purposes of other states or powers.

Protectorates: Countries that are controlled and protected by a more powerful country.

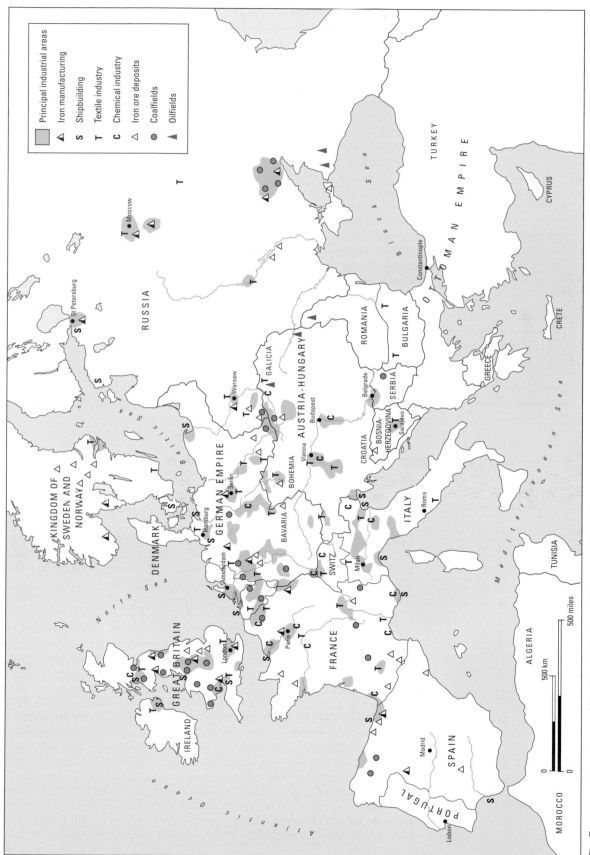

The European state system and the industrialisation of Europe, 1870–1914

Principal industrial areas

◢ Iron manufacturing
S Shipbuilding
T Textile industry
C Chemical industry
△ Iron ore deposits
● Coalfields
◤ Oilfields

TURKEY

CYPRUS

OTTOMAN EMPIRE

Black Sea

Constantinople

RUSSIA

Moscow

St Petersburg

ROMANIA

BULGARIA

GALICIA

AUSTRIA-HUNGARY

Warsaw

Belgrade

SERBIA

Sarajevo

BOSNIA-HERZEGOVINA

CROATIA

Budapest

Vienna

BOHEMIA

GERMAN EMPIRE

Berlin

Hamburg

BAVARIA

SWITZ.

Milan

ITALY

Roma

Amsterdam

KINGDOM OF SWEDEN AND NORWAY

DENMARK

Baltic Sea

North Sea

Mediterranean sea

GREECE

CRETE

GREAT BRITAIN

IRELAND

London

Paris

FRANCE

SPAIN

Madrid

PORTUGAL

Lisbon

Atlantic Ocean

MOROCCO

ALGERIA

TUNISIA

0   500 km

0   500 miles

'**Iron curtain**': A fortified border from the Baltic to the Adriatic. The states to the east of this 'curtain' were no longer independent in any meaningful sense.

Supranationalism: The belief that states should surrender their powers of action in some or in all matters of policy to an international body.

1. What were the main changes brought about in the politic map of Europe (a) by the First World War and (b) by the Second World War?

2. What are the main differences between the political map of Europe at the beginning and at the end of the period 1870–1991?

but otherwise the map of Europe looked much like that which existed 20 years earlier. In reality, this was not the case. An '**iron curtain**' divided Europe. The political and economic affairs of the states to the east were determined in accordance with the priorities and interests of the Soviet Union. Attempts by East Germany, Hungary and Czechoslovakia to assert their political freedom of action were suppressed with great brutality (see Chapter 13). The Soviet government put forward the claim that a similar form of '**supranationalism**' had developed in western Europe, based upon the capitalist interests of the USA. In reality, however, the states of western Europe retained their political independence, with borders broadly similar to those that had existed before the war.

The period 1918–1991 ended as it began, with the disintegration of a major European 'empire' into its component parts. As the late 19th century saw the steady decline of the Austro-Hungarian Empire, the 1980s witnessed the more sudden collapse of Soviet control over eastern Europe, and then of the Soviet Union itself. As some states – such as Poland, Hungary, Latvia, Estonia and Lithuania – recovered their former independent status, others disintegrated. Yugoslavia became the most unstable region of Europe, while Czechoslovakia divided in more amicable fashion into its Czech and Slovak components. With the prosperous states of the European Community exerting an influence for greater integration in the west, and nationalism still acting as a destabilising influence in the east, it remains unclear what the overall shape of the European state system will become as the 21st century progresses.

1.3 How were European states governed during this period?

Why was monarchy so widespread in Europe in 1870, and why did it subsequently decline?

In 1870, Europe was already involved in a complex and bitter debate about the most just and most effective form of government. One hundred years earlier, on the eve of the French Revolution, European government had been almost exclusively monarchical, with Switzerland the only region that was not governed by a king, queen, prince, or some similar dignitary. Despite the political disputes that had taken place since, it was still true in 1870 that, in the words of historian David Thompson, 'monarchy was, to most people, the most natural form of government in the world.' It prevailed in every major state in Europe. Even in France, where the regime of Napoleon III was soon to collapse, there was much support in the years that followed for a restoration of the monarchy.

'**Legitimacy**': The belief that in any one state one family alone had been directly entrusted with power by God.

Before the French Revolution most European monarchs would have claimed that their authority was based upon the principle of '**legitimacy**'. The Bourbons (France), the Habsburgs (Austria) and the Romanovs (Russia) all claimed the 'divine right of kings' (see Chapter 4) as the foundation of their political authority. The decision of the French revolutionaries to depose and to execute their king (1793) for crimes against the people was as radical a political gesture as could be imagined at the time. It was also a blow from which the principle of 'legitimacy' never quite recovered. It survived longest in Russia, where it still formed the basis of Nicholas II's monarchy at the opening of the 20th century. Within

20 years, however, the Tsar's incompetence had demonstrated that his power really rested upon more pragmatic foundations. Abandoned by his traditional supporters and rejected by his subjects, his own murder in 1918 marked the end of 'divine right' monarchy in Europe.

In the course of the 19th century, most monarchs had come to acknowledge that their powers were limited, and that they were obliged to govern with the consent of their subjects. By 1871, the German **Kaiser**, the King of Italy and the Queen of England all had their powers restricted by the terms of a **constitution**, and all had accepted a subtly different political role. Rather than ruling as God's representatives, they now acted as symbols of stability, as apparent guarantees of traditional values. Traditionally, monarchy received its most consistent support from the landowning nobility and from the Church. The role of the landowner is best illustrated in Prussia, where the *Junker* class (see Chapter 3) provided the staunchest support for the monarchy. In France, Italy and Spain the Catholic Church, like its Orthodox 'cousin' in Russia, aligned itself with conservative interests throughout this period. It was also relatively easy for more modern conservative interests, such as those of leading industrialists and merchants, to align themselves with constitutional monarchs. On the one hand, such support strengthened the principle of monarchy, placing it at the centre of a conservative alliance. On the other hand, it meant that Europe's monarchs would be dangerously isolated if these influential allies were ever to withdraw their support.

Whatever its theoretical justification, monarchy thrived when it was identified with success. The German and Italian monarchies, for example, increased their authority and prestige enormously through identification with the cause of national unity, a cause that in fact was based upon a completely alien set of political principles. In general, however, European monarchies did not keep pace with economic and social change, and could not expect to survive national failure or humiliation. The German Kaiser, the Austrian Emperor, the Russian Tsar, all paid the price for the disaster of the First World War, and in each case the state emerged from the war as a **republic**.

What have been the main aims and principles of liberal democracy?

From the beginning of the 19th century to the eve of the First World War, the most realistic alternative to monarchical theories of government was provided by liberal democracy. European liberalism grew out of the **rationalism** of the 18th century and was most clearly implemented in the early years of the French Revolution. Liberals differed from traditional conservatives most starkly in their conviction that humankind was essentially good, and that to allow the individual a high degree of personal freedom would lead, not to anarchy and lawlessness, but to the ordered and rational progress of society. The French Revolution provided the classic statement of liberal preconceptions about society and politics in the form of 'The Declaration of the Rights of Man and of the Citizen' (26 August 1789). Essentially an expression of middle-class individualism, the declaration established the natural rights of 'liberty, property, security and resistance to oppression'. The main political demand, both of this 'Declaration' and of all subsequent liberals, was for a constitution. The individual freedoms thus guaranteed in 19th-century constitutions were remarkably consistent: freedom of speech, of worship, of assembly, and of the press; freedom from arbitrary arrest, imprisonment and taxation; equality of opportunity. A further feature of these constitutions was a representative assembly – a parliament – elected by a large proportion of the population to express and

Kaiser: Emperor, especially the German emperor; a ruler superior to kings.

Constitution: A legal statement of limitations upon the power of government, and of the rights and freedoms of those governed.

Republic: A country whose system of government is based on the idea that every citizen has equal status, so that there is no king or queen and no aristocracy.

Rationalism: A philosophy developed in the 18th century, which stressed the ability of humankind to order its affairs, and to understand its environment, by the application of reason. Although it was not exclusively a political philosophy, it had important political and social implications, in that a rationalist could not automatically accept beliefs, such as the divine right of kings or the existence of God, which could not be directly proved by the application of reason.

to safeguard their interests against the monarch or the ruling élite. Parallel to these demands, especially in those states with more advanced industrial economies, came the request for the freedom of trade and of economic enterprise. Indeed, Karl Marx believed that in essence, all liberal thinking boiled down to these economic priorities.

By the outbreak of the First World War, such political and economic programmes as this had been accepted, either freely or under duress, by all European rulers. Even the Catholic Church had accepted that Pope Pius IX (1846–78), in condemning such ideas in his *Syllabus of Errors*, was swimming against the tide. The Tsar of Russia recognised many of these freedoms in the aftermath of the 1905 Revolution, with the proviso that they were not so much inalienable rights, as privileges granted by a benevolent monarch.

Nevertheless, liberalism was essentially a middle-class doctrine that would frequently ally itself with political conservatism. This was confirmed in many European states in the course of the 19th and 20th centuries. In some states, such as Britain and France, liberalism acquired genuine political influence, and parliamentary government became a reality. Elsewhere – in Germany and Italy for example – the rights guaranteed by the constitution were more limited, a more restricted range of citizens benefited from them, and considerable political power remained in the hand of the traditional governing élites.

By supporting a high degree of personal liberty, and of freedom of enterprise, liberals accepted that some people would prosper more than others. They accepted that European society would be unequal in material terms. By the end of the First World War, it was no longer easy to see liberalism as a radical doctrine. Increasingly, the poorer members of society cast the votes that liberalism had won for them in favour of socialist policies. Socialists borrowed many aspects of liberalism, such as popular assemblies and rights guaranteed by constitutions, but they often applied them to different purposes. Among the major purposes of socialist politics was the diversion of wealth from the rich to benefit the poor, and more radical forms of class struggle. It seemed during the 1920s and 1930s that the age of liberal democracy was fading, and that the future lay either with socialism or with the new, radical conservatism that emerged in Germany and in Italy. In this respect, the Second World War brought about a dramatic re-orientation in European politics. Although it established Communism firmly in eastern Europe for several decades, it greatly increased the influence of the USA, the greatest bastion of liberal democracy, in western Europe. Dependent for some time upon the military protection and the capital of the USA, and basing their own post-war recovery upon principles of parliamentary democracy and free trade, the states of western Europe witnessed a recovery of liberalism that could hardly have been foreseen on the eve of war.

To what extent was European government influenced by the Christian Churches?

This is a complex issue, made all the more difficult by the variety of Christian churches within Europe. The Catholic Church predominated in southern and central Europe, in Italy, Spain, Austria, southern and western Germany, and in much of France. The Eastern Orthodox Church was dominant in Greece, in much of the Balkans and, above all, in Russia. Protestantism had its greatest influence in the north – in Scandinavia, Britain, northern Germany and the Netherlands. The Churches differed from one another in details of doctrine, but traditionally they had all worked for many years in partnership with the political authorities of their

1. What were the main principles of

(a) traditional monarchy and

(b) liberalism in the late 19th and early 20th centuries?

2. Why did the principles of monarchy lose so much of its authority in Europe between 1870 and the end of the First World War?

3. How would you explain the relative strength of liberal democracy in western Europe at the beginning and end of the 20th century, and its relative decline between 1920 and 1945?

respective states. Russia was governed by a firm alliance between the Tsar and the Orthodox Church. In many states the Catholic Church had acted in similar fashion as a partner in conservative government, but this role was undermined in the 19th century by two factors.

Its traditional identification with conservative government made it a prime target for the hostility of the liberals. Anti-clericalism, hostility to the special status and privileges of churchmen, became a major feature of Italian and French liberalism.

Further damage was done to this traditional conservative partnership by Pope Pius IX, who insisted that, as God's representatives on earth, the Catholic Church had the loudest voice in political decisions. Any political practice or ideal that ran contrary to the principles of the Church should, he claimed, be rejected by Catholic citizens. This not only caused serious confrontations with liberal regimes, but also resulted in great suspicion towards the Catholic Church in such conservative regimes as that which governed Germany. By the end of the First World War, the Catholic Church had ceased to play any meaningful role as a governmental force, except perhaps in Spain. Nevertheless, its role as a moral force remained so powerful that such regimes as those in Fascist Italy, Nazi Germany and Communist Poland had eventually to include it in their political calculations.

1.4 What political ideas had the greatest influence upon Europe during this period?

What is the significance of nationalism during this period?

In part nationalism was a product of the decline of monarchy, outlined above. As it became less and less acceptable to characterise populations simply as the subjects of a particular monarch, intellectuals sought truer ways to establish their identity. Socialist thinkers such as Karl Marx argued, by the mid-19th century, that the distinctive, defining characteristic was membership of a socio-economic class. For many others, national identity appeared to be a more obvious and meaningful distinction. The fundamental principle of nationalist thinkers was that humankind was naturally divided into 'nations', which could be identified by such common features as language, culture, and perhaps by their common historical experience. Their secondary principle was that such identifiable communities should not be governed by outsiders, by foreign princes, but should be free to decide their own political destinies. For US President Woodrow Wilson, at the end of the First World War, this principle of 'national self-determination' appeared to be as natural and undeniable a democratic right as freedom of speech or freedom of religion. A third assumption of nationalists has always been that it is the natural duty of the individual to serve his or her national community, to cherish, to protect and to develop its culture and identity.

For all these common features, European nationalism flowed into a number of distinct channels in the course of the 19th century. One of these channels flowed from the French Revolution, whose 'Declaration of the Rights of Man and of the Citizen' contained the statement that 'the source of

Nation state: In the 19th century, it became the conventional belief that the most 'normal' form of political organisation should be the 'nation state'. In other words, it was assumed that the German people were entitled to be part of a single state. The same thinking assumed that multinational states were inappropriate political organisations.

Georg Hegel (1770–1831)
Professor of Philosophy at Heidelberg (1817–18) and at Berlin (1818–31). Hegel believed that all change and progress in history result from the clash of opposite ideas and forces. From such clashes between a 'thesis' and an 'antithesis' results an end-product, a 'synthesis', which contains elements of both original sets of ideas. This synthesis eventually comes into conflict with its own opposite, and so change and development continue. As an example, the French Revolution might be seen as a clash between absolute monarchy (the thesis) and radical republicanism (antithesis), producing the synthesis of Napoleon's popular, paternalistic monarchy.

---

all sovereignty resides in the nation'. For contemporary French thinkers, 'the nation' had no racial connotation. It was not necessarily based upon a common language or upon common ethnic characteristics. French nationalism was not an excuse for aggression, for the division of humanity, but a democratic bond uniting it in the spirit of fraternity. Perhaps the greatest exponent of this brand of nationalism was the Italian, Giuseppe Mazzini (1805–1872), who exerted a considerable influence upon the movement for the liberation and unification of Italy in the mid-19th century.

By that time, however, German nationalism was displaying some very different characteristics. These were derived from a number of important intellectual sources. Johann Gottfried von Herder (1744–1803), a leading German philosopher, put forward the idea that God had created each national group with its own distinct set of characteristics, its own 'spirit' (*Volksgeist*). Members of the national community were thus obliged to develop this 'spirit', rather than imitating those of foreign states. Johann Gottlieb Fichte (1762–1814) took this idea a step further, stressing the superiority of the German 'genius' to those of other nations, such as the French. It was no coincidence that his major work, *Addresses to the German Nation*, was written at the height of the German states' struggle against French invasion (1807–08). Fichte's successor at the University of Berlin, Georg Hegel, made a significant contribution to the development of nationalism. This arose in particular from his conviction that the most important end-product of dialectical historical development was the emergence of the **nation state**, and that the individual could only be fulfilled as part of that organic state. This might still have placed him closer to Mazzini than to Fichte were it not for two other factors. Hegel was convinced of the special destiny reserved for Germany, and of the role to be played in this destiny by the Prussian monarchy. Secondly, he strongly implied that conventional notions of legality and right had little meaning in relations between states. His reminder that 'men are foolish to forget the truth that lives in power' rings ominously through the history of 19th- and 20th-century Germany.

Two generations of thought thus made nationalism in Germany a doctrine centred largely upon a sense of cultural superiority, a sense of duty to the national state, and an admiration of power. Such features were not unique to Germany in the 19th century. Pan-slavism, in particular, imitated some of them (see Chapter 2). The combination of these philosophical principles, with the growing political and economic power of Germany, was to make German nationalism a particularly potent force in this period.

How did nationalism develop in the course of the 20th century?

The establishment of such nation states as Germany and Italy, the primary goal of 19th-century nationalists, did not end the appeal of nationalism. In large part, this was because nationalists had deceived themselves. One of their basic assumptions had always been that a sense of national community existed before the creation of the state, and that the establishment of state institutions would merely complete the structure. In many cases this proved to be untrue. It quickly became evident that many did not necessarily identify with the political unit that now governed them. The German Reich in 1871 was riddled with religious, economic and social differences that the Prussian-based government had to resolve. Many Italians in Naples and in Sicily resented the imposition of Piedmontese rule, and had to be persuaded by military force. Even France, a nation state for centuries, spent much of the 19th and early 20th centuries resolving differences of this kind. Historians are now aware that 'nation building' was an important process in this period, and that it largely took place after the establishment of political unity. The

German term *Sammlungspolitik* – a policy of gathering together (see Chapter 4) – summarises the task that faced such governments. In their hands, nationalism became a practical means whereby fundamental differences within the state could be reconciled. Emphasis upon the might of the national army, the growth of a colonial empire, or the wrongs suffered at the hands of other states, could all provide useful distractions from domestic economic difficulties or social tensions. Thus nationalism played a role in the years before the First World War similar to that played by economic expansion and material prosperity in western Europe after 1945, acting as the cement to bond disparate elements within the state. In this respect, it not only bore much of the responsibility for the outbreak of the First World War, but was stimulated and enhanced by that conflict.

The inter-war years marked a particularly dangerous stage in the history of European nationalism. It could be claimed that there was something essentially artificial about nationalism before 1914; that governing élites recognised it as a tool that might be used or laid aside as they wished. The experience of the First World War added bitterness and hatred to the mixture. There was no ulterior motive behind Hitler's claim that Germany had been wronged and betrayed during the war and in the drafting of the peace treaty. His belief was shared by millions of German voters. For many others, in Italy, Spain and elsewhere, national identity also provided a safe alternative to the class struggle that was advocated by communists, in the ascendant after the Russian Revolution.

In western Europe, at least, nationalism appeared to be largely discredited by the events of the 1930s and of the Second World War. It was now identified far more readily with Nazi atrocities, or with the disasters that the ambitions of Hitler and of Mussolini had brought upon their countries. Those who now advocated supranationalism (see Chapter 14) found that most Europeans were not ready for such a concept. France, West Germany and Great Britain were among the countries that embraced the principles of common economic policies in the 1960s and 1970s, without wishing to abandon elements of their nation's political and cultural identity. In eastern Europe, meanwhile, the principles of nationalism continued to thrive. The crumbling of the Soviet 'bloc' in the 1980s (see Chapter 13) made it clear that four decades of socialist ideology had failed to eliminate awareness of national identity in such states as Poland and Czechoslovakia, and even in the territories that formerly constituted the Soviet Union. Events in the Balkans in the final decade of the 20th century showed that atrocities could still be committed in the name of ethnic identity on a par with those committed in the 1940s.

Why did so many European countries follow Imperialist policies during this period?

Imperialism was not a product of the 19th century. At least five European states had established extensive overseas empires in the course of the previous three centuries, some of which continued to flourish. It is true that the best days of the Spanish, Portuguese and Dutch empires were over. However, France began to construct an important collection of colonies in North Africa, centred upon Algeria. The British Empire, despite the loss of its American colonies, still consisted of substantial possessions in Canada, the West Indies, southern Africa, Australasia and in the Indian sub-continent.

In the mid-19th century, nevertheless, it appeared that overseas colonisation by European powers was a thing of the past. The rebirth of European colonialism, in the three or four decades before the outbreak of

1. What were the main ideas put forward by European nationalists in the course of the 19th century?

2. What were the fundamental differences in the 19th century between the nationalist ideas put forward in France and those put forward by German thinkers?

3. For what reasons, and to what extent, did the popularity and appeal of nationalist ideas fluctuate in the course of the 20th century?

Imperialism: The acquisition of overseas colonies governed in the interests of the mother country.

the First World War, was therefore one of the most startling elements in contemporary international relations. Although this 'new imperialism' was not confined to one continent, the so-called 'Scramble for Africa' was its most spectacular manifestation. In 1875, only some 10% of Africa was occupied by European states; 20 years later, only 10% remained unoccupied. Another important area of imperialist expansion was eastern Asia, where France acquired significant possessions in the latter decades of the 19th century, and where many other powers exploited the decline of the Chinese empire to establish important trading interests. One of the most successful and enduring examples of European expansion was that undertaken by Russia, which absorbed vast regions of Siberia and central Asia, much of which remains its national territory today.

Why did this happen? A popular and widely accepted interpretation of 19th-century imperialism saw it as a natural result of capitalist development in Europe. In *Imperialism: a Study* (1902), the English journalist, J.A. Hobson, argued that colonies satisfied an investment need in capitalists that could not be met by markets nearer home. Imperialism, he argued, also received support from a variety of capitalist interests, such as shipping companies, armament manufacturers, and the administrative professions, which gained occupation and profit from servicing the colonies. Hobson's views were developed by Vladimir Lenin in *Imperialism: the Highest Stage of Capitalism* (1916), which became the orthodox socialist explanation of the phenomenon. Lenin, too, saw European imperialism at the turn of the century as a capitalist development, arising from the saturation of domestic markets and the subsequent quest for new resources and new markets.

In many respects, however, this kind of explanation has proved to be unsatisfactory. More recent research has made it clear that imperialist powers usually invested more heavily in other advanced economies than they did in their colonies. Russia, for instance, was a more popular target for investors, especially the French, than any African or Asian territory. Nor have historians found it easy to regard some colonising powers, such as Italy or Japan, as states that had exhausted their own domestic capacity for capitalist investment.

The most serious alternatives to economic interpretations of imperialism have been those that see it as an extension of European nationalism and national rivalries. This argument might be supported by the example of French colonial expansion in the 1880s which was, both for Jules Ferry and for Otto von Bismarck, a deliberate attempt to distract attention from the national humiliation that France had suffered in 1870–71. German imperialism in the 1880s and 1890s had been seen as a means, used by the government, to divert attention away from economic and political tensions within German society (see Chapters 3 and 4). This gives some support, therefore, to Lenin's view that imperialism was at this stage a product of class struggle.

Although they were undoubtedly secondary, a further set of motives should not be overlooked. The idea of imperialism as a moral duty – as a means of spreading western civilisation and Christian values – undoubtedly spurred on many. Some 60,000 missionaries, two-thirds of them Roman Catholic, were serving in Africa and Asia in 1900. It is also certain that curiosity, and excitement at the geographical discoveries that were made, played a role in establishing the popular appeal of imperialism.

On a more practical level, we should also note that many contemporary developments made colonial expansion a more viable proposition for European states than it had been 50 years earlier. Communications, for instance, had improved greatly, with the average duration of a voyage from England to Australia halved in the second half of the 19th century, from 83 days to 42. The invention of the telegraph was of enormous importance for communications within extensive colonial territories. Medical advances made the settlement of Europeans in Africa a much safer process than it had previously been. Military developments, such as the introduction of the machine-gun, and later of the aircraft, made it virtually impossible for native forces to resist European aggression in the long term.

Why did European imperialism decline after the First World War?

Another notable feature of this 'new imperialism' was its relatively short lifespan. By the end of the First World War one major power – the USA – was actively campaigning against it, advocating the same kind of 'national self-determination' that it applied to territorial issues in Europe. The British and French empires appeared to take on a new lease of life, making substantial gains from the wartime collapse of the German and Turkish empires. Like so many elements of the peace settlement, however, this colonial expansion was deceptive and the 1920s and the 1930s saw many powerful factors working against imperialism. These included well-co-ordinated and popular movements for independence, notably in India, Vietnam and the Arab world, socialist agitation at home against the racism and exploitation of imperialism, and severe economic difficulties that made it increasingly difficult to defend distant colonies. Within a decade of the Versailles settlement (1919), Britain at least was contemplating routes to self-government in such regions as India and Palestine. Alone among the European powers, Italy pursued a policy of serious colonial expansion in the 1930s, seizing new territory in a manner reminiscent of the 19th century. Indeed, Mussolini's invasion of Abyssinia was a conscious attempt to complete unfinished colonial business from the 1890s.

The Second World War ruined Italian hopes of a colonial empire as the First had ruined German hopes. It also made it clear that the days of the long-established empires were numbered. In the Far East, the Japanese had overrun large areas of British, French and Dutch possessions, and the nationalist movements that sprang up to resist the Japanese also made it hard for European powers to re-establish their control after the war. The war also destroyed much of the economic buoyancy upon which imperialism had been based. Finally, the politics of the 'Cold War' (see Chapter 13) caused both the USA and the Soviet Union to pose as the champions of **'third world'** peoples, and further undermined the political and moral viability of European imperialism. Some European powers, such as France and Belgium, tried to regain international prestige, lost during the war, by re-asserting their authority over their colonial empires. A series of colonial defeats in the 1950s and 1960s proved to them that this was impossible, and that their future lay with European integration. Thus the second half of the 20th century was an era of 'decolonisation'.

How should we assess the long-term impact of imperialism?
In some cases, as in those of Germany and Italy, European imperialism was a brief episode of little lasting significance. The British and the French empires, however, achieved a lasting impact, in terms of language, culture and government. It is important to avoid a strictly 'Euro-centric' view of these events. The impact of imperialism upon Europe was slight compared to the revolution that it brought about, for instance, in Africa. Its effects there are evident in governmental structures, in national frontiers that ignore former tribal boundaries, and in such major elements of technological infra-structure as railways. 'Although European empires have passed away,' the historian David Omissi has written, 'our world remains very much a world shaped by empire.'

'Third world': Those countries or parts of the world that are poor, do not have much power, and are considered to be underdeveloped.

1. What arguments have been put forward to explain the colonial expansion of European states in the late 19th and 20th centuries?

2. How valid is the claim that 'European imperialism in this period was a passing phase that had few important consequences in the long term'?

Why did Fascism have such a dramatic impact upon Europe in the 1920s and 1930s?

Probably no contemporary historical term has been so abused and misused as the word 'Fascism' (see Chapter 9). In modern political usage it has often become a term of crude abuse aimed at any political views to the right of one's own. In the strictest sense, Fascism in the 1920s and 1930s could be taken to refer only to the movement led by Mussolini in Italy. So many other movements imitated elements of Italian Fascism, however, that it is usual to apply the term to all of the authoritarian, right-wing regimes that emerged in inter-war Europe.

A number of general theories of Fascism have been put forward. For many Marxist theorists, Fascism appeared to be the last desperate and violent attempts of capitalism to prevent its own collapse. The theory appeared all the more credible because of the sympathy shown by 'big business' for the Fascist and Nazi policies pursued in Italy and Germany. On the other hand, it is not easy to see Italy, Spain or Portugal as societies in which in the 1920s capitalism had reached its highest point of development. Many western liberals, such as Hannah Arendt and C.J. Friedrich, retaliated in the atmosphere of the 'Cold War' by comparing Fascism, not with capitalism, but with Soviet Communism. Both, they claimed, were forms of the wider concept of **'totalitarianism'**. The parallels that they drew stressed the imposition of ideology and of a single party system, and the use of terror as a political tool. This line of approach is viable as long as one concentrates upon means, but is weaker when one considers ends. The preconceived end-product of the Marxist revolution – the classless society – is clearly stated by Communist theorists. The final aim of Fascism, where it is possible to identify one, was certainly not the same.

'Totalitarianism': The ideas, principles and practices of political systems in which there is only one political party. This one party controls everything and does not allow opposition parties.

Was Fascism a coherent political philosophy or a short-term response to the political problems of the inter-war years?

Whereas Marxism began life as a theory (see below), subsequently modified and adapted in practice, Fascism existed as an emotional form of political action before theories – such as those of Giovanni Gentile (1875–1944) in Italy or Alfred Rosenberg (1893–1946) in Germany – were devised to give it intellectual credibility. For all its claims to the contrary, Fascism was a negative phenomenon. It was not a 'brave new world', but a reaction against certain elements in the contemporary world. Fascism, as the historian Hugh Trevor-Roper concluded, 'is inseparable from the special experience of one generation: the generation which flourished – or failed to flourish – between the two world wars'. The political concerns of that generation had been shaped by the First World War. The collapse of well-established regimes in central Europe left in their place parliamentary regimes often unable to resolve the economic and social problems that they inherited. The economic collapse that followed in the late 1920s and early 1930s only heightened the sense of insecurity and instability. In specific cases, such as Hungary, Germany and Italy, the peace terms of 1919 left a burning sense of national injustice. At the same time, the success of the Bolshevik revolution in Russia (see Chapter 7) offered an alternative vision of the future that horrified the middle classes and those members of the working classes that aspired to middle-class standards.

Sometimes the response to these factors took the form of a philosophy determined to sweep away existing religious, social and governmental systems, as was the case with the young Mussolini. Sometimes it expressed itself in more traditional conservative forms. Most 'Fascist' regimes in the 1920s and 1930s combined the two responses; hence their divergent forms and their frequent internal tensions. On a more practical level, the war and the subsequent recession provided a further element that was to be a

Friedrich Nietzsche (1844–1900)
German philosopher, who abandoned his orthodox academic teaching and studies (1878) to elaborate a radical philosophy in which he rejected the Christian basis of existing social and moral thought. In such works as *Thus Spake Zarathustra* (1883–5) and *Beyond Good and Evil* (1886), he explored what an individual (The Superman – *Der Übermensch*) could achieve once he was liberated from the constraints of conventional morality. The later, nationalist applications of his ideas were largely the responsibility of his sister, who edited and published his work after his death.

prominent feature of all Fascist movements. The large numbers of ex-servicemen, brutalised by war and apparently robbed of security in peacetime, formed the basis of organisations, such as the SA in Germany (see Chapter 10) or the *Squadristi* in Italy (see Chapter 9), that gave Fascism its original physical impact.

Fascism drew many of its ideas from past political and social philosophies, but it borrowed them in a confused and unclear way. The prototype for the authoritarian Fascist state and for the charismatic Fascist leader can be found in the work of Hegel and of Friedrich Nietzsche. Nietzsche believed in the potential of humankind once freed from the 'slave mentality' of Christianity. Socialism, too, played a role in the origins of Fascism. Mussolini began his political career in Italy as a socialist, and on the left of most Fascist movements stood men like the Strasser brothers in Germany (see Chapter 10), who wanted to sweep away the old social and political order, and establish a new one. Nationalism, however, was undoubtedly the strongest element in Fascism. It was so strong that each movement broadly termed 'Fascist' was firmly rooted in the specific historical problems of its own country, and was dedicated to specifically national aims. In this sense, in Mussolini's words, Fascism was truly 'not for export'. Despite the many shared features in the authoritarian regimes of the 1920s and 1930s, it would be wrong to look for uniformity of aims. Instead we have to accept a broad definition such as that proposed by R.A.H. Robinson, of Fascism as 'a nationalist, anti-Marxist, mass-mobilising political movement, normally headed by a charismatic leader, aimed at the complete conquest of power by means of a single-party system.'

In what ways did Socialism challenge the traditional political and social structures within Europe?

The 19th century produced a new challenge, both to the old hierarchy of kings and landowners, and to the new one that the **bourgeoisie** sought to construct. This came from the scattered group of intellectuals who called themselves 'socialists'. The term 'socialism' is very broad. It has meant many different things to different people. Nevertheless, there were certain common bases to those movements that claimed it as their title. One was their common dissatisfaction with the system of industrial production developing in Europe during the 19th century. Its main fault, as defined by the English socialist Robert Owen, was that it laid too much stress upon the production of goods, and not enough upon their distribution. Thus, despite Europe's vast industrial resources and agricultural fertility, millions of its population could scarcely afford basic necessities.

Socialism and the rejection of capitalist society
Essentially, socialists in the 19th and 20th centuries proposed two different solutions to this problem. One was that the workers who played such a central role in industrial production should receive a greater share in its

1. What different conclusions have been reached about the general nature and the main features of Fascism?

2. Why was Fascism such a dynamic force in Europe in the 1920s and the 1930s and not at other times?

Bourgeoisie: A French term, originally indicating those who lived in cities, but increasingly being understood to mean those members of the middle classes who lived by trade, investment and speculation.

fruits, through higher wages, and therefore a greater ability to purchase the goods that industry produced. The more radical suggestion was that the workers should actually control the production and the distribution of industrial goods. One of these demands allowed for some degree of compromise between workers and capitalists, the other guaranteed confrontation.

A second common feature of socialist thinking is its optimistic view of human nature and of humankind's capacity for social virtue and co-operation. Socialists quickly rejected the conservative view of humanity as necessarily selfish and sinful and thus needing to be kept in check by the political authority of the state. Much socialist thinking in the early part of the 19th century came to the conclusion that existing forms of society in Europe were based entirely upon the desire for personal profit. Reformation, therefore, was only possible if alternative societies were constructed. Such projects were widely termed '**utopian**'.

By the middle of the 19th century, utopian socialism had largely lost credibility amongst European thinkers. Some socialists remained firm in the belief that modern, industrial society was incapable of reform, and that new forms of society had to be devised. **Anarchism**, in particular, renounced the concept of the state and of traditional authority. Instead it advocated a society based upon free association and voluntary co-operation between individuals and communities. By the same token, anarchists even rejected the centralised leadership of socialist political parties. Two French theorists, Pierre-Joseph Proudhon and Auguste Blanqui, provided rival theories as to how anarchists might achieve their aims. Proudhon believed that such an ideal situation might be brought about by peaceful means, but Blanqui was convinced that it would be necessary to undermine existing social and political structures by violent action. Proudhon's views exercised an important influence over the Paris Commune in 1871. Blanqui's view was developed by the influential Russian anarchist, Mikhail Bakunin, and acts of violence against leading government figures were a feature of Russian radical activity in the latter part of the 19th century (see Chapter 2). In this respect, anarchism made a significant contribution to the tactics of the Russian Communists as they prepared their revolution, although anarchist views were scarcely welcome in the society that the Russian Revolution established. The attractions of direct and violent action remained strong, and the over-simplified idea that acts of violence might cause the collapse of

'Utopian': The word derives from the work written by the English statesman Sir Thomas More in the early 16th century. In it, he described an ideal society in which all political and social arrangements were equal and just. Knowing that no such society existed, More named it 'Utopia', which is Greek for 'nowhere'.

Anarchism: Political belief that regards formal government as oppressive and undesirable. Anarchists advocate a society based upon free association and voluntary co-operation between groups and individuals.

Pierre-Joseph Proudhon (1809–1865)
Unusual among early socialists in that his origins were working class. He published influential works (*What is Property?* and *On the Creation of Order among Mankind*) in the 1840s in which he argued that labour is the only true form of capital. He sat in the National Assembly in 1848 and served a prison sentence for his views (1849–52) under Louis Napoleon. He subsequently conducted much of his journalistic activity from exile in Belgium.

Auguste Blanqui (1805–1881)
Son of a senior local government official, he was first active against the French monarchy in 1827. A keen advocate of revolutionary action by the working classes, Blanqui was imprisoned by successive French regimes, by Louis Philippe (1839), by the Provisional Government (1848) and by the Republican government (1870). In total, he spent 39 years in prison for his beliefs. Granted an amnesty (1877), he continued his anarchist writing and agitation until his death.

Mikhail Bakunin (1814–1876)
Born into a noble Russian family, he abandoned a military career in 1841 and emigrated to Berlin, and subsequently to Paris. Author of *Reaction in Germany* (1842) and active in the events of 1848 in Paris and in Prague. Deported to Russia, Bakunin was sent to Siberia, but escaped (1861) to return to western Europe. Subsequently, he was active in the formation of socialist political societies and journals, especially relating to Russia, and in the establishment of the First International. His expulsion by the supporters of Karl Marx represented the defeat of anarchist principles at the hands of orthodox Marxism.

conservative structures continued to attract recruits. Anarchist groups were frequently in evidence in later European history, even in the student revolts that swept western Europe in the late 1960s.

Socialism and the reform of capitalist society

In the course of the 20th century, socialism developed beyond its utopian roots in a variety of different directions. One of these was dominated by Marxism (see next section). Utopian socialists, anarchists and Marxists alike all sought ways to change society and its priorities at a time when political power was largely the preserve of traditional governing élites. None of these groups regarded democratic reform, through parliament and through the legal system, as a serious option, for none had much hope of gaining access to such channels of power. Less radical socialists, however, such as the Fabians and the Independent Labour Party (ILP) in Britain, and similar groups in continental Europe, did accept the idea that an enfranchised working class could exert sufficient influence through normal political channels to achieve many of their moderate aims. One of the most important of these groups was the German Social Democratic Party, or SPD (*Sozialdemokratische Partei Deutschlands*). Under the leadership of Eduard Bernstein, the SPD began to argue that power and reform could both be achieved through the ballot box.

Jean Jaurès (1859–1914) led French socialism in a similar direction. Indeed, some French socialists made an even greater adjustment, when they agreed to a possibility that socialists might actually accept ministerial office in capitalist governments. Such 'revisionists' were bitterly criticised by orthodox Marxists, and their judgement was called into question in 1917 with Lenin's success in Russia. Events in Russia and in western Europe in the final decades of the 20th century, however, seem to suggest that these democratic socialists saw the future more clearly.

If the success of democratic socialism is to be gauged by the actual formation of socialist governments in Europe, one would have to conclude that its achievement was small. Nothing remotely resembling a socialist government was formed before the Russian Revolution in 1917, and even afterwards the Social Democratic Party in Weimar Germany and the 'Popular Front' in France in the 1930s held power under difficult and limiting circumstances. Even in the stable conditions of western Europe after the Second World War, socialist parties have won relatively few elections. The Social Democratic Party, for instance, won only one of the 11 general elections held in the history of West Germany. On the other hand, the threat of the working classes coming to power, or creating revolutionary disturbances, was often a powerful factor in initiating reform, even under the most conservative regimes. It drove Bismarck to adopt a programme of social reform in the 1880s, and secured even more far-reaching reforms in Tsarist Russia in the years after the 1905 revolution. Ironically, although Lenin's revolutionary success in 1917 did not inspire the general revolution for which he hoped, it probably helped to ensure that every European government would subsequently feel itself bound to take working-class interests into account in its social and economic legislation.

Another manner in which socialists sought to bring about change within the existing system was through **trade unionism**. More extreme socialists attached great importance to the 'general strike', the ultimate weapon, which might threaten the very existence of capitalism if the workforce as a whole withdrew its labour. The great weakness of such a tactic lay in the fact that employers could usually survive the economic hardship of a strike more easily than the workers. These were likely to be driven back to work by the hardships that arose from the loss of their income. A further weakness arose

---

Eduard Bernstein (1850–1932)
A founder and prominent member of the German Social Democratic Party. Originally an orthodox Marxist, he abandoned that position under the influence of British socialists, and supported instead the achievement of socialist power through the ballot box. Bernstein himself served as a deputy in the Reichstag (1902–06 and again in 1912).

Revisionists: Term applied to an individual or group which takes an established belief or philosophy and adapts or revises it to suit their purposes. In the view of orthodox thinkers, this adaptation destroys or perverts the original value of the philosophy.

Trade unionism: The organisation of workers, within their workplace or in wider groupings, to promote common action. Trade unions existed to protect the interests of their members, and to threaten the capitalist system through the weapon of the strike.

from the short-term, material concerns of the majority of workers. Given the choice of far-reaching social or political reform or a bigger pay-packet, the pay-packet usually won. The fact that governments associated unions with essentially moderate demands is illustrated by their willingness to legalise such organisations. Membership of unions was legal in most western European states by 1870, and strike action was widely permitted, as long as its objective was economic, rather than political.

In the course of the late 19th and the 20th centuries, socialist politics made less headway than anticipated. The logic that socialism was bound to triumph because it represented the interests of the majority proved to be flawed. There are a number of explanations for this. Socialist thinkers frequently underestimated, for instance, the patriotism of the working classes. This was particularly evident in 1914, when hopes that war might be avoided through the refusal of workers to fight their foreign co-workers proved mistaken.

European socialism also suffered greatly from its own idealism. In the 1920s and 1930s, and even after the Second World War, socialists were often more eager to establish the correctness of their own model of party organisation, or of economic change, than to defeat the policies of conservatism. Co-operation was rare. Even when it occurred, as in the 'popular fronts' of the 1930s, it was shot through with mutual suspicion. In the final analysis, beyond the Soviet bloc, socialism achieved most in this period when its ideas were borrowed by more conservative politicians. Although in western Europe socialist governments rarely had the opportunity fundamentally to restructure the political systems of the state, the pressure that they exerted for social and economic reform was of the greatest importance. It helped to ensure that consistent and successful attacks upon such problems as unemployment, inequality, social insecurity and militarism became consistent features of contemporary democratic politics.

> ❓ 1. Why did socialist thinkers object to capitalist society, and by what different means did they seek to change it in the late 19th and early 20th centuries?
>
> 2. What arguments are there for and against the claim that socialist thinking made a major impact upon European politics during this period?

Why did Marxism make such an impact upon European politics during this period?

Karl Marx and the significance of The Communist Manifesto
By far the most important influence upon socialism in the 19th century was the publication in London in 1848 of a slim volume entitled *The Communist Manifesto*. Its authors were Friedrich Engels and the most influential thinker that socialism ever produced, Karl Marx. Engels and Marx had already founded the Communist League in 1846. Now they presented an outline of communist economic and political philosophy, which Marx was subsequently to expand in such major works as *Capital* (*Das Kapital*, 1867).

Friedrich Engels (1820–1895)
Son of a prosperous manufacturer with interests in Manchester and in the Rhineland. Worked with Karl Marx on *The Communist Manifesto* (1848) and other key works. His use of Darwin's ideas (see Chapter 10) gave Marxism a scientific element which was to influence Soviet thinking. Engels' first book was *The Conditions of the Working Classes in England* (1845). After Marx's death, Engels edited the second and third volumes of *Das Kapital*.

Karl Marx (1818–1883)
Son of a lawyer, he studied law and philosophy at Bonn and Berlin. Began his collaboration with Engels in 1844, with whom he developed the Marxist philosophy. Both joined the Communist League (German refugee organisation) and prepared its programme *The Communist Manifesto* (1848). In the wake of the 1848 revolution, Marx was expelled from Prussia. He settled in London. In 1864 the International Working Men's Association was formed, with Marx largely in control of its policies. It collapsed 8 years later owing to Marx's disputes with the anarchists, including Bakunin.

The achievement of *The Communist Manifesto* was that it placed the experiences of the working classes in the widest historical context. It replaced the vague hopes of utopian socialists and the reckless conspiracies of desperate terrorists with a coherent view of history. It explained to the workers the origin of their plight, and outlined what the authors saw as the logical development of their economic situation. It preached a hard doctrine of the need to use force to destroy a social system based upon exploitation, and it told the working classes squarely that their fate lay in their own hands.

The starting point of the Marxist argument was that history consists of a constant struggle between the classes, with political power and control of the state at any given time lying with that class which controls the means of economic production. The latest stages of this struggle had seen the steady triumph of the bourgeoisie, whose victory over the landed aristocracy was marked by such great historical events as the French Revolution. By the growth of its industrially based power, however, capitalism created the weapons of its own destruction. Firstly, capitalism strove towards **monopoly**, making competition and the defeat of one company by another an essential feature of the system. Secondly, it transformed the working classes. It concentrated them in large numbers in industrial towns, it exploited their labour, making them work for as long and for as little reward as possible, and it provoked them to unite against the abuses of capitalism. This exploitation Marx summarised in his 'theory of surplus value': the value of a product derived primarily from the labour expended on its production. Yet the wages received by the worker were always lower than the market value of the finished product, the balance passing to the capitalist in the form of profit. In effect, the profit of the capitalist amounted to the theft of the worker's labour.

Monopoly: An economic circumstance in which a single merchant or company has exclusive ownership or control of a product. Under such circumstances that owner would be able to manipulate prices to his or her own advantage.

The development of capitalism also had important international implications. Competition between companies for limited resources and markets would be reflected by similar rivalry between state and state. Thus capitalism, that appeared so strong to Marx's contemporaries, would steadily manufacture the crisis that would destroy it.

Karl Marx's other great contribution to socialist development was to stress the importance of working-class political organisation as a means of promoting **class-consciousness** and of exploiting this crisis of capitalism. In his view only the Communist Party could fulfil this role, by virtue of its more logical grasp of social and economic realities. The victory of the working class in the resultant revolutionary struggle would be followed by a historical stage that Marx described as the 'dictatorship of the proletariat'. The machinery of the state, now controlled by the workers, would be turned against the defeated classes in order to eliminate them. Only when this stage was completed could a truly communist society come into being, with public ownership of land and of all other means of production, with a heavy and progressive income tax, and with public control of all financial resources. Since its sole purpose was class exploitation and repression, the state machinery would have no further role in a classless society, and would thus 'wither away'. With its comforting doctrine of inevitable success, and its reassurance that the workers' fate lay in their own hands, the influence of *The Communist Manifesto* on socialist thought grew steadily in the second half of the 19th century.

Class consciousness: The state of being actively aware of one's position within the socio-economic class structure, and of the political implications of that position.

Marxism in the 20th century

In the course of the 20th century, Marxism has both 'boomed' and declined with surprising rapidity. The First World War provided a turning point for Marxism. While German Social Democrats decided that the time was not ripe for revolution, and backed their nation's war effort, Russia's Marxist leaders took full advantage of the war to seize power. The Russian Revolution made Marxism the official doctrine of Europe's most populous state, and its imitation elsewhere made it the official ideology of half the world's population in the course of the 20th century. Nevertheless, Lenin was essentially a 'revisionist' (see Chapter 7). His revolution had not taken place as an inevitable consequence of class struggle, but because of the desperation caused by the social and economic catastrophes of wartime. Both Lenin and his successors in Russia had to make many adjustments to their policies and to their ideology in the years that followed. It could hardly be doubted that by 1945 Stalin's regime operated in the interests of Russian power rather than in the interests of an international workers' revolution.

While the opportunism of Russian politicians did much to undermine Marxism, it was also undone to a great extent by developments within capitalism. Avoiding many of the traps into which Marx believed that it was bound to fall, capitalism made astonishing progress, especially in the years after the Second World War. Generating enough wealth to pay both for military might and for an unprecedented level of consumer comfort, it established living standards that the Soviet Union could not match. By the end of the 20th century there was no longer any Marxist regime in Europe. If this reflects weaknesses in Marxist predictions of the future, it should not be allowed to detract from the profound observations of western political and economic development that Marx himself had made in the middle of the 19th century.

1. In what respects were the ideas of Karl Marx different from those of other socialist thinkers in the 19th century?

2. Why did Marx consider that revolution was inevitable in the industrialised states of Europe?

1.5 How did the role played in international relations by military strength and by warfare change during this period?

The place of warfare in the late 19th century

One of the most striking changes within the period covered by this book is the change in European attitudes towards war, and in the role played by war within European politics. At the opening of the period, war was still regarded as a valid tool of diplomacy and as a traditional means by which to pursue the political interests of the state. Many of the assumptions that were made about warfare by European leaders in the 40 years before the First World War were established or confirmed by the Franco–Prussian War of 1870–71. There, in a campaign that was effectively decided within a matter of weeks, a coalition of German states inflicted a decisive defeat upon the forces of France, changing the continental balance of power, and transforming the map of Europe by the subsequent creation of a united German state. For a generation, this seemed to be a classic example of the effects of a successful military campaign.

The Franco–Prussian War established a number of assumptions that dominated military thinking for the next 60 to 70 years. One of these was that the days of the professional army were over. The successful Prussian army had contained many conscripted soldiers, ordinary citizens drafted into the army for a relatively short period, usually for two or three years. Once that period of service was completed they would return to civilian life, but would remain liable to service in the military reserve, and liable to be recalled to full-time military service in the event of a national emergency. Such an arrangement guaranteed a large body of trained men when it was needed, and avoided the ruinous expense of a large standing army at other times. Even so conservative a state as Russia embraced this principle with great enthusiasm in the aftermath of its defeat in the Crimean War (see Chapter 2).

Other assumptions made by European states when they planned for war were confirmed by the conflict of 1870–71. All assumed that their conflicts would be wars of movement, in which armies manoeuvred, sought one another out, and decided the issues at stake by one or two decisive battles. Thus Austrian influence in Germany had been destroyed by the defeat at Sadowa in 1866, and Napoleon III and his government fell from power in France because of the French defeat at the Battle of Sedan in 1870. Equally, it was assumed that these wars would be fought by armies commanded by officers who were largely recruited from the dominant political classes. It is not hard to see that such armies also played an important role in maintaining the domestic dominance and control of these governing élites. It was hardly coincidental that in Prussia the landowning *Junkers* (see Chapter 3) dominated both the army and the major offices of state.

Such armies sought to defeat the policies of neighbouring states but, by definition, it was never their aim to destroy ruling élites or to undermine the social structure of their enemies. It was unusual indeed for a state to pursue direct economic warfare against another, or to attack an opponent's civilian population, other than in the course of a campaign against the enemy's army. The siege of Paris by Prussian forces in 1870–71 was almost unique in European warfare in the 19th century, which made it all the more horrifying to contemporary public opinion.

This tendency towards limited warfare was confirmed in some states by their preoccupation with colonial wars. Britain, Spain and to a lesser extent France had armies which, in the second half of the 19th century, expended much of their energies in establishing imperial influence in Africa and Asia, fighting much less organised and advanced opponents than they would have encountered in Europe.

The technology of war

It was on these distant battlefields that the technology of modern warfare – machine-guns, railways and modern artillery – began to be applied for the first time. There, of course, the impact of such technology was usually irresistible.

Rapidly, the major European states became increasingly aware of the military potential of heavy industry. Between the Franco–Prussian War in 1870 and the outbreak of the First World War in 1914, the most heavily industrialised states applied modern technology increasingly to the construction of weapons of war. The gap between the armaments carried into war in 1870 and those available to the warriors of 1914 constituted a technological revolution. For land forces, the most important advances were in heavy artillery, with enormous increases in range and in destructive power. The faith placed in such weapons is clearly illustrated by the huge emphasis that was placed upon them by the commanders of the First World War. German and French forces fired nearly 24 million shells between them in the Battle of Verdun alone, and nearly 60% of all British casualties in the war were the result of artillery fire. It was widely believed when war broke out in 1914 that no army would be able to hold a fortified defensive position for long against a modern artillery bombardment.

No branch of the armed forces was so dramatically affected by this technological revolution as the navies. Here, more traditional thinkers insisted that the new technology should be applied to that most traditional of naval weapons, the battleship. Thus, this weapon increased in size, in speed, and in firepower. When the British battleship 'Dreadnought' was launched in 1906, she set new standards in each of these respects. Capable of a speed of 25 knots, she was four knots faster than any other battleship; with eight 15-inch guns, she was more heavily armed; with 11 inches of steel plate, she was more heavily protected. Other naval strategists favoured the development of less traditional weapons. At the outbreak of war in 1914, Britain was preparing a force of over 100 submarines, while Germany was approaching a force of 60.

Military chiefs were relatively slow to appreciate the potential of aircraft technology, and such projects as existed in the years before 1914 still placed more emphasis upon the dirigible airship (of which the German Zeppelins were the most famous examples) than upon the powered airplane. In other respects, however, they had fully appreciated the military importance of modern communications. Famously, railways were central to the mobilisation plans of the German army in 1914, and even the Russian army had 4,000 trains available at that time for the same purpose. Similarly, many thousands of motor vehicles saw military service for the first time in the early stages of the conflict.

The impact of two world wars

In the event, of course, the result of these technological developments, so evenly spread among the combatants, was destruction upon an unprecedented scale. It is hard to exaggerate the impact of the First World War upon attitudes to war among military leaders, politicians and ordinary citizens alike. Most of the preconceptions with which military planners approached the war were proved incorrect or inappropriate. The existing organisation of the armies quickly proved inadequate during the bloodbath of the early months of the war, and all of the combatants were forced to mobilise large numbers of private citizens, first as volunteers and subsequently as **conscripts**. Despite the enormous power of heavy artillery, the tactics of the war were predominantly defensive, and the cost in men and in material of each offensive campaign became ruinous. Faced with a military deadlock that they had not anticipated, political and military leaders extended warfare to the civilian populations, attacking merchant shipping and using **economic blockade** for the first time as a truly effective tactic. Arguably, it was the impact of the war upon their civilian populations, rather than upon their armies, that drove both Russia and Germany out of the war, destroying their governments and undermining their social and economic systems.

The result of all this was a 'semi-revolution' in attitudes towards war. To many, the First World War proved that war could no longer be regarded as an acceptable method of enforcing or preventing political change. In many countries the armed forces would never again enjoy the broad degree of prestige and popular support that had seen them off to war in 1914. The view of Russian writer Feodor Dostoevsky (1821–81) that 'war rejuvenates men, it raises the spirit of the people and the recognition of their worth,' would never again be so widely accepted. Certainly, no subsequent war would be entered into so light-heartedly. There was considerable support for the 'new diplomacy' and the 'collective security' that President Wilson proposed at the Versailles peace conference.

This remained only a 'semi-revolution', however, because others merely drew the conclusion that the war had been fought in the wrong way and for the wrong reasons. The largest European armies of the 1920s and the 1930s claimed to be motivated by ideology. They aimed to right the wrongs suffered by Germany or by Italy, or to defend and perhaps to extend the principles of Communism. Germany's military leaders drew the lesson that their national interests could best be served by applying the military lessons of the First World War to a new army. In this case the lesson

Conscripts: People, between certain ages, who are made to join the army, navy or air force, even though they have not volunteered.

Economic blockade: Preventing goods from reaching a particular country or place, with the aim of starving the opposition/enemy into submission.

Wars of attrition: Conflicts in which victory is gained by slowly wearing down the resources and resistance of the opposing power.

learned was not that there should be no more war, but rather that there should be no more lengthy and costly **wars of attrition**. Germany's military development in the 1930s, in particular, showed a desire to return to a strategy of rapid strikes and quick victories (*Blitzkrieg* – see Chapter 12). The new German armed forces would be based upon the three new weapons of the century – the tank, the airplane and the submarine. It is not coincidental that the fourth characteristic weapon of the 20th century, the rocket, also had its origins in this period.

This kind of military and technological thinking had a dual impact on the course of the Second World War. Initially, it was conceived to concentrate and therefore to shorten the impact of warfare. It was assumed that the bombing of Rotterdam, Warsaw or London would be devastating, but localised, and that it would trigger the desired political response, surrender. Towards the end of the war, the allies made the same assumption in their bombing of Hamburg and of Dresden (see Chapter 12). Germany's failure to enforce a rapid victory meant that the Second World War too developed into a 'total' war, just like the First. As a result, its destructive impact was even greater and even more widespread. Where warfare was restricted in 1914–18 to relatively small areas of the front line, the war of 1939–45 devastated Europe from end to end, destroying cities, killing more than 20 million Europeans, and displacing at least as many again.

The transformation that the Second World War brought about in the shape of warfare cannot be overstated. The last major belligerent act of the war was the destruction of the Japanese cities of Hiroshima and Nagasaki by American atomic bombs. To use the historian A.W. Purdue's neat comparison, the war that had begun 'with a German army invading Poland largely with horse-drawn supply trains, ended in the Far East with a new weapon of mass destruction, the fear of which would dominate the post-war world.' The arrival of nuclear weapons did not make war impossible, and there have been many examples since 1945 of wars fought on a more limited scale, without the use of these ultimate weapons. Until the outbreak of localised fighting in the Balkans in the 1990s, however, there had been no warfare within Europe for nearly half a century.

The Second World War also transformed the nature of great power relationships. Not only did it produce a strategic balance between two world superpowers (the Soviet Union and the USA), but it also generated unprecedented motivation among western European states to recover by co-operation and integration the prosperity that war had destroyed. In those respects, for the duration of the 20th century at least, this second great war had proved in the European context to be 'the war to end all wars'.

1. What were the main assumptions that governed military thinking and the organisation of war in the 40 years before 1914?

2. Why were European states less willing to settle their political differences by war after 1945 that they had been at the beginning of the 20th century?

The consolidation of Russian Conservatism, 1855–1894

Key Issues

● Why did Alexander II undertake an extensive programme of reforms in the 1860s?

● What was the impact of these reforms upon Russian society and upon the Tsarist regime?

● Why did the Russian regime return to conservative policies in the 1880s?

Framework of Events

1854	Outbreak of the Crimean War
1855	Death of Tsar Nicholas I; accession of Alexander II
1856	Conclusion of the Crimean War by the Treaty of Paris
1861	Emancipation of the Russian serfs
1863	Polish Revolt
1864	Introduction of *zemstva*. Reform of judiciary system
1872	Russia enters League of the Three Emperors
1873–74	Radical students institute the 'To the People' movement
1874	Introduction of Milyutin's military reforms
1877–78	Russo–Turkish War
1878	Congress of Berlin
1881	Assassination of Alexander II; accession of Alexander III
1889	Introduction of Land Commandants
1894	Death of Alexander III; accession of Nicholas II.

Overview

I N the first half of the 19th century Russia's status as a great power appeared undeniable. It rested upon the dual foundation of an autocratic political system and a strictly ordered society in which the ownership of serfs by

Tsar: Title of the emperor of Russia. Also spelled Czar and Tzar. Believed to be a shortened form of Caesar (Roman emperor).

Private enterprise: The economic activities of a country or a community which are independent of government control and directed to satisfy private wants.

Autocracy (adj. autocratic): A form of government in which the ruler (the autocrat) exercises absolute political power, unlimited by other factors such as a parliament or a constitution.

landlords guaranteed the transmission of the **Tsar's** will to the lowest ranks of society. The disadvantages of such a system lay in the fact that it severely hampered **private enterprise**. The fact that the peasants were not free to pursue greater prosperity, and that many landowners were comfortably cushioned by their privileged position, deprived Russia of the kind of growth that was generating an economic revolution in many parts of western Europe. Awareness of such disadvantages, along with a degree of ideological opposition to **autocracy** and serfdom, was already growing when defeat in the Crimean War emphasised the extent of Russia's decline as a great power. If that war sometimes appears to be little more than a footnote in French or British history, it was a key event for Tsarist Russia. The Crimean War stimulated attitudes and triggered policies in Russia that had simmered below the surface for decades.

Under these circumstances, Tsar Alexander II introduced a programme of reforms that was undoubtedly the most radical and far-reaching of any attempted by a European government in the 19th century. Over 40 million people were released from slavery, and a series of further reforms was implemented that appeared to be based upon liberal institutions in western Europe. Nevertheless, a profound paradox ran through this programme. While it introduced a degree of personal and legal freedom previously unknown in Russia, it did so by an act of the monarch's autocratic will. Indeed, the preservation of the Tsar's authority, and the consolidation of conservative interests, were among the fundamental aims of the programme. Does this mean, as Soviet historians usually claimed, that the 'great reforms' were confused and sterile? Was it all a hopeless attempt to preserve a doomed political system? Or is it better to follow the interpretation often reached by liberal, western historians, who see these reforms as steps that could have taken Russia forward into a modern age of political reform and economic progress?

The tragedy of Alexander II's great reform programme was that he and his ministers only partly understood the implications of their actions. They hoped for peace and stability in the countryside, for a more prosperous and contented peasantry, and for a degree of industrial growth that would strengthen and modernise both the economy and the army. Yet the reforms transformed most of the existing social, political and economic relationships within the state. They were bound to hasten Russia into a new world of market forces and political debate that was incompatible with the habits of command and blind obedience upon which Russian government had been based for centuries. Perceived as a short, sharp burst of radical change which would earn widespread gratitude for the 'Tsar liberator' (Alexander II), the reforms opened a troubled era of Russian history. As governments sought, alternately, to advance modernisation or to apply the brake, so various sections of the population tried to exploit the momentum towards change, or recoiled from its implications. The assassination of Alexander II in 1881 was a result of these political tensions. It guaranteed that for a generation, Russia's rulers would recognise the dangers of reform more clearly than they recognised its benefits, and that they would abandon that path. For three decades before the outbreak of the First World War, the Tsarist regime attempted to restore the effectiveness of traditional forms of government, without the bedrock institution of serfdom, upon which those traditional forms had been based.

At the same time as it struggled with the domestic problems that the Crimean War had highlighted, the Russian government also had to confront the diplomatic implications of the war. Recently regarded as the European continent's strongest military power – the 'gendarme of Europe' – Russia now found itself isolated and vulnerable. In addressing this problem, the government employed two different strategies. On the one hand, it attempted to find a working relationship with the other powers of continental Europe, especially with the new German state that emerged in 1871. On the other, in a fashion that resembled the westward expansion of the USA, it sought to exploit the vast 'virgin' regions that lay to the east. It sought power in Asia as a compensation for weakness in Europe. In the short term, there is a good case for arguing that Russia had regained its status as a great power by the end of Alexander III's reign. In the longer term, the steps taken in foreign policy led directly to Russia's disastrous involvement in the wars of 1904 and 1914. In foreign affairs, as in domestic policy, these decades prepared the ground for the traumas that Russia experienced in the first decades of the 20th century.

Tsars of Russia

Nicholas I
  1825–1855
Alexander II
  1855–1881
Alexander III
  1881–1894
Nicholas II
  1894–1917

2.1 What forces were there for continuity and for change within the Russian Empire on the eve of the Crimean War?

Autocracy

As Russia went to war in 1854, the reign of Tsar Nicholas I was nearing the end of its third decade. Throughout that period the Tsar had rigidly maintained the traditional, autocratic forms of government. Under this system, all executive political authority was concentrated in the hands of one man, and his edict (*ukaz*) was the only source of law. In principle, the Tsar's relationship with the Russian people was that of a loving, but authoritarian, father. 'His subjects,' as a senior police official explained, 'are his children, and children ought never to reason about their parents.' Just as it would be a dereliction of responsibility by a father to allow children to make decisions about the future of the family, so all political decisions lay in the hands of the Tsar. Although a variety of opinions existed in Russia on political and social issues, it remained difficult to express them, and virtually impossible to implement them unless one could enlist the support of the Tsar himself. This was the principle that was expressed by Tsar Paul I (1796–1801) when he informed an official that 'no one is important in Russia except the man who is speaking to me, and then only when he is speaking to me'.

The roles of the nobility and of the Orthodox Church

It remained a more difficult matter to implement the Tsar's authority throughout the vast Russian Empire (see map on page 48). At the centre, the main tool of government was His Imperial Majesty's Private Chancery. The Third Section of this Chancery was in charge of state security, standing at the centre of a complex web of censorship and surveillance. The work of the censors extended from the strict limitation of any reporting of events in western Europe, to the banning of any criticism of social conditions within Russia. It also involved the control of any careless or dangerous expression in any form of literature. In the reign of Nicholas I, the Third Section shadowed some 2,000 persons and dealt with around 15,000 security cases annually. In the distant provinces, the regime relied heavily upon the Russian nobility. Some of these served the Tsar as provincial governors, but all landowners had a vested interest in local law and order, ruling their estates and their serfs (peasants) almost as miniature Tsars. In the early years of the 19th century, this consensus of political and social interests provided Russian government with a considerable degree of unity. 'The landowner,' commented Nicholas I's Chief of Police, 'is the most faithful, the unsleeping watchdog guarding the state; he is the natural police magistrate.' It remained unclear how the Russian Empire could be governed if that cohesion were ever dissolved.

Throughout the 19th century the Orthodox Church, with its message of faith in God and unquestioning submission to God's will, was the major support of the Tsarist regime. It endorsed the regime's claim that its power was an expression of the Divine Will. There were numerous other religious groups within the Empire. A commission set up in 1839 reported 9.3 million non-Orthodox Christians alone. However, for most of the century it was claimed, with varying degrees of coercion, that only members of the Orthodox faith could really be true and reliable subjects of the Tsar.

The political beliefs of Nicholas I

As has already been explained, any project for political or social change in 19th-century Russia would be totally dependent upon the reaction of the Tsar himself. Several factors dictated, during the long reign of Nicholas I, that the Tsar's attitude would be rigidly conservative. Nicholas, for instance, was profoundly influenced by the dramatic Decembrist revolt that accompanied his accession in 1825. This was an unsuccessful attempt by liberal intellectuals and army officers in St Petersburg to place Nicholas' brother Constantine at the head of a constitutional monarchy. It filled Nicholas with horror. It convinced him that, despite the defeat of France in 1815, Europe was not safe from the radical ideas of the French Revolution, from blasphemous attempts to undermine the authority of monarchs who were God's representatives on earth. The fear and revulsion inspired by such **radicalism** were renewed at regular intervals: by the deposition of Charles X by the French in 1830; by the Polish revolt of 1831; and by the European revolutions of 1848. Nicholas' pretension to act as the 'gendarme of Europe' in Wallachia (1848) and in Hungary (1849) typified the role that he felt compelled to play throughout his reign – that of defender of the old discipline against the influences of 'rotten, pagan France'.

Slavophiles

The conservative principles of Nicholas I were part of a broader system of beliefs that dominated Russian thought in the 19th century. This was the conviction that Russian social organisation, religion, government, culture and philosophy were superior, by virtue of their isolation from the mainstreams of western European development. It was thus the duty of all Russians to protect these blessings against all external (i.e. western) threats. Those who wished to preserve and consolidate the essentials of Slav culture, and to spread that culture throughout the Empire, became known as 'slavophiles'. There can be no doubt that, for 30 years before the Crimean War, the Russian government shared the views of such slavophile thinkers. To the west, the reaction of Nicholas I to the Polish Revolt of 1831 showed very clearly his deep concern at the spread of western liberalism and **nationalism**. The rising was ruthlessly suppressed and many important elements of Polish national identity were subsequently attacked. The constitution was withdrawn, the universities closed and the Russian language was vigorously imposed in Polish public life. To the south, consistent attempts were made to support the Slav inhabitants of the declining Turkish Empire and to turn

Radicalism: The belief that there should be great or extreme changes in society.

Nationalism: The growth and spread of loyalty towards a nation, rather than towards an individual ruler.

them into clients of Russia. Indeed, Nicholas' attempts to exert influence over the Sultan's Orthodox Christian subjects were a major cause of the Crimean War (see later section). The most spectacular expansion of Russian culture and political influence occurred to the south and southeast. The acquisition of Persian Armenia (1828), was followed by the establishment of influence over Dagestan and the Caucasus in the 1830s and 1840s, and of control over the Uzbeks and the Kazakhs in the same decades.

Westernisers

The alternative view was that Russia would be strengthened and modernised by the adoption of some western technical and philosophical ideas. Such 'westernising' beliefs comprised the major forces for change that operated within 19th-century Russia, but they made little headway during the reign of Nicholas I. Such ideas clearly lay behind the Decembrist revolt of 1825, and their association with that event condemned them in the eyes of the Tsar. The failure of the revolt drove liberal ideas underground and for the next 30 years they found expression mainly in literature and in the discussions of intellectuals. If those intellectuals were too outspoken in their statements, they might expect severe consequences. Alexander Pushkin, arguably the greatest of Russia's poets, had his work personally censored by the Tsar. It is possible that Pushkin's political views contributed to his death in a duel (1837). Pyotr Chaadaev was officially pronounced insane after the publication of an anti-government essay in 1836.

Nevertheless, indirect criticism of the existing social system could be expressed in more subtle forms. Nikolai Gogol exposed provincial corruption in his play *The Government Inspector* (first performed in

1. Where do you think the painter of this picture stood in the contemporary debate between westernisers and slavophiles?

2. What evidence is there in this work of the artist's attitude towards Russia's past and present?

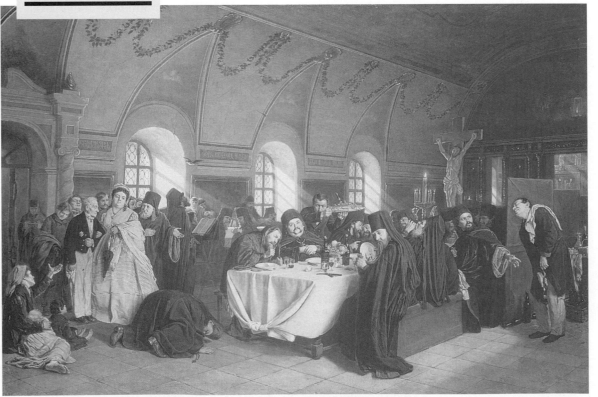

A work by the Russian artist Vasili Perov, painted between 1865 and 1875 and entitled 'A monastic refectory'.

Dmitri Milyutin (1816–1912)
His early life was divided between military and academic circles, and he had some experience of travel in western Europe. Dmitri was Deputy Minister for War (1860) and Minister for War (1861–81), introducing expansive reforms of the Russian army. Milyutin resigned upon the death of Alexander II, but continued to sit on the Council of State until 1905.

Nikolai Milyutin (1818–1872)
Younger brother of Dmitri, and prominent among the 'enlightened bureaucrats' at the end of the reign of Nicholas I. As a high official in the Ministry of the Interior, he played a major role in the drafting of the legislation for the emancipation of the serfs (see page 50), but was dismissed for the radicalism of his views in 1861.

Patrons: Those who could offer jobs, promotion or favours to other individuals.

Paternalism: 'Fatherly' attitude shown by a ruler or government. All decisions are made for the people, thus taking away personal responsibility.

1. Outline the means by which the Tsar maintained his control in Russia in the first half of the 19th century?

2. Summarise the forces that resisted liberal and modernising reforms in Russia at the opening of Alexander II's reign?

3. On what issues did 'slavophiles' and 'westernisers' disagree in 19th-century Russia?

1836) and satirised the institution of serfdom in his novel *Dead Souls* (1842). The publication of 224 new magazines from 1826 to 1854 indicates that ideas continued to circulate in Russia during the reign of Nicholas I, even if the Tsar remained unmoved by most of them. Similarly, the number of university students in Russia doubled between 1836 and 1848. This was mainly due to the government's desire to educate an administrative élite, but inevitably a proportion of this group would learn to think for themselves. Indeed, one of the most important developments of Nicholas' later years was the emergence of a group identified as the 'enlightened bureaucrats'. These younger officials emerged from the education system into official positions, fully aware of some of the weaknesses of the Russian system. They were eager to remedy them if their political masters would permit it. The Milyutin brothers, Dmitri and Nikolai, fit into this category. They found influential **patrons** in such major political figures as Count Lev Perovski, the Minister of Internal Affairs, and Nicholas' younger son, the Grand Duke Constantine Nikolaevich.

The greatest weakness of such thinkers was that they had no alternative to Tsarist autocracy, but merely sought to give it a more humane, or a more efficient form. They were powerless as long as the Tsar refused to entertain their arguments. Nicholas steadfastly refused to do so, not because he rejected change, but because he remained extremely wary about the means of change. As the historian David Saunders (1992) concludes, 'the Tsar knew that changes had to be undertaken, but was determined not to allow them to be promoted by any movement or group beyond the control of the government. He believed that reform could be achieved by the government acting alone.' Nevertheless, the last years of Nicholas I's reign remained unpromising for the westernisers. The European revolutions of 1848–49 destroyed any positive elements that remained in the Tsar's **paternalism** and he reacted sternly against any hint of liberalism within Russia. The campaign against any freedom of thought or expression was typified by the formation of the Buturlin Committee to supervise and regulate the work of the existing censors, and by the attack (April 1849) upon the intellectual circle of M.V. Petrashevsky. This circle was influenced by the works of the French socialists, and included in its ranks the young writer Feodor Dostoevsky. With the appointment of a new Minister of Education, Platon Shirinsky-Shikhmatov, school fees were duly raised, the number of university students was reduced (from 4,600 in 1848 to 3,600 in 1854), and the study of such 'dangerous' subjects as philosophy and European constitutional law was suppressed.

2.2 Was serfdom a source of strength or of weakness for the Russian state and the Russian economy?

What was serfdom?

While intellectuals debated in St Petersburg and Moscow, and while ministers issued decrees, the social and economic life of the Empire centred overwhelmingly upon the vast Russian countryside. The population of the Russian Empire in 1858 was 74 million, of whom nearly 85% worked on the land. Of these peasants, some 22.5 million were serfs; that is, they were the personal property of the landowners for whom they worked and on whose estates they lived. In addition, over 19 million were 'state peasants', tied to lands owned by the Crown. The authority of these owners, sometimes delegated to the elders of the peasant commune (the *mir*), was almost absolute. It extended over the allocation of land, labour dues, taxes and corporal punishment, to the actual sale of the serf to a new master.

The institution of serfdom constituted the most difficult domestic problem facing the government, just as it had for more than a century. The moral objections to such a system had been recognised, but swept under the carpet for more than half a century before the Crimean War. 'There is no doubt,' Nicholas told his Council of State in 1842, 'that serfdom in its present situation in our country is an evil, palpable and obvious to all, but to attack it now would be something still more harmful.' Under Nicholas I, legislation did away with some of the most inhuman aspects of the institution:

● forbidding the splitting up of families by the sale of individuals (1833)

● banning the auctioning of serfs (1841).

Such tentative reforms did little to still the peasant discontent that had been a constant feature of Russian politics for a century. There were 712 outbreaks of revolt between 1826 and 1854, half of them between 1844 and 1854. In addition to these issues of social stability, there were also increasing economic arguments in some well-informed quarters for the abolition of serfdom. As the rural population increased, and as agricultural practices in Russia slipped further behind those in western Europe, serfdom made less and less economic sense. Serf labour found it increasingly difficult to produce enough grain both to feed the local population and to provide a surplus for the landowner to put on the market. Many landowners found their debts mounting, to such an extent that, by 1860, 60% of private serfs had in fact been mortgaged to the state. Yet two compelling reasons stood out against the abolition of serfdom. One was that the monarchy scarcely dared to challenge the vast vested interest of the nobility and landowners, whose financial and social status depended upon the number of 'souls' that they owned. The other was that the monarchy itself derived great benefit, not only as the owner of the 'state peasants', but also from the role played by the landowners in the maintenance of local order and stability.

Serfdom and industrial backwardness

While slavophiles stressed the importance of serfdom in the preservation of political and social stability, westernisers emphasised its role as a brake upon Russia's economic development. Essentially, although not exclusively a rural institution, serfdom placed severe restrictions upon the development in Russia of an urban middle class, and of an urban workforce. In 1833 the total urban population was about two million. Even then, most towns were market and administrative, rather than industrial,

1. What powers did Russian landowners have over their serfs?

2. Why has serfdom usually been regarded as a force that held back economic growth in Russia?

centres. Russia lacked the basis for any serious industrial development on the scale of western Europe. The Soviet historian P.A. Khromov estimated that only 67,000 people were employed in textile manufacture in 1830, and only 20,000 in the iron and steel industries. Russia's cotton industry in 1843 had only 350,000 mechanised spindles, compared with 3.5 million in France and 11 million in Britain. Its share of world iron production dropped, as the industry developed faster abroad, from 12% in 1830 to 4% in 1859. The classic indication of Russia's industrial backwardness was the slow growth of its railways. The first, a short line for the use of the Imperial family from St Petersburg to the summer residence at Tsarskoe Selo, was built in 1837. The first train did not run between St Petersburg and Moscow until 1851.

2.3 What were the domestic political implications of Russia's defeat in the Crimea?

Allied troops landed on Russian soil at Eupatoria (14 September 1854) and within two weeks had laid siege to Sevastopol, Russia's major naval base on the Black Sea. The year-long siege showed both facets of the Russian military machine. The gallantry of the common soldiers defied all attempts to take the town, but weaknesses of strategy and supply contributed to the defeat of a number of relief operations, at Balaclava (October 1854), at Inkerman (November 1854) and at the Chornaya (August 1855). The fall of Sevastopol in September 1855 fulfilled the main objectives of the British and the French and paved the way for a peace settlement.

A superficial consideration of the peace terms concluded in Paris in 1856 suggests that Russia escaped lightly. Despite the neutralisation of the Black Sea and the loss of its influence over the Romanian principalities, Russia was never threatened with the destruction of its 'great power' status – as France had been in 1815. The nature and causes of its defeat, however, had more serious implications for the Tsarist regime. Russia's vast military strength had proved to be an illusion. Partly because of the need to maintain forces on other frontiers, but largely because of the lack of a modern system of communications, Russia was never able to muster in the Crimea more than 60,000 of its one million soldiers. Worse still, Russian industry proved largely incapable of equipping these troops properly. It could provide no more than one musket for every two men at the start of the war. It could equip only 4% of Russian troops with the newer, long-range percussion rifle, when 33% of French troops and 50% of British troops used this weapon. The implications of such failures can hardly be exaggerated. The strongest justification for autocracy, and the most persuasive argument of the slavophiles, was that the existing system guaranteed Russian stability and greatness. So its failure seemed to call into question the very bases of Russian politics and society. The defeat in the Crimea appeared to justify the crushing verdict delivered by the government censor A.V. Nikitenko: 'the main shortcoming of the reign of Nikolai Pavlovich [Tsar Nicholas I] consisted in the fact that it was all a mistake'.

In the aftermath of the defeat, one of the major preoccupations of the Tsar's government was with the state of the Russian army. Various examples of incompetence on the part of the British and French commanders could not hide the fact that they commanded superior armies, which were better equipped and more effectively organised. Bravely as Russia's serf soldiers had fought, it was clear that they could not be relied upon as the basis of an effective, modern army. Above all, the Crimean War demonstrated to the Russians the advantages of a western-style army in which soldiers served for a relatively short period, before returning to

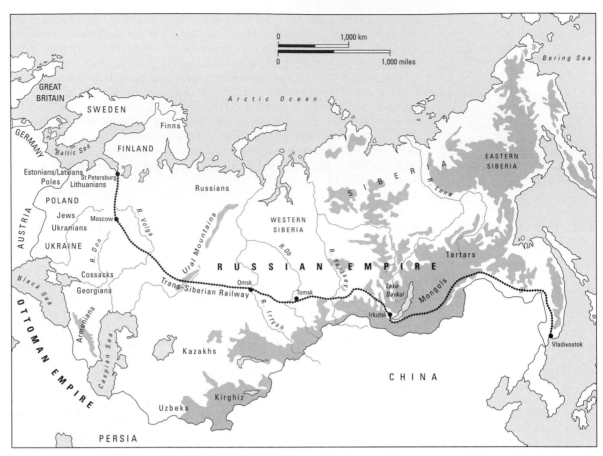

The Russian Empire and its
nationalities, 1914 – showing the
Trans-Siberian railway

1. What weaknesses were revealed by Russia's defeat in the Crimean War?

2. Why did Alexander II decide to adopt a programme of reforming measures at the end of the Crimean War?

civilian life as members of a trained military reserve. Serfdom made it impossible to implement such a system in Russia, for the traditional practice had been to free serf soldiers at the end of their marathon, 25-year stint of military service. To continue such a practice after a shorter term of service would mean the liberation of large numbers of serfs by instalments. To return men to serfdom at the end of their period of military service would mean a steady accumulation in the provinces of discontented serfs with military training. In this respect, as in many others, the Crimean War reinforced the arguments of those who saw the abolition of serfdom as an inevitable preliminary to other forms of reform and modernisation within Russia.

2.4 How effective were the measures taken from 1861 to emancipate the Russian serfs?

The process of emancipation

In the midst of the crisis of the Crimean War Tsar Nicholas I died (2 March 1855), apologising to his son for the state in which he left the empire.

Alexander II came to the throne at the age of 36, the undisputed heir, and far better prepared and trained for the succession than his father had been. It was never the intention of the new Tsar to depart from the principles of autocracy. Yet he was less of a disciplinarian than his father, more open to the arguments of others, and was convinced, by the experience of the war and by the more liberal group of ministers that he chose to consult, that fundamental changes had to be made.

The new Tsar became responsible for the introduction of the most spectacular social reform of the 19th century. Speaking to the nobility of Moscow in April 1856, and referring both to the Crimean War and to renewed peasant disturbances, Alexander said that 'the existing order of serfdom cannot remain unchanged. It is better to abolish serfdom from above than to wait for the time when it will begin to abolish itself from below.' The early months of Alexander's reign saw an unparalleled degree of discussion in intellectual, noble and administrative circles, and an unusual consensus in favour of change. The peasantry, too, was in a state of unusual agitation. Under these pressures, Alexander may appear less as a far-sighted reformer than as a dutiful ruler forced to confront challenges of great complexity.

The lapse of five years between Alexander's Moscow speech and the Edict of Emancipation of February 1861 (see panel on page 50) reflected the difficulty of the task that the Tsar had undertaken. It also provides some important clues to the forces that shaped the final Edict. Undoubtedly there were those within the government who worked for far-reaching reform that would help to reshape Russian society. Even if, as historian David Saunders concludes in *Russia in the Age of Reaction and Reform, 1801–1881* (published in 1992), 'none of the enlightened bureaucrats of the reign of Alexander II was a social revolutionary, all of them sought greater social fluidity. Like the Tsar, they were determined to maintain order, but they were also anxious to discover new sources of energy.' Few of the 232,000 serf owners were sufficiently scared to co-operate unreservedly with the Tsar. Only the Lithuanian nobility accepted his invitation to submit plans for emancipation in their region. The greatest problem was land. Land could only be granted

Women barge haulers in Russia

The terms of the Edict of Emancipation

The Edict of Emancipation was issued on 19 February 1861 and constituted a fundamental break with Russia's past.

- The serfs were granted their personal freedom over a period of two years.

- They now possessed the same legal freedoms enjoyed by other Russians, such as the freedom to own land, to marry without interference, and to use the law courts.

- The freed peasants were granted ownership of the houses in which they lived, and the plots around those houses, which they had previously worked.

- The Edict confirmed the landlords' legal ownership of the land on their estates, but provided (from 1863 onwards) for the purchase of some of that land by the peasants. Maximum and minimum prices were laid down based upon the productivity of the land in different regions, but the precise details were to be negotiated between peasant and landlord.

- The government was to compensate landlords for land transferred to the peasantry, paying them the purchase price in the form of government bonds.

- To recoup its losses, the government charged the peasants 'redemption dues' in the form of regular repayments over a period of 49 years.

- The same terms applied to state peasants, although in their case the period of transition to freedom was five years.

- Domestic serfs who had not previously worked the land did not receive land under the terms of the Edict.

to the peasants at the expense of the landlords, and such a step would come dangerously close to accepting the radical doctrine that the land truly belonged to those who worked it. To liberate the serfs without land, on the other hand, would merely have served to create a vast and dangerous mass of destitute third-class citizens. So difficult was it for the Russian landowners to grasp this that it required a direct order from the Tsar, the Nazimov Rescript (November 1857), to make it clear to them that the serfs were to receive land along with their personal liberty.

How great a reform was the emancipation?

No European government in the 19th century broke with its social and economic past so emphatically as Russia did in 1861. Yet, the political system that initiated these reforms, supposedly to strengthen its own position, had collapsed within 60 years of their introduction. It is hardly surprising that historians have found it difficult to agree about the success of the emancipation. Many have felt constrained to dismiss it as a fraud, and to show the Tsar embarking on a course of false liberalism, only to recoil from the true implications of his actions. The historian Hugh Seton-Watson, in *The Russian Empire, 1801–1917* (1988), makes a valuable comparison when he set the Tsar's reforms alongside the emancipation of the black American slaves at the same time. He stresses that the American reform was carried out less peacefully and was far less successful in guaranteeing the personal freedom of those that it supposedly liberated. A more recent authority on the Russian peasantry, David Moon (*The Russian Peasantry 1600–1930*, published in 1999) echoes this judgement, adding that the guarantee of land was a major benefit that was not shared by the American slaves. David Christian, in his book *Imperial and Soviet Russia* (1997), supports such views by emphasising that the emancipation of the serfs was in fact wholly successful in achieving its immediate objectives. 'The peasant disturbances which had continued for so long, like approaching thunder, died away to a distant rumble for 40 years after 1862. The government had succeeded in the complex task of abolishing serfdom without provoking an immediate rebellion. That was a considerable achievement.'

Much depends upon the criteria that one uses to evaluate the emancipation. If one judges it in terms of rights and liberties, it is difficult to remain unimpressed, for the legal status of some 40 million Russians was transformed at a stroke. If one considers, as most of the peasants probably did, the impact of the reform upon the wealth and the living standards of the former serfs, the short-term effects do not appear so positive. Although the reform ended an era of Russian social history, its immediate impact was lessened by a host of practical problems in its implementation. Above all, it could not be implemented in the localities without the co-operation of the landlords, and was thus often applied in ways that served their interests. The process was always slow and the land settlement made upon the ex-serfs was usually unsatisfactory. The areas granted were often too small, resulting in an average holding of about nine acres (four hectares), and the landlords rarely hesitated to compensate themselves for the loss of free serf labour by inflating the estimated value of the land. Many peasants found themselves saddled with **redemption payments** far greater than the actual productive value of the land that they farmed. David Moon estimates that peasants may have been overcharged by as much as 20% in the more fertile 'black earth' regions, and by as much as 90% in less productive regions. Besides, many peasants were convinced that the land was really theirs in the first place, and thus greatly resented the purchase by redemption payments of their own 'property'. Lastly, although freed from the landowner, the peasant often remained bound to the *mir*, which continued to exercise many restrictions upon travel and freedom of enterprise.

In the shorter run, too, emancipation did not seem to solve the problem of industrial backwardness. The inadequacy of peasant land holdings ruled out the rapid rise of a prosperous class of peasant consumers. As late as 1878 it was estimated that only 50% of the peasantry farmed allotments large enough for the production of surplus goods. This proportion failed to increase largely because of a dramatic 50% rise in the rural population of Russia between 1860 and 1897. Nor did the government's reforms help to create a landowning class with the funds for substantial agricultural or industrial investment. The majority of the landowners before emancipation were so deeply in debt that it has been estimated that 248 million of the 543 million roubles paid to them by the government by 1871 was used to pay off existing debts and mortgages.

Why did the emancipation of the serfs entail a further programme of reforms?

In some respects, the landowning nobility found it harder than the serfs did to adjust to the new economic world created by the emancipation. Many simply abandoned that world by selling their land-holdings. Thus, whereas in 1862 the nobility owned 94.8 million hectares of land in

Redemption payments: The sums of money which peasants paid every year to the government to purchase the land they had been granted in 1861.

1. What did the Russian serfs gain by the Edict of Emancipation?

2. Why did it take so long after the Crimean War to complete the legislation for the emancipation of the Russian serfs?

3. Did the emancipation of the Russian serfs accomplish what it set out to achieve?

Russia, their landed property in 1911 amounted to only 46.9 million hectares. It could be argued that, by undermining the landed interests, and the role of the nobility in local government, the emancipation struck a serious blow at the effectiveness of Tsarist government. It was inevitable, therefore, that emancipation should be followed by a wider programme of reforms aimed at repairing the damage that had been done in this respect.

The zemstva

This wider programme also owed much to the liberal thinking of those who now surrounded the Tsar. Particularly notable was a series of proposals put forward by the nobility of Tver province. The essentially liberal nature of these proposals is illustrated by the fact that they included the suggestion of a national, elected assembly to advise the Tsar. Although this notion was rejected out of hand, what Alexander accepted certainly constituted a substantial step in the direction of liberal local government. An Imperial decree of 1864 established a series of local governmental assemblies known as *zemstva*. Potentially such elected assemblies, supplemented from 1870 by similar urban assemblies, were as radical a measure in an autocracy as the emancipation of serfs itself. It is clear, however, that Alexander saw them as props for the autocracy, rather than as a step away from the traditional system of government. Thus the hopes of Russian liberals were dashed almost before they were raised. Both the system of voting and their established local reputations made it easy for the conservative nobility to dominate these assemblies, and at provincial level they occupied 74% of all *zemstvo* seats in 1865–67. Furthermore, when *zemstvo* representatives had the audacity to suggest that delegates from each assembly should gather to form a central, national body, they were sharply reminded by the Tsar of the limitations upon their powers. At this point, Alexander stood at the crossroads between autocracy and liberal reform. Having whetted the appetite for the latter, he remained committed to the former.

Legal, military and educational reforms

The emancipation of the serfs also required substantial reform of the Russian legal system, now that the summary justice of the landlord could no longer be so easily applied in the localities. From 1865 onwards measures were introduced to ensure that:

● legal proceedings were conducted in public;

● they were uniform for all classes of society;

● a jury system prevailed for the trial of all charges;

● judges were independent of the government.

Although the government retained the power to impose **martial law** in emergencies, and did so to a wide degree during the terrorist crisis of the 1870s, these were remarkable reforms. They ensured that, in Seton-Watson's words, 'the court-room was the one place in Russia where real freedom of speech prevailed'.

If all these reforms were directly or indirectly a response to the military disasters of the Crimea, then it was only logical that the Russian military establishment should also be re-examined. Army life had traditionally reflected the state of Russian society, with privileges for the noble officers and savage penalties for the peasant soldiers. The task of bringing greater equity and efficiency into this system fell to the Minister of War, Dmitri Milyutin. He was perhaps the leading liberal figure in Russia in the 1860s, and was hailed by Florinsky and other Russian historians as one of the few outstanding statesmen of imperial Russia. During his tenure of office

Zemstva (singular *zemstvo*): Elected local government institutions in rural areas, established in 1864, whose functions included the administration of primary education, public health, poor relief, local industry and the maintenance of the highways.

Martial law: Military law when applied to civilians. Normal civil rights are suspended, allowing the government to arrest individuals and detain them without trial. Suspects could be tried by military court (without a jury) and given the death penalty if found guilty.

1. What further reforms did Alexander II carry out with the emancipation of serfs?

2. To what extent were Alexander II's reforms in the 1860s motivated by a desire for a more modern state and society in Russia, and to what extent did they bring about such results?

3. How profound, and how effective, were the great reforms of the 1860s in Russia?

Milyutin reduced the term of service in the army from the 'life sentence' of 25 years to a period of six years. He also introduced universal military service (1874) to which all males were now liable at 20 years of age, without the loopholes that had frequently allowed the nobility and richer classes to escape the obligation to serve their country. The abolition of more brutal forms of punishment, and of military service as a form of punishment for criminal offences, went far to humanise conditions in the Russian army. A further victim of Milyutin's reforms were the 'military colonies' to which the sons of long-term recruits had been sent to be trained as the next generation of soldiers.

Lastly, education, always an accurate barometer of the philosophy of Russian governments, was liberalised. The Minister of Education, A.S. Norov, reversed most of the repressive measures of the previous reign. The numbers of university students were allowed to rise (1855) and lectures were permitted once again on European government (1857) and on philosophy (1860). A new University Statute (1863) gave the universities more autonomy in the conduct of their affairs than at any previous point in their history.

Source-based questions: The impact of emancipation

SOURCE A

The Tsar outlines his expectations of the emancipated peasants

The serfs will receive in time the full rights of free rural inhabitants. At the same time, and with the consent of the nobility, they may acquire in full ownership the arable lands and other properties which are allotted them for permanent use.

And now We confidently expect that the freed serfs will appreciate and recognise the considerable sacrifices which the nobility has made on their behalf. They should understand that by acquiring property and greater freedom, they have an obligation to society and to themselves to live up to the letter of the new law. Abundance is acquired only through hard work, wise use of strength and resources, strict economy, and above all, through an honest God-fearing life. And now, Orthodox people, make the sign of the cross, and join with Us to invoke God's blessing upon your free labour.

Part of the Emancipation Edict, 1861

SOURCE B

A British traveller and journalist comments upon the economic impact of emancipation upon the Russian peasants

If the serfs had a great many ill-defined obligations to fulfil [before emancipation], they had, on the other hand, a good many ill-defined privileges. They grazed their cattle during part of the year on the manor lands; they received firewood, and occasionally logs for repairing their huts; and in times of famine they could look to their master for support. All this has now come to an end. Their burdens and their privileges have been swept away together, and been replaced by clearly-defined, unbending legal relations. They now have to pay the market price for every stick of firewood that they burn, and for every acre of land on which they graze their cattle. If a cow dies, or a horse is stolen, the owner can no longer go to the proprietor in the hope of receiving a present.

From a contemporary account written by Sir Donald McKenzie

Source-based questions: The impact of emancipation

SOURCE C

A radical landowner describes the peasants' response to emancipation on one of his estates

I was in Nikolskoye in August 1861, and again in the summer of 1862, and I was struck by the quiet, intelligent way in which the peasants had accepted the new conditions. They knew perfectly well how difficult it would be to pay the redemption tax for the land, which was in reality an indemnity to the nobles in place of the obligations of serfdom. But they so much valued the abolition of their personal enslavement that they accepted the ruinous charges – not without murmuring, but as a hard necessity – the moment that personal freedom was obtained.

Peter Kropotkin, Memoirs of Prince Kropotkin *(published in 1930)*

(a) Study Source C.

From this Source and your own knowledge, explain the reference to 'the redemption tax for the land'. [20 marks]

(b) Study Sources C and D.

To what extent do the figures in Source D confirm the impression stated in Source C that the emancipated peasants would find it difficult to pay the redemption dues imposed upon them? [40 marks]

(c) Study all of the Sources.

Using all of these Sources and your own knowledge, examine the view that the Russian peasantry lost more than they gained through the Edict of Emancipation. [60 marks]

SOURCE D

Statistics for the repayment of redemption dues in different regions of Russia
(The table covers the years 1876–80.)

	Sums due*	Arrears*	Arrears as % of sums due
Northern provinces	8,527	3,968	46
Baltic provinces	1,686	161	10
North-western provinces	11,999	2,646	22
South-western provinces	12,928	1,125	9
Industrial regions	24,344	5,402	22
Central black-soil provinces	40,574	6,443	15
Eastern provinces	22,220	7,975	36
Southern provinces	9,329	3,128	33
Ukraine	11,408	1,021	9

*(thousands of roubles)

Taken from: E. Wilmot, The Great Powers 1814–1914

OCR 2582

2.5 To what extent does Alexander II deserve the title of 'Tsar Liberator'?
A CASE STUDY IN HISTORICAL INTERPRETATION

There can be no doubt that Alexander II bore direct responsibility for the great reforms that occurred in Russia during his reign. One of the peculiarities of Russian government, as we have seen, was the fact that all executive power lay in the hands of the Tsar, and that there were simply no means by which political initiatives could be implemented without his authority. Whatever pressures might be generated by economic or social forces, only the Tsar could trigger change. Reform, therefore, took place in the 1860s for two reasons. While the impact of defeat in the Crimean War was an extremely important factor, nothing could have been achieved in Russia without a new ruler whose response to that defeat was to listen to reformers. The accession of Alexander II raised great hopes for an end to blank and sterile reaction, and the first actions of the new Tsar seemed to justify those hopes. Political prisoners were released, censorship was relaxed, tax arrears were cancelled, and some of the liberties of Poland and of the Catholic Church were restored.

Yet it is impossible to view Alexander II as a liberal in any real sense. Coming to the throne at the age of 36, he was less of a soldier and less of a disciplinarian than his father. Also he was made more aware by the Crimean War of the faults in the social and governmental systems of Russia. Yet his reforms were motivated by a desire to strengthen autocracy rather than to replace it. Those historians who have denied Alexander credit as a great reformer have often done so on the grounds that at the end of his reign, 'the concept of the state embodied in the person of the autocrat was in no way altered' (the words of W. Bruce Lincoln in *The Great Reforms, Autocracy, Bureaucracy and the Politics of Change in Imperial Russia*, 1990).

What then were Alexander's motives? Did he act predominantly in the interests of the traditional political establishment? Russian Marxist historians insisted that the Tsar was motivated by the desire to benefit his noble supporters rather than the serfs, and that emancipation was mainly a means of putting money in the pockets of a regenerated land-owning class. Others have emphasised other motives, equally beneficial to the establishment. Dmitri Milyutin, one of the most prominent of Alexander's reforming ministers, consistently stressed the beneficial impact that emancipation would have upon the army, perhaps because he felt that this was the kind of argument to which his master would be most susceptible.

Machiavellian: A term describing a form of political activity which is guided by cynical self-interest and advantage, rather than by any form of abstract principle. The term derives from the 15th-century Italian, Niccolo Machiavelli, who was an advocate of such political activity.

Anarchist: One who believes in 'anarchy', or the absence of government. This philosophy believes that society should be self-ordering, and should not be directed by orders and sanctions decreed by a central government.

This is probably unfair to Alexander, for there is little in his life to suggest that he was cynical or **Machiavellian**. Most historians agree that he did not have the mental agility to operate in that way, and none suggests that the reforms of the 1860s sprang from Alexander's superior political vision. He was not a clever man, and was not at ease in the company of clever people. As a contemporary cruelly noted, 'when the Emperor talks to an intellectual he has the appearance of someone with rheumatism who is standing in a draught'. The most satisfactory explanation may be to view Alexander's reforms as arising from the specific strengths and weaknesses in his personality. The **anarchist** Pyotr Kropotkin, who served at court before embracing radical politics, observed that the Tsar was a complex and confusing man:

'Two different men lived in him, both strongly developed, struggling with each other. He was possessed of a calm, reasoned courage in the face of a real danger, but he lived in constant fear of dangers that existed only in his brain.'

Such a personality is well reflected in the inconsistent nature of the Tsar's reforms. As an autocrat, he recognised it as his duty to rectify a system that had manifestly failed Russia in the Crimea, yet he was uncertain how best to go about the task, and apprehensive whenever he glimpsed the more radical implications of his policy. A number of recent historians have based their evaluation of Alexander's policies upon this sort of contradiction. Perhaps David Saunders, in *Russia in the Age of Reaction and Reform, 1801–1881* (1992), captures the Tsar's state of mind most accurately when he concludes that 'the laws which freed the serfs emerged from a process that the Tsar barely understood and over which he had only partial control.'

A little earlier, both W.E. Mosse in *Alexander II and the Modernisation of Russia* (1958) and Hugh Seton-Watson in *The Russian Empire, 1801–1917* (1967) had seen Alexander II confronting the choice between autocracy and modern constitutional development. They saw him refusing to abandon the former, and failing mainly because he sought to reach an unrealistic compromise between the two.

In the final analysis, however, it seems harsh and unhistorical to criticise Alexander II because he could not or would not turn his back on the philosophy of his ancestors. Even if they did not solve the problems that they addressed as thoroughly as the government anticipated, and even if they did not quite address the right problems, the reforms of the 1860s were staggering in the breadth of their conception and extremely far-reaching in their impact. Historian David Saunders grudgingly accepts this in his judgement that although they were 'conceptually limited, poorly executed, incomplete, unsustained and insecure, the measures enacted by Alexander II nevertheless transformed the Russian Empire'. Some might prefer this more charitable judgement made at the time by the Russian liberal, B.N. Chicherin:

> 'Alexander was called upon to execute one of the hardest tasks that can confront an autocratic ruler: to completely remodel the enormous state which had been entrusted to his care, to abolish an age-old order founded on slavery, to replace it with civil decency and freedom, to put a repressed and humiliated society on its feet and to give it the chance to flex its muscles.'

The kind of political and social liberation that emerged from all this may not have been the kind that either Alexander or Chicherin envisaged, but it was liberation nevertheless.

1. Why have historians found it difficult to decide how much credit should be given to Alexander II for his domestic reforms?

2. Comment upon the view that Alexander II's reputation as a reformer has been greatly exaggerated.

2.6 How seriously was the Tsarist regime threatened by the opposition that arose during Alexander II's reign?

Instead of strengthening and stabilising the regime, and earning universal acclaim for the 'Tsar Liberator', the reforms of Alexander II drew fierce criticism from many sections of the political spectrum. The Tsar suffered the classic fate of those who try to enjoy the best of both worlds, and became trapped in a cross-fire of criticism. Conservatives resented the loss of influence and privilege, while liberals became frustrated at the Tsar's refusal to take his reforms to their logical conclusion. Many governmental departments became the scenes of bitter personal and political rivalries, such as that between Dmitri Milyutin and P.A. Shuvalov at the Ministry of War. The disappointment of conservatives and liberals alike, however, was muted by the need to rally against the more radical and revolutionary forms of opposition that developed as Alexander's reign progressed. This opposition was, in some cases, fuelled by a fierce ideological hatred of the regime, and encouraged by the freer political atmosphere created by the Tsar's reforms.

The Polish Revolt

The bitter disillusion that Alexander II felt at the reaction to his role as the 'Tsar Liberator' was quickly fuelled by the revolt of his Polish subjects in 1863. Poland had fallen under the power of the Tsars as a result of a compromise made at the Congress of Vienna in 1815. Rather than allow the former independent kingdom of Poland to become part of the Russian Empire, the allies had preserved its nominal independence. However, they had allowed the Tsar to rule as King of Poland, thus effectively combining the two states. This special status, and the vague paternalism of Alexander II, had combined to give Poland rather freer institutions than existed anywhere else in eastern Europe. Poland enjoyed a constitution, a parliament, and the use of Polish as an official language. The first Polish rebellion (1831) had resulted, however, in the suppression of many of these liberties by Nicholas I. Poland nevertheless, like other parts of the Empire, had reason to greet the accession of Alexander II with optimism. The Tsar's gestures included the filling of the vacant Catholic archbishopric of Warsaw (1856) and the formation of a new Agricultural Society (1857) to promote new techniques of cultivation.

On the surface it appeared that the question of land reform was the most pressing of Poland's problems. Unlike the rest of the Empire, however, the demand for such reform was directly connected with the desire to re-establish Polish nationhood, a desire to which no Tsar could agree. It was nationalist demonstrations in Warsaw that set off a train of events in February 1861. In April the Agricultural Society was dissolved on account of its links with nationalist unrest, and in the demonstrations which resulted up to 200 were killed. In May 1862 the Tsar's brother, Constantine, a liberal by reputation, was appointed **viceroy** in an attempt to defuse the situation. He came close to assassination in his first month in office. Further concessions were proposed, including the emancipation of Polish Jews and the opening of a university in Warsaw. A proposal for the conscription of Poles into the Russian army nullified any calming effect, and armed insurrection broke out in January 1863.

Viceroy: Governor of a country or province acting in the name and the authority of the ruler (i.e. a vice-king; from 'roi', French for king.)

This was largely a rural rebellion, with the majority of the landowners more or less favourable to the rebels, but with the attitude of the peasants remaining highly **ambiguous**. It took nearly a year to control and was not properly over until August 1864. In that year **agrarian** reform was at last carried through, giving **freehold tenure** to 700,000 peasant families, without any redemption payments to the Russian government. Although some historians have seen the reform mainly as an attempt to separate the peasants from the nationalist landowners, it was consistent with Russia's relatively liberal treatment of Poland between 1855 and 1863. The Tsar saw its general failure as further evidence of ingratitude and of the futility of conciliatory gestures. In reality, the failure demonstrated the impossibility of reconciling such beliefs as Polish nationalism with Tsarist autocracy. Henceforth Russian policy towards all the nationalities of the Empire would be one of Russification (see later section).

Ambiguous: Unclear or confusing because it can be understood in more than one way.

Agrarian: Relating to the ownership and use of land, especially farmland.

Freehold tenure: Originally a form of ownership which required a tenant to give only services and obligations as were worthy of a freeman (i.e. not a serf).

The growth of radical opposition; from Herzen to Nihilism

The most important names on the Russian left in the 1850s and 1860s were those of Alexander Herzen, Nikolai Chernyshevsky and Dmitri Pisarev. Herzen, already an exile from Russia by 1848, had moderated his stance as a result of the revolutions of that year and became more willing to accept and applaud reforms, even if they came from the Tsarist government. His journal *The Bell* (*Kolokol*) was published from London and regularly reached influential persons in Russia by unofficial channels.

Chernyshevsky took the opposite path. Originally part of the literary radicalism of the 1850s and enthusiastic about the emancipation of the serfs, he came to realise that further worthwhile reform was impossible without a fundamental alteration of Russia's political and economic bases. Thus he stands on the threshold of a new generation of Russian radicals who paved the way for the philosophy of the 1917 revolution. Chernyshevsky himself was largely dismayed by the increasing use of violence by those who claimed to be his disciples. Nevertheless his novel

What is to be Done? (1862) inspired the next generation and provided the title for one of Vladimir Lenin's most important works.

To a limited extent, Pisarev supplied an answer to Chernyshevsky's famous question. Rejecting revolution as impossible for the present, Pisarev advocated a thorough examination and revision of the moral and material bases of society, in order to provide a better future basis for justice and equality. His followers were advised not to 'accept any single principle on trust, however much respect surrounds that principle'. From this desire to accept nothing of the existing society without question, the novelist Ivan Turgenev (1818–1883) named this philosophy '**nihilism**'. Pisarev liked the term and accepted it.

'**Nihilism**': Belief that rejects all political or religious authority and current ideas, in favour of the individual. From the Latin *nihil* – nothing.

Populism: Belief that all political activities or ideas are based on the interests and opinions of the ordinary people.

Populism

Many young radicals were reluctant, however, to wait for revolution – as Pisarev thought necessary. Broadly, they envisaged two possible answers to the question 'What is to be done?' One of these was **populism**, a movement that dominated Russian radicalism in the mid-1870s. The founders of populism, Nikolai Mikhailovsky and Pyotr Lavrov, viewed the Russian peasantry not as a force of great revolutionary potential, but as one which needed thorough re-education. Thus in 1874–75 some 3,000 young radicals invaded the countryside to open the eyes of the population to their plight and to the sources of their salvation. This movement – 'To the People' (*v narod*) – was a depressing failure. Hugh Seton-Watson notes that 'some peasants listened with sympathy, many were hostile, and most understood hardly anything of what they heard'. Over 1,600 of these populists (*narodniki*) were arrested between 1873 and 1877, often handed over to the police by the very peasants, blindly loyal to the Tsar, that they sought to help. Learning from these failures, a breakaway group calling itself 'Land and Liberty' (*zemlya i volya*) made some progress in the following years with a revised plan that involved living with the peasants for longer periods to understand their mentality better. Perhaps the most lasting legacy of populism was the foundation by members of 'Land and Liberty' of the first unions for Russian industrial workers in Odessa (1875) and in St Petersburg (1878).

The rise of terrorism

For those with equal conviction but less patience, the more attractive alternative was conspiracy and terrorism. The first attempt on the life of the Tsar occurred in 1866 when a student named Karakozov shot at him in the streets of St Petersburg. The best claim to be the founder of the conspiratorial activism that triumphed in 1917 belongs, however, to Sergei Nechayev. Apparently motivated by a mixture of idealism and ambition, he created a complex system of revolutionary cells up to 1869 by ruthless methods. This system collapsed when internal arguments caused him to murder a fellow conspirator, and the trial that followed gave full publicity to Nechayev's unsavoury aims and methods. The real 'heyday' of terrorism as a means towards political change followed a split in 1879 in the ranks of 'Land and Liberty'. One wing, led by Georgi Plekhanov and Pavel Axelrod and calling itself the 'Black Partition' (*chorny peredyel*), favoured further peaceful work among the peasants. The other, 'The People's Will' (*narodnaya volya*), advocated violence as the trigger to general revolution. Although other government officials were among their early victims, their chief target was always the Tsar himself. Within a period of a year, Alexander survived: another attempt to shoot him (April 1879); an attempt to dynamite the royal train, which blew up the wrong train (December 1879); and an explosion in the banqueting hall of the Winter Palace (February 1880).

Although by the end of 1880 the radical opposition within Russia had achieved nothing of worth, many of the methods and preconceptions of the 1917 revolutionaries can be seen in the process of formation during the reign of Alexander II.

Conclusion

No member of the Tsar's government could have remained complacent about the wave of violence that Russia experienced between 1878 and 1881. When the Tsar himself was added to the list of the terrorists' high-ranking victims in March 1881, it became clear that the revolutionaries could indeed strike successfully at any member of the political establishment. The Tsar's assassination made it equally clear, however, that they could neither destroy nor replace that establishment. It remained as true as ever that social and political power lay in the hands of a narrow élite, and that no political change could be brought about by anyone outside that group.

Alexander II's son succeeded peacefully to the throne and pursued policies that crippled the revolutionary organisations for a generation. Terrorism failed to destroy Tsarist government for at least three reasons.

1. By its very nature – intellectual, exclusive and secretive – it could not mobilise the considerable resources of peasant discontent that constituted the major threat to political stability.

2. It offered no practical alternative to the existing government, no regime that could replace Tsarism if indeed it did collapse under the weight of the terrorist assault.

3. It failed because conservative interests in Russia were far too strong. If those interests were less automatically sympathetic to the Tsar than they had been before the emancipation, they could never support the violent and ill-defined alternatives that the terrorists seemed to propose. If the Tsar's government could, in future, form a stronger alliance with those conservative interests, it was highly likely to survive the onslaught of the radicals.

1. What alternatives to Tsarist rule were offered by Russian radicals during the reign of Alexander II?

2. How effective were opposition groups (both Russian and non-Russian) within the Tsarist Empire in the period 1855–1890?

2.7 Why did Tsarist policy change between reform and reaction in the years 1879–1894?

Alexander II's return to reformism

By the beginning of the 1880s Alexander II was, according to the historian W.E. Mosse, 'isolated from the Russian people, unpopular with the educated public, and cut off from the bulk of society and the Court. His fate had become a matter of indifference to the majority of his subjects.' This was largely the result of his indecision between the two policies of reform and conservatism. Even at Court he was increasingly unpopular because of his embarrassing passion for a much younger woman, the Princess Dolgoruky. She bore Alexander a number of illegitimate children, and he married her with indecent haste upon the death of his first wife in 1880. The passion contributed directly to the further confusion of imperial policy in the last years of Alexander's life. While the Tsar grew more and more disillusioned and conservative, the princess remained the friend and patron of a number of liberal politicians. Thus the government's reaction to the violence of 1879–80 was a mixture once again of repression and concession. Executions took place, but the major political event was the appointment as Minister of the Interior of Mikhail Loris-Melikov, a member of Princess Dolgoruky's liberal circle.

The Loris-Melikov ministry

Despite the misgivings of the Tsar, within a year (January 1880 – February 1881) Mikhail Loris-Melikov had abolished the Third Section, replaced the reactionary Dmitri Tolstoy at the Ministry of Education, and steered Alexander II to the verge of the most fundamental reform of his reign. By February 1881 plans were prepared for the calling of a national assembly, partly of nominated members, but partly of elected representatives of the *zemstva* and the town councils. It was thus a limited body, but a logical and significant step away from total autocracy. The Soviet historian P.A. Zaionchkovsky, in *The Abolition of Serfdom in Russia* (1978), conceded that 'in the conditions of an increasingly complex situation it might have been the beginning of the establishment of a parliamentary system in Russia'. The Tsar had just given his personal approval to the measure when the luck of the 'People's Will' changed, and on 13 March Alexander was killed by the second of two bombs thrown at his sledge in a St Petersburg street.

Alexander III and the return to reaction

The heir to the throne was Alexander's son by his first marriage, who succeeded as Alexander III. The death of his father did not initiate the conservatism of the son, but the horrible circumstances of that death, and the cruel irony of its timing confirmed it most strongly. The greatest influence on the views of the new Tsar was that of his former tutor and trusted adviser, Konstantin Pobedonostsev. Pobedonostsev's sympathies

> **Mikhail Loris-Melikov (1825–1888)**
> Originally a professional soldier with distinguished service in the Russo–Turkish War. Military governor of the Ukraine (1879), where he gained a reputation for firm administration based upon the rule of law. Appointed Minister of the Interior (1880–81) through the patronage of Princess Dolgoruky. Retired from public life after the assassination of Alexander II.

Members of the 'People's Will' movement on their way to be executed for the assassination of Alexander II.

Alexander III (1845–1894)
Married Dagmar (1847–1928), daughter of Cristina IX of Denmark and sister to Queen Alexandra of Britain, in 1866. Succeeded his father, Alexander II, as Tsar of Russia in 1881. Pursued a reactionary policy, persecuting Jews and promoting Russification (see page 62). In foreign affairs, Alexander III followed a policy of peace and non-intervention.

Konstantin Pobedonostsev (1827–1907)
Leading theorist of Russian conservatism and autocracy. Professor of Civil Law at Moscow University (1858). Procurator of the Holy Synod (leading government official responsible for the Orthodox Church) from 1880. Tutor to the sons of Alexander II and Alexander III.

Democracy: A system of government in which people choose their rulers by voting for them in elections.

Universal manhood suffrage: The right that all males over the age of consent have to vote, in order to choose a government or a national leader.

Pan-slavism: A political doctrine which advocated the political union of all Slav peoples. This was widely viewed in other European states as a cover for the political ambitions of Russia.

lay with autocracy against **democracy**, with Orthodoxy against all other sects, and with Russians against all other nationalities of the Empire. For him **universal manhood suffrage** was 'a fatal error'; the principle of the sovereignty of the people was 'among the falsest of political principles'; parliamentarianism was the 'triumph of egoism'; the freedom of the press was 'one of the falsest institutions of our time'. As Pobedonostsev also served the new Tsar as tutor to his eldest son, Nicholas, his influence stretched unbroken from 1881 to the turmoil of 1905.

Although of less direct influence, another major 'prophet' of the new temper in Russian thought, and especially in Russian foreign policy, was Nikolai Danilyevski. In his most influential work, *Russia and Europe* (1871), he rejected the enthusiasm of westernisers for Western philosophy and technology. Instead he argued that as Russia had a quite different history and development, it should ignore the Roman and Germanic worlds and concentrate upon its Slav nature and inheritance. This view differed from the old slavophile notions in that it was more aggressive, preaching a union of all Slav nations under Russian leadership stretching from the Baltic to the Adriatic. This regeneration of aggressive, autocratic nationalism was called '**pan-slavism**'.

Conservative legislation, 1882–1892

It was scarcely surprising that the bomb that killed Alexander II also destroyed the careers of his more liberal ministers and the policies that they advocated. Mikhail Loris-Melikov was replaced as Minister of the Interior by Nikolai Ignatiev, who later gave way to Dmitri Tolstoy. At the heart of the new policy lay the hope of restoring the Russian nobility to the position of strength and influence that it had held before the emancipation. In July 1889 the office of justice of the peace was abolished in local government and a new office, that of Land Commandant (*zemsky nachalnik*), was created. The essential qualification for this office was membership of the nobility, and the holder enjoyed senior administrative and judicial power in the locality, over-riding the authority of the *zemstva*. The partly elective *zemstvo* became a prime target for the reactionaries. Laws of 1890 and 1892 revised the franchise in rural and urban assembly elections to restrict the popular vote. In St Petersburg the combined effect of the laws was to reduce the electorate from 21,000 to 7,000. Furthermore, the assemblies frequently found their most apolitical proposals obstructed and undermined by the objections of a government fundamentally opposed to the principle of elected assemblies.

Russian intellectual life in a period of reaction

Illiteracy: State of not knowing how to read or write.

1. By what means did Alexander III attempt to stabilise government and society in Russia?

2. In what respects did Alexander III's response to Russia's internal problems differ from that of Alexander II?

Naturally, educational policy also felt the impact of this revision of government thinking. The Minister of Education from 1882 to 1898 was I.V. Delyanov, a man essentially opposed to any 'dangerous' advance in education such as had been proposed in the reforms of Alexander II. Policies towards the universities included the limitation of their administrative autonomy (1884) and the raising of their tuition fees (1887). The raising of fees was also a useful method in primary and secondary education to ensure that the 'children of coachmen, servants, cooks, washerwomen, small shop-keepers, and persons of similar type should not be brought out of the social environment to which they belong'. Only parish elementary schools, safely under the influence of the local clergy, were allowed any real expansion during Delyanov's term of office. Consequently, by the end of the 19th century Russia presented an educational paradox. Its élite contained some of the most famous figures of the century: scientists (Pavlov, Mendeleiev), writers (Chekhov, Tolstoy, Gorky), historians (Klyuchevsky), musicians (Tchaikovsky) of world repute. Yet this brilliant surface of Russian society hid a substructure of rottenness and ignorance represented as late as 1897 by a staggering **illiteracy** rate of 79%.

2.8 Why and with what consequences did the Tsarist government pursue a policy of Russification?

What was Russification?

Referring specifically to Poland, the conservative writer Y.F. Samarin described nationalism in the 1860s as 'a dissolving agent as dangerous, in a different way, as the propaganda of Herzen'. The policy of Russification – that is, of attempting to suppress the local characteristics of various regions within the Empire, and to spread Russian characteristics to all the Tsar's subjects – was not an invention of Alexander III but was applied by his government with fresh vigour and determination.

The Russians were, in fact, in a minority within their vast empire, 55% of the total population belonging to other racial groups. The largest groups within the population were as shown in the table below.

Nationalities of the Russian Empire (according to the 1897 census)	
Great Russians	55.6 million
Ukrainians	22.4 million
Poles	7.9 million
White Russians	5.8 million
Jews	5.2 million
Tartars	3.4 million
Germans	1.8 million
Armenians	1.2 million
Georgians	0.8 million

'Disloyal' subjects

The total population of the Empire at that time was a little over 125 million. The historian J.N. Westwood has divided these racial groups into three main political categories, which he labels 'mainly loyal, mainly disloyal and the Jews'. In the 'disloyal' category it was the Poles who, after the nationalist outbreak of 1863, could most expect to be the subject of rigid Russification. The measures taken by the subsequent governors of defeated Poland, F.F. Berg (1864–1874) and P. Kotzebue (1874–1880), set the pattern for future policies elsewhere. The property of the Polish Roman Catholic Church was seized (1864) and Warsaw's university was closed (1869). Russian replaced Polish as the administrative language, and more and more Russians replaced Poles in the ranks of the administrators. Similar measures were adopted in the Ukraine, but as there had been no comparable nationalist demonstrations there, they were mainly directed against a small group of radical intellectuals. The other main components of the 'disloyal' group were the Tartars and the Georgians. In both cases the Orthodox Church played a leading role on behalf of the state. By 1900, it had converted an estimated 100,000 Tartars. It also fought a fierce conflict, that went as far as political assassination in some cases, against the Georgian Church. Islam and the Georgian Church both put up fierce resistance, however, and the problem of separatism among the Tartars and the Georgians was still very much alive in 1917.

Finland, Armenia and the Baltic provinces

Much more damaging to the autocracy of the Tsar were the counter-productive efforts to 'russify' areas whose loyalty had not previously been in doubt. Into this category fell Finland, Armenia, and the Baltic territories of Estonia, Latvia and Lithuania. The Finns had been especially well treated under Alexander II and the use of their own language had not merely been permitted, but was actually made compulsory in local administration. Now disadvantageous trade tariffs were imposed. Russians and their language intruded more and more into Finnish government. The process culminated in 1903 with the suspension of the Finnish constitution, a direct breach of the terms upon which Alexander I had absorbed Finland into the Empire in 1815. The Armenians, too, were essentially well disposed to Russian rule, for it had done much to protect them from their major enemy, the Turks. Their reward, under Alexander III, included the confiscation of the property of the Armenian Church and the suppression of the Armenian language. Similarly, the Baltic Germans had enjoyed privileged treatment at the hands of the two previous Tsars, who employed several high-ranking ministers from that region. Now, in contrast, the reconstruction of the great Orthodox cathedral in Riga (1885) and the increasing proportion of Russian students at the famous University of Dorpat (now officially known by its Russian name of Yuriev) constituted symbols of uncompromising Russian domination.

The Jews

The 'pale': The area in western Russia to which Jewish settlement was legally restricted. It had been established in the 18th century by Catherine the Great. Also known as the Pale of Settlement.

Anti-semitism: Hostility to Jews or the Jewish religion (Judaism).

Propaganda: Information, often exaggerated or false, which is spread by political parties in order to influence the attitudes of the general public.

Pogroms: Violent attacks upon Jewish communities and upon their property.

Characteristically, the worst blows fell upon the Empire's long-suffering Jewish population. Even the Jews had experienced some improvement in their conditions under the previous reign. Recruitment of Jews into the army had been put on the same basis as that of Russians and the laws forbidding settlement beyond the '**pale**' had been relaxed. Now, however, Alexander III's regime combined the 'official' religious **anti-semitism** of the Orthodox Church with the crude, popular hostility that arose from the Jews' economic role. Associating the Jews in **propaganda** with the Polish rebellion and with the assassination of Alexander II, but also happy to use them as scapegoats on which popular discontent could be vented, the Russian government permitted and even encouraged **pogroms**. An estimated 215 such disturbances occurred between the first outbreaks in May 1881, in the Ukraine, and the 'great' pogrom of 1905 in Odessa in which nearly 500 Jews were killed. As Minister of the Interior, Dmitri

Zionist movement: A form of Jewish nationalism, which advocated the establishment of a Jewish state.

1. Which groups within the Russian Empire felt the impact of the policy of 'Russification'?

2. Did the policy of 'Russification' do more to strengthen or to undermine the authority of the Tsarist regime?

Tolstoy was less keen to countenance such actions, not out of any concern for the victims, but out of a general uneasiness at the idea of civil disorder. In their place he instituted a series of less violent, but equally discriminatory, measures. No new Jewish settlers were allowed in rural areas, even within the Pale of Settlement. Jews were forbidden to trade on Christian holy days. As they already closed on Jewish holy days, this made it hard for them to compete with non-Jewish rivals. Strict quotas for Jews were set in schools and universities, which never rose above 10% even within the Pale. In 1886 in Kiev, and in 1891 in Moscow, all 'illegal' Jews were expelled, which provided a useful opportunity to harass 'legal' settlers as well.

Apart from emigration, two other courses presented themselves for Jews who had had enough of such treatment. One was militant nationalism, which took the form of the **Zionist movement**. The other was revolutionary agitation as seen in the formation of the Bund (1897), a Jewish socialist organisation which was to play an important part in the development of revolutionary socialism in Russia in the next two decades. Thus, in the long run, the policy of Russification proved to be an even more dangerous 'dissolving agent' than the nationalism that it originally set out to combat.

Source-based questions: Alexander II as 'Tsar Liberator'

SOURCE A

How successful were the 'Great Reforms'? The government had undertaken a radical overhaul of the social, economic, political and military structure of the Russian Empire. This was a complex and potentially dangerous task. So the best measure of the government's success is the fact that it survived the reforms unscathed, unlike the reforming government of Mikhail Gorbachev 130 years later. However, the reforms left serious problems for future governments. In trying to balance the interests of nobles and peasants, while retaining its own powers intact, it alienated both the major classes of traditional Russian society. For Russian society as a whole, the reforms marked an important, though painful, step towards modernity.

From Imperial And Soviet Russia *by David Christian (1997)*

SOURCE B

Norman Pereira [in *Tsar Liberator: Alexander II of Russia,* 1983] has drawn attention to four points between 1856 and 1861 at which, but for the Tsar, forward movement might have come to an end. First, the publication of the Nazimov Rescript at the end of 1857. Second, on a tour of the provinces in 1858 Alexander made plain to backwoodsmen that their committees should take a positive view of the reform. Third, when the provincial gentry still did not take up the cause of reform with alacrity, the Tsar bypassed them by appointing a majority of reformers to the Editing Commissions. Fourth, when draft legislation came before the Main Committee in 1860 Alexander stood firm for change in the face of obdurate resistance from aristocrats.

The determination that Alexander showed as a war leader undoubtedly resurfaced on a number of occasions, but explaining the emancipation of the serfs by depicting him as a latter-day Peter the Great oversimplifies Russian politics between 1855 and 1861. It was 1859 before Alexander gave reformers their head by granting them control of the Editing Commissions, and by then the prestige of the throne would have suffered far more from the abandonment of emancipation than from allowing a version of it to go through. The laws which freed the serfs emerged from a process which the Tsar barely understood and over which he had only partial control. The complicated narrative of the emancipation cannot be reduced to the proposition that Alexander sensed he was facing a crisis and believed that attack was the best form of defence.

Adapted from Russia In The Age Of Reaction And Reform, 1801–1881 *by David Saunders (1992)*

Source-based questions: Alexander II as 'Tsar Liberator'

SOURCE C

Alexander was subject to liberal influence in his closest circle. His brother Constantine had become an ardent supporter of emancipation. Possibly even more effective was his aunt, the Grand Duchess Elena Pavlovna. Her magnificent work for the wounded during the [Crimean] war had increased her standing in Russian public life. Her palace was a centre of liberal ideas, and she herself gave her protection to liberal officials such as N.A. Milyutin. The influence of these two members of the Imperial family is not so well documented as that of the officials who carried out the reform, but it cannot be doubted that it was very great. The experts prepared the legislation, but it was largely due to the advice of Constantine and Elena that the Tsar was induced to force it through.

From The Russian Empire 1801–1917
by H. Seton-Watson (1967)

SOURCE D

Certainly Dmitri Milyutin's path would have been much easier if Alexander II had been a more consistent and a wiser man. The War Minister's own conviction that the autocracy was the absolutely necessary agent for Russia's progress was based upon the principle that the autocrat was the partner of the Russian people and, standing above the interests of all groups, he was able to ensure the organic unity and the equality of the entire nation. Quite on the contrary, Alexander allowed himself to be insulated from reality by [conservative politicians such as] Shuvalov, and in these years often served the interests of the gentry. Certainly one gets the impression that Alexander was never really a reformer except for his conviction that the serfs had to be freed and that all subsequent reforms were dictated by circumstances.

From Dmitri Milyutin, *by Forrestt A. Miller (1968)*

(a) *Use Source A and your own knowledge.*

Explain what is meant by the statement that, in the Edict of Emancipation, Alexander II tried to 'balance the interests of nobles and peasants'.

[5 marks]

(b) *Compare Sources B and C and use your own knowledge.*

How fully do Sources B and C explain the political problems that faced Alexander II as he sought to emancipate the serfs? *[10 marks]*

(c) *Use Sources A, B, C and D and your own knowledge.*

With reference to these sources and your own knowledge assess the view that 'the reputation of Tsar Alexander II as a reformer has been considerably exaggerated'. *[15 marks]*

AQA Unit 4

2.9 To what extent was Russia's international prestige restored in the reigns of Alexander II and Alexander III?

Just as the end of the Crimean War signalled a turnabout in domestic policy, with substantial reform taking the place of rigid reaction, so a change of equal proportions came about in the foreign policy of the Russian Empire. The defeat, the evidence that it provided of Russian weakness, and the preoccupation of the government with domestic changes all limited the one-time 'gendarme of Europe' to a largely passive role from 1856 until the early 1870s.

Russia's relations with the western European powers

Nevertheless, Russian diplomacy did have one major aim during this period, and it was an uncharacteristic one. The defeat in the Crimea had

Black Sea clauses: Those clauses of the Treaty of Paris (1856) which forbade Russia to maintain a fleet in the Black Sea. Their aim was to limit Russian influence in the affairs of the Ottoman Empire.

Alexander Gorchakov (1798–1883)
Ambassador to Vienna (1854); Foreign Minister (1856–82); Tsar Alexander II's chief minister from 1866. Gorchakov was the chief Russian representative at the Congress of Berlin (1878).

transformed the greatest conservative power into a revisionist power, eager especially to revise the **Black Sea clauses** of the Treaty of Paris that placed such humiliating restrictions upon its naval power in that area. Between 1856 and 1863, the best means of achieving this end seemed to be to cultivate the friendship of France with a view to gaining a diplomatic agreement at some future date. Thus at the Paris conference (May–August 1858), which effectively formed Wallachia and Moldavia into an independent Romanian state, Russia eagerly co-operated with the French 'line'. In March 1859 Russia even agreed to remain neutral in the event of French action in northern Italy, in stark contrast to its attitude to disturbances in the Austrian Empire ten years earlier. By the early 1860s, however, the understanding with France was on its last legs. French interference with the 'legitimate' regimes of Italy was more than Alexander II could tolerate, and the breaking point came with evidence of French sympathy for the liberalism and the Catholicism of the Polish revolt in 1863.

For ten years from 1863 Russia was almost wholly isolated in European diplomacy. The sole exception was its relations with Prussia, which were improved by General von Alvensleben's mission in that year to offer aid against the Polish rebels. If it was beneath the Tsar's dignity to use the forces of a lesser power to control his own subjects, the friendly gesture was appreciated in contrast to French, Austrian and British hostility. Russia extended benevolent neutrality towards Prussia in its anti-Austrian adventures of the 1860s. Indirectly, Prussia's adventures led to the achievement of Russia's main ambition. With Europe preoccupied with the Franco–Prussian War from July 1870, Russia sensed that this was the moment to renounce the Black Sea clauses. The foreign minister, Alexander Gorchakov, informed the powers in November 1870 that Russia no longer accepted this section of the Treaty of Paris. Although the action was condemned at a conference in London two months later, the powers were forced to recognise that no retaliatory action could be taken.

In the longer term, the main result of the Franco–Prussian War was that Russian diplomacy had to come to terms with the new German Empire, a more powerful neighbour than it had ever known before. The conclusion of the League of the Three Emperors between the rulers of Russia, Austria and Germany gave a false air of stability to the politics of eastern Europe. Behind its facade, a series of factors kept alive Russian resentment at rising German power and at Austrian pretensions in the Balkans. The settlement engineered by Bismarck at the Congress of Berlin, which limited Russia's gains from its conflict with Turkey, struck a serious blow to Russo–German relations. Shortly afterwards, in 1883, Romania formally associated itself by treaty with Germany and Austria. It was a measure of the tension between Russia and Austria that Alexander III refused (April 1887) to renew the Three Emperors' Alliance, as the League had become in 1881. The Reinsurance Treaty concluded with Germany alone two months later (see Chapter 3) maintained the facade of stability. It was a dubious piece of opportunism, partially at odds with Germany's undertakings towards Austria, but it provided an encouraging indication of Germany's desire to maintain good relations with Russia. Thus the refusal of a new German Kaiser to renew the Reinsurance Treaty in 1890 seemed to be a specific rejection of Russian friendship, and starkly renewed Russia's international isolation.

The result was a revolution in Russian diplomacy whereby it turned towards republican France, different in every important aspect of recent history and culture, but well placed strategically to the west of Germany. The process by which France and Russia passed from financial to military understanding is described in Chapter 6. Russian approaches to Germany in 1893 have suggested to some historians that the exercise may have been planned as a lever to force Germany into warmer relations. There being no

Entente: Friendly agreement
between two or more countries.

favourable reaction from Berlin, an *entente* with France became the main-stay of Russian foreign policy, for want of anything better.

Russian foreign policy in the Balkans

The renunciation of the Black Sea clauses gave Russian policy in the Balkans a new lease of life. This policy continued to be motivated by the familiar blend of concern for national security and the search for prestige in the face of domestic difficulties. This time, extra spice was added by the doctrine of pan-slavism, although Gorchakov's policies in south-east Europe in the early 1870s were conducted more in a spirit of cautious realism. In 1875, however, a series of revolts began among the Serbian and Bosnian subjects of the Turkish Sultan, which set off much pan-Slav agitation for the dispatch of Russian aid. The brutal suppression of the associated Bulgarian revolt in 1876 further excited both Russian feelings and foreign suspicion. Gorchakov quietened Austrian misgivings by an agreement concluded at Reichstadt (July 1876) whereby Russia would regain southern Bessarabia, lost in 1856, and Austria would receive part of Bosnia and Herzegovina in the event of a successful Russian clash with Turkey. Such a war was brought closer, as it had been in 1854, by the inflexible attitude of Turkey. In the first three months of 1877 the Sultan rejected proposals for reform from several of the major European powers, and Russia formally opened hostilities in April of that year.

The Russo–Turkish War was fought on two fronts. In the Caucasus the Turks used the tactic of stirring up local rebellion to keep the Russian forces occupied, and not until late in the year did the latter gain decisive successes. They won a major victory at Aladja Dag in October and captured their main objective, the fortified town of Kars, in November. In the European theatre the initial Russian advance was checked at Plevna, which held out from mid-July until early December 1877. The fall of that town paved the way to a victory that Russia sealed at the decisive battles of Plovdiv and Shipka (January 1878). It had been, as Lionel Kochan notes in *The Making of Modern Russia* (1997), 'a war between the one-eyed and the blind – so many errors of strategy and judgement were committed'.

Nevertheless, Russia briefly enjoyed considerable gains. The Treaty of San Stefano (3 March 1878) ignored its Reichstadt undertakings to Austria and created a large Bulgarian state, wide open to Russian influence. The diplomatic hostility caused by such success, however, forced Russia to agree to a revision of the treaty formulated at an international congress in Berlin. The size of Bulgaria, and thereby the extent of Russia's influence in the Balkans, was reduced. Russia was, nevertheless, left with southern Bessarabia and the Caucasian gains of Kars and Batum. It was a clever settlement, but left pan-Slavs and Russian nationalists bitterly offended, especially with Bismarck whose 'honest broker' stance seemed to them to hide anti-Russian and pro-Austrian intent. In the development of Russian relations with its central European neighbours, the events of 1877–78 foreshadowed greater conflicts to come.

Russian penetration into Asia

If the aftermath of the Crimean War left Russia badly placed to take initiatives in European affairs for several decades, no such restrictions existed along its eastern frontiers. These regions are described by Lionel Kochan as 'the happy hunting-grounds of Russian imperialist adventurers, dubious carpetbaggers, and pseudo-viceroys'. Some voices were indeed raised in St Petersburg against the risks and costs of such uncontrolled expansion, but it proved impossible to check the ambitions of provincial generals and their followers. Motivated by **chauvinism**, by a sense of a civilising

Chauvinism: Aggressive and unreasoning patriotism.

1. *What were the main aims of Russian foreign policy during the reigns of Alexander II and Alexander III?*

2. *Compare the degrees of success achieved by Russian foreign policy in this period in:*

(a) eastern Europe

(b) Asia.

mission, and often by pure greed, Russian control spread steadily into the Caucasus region, across the Caspian Sea, and into Siberia. Turkestan was penetrated by stages that included the taking of Tashkent (1865) and of Samarkand (1868), and the Khanate of Bokhara acknowledged indirect Russian rule in 1875. The integration of these areas into the Empire was slowly effected by settlement by Russian peasants, especially during Pyotr Stolypin's period as premier, and by a number of ambitious communications projects, such as the construction of the Transcaspian railway in 1886–98.

The spreading of Russian influence in Siberia was a longer process. Substantial areas of territory were gained from China by the treaties of Aigun (1858) and Peking (1860), and the foundation of Vladivostok in 1861, on the shores of the Pacific itself, completed the most successful example of European territorial expansion in the 19th century. Here, too, great feats of communication were undertaken. Work on the Trans-Siberian railway – one of the great engineering feats of the 19th century – was begun in 1892.

2.10 What was the extent of Russia's economic development during the reigns of Alexander II and Alexander III?

Stimuli to industrial expansion

Although the great social reforms of the 1860s did not immediately stimulate general economic growth, the reigns of Alexander II and Alexander III did form a period of overall industrial development. This development was, however, uneven and fluctuating. In the 1860s the difficulties of the emancipation of the serfs, and the 'cotton famine' that resulted from the civil war in America, were retarding factors. In the 1870s, however, the Russian economy benefited from the increase in railway building and from the policy of low **tariffs**, which facilitated the import of raw materials. The economic historian, A. Gerschenkron, has written of the former that Russia's 'greatest industrial upswing came when the railway building of the state assumed unprecedented proportions and became the main lever of the rapid industrialisation policy'. The development of Russia's railways was not only substantial in quantity, but also showed much greater economic logic than the earlier lines had displayed. Lines such as those between Moscow and Kursk, Moscow and Voronezh and Moscow and Nizhni Novgorod linked major areas of industrial production to important markets. Similarly, the Kursk–Odessa and Kharkov–Rostov lines linked these towns, and areas of agricultural production, to the ports of the Black Sea. The Batum–Baku railway (1883) linked the Caspian with the Black Sea, and served greatly to increase oil production. The steady growth of the Russian railway system is illustrated in the table opposite.

Following the initial policy of freer trade, tariffs began to rise steadily as it became clear that low tariffs were causing a heavy influx of foreign goods and creating a substantial trade imbalance. The first major increase came in 1877, followed by further acts in 1881 and 1882. The policy culminated in the great protective tariffs of 1891, which especially affected iron, industrial machinery and raw cotton. The beneficial effect on domestic coal and pig-iron production is shown in the table.

In judging the level of Russia's industrial development one certainly sees the truth of the judgement that Lenin passed in 1899: 'If we compare the present rapidity of development with that which could be achieved with the modern level of technique and culture, the present rate of development of

Tariffs: Customs duties; applied to goods coming into the country as a percentage of the value of the goods.

The development of Russia's railway system	
Date	**Kilometres constructed**
1861–1865	443 km
1866–1870	1,378 km
1871–1875	1,660 km
1876–1880	767 km
1881–1885	632 km
1886–1890	914 km

Russian coal and pig-iron production

Date	Coal (poods)	Pig-iron (poods)
1860–1864	21.8 million	18.1 million
1865–1869	28.4 million	18.9 million
1870–1874	61.9 million	22.9 million
1875–1879	131.3 million	25.9 million
1880–1884	225.4 million	29.2 million
1885–1889	302.6 million	37.6 million
1890–1894	434.3 million	66.9 million
1895–1899	673.3 million	120.9 million

1 pood = 36 lb = 16.3 kg

From M. E. Falkus, *Industrialisation of Russia* (1972)

1. In what respects was the Russian economy modernised during this period?

2. How convincing is the argument that the reigns of Alexander II and Alexander III saw the emergence of Russia as an industrial power?

capitalism in Russia really must be considered slow.' In the longer term, one can also appreciate the judgement passed by a later economic historian, W.O. Henderson. 'If the Russian economy was still backward in some respects, it was also true that vigorous state action, foreign capital and foreign machinery had given Russia a powerful impetus on the road to industrialisation.'

Source-based questions: Terrorism and the State

SOURCE 1

The purpose of terroristic activities is to break the spell of government power, to give constant proof of the possibility of fighting against the government, to strengthen in this way the revolutionary spirit of the people and its faith in the success of its cause, and, finally, to create organisations suited and accustomed to combat.

(From the manifesto of the 'People's Will' organisation, January 1880)

SOURCE 2

Recent events have clearly demonstrated the existence in Russia of a gang of evildoers which, if not very numerous, nonetheless persists in its criminal delusions and strives to undermine all the foundations of the structure of state and society. Not confining themselves to propagating, by means of secretly printed and circulated proclamations, the most revolting doctrines aimed at subverting religious teaching, family ties, and property rights, these scoundrels have made repeated attempts on the lives of the highest dignitaries of the Empire.

(From the Tsar's emergency decree, April 1879)

(a) Study Sources 1 and 2.

How far do these two sources agree in their view of the threat that terrorism posed to the Russian state? [5 marks]

(b) What means did radicals use in the 1870s, other than terrorism, to bring about social and political change in Russia? [7 marks]

(c) What, if anything, had Russian radicals achieved up to the death of Alexander III in 1894? Explain your answer. [18 marks]

Edexcel, Unit 3

Germany under Bismarck, 1871–1890

Key Issues

- *What problems confronted Bismarck in the government of united Germany, and how effectively did he deal with them?*

- *In what ways did Germany's economy and society develop in the years after unification?*

- *How well did the diplomacy of the united Reich serve the interests of Germany and of European peace?*

3.1 What were the main political features of the Bismarckian state?

3.2 Why, and with what results, did Bismarck enter into an electoral alliance with the National Liberals between 1871 and 1878?

3.3 What was the purpose of the *Kulturkampf*, and to what extent was it achieved?

3.4 Why did Bismarck abandon the National Liberals for a more conservative stance in 1878?

3.5 How successful was Bismarck in his attempt to combat socialism?

3.6 Historical interpretation: To what extent was Bismarck responsible for the authoritarianism and intolerance of the German state in the early 20th century?

3.7 To what extent did Bismarck's foreign policy succeed in defending German interests in the 1870s?

3.8 Did Bismarck's alliance with Austria after 1878 represent the failure of his diplomatic system?

3.9 Why did Bismarck launch a German colonial policy in his last years in power?

3.10 What was the impact of unification upon German economic development?

Framework of Events

1871	(January) Proclamation of German Empire
	(May) Franco–Prussian War concluded by Treaty of Frankfurt
1872	(June) Expulsion of Jesuits from Germany as part of *Kulturkampf*
	(September) Formation of 'League of the Three Emperors'
1874	Introduction of May Laws, limiting the independence of Catholic clergy
1875	(March) Publication of **papal bull** *Quod Nunquam* attacking May Laws
	(April) 'War in Sight' crisis
1878	(June–July) Congress of Berlin resolves the international crisis arising out of the Russo–Turkish War
	(July) Major conservative gains in Reichstag elections at expense of National Liberals
	(October) Introduction of anti-socialist laws
1879	(July) Passage of new tariff laws, introducing economic protectionism
	(October) Conclusion of Dual Alliance between Germany and Austria
1880	Conclusion of revised Three Emperors' Alliance between Germany, Russia and Austria
	Introduction of accident insurance – part of Bismarck's 'state socialism'
1882	Formation of Triple Alliance, involving Germany, Austria and Italy
1883	Introduction of sickness insurance as part of Bismarck's policy of 'state socialism'
1884	Renewal of Three Emperors' Alliance

Papal bull: Decree issued by the Pope.

1885	German East Africa Company created. Annexation by Germany of Tanganyika and Zanzibar
1886	Anglo–German agreement on spheres of influence in East Africa
1887	Conclusion of Reinsurance Treaty between Germany and Russia
1888	(March) Death of Emperor Wilhelm I; succession of Friedrich III
	(June) Death of Friedrich III; succession of Wilhelm II
	(March) Dismissal of Bismarck as Chancellor of Germany.

Overview

I N order to understand the methods by which Otto von Bismarck governed the German Empire between 1871 and 1890, it is necessary to understand the complex origins of that Empire. Important as the personal role of Bismarck was in bringing about German unification, other forces impersonal and perhaps more powerful were also at work. Since the 18th century nationalist theorists had preached that it was Germany's destiny to rise above the selfish interests of individual German princes and to create a united state that might allow Germans at last to play a positive and dominant role in European affairs. Such beliefs had been stimulated by the disturbances of 1848, which seemed to promise the collapse of the old political order in Europe, and by events in Italy in the 1850s, which began to undermine the conservative influence of the Austrian Empire. Alongside such theories, the advance of industrialisation in Germany created economic interests that orthodox politicians found difficult to ignore and impossible to resist. The advantages of easier trade and communications between the states were such that, as early as 1834, a range of north German states had associated themselves in a customs union, the *Zollverein*, that involved a high degree of economic co-operation decades before any political union was envisaged.

Legitimist: A theory of monarchy which considers that each state has a ruler, or ruling family, designated by God as the only 'legitimate' or true ruler. Thus the Hohenzollern family were the 'legitimate' rulers of Prussia.

Junkers: The aristocratic landowners, with extensive estates predominantly in East Prussia, who formed the governing class of the Prussian state.

These forces were confronted by other, more conservative, interests. Austria and Russia had enormous traditional interests to defend in central and eastern Europe. Not only were the rulers of both states dedicated to the defence of **legitimist** interests, including those of the individual German princes, but both governed such a mixture of racial groups that the very existence of their empires was threatened by the principles of nationalism. In Prussia, too, conservative instincts were likely to oppose any attempt to establish a unitary, popular German state. Under Friedrich Wilhelm IV (1840–61), and under his brother and successor Wilhelm I (1861–88), the Prussian monarchy was equally devoted to legitimist principles, and equally hostile to the notion that political power should lie in the hands of the nation. In Prussia's feudal landowning class, the **Junkers**, the kings of Prussia found ample support for such conservative ideas.

Otto Edouard Leopold von Bismarck (1815–1898)
Born in Brandenburg, Bismarck studied law and agriculture before becoming a member of the Prussian parliament in 1847. He was Prime Minister of Prussia (1862–90) and Chancellor of the German Empire (1871–90). He became Prince von Bismarck in 1871. After successfully waging wars with Denmark in 1863–64, he went to war with Austria and its allies (the Seven Weeks' War, 1866). His victory forced the unification of the north German states under his own chancellorship (1867). He was then victorious against France, under the leadership of Napoleon III, in the Franco–Prussian War (1870–71), proclaiming the German Empire and annexing Alsace-Lorraine. His priorities as Chancellor were to preserve Prussian leadership within Germany, and to guarantee German security through alliances with Russia and Austria. He was forced to resign by Wilhelm II on 18 March 1890.

From 1862, Bismarck himself acted as the leading servant of this conservative Prussian monarchy, and as the willing representative of Junker interests. As such, he had little sympathy for the causes of national unity or of liberal reform, yet he was equally hostile to the authority of Austria within the **German Confederation**, and to the claims of the Austrian Emperor to be able to dictate to Prussia over the affairs of Germany. Bismarck's primary aim in the 1860s was to readjust the political balance within Germany, guaranteeing the security of Prussian interests, while controlling those political forces within Prussia that threatened the interests of the governing class. If his aims were essentially conservative, Bismarck's methods were subtle and imaginative. Contemporary diplomatic circumstances in Europe enabled him to isolate and confront Austria, and the promise of significant changes in German politics won the consent of liberals within Prussia and other German states.

German Confederation:
The alliance of German states, under the presidency of the Austrian Emperor, established in 1815 to guarantee the security of its members in the aftermath of the Napoleonic Wars.

How successful was Bismarck in the 1860s? It is quite possible that he had achieved all that he aimed for by 1866. At that stage, he had isolated and defeated Austria, effectively ending its influence over the affairs of northern Germany. It may well be the case that Bismarck visualised the **North German Confederation**, under Prussian leadership, as the ideal outcome of this struggle. Other factors, however, forced him to go further. Unsuccessful in his attempts to appease or to deflect French suspicions over the growth of Prussian influence, Bismarck accepted an unlikely alliance with nationalist enthusiasm in the course of the Franco–Prussian War (1870–71). The most important outcome of the war was the transformation of the wartime coalition of German states into a formal and permanent political union. By 1871, his achievement was not so much that a united German **Reich** emerged from that war, but that it emerged in a form acceptable to the conservative forces that Bismarck represented:

North German Confederation: A revised version of the German Confederation, established as a result of Prussia's victory over Austria in 1866. It comprised those German states north of the river Main, and Prussia was the dominant political influence within the confederation.

Reich: The German state or Empire.

- Austria was excluded.

- The existence and independence of the German princes were maintained to a degree. Indeed, the Imperial authority of the Kaiser was based upon the support and acclamation of the German princes.

- The Imperial constitution guaranteed the political interests of Prussia's governing classes in all important respects.

Inevitably, one of the dominant themes of German domestic politics during the 1870s and the 1880s was the government's attempt to keep political power predominantly in the hands of these traditional, conservative classes. However strong nationalist sympathies may have been in some areas of German politics, Bismarck's domestic policies were directed more by considerations of class struggle. Aware of the potential challenge from middle-class interests and from the increasing political organisation of the working classes, Bismarck worked to ensure that no direct political power fell into the hands of these groups. In this undertaking he was only partly successful. Appearing to work with the National Liberals in the 1870s, Bismarck successfully placed his emphasis upon policies that consolidated the Bismarckian state, rather than any that strengthened the direct political interests of the Liberals. Bismarck's great political re-alignment in 1879, however, represented a shift to a **coalition** in which he was no longer the undisputed senior partner. In a climate of economic recession he could not

Coalition: A government or a parliamentary majority consisting of people from two or more political parties who have decided to work together.

afford to ignore the demand of Junker agriculturalists, and of industrialists, for economic protection. Although it was not wholly distasteful to Bismarck to abandon the Liberals for more conservative allies, the move demonstrated the limits of his success in the long term. While he could control the parliamentary aspirations of the industrial middle classes, he could not ignore their economic power, for that formed a fundamental basis of the power and prosperity of the German state. Able to manipulate the **Reichstag**, but not the economic might of the Ruhr, Bismarck was forced now to seek a path equally acceptable to Junkers and industrialists. In the course of the next three decades, this 'alliance of rye and steel' would lead German policy into paths that Bismarck would never willingly have contemplated. He had indeed ensured that the united Reich would be based upon conservative interests, but not exclusively upon those of the Prussian Junkers.

Bismarck's attitude towards the other major component of German industrialisation – the urban working class – was much clearer. He regarded them as a consistent threat to the aristocratic society, from which he came, and remained unconditionally hostile to their political ambitions. Bismarck was a sufficiently subtle politician, however, to know that such ambitions had to be deflected, rather than suppressed. He therefore pursued a dual policy that sought to obstruct the growth of the leading socialist parties, while introducing a programme of social reforms promoted and funded by the state.

How successful was Bismarck in these domestic policies? To a remarkable extent, he succeeded in preserving the political structures that he valued. At the end of his career, the Prussian monarchy and the army were stronger than they had ever been, and the Junker class continued to dominate the high offices of state. The economic and social structure of Germany, however, had not stood still. German industry had continued to develop, its growth directly stimulated by political unification. Bismarck contributed to this growth by his strategy of coalition, compromise and concession to these economic forces. At his fall from power, he left one of the most modern and dynamic economies in Europe in the hands of rulers and politicians whose attitudes and political priorities were those of the mid-19th century.

The newly unified German state also faced another major challenge. Unification brought about a transformation in the European balance of power. Germany had to confront the mistrust, if not the downright hostility, of states whose interests had been damaged or threatened by this transformation. Although three wars were fought in the process of unification in the 1860s, Bismarck had little to gain from further warfare. Utterly opposed to a *grossdeutsch* union that would bring Austria back into German politics, he had no further territorial ambitions. German diplomacy in the 1870s and 1880s was dominated by the desire to isolate France, the state most likely to challenge the new Germany, and to maintain a system of alliances that would prevent conflict between Austria and Russia. For all his shifts and compromises in the course of two decades, that system remained essentially intact at the end of Bismarck's career. It is tempting to view the fall of Bismarck in 1890 as a key factor in the transformation of European diplomacy from stability and balance to ambition and confrontation.

Reichstag: The parliament of the united German Empire (Reich).

Grossdeutsch ('Great German'): Term used to describe the concept of a united Germany in which all ethnic Germans are included.

1865: Prussia

1871: Territory included in German Empire

1867–71: Limit of North German Confederation

The German Empire functioned as a federation of 25 states (18 lesser states + free cities + Alsace-Lorraine). Each possessed its own representative assembly and was responsible for specific local provisions.

The German Empire in 1871

3.1 What were the main political features of the Bismarckian state?

In theory, the German Empire created in 1871 was a voluntary association of German states, governed by as free a constitution as existed anywhere in Europe. The Empire was a federal state, consisting of four kingdoms (Prussia, Bavaria, Württemberg and Saxony), 18 lesser states, three free cities, and the imperial territory (Reichsland) of Alsace-Lorraine. Each of these, with the exception of Alsace-Lorraine, retained a great deal of its former autonomy in regard to its own domestic administration. Yet Prussia was by far the largest and most powerful of Germany's constituent parts. It comprised over 60% of the area of the Reich (134,000 out of 208,000 square miles) and a similar proportion of its population (24.7 million out of 41 million). It was hardly surprising, therefore, that the power and influence of Prussia lurked behind each article of the German constitution.

The Reichstag

The basis of the Reich's parliamentary constitution was adapted directly from that of the North German Confederation. The Imperial Assembly (Reichstag) was elected by universal manhood suffrage, but was subject to a number of limitations which prevented its growth into a true parliamentary body. It had the power to question the Chancellor (which office fell of course to Bismarck) and to initiate debate upon any point of his policy, but neither he nor any other minister was responsible to the assembly for their actions. The Reichstag had theoretical control over any alteration to the military budget, but largely sacrificed this weapon by agreeing in 1874, mainly through fear of starting a new constitutional conflict, to approve that budget for a period of seven years. It repeated this process in 1881 and 1887. This 'loss of the full right of budget approval', argues historian Hajo Holborn, 'blocked the growth of a parliamentary system in Germany.' Furthermore, the bulk of the remainder of the Reich income, from indirect taxation, posts and from the contributions of member states, lay wholly beyond the control of the Reichstag.

The Bundesrat and the Emperor

Bundesrat: Upper house of the Reichstag which represented the independent interests of the states.

In reality, political power lay outside the Reichstag. In part, it lay with the upper house, the *Bundesrat*, but for the most part it rested with the Prussian hierarchy. The *Bundesrat* had the power to initiate legislation. Also, with the assent of the Emperor, it had the authority to declare war and to settle disputes between states. With the interests of the Reich and of the individual states thus balancing each other out, real power lay with Wilhelm I and his ministers. Wilhelm was by hereditary right German Emperor, with full powers over the appointment and dismissal of ministers, who were responsible only to him. He also had full control over foreign affairs, and had the

Veto (Latin – 'I forbid'): A negative vote exercised constitutionally by an individual, an institution or a state. It has the effect of automatically defeating the motion against which it is cast.

right to the final say in any dispute over the interpretation of the constitution. By virtue of its size, Prussia possessed 17 of the 58 seats in the *Bundesrat* at a time when 14 votes constituted a **veto**. The body therefore served the important dual purpose of maintaining the separate political

**Kaiser Wilhelm I
(1797–1888)**
Saw action in the Napoleonic Wars, and developed a reputation in Prussia as a conservative and militarist. He became regent of Prussia upon the breakdown of his brother, King Friedrich Wilhelm (1858), and succeeded as king upon his brother's death (1861). He appointed Otto von Bismarck as Minister President (1862) to stave off constitutional challenges, and supported his minister through successful wars with Denmark, Austria and France. Upon the formation of the German Reich in 1871, Wilhelm became the first Kaiser (Emperor) of united Germany. He remained a symbol of conservative values, and of the dominance of the Prussian elite within united Germany until his death at the age of 91.

identity of Prussia within the Reich, and of blocking any steps towards a radical, unitary state. Indeed, the balance of forces in the German constitution as a whole indicated clearly that it was designed to block and to prevent any major constitutional change or development in the future.

The Treaty of Frankfurt and the annexation of Alsace-Lorraine

War indemnity: A payment made by the defeated side in order to pay the costs occurred by the victors in the war.

The outcome of the Franco–Prussian War and the ultimate shape of the German Reich were decided simultaneously by the terms of the treaty signed at Frankfurt on 10 May 1871. France was compelled to pay a **war indemnity** of 5 billion francs over a period of three years. It also had to accept substantial territorial losses. German nationalists had claimed Alsace unsuccessfully in 1815, in the 1820s and again in 1848–49, and now that desire was supplemented by power, annexation was perhaps inevitable. 'This territory,' wrote the nationalist historian von Treitschke, 'is ours by right of the sword, and annexation follows from the right of the German nation to prevent the loss of any of its sons.'

Northern and eastern Lorraine, with the great fortress of Metz, also became German territory. There was far less justification for regarding these as German lands, and for many years the standard view on this issue was that Bismarck bowed reluctantly to the pressure of the army, the king and the nationalists. More recent research has suggested that Bismarck may have had some role in the formation of this public mood. His motives, however, are unlikely to have been ideological. On a practical level, historian Gordon Craig points out in *Germany 1866–1945* (published in 1981) that French bitterness was likely to be just as great, whatever the terms of the surrender, and Bismarck himself wrote in similar vein to his ambassadors abroad. 'We cannot look to the French temper for our guarantees. What the French nation will never forgive is their defeat as such. In German hands Strasbourg and Metz will take on a purely defensive character.'

Political parties

Pressure groups: Political organisations who wish to influence political decision making but do not wish to gain political power.

The parties that competed for seats in the Reichstag were very different organisations from their English counterparts. They were predominantly **pressure groups** representing the sectional interests of one part or another of the diverse German nation, and they remained social phenomena rather than instruments for winning the struggle for power.

The Conservatives
On the right wing of the Reichstag stood two major groups, the

Composition of the Reichstag, 1871–1890

	1871	1874	1877	1878	1881	1884	1887	1890
German Conservatives	57	22	40	59	50	78	80	73
Reichspartei	37	33	38	57	28	28	41	20
National Liberals	125	155	141	109	47	51	99	42
Progress Party	46	49	35	26	60	–	–	–
Centre Party	61	91	93	94	100	99	98	106
Social Democrats	2	9	12	9	12	24	11	35
Guelphs	9	4	10	4	10	11	4	11
National groups (Alsatians, Poles, Danes)	14	30	30	30	35	32	29	27

Total seats = 397 (1871: 382)

Ludwig Windthorst (1812–1891)	Wilhelm Liebknecht (1826–1901)	August Bebel (1840–1913)	Ferdinand Lassalle (1825–1864)
Deputy (1849) and Minister of the Interior in Hanover, and hostile to the Prussian annexation of that state. Leader of the Centre Party (*Zentrum*) in the Reichstag after unification, fiercely opposing Bismarck in the course of the *Kulturkampf*.	A socialist, active in 1848, and subsequently in contact (1850) with Karl Marx. One of the founders of the First International (1865) and of the German Social Democractic Party (1869). Deputy in the Reichstag from 1874 to 1900.	Worked with Liebknecht on the foundation of the First International (1865) and of the German Social Democractivc Party. Subsequently, leader of the SPD and a prominent member of the Second International.	Radical socialist, a friend of Karl Marx. Active in the Ruhr in 1848–49 and subsequently founder of the first German trade union.

Kulturkampf: German term meaning 'struggle for civilisation': the clash with the Catholic Church in Germany in the 1870s. For German liberals, the Catholic Church was the 'old enemy'. For Bismarck, it was not so much a struggle between belief and unbelief, more a 'matter of a conflict between monarchy and priesthood. What is as stake is the defence of the state.'

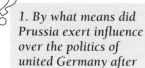

1. *By what means did Prussia exert influence over the politics of united Germany after 1871?*

2. *What different interests were represented by the political groups within the Reichstag between 1871 and 1890?*

3. *How convincing is the claim that 'the constitution of the German Reich in 1871 was one of the most democratic in Europe'?*

Conservatives (from 1876 the 'German Conservatives') and the Imperial Party (*Reichspartei*). The former had its strength in Prussia itself, among Protestant, aristocratic landowners. Concerned at, and sometimes openly hostile towards, Bismarck's flirtations with liberalism and nationalism, it remained a moderate force in the Reichstag, but a major one in the Prussian Landtag, which it dominated through local influence. The *Reichspartei* enjoyed a broader geographical basis of support, among landowners and industrialists alike. Also, its support for the Imperial Chancellor was much more consistent, in admiration of his great achievement in the foundation of the Reich.

The Centre Party

The Centre Party (*Zentrum*), founded in 1870, still tends to be described as the party of Germany's large Roman Catholic minority. In fact it was more than that. Primarily dedicated to the defence of the interests of the Catholic Church, it also attracted others with a partisan objection to the recent work of Bismarck, such as the Protestant 'Guelphs', who were embittered supporters of the deposed King George of Hanover. Particularly strong in Bavaria and in the Rhineland, the Centre Party was led in the Reichstag by a Catholic Hanoverian, Ludwig Windthorst. One of the few great parliamentarians of the 'Bismarck era', greatly respected even by those who loathed his views, Windthorst has been characterised by historian Golo Mann as 'a sly idealist, a devout fox, a man of principles and a very clever politician, dignified and cunning'.

The Liberals

In the 1870s the National Liberals were Bismarck's most enthusiastic supporters in the Reichstag. They were at one with him in their enthusiasm for a centralised state, if increasingly at odds with him in their support for progressive social and constitutional legislation. To their left stood the Progress Party (*Fortschrittpartei*), diminished but unbowed by the liberal split of 1866. They shared the National Liberals' enthusiasm for free trade and the rule of law, but were opposed to the centralism and militarism of the Bismarckian state. In Eugen Richter and Eduard Lasker they had effective parliamentary leaders, the latter so consistent a critic of the Chancellor as to be described by Bismarck as 'even more of a vile louse than Windthorst'.

The Left

German socialism in 1871 was as yet a modest force, based upon Ferdinand Lassalle's General Workers' Association (*Allgemeiner Arbeiterverein*) founded in 1863, and the Social Democratic Workers' Party formed by Wilhelm Liebknecht and August Bebel at Eisenach in Saxony in 1869. Its day was, however, soon to come.

3.2 Why, and with what results, did Bismarck enter into an electoral alliance with the National Liberals between 1871 and 1878?

How much common ground existed between Bismarck and the National Liberals?

The first seven years of Bismarck's government of a united Germany, 1871–78, are frequently described as his 'liberal era'. While Bismarck was by no stretch of the imagination a true liberal, he found it convenient during this period to co-operate in the Reichstag with the National Liberal party. In the first place, they were the dominant party in an assembly where the Chancellor had no party of his own. Secondly, the spirit of conciliation that had motivated the **indemnity of 1866** remained alive. The National Liberals remained broadly sympathetic towards Bismarck as the architect of their major policy aim, national unity. Most important, their immediate aims coincided with Bismarck's in such areas as the consolidation of that national unity and the centralisation of the administration of the Reich.

To conservative critics it often seemed that the alliance with the National Liberals was carrying Bismarck too far to the left. Lothar Gall, in *Bismarck, the White Revolutionary* (1986), describes Bismarck as being 'the stirrup-holder of liberalism'. In fact it is clear that the Chancellor gave his 'supporters' nothing that involved any immediate political power. The Press Law (May 1874) provided little protection for editors against government prosecution. Attempts in the Reichstag to limit the influence of the Junkers in Prussian local government achieved little of practical value. Also, as we have seen, the Reichstag failed to maintain control over the vital area of government military expenditure.

It is equally important to establish, however, that the measures undertaken in 1871–78 should not merely be written off as 'sops' offered by Bismarck to 'fool' the National Liberals and to maintain a convenient political understanding in the short term. The economic and administrative legislation of his 'liberal era' was of the greatest importance in the formation of the German state. It illustrates very clearly the complex relationship between Bismarck and the German liberals. The period produced, in the words of historian Geoff Eley, 'an impressive concentration of forward-looking economic legislation [and] an elaborate framework of capitalist **enabling laws**'. Although Bismarck refused to grant the liberals the kind of political framework that they desired for Germany, the *kleindeutsch* state of 1875 was, in economic terms, very much what liberal thinkers had always envisaged. Only time would tell whether this delicate balance of socio-economic progressiveness and political conservatism could be maintained.

Administrative and financial consolidation

The state created by Bismarck was a curiously disunited entity. It lacked religious unity and unity of economic interests. It contained national minorities with little or no desire to be part of the German Empire. There is thus much truth in the historian A.J.P. Taylor's description of the Reich in 1871 as merely a 'wartime coalition'. Such were the separatist feelings of the states, for instance, that Germany had no national flag until 1892 and no national anthem until after the First World War. For Bismarck, with his desire for closer political control, and for the National Liberals, with their enthusiasm for national unity, it was vital that this situation be improved. The first session of the Reichstag, therefore, saw the passage of over 100 acts to this end. The currencies of the states were unified into a national currency, all tariffs (taxes) on internal trade were abolished, and a uniform

Indemnity of 1866: One of Bismarck's first actions upon coming to office in 1862 was to ignore liberal objections to taxation needed by the state to increase the size of the army. The taxes were levied without parliamentary permission, in defiance of all liberal and constitutional principles. Following his success against Austria in 1866, and the creation of a North German Confederation, Prussian liberals voted to 'pardon' Bismarck for this action. This is widely interpreted as a sacrifice of constitutional principles in the interests of nationalism.

Enabling Laws: Laws which confer the legal freedom to take certain actions, although they do not make these actions obligatory.

Kleindeutsch ('Little German'): Term used to describe the concept of a united Germany (favoured by Prussia) from which Austria is excluded.

Edwin von Manteuffel (1809–1885)
One of the main influences behind Prussian army reform in the early 1860s and active in the wars against Denmark, Austria and France. Commanded army of occupation in France (1871–73). Governor of Alsace-Lorraine (1880–85).

Chlodwig von Hohenlohe (1819–1901)
Prime Minister of Bavaria (1866–70) in which office he supported the idea of German unity under Prussia. German ambassador to Paris (1874–85); Governor-General of Alsace-Lorraine (1885–94); Chancellor of Germany (1894–1900).

Plebiscite: A direct vote of all of the electors of a state to decide a question of public importance. Otherwise known as a referendum.

1. What measures were taken in the 1870s to consolidate the unity of the German state?

2. How accurate is the description of the years 1871–78 as a 'liberal era' in the government of Germany?

body of commercial law was introduced. The Prussian State Bank became the Reichsbank, and Germany adopted the gold standard. Uniformity of legal procedures was achieved in 1877. A national Appeals Court was established by 1879, although the codification of German civil law did not come into effect (January 1900) until long after Bismarck's fall from power.

The problem of the national minorities

After administrative separatism, the second major area of disunity concerned the national minorities within Germany's borders. For nearly 20 years, by a mixture of coercion and conciliation, Bismarck attempted to tie these minorities more closely to the German state, but had no significant degree of success. In Alsace-Lorraine the decision to allow French or pro-French elements to leave the territories resulted in the migration of 400,000 people between 1871 and 1914. The remainder found themselves governed by Prussian civil servants, with the German language imposed in schools and in local administration. From 1874 they were represented in the Reichstag, and the choice of governors for the territories showed some tact and commonsense. Edwin von Manteuffel (18791885) was a humane and conscientious administrator. His successor, Prince Chlodwig von Hohenlohe, was a south German Catholic and had more in common with the people of Alsace than with many Protestant Prussians. The consistency with which the people of Alsace voted for deputies in favour of separation from the Reich showed, however, that such attempts at conciliation were largely unsuccessful.

In the case of the Poles, conciliation was much less in evidence. When the state sought to reduce the influence and independence of the Catholic Church within Germany, Polish clergy in the eastern provinces were particularly hard hit. Their leader, Cardinal Ledochowski, was imprisoned and his office left vacant for 12 years. The use of the Polish language was outlawed in education and in the law courts. State funds were used to finance the purchase of lands in Polish hands for the purpose of settlement by Germans, although the Poles were rather more successful in raising funds for the reverse purpose. It is scarcely surprising that, given these tactics, the Polish problem remained unsolved.

Finally, the problem of the Schleswig Danes was largely ignored. In 1879, on the eve of the Dual Alliance, Austria agreed to allow Germany to abandon the **plebiscite** in North Schleswig promised by the Treaty of Prague in 1866. It took a world war to revise the status of North Schleswig and of Alsace-Lorraine, and to resolve the problems of Germany's Polish subjects.

3.3 What was the purpose of the Kulturkampf, and to what extent was it achieved?

German liberalism and the Catholic Church

The first decade of domestic politics in the German Reich was dominated by the clash with the Catholic Church. It was branded at the time as the 'struggle for civilisation' (*Kulturkampf*). It is difficult for us to grasp today, in a generally more secular age, the feelings aroused by this legal assault upon Germany's substantial Catholic minority. We shall miss its significance altogether unless we accept that, as historian Erich Eyck tells us in *Bismarck and the German Empire* (1968), 'in those years many of the most enlightened and highly educated men believed that the future of mankind was at stake'.

The view that Bismarck artificially engineered this confrontation as a means of uniting various strands of German opinion against a common enemy is no longer tenable. The roots of the *Kulturkampf* stretch deep into German history, certainly back to Prussia's acquisition of the largely Catholic Rhineland in 1815, and possibly to the Reformation. This was not even exclusively a German issue, for reforming politicians in Italy, and in France during the Third Republic, had also felt obliged to confront the conservative principles of the Catholic Church. In those states, too, it seemed to many that the authority and the teachings of the Church were incompatible with the principles of a modern society based upon national identity. In the case of Germany in the early 1870s the struggle was really made up of two separate clashes. For the German liberals, the Catholic Church was an old enemy. Precursors of the *Kulturkampf* can be seen even in the southern states, as in the Church Law (1860) and the Elementary School Law (1868) passed in Baden. The offence of the Catholic Church had been compounded in 1864 with the publication of Pius IX's *Syllabus of Errors*, in which the Pope condemned every major political and social principle for which German and Italian liberals stood. Pius had declared moral warfare, and for the liberals the battle appeared to be one for the future of human thought.

Bismarck and the Catholic Church

For Bismarck the issue was less abstract. Despite the fact that he and most of the Prussian Junkers were Protestant, his battle had little to do with doctrine. 'It is not a matter of a struggle between belief and unbelief,' he declared. 'It is a matter of the conflict between monarchy and priesthood. What is at stake is the defence of the state.' For him the origins of the *Kulturkampf* lay in the events of 1866–70, during which Prussia had replaced Austria as the dominant force in German politics. In the process, tens of thousands of German Catholics had been transformed from sympathetic *grossdeutsch* supporters of the Habsburg monarchy into reserved followers and subjects of Prussia. Its origins also lay in the recently declared doctrine of **Papal Infallibility** (July 1870). By aiming to tie Catholic loyalties directly to the Papacy, instead of to the national state, the doctrine was a clear challenge to state power. The launching of this struggle offered Bismarck other political advantages, such as closer ties with the anti-clerical Italian government, with Russia, themselves greatly troubled by Catholic Poles, and with the National Liberals. His major motive, however, was probably the desire to combat those whom he felt genuinely to be 'enemies of the Empire' (*Reichsfeinde*). The Catholics were thus the first of many minority groups to play this role in 'united' Germany.

The May Laws

The spearhead of the attack upon the Catholic Church was formed by legislation framed, under Bismarck's instructions, by Adalbert Falk, the Prussian Minister of Religious Affairs. First, in 1872, came the cutting of diplomatic relations with the Vatican (May) and the expulsion of the **Jesuit order** from German soil (July). In the following year came the main onslaught in the form of Falk's notorious 'May Laws'. The education of clergy, clerical appointments and the inspection of Church schools were all brought under state control. Appointments to German ecclesiastical positions were limited to those educated in Germany, and priests were forbidden to use the threat of **excommunication** as a means to compel opponents. In a further series of measures civil marriage – strenuously opposed by Bismarck – in 1849 became compulsory in the Reich, and most religious orders in Germany were dissolved (1875).

Papal Infallibility: The principle defined by Pope Pius IX in 1870, whereby the Pope, as God's representative on Earth, was inevitably correct in any doctrinal statement that he made. As a denial of freedom of opinion, and as a potential challenge to the authority of national governments, this doctrine isolated the Catholic Church from most of the other major political and philosophical forces in western Europe.

Jesuit order: A religious order founded by St Ignatius Loyola in the 16th century. The founder's principle that members owed direct obedience to the Pope alone caused the order to be viewed with great suspicion in most European states. The order's close association with education also caused it to be viewed as a major channel by which the influence of the Catholic Church might be spread.

Excommunication: Expelled from the Church; destined for eternal damnation.

The results of the **Kulturkampf**

In 1874–75, Church and state remained locked in conflict. Eight of the 12 Catholic bishops in Prussia were deprived of their offices and more than 1,000 priests were suspended from their posts. However, the desired political effect was not achieved. Spiritually the Church thrived upon its 'martyrdom', and politically the increase in the representation of the Centre Party in the Reichstag frustrated Bismarck's hopes of a quick surrender. There were also other unhappy side-effects. The anti-Catholic stance endangered good foreign relations with Austria and the threat of an Austro–French understanding grew. Prussian conservatives, although staunchly Protestant, disliked the liberals' hostility to all religious instruction in schools and distrusted Bismarck's liberal 'alliance' in general. Indeed, the price demanded by the liberals for their further support – the extension of free trade and ministerial office for members of their party seemed to Bismarck himself to be unreasonably high. The death of Pius IX (1878) and the election of the more conciliatory Leo XIII provided an opportunity that Bismarck seized with enthusiasm. With the repeal of the bulk of the May Laws (1878) and the symbolic dismissal of Falk (July 1879), the *Kulturkampf* came to an abrupt end. Of the great 'struggle for civilisation', only the laws on civil marriage, state supervision of schools and those against the Jesuits remained.

Did Bismarck, therefore, lose the *Kulturkampf*? Certainly the struggle did much to damage his earlier work of unification, and made the majority of German Catholics more sympathetic to Papal authority than they had been before. On the other hand, reconciliation did largely transform the Centre into a purely religious party. If we see Bismarck's aim as the preservation of his state in the longer term, then perhaps we should accept the verdict of historian C. Grant Robertson that 'Bismarck deliberately sacrificed victory in the *Kulturkampf* to victory in other issues, more important in his judgement.'

1. What measures were taken against the Catholic Church in Germany in the course of the Kulturkampf?

2. Why did Bismarck launch the Kulturkampf in the 1870s?

3. What, if anything, did Bismarck gain by his measures in the 1870s against the Catholic Church in Germany?

3.4 Why did Bismarck abandon the National Liberals for a more conservative stance in 1878?

The 'Great Depression' and its impact upon German politics

For all the issues of principle at large in the 1870s, German politics did not operate by ideology alone. For much of the so-called 'Bismarck era' the political life of Germany was played out against a background of economic anxiety and depression. Germany's 'Great Depression' was a classic case of economic recession. The economic history of the Reich opened with a short period of 'boom', fuelled by over-generous credit policies on the part of German bankers, and by the large amounts of capital pumped into the economy by French **war reparations**. These stimuli set off a wave of unsound investment projects whose eventual collapse, in the same fashion as the Wall Street Crash, struck a blow to business confidence whose effects could still be felt nearly 20 years later. It is important to appreciate the exact nature of the impact made by this 'Great Depression'. In terms of production and of economic growth, Germany recovered relatively quickly. The production levels of 1872–73 had been restored by 1880; urban growth continued unabated, especially in Berlin and in the Ruhr; the development of **cartels** allowed major industrial enterprises to maintain their stability. After 20 years of uninterrupted economic growth, however, the psychological impact of the slump was considerable, and the effect of the depression on political mentalities was to last well beyond

War reparations: Payments made by a defeated state to compensate the victorious state(s) for damage or expenses caused by war.

Cartels: Economic arrangement whereby major manufacturers agree to share markets, rather than to compete for them. The aim is usually to fix prices for the benefit of the manufacturers and to guarantee levels of sales and profits.

1880. Its main political impact was to mobilise and to polarise conservative economic thinking, and to create a powerful lobby in favour of economic protection. The rejection of liberal, free-trading policies by the leaders of German industry soon became evident in the formation of such pressure groups as the League of German Iron and Steel Manufacturers (1873) and the Central Association of German Industrialists (1876). When Junker agriculturalists also became convinced that their interests were threatened by free trade, Bismarck was faced by an enormously powerful coalition in favour of protective tariffs.

The real impact of the depression, therefore, was that it undermined the political basis upon which Bismarck had founded his power in the early 1870s. It forced him to adapt once more to the prevailing circumstances within Germany. As historian D.G. Williamson puts it, in *Bismarck and Germany, 1862–90* (1986), the economic developments of the later 1870s 'discredited both economic and political liberalism and enabled the conservatives and the survivors of the pre-capitalist era successfully to attack the liberal ethos'.

The significance of the reforms of 1878–1879

The ending of the *Kulturkampf* cannot be seen merely as a tactical withdrawal, cleverly calculated by a master politician. In 1878–79, Bismarck was faced once again with a crisis of the utmost gravity, which forced him to adapt and revise his policies. The change of direction that he undertook at the end of the 1870s has often been interpreted as political opportunism. More recently, historians have come to view this period as a key stage in the development of the German Reich, as significant in its way as the events of 1870–71. Helmut Böhme, for instance, argues in *An Introduction to the Social and Economic History of Germany* (1978) that the Franco–Prussian War established a viable form of unity between the German states, but did not establish a satisfactory socio-economic balance within the new Reich. It became increasingly clear in the course of the 1870s that Bismarck's alliance with German liberalism failed to meet the interests of many influential groups within the Reich. The dramatic switch to economic and political conservatism at the end of the decade represented an acceptance on Bismarck's part of conservative social and economic values more closely in keeping with the conservative structure of the state. Historian Agatha Ramm confirms this interpretation in describing these reforms as a 'coherent and systematic revision of policy in relation to the economic, social and financial needs of the Reich'.

The introduction of protectionism

Protectionism: The economic practice whereby a country's domestic industries are protected from foreign competition by the imposition of high import duties placed upon foreign goods.

Bismarck now felt compelled to meet the growing demand for measures of economic **protectionism**. While free trade remained an essential principle of the National Liberals, demands for higher protective tariffs increased from other quarters. These demands had been heard from the iron and steel industries from the mid-1870s, but now Prussia's Junker landowners added their voices to the argument. Instead of aiming at free access to the markets of Britain and France, they now found themselves threatened by the cheap grain arriving from the United States of America. The adoption of protective tariffs by France, Russia and Austria–Hungary over this same period seemed to make it all the more desirable for Germany to follow suit. Apart from this impressive array of industrialist and Junker opinion, the government itself had pressing motives. Protection would aid the growth of national self-sufficiency in the event of a future crisis, and tariffs provided the government with a valuable source of income independent both of the Reichstag and of the member states.

Rudolf von Delbrück (1817–1903)
Prussian statesman. Active (1864–66) in the reorganisation of the *Zollverein*. As President of the Imperial Chancellery (1871) he was prominent in the drafting of Reich laws.
A supporter of free trade, he resigned in 1876 over Bismarck's promotion of protective tariffs.

1. In what ways were the economic policies of the German Reich changed in the late 1870s?

2. Who gained and who lost from the introduction of economic protectionism in Germany in the late 1870s?

From 1876, the path chosen by Bismarck became clearer. In April of that year he accepted the resignation of Rudolf von Delbrück, head of the Chancellor's Office and architect of the earlier free-trade policies. In early 1878, the refusal of the Liberal leaders to join Bismarck's government unless they were given guarantees over ministerial appointments and policy decisions, sealed their fate in the eyes of the Chancellor. When the new tariff laws were enacted in the Reichstag (July 1879) they imposed duties of between 5% and 7% on imported foodstuffs, and of 10%–15% on imported industrial goods. An amendment proposed by Freiherr zu Frankenstein limited Bismarck's triumph: it fixed an upper limit of 180 million marks in tariff income to be retained by the Reich, and ensured that any surplus would be distributed among the states. If this provided those states with some little satisfaction, there was none for German liberalism. A substantial step had been taken back to the path of conservatism, and the 'liberal era' in the history of united Germany was effectively at an end. In the view of one of the most influential of recent German historians, Helmut Böhme, these measures constituted the establishment of an interest-based coalition that would dominate the politics of Imperial Germany up to 1918. So important was this step, Böhme believed, that it amounted to nothing less than a 're-founding of the German Empire.'

3.5 How successful was Bismarck in his attempt to combat socialism?

Bismarck's fear of socialism

Reichsfeind (German – 'enemy of the Empire'): In Bismarck's Germany this came to indicate the deliberate policy whereby one particular group (e.g. Catholics or Socialists) was held up as an enemy in order to unite other groups against them and in support of the state.

Paris Commune: A radical political regime set up in Paris (March 1871) in the aftermath of France's defeat in the Franco–Prussian War. It lasted only until May 1871, when it was brutally crushed by French troops, but it created such an impression that it remained a powerful symbol of radical, socialist excesses for more than a generation.

The second compelling motive for Bismarck's change of course in the late 1870s was his desire to combat what he saw as the menace of socialism within Germany. Although the weakness of the socialists in the Reichstag might seem to make them unlikely candidates for the role of *Reichsfeind*, Bismarck, like most European statesmen, was genuinely shaken by recent events such as the **Paris Commune**. The 'Eisenach' socialists had, after all, refused their support for the war in 1870. Many remembered August Bebel's claim in the Reichstag in May 1871 that 'before many decades pass the battlecry of the proletariat of Paris will become that of the whole proletariat of Europe'. It seems probable that if Bismarck's opposition to Catholicism was not primarily ideological, his opposition to socialism was. In A.J.P. Taylor's words, he 'genuinely believed in the turnip-ghost which he conjured up'.

The anti-socialist law

Bismarck's opportunity came in mid-1878 when two attempts upon the life of the Kaiser gave him the chance to raise the cry of 'the Fatherland in danger', to dissolve the Reichstag and to hold fresh elections. Although neither would-be assassin had any clear association with the Social Democratic Party, the mood of the electorate was patriotic and conservative. 'The Emperor has the wounds, the nation the fever,' commented a liberal observer. The Social Democrats themselves had few seats to lose and the real losers of the election were the National Liberals. A majority was returned in favour of economic protection, the repeal of the 'May Laws', and the passage of Bismarck's anti-socialist measures (*Sozialistengesetz*). This law (19 October 1878) did not ban the Social Democratic Party directly, but crippled its organisation by banning any group or meeting aimed at the spread of socialist principles, outlawing trade unions, and closing 45 newspapers. It was originally in operation, thanks to a liberal amendment, for only two and a half years, but was renewed regularly until 1890.

'State socialism'

It was clear to Bismarck that socialism could not be conquered by oppression alone. The second string of his anti-socialist policy was thus a programme of 'state socialism'. This involved a series of measures to improve the conditions of the German workers. In 1883, medical insurance and sick pay were introduced. Although these were largely financed by the workers themselves, the employers were responsible for the funding of the scheme of insurance against industrial injuries introduced in the following year. Finally, in 1889, old age pensions were introduced, some two decades before their appearance in Britain.

Did such measures bring Bismarck more success against socialism than he had enjoyed against Catholicism? Historians have differed in their assessments of 'state socialism'. Some, like Erich Eyck, have seen the policy as a fraud, pursued for short-term political advantage. They point out how much more advantageous it would have been to relax the restrictions upon trade unions to allow workers to fight their own battles. They note that old age pensions were paid only to those who reached the age of 70, a ripe old age indeed for an industrial worker. Certainly, Bismarck failed to check the growth of the Social Democratic Party. Its membership increased from 550,000 in 1884 to 1,427,000 in 1890, suggesting that the workers saw 'state socialism' as a fraud and gave their support to the left. Gordon Craig, however, believes that it is possible to trace such paternalism in Bismarck's policies right back to 1862. 'State socialism', therefore, was based upon genuine conviction. Certainly Bismarck gained enthusiastic support from 'academic socialists' (*Kathedersozialisten*), such as Franz Brentano and Max Weber. He also horrified some liberals who accused him of attempting to found communism in Germany.

The historian A.J.P. Taylor regarded Bismarck's policies as successful in some important respects. He noted how subservient the German working class was to government policy in the years leading up to 1914 and concluded that Bismarck's policy had at least defused the threat of working-class opposition to the state. More recently David Blackbourn has reinforced this observation in slightly different terms. In *The Fontana History of Germany 1780–1918: the Long Nineteenth Century* (1997), Blackbourn notes that 'more generally, organised German workers wrestled with their desires to be good socialists and good Germans – what historians refer to as the problem of "double loyalty".'

1. By what means did Bismarck check the political influence of socialism within Germany in the 1880s?

2. Did Bismarck succeed in containing the threat of socialism to the German state?

3.6 To what extent was Bismarck responsible for the authoritarianism and intolerance of the German state in the early 20th century?
A CASE STUDY IN HISTORICAL INTERPRETATION

Historiography: Different historical views by historians. Another term for historical interpretation.

Few 19th-century figures have attracted the attention and controversy that surround the achievement of Otto von Bismarck. This is easy to understand when one considers the tremendous impact of German unification upon European history in the 75 years after 1871. Even in his own lifetime, the perception that Bismarck's work was central to that unification created a strand of German **historiography** that portrayed him as the master statesman, successfully manipulating events in order to lead Germany to its rightful destiny. Prominent in this school of thought was the Prussian academic Heinrich von Treitschke, whose monumental *German History in the Nineteenth Century* (1879–94) traced the 'inevitable' rise of Prussian mastery, with Bismarck portrayed as the chosen instrument of Germany's fate. Two ruinous world wars naturally had a considerable effect upon Bismarck's reputation among historians, within Germany and abroad. If he was indeed so great and successful a statesman, and if the Germany that he governed was his conscious and deliberate creation, then he should naturally assume much responsibility for the actions, and the subsequent development, of that state.

This view was widespread in the years after the Second World War. As historians in Germany and abroad searched for the origins of the disasters caused by Nazism (see Chapter 8), they looked to the growth of the German state before the Hitler era. They examined the role of Bismarck in the political development of that state. German liberals such as Erich Eyck, in *Bismarck: Life and Work* (1941–44), and the academic Friedrich Meinecke, in *The German Catastrophe: Reflections and Recollections* (1960), led the attack by stressing Bismarck's repression of political freedom after 1870. By crippling the development of democratic institutions in Germany, Bismarck had laid the country open to future dictatorships. Such views were understandably popular with Germany's wartime opponents. In one of the most popular English summaries of modern German history (*The Course of German History*, 1945) A.J.P. Taylor wrote that 'during the preceding 80 years the Germans sacrificed to the Reich all their liberties; they demanded as reward the enslavement of others'. Led by Gerhard Ritter, in *Europe and the German Question* (1948), German conservatives continued to argue that Bismarck could not be held responsible for later developments. His semi-feudal brand of conservatism, they argued, along with his religion and his *kleindeutsch* views, all distanced him greatly from the principles of Nazism. As Hans Rothfels put it, in *Bismarck and the State* (1954), 'we may criticise Bismarck for paving the way to some fatal trends of our day, but we cannot very well overlook the fundamental fact that Hitler did precisely what the founder of the Reich had refused to do'.

Did Bismarck create an authoritarian state?

If we try to answer this question by examining the constitution of the united Germany, we find that the evidence is ambiguous. On the one hand, the Reichstag displayed some democratic features.

- It was elected by universal manhood suffrage, and its assent was required for all legislation, including the periodic renewal of the military budget.

- It contained a wide variety of independent political parties, representing the full range of German political interests.

Yet the assembly lacked many of the powers of a full parliamentary democracy.

- Its members had no direct control over the actions of the Chancellor, nor over foreign policy, nor – beyond the voting of the army grant – over the conduct of the army.

- With the Chancellor and other leading ministers standing aloof from the party system, the political parties could not play any direct role in the formulation of government policy.

In short, the constitution embraced two different political mentalities: one with its roots in German liberalism, and the other with its roots in the authoritarian government that had been the norm within the individual German states. Its future depended upon which would emerge supreme.

Clearly, in the course of the 40 years after 1871, conservatism came out on top. In part, this was due to the preferences of Bismarck himself. It is clear that he saw the Reichstag as a body to be manipulated, rather than as a mirror in which to discover the will of the German people. His primary aims were not to advance German democracy, but as the historian Wolfgang Mommsen puts it, in *Imperial Germany 1867–1918* (1995), to 'preserve the pre-eminence of the traditional élites despite the changes that were taking place in German society'.

One influential view of German history, however, credits Bismarck with much less direct influence over the political development of the infant Reich. Helmut Böhme, in *Germany's Path to Great Power Status* (1966), not only placed economic trends at the heart of the process of German unification, but also saw in economics the main factors behind the shaping of politics within the new state. For Böhme, the crucial factor was the great economic depression that affected Germany between 1873 and 1879. From this crisis emerged a coalition of conservative interests, linking industrial and Junker agrarian interests, that would dominate the Reich until 1918. Liberalism was thrust into the margins of German politics, and such 'anti-modern' notions as anti-socialism and anti-semitism thrived in so conservative an environment. Socialism, in particular, was a direct product of the economic depression, and an obvious threat to the interests of these economic élites. Political oppression of the German socialist movement, therefore, was a logical product of these forces and not merely a whim or a political expedient employed by Bismarck. Geoff Eley concludes in 'Bismarckian Germany' in *Modern Germany Reconsidered 1870–1945* (1992), that 'the politics laid down in the Bismarckian period cast a long shadow. They established powerful continuities that extended through the imperial period to that of Weimar and played the key part in rendering German society vulnerable to Nazism.'

This impersonal emphasis, however, does not get Bismarck off the hook altogether. It must be pointed out that fear of revolution and of social radicalism was a fundamental element in Bismarck's political make-up and that he thus served as a major component in this conservative alliance, and a driving force behind its political measures. Several of the political elements within this alliance – leading industrialists for example – might have been identified in other states with more advanced causes. In Germany, however, under Bismarck's influence, they assented to authoritarian government, they contributed to the hostility that existed in educational and other professional circles towards democracy, and they helped to emphasise the authority and the mystique of the state. It seems necessary, therefore, to accept a consensus which, as Geoff Eley puts it, 'casts German state making in the light of social and economic history, but without turning Bismarck into the cipher of impersonal forces'.

Viewed in this way, the indictment against Bismarck is not that he created political conditions that were later used by German dictators, but that he used political forces and conditions that already existed, and which continued to exist in subsequent generations. It is hard to resist the conclusion that he did so willingly and eagerly, and that in the 1880s he presided deliberately over a political system based upon narrow conservative interests, and upon the restriction of the political activities of certain groups identified as 'enemies of the state'. The notion that German prosperity and security were threatened by hostile groups within Germany or abroad was central to Bismarck's political style. It is scarcely surprising that the next generation accepted so readily the claim that neighbours sought to restrict and restrain

Germany's legitimate growth. Although Bismarck may not have approved of some of the ends to which Wilhelm II turned his political authority from 1890 onwards, he was directly responsible for the fact that the new Kaiser possessed the political authority, and the necessary political support, in the first place. It is far less credible to blame Bismarck for the power that fell into Hitler's hands in the 1930s. Where Wilhelm II acted largely within the structure of the Bismarckian constitution, and of the conservative coalition that Bismarck bequeathed to him, Hitler began his period in power by deliberately demolishing large portions of the Bismarckian structure. Not only was the Reichstag undermined by his assumption of emergency powers in 1933, and rival political parties banned, but the more traditional elements of the conservative coalition were steadily excluded from political influence. Above all, the federal structure of the Reich, so important for the preservation of Prussia's distinct political identity, was demolished and replaced by a centralised state system. *Anschluss* – the integration of Austria into a greater German state (see Chapter 11) – was, of course, the opposite of everything that Bismarck had worked for in the 1860s.

3.7 To what extent did Bismarck's foreign policy succeed in defending German interests in the 1870s?

Before 1870, Bismarckian foreign policy had aims, more or less specific, that were pursued and eventually achieved by the skilful exploitation of external circumstances. Chief among these were the desire to substitute Prussian influence for that of Austria in the affairs of the German states, and subsequently to deflect the hostility of France, aroused by Prussia's success. After 1871 the essential principles of German foreign policy underwent a substantial change. In the eyes of Bismarck the *kleindeutsch* settlement of that year was final, and Germany was a state without further territorial ambitions. As he himself remarked, 'when we have arrived in a good harbour, we should be content to cultivate and hold what we have won'. It was now Bismarck's primary aim to prevent external events from disrupting the settlement that he had created. In this undertaking he was to achieve far less success than he had enjoyed in the first decade of his diplomatic career.

The Dreikaiserbund

For some years after 1872 the mainstay of Bismarck's delicate diplomatic balance was the understanding between the rulers of Germany, Russia and Austria–Hungary, known as the 'League of the Three Emperors' (*Dreikaiserbund*). First projected at a meeting of the monarchs in 1872, it was confirmed the following year (22 October 1873). It was given a more solid form by a series of military agreements promising aid to any party attacked by a fourth power.

In concluding this general and formless agreement, Bismarck probably had three main motives, although authorities disagree as to where the main emphasis should be placed. Firstly, the *Dreikaiserbund* represented a natural union of conservative ideals against disruptive forces such as nationalism and socialism. Secondly, the League ensured that neither Austria–Hungary nor Russia was available as an ally for France. A.J.P. Taylor preferred to emphasise the third potential benefit to Germany from the League. 'Its object insofar as it had one, was to prevent a conflict between Austria–Hungary and Russia in the **Eastern Question**.' Preoccupied by domestic issues for much of the decade, Bismarck sought to ensure that Europe remained peaceful by leading a combination of three of Europe's five main powers.

Eastern Question: A term used to describe the political and diplomatic problems posed by the decline of the Turkish Empire. This decline raised the prospect of Russian expansion in the eastern Mediterranean, the Middle East and the Balkans. Such prospects threatened the interests of Great Britain, France and Austria–Hungary.

The 'war in sight' crisis

Behind the superficial unity of the *Dreikaiserbund* lay self-interest and mutual suspicions that were always likely to undermine it. Two crises in the 1870s demonstrated the instability of the League. The first, the so-called 'war in sight' crisis of 1875, was the result of a major diplomatic miscalculation on the part of Bismarck. He had estimated, since 1871, that his purposes were best served by the survival of a republican government in France, as this would strengthen Russian and Austrian suspicions of France and keep that country in isolation. Bismarck even went so far as to dismiss and humiliate his ambassador in Paris, H. von Arnim, when the latter disagreed and promoted royalist interests. In 1875, however, political developments in France indicated a rise in royalist support and there were disturbing signs of military preparations. Bismarck's reaction was to allow threats of a preventative war, which he certainly never intended to fight, to circulate from unofficial sources. These came to a head with an article in the *Berliner Post* (9 April 1875) entitled 'Is war in sight?' Far from leading to the desired French embarrassment and retreat, the article caused France to appeal to the other powers to prevent a further German assault upon it. Britain and Russia led the protests to Berlin, and the crisis ended as suddenly as it had begun, with a German retreat. The limits of Russia's confidence in Germany had been clearly illustrated.

The Eastern Crisis

The second crisis, the Eastern Crisis of 1875–78, was not of Bismarck's making. It arose from the general revolt of the South Slav peoples, with Bulgarian support, against their Turkish overlords in 1875–76. Panslavism (see Chapter 2) and practical political interests encouraged successful Russian intervention and resulted in the Treaty of San Stefano (3 March 1878). By the terms of this treaty European Turkey was substantially reduced in size by the creation of large Russian **client states** in Bulgaria, Romania, Serbia and Montenegro. Bismarck had disclaimed any interest in the Eastern Question, using the famous phrase that no Balkan issue was 'worth the healthy bones of a single Pomeranian musketeer'. Even so, he could not fail to be concerned at the prospect of a clash between Russia and Austria–Hungary, which now saw its only remaining sphere of influence in the Balkans threatened. The only alternative to war was a conference of the great powers, and this met in Berlin (June–July 1878) under the presidency of Bismarck. There he played the role of the 'honest broker', not aiming for personal profit, but for a peaceful settlement between his 'clients' Russia and Austria–Hungary. The interests of the other major powers, including Britain, ensured that Russia would not be able to maintain the San Stefano settlement.

Superficially, the Congress of Berlin marked a highpoint in Bismarck's diplomatic career. In the short term, he had preserved peace and confirmed Berlin as the centre of European diplomacy. Erich Eyck, on the other hand, was one of those historians who preferred to see the congress as marking the beginning of the end of the Bismarckian system. Russian opinion was bitter at the loss of Slav territory, won at the cost of Russian blood, even though they kept their substantial Asian gains from Turkey. Tsar Alexander II was not alone in seeing the Congress of Berlin as 'a European coalition against Russia under the leadership of Prince Bismarck'. The introduction of protective tariffs against Russian agriculture in 1879 only confirmed this impression. Quite apart from the chill that entered into Russo–German relations, the *Dreikaiserbund* was further undermined by the occupation of Bosnia and Herzegovina by Austria–Hungary against the will of the local population.

Client states: Nations receiving support in the form of money, services and weapons from a more powerful nation.

1. What diplomatic steps did Bismarck take to defend German interests between 1871 and 1878?

2. How successful was the Congress of Berlin from Bismarck's viewpoint?

3.8 Did Bismarck's alliance with Austria after 1878 represent the failure of his diplomatic system?

German and Austrian motives behind the Dual Alliance

Anti-German feeling in Russia arose after the Congress of Berlin as a result of thwarted pan-Slav ambitions and of the wounded pride of Alexander Gorchakov, the Russian premier, rather than as the result of any deliberate re-orientation of German policy. It had great, long-term importance in that it confirmed the impressions that Bismarck had derived from the events of 1875–78. He felt that the time had come to put Germany's relations with Austria–Hungary on a surer footing. His motives were undoubtedly complex, but were dominated by the desire to avoid diplomatic isolation, and perhaps by the hope of frightening Russia back on to better terms with Germany by the prospect of its own isolation. It was also certain that a clear commitment to Austria would be the most popular of the diplomatic options within Germany, especially at a time when his own domestic policy relied so heavily upon conservative support. As Bismarck wrote to the reluctant Kaiser Wilhelm: 'German kinship, historical memories, the German language, all that makes an alliance with Austria more popular in Germany than an alliance with Russia.' Nevertheless, it was only with great difficulty that the Emperor's scruples about the 'betrayal' of Russia and of his fellow monarch were overcome.

In Austria, on the other hand, the prospect of an alliance was greeted with great enthusiasm. The chief minister, Count Andrassy, was reported to have 'jumped for joy' at news of the German proposals. By the terms of this Dual Alliance (October 1879), both powers committed themselves to aid the other in the event of a Russian attack, but only to neutrality if the attack came from another power. Austria–Hungary, therefore, was not committed to aid Germany in hostilities against France – an inequality that drew further criticism from the Kaiser.

In the following years the Dual Alliance became the centre of a system of German diplomacy. The agreement has been variously interpreted by different historians, some seeing it as the salvation of European peace in the 1880s, and others seeing it as confused and contradictory. In May 1882, the alliance became the Triple Alliance through the association of Italy with Germany and Austria–Hungary. This extension of the Bismarckian system had real advantages for Germany in that its mutual undertakings with Italy were specifically anti-French. This provided Germany for the first time with a committed ally against that country. On the other hand, Austria's alliances with Serbia (June 1881) and Romania (October 1882) drew Germany even deeper into areas where it had no direct stake or interest.

The Reinsurance Treaty and its significance

Meanwhile, what of Russia? In the short term, Germany was able to maintain friendly relations with its neighbour. Fear of diplomatic isolation encouraged Russia to agree to the renewal of the *Dreikaiserbund* on a more formal basis (June 1881). The three powers agreed to remain neutral in the event of one of their number going to war with a fourth power. Russia and Austria–Hungary also defused tension in the Balkans for the time being, by acknowledging each other's spheres of influence in the region.

In the late summer of 1886, however, a new crisis arose over Russia's virtual deposition of Bulgaria's independent-minded King Alexander (August–September 1886). It raised the likelihood of an Austro–Russian clash more starkly than at any time since 1878, and the resultant collapse of the *Dreikaiserbund* threatened the whole basis of Bismarckian diplomacy. In an attempt to plug the gap and to retain some influence over Russia's actions, the Chancellor was able to conclude (June 1887) a secret agreement with Russia, known as the Reinsurance Treaty. By its terms, both powers agreed to remain neutral in the event of a dispute with a third power. Germany also recognised Russia's greater interest in Bulgaria. As these neutrality clauses did not apply in the event of a German attack on France, or of a Russian attack upon Austria–Hungary, Bismarck did in fact gain some means of preventing the latter eventuality. Much controversy has centred upon the question of whether the Reinsurance Treaty was compatible with the Dual Alliance. In fact, there was no contradiction in the letter of the two agreements. They placed Germany in the position of having to decide, in the event of a clash between Russia and Austria–Hungary, who was truly the aggressor and thus which treaty Germany would honour. Bismarck's achievement in the Reinsurance Treaty was that he preserved Germany's power to arbitrate between the two powers.

The 'balance sheet' of Bismarckian diplomacy

What, then, was Bismarck's diplomatic legacy? The historian John McManners, in *Essays in Modern European History*, concludes that, by his commitment to Austria–Hungary, Bismarck bequeathed potential political disaster. 'Two years before Bismarck's fall from office, his system was shaking and the shadow of a Franco–Russian alliance was creeping into the horizon.' This judgement is harsh in that it attaches too little importance to the forces driving Bismarck in his decision in 1879, and underestimates the subtlety of the Reinsurance Treaty. It was, after all, Wilhelm II who allowed the treaty to lapse in 1890 when Russian enthusiasm for its renewal remained high. Nor did Bismarck create the eastern European tensions that erupted in 1914. If Bismarck's work as a diplomat can be criticised it is perhaps on the grounds that he monopolised power to such an extent that, after his fall, the diplomatic future of Germany would inevitably lie in the hands of less able men.

1. What changes took place in Germany's relations with Austria and with Russia in the years between 1878 and 1890?

2. Does Bismarck's foreign policy after 1871 suggest that he was more concerned to consolidate German power in Europe than to expand it?

3. How secure was Germany's position in European diplomacy by the time Bismarck left office in 1890?

3.9 Why did Bismarck launch a German colonial policy in his last years in power?

The acquisition of colonies

In the mid-1880s, the otherwise consistent course of German foreign policy took an unprecedented twist. Bismarck gave his government's support to the formation of a far-flung, but important, body of German colonial possessions. This contrasted starkly with the fact that in 1871 he had refused to annex French colonial possessions in place of Alsace-Lorraine, and that as late as 1881 he had declared that 'so long as I am Chancellor we shall pursue no colonial policy'. Germany's part in the 'scramble for Africa' was concentrated in the years 1884–85, establishing sovereignty in areas where German trading interests had been developed by private firms over the previous decade or so. In April 1884, the state agreed to 'protect' a strip of territory at Angra Pequena, in what is now Namibia, which had been secured from the Nama tribesmen by the Bremen merchant, Franz Lüderitz. Within the year, to the deep concern of British interests in southern Africa, this had grown into the colony of South-West Africa. In July of the same year the government appointed Gustav Nachtigal as German Consul-General in Togoland and the Cameroons, where he had previously been representing a group of

Hamburg businessmen. Karl Peters, a businessman and adventurer of dubious reputation, acquired most of German East Africa (now Tanzania) for the Reich, in February 1885, through a series of shady deals with local chiefs. Further afield, the establishment of Imperial control over northern New Guinea (May 1885) and over the Samoan Islands in the Pacific (1899) completed the shape of the German colonial empire.

What were Bismarck's motives?

The reasons for this abrupt departure from tradition have exercised historians ever since, and there is still no general agreement as to Bismarck's motives. The traditional view of nationalist historians was that Bismarck had always hoped for imperial greatness, and was merely awaiting his opportunity. More recently, the most widely accepted explanation has been that the German Chancellor had to conform to dominating trends in German society. German industry was now powerful enough to seek new outlets and new sources of raw materials abroad. It was perhaps natural that, after the introduction of protective tariffs in 1879, many businessmen should seek similar protection for their interests abroad from the state. This enthusiasm found expression in the formation of such successful pressure groups as the German Colonial Union (*Deutscher Kolonialverein*, 1882) and the Society for German Colonisation (*Gesellschaft für Deutsche Kolonisation*, 1884). Nationalist feeling also proclaimed that the German state, having established its European position, now had to make its power felt in the wider world. Lastly, Bismarck may have been influenced by the arguments of the political conservatives, who saw foreign adventures as a welcome distraction from domestic tensions at a time when the struggle against socialism was in full swing.

Imperialism: The practice whereby a state acquires economic and/or political power over other territories, usually with a view to commercial/industrial expansion.

Whatever the rationale behind it, German colonial policy was generally sterile. Bismarck had hoped that colonisation would not become a financial burden upon the Reich, but would be financed by private enterprise. 'I do not wish to found provinces,' he told the Reichstag in 1884, 'but to protect commercial establishments in their development.' These hopes were ill founded. By 1913 colonisation had cost the German taxpayer over 1,000 million marks in direct government aid. Only Togoland and Samoa had proved to be self-supporting. In almost every respect the results of 30 years of **imperialism** had been a disappointment. The total German population of the colonies amounted to only 24,000, most of them officials. Only South-West Africa, where diamonds were discovered in 1907, fulfilled hopes of valuable natural resources. The native populations, poor and under-developed, were unable to play the role of consumers of German industrial produce. Worst of all, the limited colonial experiment of 1884–85 provided the basis for German pretensions to a 'world policy' in the next decade, and thereby played no small role in the events that led to war in 1914.

1. What colonial territories did Germany acquire in the 1880s?

2. What benefits and what disadvantages did Germany derive from the acquisition of colonies in the 1880s?

3.10 What was the impact of unification upon German economic development?

The stimulus of unification

The establishment of the Reich in 1871 provided a number of direct stimuli to an economy that already possessed a substantial base for prosperity. Alsace-Lorraine, for example, contained Europe's largest deposits of iron ore. Production increased rapidly under German control, from 684,000 tons in 1872 to 1,859,000 tons in 1882. The injection of part of the French indemnity payments into the national economy caused a spectacular, if short-lived, boom in 1871–73. This was felt especially in the building and railway industries. Lastly, unity provided the opportunity for a burst of legislation designed further to unify the economic life of the Reich.

Simply in terms of output, the 'Bismarck era' provided further dramatic advances for the German economy. Coal production soared, steel production increased by some 700%, and the German merchant marine advanced from virtual non-existence to the position of second largest in the world. The table below, by contrasting German development with that of Great Britain and France, gives an impression of its advance as a world industrial power. Apart from the doubling of the railway network, it is also important to note the extent of nationalisation that took place during these decades. Out of Prussia's 28,000 kilometres of track, 24,000 kilometres passed into state ownership between 1879 and 1884.

Economic comparisons between Great Britain, France and Germany, 1870–90

	1870	1890
Population (millions)		
Germany	41	49
Britain	32	38
France	36	38
Coal production (million tons)		
Germany	38	89
Britain	118	184
France	13	26
Steel production (million tons)		
Germany	0.3	2.2
Britain	0.6	3.6
France	0.08	0.6
Iron ore production (million tons)		
Germany	2.9	8
Britain	14	14
France	2.6	3.5

Banking, finance and industrial cartels

In these respects the 1870s and 1880s formed part of a steady and consistent development. What was unique to this period was the development of two important features in the economy. Firstly, the post-war boom provided a considerable stimulus to the German banking industry. By the mid-1870s, Germany had a remarkably well-endowed system. Apart from the Reichsbank, there were six other banks which dominated commerce and industry with a combined capital of 2,500 million marks. They participated widely in the arrangement of private loans to industry and of public loans to the state, in the encouragement of new industries such as electricity and chemicals, and in the development of foreign and colonial ventures. With their representatives sitting on the boards of many leading companies, the co-operation between bankers and industrialists – known as 'finance capitalism' – reached a high stage of development during this period. Such bankers could also provide important services for the state. Bismarck's own banking adviser, Gerson Bleichröder, helped to finance the expensive military campaigns of 1863–66 at a time when state reserves

The Krupp factory at Essen – the basis of German industrialisation

1. What were the major features of Germany economic and commercial development in the 1870s and the 1880s?

2. In what ways did German economic developments in the 1870s and the 1880s change the state and the society that Bismarck had created in 1871?

were low, and later stage-managed the policy of railway nationalisation in the 1870s and 1880s.

The second distinctive feature of contemporary economic development was the growth of cartels. There were four such cartels in 1865, and only eight a decade later. Harder times made such arrangements more attractive and Germany boasted 90 in 1885 and 210 five years later. The largest cartels, such as the Rhenish Steel Syndicate and the Ruhr Coal Syndicate, headed by such men as Alfred Krupp, Hugo Stinnes and Fritz Thyssen, exercised enormous influence over the economic and political development of the Reich. Their demands for protective tariffs in the 1870s, and their later campaigns for naval and colonial development, clearly demonstrate this influence. A further result of these cartels was that safe home markets enabled German industrialists increasingly to break into foreign markets by 'dumping' goods cheaply.

Therein lay the seeds of the ultimate failure of Bismarck's conservative system. For all his fear of Catholics or Socialists, the greatest danger to Junker, Prussian Germany arose from the increasing demands and ambitions of German financiers and industrialists.

Source-based questions: Bismarck as pragmatic politician

Study Source 1 below and then answer questions (a) to (c):

SOURCE 1

(Bismarck explains the motives behind his policies in a speech to the Reichstag, 1881)

I have often acted hastily and without reflection, but when I have had time to think I have always asked: what is useful, effective, right for my fatherland, for my dynasty – so long as I was merely in Prussia – and now for the German nation? I have never been a doctrinaire. Liberal, reactionary, conservative – these I confess seem to me to be luxuries. Give me a strong German state, and then ask me whether it should have more or less liberal furnishings, and you'll find that I answer: Yes, I've no fixed opinions. Make proposals, and you won't meet any objections of principle from me. Sometimes one must rule liberally, and sometimes dictatorially, there are no external rules.

(a) Study Source 1.

What, according to Source 1, were Bismarck's main priorities in his government of Germany between 1870–90? [5 marks]

(b) On what issues did Bismarck most strongly disagree with the German liberals? [7 marks]

(c) What are the main arguments for and against the claim that 'Bismarck was primarily a conservative influence upon German politics between 1870–90'? [18 marks]

Edexcel Unit 3

Wilhelmine Germany, 1888–1918

4.1 What was the impact upon German politics of the accession of Wilhelm II in 1888?

4.2 What was the extent and what were the consequences of German economic growth between the accession of Wilhelm II and the outbreak of the First World War?

4.3 To what extent did Chancellor von Caprivi pursue a 'new course' in German domestic politics?

4.4 How effective were the major institutions of government within Wilhelmine Germany?

4.5 What were the main aims of German domestic policies between 1890 and 1914?

4.6 Was social democracy a serious threat to the stability of Wilhelmine Germany?

4.7 What were the results of Germany's decision to pursue a 'world policy'?

4.8 Was Germany's position in European diplomacy strengthened or weakened by its policies between 1894 and 1905?

4.9 What was the impact of the First World War upon German domestic politics?

4.10 Historical interpretation: What forces shaped the political policies of Wilhelmine Germany?

Key Issues

● *How important were the personality and priorities of Wilhelm II in shaping German politics in this period?*

● *What pressures and priorities guided German government in this period?*

Framework of Events

1888	(February) Publication of German commitments to Austria-Hungary in the Dual Alliance
	(March) Death of Kaiser Wilhelm I
	(June) Death of Kaiser Friedrich III; accession of Wilhelm II
1890	(January) Reichstag refuses to renew Anti-Socialist Laws
	(March) Resignation of Bismarck as Chancellor of Germany
	(June) Reinsurance Treaty between Germany and Russia allowed to lapse
	(October) Expiry of Anti-Socialist Law
1891	Renewal of Triple Alliance between Germany, Austria and Italy for 12 years
1894	Dismissal of Caprivi. Hohenlohe appointed Chancellor of Germany
1897	von Tirpitz is appointed as German naval secretary
1898	First German Naval Bill
1900	von Bülow replaces Hohenlohe as Chancellor of Germany
1904	German attempts to initiate an alliance with Russia fail
1905	First Moroccan crisis, started by Kaiser's visit to Tangier
1906	Third German Naval Bill
1908	Fourth German Naval Bill. Publication of interview in *Daily Telegraph* causes embarrassment for Kaiser
1909	Germany recognises French interests in Morocco
	von Bülow is replaced as German Chancellor by Bethmann-Hollweg
1911	Second Moroccan Crisis

1912	Elections leave Social Democrats as strongest party in Reichstag
1913	'Zabern Incident' in Alsace-Lorraine embitters Franco–German relations
1914	(June) Assassination of Archduke Franz Ferdinand in Sarajevo
	(July) Austria-Hungary declares war on Serbia
	(August) Germany declares war on Russia and on France
1916	Hindenburg becomes Chief of the General Staff
1918	Armistice ends the First World War.

Overview

A key issue in any political appraisal of Wilhelmine Germany is to establish whether or not the events of 1890 really constituted a new departure in German history. In that year Wilhelm II, only 18 months into his reign, dismissed Otto von Bismarck from his post as Chancellor. The traditional view of historians is that the removal of Bismarck's caution and realism, and of his fundamental concern for a peaceful diplomatic balance in Europe, set Germany and Europe on the road to the disaster of 1914.

Yet it may also be argued that little changed in 1888 in terms of the fundamental forces that drove German politics. These emerged in the late 1870s when, against a background of severe economic depression, Bismarck formed a formidable conservative alliance to resist the economic and political demands both of liberals and of the working classes. Industrialists and Junker landowners alike demanded policies that resisted the growth of genuine political freedom, which favoured the protection and development of their own economic interests, and which deflected the demands of the lower orders in German society. The emergence of a colonial programme, largely at odds with most of the principles that Bismarck had followed earlier in his political career, may be taken as a prime example of such policies. The departure of Bismarck, the argument continues, had little impact upon this situation. The essential conservative power-base of the German government, and the essential threats to that power-base, remained unchanged, and future Chancellors came under equal pressure to respond to these factors.

On the other hand, in social and economic terms, a great deal changed in Germany after 1888, and it changed very quickly. In the first decade of the 20th century the German Reich was barely recognisable as the state that Bismarck had founded in 1871. Its industrial economy had grown spectacularly, becoming the strongest in Europe, employing some 60% of the working population. In combination with this development, trade unionism expanded rapidly and the Social Democrats (SPD) attracted votes at such a rate that, by 1912, they constituted the largest single party in the Reichstag. Despite the enormous political and economic successes that Germany had achieved in the past few decades, or perhaps because of them, the Reich that entered the 20th century was full of contradictions. Economically and socially it was a modern and dynamic state; in political terms, however, it remained dominated by traditional élites who clung to their power and privileges, with little sympathy for political reform. Unsurprisingly, these élites supported policies that might have the widest appeal to the population, which might attract or at least isolate those who would otherwise favour more radical politics. The most striking political features of the Wilhelmine period, therefore, were not constructive measures of social development and reform, but measures and gestures designed to promote Germany's international status and prestige.

Sammlungspolitik (German – 'policy of gathering together'): Term used to describe the attempt by the German government in the 1890s and 1900s to pursue policies that would have an equal appeal to the many different political and economic interest groups that existed within the Reich.

Superficially, Wilhelm II was well suited to act as the focus for this *Sammlungspolitik*. He relished military affairs, and delighted in grand gestures which made him the centre of public attention. Unfortunately, he was not a good judge of such gestures, and failed to appreciate the impact that they might have upon Germany's neighbours. It was one of the great ironies of the Wilhelmine period that Germany – perhaps the most secure and prosperous state in Europe – appeared to believe itself threatened and restricted on all sides by jealous enemies. The most dangerous and damaging elements of this *Sammlungspolitik* were the building of a German battle fleet, and the decision to pursue *Weltpolitik*. Even if the aim in both cases, as many historians now argue, was to win popularity at home, rather than really to challenge foreign powers abroad, the very nature of that policy made it impossible to reassure those foreign powers. In attempting to avoid the consequences of domestic instability, therefore, Germany made a substantial contribution to international instability.

Weltpolitik (German – 'world policy'): Term used to describe the policy of the German government in the 1890s and 1900s whereby it sought to establish and advance German interests in all parts of the world, rather than concentrating upon European affairs.

In both international and domestic terms, the First World War provided an enormous test for the German state and society. In retrospect, the decision to enter the war, in the hope of a quick and rewarding victory, was disastrous, for the impact of the war upon domestic politics was exactly the opposite of that which Germany's leaders had envisaged in 1914. The economic prosperity of the country was wrecked by the enormous costs of the war and by the economic blockade which was imposed by Germany's enemies. The political differences that the war was intended to heal, or at least to mask, opened wider than ever. In the final stages of the war Germany was a country in crisis: the rift between the most conservative and the most left-wing elements in German politics were such that the state stood on the verge of civil war. In addition, the economic confidence and security that had been the most striking features of pre-war Germany lay in ruins. Although the Kaiser abdicated and fled into exile, the military and industrial conservatives who had supported him remained, eager to preserve their pre-eminence, and to shift the blame for the disaster onto other shoulders. The scene was set for the darkest decades in German history.

4.1 What was the impact upon German politics of the accession of Wilhelm II in 1888?

The long reign of Wilhelm I ended in March 1888, in the Kaiser's 92nd year. His son, briefly Kaiser as Friedrich III, had only months to live. He had suffered for a year from cancer of the throat, which had already deprived him of speech, and which ended his life in June. The imperial throne of Germany thus passed to his own son, and the 30-year reign of Wilhelm II began.

The personality and aims of Wilhelm II

The personality and psychology of the new Kaiser, now 29 years of age, have been a source of fascination for historians. His relationship with his parents, especially with his English mother, was tense and uneasy, and his personal sensitivity was undoubtedly increased by an accident at birth which left him with a withered arm and partially deaf. At Bonn University

Delusions of grandeur: a photograph of Wilhelm II, dated 1880.

Aristocrats: People whose families have a high social rank, especially those who hold a title. Their wealth is passed down the generations by inheritance.

Divine Right of Kings: The political view that claims that royal authority derives directly from God. As a consequence, a particular family or individual is designated by the will of God as ruler in a particular state.

Alfred von Kiderlen-Wächter (1852–1912)
Prominent German diplomat. Ambassador to Denmark (1894), to Romania (1900) and to Turkey on several occasions. Foreign Minister (1910) under Bethmann-Hollweg's administration. An enthusiastic supporter of *Weltpolitik* in general, and of the Triple Alliance in particular.

he showed far less interest in systematic study and learning than in the company of student **aristocrats**, and discovered the true passion of his youth in his years as an officer in the Potsdam Guards. Dismissed by his own father as 'inexperienced, immature and presumptuous', Wilhelm has not been kindly treated by historians. A typical judgement is that of Gordon Craig, in *Germany 1866–1945* (1978). 'Wilhelm had as much intelligence as any European sovereign and more than most, but his lack of discipline, his self-indulgence, his overdeveloped sense of theatre, and his fundamental misreading of history prevented him from putting it to effective use.'

The age of the young Kaiser was also significant. He belonged to a new, confident generation unaware of the dangers that German conservatism had narrowly survived in 1848 and in 1862. As historian Golo Mann put it, 'his memories began in 1870. He regarded the position which he owed to brilliant manoeuvres and clever acts of violence as the gift of God, as the natural order of things.'

What did the personality of the new Kaiser mean for the conduct of the German government? Firstly, it meant that Wilhelm II would not be content with the passive role played by his grandfather. He believed passionately in the **Divine Right of Kings**, and from this derived a notion of the mystical link between the ruler and his people. Not for him a reign based upon the narrow interest of Junker landowners, or dictated by the advantage of Prussia alone. Wilhelm, in the words of the historian A.J.P. Taylor, 'desired an absurdity – to be Emperor of all of the Germans'. In a state built by Bismarck upon division and confrontation, the prospects of harmonious relations between monarch and Chancellor were dim.

Strong though he was on principle, the new Kaiser's style of government was hectic, spectacular and shallow. He travelled obsessively, rarely spending as much as half the year in his capital and earning the nickname of *Der Reise-Kaiser* ('the travelling Emperor'). He had views on everything, but rarely bothered to back his 'inspiration' with hard information. 'He just talks himself into an opinion,' remarked the German diplomat Alfred von Kiderlen-Wächter in 1891, while Wilhelm's biographer M. Balfour has remarked that 'his fluency in speaking meant that he approached all questions with an open mouth'. It was a fair summary of the man and the monarch that he openly boasted that he read neither the newspapers nor the German constitution. The outcome was a 30-year reign of great spectacle, constant motion, but little positive content. It amounted, in the words of the future Weimar minister, Walter Rathenau, to a 'dilettante foreign policy, romantic conservative internal policy and bombastic and empty cultural policy'.

The collapse of Bismarck's political system

For all the monumental achievements of the previous three decades, Bismarck's position as Chancellor of the Reich had remained dependent, in practice, upon the goodwill of the monarch. That position had appeared for some years to be threatened by the prospect of the succession of Crown Prince Friedrich, with his allegedly liberal sympathies, and his English wife, the Crown Princess Victoria. The death of Friedrich saved Bismarck from one challenge to his authority only to confront him with another. The political sympathies of Wilhelm were less liberal, but he differed fundamentally with his Chancellor as to methods of government.

The issues that divided the two men in 1888–90 were, in reality, merely symptoms of their different interpretations of the Reich and of the role of the Kaiser. A strike by miners in the Ruhr (May 1889) gave Wilhelm the chance to display his brand of paternalism towards the

German working class. While he prepared a programme of social reforms, including a ban on Sunday working, Bismarck rejected the principle of conciliation and concession. Instead he aimed to continue a policy of hostility and confrontation. Bismarck's plans to make the renewable Anti-Socialist Laws permanent not only provoked a clash in the royal council (January 1890), but had severe repercussions in the Reichstag elections in the following month. Bismarck's coalition of Conservatives and National Liberals lost 85 of their 220 seats, and the Social Democrats nearly doubled their share of the vote. Deprived of the support of both monarch and Reichstag, Bismarck had only intrigue to fall back on. His attempts to force through a package of measures to revise the constitution, to help his political control, forced the Kaiser's hand. Wilhelm chose the path of conciliation, demanded Bismarck's resignation, and received it on 18 March 1890.

Bismarck's legacy

For all his earlier achievement, Bismarck bequeathed to Germany a legacy of tension and troubles. The concentration of power in his own hands meant he had consistently obstructed the growth of truly representative institutions in Germany. As Max Weber commented, 'Bismarck left behind him as a political heritage a nation without any political education ... a nation without any political will, accustomed to allow the great statesman at its head to look after its policy for it.' Undoubtedly, Bismarck had governed with great shrewdness, but the sad result of his political egoism was that his great power now passed into the hands of an irresponsible and unstable monarch. Furthermore, Wilhelm inherited a variety of thorny problems, especially in colonial and foreign policy, which Bismarck had allowed to develop for reasons of short-term political advantage. Despite his famous announcement upon Bismarck's resignation that 'the ship's course remains the same; "Full steam ahead" is the order', Wilhelm's fundamental misunderstanding of recent German and European history was to guarantee the destruction of most of the essential principles of Bismarckian Germany within the next 30 years.

1. What were the main political beliefs of Kaiser Wilhelm II?

2. Why did Otto von Bismarck fall from power in 1890?

4.2 What was the extent and what were the consequences of German economic growth between the accession of Wilhelm II and the outbreak of the First World War?

The years of Wilhelm II's reign to 1914 saw German industry build upon its Bismarckian foundations (see Chapter 3) to take its place among the foremost industrial economies of the world. In this respect, the character of the country matched that of the Kaiser. It was young, dynamic, and outwardly confident.

Population growth, heavy industries and communications

Underlying Germany's economic acceleration was a continued rapid growth in population, providing native industries with a greater labour force and with more consumers. Between 1870 and 1890, Germany had experienced a population rise of 21%, from 40.9 to 49.5 million. In the next two decades, the rate of increase was half as great again, leading to a population of 65 million.

The traditional heavy industries of the Reich maintained the direction that they had followed in 1870–90, but they experienced a spectacular acceleration in the pace of output. Coal production was challenging that of

Key economic indicators, 1890–1913

	Coal and lignite (million tons)	Pig iron (million tons)	Steel (million tons)	Exports (£ million)	Imports (£ million)
1890	89.1	4.66	3.16	170.5	213.6
1900	149.8	8.52	7.37	237.6	302.1
1910	192.3	14.79	13.15	373.7	446.7
1913	279.0	–	–	504.8	538.5

Britain by the outbreak of the First World War, while steel output had surpassed that of Great Britain in 1900, and was nearly double that of its rival by 1910. The necessary corollary of these increases in German production was the expansion of its communication system. The Wilhelmine period saw a steady continuation of the growth in the railway system that had been a central feature of economic expansion since the foundation of the Reich. A system that extended 19,480 kilometres in 1870, and 41,820 kilometres in 1890, had grown to 59,016 kilometres by 1910.

The development of a German merchant navy was even more spectacular. The total tonnage of steamships registered at Hamburg rose from 99,000 in 1880 to 746,000 in 1900, while the figures for Bremen in the same period were 59,000 and 375,000. Germany's total merchant marine in 1914 amounted to 3 million tons, only a quarter of the British total, but nearly three times that of the USA.

The 'new' industries

Nor was German expansion limited to traditional industries. By the outbreak of the First World War, Germany had established a substantial lead over all other European powers in the new chemical and electrical industries. Germany came to produce 75% of the world's output of chemical dyes by 1914, and played a prominent role in the development of agricultural fertilisers, pharmaceutical products and the industrial uses of sulphuric acid, sodium and chlorine. In electronics, Werner von Siemens had already contributed the electric dynamo (1867), and important work on electronic traction (1879 onwards). There was also the development of the two biggest electricity combines in Europe, Siemens/Halske, and AEG (*Allgemeine Elektrizitäts Gesellschaft* – General Electricity Company). By 1913 half of the world's electro-technical trade was in German hands. Such household names as Daimler and Diesel also attest to German achievement in engineering. In short, Germany's economic position within Europe was being transformed, not merely by industrialisation, but by the creation of 'young' industries, emerging at a time when older industrial economies were beginning to feel the need for reinvestment and modernisation.

National wealth and living standards

The total wealth of the German Reich increased in the peaceful years of the Wilhelmine era, according to the contemporary economist, Karl Helfferich, from 200,000 million marks to 300,000 million. The table opposite relates to Prussia alone. It indicates the increase in the number of great personal fortunes in this period. Other evidence suggests that the increase in German prosperity was more generally felt. For example, per capita income doubled in the course of 40 years. It rose from 352 marks per year (1871–75), through 603 marks per year (1896–1900) to 728 marks per year in 1911–13.

The rise in incomes – in the German Imperial currency of Reichmarks (RM)		
Total fortune of:	**1895**	**1911**
Between 100,000 & 500,000 RM	86,552	135,843
Between 500,000 & 1 million RM	8,375	13,800
Between 1 and 2 million RM	3,429	5,916
Over 2 million RM	1,827	3,425

The dramatic decrease in the rate of emigration, from 134,200 in 1880–89, to 28,000 in 1900–10, also indicates the relative rise in German living standards by the latter decade.

It should be noted, however, that this overall prosperity was not shared by German agriculture. It was not that agriculture stagnated: scientific methods of cultivation had spread rapidly since 1870, with an estimated fourfold increase in mechanical harvesting between 1882 and 1907 alone. Yet German grain producers could not compete adequately with American imports, especially when large ocean-going steamers and low freight charges cheapened imports further. By 1900, it was cheaper to import grain from America than to transport it 400 kilometres within Germany. Grain prices dropped and heavy internal tariffs were needed to enable the Junker farmers of East Prussia to pay their debts. Economically, therefore, the Germany of Wilhelm II presented a subtly contrasted picture of modern dynamism and embattled conservative interests.

Inevitably the dramatic expansion of German industry involved substantial changes in the distribution and the living standards of the working population. Already evident in Bismarckian Germany, these changes accelerated dramatically in the decades that immediately preceded the First World War. In particular, they took the form of a large-scale movement of the population to urban centres, and from agricultural to industrial employment. In the four decades up to 1907, it has been estimated, something like 40% of the population of united Germany moved from one region of the Reich to another, and the proportion of the population employed in industrial production increased from 31% to 40%. Some spectacular examples of urban growth had occurred in the years since unification. Between 1870 and 1910, for example, the population of Leipzig grew from 107,000 to 679,000. Equivalent figures for Cologne (129,000 to 517,000), Essen (52,000 to 295,000) and Duisburg (32,000 to 229,000) tell the same story, and must be placed in the context of an overall rise in the German population of only 44%. Apart from the growth of individual towns, the nature and function of whole regions were sometimes transformed. In the Ruhr, in the Saarland, in Upper Silesia and elsewhere, new industrial conglomerations had been created as villages developed into towns, and merged with each other in the process of industrial growth. Such regions naturally experienced the same social problems that had arisen in other parts of Europe where rapid industrialisation had taken place. 'Overcrowding,' writes David Blackbourn (*Germany 1780–1918: The Long Nineteenth Century*, 1997), 'was exacerbated by the conditions to which the occupants of attics, cellars and tenements were exposed – damp, lack of natural light, primitive sanitary conditions that made the perfect breeding ground for infectious diseases. Periodic outbreaks of cholera and typhus were the most vivid symbol of dangerous, degraded living conditions.' A major outbreak of cholera in Hamburg in 1892 was the worst of many such epidemics.

1. In what respects did the German economy make the most spectacular progress between 1890 and 1914?

2. Who benefited most and who benefited least from the trends in the German economy during these years?

What were the political implications of such developments?

It would be easy to see these developments as a classic case of industrial expansion alienating the industrial workforce, and preparing the ground for class conflict. In the case of Germany, however, the effects may have been more complex. The nature of Germany's economic growth in the Wilhelmine years, for instance, also produced a rapidly expanding lower middle class, with less radical political aspirations, alongside the industrial workers. It has been estimated that, in the 25 years leading up to 1907, the number of 'white collar workers' (clerical, rather than manual workers) roughly tripled in Germany to a total of 3.3 million. At the time of unification there were more than ten manual workers to each clerical worker. On the eve of the First World War the ratio had been reduced to 3.5 to 1. A number of social historians have also stressed that regional and religious identities remained strong in Germany, often cutting across traditional conceptions of class-consciousness. A further factor to be taken into account is the fact that the vast bulk of this urban population found work during the Wilhelmine period. In only one year between 1900–14 did unemployment rates in Germany rise above 3%. Wilhelmine Germany never had to cope with the impact of economic depression upon this industrial population. There can be little doubt that the governing élites of the period regarded the industrial masses with suspicion, and often with fear. Whether they were right to do so is a question on which historians have yet to reach agreement.

4.3 To what extent did Chancellor von Caprivi pursue a 'new course' in German domestic politics?

The search for a German consensus

Leo von Caprivi (1831–1899)
Entered the Prussian army in 1849 and fought in the conflicts with Denmark (1864), Austria (1866) and France 1870–71). Head of Admiralty (1883–88). Imperial German Chancellor (1890–94).

Bismarck's successor as Chancellor of the Reich and as Prime Minister of Prussia was General Leo von Caprivi. He brought to these offices the prestige of high military rank, personal honesty and modesty, but none of the political experience or deviousness necessary to master the complexities and contradictions of the Bismarckian state. 'The primary problem of the Caprivi Era,' in the opinion of historian J. Alden Nichols (*Germany after Bismarck*, 1958), 'was how to handle a complex political creation that had finally escaped from the control of its creator.' The new Chancellor, like the Kaiser, desired greater conciliation and less confrontation in domestic politics. He refused to regard any political grouping as a *Reichsfeind* (see Chapter 3) and was willing to accept the assistance of any group in furthering his projects. Both Caprivi and the Kaiser claimed not to be initiating a 'new era', an indication of how little they understood of Bismarck's rule.

Reform of the Bismarckian system

The years 1890–94 saw systematic inroads made into the domestic system established by Bismarck.

● The Anti-Socialist Laws were allowed to lapse.

● Attempts were made to win the working classes over to the Reich with a series of reforms that included:
  – a ban on Sunday working
  – the limitation of working hours for women and children
  and the establishment of courts for industrial arbitration.

● Confrontation with national minorities in Posen and in Alsace-

Lorraine was eased by the relaxation of rules governing the use of German in administration and education.

● A moderate reduction was sought in the privileges of Prussia within the Reich. Prussia's independent foreign ministry was abolished, its tax system reformed and a graduated income tax introduced.

Of much more direct offence to the Prussian Junkers was Caprivi's new economic course. In the interests of increased trade and of cheaper food, he abandoned Bismarckian protectionism, that great guarantee of the Junkers' agricultural prosperity. A series of trade treaties – with Austria-Hungary and Italy in 1892, with Belgium, Switzerland and Romania in 1893, and with Russia a year later – greatly stimulated Germany's industrial progress but involved, as their price, the reduction of German agricultural tariffs. The unfortunate coincidence of these measures with the increase in cheap American corn exports drove not only the Junkers, but also most farmers into opposition to the government. The Federation of Agriculturalists (*Bund der Landwirte*), founded to organise this opposition (February 1893), boasted 250,000 members within the year and constituted one of several new conservative forces in German politics.

The fall of Caprivi and the return to conservatism

The fate of two pieces of projected legislation illustrated the deterioration of Caprivi's political position. A bill by the Prussian Ministry of Education, proposing religious segregation of schools, and closer control of religious education by the Churches (1892), was defeated by the opposition of all liberal groups in the Reichstag. The defeat brought about Caprivi's resignation as Prime Minister of Prussia, which further weakened his political base. More surprisingly, a new Army Bill also ran into opposition. Presented to the Reichstag in 1892, it was only passed after a dissolution and new elections in which the conservative parties and the Social Democrats prospered at the expense of the Liberals.

Four years in office served to convince Caprivi that he had underestimated the selfishness of the various political interests in the Reichstag. In the same period, the initial, superficial 'liberalism' of the Kaiser had faded. Wilhelm accepted his Chancellor's resignation in October 1894. He was disillusioned at the failure of the workers to desert the Social Democrats and rally to him, perturbed at the resurgence of political violence especially evident in the assassination of the French president by anarchists, and perplexed at the rift between the government and Junker conservatism.

Did Caprivi abandon Bismarck's foreign policy?

Friedrich von Holstein (1837–1909)
Entered the Prussian diplomatic service in 1860. Became a *protégé* of Bismarck, but lost favour through his disagreement with the Chancellor's policy of alliance with Russia. Returned to prominence after Bismarck's fall. Head of Foreign Ministry (1900–06), losing office in the aftermath of the Moroccan crisis.

It is a more complex matter to decide whether Caprivi departed from the traditional Bismarckian course in handling Germany's foreign affairs. Certainly he presided over the destruction of a central element in the Bismarckian diplomatic system when in March 1890 he refused to renew the Reinsurance Treaty with Russia. In this, he was not acting with any anti-Russian motive; instead he hoped to maintain friendly relations with the great eastern power. Caprivi was influenced, however, by personalities in the foreign office, such as Friedrich von Holstein whose general leanings were anti-Russian. Their convincing arguments concerned the incompatibility of sections of the treaty with German undertakings to Austria and to Romania, and the undoubted fact that its terms gave far greater advantages to Russia than to Germany. In short, Caprivi acted honestly where deviousness might have served better. The result of his action was the almost immediate confirmation of Bismarck's nightmare, a diplomatic understanding between Russia and France. Furthermore, by agreeing to the renewal of the Triple Alliance with Austria and Italy in 1891 he made a contribution to the formation of hostile camps in Europe that eventually undermined the peace.

Caprivi remained Bismarckian in the sense that he continued to resist the considerable pressures within Germany for a 'world policy' (*Weltpolitik*). He saw little realistic future in the acquisition of colonies. The essence of his policy remained European, to consolidate and improve Germany's position in Central Europe. This aim was served by his system of economic agreements with Germany's neighbours and by the confirmation of the Triple Alliance.

It had its most controversial display in the Anglo–German treaty of July 1890. By this treaty Germany transferred to Great Britain all rights to the island of Zanzibar, and to large areas of the adjacent African mainland, in return for the strategic North Sea island of Heligoland. If, however, the Zanzibar agreement was an opening move in a plan to tempt Britain into closer relations with Germany in place of the Russian alliance, it was a failure. Caprivi underestimated the reluctance of the British to get involved in binding continental commitments. He also found that his concept of Germany's continental future was not widely popular at home. The **Pan-German** League (*Alldeutscher Verband*), which took form between 1891 and 1894, was a deliberate attempt to encourage the Reich to pursue a more energetic, prestigious and cosmopolitan foreign policy. Thus, although Caprivi rejected some of the methods most dear to Bismarck, the brief span of his government did represent the last attempt to limit Germany to European commitments before his opponents launched it on the ultimately disastrous course of 'world policy'.

Pan-German: The policy which dictates that all those of German racial origin should be united in a single German state. This naturally involved the union of Germany with those parts of the Austro-Hungarian Empire whose population was ethnically German.

1. Which of Bismarck's policies were abandoned when Caprivi held office?

2. In what ways did the priorities of Caprivi's government differ from those of Bismarck's government?

4.4 How effective were the major institutions of government within Wilhelmine Germany?

Bernhard Prince von Bülow (1849–1929)
Chancellor of the German Empire (1900–09) under Kaiser Wilhelm II. Having risen through the Foreign Office, where he had been Minister since 1897, von Bülow was closely identified with German colonial expansion and seemed to share the Kaiser's enthusiasm for a 'world role'. He had a reputation for brilliance, but superficial polish was not backed by firm principles or broad vision, and he deserved the nickname of 'the eel' bestowed upon him. Bülow adopted attitudes to France and Russia that unintentionally reinforced the trend towards opposing European power groups. He resigned after losing the confidence of Wilhelm II and the Reichstag.

The office of Chancellor

The German Reich was to have three more chancellors between the fall of Caprivi and the outbreak of war in 1914. The first of these was a Catholic, Bavarian aristocrat, Prince Chlodwig von Hohenlohe-Schillingsfürst (1894–1900). After a lifetime in state service, he reached the highest office at the age of 75. He was, frankly, a stop-gap. His conservative views on domestic matters and his pro-Russian sympathies recommended him to the German right, and his lack of any coherent programme of his own fitted in well with Wilhelm's ambitions of personal government. Primarily, in the words of the contemporary German politician Friedrich Naumann, Hohenlohe was 'an artist in the avoidance of catastrophe'. His years in office constituted, in retrospect, a lull before the diplomatic storm of the new century.

Hohenlohe's resignation in 1900 was precipitated by the Kaiser's persistent failure to consult him on important policy matters. His successor was to be a prime accessory in Wilhelm's irresponsible political meddling. Bernhard von Bülow (1900–09) was a more cosmopolitan and, it was felt, more modern man than Hohenlohe. There was too much of the flattering courtier about Bülow for him to have been a safe, moderating influence on the Kaiser, as Hohenlohe had been.

Many historians have laid upon Bülow much of the blame for Germany's diplomatic irresponsibility during the period. The circumstances of Bülow's fall are thus ironic. Although his resignation in June 1909 was ostensibly due to the defeat in the Reichstag of his project for a tax on inherited wealth, the

**Theobald von Bethmann-
Hollweg (1856–1921)**
Started his career as a civil
servant in Brandenburg,
served in the Prussian Ministry
of the Interior, and became
Secretary of State in the
Imperial Office of Internal
Affairs (1907). Bethmann-
Hollweg was appointed
Chancellor in 1909. He was a
competent administrator, but
lacked knowledge and
experience of foreign and
military affairs. He became
increasingly dependent on
non-Parliamentary centres of
influence such as the court,
army and bureaucracy.

Alfred von Tirpitz (1849–1930)
Founder of the German navy.
Served in the Prussian navy
from 1865. Chief of Staff of
Navy High Command; Rear
Admiral (1895); Secretary of
State of Imperial Navy
Department (1897–1916), in
which capacity he was an
advocate of submarine
warfare. Drafted Germany's
first Navy Law (1898) and the
many subsequent laws. He
became an admiral in 1903;
Grand Admiral in 1911. Tirpitz
was a nationalist deputy in the
Reichstag (1925–28).

real cause of his downfall was, like Bismarck's, the loss of the monarch's confidence. This arose from Bülow's carelessness the previous year in allowing the publication of an interview given by Wilhelm to the British newspaper *The Daily Telegraph*. Characteristic irresponsibility on the Kaiser's part led to utterances offensive to Britain and to Russia, and highly embarrassing to Germany. Most Germans, he suggested, were hostile to Britain, and he was the only force that restrained their hostility. An outcry in the Reichstag brought Wilhelm to the verge of a nervous breakdown and ended the 'golden age' of his personal government. In the long run, as many foreign observers have pointed out, the Reichstag missed the opportunity for long-term constitutional change afforded by the *Daily Telegraph* incident, and Bülow alone paid a high price for the affair.

The last peacetime Chancellor of Imperial Germany was Theobald von Bethmann-Hollweg (1909–17). A man of personal courage and honour, he seemed an ideal choice from the point of view of domestic affairs. However, his crippling disability was his total inexperience in foreign or military affairs. While this certainly recommended him to a Kaiser who desired supremacy in those areas, it was part of Germany's tragedy that such a man led the government at the time when the fate of Europe depended upon such matters.

In a sense such changes in personnel were of secondary importance. Of greater significance in the years 1894–1914 was the erosion of the overall power of the Chancellor, perhaps the most important of all the departures from Bismarck's system of government. In part, this was due to an 'invasion from above', to the Kaiser's consistent desire for personal rule. At the same time the power of the Chancellor was eroded from below, by the loss of control over various, previously subordinate, ministries. Caprivi had allowed far greater freedom to other departments than Bismarck had ever tolerated, and Admiral Tirpitz at the Naval Ministry provided a good example of an independence of action inconceivable before 1890.

The Reichstag

Although it is clear that Wilhelmine Germany was not a true constitutional monarchy, it would be inaccurate to dismiss the Reichstag as an ineffective sham. There is much evidence of improved party organisation in the assembly after 1890, and evidence too of occasions when the Reichstag showed concerted opposition to the government. The most notable example occurred in 1913, when deputies were united in outrage over the behaviour of the military in the Zabern Affair. Yet the fact remains that the government was able largely to ignore such pressure and the Reichstag was never able to bring down a government or to restrict its actions, as its British or French equivalents might have done.

In part this was because the Chancellor was not a parliamentary party leader and could not be undermined by the reduction of his majority. There were also other serious weaknesses in the German parliamentary system, which prevented it from playing a more positive role in government. As a representative assembly, it was unsatisfactory in several respects. Its constituencies, for instance, were notoriously uneven, their boundaries remaining unchanged between 1871 and 1914. By the time of the 1912 elections, the largest were ten times the size of the smallest. They did not reflect population changes, and it took far more votes to elect a Social Democratic representative in an industrial region than to elect a conservative or a member of the Centre Party in a rural constituency.

Yet the Social Democratic Party steadily increased its parliamentary representation. Why then could parties not put effective pressure upon the government in the Reichstag? To a large extent, this was due to their inability to form effective coalitions. This, in turn, was due to divisions and resentments arising from the party politics of previous decades. The National Liberals had supported Bismarck's anti-socialist laws and had been enthusiastic promoters of the *Kulturkampf* (see Chapter 3). The Social Democratic Party and the Centre Party could not easily forget or forgive this. Such differences were eventually overcome under the pressures of war, and a coalition emerged between these groups that formed the basis of the Weimar Republic (see Chapter 11), but there was no such urgency in the 1890s or the 1900s. Historian David Blackbourn, in *The Fontana History of Germany 1780–1918: the Long Nineteenth Century* (1997), emphasises how these parties never had to concern themselves with practical issues or effective compromises. This was because they were never in power in this period, or seriously in pursuit of power. Instead, they could afford the luxury of ideological rhetoric, which distanced them from each other. This was especially true of the Social Democratics. Theoretically a Marxist party, it turned its face against alliances with 'bourgeois' parties, and preached radical social and political change to an extent that created fear and hostility among political groups with whom the Social Democratics might profitably have formed an electoral alliance. It must also be remembered that the German state was **federal**, and that significant differences existed between political conditions in one state and in another. Party co-operation on a national level became even more difficult when party attitudes and relations differed greatly in the provinces.

Federal: A system of government which consists of a group of states controlled by a central government. The central government deals with things concerning the whole country, such as foreign policy, but each state has its own local powers and laws.

The army in the German mentality

The decline of the Chancellor's office, the personal unreliability of the monarch and the failure of the Reichstag to seek fundamental political change, were different elements in the severe weakening of civil government in Germany. The most important result of this was that the German army occupied a status unparalleled in Europe. In part, it owed this status to the role that it had played in Germany's growth. The nation suffered from what the historian A.J.P. Taylor called a 'Sadowa–Sedan complex', based on the memories of the great victories of the past. Glorification of war and conquest was commonplace in contemporary German thought and writing. 'The whole nation,' remarked the socialist August Bebel, 'is still drunk with military glory and there is nothing to be done until some great disaster has sobered us.'

Two illustrations may help to indicate the independence of the army from German government. In November 1913, a series of disturbances broke out in the garrison town of Zabern (Saverne) in Alsace. They were evidently triggered by the arrogant behaviour of garrison troops, and resulted in arbitrary arrests, the use of force to disperse crowds, and the declaration by the military authorities of a state of siege. Fearful for public order, the civil authorities sought to discipline the soldiers involved, but were directly overruled by the Kaiser himself. The 'Zabern Affair' escalated and caused an outcry in the Reichstag comparable with that over the *Daily Telegraph* interview. The vote of censure against the government and its support of the military authorities was carried by 293 votes to 54. Yet the matter ended there. As in 1908, the Reichstag hesitated to take further action, and the Kaiser and his ministers firmly maintained their support of the army. The failure to take any effective action against excesses illustrates the virtual immunity of the army from political control.

A similar point is made by a study of the contemporary development of military strategy. Under Count von Schlieffen (Chief of the General Staff 1891–1906), the army command had come to terms with the problems of

1. What evidence is there of the political influence and independence of the German army during the reign of Wilhelm II?

2. What were the strengths and weaknesses of the Chancellors who served Wilhelm II between 1894 and 1914?

3. In what respects can it be argued that the government of Germany during the Wilhelmine period was undemocratic?

war on two fronts. Their strategy – the 'Schlieffen Plan', formulated in 1897 – called for a rapid outflanking movement through Belgium and Luxembourg to eliminate France from the war before Russian mobilisation was completed. Sections of that force could then be transferred to the Eastern Front to meet the Russians. Militarily, it was a daring plan, yet it was politically indefensible, as Germany was among those nations who guaranteed Belgium's neutrality. Nevertheless, the strategy became the basis of German military planning for the next 15 years. Gerhard Ritter, who saw the growth of unrestrained military independence in Germany as one of the main causes of the disaster of 1914, has outlined the reason for this. 'To raise political objections to a strategic plan worked out by the General Staff would have appeared in the Germany of Wilhelm II unwarranted interference in a foreign sphere.' In the years preceding 1914, and in that fateful year itself, the German military establishment differed from those of other European powers, not in the degree of its preparedness for war, but in the degree of its freedom from civil governmental restraint.

4.5 What were the main aims of German domestic policies between 1890 and 1914?

For many years after the collapse of the German Reich in 1918, it was usual for historians to conclude that the policies of Wilhelmine Germany had been shaped primarily by foreign aims and ambitions. In recent years, however, a new 'school' of German historians has insisted upon the 'primacy of domestic affairs'. They argue that domestic struggles were the prime preoccupation of German politicians, and that even the great adventure of *Weltpolitik* was in truth only a foreign means to a domestic end. Hans-Ulrich Wehler, in *The German Empire 1871–1918* (1985), states that the true theme of Wilhelmine, and indeed of Bismarckian, politics was 'the defence of inherited ruling position by pre-industrial élites against the onslaught of new forces – a defensive struggle which became even sharper with the erosion of the economic foundations of these privileged leading strata'.

Government through repression or through national consensus?

Certainly, the years of Caprivi's chancellorship had seen the vested interests of the Junker class threatened by the benevolent attitude of the Kaiser towards social problems, and by the sympathy of the Chancellor for industrial economic interests. The fall of Caprivi, largely the work of the Junkers themselves, forced future chancellors to seek new tactics against the dual threats of socialism and industrialism. The first tactic was repression. After 1894, the expressed desire of Wilhelm II to be 'King of the Beggars' was rarely in evidence. Instead, the Kaiser pointedly withdrew his original instructions to Protestant pastors to concern themselves with social questions. The five years between 1894 and 1899 witnessed a stream of anti-socialist and anti-union legislation proposed in the Reichstag, mostly without success.

The refusal of the Reichstag – in which conservative representation dropped 21% between 1893 and 1898 – to support a policy of repression, forced a change of tack. Under Bülow's administration, the government embraced a principle defined in 1897 as *Sammlungspolitik*. In other words, it sought to 'gather together' behind a common policy all the major propertied and conservative interests in the Reich. If the hostility between Junker and industrialist could be bridged, a formidable front could be presented to social democracy. Bülow's policy had two 'prongs':

1. The reorientation of economic policy, evident in 1902 when Bülow abandoned Caprivi's system of trade treaties, to replace them with a set of high tariffs protecting agriculture and certain key German manufactures from foreign competition. Russian corn, incidentally, was largely excluded thereby from the German market, to the relief of the Junkers. The discontent of German heavy industry, meanwhile, was relieved by the start of Germany's massive naval construction programme. Aptly this conciliation of conservative economic interests became known as the 'Alliance of Rye and Steel'.

2. Meanwhile, the wider policy of *Weltpolitik* played the same role. Bülow's explanation of his policy in 1897, while superficially declaring the 'primacy of foreign affairs', in fact betrayed the true nature of *Weltpolitik*. 'I am putting the main emphasis on foreign policy. Only a successful foreign policy can help to reconcile, pacify, rally, unite.'

Parties in the Reichstag, 1890–1912

	1890	1893	1898	1903	1907	1912
Conservatives	93	100	79	75	84	57
National Liberals	42	53	46	51	54	45
Left Liberals	76	48	49	39	49	42
Centre	106	96	102	100	105	91
Social Democrats	35	44	56	81	43	110
National minorities (e.g. Poles, Danes, Alsatians)	38	35	34	32	29	33
Anti-Semites	5	16	13	11	21	13

Germany and its minorities

A lesser, but nevertheless significant, feature of the domestic politics of 1894–1914 was the reversal of Caprivi's policies towards national minorities within the Reich. In Prussia, for example, Bülow rigorously enforced the laws banning the use of Polish in education, and passed a law in the Landtag (1908) allowing the confiscation of Polish estates for the settlement of German farmers. It is true that in 1911 Alsace and Lorraine received a new constitution integrating them more closely into the normal political system of the Reich. However, the 'Zabern Affair' of 1913 showed clearly that the brutal mentality of military occupation still predominated.

The position of Germany's Jewish population during the Wilhelmine years is not easy to define. **Assimilation** had produced some impressive success stories. Families such as the Warburgs, the Rothschilds and the Ballins had established themselves with enormous success in banking and in shipping. Middle-class Jews had little difficulty carving out successful

Assimilation: The process by which one group adapts itself to the culture and traditions of the society in which it lives. In particular, this has come to be associated with European Jewish communities who have faced the choice of adapting to become part of national communities, or of maintaining a distinct cultural identity.

careers in medicine, science or journalism. On the other hand, more traditional career areas, such as government, the army and the judiciary, remained closed. Wilhelmine Germany also boasted a variety of anti-semitic political parties, who admittedly won relatively few votes, but provided fertile soil for a growing tradition of pseudo-intellectual anti-semitism. Ernst Haeckel's *Riddle of the Universe* and Houston Stewart Chamberlain's *Foundations of the Nineteenth Century* were both published in 1899. Both adopted a pseudo-scientific approach to the question of race, 'proving' the superiority of Germanic races, and that this superiority would be undermined if Jews were allowed to 'dilute' German racial characteristics by intermarriage.

1. What was Sammlungspolitik, and why did the German government pursue such a course during this period?

2. What evidence is there of intolerance towards minority groups within Germany at this time?

Even so, recent historical research has suggested that such 'scholastic' reasoning played little part in the growth of German anti-semitism. Jack Wertheimer and Egmont Zechlin have both suggested that a more significant role was played by the influx of some 79,000 Jews from eastern Europe who flooded into Germany from Russian territory in the years shortly before the First World War. The element of class threat posed by these poor and unassimilated Jews, together with the element of patriotic mistrust generated by the war, formed the true basis of the anti-semitic explosion of the 1930s.

4.6 Was the rise of social democracy a serious threat to the stability of Wilhelmine Germany?

The growth and development of social democracy

We have already seen that this was a period of dramatic social and economic change in Germany, and that these changes caused alarm among the governing classes. Alongside those changes, and perhaps because of them, electoral support for the Social Democratic Party also increased considerably. As the table on page 108 shows, a temporary lapse in Social Democrat support in 1907 was reversed so effectively that by 1912 the party was the most powerful in the Reichstag. If one were to judge from these figures alone, one would conclude that *Sammlungspolitik* failed to secure the state against the threat of socialism. Their triumph certainly had an effect upon the Kaiser and his government. 'The German parliamentarian,' Wilhelm declared in 1913, 'becomes daily more of a swine.' Yet how much of a threat did **social democracy** pose to the Imperial system of government? For all its Marxist origins, the German socialist movement by 1912 was broadly committed to the 'revisionism' proposed by Eduard Bernstein in 1898 in his work, *The Presuppositions of Socialism and the Tasks of Social Democracy*. Bernstein's conclusion was that Marx had been mistaken about the approaching crisis of capitalism, as the rising living standards of German workers proved, and that change should not be sought through the active promotion of revolution. Historian David Blackbourn summarises the position of the Social Democratic Party neatly: 'It believed that history would deliver the future into its lap. Waiting for revolution, it was caught between accommodation and action.' From 1906 onwards, leading social democrats were willing to make electoral pacts with the Liberals to forward desirable social policies. They were willing, in general, to subscribe to an Imperial foreign policy which they interpreted as primarily opposed to reactionary Tsardom. They even supported the financial provisions of the Army Bill in 1913, because of the government's proposal that these should be paid for by a property tax.

Social democracy: A kind of socialism in which people are allowed a relatively large amount of freedom.

Karl Liebknecht (1871–1919)

Son of Wilhelm Liebknecht, founder of the Social Democratic Party. After an early career as a radical lawyer, Karl Liebknecht was active in the Social Democrats resisting moves to direct the party away from its Marxist roots. Entered the Reichstag (1912), voted against war credits (1914), and served during the war as a non-combatant. Expelled from the Social Democrats (1916), he helped to found the Spartacus League. A leading figure in German communism at the end of the war, Liebknecht was killed in the course of the Spartacist rising.

Rosa Luxemburg (1871–1919)

Born in Poland and active in Polish radical politics before emigrating to Switzerland in 1889. Joined German Social Democratic Party, and actively resisted Bernstein's revision of its Marxist doctrine. An advocate of the general strike as a revolutionary weapon. Formed the Spartacus League with Karl Liebknecht (1916), and like him was killed in the course of the Spartacist rising.

The 'threat' of social democracy

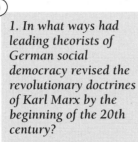

1. *In what ways had leading theorists of German social democracy revised the revolutionary doctrines of Karl Marx by the beginning of the 20th century?*

2. *How realistic were the fears felt by the German governing classes at the increase in support for the Social Democrats?*

Nevertheless, it is possible to understand the apprehension of the ruling classes at the electoral success of social democracy which destroyed the conservative 'Bülow bloc' of parties, and replaced it with a bloc effectively able to resist any unpopular government legislation. The 1912 elections, wrote Wolfgang Mommsen (1995), thus created the 'stalemate of the party system'. The Zabern incident, although it demonstrated the practical weaknesses of the Reichstag, also provided a disturbing illustration of the fact that massive anti-government feeling could now be mobilised within that assembly. The Social Democratic Party, furthermore, did possess an active left wing, led by Karl Liebknecht and Rosa Luxemburg. It maintained an orthodox Marxist line, and was to show its revolutionary potential in 1918. Lastly, we should not ignore the fact that the prospect of power in the hands of industrial workers appeared outrageous and highly dangerous to many conservatives, regardless of the uses to which those workers might turn their power. With or without justification, therefore, the election results of 1912 ensured that domestic political tensions were as high as ever as the conservatives of the German government and General Staff approached the international crisis of the last years of peace.

4.7 What were the results of Germany's decision to pursue a 'world policy'?

The nature of Weltpolitik

In the years that followed the fall of Caprivi, a revolutionary new factor came to dominate the foreign policy of the Reich. That policy departed from the essentially European concerns of Bismarck and came, more and more, to demand a world role for Germany. By enlarging its interests in non-European affairs Germany was to become a 'world power' (*Weltmacht*). The reasons for this fundamental change were complex and varied, yet on the whole this 'world policy' (*Weltpolitik*) must be seen as an external reflection of internal German developments.

Firstly, it undoubtedly reflected the mentality and personality of the Kaiser. *Weltpolitik* consisted of a headstrong and incoherent insistence that Germany should have a say in all major issues, just as Wilhelm intruded his half-formed opinion into all aspects of domestic government. As the historian Imanuel Geiss puts it, in *German Foreign Policy, 1871–1914* (1976), 'German foreign policy during this time bore the personal stamp of the Kaiser. He found it more or less congenial and in keeping with his personal ambitions and his style of behaviour.' Certainly, Wilhelm made a direct practical contribution to this policy by his appointment to high office of its enthusiastic supporters. In 1897 alone, the promotions of Johannes von Miquel to the vice-presidency of the Prussian ministry, of Alfred von Tirpitz to the naval ministry and of Bernhard von Bülow to the head of the foreign ministry provided the core of the *Weltpolitik* 'crew'.

Weltpolitik was not merely a result of the Kaiser's whim. The expansion of German industry had renewed and increased the national sense of power, and many leading figures expressed the fear that existing resources and markets would soon prove insufficient and that emigration to the USA might rob Germany of its most dynamic sons. 'Our vigorous national development,' claimed Bülow himself, 'mainly in the industrial sphere, forced us to cross the ocean.' The historian Treitschke and the statesman Delbrück publicised a variation upon this theme. Since German unification, the colonial expansion of other powers had cancelled out Germany's advance in status. Germany was faced with the choice of colonial expansion or stagnation as a major power. This theme of world expansion as a logical sequel to unification was most eloquently expressed by the sociologist Max Weber in his inaugural lecture at Freiburg University in 1895. 'We have to grasp,' he stated, 'that the unification of Germany would have been better dispensed with because of its cost, if it were the end and not the beginning of a German policy of World Power.'

Lastly, many recent historians concentrating upon the domestic affairs of the Reich have interpreted *Weltpolitik* as essentially an element in the solution of Germany's internal political problems. At a time when the apparent factional divisions in German politics were widening, it provided a means of uniting national opinion and neutralising the disruptive opposition of the Social Democrats. The patriotic stance of the Social Democrats in 1914 certainly suggests that *Weltpolitik* succeeded where the reform programmes of Bismarck and of Caprivi had failed. Most historians would now agree with the conclusion stated by Imanuel Geiss, that '*Weltpolitik* came into existence as a red herring of the ruling classes to distract the middle and working classes from social and political problems at home'. Where Bismarck (in 1890) and Wilhelm II (in 1894) had toyed with the idea of a *coup d'état* as the answer to domestic pressures, Germany now turned to the glamour and excitement of *Weltpolitik*.

Coup d'état: The process whereby a small political group seizes control of the state by force.

The acquisition of colonies

In the last four years of the 19th century the mentality of *Weltpolitik* manifested itself in all those quarters of the globe subject to European penetration. In Africa it took the form of a masquerade as protector of the Boers in their confrontation with British imperialism in the Transvaal, under President Kruger. After the Boers had thwarted an ill-organised, British-backed coup, Wilhelm dispatched his famous 'Kruger Telegram' congratulating them on maintaining their independence 'without having to appeal to friendly powers for assistance'. With German naval power in its infancy, it was an empty gesture, whose only lasting effect could be to cause offence to a potentially friendly European power.

The first tangible reward of *Weltpolitik* was reaped in China in 1897. There, alarmed at the extent of Japan's success in its war against China (1894–95), Germany acted, together with Russia and France, to modify the original Japanese gains, and to ensure that China remained open to European penetration. Its own private gain was a 99-year lease of the port of Kiaochow as a trading and naval base. The following year the small groups of Pacific Islands, the Carolines and the Marianas, were purchased from Spain. In 1899, Germany declared that its joint control with Britain and the USA over the islands of Samoa was dissolved, and assumed possession of the eastern portion of the islands.

Patently trivial as such gains were, the extension of German interests in the Middle East had more serious international implications. As early as 1888, the Deutsche Bank had agreed with the Turkish government to finance the projected railway from Baghdad to the Persian Gulf. It was clearly a region sensitive to both British and Russian interests. While Bismarck had specified at that time that German money implied no direct German political interest, Wilhelm II showed none of his restraint. In a typically pretentious speech (1898) he referred to himself as 'the protector of 300 million Muslims', and openly referred to 'my railway'. The compensation for strained relations with Britain and Russia was the attraction of the Turkish Empire into the German orbit – yet the First World War proved Turkey to be an ally of doubtful worth.

The birth of the German navy

The most spectacular and damaging manifestation of Germany's new ambitions was the growth of its naval power. The development of a mighty battle fleet, like *Weltpolitik* itself, served several purposes. For many, like its founder Admiral von Tirpitz, it was an assertion of the nation's new status. 'The fleet, he declared, 'is necessary to show that Germany is as well born as Britain.' In so saying, he betrayed the essential feature of naval development. It was aimed at, and bound to offend, Great Britain. It was the one major European power with whom Germany had no potential continental argument, and whose friendship might have offset the Franco–Russian alliance. Equally, the decision to develop the fleet provided a huge new outlet for German heavy industry. It was no coincidence that so great an industrialist as Alfred Krupp was a leading member and backer of the Naval League (*Flottenverein*), founded in 1898. To the politically-minded middle classes, the fleet represented a national weapon relatively free from the influence of the Prussian Junkers.

The first Naval Bill, of March 1898, envisaged an eventual force of 19 battleships, 12 heavy cruisers and 30 light cruisers. The launching of the revolutionary British battleship, 'HMS Dreadnought' (February 1906), had a double impact upon the naval question. By rendering obsolete all existing battleships, it opened up the real possibility that a German fleet could compete with its British counterpart. At the same time, it necessi-

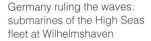

Germany ruling the waves: submarines of the High Seas fleet at Wilhelmshaven

tated an urgent rebuilding of the German fleet. In retrospect, further German bills in 1906, 1907 and 1908 constituted a double misfortune for the German state. They resulted in a tremendous financial undertaking, and signalled the beginning of a naval arms race between Britain and Germany. It is in these respects that we may accept the verdict of historians Ian Porter and Ian Armour, in *Imperial Germany 1890–1918* (1991), that 'the whole naval programme was an expensive failure'.

Weltpolitik: *the balance sheet*

With the exception of the new battle fleet, the physical results of *Weltpolitik* were meagre, even absurd. By 1914, Germany possessed a colonial 'empire' of only about a million square miles. Total German investment in those colonies was only 505 million marks. The colonies were dotted about the globe, almost indefensible and totally vulnerable to the attack of an enemy – as their fates in 1914 were to prove. In terms of Germany's overall diplomatic position, the decision to move towards 'world power' was of enormous negative importance. It completed the destruction of the Bismarckian European balance and prepared the way for Germany's isolation and encirclement. The historian Bernadotte Schmitt summarised the error of *Weltpolitik* as follows:

'A policy of naval expansion, the development of an African empire, commercial and financial penetration of the Near East could each be justified. But to pursue all three courses at the same time was the worst possible policy, for it kept alive the distrust and suspicion of the *Entente* powers, convinced them of the dangerous reality of German militarism, and made them more anxious than ever to act together.'

1. Into what areas did German influence spread as a result of Weltpolitik?

2. Summarise the impact of Weltpolitik upon Germany's diplomatic relations with other European powers.

3. Why did Germany decide to build a major battle fleet at the end of the 19th century?

Source-based questions: The construction of the German navy

Study the following source material and then answer the questions which follow.

SOURCE A

Record of a conversation between the Chancellor, Hohenlohe-Schillingfürst, and the Kaiser, March 1897

His Majesty received me with great affability, listened approvingly to my explanation, and then indulged himself in a highly detailed lecture on the navy. He enumerated the ships that we have and the ones we would need in order to survive a war. He emphasised that we had to have an armoured navy to protect our trade and to keep ourselves supplied with provisions; and was of the opinion that our fleet would have to be strong enough to prevent the French fleet cutting off food supplies that we needed. If the Reichstag didn't approve this, he would nevertheless carry on building, and would present the Reichstag with the bill later. Public opinion didn't concern him.

SOURCE B

Part of an article in Nauticus, *a journal published to promote the German navy (published in 1900)*

The concept of the navy has indeed been the hearth around which the German attempts at unity have clustered and warmed themselves. Thus it has already helped to fulfil a great national mission. It has also, however, been allotted the further task of overcoming the discord between the parties in the united German Empire, and directing the minds of the disputants towards the greatness and the glory of the Fatherland. Today millions of our compatriots are spiritually alienated from the state and the prevailing economic order: the concept of the navy possesses the power to revive the national spirit of the classes and fill them once again with patriotic loyalty and love for Kaiser and Reich.

AQA Unit 1

Source-based questions: The construction of the German navy

SOURCE C

Part of a secret communication from the German ambassador in London to the Chancellor, von Bülow. He reports conversations with senior British ministers. (The comments in brackets are those written by the Kaiser in the margins of the original document.) July 1908.

Both ministers considered that the situation between England and Germany turned on the question of the fleet. Expenditure on the British navy had risen as a result of the German programme ('False! As a result of British greed for power, and their fear of bogeymen.'), and in proportion to the increased speed of construction ('There has been no increase'). Every Englishman would spend his last penny to maintain naval superiority ('According to *Nauticus* they have it threefold'), on which depended England's existence as an independent state.

I replied that a 'German invasion' existed only in the British imagination. No reasonable being in Germany thought of it ('Very good'). The invention of the Dreadnought had unfortunately made ship-building dearer and had caused Britain to forfeit her immense advantage, but whose fault was that?

(a) Use Source C and your own knowledge.

Explain briefly the reference made in Source C to 'the invention of the Dreadnought'. [3 marks]

(b) Use Sources A and B and your own knowledge.

Explain how Source A differs from Source B in its explanation of the motives behind the development of a German navy. [7 marks]

(c) Use Sources A, B and C and your own knowledge.

Explain the impact of the German decision to build a navy upon German domestic and foreign politics in the years between 1897 and 1914.

[15 marks]

4.8 Was Germany's position in European diplomacy strengthened or weakened by its policies between 1894 and 1905?

Germany and Russia

The weakening of the Bismarckian system of alliances left Germany's European diplomacy with two central themes in the decade after the fall of Caprivi. The first was the desire to maintain friendly relations with Russia in the hope of detaching it from its new-found friendship with France. The year 1894 provided two sources of hope in this respect, with the replacement of Caprivi by the more conservative and 'Bismarckian' Hohenlohe, and with the accession of Nicholas II. The new Tsar, a cousin of the Kaiser, enjoyed friendly personal relations with his fellow Emperor, and was susceptible to Wilhelm's entreaties to pursue a civilising mission against the 'yellow peril' in eastern Asia. The 1890s saw common action against excessive Japanese gains from China, but the logical outcome of Russian commitment was its involvement in the Russo–Japanese war of 1904. Although such distractions suited Germany's purposes, the conviction in St Petersburg that such a war had always been the German goal merely compounded the damage done by the cancellation of the Reinsurance Treaty. Nevertheless, Wilhelm came close to success in a final effort to separate Russia and France. In a meeting at Björkö (July 1905) he persuaded the Tsar to conclude an agreement whereby both states undertook to aid the other in the event of an attack by another European power in Europe. The success was, however, merely superficial. The Tsar had undertaken more than his ministers would allow him to fulfil. The implications for the loss of French economic aid alone were so serious that they refused to endorse the agreement, and the Treaty of Björkö remained a 'dead letter' from the moment of its signature.

Germany and Britain

A logical response to the growing intimacy of Russia and France would have been to cultivate relations with Great Britain more closely. German attitudes to Britain, though, remained highly ambiguous. The ambassador to London, von Hatzfeldt, hoped and believed Britain might be drawn into the Triple Alliance and consistently condemned *Weltpolitik* as a tactless means of alienating a valuable ally. The Kaiser himself was certainly attracted to some elements of British society, but had an intense dislike for others, such as its constitutional monarchy. Such ambiguity was mirrored in the diplomatic history of the 1890s. The promise of the agreement over Heligoland and Zanzibar contrasted with the lively hostility created by the 'Kruger Telegram'. Germany's official, and vaguely benevolent, neutrality during the Boer War (1899–1900) was offset by the violently anti-British propaganda of the Pan-German League and the Naval League. Thus, when a Conservative government in Britain abandoned the **isolationism** of the Liberals and put out feelers for a formal alliance, the opportunity was missed.

The first British approach (March 1898) collapsed because of German fears that a treaty might fail to achieve parliamentary ratification, and that relations with Russia might be strained to no avail. The second approach (January 1901) was killed by a series of miscalculations by the German Foreign Office. In the first place, senior officials remained convinced that a German alliance was Britain's only option. Speaking of British hints of an approach to France, Bülow declared that 'in my opinion we need not worry about such remote possibilities'. Secondly, Germany set excessively strict conditions upon an understanding with Britain. It was to tie itself, not simply to Germany, but to the Triple Alliance as a whole. Finding the prospect of commitment to the maintenance of Austria-Hungary quite unacceptable, Britain had within three years informally associated itself with the Franco–Russian Entente.

The so-called 'free hand' policy of the German Foreign Office, by rejecting British overtures, and by overestimating the significance of the Björkö agreement, had by 1905 left Germany isolated but for its partners in the Triple Alliance. Given the vacillation of Italy and its improving relations with France, this effectively meant dependence upon Austria–Hungary as Germany's sole reliable ally.

Isolationism: The policy by which a state withdraws from international commitments to pursue the development of its own domestic interests.

1. What changes occurred in Germany's diplomatic relations during this period

(a) with Russia and

(b) with Great Britain?

2. Compare the strengths and weaknesses of Germany's diplomatic position in 1890 and in 1910.

4.9 What was the impact of the First World War upon German society and politics?

In Germany, as in other combatant states, the war provided an unprecedented test of national unity and of national identity. Indeed, like conservatives all over Europe, many German politicians led their country into the conflict in the hope that the crisis would submerge differences and tensions, and would unite the population behind the governmental system. In the early stages of the war the gamble appeared to be justified.

Governmental claims that this was a defensive war, necessary to prevent Germany being stifled by jealous neighbours, seemed generally to be accepted, and Germans of all political persuasions rallied to the cause. The SPD, so critical recently of most aspects of the Kaiser's policy, voted in favour of war credits, and intellectuals who should have known better issued manifestoes in which they justified the war as a necessary defence and safeguard of superior German 'Kultur'. Programmes demanding large-scale territorial annexations after Germany's inevitable victory were extremely popular, as the historian David Blackbourn has indicated:

> 'Annexationist ambitions were not confined to soldiers like Hindenburg and Ludendorff, or to Pan-Germans or other super-patriots. They were shared by civilian ministers, civil servants, Catholic and liberal politicians, liberal intellectuals, even by some Social Democrats. The point is not that there were no differences between extreme annexationists and moderates – there were – but that the moderates were not really so moderate.'

Burgfriede (literally, 'Castle peace'): The term refers to the way in which the garrison of a besieged castle puts aside its differences in the face of a common threat. The term comes to mean, therefore, a political truce at a time of crisis.

Germans of all descriptions appealed to the concept of *Burgfriede*, the abandonment of differences that occurs within a castle that is under siege.

Why did the political unity of 1914 degenerate as the war progressed?

The maintenance of this *Burgfriede* depended upon a speedy victory and, as the war entered its second year, the first cracks in the political solidarity of 1914 began to appear. In particular, these were provoked by the economic effects of the war, which were complex and far-reaching. Problems quickly arose in terms of manpower and of its organisation. By the end of 1914, one-third of Germany's pre-war industrial labour force was in uniform, and with little prospect of their immediate return, new sources of labour had to be found. The number of women employed in factories rose by 50%, foreign labour was conscripted from occupied areas, especially from Belgium and Poland, and new industrial workers were recruited from the countryside. These new urban workers were subjected to an increasing level of governmental regulation. The War Raw Materials Office (KRA – *Kriegsrohstoffabteilung*) was quickly established (August 1914), co-ordinating the private companies that were to produce and distribute the raw materials required for the war effort, and this set the pattern for increasing government intervention in the economic life of the state. In 1916, the introduction of the Auxiliary Labour Law made it obligatory for all German males between the ages of 17 and 60 to work for the war effort if so required, and left them with little independent choice as to where and how they would be employed. Although arbitration boards were established to resolve disputes, and trade unions were allowed an unprecedented role, there can be no doubt that these developments represented a substantial extension of military control over the working population. Political tensions arose from a variety of associated factors. Little seemed to be done to limit the profits made by key war industries, and no minister dared to reduce the fiscal privileges of the Junker agriculturalists. Inflation eroded wage levels in all industries, and government attempts to requisition food from the countryside caused considerable resentment among farmers. There is evidence of growing opposition to the war in the countryside some time before it manifested itself in the cities.

In addition, the attempts by the allies to blockade Germany, and to cut off imports of food and raw materials, were hugely effective. The impact upon a country that imported a third of its foodstuffs was bound to be serious, and problems of malnutrition were widespread even before the notorious 'turnip winter' of 1916–17. Over the whole course of the war, it is believed, as many as 750,000 German deaths could be attributed to starvation. In addition to the material hardships, the government's attempts to regulate food supplies caused considerable bitterness and political division. Rationing was not implemented efficiently, with different official levels applying in different areas, and a flourishing black market existed throughout the war.

The waning of popular enthusiasm coincided directly with the tightening of conservative, military control over the direction of the war. The disastrous losses at Verdun (see Chapter 6) led to the dismissal of Field Marshall von Falkenhayn, and control of the Supreme Command (OHL – *Oberste Heeresleitung*) passed into the hands of Paul von Hindenburg and his second-in-command Erich von Ludendorff. This was of the greatest importance in terms both of German military strategy and of the direction of domestic politics. Both men set their faces against any suggestion of a compromise peace, and sought to prosecute the war by all available means to a successful conclusion. Some of the available means, such as unrestricted submarine warfare in the west, or a draconian peace settlement with Russia in the east, had serious military and political implications. On the domestic front, meanwhile, it became increasingly clear that political power had fallen into military hands to an extent that was unprecedented even in recent German experience. In July 1917, Bethmann-Hollweg, increasingly aware that it was in Germany's interests to seek a negotiated peace, lost the confidence of the military leaders and was forced out of office. His fate was later shared by the Secretary for Foreign Affairs, von Kühlmann, who was forced to resign as late as July 1918 for suggesting in the Reichstag that the allies might be approached for a negotiated peace.

It was clear that the tripartite governmental structure of Wilhelmine Germany no longer existed. The new Chancellor, Georg Michaelis, was effectively controlled by the army, and the Kaiser no longer exercised any realistic authority. The army was now in control, to the extent that historian Martin Kitchen refers to this period as the 'Hindenburg dictatorship'. The army acquired domestic powers, restrictions upon public assemblies, supervision of political meetings, the use of troops as strike-breakers, which were not at all what left-wing politicians had originally envisaged as the results of their cooperation with the war effort. The German experience of war now aggravated the very divisions that it had been intended to heal. The SPD, for example, was increasingly at odds with the military leadership. As early as December 1915, some members had proposed a motion in the Reichstag opposing annexations in Belgium at the end of the war, and threatening to oppose the voting of further war credits. That threat surfaced once more in July 1917 when the fall of the Tsarist government in Russia raised the possibility of moderate peace proposals which might encourage Russia to leave the war. April 1917 saw major strikes in several German cities and, while the SPD in general remained loyal to the patriotic cause, some of its more radical members took a different route. At a conference in Gotha in April 1917, Hugo Haase, former chairman of the party, led a group of dissidents to form a new party, the Independent Social Democrats (USPD – *Unabhängige Sozialdemokratische Partei Deutschlands*). Three months later the SPD renewed its threat to vote against further war credits. Then, in January 1918, at least a million workers participated in the biggest strike that Germany had witnessed during the war.

At the same time, this movement to the left was offset by a rallying and consolidation of right-wing patriotic elements. 1917 also witnessed the formation of the Fatherland Party, a coalition of traditional conservative groups, which quickly boasted 1.25 million members and included some prominent conservative names among its membership. Admiral Tirpitz was its chairman, and Wolfgang Kapp, soon to give his name to one of the most dangerous assaults upon the Weimar Republic, was one of its primary administrators. A much less prominent member, Anton Drexler, was shortly to found another extreme nationalist organisation, the National Socialist Party. By early 1918, the battle-lines within domestic German politics had become more rigidly defined than they had ever been before the war.

What was the significance of the wartime experience for Germany's political future?

The political polarisation that took place in the course of 1917–18 serves to illustrate how important Germany's wartime experience is in understanding the events of the next two and a half decades. It is commonplace to emphasise the role played by the 1919 peace settlement in creating the divisions that crippled the Republic and eventually brought Adolf Hitler to power. More recently, however, historians have been eager to stress that most of these factors had their origins in the war itself. Edgar Feuchtwanger (*Imperial Germany 1850–1918*, 2001) has explained how most of the major difficulties facing Weimar politicians (see Chapter 10) had their genesis in the war. By an early stage in the war the small business man, later the target of much Nazi propaganda, already felt himself severely damaged by the privileges and incentives offered by the military and the government to large-scale industrial producers. The crippling inflation that constituted one of the most spectacular problems of the 1920s was the direct result of inadequate financing of the war. The fact of an extended conflict left the German government with severe financial problems. Able to cover only 16% of the costs from taxation, and unwilling to extend the tax liability of the privileged classes, the German government gambled on other means. On the assumption of eventual victory, and subsequently of imposing heavy reparations upon their opponents, they printed extra cash to finance the war, so that 'Germany floated through the war on a sea of paper money' (Ian Porter and Ian Armour, *Imperial Germany 1890–1918*, 1991). Another method of financing the war was through the large-scale issue of war bonds. Prosperous members of the middle classes invested patriotically in such bonds, only to find that the prospects of repayment receded with the prospects of victory. For many such Germans the war destroyed the social status and the financial security to which they had been accustomed, and left them adrift in an uncertain and threatening world. In effect, the Weimar Republic in 1919 inherited an economic situation that was more or less hopeless, not because of the terms of the peace, but because of the nature of the war itself.

4.10 What forces shaped the political policies of Wilhelmine Germany?
A CASE STUDY IN HISTORICAL INTERPRETATION

One of the most important and persistent themes in historical revisionism in recent decades has been the tendency to question the roles and the importance of 'great men' in shaping historical events. This tendency has been particularly evident in recent work on German history, where traditional interpretations have laid great emphasis upon the roles of such individuals as Otto von Bismarck and Adolf Hitler. Although historians have rarely accorded him the same status as these men, Kaiser Wilhelm II was also believed to have made an important impact upon the course of German politics in the two decades before the outbreak of the First World War. His accession to the throne in 1888 was held to signal a significant change in the exercise of state power within the Reich. Where his grandfather, Wilhelm I, had largely entrusted Bismarck with his executive authority, and had allowed his Chancellor a wide freedom of action, the young Kaiser insisted upon direct, personal control. Distinct differences were therefore discernible between the priorities of 'Bismarckian' and of 'Wilhelmine' Germany. Tentative and insincere colonialism, for instance, gave way to full-blown *Weltpolitik*. The alliance with Austria, once a tool for maintaining the balance of Europe, became the basis for a wartime alliance. J.G. Röhl, in *Germany without Bismarck: the Crisis of Government in the Second Reich, 1890–1900* (1967), made a characteristic case for this point of view when he wrote that between 1897 and the crisis of the *Daily Telegraph* interview, Wilhelm 'dictated policy to an amazing extent. All appointments, all bills, all diplomatic moves were made on his orders.' This emphasis upon the personal authority of the Kaiser was widely accepted, both by contemporaries and by historians. In 1918, the army's Junker commanders believed that they could convince enemy politicians that fundamental change had taken place in the political structure of Germany simply by forcing the abdication of the Kaiser.

This comfortable consensus was one of the casualties caused by the important work of the German historian Fritz Fischer. In such books as *War of Illusions: German Politics, 1911–1914* (1969) and *World Power or Decline: The Controversy over Germany's War Aims in the First World War* (1975), he claimed that elements in German society pressed the state into policies which made Germany directly responsible in large part for the outbreak of war in 1914. It was not satisfactory either to pin blame solely upon the Kaiser's erratic personality, or to deny Germany's overall responsibility. Although Fischer's main concern was with the origins of the war, his conclusions had important implications for the writing of Wilhelmine history. In the place of a stable society, dominated by a powerful Kaiser, Fischer portrayed a society in crisis, whose governors sought desperately for policies that might provide a degree of national unity.

The body of work that followed in support of the 'Fischer thesis' was largely synthesised by Hans-Ulrich Wehler in his influential book, *The German Empire* (1973). Wehler, too, portrays Wilhelmine Germany as a cynically anti-democratic state, in which élite groups, industrialists, Junkers, and certain agencies in which their influence was entrenched, such as the army and the diplomatic corps, placed enormous pressures upon the Kaiser and his government to protect their vested interests. The Zabern Incident in Alsace-Lorraine in 1913, or the wide acceptance of the dangerous and irresponsible Schlieffen Plan, might be taken to represent one strand of these influences. The authority of Friedrich von Holstein in the Foreign Ministry (1900–06) might be taken to represent another.

In its turn this 'new orthodoxy' has been challenged in recent years, especially by the work of a school of British historians that includes Richard Evans (editor, *Society and Politics in Wilhelmine Germany*, 1978), David Blackbourn and Geoff Eley (co-authors of *The Peculiarities of German History: Bourgeois Society and Politics in Nineteenth-century Germany*, 1984). Their main criticism of Wehler and his school is that they have underestimated the complexity of Wilhelmine society, and have thus overestimated the ease with which that society could be manipulated by the government. They have concentrated less upon the upper strata of German society, and are less convinced of the coherence and control of its governing élites. Instead their emphasis falls upon non-élite groups in the lower-middle or working classes, which they see as exerting enormous and disruptive pressures, to which the governors of Germany were forced to respond. The growth of the Social Democratic Party in the Reichstag in the last years of peace provides specific evidence of the pressure emanating from the industrial working classes. David Blackbourn's work on the Centre Party at this time also indicates that it was no longer a strictly clerical party, but increasingly a party that reflected middle-class and lower-middle-class interests. The government was forced to adopt policies that would court the parliamentary representatives of these classes, or which would deflect them from social and economic demands more threatening to the interests of the political élites. In particular, this might be seen in the more active and expansionist foreign policy of the Wilhelmine period. Volker Berghahn also placed the history and development of the German navy in this context, seeing it as a focus for popular, patriotic emotion, rather than as a strategic military weapon in its own right.

Where once the German Reich between 1890 and 1914 was seen as a stable and orthodox, semi-autocratic state, the question of political control now seems to be more difficult and confused. No new consensus has emerged to replace the traditional interpretation, and the picture created by recent research is rather of lack of control, of a state attempting to reconcile many conflicting forces and interests. This is the view and the social diversity that James Retallack refers to, in *Modern Germany Reconsidered* (1992), when he writes that 'the Empire was not entirely bad. It was neither completely urban nor completely rural. Aristocrats did not exclusively set the tone of everyday life – but neither did the Social Democrats. Manipulative strategies to deflect change did not always work as planned [and] often they went disastrously wrong.'

? Source-based questions: The government role of Wilhelm II

Study the following four passages and answer both of the sub-questions that follow.

SOURCE A

From: Edgar Feuchtwanger, Imperial Germany 1850–1918, *published in 2001. This historian ascribes an important role to the Kaiser, at least in the early stages of his reign.*

The first three years of Hohenlohe's chancellorship saw the 'personal regime' at its height. Most of the Kaiser's assertions of self-will had to do with personalities, the 'fight against revolution', and most importantly with the complex of foreign and defence policy, including the building of an ocean-going fleet. In fact the Kaiser interfered often decisively in most major decisions and the only limit to the personal regime was his own ignorance, inconsistency and lack of a coherent plan. This still left the chancellor and the bureaucracy room for manoeuvre.

SOURCE B

From: Katherine Anne Lerman, Kaiser Wilhelm II. Last Emperor of Imperial Germany, *published in Heinemann History Briefings, 1994. This historian largely rejects the idea that historical events are determined by the influence of one man.*

Many historians have been understandably reluctant to accept the thesis that the Kaiser personally ruled Germany before 1914. Not only does this thesis seem perilously close to the 'great man' theory of history, but it also appears to underestimate the complexity of the imperial German political system, the influence of the other states and political institutions within the Empire, and the inevitable constraints on the exercise of monarchical authority. Moreover, on close examination of policy issues, it is quite clear that the Kaiser did not rule Germany on a day to day basis or have command of the details of government work. His knowledge and understanding of political matters was always very superficial; he disliked routine work and read newspaper cuttings in preference to political reports. The one major issue on which Wilhelm II's will is generally seen to have been decisive is in

Source-based questions: The government role of Wilhelm II

the building of a German navy. A preoccupation with the Kaiser's political initiatives and actions tends to encourage the conclusion that his 'personal rule' was a myth, and that the monarchy merely interfered with or meddled in political decision-making, thereby contributing to, but in no sense determining the erratic course of German policy before 1914.

SOURCE C

From: Hans-Ulrich Wehler, The German Empire 1871–1918, *published in 1985. This historian suggests that no individual or interest was able to dominate German politics during this period.*

A power vacuum was created [by the fall of Bismarck] and subsequently a climate arose in which various personalities and social forces appeared in an attempt to fill it. Since neither they nor Parliament succeeded, there existed in Germany a permanent crisis of the state behind its façade of high-handed leadership. This in turn resulted in a variety of rival centres of power. It was this system that caused the zigzag course so often followed by German politics from that time on. First the young Kaiser tried to be both Emperor and Chancellor in one, in Bismarck's mocking phrase a brand of 'popular absolutism'. But this never received constitutional sanction: nor did Wilhelm II succeed in changing constitutional reality for any length of time, however much his clique of advisers tried to surround the decision-making process with the illusion of monarchical power.

SOURCE D

From: D. Blackbourn, Germany 1780–1918; the Long Nineteenth Century, *published in 1997. This historian emphasises the role that Wilhelm was able to play in German government by his indirect influence, rather than by direct constitutional authority.*

Recent writers have devoted much attention to the Kaiser's state of mind. Whether he suffered from arrested development, megalomania or manic-depression, the point is that his personal flaws mattered because he mattered. The Kaiser exercised an influence on German politics in many different ways. He was a powerful symbolic figure who helped to set the tone of public life and seduced many younger middle-class Germans by acting out the role of 'strong man'. The Kaiser also exercised his prerogatives. He took his power of appointment seriously, and used it, often against the advice of responsible ministers. He absorbed the influence of courtiers and favourites, and he interfered in decision-making by personal vetoes, marginal notes on official documents, and endless policy pronouncements. While ministers dealt with elected politicians, they also had to cope with demands and initiatives that came directly or indirectly through the Kaiser from various sources – powerful economic interests, court favourites, aides-de-camp and generals.

(a) Compare the views put forward in Sources B and D on the role played by Wilhelm II in the direction of German government. [15 marks]

(b) Using these four passages and your own knowledge, evaluate the claim that 'the major problem in German politics between 1890 and 1914 was not the power of Wilhelm II, but the absence of any dominant political power'.

[30 marks]

The crisis of Russian autocracy, 1894–1914

5.1 How well suited was the new Tsar to tackle the problems that confronted Russia in the 1890s?

5.2 In what respects and with what success was Russia's industrial economy modernised between 1892 and 1905?

5.3 To what extent did political opposition to the regime become more dangerous during this period?

5.4 What were the causes of the Russo–Japanese War?

5.5 Why did Russia lose the Russo–Japanese War and what were the consequences of its defeat?

5.6 Why did revolution break out in Russia in 1905?

5.7 How did the government survive the 1905 Revolution?

5.8 Did the Dumas represent a real constitutional advance in Russia?

5.9 What impression of Russian society is conveyed by scientific and cultural developments in the two decades before the outbreak of war?

5.10 Historical interpretation: How stable and how strong was the Russian regime on the eve of world war?

Key Issues

● *What political and economic problems faced Russia at the beginning of the 20th century?*

● *What problems contributed to the outbreak of revolution in Russia in 1905, and how did Tsarism survive?*

● *How strong was the Tsarist regime on the eve of the First World War?*

Framework of Events

1892–1903	Witte in office as Finance Minister
1894	Accession of Nicholas II
1897	Russian currency placed upon gold standard
1900	Formation of Socialist Revolutionary Party
1903	Formation of Russian Social Democratic (communist) Party, which splits into Bolshevik and Menshevik factions
1904–05	Russo–Japanese War
1905	(January) 'Bloody Sunday' massacre
	(May) Formation of first Soviet
	(October) Major strikes in St Petersburg. Issue of October Manifesto
1906–11	Stolypin in office as chief minister
1906	(April–July) First Duma
	(November) Stolypin's agrarian reforms
1907	(February–June) Second Duma
1907–12	Third Duma
1911	Assassination of Stolypin
1912–17	Fourth Duma
1914	Outbreak of First World War.

Overview

Nicholas II (1868–1918)
Tsar of Russia (1894–1917). He was dominated by his wife, Tsarina Alexandra, who was allegedly under the influence of Rasputin (see page 189). Nicholas' mismanagement of Russian internal affairs and of the Russo–Japanese war led to the revolution of 1905. Although the revolution was suppressed, the Tsar was forced to grant limited constitutional reforms. Nicholas took Russia into the First World War, but was forced to abdicate in 1917 after the Russian Revolution (see Chapter 7). The Tsar and his family were executed in 1918.

Romanov dynasty: The imperial crown of Russia had been passed from generation to generation of the Romanov family since Michael Romanov had been proclaimed Tsar in 1613.

Duma: The semi-constitutional assembly in Russia between 1906 and 1917.

I N 1894 a new Tsar came to the Russian throne to be confronted by some familiar problems. Like his immediate predecessors, Nicholas II had to decide upon the balance that his government would strike between the traditional political structure of Tsarist Russia, and the massive socio-economic forces that were operating within the Russian Empire. In some respects, the problems that he faced were more acute than those faced by his predecessors, for the forces unleashed by the great reforms of the 1860s were now making an increasing impact upon the economic and political life of his Empire. Although Russia could scarcely rival the great industrial economies of western Europe, it was no longer the exclusively agrarian society that it had been 50 years earlier. It was also now clear that Russia's international status depended heavily upon continued industrial growth. At the same time, the majority of Russian workers were still engaged in agricultural production, and there remained many agrarian problems to be solved before the aim of the Edict of Emancipation – a freer and more prosperous peasantry – was achieved. On a domestic, political level, several decades of freer expression had given rise to a variety of political groupings for whom unquestioning obedience of the Tsar's autocratic will was no longer acceptable.

Alexander III's response to these pressures had been to dig in his heels and to resist social and political change wherever possible. The response of Nicholas II suggests that he had more in common with his grandfather, Alexander II. Nicholas listened to ministers who recognised the need for economic modernisation, but he too failed to appreciate that this was likely to entail a significant degree of political change. There is little doubt that Nicholas' ideal vision of Russia's future included a more modern and efficient economy, combined with a political system that retained the traditional features of autocracy. The great revolutionary outburst of 1905 was largely the result, therefore, of the government's failure to adapt politically to the substantial social and economic changes that had taken place.

The 1905 revolution was the most concentrated outburst of domestic opposition that the **Romanov dynasty** had so far faced. It indicated that the regime faced opposition, not only from the peasantry and the rapidly expanding urban workforce, but also from significant sectors of the educated middle class who were no longer willing to tolerate government by an autocratic Tsar and his closed bureaucracy. Yet the government survived because it had some important cards to play. Faced with mounting crisis, Nicholas again accepted the need for reform, or at least for the appearance of reform. The measures implemented by his chief minister, Pyotr Stolypin, aimed to win back the support of his more moderate opponents, and to create a viable, conservative base of support for the monarchy. Constitutional reforms, of which the most important was the establishment of a **Duma** (parliament), offered the educated classes some real hope that they might now be involved in the processes of government. At the same time, Stolypin's agrarian reforms offered concessions and encouragement to the more prosperous and enterprising of the peasants, who might fulfil similar, conservative functions in the countryside.

In short, the reforms proposed a new power base for the Russian monarchy in place of that which had been undermined by the great agrarian reforms of the 1860s. In 1905, as in 1861, the monarchy stood at the crossroads between limited but significant reform, and stubborn reaction.

It is easy to write off Stolypin's experiment as a failure. There is much evidence that the Tsar saw it only as a temporary expedient, as a way of warding off the immediate danger. Within 10 years, the First World War set off the train of events that would destroy the Romanovs forever. The fact remains, however, that by 1906 the Russian monarchy had introduced a constitution, and had embraced some of the most important economic implications of the emancipation of the serfs. These were remarkable advances from the situation that had existed at the end of the Crimean War, just 50 years earlier. For many years the dominance of communism in Russia made this brief period of 'constitutional monarchy' appear a pathetic and doomed response to the great determinist forces that were bearing down upon the Russian conservatives. With the recent collapse of the Union of Soviet Socialist Republics (USSR), many historians find it meaningful once more to consider whether this period really formed a viable basis for the long-term survival of a reformed Romanov monarchy.

5.1   How well suited was the new Tsar to tackle the problems that confronted Russia in the 1890s?

The death of Alexander III in October 1894 brought his 29-year-old son, Nicholas, to the throne. A determined and dominant father had produced a shy and less assertive successor. There is a rare agreement among historians that the new Tsar was not equal to the tasks that confronted him. Hans Rogger speaks for many when he writes, in *Russia in the Age of Modernisation and Revolution 1881–1917* (1983), that:

> 'Nicholas had no knowledge of the world or of men, of politics or government, to help him make the difficult and weighty decisions that the Tsar alone must make. The only guiding stars that he recognised were an inherited belief in the moral rightness of autocracy, and a religious faith that he was in God's hands, and his actions were divinely inspired.'

In an attempt to achieve a balanced assessment, many commentators have drawn attention to Nicholas' private qualities, especially those as father and husband. However, as historian J.N. Westwood comments, in *Endurance and Endeavour: Russian History 1812–1980* (1981), 'family happiness has never yet saved a dynasty'.

The main influences on the Tsar had been conservative in the extreme. Such factors as the assassination of his grandfather in 1881, and his education at the hands of Konstantin Pobedonostsev, had left the new Tsar determined to maintain the autocracy of his predecessors. In the year of his succession, Nicholas was married to Princess Alice of Hesse-Darmstadt, and this only compounded the difficulties of the reign. Alexandra, as she became upon conversion to the Russian Orthodox faith, shared her husband's political incompetence. Being a stronger character and equally devoted to the principle of autocracy, she was better able to resist the good advice of those who might have saved the monarchy.

The probable course of the reign was indicated at an early stage. Meeting representatives of the *zemstva* and the town councils in January 1895, Nicholas dismissed their hopes 'for public institutions to express

1. What factors formed the political views of Nicholas II?

2. How similar were the personality and political philosophy of Nicholas II to those of Alexander III?

'**Land hunger**': A term used to describe the problem encountered by the Russian peasantry, who had no other means of livelihood than agriculture, but who did not always farm enough land to make an adequate living. As the population increased, the demand for more land to farm grew dramatically.

'**Virgin land**': Land that has not previously been farmed or exploited.

their opinion on questions which concern them' as evidence that they were 'carried away by senseless dreams'. To the horror of those who hoped for some relaxation of the oppression of his father's reign Nicholas pledged himself to 'uphold the principle of autocracy as firmly and unflinchingly as my late, unforgettable father'. In terms, however, of the social and economic development of Russia, and of the development of foreign affairs, Nicholas was on the verge of a very different world from his father's.

How had Russia's agrarian problems developed by the 1890s and by what means did the government of Nicholas II address them?

The peasant problem

The early years of Nicholas II's reign brought little respite for the peasantry, or for many of the smaller gentleman landowners, from the problems that had beset them since the emancipation of the serfs. The official government policy of low bread prices meant a low income for the farmers even when harvests were good, and harvest failures were frequent (notably in 1891, 1892, 1898 and 1901). Steady population growth in European Russia also increased the pressure upon peasant holdings that were already inadequate. It has been estimated that the average peasant holding shrank from 35 acres (14.5 hectares) in 1877 to 28 acres in 1905 due to subdivision within the growing family. The result, quite apart from frequent outbreaks of agrarian violence, was that arrears in taxation and in redemption payments accumulated rapidly.

Government initiatives

Motivated by concern for its own income, and for the future of the landed gentry and nobility, the government attempted two solutions to these problems. One was the formation of an improved Land Bank in 1886. The bank was equipped with funds and with reserves of land, much of it former state land, to encourage the purchase of holdings that might satisfy the pressing '**land hunger**' of the peasants. Within two years of its formation the interest rates charged by the bank upon its loans were as low as 4%. The second was to exploit a larger proportion of Russia's vast land resources by encouraging settlement on '**virgin land**' in the east. In 1896, the government founded its Resettlement Bureau to stimulate migration to Siberia. As a further encouragement, and to improve the public image of Siberia, the shipment of criminals there was suspended in 1900.

Neither project was wholly unsuccessful, but neither could hope to do more than scratch the surface of an enormous problem. It is true that the total amount of land in peasant hands increased substantially, by over 26 million hectares between 1877 and 1905, but that in the hands of the nobility declined by nearly 21 million. Equally, the fact that 750,000 peasants migrated to Siberia in the last four years of the 19th century needs to be set against the huge total peasant population of nearly 97 million reflected in the census of 1895.

The survival of agrarian problems

By the revolutionary year of 1905 there were still several obstacles between the peasant and a lasting solution to the land problem. One was the continuing existence of the peasant commune, the *mir*, to which many were still bound by the legislation of 1861. In many cases the *mir* continued to impose restrictions upon travel and freedom of enterprise that counteracted government initiatives. Secondly, the consistent lack of direct financial investment in agriculture meant that the Russian peasant was still using primitive farming methods totally outdated by comparison with western Europe. The magnitude of Russian agricultural production was a reflection of its land resources, and not of the efficiency

1. What were the main difficulties facing Russian agriculture at the end of the 19th century?

2. How justified is the statement that, at the start of the 20th century, the Russian government was taking realistic and effective steps to solve the state's agrarian problems?

with which they were exploited. In 1898–1902, for example, an average acre of Russian farmland produced 8.8 bushels, compared with 13.9 in the USA and 35.4 in Great Britain.

The fact, therefore, that Russia became the world's largest supplier of wheat to foreign markets in 1913 by exporting 3.33 million tons, conceals the truth that much of this was what came to be referred to as 'starvation exports'. The phrase reflects the fact that wheat was often exported despite domestic demand for the product, in order to pay for the industrial raw materials and machinery upon which the government, by the late 1890s, was staking the future of Russia.

5.2 In what respects and with what success was Russia's industrial economy modernised between 1892 and 1905?

Count Sergei Witte (1849–1915)

Russian statesman of Dutch origin. His family had achieved noble status by service to the state, and Sergei rose to high office by the unusual route of outstanding service in railway administration (he oversaw the construction of the Trans-Siberian railway). He was thus highly unusual among Russian ministers in that he was attuned to the needs and priorities of business and industry. Minister of Finance (1892–1903). Witte urged the rapid industrialisation of Russia, and took measures to stabilise the rouble and to attract foreign loans. Removed from office as a result of criticism of the results of his policies, but was recalled in the summer of 1905 to help negotiate peace with Japan and to quell revolution at home. After a six-month spell as Prime Minister, he was again dismissed from office.

Sergei Witte's view of the future of Russia

For all the political shallowness of Nicholas II, he was served by two ministers who might have saved the monarchy, given the right circumstances and consistent support. The first of these was Sergei Witte, who became Minister of Finance in August 1892 and held office until 1903. Witte did not regard himself as a narrow financial specialist. Self-confident and dynamic, he regarded the ultimate aim of his policies as being the salvation of Russia and the creation of a strong, modern state, but his political views were confused and uncertain. Although he professed himself dedicated to the maintenance of the autocracy, he cannot wholly have failed to foresee the political effects that the economic transformation of Russia would have. This curious mixture of energy and miscalculation naturally made Witte a controversial character among contemporaries and historians alike. Political opponents accused him of extravagance and of unpatriotic concessions to foreign capitalists. A number of more recent historians have criticised him for being insufficiently aware of the need for agricultural reform. Others have been impressed by the extent of his practical ability, and by the vision that he showed in advocating, for the first time in Russia's history, a coherent programme of industrial growth. Historian Hugh Seton-Watson, in *The Russian Empire, 1801–1917* (1988), is not alone in regarding Witte as 'one of the outstanding statesmen of the 19th century'.

Witte's measures

Witte understood that the key to Russia's future greatness lay in industrialisation. Russia's only alternative was to become a 'European China', a vast market unable to supply its own needs and thus 'the eternal handmaiden of states that are economically more developed'. His views were not original, being largely those of the previous Minister of Finance, I.A. Vyshnegradsky (1887–92). Witte was also influenced by Bismarck's policies in Germany. His real contribution was the coherent programme that he proposed in the 1890s to carry out this desired industrialisation. The basis of the policy was the strengthening of protective tariffs to guard infant Russian industries against the destructive competition of stronger European economies.

But how was Russian industry to develop when the vital investment capital was lacking, when the total amount of capital lying in Russian banks amounted to only 200 million roubles? How would foreign powers react if their access to so valuable a market were to be restricted? Witte's solution was to invite these foreign powers to continue to participate in the Russian economy, but by investing capital in it rather than by off-loading their consumer goods on to it. Thus the capital would be provided for the development of Russian industry. Industrial growth would also safeguard the government against social unrest by providing fuller employment and, in the long run, higher wages and cheaper goods. Protective tariffs, the attraction of foreign capital and the placing of the Russian currency on the **Gold Standard** (January 1897) – in order to inspire greater foreign confidence – were the three prongs of Witte's policy to create a great industrial Russia.

Gold Standard: A system whereby a state regulates the value of its currency, and the amount of currency in circulation, according to the quantity of gold that it has in its reserves. The object is to create greater international confidence in the national currency.

The development of heavy industries

At the time of the outbreak of the First World War, Russia was still a modest industrial power by comparison with much of Europe and with the USA. For example, in 1912 it produced only 5.6% of the world's pig iron, and only 3.66% of its steel. In 1910 only 30% of Russia's total national production was industrial, compared with 75% in Britain, 70% in Germany, and even 47% in Austria-Hungary. In purely Russian terms, nevertheless, progress had been rapid. An annual industrial output valued at 1,502 million roubles in 1890 had increased to 5,738 million by 1912. It should be remembered that this period included a major economic slump (1899–1902) and serious foreign and domestic disruptions (1904–06). Development differed from area to area and from industry to industry. Industrial production was largely concentrated in four regions: in St Petersburg and the shores of the Baltic, in Moscow and the provinces of Nizhni Novgorod and Vladimir, in Poland, and in the Donbas and Krivoi Rog regions of the south. Textile production continued to dominate, accounting in 1910 for 40% of Russia's industrial output. The table shows that, although they may not have compared so favourably with their more developed world rivals, other industries made impressive advances.

Russian industrial production (thousand tons)

	Coal	Petroleum	Iron ore	Steel
1880	3,290	382	–	307
1885	4,270	1,966	–	193
1890	6,010	3,864	1,736	378
1895	9,100	6,935	2,851	879
1900	16,160	10,684	6,001	2,216
1905	18,670	8,310	4,976	2,266
1910	25,430	11,283	5,742	3,314

From Cook and Paxton, *European Political Facts, 1848–1918*

Attracting foreign investment in Russian industry

Certainly, those industries detailed in the table above were among those that benefited most from the influx of foreign capital stimulated by Witte's policies. There is no recent study of the exact extent to which foreign powers and individuals involved themselves in Russian industry, but older studies show that it was vast. A Soviet commentator, P. Ol, showed 214.7 million roubles of foreign capital invested in Russia in 1890, 280.1 million in 1895, and then a very substantial upsurge to reach 911 million in 1900, and 2,000 million before the outbreak of war in 1914. About half of this went into the mining and metallurgical industries of the south, and it is possible that by 1900 as much as 90% of the finance behind these sectors of the economy came from foreign investment. Oil production and banking were the next largest recipients of foreign funds. The greatest financial friend to Russia was its closest political ally, France, whose investment was about 33% of the total in 1914. The other most important suppliers of capital were Great Britain (23%), Germany (20%), Belgium (14%) and the USA (5%).

Railway development and foreign trade

The development of Russian railways also produced some impressive growth statistics, although these pale by comparison with those of more advanced countries. While Russia had built only 5,800 kilometres of track between 1861 and 1890, the rate of railway construction accelerated to produce a national system of 59,616 kilometres by 1905. The imagination of the world was captured by the vast engineering feat of the construction of the Trans-Siberian Railway, linking European Russia to its most easterly outpost of Vladivostok (1891–1904). The greatest years of industrial expansion, however, coincided with a tailing-off of railway construction. The five years between 1908 and 1913 saw the slowest rate of growth since the 1880s, and although Russia boasted the world's second largest railway network in 1913, there was a substantial gap between Russia and the only state of comparable size. Its network totalled 62,200 kilometres, compared with 411,000 kilometres in the USA. Other forms of communication in Russia remained wholly inadequate. Only the major inter-city roads of European Russia matched up to general European standards, and the merchant marine was remarkably small, nearly all of Russia's substantial foreign trade travelling in foreign ships.

This foreign trade formed the last major feature of Russia's pre-1914 industrialisation. The table below indicates the steady increase in trade in both directions. It should be remembered, however, that while the balance remained favourable to Russia, its exports were mainly of agricultural produce. The balance in industrial goods, therefore, remained very much to Russia's disadvantage. Russia was most heavily involved with Germany, to whom it exported 453 million roubles' worth of goods in 1913, and from whom it received 652 million roubles' worth. Great Britain held second place in both respects.

Russia's balance of trade (million roubles)

	Imports	Exports
1904	651.4	1,106.4
1906	800.6	1,094.8
1908	912.6	998.2
1910	1,084.4	1,449.1
1912	1,171.7	1,518.8

The growth of an urban proletariat

The steady industrialisation of the Russian economy accentuated the breakdown of the traditional social structures that had begun in 1861. It combined with Russia's continuing agrarian problems to accelerate the drift of workers from the impoverished countryside to the developing centres of industrial production. In 1900, 2.5 million workers were employed in factory or workshop production. Taking into account their families and dependants, this probably meant that 10–13 million Russians were now reliant upon an industrial wage. This was a relatively small proportion of Russia's total population of 116.5 million (1895), but was probably three times the figure that had applied in 1880.

Of equal importance was the increase in the size of units of production. The next table, indicating an increase of about 30% in the number of factories while the workforce doubled, makes it clear that the workforce of the average factory grew substantially. Nearly half of Russia's industrial workforce in 1902 worked in factories employing 1,000 men or more.

Russia's industrial workforce

	Factories	Workers
1887	30,888	1,318,000
1890	32,254	1,434,700
1897	39,029	2,098,200
1908	39,856	2,609,000

1. What steps did Sergei Witte propose to modernise Russian industry?

2. How convincing is the claim that, at the start of the 20th century, industrial development was making Russia a more stable and prosperous country?

3. In what ways did the state of the Russian economy in 1900 pose problems for the Tsarist government?

The results of these changes were typical of the early stages of industrialisation elsewhere in Europe. The dramatic growth rates of the major towns between 1867 and 1997, such as Moscow (197%), Warsaw (253%), Baku (702%) and Lodz (872%), suggest the problems of urban overcrowding that now developed. Living and working conditions are suggested by the trickle of social legislation wrung from a reluctant government by a wave of strikes at the turn of the century.

- The employment of children under 12 was forbidden (1892).

- Female labour was banned in mines (1892).

- An eleven-and-a-half-hour working day was legally instituted (1896), although the law was widely ignored by employers.

- Factory inspectors were finally introduced in 1903.

Nevertheless, major problems persisted, such as overcrowding in factory barracks, and the illegal payment of part of the worker's wages in kind. Strikes, although illegal until 1905, were frequent: 68 were recorded in 1895, 125 in 1900, culminating in 14,000 outbreaks in the revolutionary year of 1905.

5.3 To what extent did political opposition to the regime become more dangerous during this period?

Given the ultimate success of the Marxists in 1917, it is easy to understand how a number of western historians, as well as their Soviet counterparts, should have emphasised their importance in the years before 1914, and diminished the importance of other radical groups. The later collapse of Soviet communism makes it easier to appreciate, however, that this was not the inevitable outcome of contemporary Russian politics, and that there were other forces at work which might have moderated, or even replaced, the power of the Tsar. In the context of the time, at least two other opposition movements had far greater support and played a far more positive role in the events of the years 1905–14.

Russian liberalism

The events of 1905–14 provided encouragement above all for Russian liberalism. This was a diverse movement, made up of many different groups, of varying degree of radicalism. Prominent among them were the liberal politicians who had been active in the localities as members of the *zemstva*. Some of these, led by D.N. Shipov, persisted in their hopes for a representative assembly that would provide some form of consultation between the Tsar and his people on the lines of the old *Zemsky Sobor*. Many *zemstvo* politicians, supported by a more radical group known as the 'Third Element', expressed less interest in political institutions than in practical reforms within the existing social system. Among their demands were the abolition of corporal punishment and of the power of the Land Commandants over the peasantry, and the introduction of primary education for all children. In the light of the events of the decade 1905–14, these liberals might claim to have been the most successful of the opposition groups within Russia.

Until 1905, the two courses of action proposed by liberals had borne little fruit. For a while it had seemed that direct representations to the government might work. The then Minister of the Interior, Ivan Goremykin, seemed willing to introduce *zemstvo* institutions into Lithuania, Byelorussia and other areas where none existed. By 1902, however, he had lost both the debate on the subject within the council of ministers and his official post. The other course, common to many opposition groups, was to found a party and a journal in the safety of foreign exile. Both the influential liberal newspaper *Liberation* (*Osvobozhdeniya*) and the Union of Liberation (*Soyuz Osvobozhdeniya*) were established in 1903. The dramatic realisation of several liberal demands was, however, to be brought about by events of a quite different nature.

The Socialist Revolutionaries

To the left of such liberal politics, the largest and most dangerous socialist grouping was the Socialist Revolutionary Party, founded in 1901. The SRs, as they came to be called, were essentially second-generation populists (see page 58), their cause revived by agrarian distress in 1891 and by the release of some earlier leaders from Siberia. They followed a path recognisable to the earlier generation, but modified to meet changed circumstances, such as the undeniable development of Russian capitalism. It is common for historians to refer to the Socialist Revolutionaries as 'the party of the peasants', but their views and policies extended beyond purely agrarian concerns. This enabled the SRs to build up a much broader membership. The various groups established in Moscow, in Saratov and in the Ukraine in the 1890s placed a common emphasis upon the need to spread their views among the urban workers. They differed, however, in the confidence that they placed in the peasantry, and in the importance that they attached to terrorism as a revolutionary weapon. As agrarian discontent spread, especially in the Ukraine in 1902, the revolutionary role of the peasantry became a more prominent element in party theory. When party policy was officially formulated, the peasantry was placed in the role of the army that would follow the 'vanguard' of the **urban proletariat**. The main plank of the party's platform was the redistribution of agricultural land to the peasantry on the basis of how much each could profitably use.

The terrorist branch of the SRs also achieved spectacular, if sterile, successes. The deaths of the Minister of Education, Bogolepov (1901), the Minister of the Interior, Sipyagin (1902), his successor Plehve (1904), and the governor of Moscow (1905), were all the work of its members. The apparent success of peasant agitation and terrorist conspiracy thus made

Zemsky Sobor (Russian – Assembly of the Land): A representative assembly that sometimes assembled in 16th- and 17th-century Russia. It had some of the characteristics of an early form of parliament.

Ivan Goremykin (1839–1917)
Minister of the Interior (1895–99). Prime Minister (1906 and 1914–16). Arrested and executed by the Bolsheviks in the course of the revolution.

Vyacheslav Plehve (1846–1904)
Director of Police in Russia (1880–84). State Secretary for Finland (1889–1902), where he pursued a policy of strict Russification. Minister of the Interior (1902). Assassinated by Socialist Revolutionaries.

Urban proletariat: Term used by Marx to describe those who lived in towns and cities who owned no property and had to sell their labour to survive. Sometimes used more closely to mean 'working class'.

the SRs a party of action, while the Marxists seemed to remain a party of faction and theory. 'More than any other party,' wrote Richard Charques, 'it was the party of youth.' This immediate, superficial appeal made the SRs the most popular of the radical opposition groups until 1917.

The limited scale of Russian Marxism in the 1890s

Meanwhile, the ideas of Karl Marx had made only slow progress in Russia. That the arguments of a German socialist thinker advanced at all was partly due to the enthusiasm of Georgi Plekhanov, but also in part to the curious leniency of the Russian censors. Plekhanov was originally a populist prominent in the 'Land and Liberty' movement. Observing the growth of Russian industry, he became convinced that Marx, and not those who concentrated upon the Russian peasant and his commune, held the key to Russia's future. Vera Zasulich and Pavel Axelrod were other figures who formed a bridge between populism and Marxism. By 1894 the writings of Plekhanov had given Russian readers their most coherent summary of Marx's thought. That they were able to read it at all was largely due to censors who allowed Marxist works in the belief that they would weaken the terrorist threat of populism. *Das Kapital* was thus available in a Russian translation as early as 1872.

It is only with hindsight that any political importance can be given to the earliest Marxist groups in Russia. A number of very small cells existed from 1889 in St Petersburg, Moscow, Vilna and Kiev. Their only real claim to fame at this point was that one of the St Petersburg groups was joined in August 1893 by a young lawyer from Simbirsk named Vladimir Ilyich Ulyanov. He was later to adopt the 'cover' name of V.I. Lenin (see page 194). Not until March 1898 did representatives of the various groups meet secretly in Minsk to found the Russian Social Democratic Labour Party (RSDRP). Even then the immediate arrest of eight of the nine delegates rendered Marxism a modest force in Russian politics at the turn of the century.

At this stage the Russian Marxists rejected the use of terror as counter-productive and chose to concentrate instead upon industrial agitation and propaganda. Marxists were active alongside other opposition groups in the industrial disturbances in St Petersburg in 1895, 1896 and 1897.

Vera Zasulich (1849–1919)
Populist activist. Attempted assassination of governor of St Petersburg (1877), was arrested but acquitted by jury. Abandoned terrorism in favour of Plekhanov's early Marxist movement.

Pavel Axelrod (1850–1928)
Prominent in the movement 'To the People' (1875). Co-founder of *Iskra* (1902). Consistently supported Menshevik faction of communists, and fiercely opposed the October Revolution.

1. *What were the main political objectives of (a) the Russian liberals and (b) the Socialist Revolutionaries at the start of the 20th century?*

2. *How convincing is the claim that Marxism posed the most serious threat to the Tsarist government by 1905?*

5.4 What were the causes of the Russo–Japanese War?

The colonial collision in the Far East

The Russo–Japanese War was the direct result of the clash of two sets of imperialist ambitions attempting to expand into the same **power vacuum**. Russian economic activity in the Far East had a long history. The development of Vladivostok dated from the 1860s but, although important, the port was of limited value as it was closed by ice for three to four months of the year. The decision to begin the Trans-Siberian Railway in 1891 represented a more substantial commitment to eastward expansion. Between 1891 and the turn of the century, Russia gained substantial advantages from the collapse of the Chinese Empire. The construction of the Chinese Eastern Railway across Manchuria (1897) brought valuable political and economic penetration of that region. In 1898, to offset German gains in China, Russia demanded and received a 25-year lease on the ice-free port of Port Arthur, together with its **hinterland**, the Liaotung **Peninsula**. When Chinese resentment of foreign encroachment made itself felt in the Boxer Rebellion (1900), Russian troops were most prominent in the

Power vacuum: A term used to describe a region in which no state exercises effective control. Such areas are always liable to be occupied by expansionist powers.

Hinterland: The area behind a coast, which is linked to it economically.

Peninsula: A body of land surrounded on three sides by water.

protection of European lives and interests, creating a dangerous confidence in their ability to defeat any oriental foe.

Japan watched Russian progress with apprehension and resentment. Japan's recent modernisation and westernisation contrasted starkly with China's decay, and it had taken advantage of that decay to prosecute long-standing territorial claims. The Chinese–Japanese War of 1894–95 had established Japanese control over Korea, Port Arthur and the surrounding Manchurian territory, much of which it had been forced to relinquish by pressure from the European powers established in China. Russia's subsequent acquisition of much of this territory was naturally a source of great indignation among nationalists in Japan.

The collapse of Russo–Japanese relations

Two years of effort (1901–03) by Japan to reach an understanding about spheres of influence in Manchuria and Korea failed, largely due to Russian apathy. When, in February 1903, Russia failed to remove its 'temporary' garrison from Manchuria, it looked suspiciously as if it had ambitions to dominate both regions. There is little evidence to suggest a deliberate desire for aggression on Russia's part, but many factors left it inclined to accept a

> *1. What factors caused Russia and Japan to clash in the Far East in 1904?*
>
> *2. Were the causes of the Russo–Japanese War mainly political or economic?*

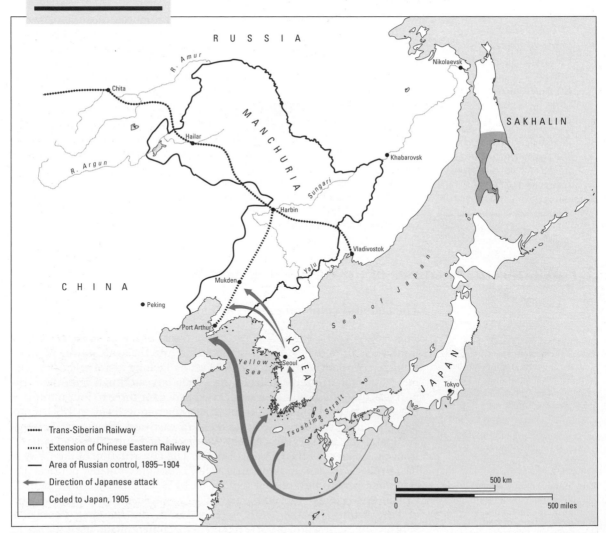

Far East at the time of
Russo–Japanese War, 1904–05

military solution if the necessity arose. The so-called 'Bezobrasov Theory', whereby Russian arrogance in the Far East was largely due to the work of an adventurer of that name, is no longer widely held. The historian G. Katkov, for example, has helped to show that the government was more closely connected with eastern financial adventures than was originally thought. The blame placed upon Bezobrasov and his like was partly a campaign by prominent politicians, including Witte, to distract attention from their own role. Nevertheless, influential figures did have large financial interests in economic ventures such as the Russian Timber Company of the Far East. Furthermore, the Tsar received considerable personal encouragement for adventures in the east from the German Kaiser, happy to see Russian attention diverted from eastern Europe by a cultural 'crusade' against the 'Yellow Peril'. Last, but not least, the domestic political tensions in European Russia made a foreign distraction welcome to the Tsar and his ministers. There were doubtless many in high places who shared Plehve's judgement that 'to stem the tide of revolution, we need a successful little war'.

In February 1904, their patience exhausted, and aware of the lack of Russian preparation, the Japanese launched a naval attack on Port Arthur without a formal declaration of war. They laid mines to blockade the Russian fleet in the port.

5.5 Why did Russia lose the Russo–Japanese War and what were the consequences of its defeat?

What images of Russia and Japan are projected in this cartoon?

The balance of military power

The general assumption of international observers was that Russia could expect a quick and easy victory over a minor power such as Japan, yet such expectations should not have survived intelligent and detailed examination. Although Russia's population was three times that of Japan

A cartoon by the French commentator, Caran d'Ache, which appeared in *Le Figaro* in 1904. It shows the Russian bear impertinently challenged by Japan.

and its territory was vastly greater, Japan enjoyed much easier access to the theatre of war (see map). Russian communications were dependent upon the Trans-Siberian Railway, which operated on a single track for much of its length and which still had a gap of 150 kilometres in it in the region of Lake Baikal. Russian forces in the Far East totalled only 100,000 men at the beginning of hostilities, which the railway could only reinforce at the rate of 35,000 per month. Political developments in the west made it desirable to keep large numbers of experienced and reliable troops available for action there. Naval reinforcements posed even greater problems with the Black Sea fleet effectively 'locked up' there by the terms of the Straits Convention of 1841. Lastly, the Russian command structure was crippled by the rivalries between the regular army commanders and the court favourites who directed political affairs in the Far East.

Japan, on the other hand, had the capacity to put 180,000 men into the field immediately and to reinforce them by a short sea route. For all the endurance and bravery that they showed, the Russian troops never fought with the nationalistic and semi-religious fanaticism that the Japanese soldiers frequently displayed.

The loss of Port Arthur

On land, the Russian forces quickly found themselves unable to contain the numerically superior Japanese, and by May 1904 Port Arthur was cut off. The land campaign then centred upon the respective needs to take or to relieve the port. The eventual surrender of Port Arthur in January 1905 followed a siege of 156 days and cost the Russians 17,200 casualties. Japanese casualties, however, totalled 110,000. As stores and ammunition remained in fair supply, the surrender led to subsequent charges of treason against the Russian commander, General Stoessel. Russian hopes of regaining the vital port faded when they failed to break Japanese forces at the Battle of Mukden (February–March 1905), a larger battle than any in the 19th century, involving some 600,000 men.

The establishment of Japanese naval supremacy

Admiral Stepan Makarov (1849–1904)
Saw distinguished service in the Russo–Turkish War (1877–78). Commander of the Baltic Fleet (1897), then Commander of Russian naval forces in the Far East during the Russo–Japanese War.

Even so, as Russia still had the potential for reinforcement while Japan's resources were quickly stretched to their limits, the truly decisive factor in the war was the naval campaign. Without command of the sea Japan would have been unable to supply or to reinforce its troops on the Korean mainland, but Russian attempts to wrest the initiative were spectacularly unsuccessful. In April 1904 the most popular and successful of the Russian commanders, Admiral Makarov, died when his flagship, the 'Petropavlovsk', struck a Japanese mine. Only twice afterwards did the fleet stationed at Port Arthur venture out to sea before the surrender of their base.

In May 1905 the powerful Baltic fleet arrived in eastern waters, having completed an epic voyage around the globe, without rest at anchor, and refueling its huge coal-burning battleships at sea. To reach the theatre of war was a great achievement in itself, but it was the fleet's only achievement. On 27 May 1905, attempting to pass the Straits of Tsushima to reach Vladivostok, it encountered the Japanese battle fleet under Admiral Togo. It lost 25 of its 35 ships in battle. Most of the survivors were held in neutral ports for the duration of the war.

The peace settlement and its impact

The Russians had lost largely as a result of numerical and strategic disadvantages. Equally, the incompetence of their officers and administrators contrasted, as it had done in the Crimea, with the bravery and sacrifice

1. *What advantages did Japan have in the campaigns of 1904–05?*

2. *How true is it that Russia lost the Russo–Japanese War largely because the government under-estimated the difficulties of fighting a campaign in the Far East?*

3. *Would you agree that Russia's defeat in the Russo–Japanese War was neither very surprising nor very serious?*

of the common soldier. The greater effectiveness of Japan's modern equip-ment has caused historian J.N. Westwood to ask 'which of the two belligerents was western and which oriental?' Despite these factors, Europeans' convictions of their own racial superiority rendered the outcome of the war acutely embarrassing for the Russian state.

On the face of it the peace settlement arrived at through American mediation at Portsmouth, New Hampshire (August 1905) let the Russians off lightly. Although Port Arthur and the Liaotung Peninsula were surrendered to Japan, Witte's tough negotiations ensured that Russia paid no war indemnity, kept half of the island of Sakhalin, and retained its dominance in Manchuria. The Treaty of Portsmouth, never-theless, marked a turning point in the foreign policy of Tsarist Russia. Russian interests in the Far East were not ended, but strict limitations were placed upon them. The result was that for the first time in nearly 25 years the foreign prestige of the Russian Empire depended mainly upon developments in Europe.

5.6 Why did revolution break out in Russia in 1905?

Sergei Zubatov (1863–1917)
Abandoned radical activity to join the *Okhrana* (1886). Chief of Moscow *Okhrana* (1895). Leading police official in St Petersburg (1902).

Georgi Gapon (1870–1906)
Orthodox priest and social and political activist. Founded Assembly of Russian Factory Workers (1903). Organised strikes and petitions that culminated in 'Bloody Sunday' massacre (1905). Discredited, he was murdered by Socialist Revolutionaries (1906).

The union movement and 'Bloody Sunday'

Military failure and humiliation added to the revolutionary pressure already upon the Tsarist government at the end of 1904. Most of the ingre-dients for a flare-up were now present. Peasant unrest had recurred sporadically since 1902, industrial strikes had occurred between 1902–04 in most cities, and several explosions of student unrest had taken place in Moscow and St Petersburg in the same years. The spark that set them all off was provided by the 'Bloody Sunday' massacre of 22 January 1905.

'Bloody Sunday' marked the spectacular failure of a daring experiment in the control of revolutionary elements. Sergei Zubatov, the chief of police in St Petersburg, had proposed the concept known as 'police socialism' in 1902. Under this scheme the police provided semi-official encouragement of moderate workers' organisations, aiming at genuine improvements in wages and working conditions, in the expectation that members would then refrain from more dangerous political demands. One of the largest of these organisations was the Assembly of Russian Factory Workers, founded in 1903 and boasting 8,000 members within a year. Its leader was the Orthodox priest, Georgi Gapon, a controversial figure. After 1905, left-wing suspicion of Gapon's motives was so bitter that he was 'executed' by SR agents (1906). Definite evidence of treachery, however, has never been uncovered. Strict control over the activities of his society was difficult, and the plan to present a loyal petition for redress of grievances to the Tsar in St Petersburg on 22 January 1905 carried Gapon along with it.

The demonstration of more than 150,000 people in front of the Winter Palace was perhaps the last occasion on which the Russian people genuinely approached the Tsar in his traditional role as the 'Little Father' of his people. The panic that led the Imperial troops to fire upon the crowd, killing an estimated 1,000, finished off 'police socialism', mortally wounded the reputation of the autocracy and triggered the 1905

Tsarist troops fire on the crowd, St Petersburg, on 'Bloody Sunday', 22 January 1905. This image is from a 1925 film.

revolution. 'It did more than perhaps anything else during the whole of the reign,' wrote the historian Richard Charques, 'to undermine the allegiance of the common people to the throne.'

The popular response to 'Bloody Sunday'

Gapon's subsequent denunciation of the Tsar summed up the hatred felt by much of the Russian population. 'The innocent blood of workers, their wives and children lies forever between you, the murderer of souls, and the Russian people. May all the blood that must be spilled fall on you, you hangman.' In Russian industry this anger was reflected in an unprecedented strike movement. In February 1905, 400,000 workers went on strike, and the total exceeded 2.7 million by the end of the year. No strike had greater effect than that of the railway workers in October, as a result of which the Russian cities were in imminent danger of starvation and the Russian economy was brought to the verge of collapse. No major city in European Russia escaped the dislocation of its fuel supplies and of its administration.

The relatively small size of Russia's urban proletariat made its revolt, although serious, a problem that might be contained. A general revolt of the peasantry, however, was a much more serious prospect. The first peasant revolt broke out in the Kursk Province in February and by April discontent had spread to most of the prime agricultural regions of European Russia. The peasant unrest was originally spontaneous, but was subsequently exploited by the radical political parties. Thus the All-Russian Peasant Union, formed by regional delegates in May 1905, put forward views similar to those of the SRs.

At a local level, demands and action were far less coherent, inspired by the hatred of past wrongs and by hope of present gain, especially in the form of land. Of these localised disturbances, 3,228 were serious enough to require the intervention of troops, and damage to an estimated value of 29 million roubles was inflicted upon Russian landowners in the course of the year.

Further afield, the separatist demands of various national minorities within the Russian Empire provided another threat to its survival. Socialist and nationalist tendencies combined to produce a rash of nationalist parties and groups, including the Ukrainian 'Enlightenment' group (1905), the Ukrainian Social Democratic Party (1905), the White Russian Community (1903), the Moldavian Democratic Party (1906) and the All-Estonian Congress (1905). Their activities and demands varied from the publication of books and journals, through the desire for a representative assembly within the Empire, to the demand for complete independence.

The armed forces

The key to the success or failure of the revolution lay in the attitude of the armed forces. An ominous element in the 1905 disturbances was the sporadic outbreak of mutinies in army units, but more especially in the navy. Rebellions occurred at Kronstadt in the Baltic and at Sevastopol on the Black Sea. Perhaps the most famous was the mutiny on board the battleship 'Potemkin', in the Black Sea in June. Rebelling against the squalor of their conditions of service and the harshness of their officers, the crew seized control of the ship, killed a number of the officers and bombarded Odessa. The prospect of general mutiny posed a grave threat to the survival of the regime, but it did not materialise. The 'Potemkin' was forced to seek asylum in a Romanian port, and mutinies on other ships were suppressed. The larger part of the army remained loyal. The Imperial manifesto published in December, promising better pay and fairer treatment, had the desired effect upon troops mainly of peasant origin. By clever use of non-Russian troops against Russian mutineers, and vice-versa, the government had largely restored military discipline by the end of the year.

The political response to 'Bloody Sunday'

The summer of 1905 witnessed a rapid crystallisation of opposition groups as each came to believe that its hour was at hand. Two main liberal groups emerged. In October the Union of Liberation, supported by some of the *zemstvo* politicians, established the Constitutional Democratic Party, soon known by the abbreviated title of the 'Kadets'. Its demands included an assembly elected by direct and universal suffrage and the restoration of ancient national rights to Poland and Finland. They were rather more radical than the Union of Unions formed in February by representatives of a number of professional bodies.

The Russian left was caught unawares and in a state of disarray by the events of 1905. The emergence in October of a Council (**Soviet**) of Workers' Deputies in St Petersburg was not the work of established socialist leaders, but a direct action by politically conscious workers to co-ordinate their strike action. Its 400–500 members represented five trade unions and 96 factories. Once the established leftist groups stirred themselves to tap the potential of the organisation, the Soviet came to represent mainly the **Menshevik** tendency of the RSDRP, with **Bolsheviks** and SRs in a distinct minority. Of those who returned from exile, none made a greater impact than Leon Trotsky, an associate of Lenin, but more sympathetic at

Soviet (Russian – Council): The term has come to be understood particularly as referring to the councils of workers' representatives favoured by Russian socialists from 1905 onwards.

Menshevik: A term used to describe the people who belonged to that branch of the Russian communist movement which favoured a more popular, loose-knit form of party organisation and discipline, with more democratic leadership.

Bolsheviks: Used to describe the supporters of the ideas and the political system that Lenin argued for and introduced in Russia after the Russian Revolution in 1917.

Leon Trotsky (1879–1940)
Born Lev Davidovitch Bronstein. Became involved in revolutionary activities as a teenager. Exiled to Siberia, from where he escaped (1902) and joined the Social Democratic Party. He opposed Lenin's call for a united group of revolutionary leaders; instead he worked abroad, earning his living as a left-wing journalist (1905–17). Joined the Bolshevik Party on his return to Russia and played a major role in the October Revolution. Became Commissar for War and was involved in a power struggle with Stalin after Lenin's death in 1924. He was ousted from the Communist Party and expelled from Russia (1929).

1. What groups
opposed the authority
of the Tsar's
government in the
course of 1905?

2. Did any of the
elements that rebelled
against the Tsar in
1905 seriously
threaten his control of
the country?

3. 'The 1905 revolution
represented every
element of discontent
within the Russian
Empire.' Did this make
the revolutionary
movement stronger or
weaker?

this point to the more democratic Menshevik views. Trotsky's intellectual and oratorical skills made him one of the leading figures in the political chaos that reigned in the Russian capital.

How much importance should one attach to this first Soviet? To the historians of the USSR its significance was as a 'dress rehearsal' for 1917. On the other hand, the Soviet in St Petersburg lasted only 50 days. It was not responsible for the huge strike in October, and the second general strike that it called in November fizzled out into anti-climax. It is true that its importance outside St Petersburg was negligible, but its significance is in the lead that it gave to later revolutionaries and in the brief influence that it enjoyed in the capital.

5.7 How did the government survive the 1905 Revolution?

Concessions to the liberals and to the peasantry

Frightened by his government's loss of control, the possibility of further military disobedience, and the actuality of peasant rebellion – which was the oldest fear of the Russian nobility – the Tsar had the choice of two courses of action. In early October he seemed ready to resort to outright military dictatorship but, faced with the objections of most senior ministers and some prominent members of the royal family, he finally recognised the need for concessions. The October Manifesto (30 October 1905) was, superficially, an acceptance of most of the classic liberal demands. It granted freedom of person, of speech, of religion, of assembly and of organisation. Above all, it confirmed the proposal made in August for the summoning of an elected parliament, or 'duma'.

In direct response to the agrarian unrest, a further set of concessions in November cancelled redemption payments and called for the peasants in return 'to preserve peace and order, and not violate the laws and rights of others'. Neither the November nor the October Manifesto really touched upon the true nature of Russia's social and political problems. The former made no concession to the peasants' desperate need for land and the latter set no real limitation upon the autocratic power of the Tsar. Russia faced the last nine years of peace with a liberal facade resting uneasily upon incompatible absolutist foundations. 'A constitution has been given,' remarked Trotsky, 'but the autocracy remains.'

Stolypin and repression

In another of his characteristically vivid phrases, Trotsky described the October Manifesto as 'the whip wrapped in the parchment of a constitution'. Indeed, the government had sufficiently recovered its nerve to set about the restoration of its authority by the dual policy of consistent repression and inconsistent reform. In November, the members of the St Petersburg Soviet and those of the Union of Peasants were arrested. In December, a last desperate rebellion in Moscow was crushed by regular troops with the loss of about 1,000 rebel lives, while loyal troops suppressed mutinous veterans of the eastern war along the route of the Trans-Siberian Railway. The efforts of the government were aided by the activities of extreme right-wing groups hostile to the liberalisation of 1905. A legal political party, the Union of the Russian People (October 1905), was supplemented by terrorist gangs known as the 'Black Hundreds' which attacked known reformists and specialised in anti-semitic pogroms.

In the course of the next few years, counter-terror became a longer-term government weapon in the hands of Pyotr Stolypin. A newcomer to the Council of Ministers in 1906, he was appointed its chairman in 1907. His credentials as a ruthless governor of the province of Saratov during the revolutionary year were perfect for his new task. He has been widely regarded as the second of the two men, after Sergei Witte, who might have saved the regime, had the Tsar had the wit to listen to his advice. Stolypin's plans for the regeneration of Russia were based on counter-terror and reform. He waged an unrelenting war against violent political opposition, a tactic made more necessary than ever by the resurgence of revolutionary violence in the summer of 1906. In 1907, an estimated 1,231 officials and 1,768 private citizens died in terrorist attacks. To this Stolypin replied with terror of his own. His 'field courts martial', operating under Article 87 of the Fundamental Laws, carried out 1,144 death sentences in the nine months preceding May 1907.

The bases of radical politics were also attacked through pressure upon unions and upon the press. Between 1906 and 1912, 600 unions closed and 1,000 newspapers ceased to publish. Seemingly, the policy was a success. In 1908 the number of political assassinations dropped to 365. From Alexander Guchkov, leader of the Octobrists in the Duma, came the grudging compliment that 'if we are now witnessing the last convulsions of the revolution, and it is undoubtedly coming to an end, then it is to this man that we owe it'.

Stolypin and reform

Stolypin was not such a reactionary as to imagine that counter-terror alone could stabilise the Tsarist regime. Reform, too, was essential and where Witte had set himself the task of modernising Russian industry, his successor turned to the more deep-rooted problem of the Russian peasantry. The key to Stolypin's agrarian policy was his belief that the surest basis for the regime was the support of a prosperous and contented peasantry. To achieve this without damaging the interests of the landlords he sought primarily to free the peasant from the communes created by the 1861 emancipation. Acting again through the government's emergency powers, he formulated a law (November 1906) whereby any peasant had the right to withdraw himself and his land from the commune. A further law (June 1910) dissolved all those communes where no redistribution of land had taken place since the emancipation. These laws were the culmination of a programme that had also granted equal civil rights in local administration (October 1906) to peasants and had transferred substantial amounts of state land to the Peasants' Bank (September 1906) in an attempt to satisfy 'land hunger'.

The subsequent growth of private peasant ownership was substantial. An estimated 20% of the peasantry enjoyed hereditary ownership of their land in 1905, while the proportion had risen to nearly 50% by 1915. Consolidation of scattered strips of land into viable farms was a slower

---

Alexander Guchkov (1862–1936)

Leading industrialist, prominent in the constitutional politics of the early 20th century. Chairman of Octobrist Party (1905). Speaker of Third Duma (1907–12). Guchkov became a leading member of 'Progressive Bloc' (1915), before promotion to Minister of War in Provisional Government (1917).

1. *By what means did Stolypin attempt to solve the problems that were evident in the 1905 revolution?*

2. *To what extent did the Tsar actually surrender any of his power as a result of the 1905 revolution?*

3. *How true is it to claim that Tsarism survived the revolution of 1905 unscathed?*

process, and less than 10% of peasant holdings had been thus improved by 1915. Three million cases, however, were awaiting the attention of land officials when the advent of war slowed their work rate almost to a halt. The lowering of interest rates in the Land Bank and the offering of migration facilities to 3.5 million peasants in Siberia between 1905 and 1915, bear further witness to the concern of the Tsar's senior ministers with the agrarian problem.

The greatest weakness in Stolypin's reforms, like those of Witte, was that they did not enjoy the complete support of the Tsar. Strongly influenced by extreme right-wing factions resentful of any such changes, Nicholas II was probably on the verge of dismissing Stolypin when the latter was assassinated in Kiev (September 1911). The murderer, Dmitri Bogrov, had links with both the SRs and the secret police. The confusion that has always surrounded his motives for the crime is a measure of how Stolypin's 'enlightened conservatism' had attracted the hatred of both political extremes.

5.8 Did the Dumas represent a real constitutional advance in Russia?

The Russian constitution in 1906

Outwardly Russia entered 1906 with a radically revised and modernised constitution. In effect, this constitutionalism was limited in many respects. The revived Council of Ministers, presided over at first by Sergei Witte, had the appearance of a cabinet. In fact, the ministers were entirely dependent upon the Tsar for their appointment, direction and dismissal, and thus merely continued to serve the autocracy. The upper house of the assembly (Council of State), was half elected, by *zemstvo*, Church, noble and university bodies, but was also half appointed by the Tsar. The lower house, the State Duma, was wholly elective but from its birth in February 1906 it was tied hand and foot by a series of limitations upon its powers. It had no control over military expenditure, nor over the Tsar's household finances, and in any case an enormous French loan of 2,250 million gold francs (April 1906) rendered the Crown financially independent. The Duma had no means of controlling or even of censuring ministers. Most important of all, Article 87 of the Fundamental Laws (April 1906), drawn up without consultation with the Duma, left the Tsar with the power to govern by decree whenever the assembly was not in session.

The composition of the Duma

The representative nature of the Duma was further limited by the decision of all major left-wing groups to boycott the first set of elections. Thus the elections in early 1906 were mainly contested by the Kadets and two other groups:

● The Octobrists were moderate conservatives, taking their name from their acceptance of the October Manifesto.

● The Labour Group (*Trudoviki*) was a faction largely reflecting the views of the SRs, despite the fact that the SRs were not officially involved in the contest.

The relative fortunes of these and other groups in the elections to the four Dumas that met between 1906 and 1917 are reflected in the table.

Composition of the Dumas, 1906–17

	1st Duma	2nd Duma	3rd Duma	4th Duma
Social Democrats	–	65	14	4
Socialist Revolutionaries	–	34	–	–
Trudoviks	94	101	14	10
Progressives	–	–	39	47
Kadets (also known as the Party of the People's Liberty)	79	92	52	57
Non-Russian national group	121	–	26	21
Centre Party	–	–	–	33
Octobrists	17	32	120	99
Nationalists	–	–	76	88
Extreme Right	15	63	53	64

The changes in composition from Duma to Duma reflect two factors. One was the eventual decision of groups on both political extremes to participate in elections, if only to change the nature of the assembly. The more important factor was that election was by indirect 'college' voting, whereby communities of differing sizes nominated a delegate to exercise a single vote for them. This has been variously interpreted as an administrative necessity, given Russia's vast size, and as a cynical trick to rig election results. Certainly it gave the government the chance to limit or increase the influence of sections of the population by changing the size of the community exercising one 'college' vote.

The failure of the first and second Dumas

The task facing the Duma was nearly impossible. It faced, in historian Gerald Fischer's words, 'the dilemma of attaining complex, specifically western objectives in an illiberal, underdeveloped society'. Much compromise would have been needed if it were to reach these goals, and little was forthcoming. The Tsar was never more than coldly formal towards the Duma, but a number of historians have also laid blame upon the liberal majority in the early Dumas for their inflexibility and their insistence upon unrealistic demands.

The first Duma (April 1906) was unmistakably hostile to the government in its major demands – for land reform and for an amnesty for political prisoners – and it was dissolved after only 73 days. The second Duma (February 1907) suffered from a transfer of influence from the centre to the extremes. The number of Kadets was greatly reduced after their irresponsible and impulsive 'Vyborg Manifesto' (July 1906) in which 120 of their members broke the law and disqualified themselves from future elections by calling for civil disobedience against the government. On the other hand, groups from both the extreme right and the extreme left of Russian politics now decided to participate in the elections and to use the Duma for their own forms of propaganda. The second Duma, therefore, amounted to three and a half months of continuous uproar.

The third and fourth Dumas

The longer lives of the third and fourth Dumas (November 1907 and November 1912) resulted from Stolypin's dual decision to work with a suitably conservative assembly, and to revise the electoral laws to that end. While the electoral law of 1905 had blatantly favoured the conservative forces of landowners and peasants, the new one (June 1907) manipulated the electoral 'colleges' even further. In effect it left some 50% of the final votes in the hands of the landowners (up from 31%), 23% in the hands of the peasantry (down from 42%), while the growing urban proletariat exercised only 2% of the votes (down from 4%).

The result was the election of two assemblies that hovered between reform and reaction. Historians are divided as to whether or not these Dumas should be seen as successes. Certainly the third and fourth Dumas were thwarted on many important reformist issues. Bills for the extension of the *zemstvo* system into Poland and for religious toleration were defeated in the Council of State. When Stolypin used his emergency powers to pass the former measure it was a triumph for the Fundamental Laws rather than for the Duma. On the other hand, the hated Land Commandants (see Chapter 2) were replaced by reinstated Justices of the Peace, compulsory health insurance for industrial workers was introduced (June 1912) and, with local co-operation from the *zemstva*, much progress was made in Russian education. Universal primary education within ten years was adopted as an official policy (May 1908) and by 1914 it was 50% of the way towards completion, involving 7.2 million children. Figures for attendance at secondary schools (510,000) and at universities (40,000) in 1914 do not, unfortunately, reflect a uniform advance.

As historian Hugh Seton-Watson has pointed out, the achievement of the Dumas should not only be estimated in terms of the measures that they passed. It had not become a truly representative assembly because the government had never wanted such an assembly. However, by 1914 political parties were legally established and, while rebellion was punished, open political discussion was tolerated and was allowed to appear in the press. All of these factors represented advances scarcely dreamed of before 1905.

1. What powers did the Russian Duma have between 1906 and 1914, and what powers did it lack?

2. Why did the third and fourth Dumas last longer than the first and second Dumas?

3. In what ways, if any, had the work of Pyotr Stolypin strengthened the Tsarist regime in Russia by 1914?

5.9 What impression of Russian society is conveyed by scientific and cultural developments in the two decades before the outbreak of war?

The sciences

Émigré: One who has emigrated. In this case, a political refugee who has left his/her own country, usually for political reasons, to live and work abroad.

Those historians who take an optimistic view of Russia's development in the 20 years before the First World War have often emphasised the advances that were achieved in scientific and cultural terms. 'Not only the body of Russia but the soul as well,' commented the *émigré* M. Karpovich, 'was growing stronger in the decade that preceded the World War.' Indeed, considering how few Russians were highly educated and the limitations of its facilities for higher education, its contribution to science and technology in the 20 years before 1914 was quite remarkable. In most scientific fields, Russia produced men of genius. Ilya Mechnikov was a leading figure in the study of infection and immunisation, running the Pasteur Institute in Paris and winning a Nobel Prize in 1908. An earlier Nobel Prize (1904) went to perhaps the most famous of all Russian scientists, Ivan Pavlov, whose work on digestive enzymes and on conditioned reflexes in dogs makes him a household name today. In chemistry, Dmitri Mendeleyev evolved the Periodic Table and described a number of new elements, while in agricultural sciences K.A. Timiryazev was the foremost soil scientist of his day.

In applied technology, Russia suffered rather more from its material backwardness, but led the world in two important respects. Alexander Popov's work on radio communications ran parallel to, and sometimes ahead of, that of Guglielmo Marconi, while Russia's contribution to aerodynamics was of the greatest importance. The work of N.Y. Zhukovsky and S.A. Chaplygin on airflow, important as it was, gives precedence to that of K.E. Tsiolkovsky whose developments in the fields of design and fuel make him one of the most important figures in the history of rocket technology.

The arts

In most of the arts, a golden age had ended in Russia by 1914. The major exception to this rule was in the performing arts. In ballet, Sergei Diaghilev's *Ballets Russes* (1909) maintained its supremacy for decades. In its choreographer, Mikhail Fokine, its dancers, Vacheslav Nijinsky and Anna Pavlova, and in its primary composer, Igor Stravinsky, it boasted the world's best. The Moscow Arts Theatre, with Konstantin Stanislavsky as its major director, and Russian opera, with Feodor Chaliapin as its leading performer, also raised Russia to a level of unprecedented cultural brilliance. The greatest Russian writers of the age, however, were recently dead – Anton Chekhov in 1904 and Leo Tolstoy in 1910. Although not primarily political writers, both were obsessed in their last works – as in Chekhov's *The Cherry Orchard* (1904) and Tolstoy's *Resurrection* (1900) – with the stagnation and sterility of Russian society. Their successor was Maxim Peshkov who, writing under the pen-name 'Gorky' (meaning 'bitter'), had already produced a stream of novels and plays by 1914. These were more specifically political than those of his predecessors, exposing the squalor and hopelessness of society's 'lower depths'. Historian Lionel Kochan describes Gorky, in *The Making of Modern Russia* (1979), as 'the first consciously proletarian novelist', and these works were to make him the doyen of Soviet literature in the 1920s and early 1930s.

5.10 How stable and how strong was the Russian regime on the eve of world war?
A CASE STUDY IN HISTORICAL INTERPRETATION

Perhaps more than any previous period in Russian history, the 'Stolypin era' has provoked controversy among historians. This controversy has centred around the overall evaluation of Stolypin's work, but focuses upon the question of whether his reforms, with those of Witte, had created a viable basis for the survival of the Tsarist regime in Russia by 1914.

As is the case with many aspects of recent Russian history, such assessments have often followed partisan political lines. Soviet historians, following the Marxist–Leninist assumption that proletarian revolution was inevitable, naturally concluded that any attempt to reform or to save the Tsarist regime was doomed to failure. Such writers as Aron Avrekh, in *Stolypin and the Third Duma* (1968), concentrated upon the suppression of revolution, upon the 200,000 political prisoners of 1908, and the 5,000 death sentences passed in 1907–09. To Avrekh, the 'Stolypin course' was 'the inescapable situation of reaction, the historic destiny of the rotten regime', for revolution was still the only logical outcome of the social and economic forces at work.

In general, western historians have been less ready to accept this thesis of 'inevitable' revolution, but have viewed the period immediately before the war as one that was open to many possibilities. Their appraisals of Stolypin's work have usually been kinder, sometimes excusing his use of terror by reference to the revolutionary terrorism with which he was faced, and sometimes, like the American-Russian *émigré* Leonid Strakhovsky, viewing Stolypin as a most positive reformer and as the brightest hope of the Tsarist regime.

On the broader question of the adequacy of Russian modernisation, commentators have divided into 'optimistic' and 'pessimistic' schools, respectively confident and doubtful about Tsarist Russia's prospects had it avoided involvement in the European war. For the optimists, the economic historian A. Gerschenkron has been a prominent spokesman, especially in his book *Economic Backwardness in Historical Perspective* (1962). He saw the increasing economic maturity of Russia, based upon industrial development and sound agrarian reform, as a guarantee of peacetime stability. 'One might surmise,' Gerschenkron concludes, 'that in the absence of war Russia could have continued on the road of progressive westernisation.' Others have concluded that, even under the extraordinary pressures of war, the Russian economy performed impressively, and provided evidence that the 'Stolypin Era' had given the regime a strong economic foundation. This argument was first put forward by Norman Stone, in *The Eastern Front 1914–1917* (1974), who contended that Russia's wartime weaknesses arose from problems of distribution, rather than of production. More recently it has been forcefully stated by Dominic Lieven, who concludes that, at the height of its wartime operations, 'the Russian defence industry performed miracles'.

E.H. Carr provided a clear statement of the 'pessimistic' interpretation in his classic work, *The Bolshevik Revolution* (1950–53). He drew attention to the limitations of Stolypin's reforms over Russia in general and stressed the possibility that his sacrifice of the weaker peasant to 'the sober and the strong' would, in the end, only have added to the ranks of the revolutionary proletariat.

It is certainly not easy to assess the long-term prospects of Stolypin's agrarian reforms. His central aim, of course, was to establish a class of prosperous, conservative peasants, which would provide a basis of rural support for the Tsarist regime. It is clear that the majority of Russian peasants did not withdraw themselves and their land from the *mir*. About 20% had done so by 1916, yet it might reasonably be argued that such a proportion, amounting to some two million families, might have been sufficient to provide the conservative foundation that Stolypin sought. At the same time, another 3.5 million peasants were persuaded to migrate to virgin lands in Siberia.

The pessimists counter such figures with the fact that the Russian population increased by 21% between 1900 and 1910, adding nearly 30 million to the total population. Thus, they argue, a further imbalance was created between prosperous peasants and their poverty-stricken neighbours. The picture is also blurred by the fact that Russia enjoyed outstandingly good harvests between 1909 and 1913. Perhaps rural stability was the product of an ample food supply, rather than of Stolypin's reforms.

One way or another, the Russian countryside was peaceful on the eve of the First World War, and Lenin, in distant exile, expressed fears that Stolypin had taken an effective course. 'If Stolypin's agrarian policy was maintained for a very long period, and if it succeeded in transforming the whole structure of rural landholding, it could make us abandon any attempt at an agrarian policy in a bourgeois society.' It might be added that, a generation later, Stalin viewed the prosperous peasant class, the *kulaks*, as the greatest obstacle to the establishment of a communist economic system, and went to great lengths to destroy them (see Chapter 8).

Kulaks: Richer, semi-capitalist peasants. The term literally means a 'fist', as a symbol for money-grabbing.

The years immediately before the First World War also provide some ambiguous indicators of the prosperity and stability of Russia's industrial towns. On the one hand, due in particular to the manufacture of armaments, industrial production grew at the rate of 6% per year between 1907 and 1914. The membership of trade unions and of the most radical political parties dropped considerably. Russia had only 40,000 union members in 1913, compared with 300,000 in 1907. Whether this was due to government reform or to government repression, it meant that the industrial working classes had less scope to express their discontent than they had enjoyed in 1905. Strike action, peaking in 1905–06, declined steadily over the next six years, only to explode once again in the last year of peace. It is no easy matter to predict what might have happened in the next decade, had Russia remained at peace. However, a simple observation of the facts leads to the conclusion that, as things stood in 1914, the Tsar's government was able to rely upon the army, and was able to control current levels of unrest among the urban workers.

Undoubtedly, political support for Tsarism was stronger in 1914 than it had been in 1905, in that Nicholas received grudging support from middle-class elements for whom proletarian revolt was the greatest fear. It is by no means clear, however, that the Tsar would have built upon that support in the long term, to create a genuine coalition of conservative interests. The decisive factor in this controversy may well be that which was stressed by historian Donald Treadgold in *Lenin and his Rivals* (1955). He emphasised the implacable hostility towards change of much of the Russian ruling class. This was especially true of the Tsar himself, who regarded good government not as 'an ideal to be sought, but [as] an irrelevance compared to the maintenance of the loyalty of the Russian people to his own person'.

It is also important to remember how completely, even at a time of political reform, Russian ministers remained the 'creatures' of the Tsar, with no significant scope for personal initiative. This is illustrated by the fact that Nicholas was served between 1905 and 1917 by eight different ministers for trade and industry and by 11 different ministers of the interior. Stolypin himself was succeeded in office by much less able men. His post was held in 1914 by Ivan Goremykin, 74 years of age, and almost certainly appointed by the Tsar in order to ensure that no disturbing programmes of further reform emerged from the Prime Minister's office. In *Russia in the Age of Modernisation and Revolution, 1881–1917* (1983), the historian Hans Rogger describes how Sergei Witte, 'perhaps the ablest man to serve the last two tsars, at times behaved in their presence like a junior officer – bowing excessively, his hands at the seams of his trousers, and displaying little of his bold and independent mind'. The same author reminds us that 'only an exceptional Tsar could long tolerate an exceptional minister,' and Nicholas, of course, was by no means an exceptional man. Perhaps, in the final analysis, progress towards a more modern Russia might still have been blocked by a narrow-minded and reactionary autocracy.

1. What different conclusions have been reached by historians about the potential, long-term success of Stolypin's reforms?

2. What arguments are there for and against the claim that by 1914 revolution in Russia was effectively inevitable?

Source-based questions: The political achievement of Pyotr Stolypin

Study the following source material and then answer the questions which follow.

SOURCE A

An analysis of Stolypin's policy, written by the contemporary British authority, Donald McKenzie Wallace, in 1912

Mr Stolypin formed two resolves, and he clung to them with marvellous tenacity: to suppress disorders relentlessly by every means at his disposal, and to preserve the Duma as long as hopes could be entertained of its doing useful work. Until the assembling of the third Duma he found no cordial support in any of the parties. All were leagued against him. For the conservative and reactionary Right, he was too liberal. For the revolutionary Left, he was a pillar of autocracy, an advocate of police repression and of drum-head courts martial.

SOURCE B

A judgement on Stolypin's policy by the Russian politician Alexander Izvolski, in his Memoirs, *published in 1920*

Mr Stolypin's agrarian reforms met with extraordinary success, surpassing the most optimistic expectations. The Russian peasant, prone as he is to listen to revolutionary propaganda when it appeals to his dominant passion for more land, is nevertheless possessed of a keen intelligence. He is not slow in going ahead of the measures decreed for facilitating the ownership of land which he farmed, and finding means of acquiring additional land by proper and legal methods. These results were so satisfactory that, on the eve of the revolution of 1917, it is safe to say that the entire agrarian problem was on the way to being solved definitively.

SOURCE C

Adapted from Imperial and Soviet Russia, *David Christian, 1997*

The reforms had least effect in the overcrowded central regions, where land shortage and peasant discontent were at their worst. In these areas the commune [*mir*] provided considerable protection for poorer peasants, and most households clung to it desperately. The agrarian reform did not create the politically conservative rural society that Stolypin hoped for, as the renewed peasant insurrections of 1917 proved. Nor had the constitutional reform helped to bridge the gap between the government and Russia's rapidly changing educated élite. As a result, the government remained as isolated as in 1905.

(a) *Use Source A and your own knowledge.*

Explain briefly the reference made in Source A to 'drum-head courts martial'.   [3 marks]

(b) *Use Sources B and C and your own knowledge.*

Explain how Source B differs from Source C in the conclusions that it draws about the success of Stolypin's policies.   [7 marks]

(c) *Use Sources A, B and C and your own knowledge.*

To what extent had the reforms carried out by the Russian government during Stolypin's period in office increased the stability of the Tsarist regime?   [15 marks]

AQA unit 1

Source-based questions: How realistic were the prospects of liberal reform in the reign of Nicholas II?

Study sources 1–5 below and then answer questions (a) and (b) which follow.

SOURCE 1

(From Bernard Pares, The Fall of the Russian Monarchy, *published in 1939)*

The third Duma, though its horizon was much more limited, did come to stay, and its membership was better qualified to take practical advantage of the education which it offered. Some seventy persons at least, forming the nucleus of the more important commissions, were learning in detail to understand the problems and difficulties of administration and therefore to understand both each other and the Government. One could see political competence growing day by day. And to a constant observer it was becoming more and more an open secret that the distinctions of party meant little, and that in the social warmth of their public work for Russia all these men were becoming friends.

The Duma was establishing itself as an indispensable part of the organisation of public life, and the Emperor himself took a certain pride in it as his own creation. Those surrounding him continued their attempts to prejudice it in his eyes, but having once rejected the occasion to abolish it in his *coup d'etat* of 1907, he was increasingly less likely to do so now. In 1912 he said to me: 'the Duma started too fast; now it is slower, but better'. That was the general judgement of others, and the result was a growing vigour of initiative not only in practical affairs, but also in thought and expression.

SOURCE 2

(From R.B. McKean, The Russian Constitutional Monarchy 1907–17, *published in 1977)*

The Duma parties also suffered from severe defects of organisation. Although they claimed to represent the interests of social groups throughout the Empire, the Duma parties lacked truly national structures. Continual government restrictions upon political activities and the indifference of the educated public to party politics after 1907 promoted the decay of the parties' provincial branches. By 1913 the Octobrist party structure was almost defunct. The Kadets possessed a mere nine branches in the provinces and the Progressists none. In effect the Duma parties and politics were confined to the educated society of St Petersburg and Moscow. The nature of the electoral system and the class composition of the liberal parties meant that the opposition lacked any organic ties with the peasantry and the working class. As P.N. Durnovo observed, 'between the intelligentsia and the people there is a profound gulf of mutual misunderstanding and mistrust'.

SOURCE 3

(From Orlando Figes, A People's Tragedy, *published in 1996)*

The 'zemstvo men' were unlikely pioneers of the revolution. Most of them were noble landowners, progressive and practical men like Prince Lvov, who simply wanted the monarchy to play a positive role in improving the life of its subjects. They sought to increase the influence of the zemstvos in the framing of government legislation, but the notion of leading a broad opposition movement was repugnant to them. Prince Lvov's mentor, D.N.Shipov, who organised the zemstvos at a national level, was himself a devoted monarchist and flatly opposed the demand for a constitution. The whole purpose of his work was to strengthen the autocracy by bringing the Tsar closer to his people, organised through the zemstvos and a consultative parliament.

There was plenty of ground, then, for the autocracy to reach an accommodation with the 'zemstvo men'. But, as so often in its inexorable downfall, the old regime chose repression instead of compromise and thus created the political hostility of the zemstvos. The chief architect of this suicidal policy was the all-powerful Ministry of the Interior, which regarded the zemstvos as a dangerous haven for revolutionaries and subjected them to a relentless campaign of persecution. Armed with the statute of 1890, the provincial governors capped the zemstvos' budgets, censored their publications and removed or arrested the elected members of their boards.

Edexcel Unit 6

SOURCE 4

(From Hans Rogger, Russia in the Age of Modernisation and Revolution, 1881–1917, *published in 1983)*

The political contest between the government and its critics, which looked so menacing in 1914, was confined largely to the Duma. Since the death of Stolypin it had been growing more troublesome in face of the government's disregard. Ministers refused to appear before it for months on end; they tried to whittle away its rights of interpellation, of budgetary control, of legislative initiative, and of immunity for statements made from its rostrum. The reactionary Minister of the Interior, Nikolai Maklakov, even favoured the idea, taken up by Tsar Nicholas, that the legislature should be reduced to submitting minority and majority opinions for the Tsar's decision.

SOURCE 5

(Part of the speech of Nicholas II at the dissolution of the second Duma, June 1907)

To our sorrow, a substantial portion of the representatives to the second Duma has not justified our expectations. Many of the delegates sent by the people approached their work, not with sincerity, not with a desire to strengthen Russia and to improve its organisation, but with an obvious desire to increase sedition and to further the disintegration of the state. The activity of these people in the State Duma has been an insuperable obstacle to fruitful work. A spirit of hostility has been brought into the Duma itself, preventing a sufficient number of its members, desirous of working for the good of their native land, from uniting for such work.

Answer both questions (a) and (b).

(a) Using your own knowledge and the evidence of Sources 2, 4 and 5, what do you consider to have been the main weaknesses in the Russian Duma between 1906 and 1914?   *[10 marks]*

(b) 'The prime reason for the failure of liberal and democratic political movements in Russia before the First World War was the opposition of the Tsar and his government.' Using your own knowledge and the evidence of all five sources, explain how far you would agree with this interpretation.   *[20 marks]*

6 The First World War: causes and course, 1900–1918

Key Issues

● Why did war break out in Europe in 1914?

● Why was neither side able to gain a rapid victory in the war?

● Why did the western allies emerge victorious in 1918?

6.1 In what ways did relations between the major European powers develop during the last 30 years of the 19th century?

6.2 What were the main sources of tension between the Great Powers in the decade before 1914?

6.3 Why did the Balkan crisis become so severe in 1912–13, and what impact did it have upon European diplomacy?

6.4 How did the July crisis of 1914 lead to general war in Europe?

6.5 Historical interpretation: Was Germany to blame for the outbreak of war in 1914?

6.6 What were the war aims of the respective powers at the outbreak of the conflict?

6.7 Why did the war become static between 1914 and 1916?

6.8 What impact did this prolonged war make upon the domestic populations of the combatants?

6.9 What prospects did either side have for success in 1917?

6.10 Why did the war effort of Germany and its allies collapse in 1918?

6.11 What was the impact of the First World War upon Europe?

Framework of Events

1902	(June) Renewal of Triple Alliance between Germany, Austria and Italy for six years
	(November) Franco–Italian Entente
1904	(February) Outbreak of Russo–Japanese War
	(April) *Entente Cordiale*: Britain and France resolve colonial tensions
1905	Russian defeat in Russo–Japanese War
1906	First Moroccan crisis resolved in favour of France
	(June) Third German naval bill
1907	(July) Further renewal of Triple Alliance
1908	(June) Fourth German naval bill
	(October) Austria annexes Bosnia and Herzegovina
1911	(July) Agadir Crisis
	(August) Military conversations between France and Russia
	(September) Outbreak of war between Italy and Turkey
1912	(October) Outbreak of First Balkan War
1913	(June) Outbreak of Second Balkan War
	(November) Zabern incident in Alsace-Lorraine heightens Franco–German tensions
1914	(June) Assassination of Archduke Franz Ferdinand in Sarajevo
	(July) Austro-Hungarian ultimatum to Serbia, followed by declaration of war. Russian mobilisation.
	(August) German declaration of war on Russia. French mobilisation. German ultimatum to France, followed by declaration of war. German invasion of Belgium, followed by British declaration of war on Germany. Russian defeats in East Prussia.

1914	(September) Germany's Schlieffen Plan thwarted by French victory in First Battle of the Marne and by British resistance in First Battle of Ypres
1915	(February–December) Allied offensive against Turkey at Gallipoli
	(April) Second Battle of Ypres
	(May) Italian declaration of war on Austria-Hungary
	(August) German forces capture Warsaw
1916	(February–November) Battle of Verdun
	(May) Battle of Jutland
	(June–September) Brusilov Offensive on Eastern Front
	(July) Major allied offensive on the Somme
1917	(March) Revolution in Russia forces abdication of Nicholas II
	(April) USA declares war on Germany
	(July–November) Third Battle of Ypres
	(November) Bolsheviks seize power in Russia
1918	(January) Woodrow Wilson publishes 14 Points
	(March) Treaty of Brest-Litovsk. Beginning of German Spring Offensive
	(July) Second Battle of the Marne
	(September) German retreat to Siegfried (Hindenburg) Line
	(3 November) Austria-Hungary withdraws from the war
	(11 November) Germany signs armistice.

Overview

I N the 25 years before 1914 the conduct of international relations between the major states of Europe underwent an important change. They now appeared to attach much less importance to the maintenance of an atmosphere of balance and compromise in European diplomacy. In Germany, Austria-Hungary and Russia, in particular, the social and economic modernisation of the state created tensions that appeared to threaten the interests and the political supremacy of the traditional élite groups. This was most evident in the sensational events of 1905 in Russia. Increasingly, international prestige came to be seen as the 'cement' by which the political unity of the state might be maintained. The nationalism that had been feared and rejected by conservative rulers in the mid-19th century now came to be regarded as a valuable tool in the maintenance of their domestic political control. If Britain and France had rather less reason to fear domestic instability, they too perceived threats to their security arising from this new international assertiveness. France's insecurity had a relatively long history, dating back to its defeat at the hands of Prussia in 1870. Britain, on the other hand, stood aloof from continental politics for much of the 19th century, until a crisis in its imperial politics, and the rapid growth of the German navy, focused its attention once more upon the eastern shores of the English Channel. Whether for reasons of domestic tension, or because they perceived significant threats from abroad, the great European powers ended the first decade of the 20th century with uniform feelings of insecurity.

With the benefit of hindsight it is possible to see these factors as contributing to the outbreak of the First World War in the longer term. They did not make the conflict inevitable, however, and few European politicians at the beginning of 1914 anticipated that they were on the verge of a disaster. In the middle of that year, one significant event – the murder of the heir to the thrones of Austria-Hungary – created a general crisis that posed serious questions for each of the major powers.

Some of them took irresponsible gambles, most obviously the Austrians, in thinking that they could settle their differences with Serbia without any wider consequences. Other states were then forced to decide whether their relatively insecure status as great powers could survive a decision to remain inactive. In opting to intervene they all made the same two crucial mistakes. They all believed their own propaganda about their military preparedness, and about their own superiority. In addition, they had all been deceived into believing that they were embarking upon a war of movement and attack, in which a few, sharp blows would lead to a rapid and advantageous diplomatic conclusion.

The narrative details of the war are not complicated. On both sides, the military commanders proved that they understood little about the capacity and resources of their opponents, and that the contingency plans that they had prepared for such a conflict had little basis in reality. German hopes for a victory based upon swift, co-ordinated action, and Russian plans based upon bludgeoning brute force, proved equally absurd. In the west, the result was a stalemate that lasted four years. In the east, the Russian Empire was slowly worn down by a grinding **war of attrition** that entailed a vast cost for Germany and destroyed the Austro-Hungarian Empire into the bargain. On both fronts, military leaders who had enjoyed enormous social and political prestige before the war failed utterly to devise any effective means by which the deadlock might be broken.

War of attrition: A conflict in which victory is gained by slowly wearing down the resources and resistance of the opposing power.

The politicians scarcely did any better. As national status and prestige had been such important factors in starting the conflict in the first place, no national leader dared to sacrifice these elements by seeking a compromise peace. Only Lenin, who represented a political and economic system completely alien to those that existed in 1914, dared to turn his back upon the disaster that traditional politics had created. In the end, European politics proved to be altogether incapable of resolving the chaos. A decision was only achieved in 1918 by the intervention of a new power – the United States of America – with military and economic resources that were far too powerful for exhausted opponents to resist.

The consequences of the 'Great War' were so extensive that it is impossible to do justice to them in a brief 'overview'. The war was undoubtedly the single greatest formative event of the 20th century, and although a summary of its results is attempted in this chapter, they will clearly be detected, directly or indirectly, in each of the subsequent chapters of this book.

6.1 In what ways did relations between the major European powers develop during the last 30 years of the 19th century?

The First World War was a catastrophe on a scale that Europe had never previously experienced. Quite apart from the impact that it had upon individual human lives, its impact upon the political and economic lives of European states was so far-reaching that its implications had barely been worked out 80 years after its outbreak. It is unsurprising, therefore, that some commentators should have looked for far-reaching causes behind an event that reached so far. It is equally understandable that some should have examined the foreign policies of the great European powers during the 40 years or so before 1914 to discover how their leaders could have made such fateful decisions. In recent years, nevertheless, historians have become increasingly sceptical of this view of the war as the product of long-term tensions, hostilities and mentalities. Instead, they see it as arising from a short-term crisis, its form influenced of course by pre-existing diplomatic circumstances, but without any sense of long-term inevitability. It is important, therefore, to know something of the formation of the alliances that existed in the early years of the 20th century, but it should not be assumed that these explain in any direct way the outbreak of the First World War.

The 'Bismarckian System' and its decline

The most important influence upon European diplomatic alignments in the period between 1860 and 1890 was Otto von Bismarck. His role was two-fold: in the course of the 1860s he played a major part in the destruction of the existing European diplomatic system by his role in the unification of Germany, and the military defeats that were imposed upon France and Austria in the process. Secondly, as is explained in Chapter 3, he was the architect of a new balance, which dominated European diplomacy for the next 20 years. It is clear that this 'Bismarckian system' was conceived by its author as a means of avoiding dangerous diplomatic alignments, and as a means of preserving the advantageous 'status quo' that Bismarck had achieved by the early 1870s. Put briefly, the system sought to avoid tensions between Russia and Austria-Hungary in eastern Europe, and to ensure that France could not organise a diplomatic alliance for the purpose of avenging its defeat at German hands in 1870–71. It sought to achieve these aims by associating Germany with Russia and Austria-Hungary in such a way that Germany's leaders could restrain the leaders of the other two powers. By this very association, France would be isolated and deprived of any ally sufficiently powerful to threaten German interests. It was a natural, and wholly justifiable assumption of this policy that Great Britain, with its extensive colonial interests, had little reason to become involved in continental alliances.

Bismarck fell from office in 1890, and it is certainly true that his diplomatic system largely collapsed in the course of the next decade. In this period, several factors undermined the stability of the Bismarckian system of alliances. Germany's refusal to renew the Reinsurance Treaty with Russia meant that Germany was no longer '*à trois* **in a Europe of five powers**'. Increasingly, Germany became distanced from Russia and more closely associated with Austria-Hungary. Its own decision to pursue a 'world policy' (from 1896), and its construction of a battle fleet (see Chapter 4), meant that Germany was no longer able to count upon the neutrality of Great Britain in continental matters, as Bismarck had done. Nor could Germany count upon the isolation of the other powers from each other. Apprehension over German ambitions enabled France and Russia to sink ideological differences, as France and Britain sank their colonial disagreements in the Entente that formed the embryo of their 1914 wartime alliance.

By the close of the 19th century, therefore, the restraints provided by Bismarck's diplomatic system had largely been removed. This is not in any way to suggest that Europe would now slide towards the abyss of war. Their removal, nevertheless, did provide greater scope for the pursuit by some states of political agendas that had considerable potential to disrupt the diplomatic stability of Europe. The agendas pursued by Germany during the reign of Kaiser Wilhelm II have already been discussed in Chapter 4. Two other states, however, felt a pressing need to revise their diplomatic status, and were provided with the opportunity to do so by the changed diplomatic circumstances in Europe. It is important to acquire some background knowledge, therefore, of the circumstances that determined the foreign policies of Austria-Hungary and of France in the decades before the outbreak of the First World War.

'*À trois* **in a Europe of five powers**': Otto von Bismarck's assumption was that there were five major European powers (Germany, Russia, France, Austria-Hungary and Britain) and that Germany's security would be guaranteed if it maintained an alliance with two of them. That alliance of three powers would therefore be stronger than the strongest coalition that could be organised against it.

What factors determined the foreign policy of the Austro-Hungarian Empire?

The key date in the political history of the Habsburg Empire in the 19th century was 1866, the year in which the Empire was defeated in the Austro–Prussian War. Defeat undermined the international status of the Empire and threatened its very existence. It ended the roles that it played as a German power and as an Italian power. The German Confederation – the institution through which Austria had exerted its influence over Germany for 60 years – ceased to exist, and the ascendancy of Prussia in German politics was shown to be irresistible. Worse still, it seemed possible that the defeat would bring about the collapse of the **Empire's multinational structure** and thus hasten its disintegration. That this did not happen was the result of timely concessions granted to the Hungarians, the one nationality capable of destroying the integrity of the Empire. Under the terms of the Compromise (*Ausgleich*), concluded in 1867, the Habsburg Empire entered upon a new lease of life as Austria-Hungary, or the **Dual Monarchy**. By its terms Hungary became a separate kingdom, with a variety of political links with its Austrian neighbour. The Hungarian crown was to be worn by the Austrian Emperor and the states shared a common foreign policy and common armed forces.

The failures suffered by the Habsburg Empire between 1859 and 1866 reduced its foreign policy in effect to a Balkan policy. Despite the defeat of 1866, Austro-Hungarian foreign policy in the 1870s and 1880s became increasing pro-German and anti-Russian. Fearing Russian expansion, the Empire saw its future as depending largely upon economic penetration of the Balkans. Important railway links were constructed between Austria-Hungary, Constantinople and the Aegean port of Salonika. From the Austro-Hungarian point of view it was perfectly logical that the League of the Three Emperors should gradually develop into a defensive alliance with Germany against Russia, the Dual Alliance (see Chapter 3). Imperial interests in the Balkans, after all, were not merely a matter of expansion and prestige. Control of the River Danube and access to the Adriatic coast were of fundamental economic importance to the Empire, and the rise of Slav nationalism could never be a matter of indifference to a state with so large a Slav population.

Three distinct stages may be identified in Austria-Hungary's political involvement in the Balkans. The first of these began with the Congress of Berlin (see Chapter 3), where it was decided that Austria-Hungary was permitted to occupy and administer the Turkish provinces of Bosnia, Herzegovina and Novibazar. These remained under the nominal rule of the Ottoman Empire, but in reality gave Austria-Hungary a substantial stake in Balkan affairs. Three diplomatic developments showed Austria's determination to preserve its 'great power' status in the Balkans. Two of these were the renewal of the Triple Alliance (February 1887) with Germany and Italy, and the publication (February 1888) of Germany's commitments to Austria-Hungary under the Dual Alliance. In addition, March 1887 saw the conclusion of an agreement between Austria-Hungary, Italy and Britain to preserve the status quo around the shores of the Mediterranean.

The second stage was opened in 1903 by the assassination of King Alexander of Serbia and the accession to the Serbian throne of the pro-Russian Karageorgevich dynasty. This constituted a severe blow to Austro-Hungarian aspirations in the Balkans. The new king, Peter I, and his foreign minister, Pasic, quickly made it clear that they favoured a policy of 'South Slavism' (Yugoslavism), whereby Serbia aspired to economic, and perhaps eventually to political leadership of the Balkan Slavs. The customs union concluded in 1904 between Serbia and Bulgaria encouraged the

Empire's multinational structure: Because the Empire was made up of diverse territories traditionally ruled by the Habsburg Dynasty, it contained a wide variety of ethnic groups. Of these, the Germans, the Hungarians and the Czechs were the most important, but Slovaks, Croats, Poles and others also formed significant minorities. The government naturally feared that if these groups sought to form their own political units, as many European nationalists did, this would lead to the disintegration of the Empire.

Dual Monarchy: Because of its complex political and ethnic structure, contemporaries used a variety of names when referring to the state. Before 1866, it was often referred to as the 'Austrian Empire' despite the fact that modern Austria was only one of its territorial elements. Alternatively, it was known as the 'Habsburg Empire' after the name of its ruling house. This accurately reflected the fact that this was a dynastic state, rather than a nation state (see page 168). After 1867, the changed constitutional circumstances of the state were reflected by the use of the names 'Austro-Hungarian Empire' or the 'Dual Monarchy'.

'The Piedmont of the South Slavs':
Between 1815 and 1866, the
northern Italian state of Piedmont
was a main focus of Italian
nationalism, and of the desire for
Italian independence from Austrian
influence. Between 1859 and 1866,
indeed, Piedmont became the
dominant element in the newly
independent Kingdom of Italy. The
Austro-Hungarian authorities
naturally feared that Serbia might
play the same role in the
establishment of an independent and
anti-Austrian Yugoslavia.

view in Vienna that Serbia was **'the Piedmont of the South Slavs'**. Furthermore, at the instigation of Hungarian economic interests, the Empire imposed prohibitive tariffs upon Serbian agricultural produce, especially livestock. Between 1904 and 1908, this so-called 'Pig War' helped to maintain an atmosphere of hostility and mistrust between Serbia and the Dual Monarchy. Only at the latter date did the formal annexation by Austria-Hungary of the provinces of Bosnia and Herzegovina (see page 157) lead its Balkan policy into its third and fatal stage.

How did France recover from diplomatic isolation after her defeat in 1870–71?

Between 1871 and 1894, France faced foreign policy problems that were very similar to those of Austria-Hungary. Heavily defeated in the Franco–Prussian War in 1870–71, France was another victim of the rise of Bismarckian Germany. In principle, French governments after 1871 inherited a clear foreign policy agenda: to reverse the humiliation suffered during the Franco–Prussian War in 1870–71, to protect French security, and to restore France to a position of influence in international politics. It was less easy to agree how these aims were to be achieved.

In 1871, France found itself in total diplomatic isolation. Humiliated in war, and showing signs of considerable domestic instability, the French Third Republic had little to recommend it as an ally. Despite the demands of the more hot-headed French nationalists for the regeneration of the French army, there was little realistic chance that France could challenge Germany alone, for the return of Alsace and Lorraine, the territories lost in 1871. Nearly two decades later, there was little improvement in this situation. By the Triple Alliance and the Reinsurance Treaty (see Chapter 3), Austria-Hungary, Italy and Russia all remained tied to the Bismarckian system of alliances, which had as its cornerstone the isolation of France. The chances of improvement seemed slight, for an ideological chasm still existed between French democracy and the autocracy of the Tsars. As regards Italy, the declaration of a French protectorate over Tunisia (1881), where Italy also had historic ambitions, led to a decade of bitterness. This was aggravated by the anti-French economic policies of the Italian premier, Francesco Crispi.

For many French politicians, a more realistic basis for renewed international power lay in the extension of France's colonial empire, rather than dreaming of those territories that had been lost in Europe. They never quite convinced the French public, however, that colonial power in North Africa or in Indo-China was an acceptable alternative to the recovery of Alsace and Lorraine. After considerable activity in Indo-China in the 1880s, French influence in Africa was substantially increased by a series of acquisitions: the conquest of Dahomey (1890), the colonisation of the Ivory Coast (1893), the occupation of Timbuctoo (1894) and the annexation of Madagascar (1896). In terms of European politics, however, such expansion had a negative effect upon France's diplomatic position. Apart from the tensions that arose with Italy over Tunisia, Britain looked upon French colonial expansion with great suspicion. Anglo-French tension reached its peak in September 1898, when a confrontation between a French expeditionary force and a British force at Fashoda in the Sudan brought the countries to the brink of war.

In the course of the 1890s, however, a remarkable transformation took place in French foreign relations. This owed much to errors in German diplomacy, and especially to Wilhelm II's refusal to renew the Reinsurance Treaty, which left Russia in a state of isolation. The two isolated powers were by no means natural allies, but France now had much to offer. An agreement

Nihilists: People who believed in 'nihilism', rejecting all political or religious authority and current ideas, in favour of the individual.

to curtail the activities of Russian **nihilists** in France was followed by the more important step of opening the French money market to Russian borrowing, a move that was worth the equivalent of over 400 million pounds to Russia within the next decade. More ominously, a military understanding began to take shape. In 1892, meetings between the respective chiefs-of-staff resulted in an agreement on joint military action. In January 1894, the Tsar finally consented to regard this as the basis of an official Franco–Russian alliance. Russia undertook to attack Germany if that country attacked France, or aided Italy in such an attack. France was similarly committed if Germany attacked Russia, or aided an Austro-Hungarian attack. France had pulled off one of the great diplomatic coups of the 19th century. The popularity of the alliance was enormous, and was in stark contrast to public indifference to colonial successes. Russia became 'the first love of the Third Republic'.

Remarkable as it was, the Russian alliance was only one element in France's diplomatic success at the turn of the century. Within eight years a new relationship had been forged with Italy. The key to this lay in Italy's disastrous colonial defeat at Adowa in 1896 (see Chapter 9). Italian disillusion with African adventures diminished the importance of the dispute over Tunisia, and the two states were able to conclude a series of agreements about spheres of influence in North Africa. In November 1898, a Franco–Italian trade agreement was concluded, replacing the one renounced by Crispi's government in 1887. It must be remembered that Italy remained a member of the Triple Alliance, but it was clear that, while remaining betrothed to Germany, Italy was clearly intent upon serious flirtation with other suitors.

The Boers: Settlers of Dutch origin who resisted the extension of British rule in South Africa. Their resistance led to two wars by which the British eventually, and with great difficulty, established their control over the region. The resistance of the Boers was viewed with great sympathy by other European powers.

It took longer to bridge the gap that separated French and British interests, but that too began to close in the opening years of the 20th century. Germany's decision to enter into naval rivalry with Britain, its tactless support of **the Boers**, and Britain's own sense of isolation at the end of the Boer War, all helped to provide a basis for better Anglo–French understanding. The keys to improved relations were provided by the tactful diplomacy of Paul Cambon, ambassador to London from 1898–1920, and Britain's new monarch, Edward VII, whose visit to Paris in 1903 did much to break down French dislike of Britain. April 1904 saw the conclusion of a comprehensive agreement on outstanding colonial questions, resulting especially in confirmation of British interests in Egypt and those of France in Morocco. This so-called *Entente Cordiale* had strict limitations and contained absolutely no military commitments by either side. However, it did conclude a remarkably fruitful decade for French diplomacy, at the end of which the Republic could face any political development within Europe with greatly increased confidence.

To what extent had firm diplomatic alliances been formed between the major European powers in the early years of the 20th century?

With a substantial amount of hindsight, it is possible to see the armed camps that clashed so violently in the First World War in the process of formation by 1904. This is not to say, however, that a general European war was in any way inevitable. On the contrary, many factors stood in the way of such an eventuality. Even within Germany's alliance with Austria-Hungary, the firmest element in European diplomacy, it was far from certain that Germany would back its partner unconditionally in a Balkan adventure. Within the Triple Alliance between Germany, Austria-Hungary and Italy, the attitude of Italy was extremely ambiguous. The Triple Entente between Russia, France and Great Britain was a very loose arrangement. As late as 1911 the relations between the three partners were so uncertain that the historian A.J.P. Taylor has considered the Entente to be virtually 'in the process of disintegration'. The Russo–Japanese war (see Chapter 5), if it had turned Russian attention more firmly back to European affairs, had also cast severe doubts upon its value as an ally. If its army could not defeat the Japanese, what value could it have in a war with Germany? Colonial disputes, notably in Persia, still soured Britain's relations with Russia. In addition, the Franco–British Entente, while representing a great improvement in the relations between the old rivals, contained no element of military commitment whatsoever.

Even if we accept that two broad alignments of European powers existed in 1904, we must ask what issues these alignments were likely to fight over? France's cautious new friends were unlikely to back it in a reconquest of Alsace-Lorraine, and a series of international agreements had reduced the tensions generated by the Eastern Question. Although there was renewed scope for international tension in the Balkans by 1904, it remained highly uncertain that France would see this as a cause for war, and virtually impossible that Britain would do so. Even if the atmosphere of European diplomacy remained uneasy in 1904, many more errors and miscalculations were still required to lead the continent to the catastrophe of 1914.

> 1. What alliances and what rivalries existed between European states in the opening years of the 20th century?
>
> 2. Is it justifiable to speak of the existence of 'two armed camps' in European diplomacy by 1905?

6.2 What were the main sources of tension between the Great Powers in the decade before 1914?

The origins of the first Moroccan crisis

Sultanate: A state or country subject to a sultan (king or chief ruler of Moslem country).

Between 1905 and 1914, tensions between the European powers centred upon two disputed areas: the North African **sultanate** of Morocco, and the Balkan states that had emerged from the wreckage of the Turkish Empire. Attention was first focused on Morocco by a German initiative that typified the incoherence and illogicality of *Weltpolitik* (see Chapter 4). In the course of a Mediterranean cruise, the Kaiser was prevailed upon by his chief ministers to land at Tangier (31 March 1905). There, his public speeches and behaviour implied that he recognised the Sultan of Morocco as an independent monarch, and called into question the recent Anglo–French agreements over the colonial status of these territories.

The motives of the Kaiser and his ministers are not altogether clear. They were probably keen to demonstrate, as was now usual, that no international question could be resolved without reference to Germany. They possibly also entertained hopes, by forcing France to give ground, of weakening its credibility as an ally in the eyes of Great Britain and Russia. The Kaiser's coup was followed by the formal demand that the status of Morocco should be referred to an international conference of the major powers. As that status was formally governed by an international agreement of 1880, Germany looked to be in a strong position, and the prospects of a notable triumph seemed bright. Indeed, when Théophile Delcassé, France's anti-German Foreign Minister and architect of the Anglo–French Entente counselled resistance to German projects, he failed to win general support and resigned his office.

The outcome of the conference convened at Algeçiras in Spain (January–March 1906) was, however, very different from that anticipated by Germany. Far more impressed by the bullying manner of the Germans than by the justice of their case, Spain, Italy, Russia, Great Britain, and even the USA, all supported French rights in Morocco. Isolated but for the

Théophile Delcassé (1852–1923)
French Radical deputy (1889). Colonial Minister (1894–95). Foreign Minister (1898–1905), during which time he played a major role in developing French understanding with Italy (1898) and Russia (1900) and in instigating the *Entente Cordiale* with Britain. He was forced to resign in 1905, largely to satisfy German opinion. Subsequently Naval Minister (1911–13), Ambassador to Russia (1913–14), and briefly Foreign Minister once again in 1914.

faithful support of Austria-Hungary, Germany had to accept confirmation of French predominance in the sultanate, now strengthened by its control over the Moroccan police.

How significant was the outcome of the Algeçiras Conference for the future growth of international tension?

The Algeçiras Conference played only a limited role in preparing the ground for international conflict. No military preparations were made by any power, British public opinion showed a marked lack of concern over Morocco, and subsequent Anglo–French military conversations come to nothing. Nevertheless, the impact of this diplomatic defeat upon Germany should not be underestimated. It ended Holstein's career and left Bülow in a state of physical collapse. More important, the rebuff did much to confirm German fears that the unreasonable jealousy of its neighbours was leading them to pursue a deliberate 'policy of encirclement' (*Einkreisungspolitik*), aimed at stifling Germany's natural growth and vitality. From this point, the historian Imanuel Geiss claims, in *German Foreign Policy, 1871–1914* (1976), Germany turned its back upon international conferences as a means of settling international disputes.

Lastly, it should be noted that diplomatic co-operation between the French, the British and the Russians at Algeçiras also had a number of side-effects. The discussions between the **General Staffs** of Britain and France were inconclusive. Colonial discussions between Britain and Russia ended, however, with an agreement (August 1907) that solved many of the outstanding disagreements over rival spheres of influence in Persia. British control over south-eastern Persia kept Russia at a safe distance from Afghanistan, and thus from India, and thus did much to remove the Asian tensions that had dogged Anglo–Russian relations at the time of the Russo–Japanese War.

General Staffs: The groups of senior officers responsible for the planning, organisation and overall command of their national armies.

Why did a crisis arise over Bosnia in 1908–1909?

By 1908, the Balkans had been free of major political crises for a little more than a decade, despite the emergence of an ambitious and expansionist government in Serbia. In July of that year, however, revolution by the 'Young Turk' movement overthrew the corrupt rule of Sultan Abdul Hamid and offered the prospect to other powers of easy gains in the Balkans while Turkey was preoccupied with domestic upheavals.

The opportunity coincided broadly with the appointment to high office in Austria-Hungary of men eager to re-establish the prestige of the Dual Monarchy. Conrad von Hötzendorf had been Chief of Staff since late 1906, much more confident than his predecessor, General von Beck-Rzikowsky, of the Empire's military capacity. At the same time, Aloys von Aehrenthal had succeeded Count Goluchowski as Foreign Minister. Aehrenthal came to office envisaging an energetic foreign policy as a useful means of submerging the nationalist tensions within the Dual Monarchy. The joint project of these two men for the re-establishment of Habsburg prestige involved the formal annexation of the Turkish provinces of Bosnia and Herzegovina that had been under Austrian administration since 1878. Certainly this was seen as a counter to growing Serbian influence over the Empire's Slav population, and it may even have been envisaged as the first move in a programme leading ultimately to the eventual partition of Serbia itself.

The annexation of Bosnia-Herzegovina

In September 1908, Aehrenthal sought the compliance of Russia. Meeting its Foreign Minister, Alexander Izvolski, at Buchlau, he concluded an

Conrad von Hötzendorf (1852–1925)
Chief of Staff of the Austro-Hungarian army (1906). Highly suspicious of Serbia and of Italy, he devised plans for war in the Balkans, catering for Russian involvement. His wartime campaigns in the Balkans failed, although he enjoyed some success against Russia and against Italy. Dismissed from overall command upon the accession of the Emperor Charles (1916).

Aloys von Aehrenthal (1854–1912)
Austrian diplomat. Ambassador to Romania (1895) and to Russia (1899). Foreign Minister (1906), responsible for expansionist policies, including the annexation of Bosnia-Herzegovina (1908).

Dardanelles: The straits linking the Black Sea and the Mediterranean.

Annexation: Taking possession of territory, and adding it to another, existing state. The annexed areas are then integrated into the state, and ruled as part of the state.

Alexander Izvolski (1856–1919)

Russian statesman and diplomat. Foreign Minister (1905). Sought improved relations with Britain and Japan, but was outmanoeuvred by Austria over the Balkan crisis in 1908–09. As ambassador to Paris (1910–16) he was a key figure in the construction of the wartime alliance between the two states.

---

agreement. By this agreement Russia would accept the new status of Bosnia and Herzegovina in return for Austro-Hungarian support for Russian designs on the **Dardanelles** (see map on page 160).

By accepting this agreement, Izvolski committed a diplomatic blunder of the first order. Evidently, he had expected the matter to be referred first to an international conference on the lines of 1878. On 5 October, however, Aehrenthal proclaimed the annexation of Bosnia and Herzegovina, leaving Izvolski to seek his part of the bargain single-handed. In this, he not only encountered hostile reactions in London and Paris, but had his policy disowned by his own prime minister as outdated and irrelevant to current Russian priorities. Izvolski's attempts to soften his defeat, by demanding that a conference be convened to discuss the annexation, only increased and broadened the international tension. In response, Austria-Hungary sought clarification of the position of its German ally, and received assurances of support. 'I shall regard whatever decision you come to as the appropriate one,' wrote Bülow to Aehrenthal at the end of October, while Hötzendorff received assurances from his German opposite number that Germany was prepared to mobilise in support of the Dual Monarchy.

These assurances represented a significant deterioration in the international situation. Motivated primarily by the hope of humiliating Russia, and perhaps of weakening its links with France, Germany was sacrificing another essential Bismarckian principle. It was involving itself in the Eastern Question where no fundamental German interest was involved, and where Austria-Hungary had acted without any consultation with its ally whatsoever.

The humiliation of Serbia and Russia

Thus emboldened, Germany and Austria-Hungary felt strong enough to rub both Serbia's and Russia's noses in their defeat by demanding from them a formal acknowledgement of Habsburg authority over Bosnia and Herzegovina. In March 1909, both states gave such an acknowledgement, and the crisis was over. Its legacy, nevertheless, was substantial. Russia suffered a humiliation far greater than that suffered by Germany over the Moroccan question. It could ill afford a further reverse if it was to retain any influence in the politics of the Balkans. Aware of its weaknesses in 1908–09, Russia was to embark upon a programme of military reconstruction to ensure that a future confrontation would not find it wanting.

Austria's success and the unconditional nature of German support for its aims were to embolden it in future Balkan adventures. Serbia's reverse, meanwhile, was to stimulate the growth of nationalist terrorist organisations of the kind responsible for the assassination at Sarajevo in 1914. Although the crisis had given rise to little in the way of serious military preparations, we may accept the logic of Imanuel Geiss's judgement, in *German Foreign Policy, 1871–1914* (1976), that 'the Bosnian crisis in the East was a kind of dress rehearsal for the First World War'.

The occupation of Fez and the Agadir crisis, 1911

Protectorate: A country that is controlled and protected by a more powerful country.

In May 1911, the focus of European tension switched once more to Morocco. The cause was the French occupation of Fez, the major city of the territory – a move that was widely thought to indicate that France was preparing to establish an overall **protectorate**. Given that France was exceeding the limits of its agreed role in Morocco, and that relations between its international partners, Britain and Russia, were once again strained, the prospects for German compensation seemed good. It has been argued that Germany's Foreign Minister, Alfred von Kiderlen-Wächter, was interested in more than compensation. Historian Fritz Fischer stresses the enthusiasm of expansionist elements in Germany for the establishment of permanent influence in North Africa, and has attached sinister importance to Kiderlen's apparent willingness to use force to gain Germany's ends. Similarly, a great community of interest and aims existed between Kiderlen-Wächter and the Pan-German League. Whatever its motives, the German Foreign Ministry once again acted aggressively and clumsily. The dispatch of the gunboat 'Panther' to the Moroccan port of Agadir, seemingly to protect German interests there, immediately resurrected British fears of a hostile naval presence in the Mediterranean, and of a threat to Gibraltar.

Unambiguous statements of British support for France, such as that contained in Lloyd George's Mansion House speech (21 July 1911) weakened the resolve of the less chauvinistic elements in Germany, including that of the Kaiser himself. A compromise settlement in November did grant Germany compensation in the form of territory in the French Congo. However, the maintenance of French influence in Morocco, culminating in the establishment of a formal protectorate (March 1912), clearly demonstrated that German aims in the crisis had failed.

What was the impact of Agadir upon the alliance system?

This second Moroccan crisis was unlikely to lead to a general war, mainly because of the lack of Russian interest in the affair. 'Russian public opinion,' Izvolski informed the French, 'could not see in a colonial dispute the cause for a general conflict.' Nevertheless, the crisis contributed to the likelihood of a future breakdown of international relations in several important ways. Firstly, it worsened relations between Britain and Germany for no good reason, and weakened the support in both countries for reductions in naval building programmes. Indeed, the next two years were to witness the height of the naval 'arms race'.

Secondly, French reaction to the compromise settlement destroyed the administration of Joseph Caillaux (January 1912), whose main aim had been to achieve some measure of reconciliation with Germany. 'The events of 1911', in the opinion of historian Eugen Weber, in *The Nationalist Revival in France* (1959), 'persuaded many of the pacific, the hesitant and the indifferent that the threat to France was real and that war was only a matter of time.' The succession of the more aggressively patriotic Raymond Poincaré can be seen as the beginning of the 'national awakening' that led France into war by 1914.

Thirdly, stimulated by the increased German naval estimates of 1912, the crisis led to a degree of formal military co-operation between Britain and France. This took the form primarily of the naval agreement of March 1912 whereby Britain confided its central Mediterranean interests to the protection of the French fleet, and concentrated its resources in home waters and at Gibraltar. Such an agreement still did not amount to a formal alliance, but indicated clearly Britain's awareness of the German threat to its interests.

Lastly, the Agadir crisis dealt a blow to the prestige of the German government similar to that suffered by the Russians in the Balkans. Germany, too, if faced with a similar crisis, might feel that the cost of further compromise might justify the risk of war.

1. *What issues were at stake between the great European powers in the years 1900–14 (a) in North Africa and (b) in the Balkans?*

2. *Why did the confrontations between France and Germany over Morocco in 1905 and 1911 not lead to a European war?*

3. *Would you agree that the crisis in the Balkans in 1908–09 was more dangerous than the crisis over North Africa? Explain your answer.*

6.3 Why did the Balkan crisis become so severe in 1912–13, and what impact did it have upon European diplomacy?

The Agadir crisis brought European politics to a pitch of tension from which it was not released before the outbreak of general war. Its implications spread eastwards down the Mediterranean. A direct result of the extension of French influence in Morocco was Italy's attempt in 1911 to improve its own standing in North Africa. To this end it launched an unprovoked attack upon the Turkish possession of Tripoli. This stretching of Turkish resources provided an irresistible temptation to the Balkan states to free themselves forever from the influence of Turkey. From this temptation there emerged, in the early months of 1912, the Balkan League of Serbia, Bulgaria, Greece and Montenegro.

The First and Second Balkan Wars

The First Balkan War, between the Balkan League and Turkey, began in October 1912. By the end of that month the Turks had suffered a string of defeats and had been driven out of their European possessions, apart from

The Balkans in 1914

Constantinople, the peninsula of Gallipoli and the fortresses of Scutari, Adrianople and Janina. Renewed hostilities in early 1913, however, transferred those last two strongholds to the Bulgarians and the Greeks respectively. Now tension centred upon the division of the spoils. Already, in late 1912, Austria-Hungary had attempted to maintain its prestige and security by insisting upon the establishment of an independent Albanian state, and upon the exclusion of Serbia from the Adriatic coastline.

More immediate tensions arose, however, between the victors. Serbia, thwarted over designs on Albania, and acting in partnership with Greece, occupied territory in Macedonia originally earmarked for Bulgaria. Bulgaria's attempts to clear Macedonia of Serbian and Greek forces in June 1913 started the Second Balkan War. The move was disastrous for Bulgaria. By the Treaty of Bucharest (August 1913), it had to cede territory to Serbia, Greece and Romania, which had seized the opportunity to intervene. Even Adrianople, won earlier at great cost from the Turks, was now returned to its former masters.

The status of Serbia and Austria-Hungary

The renewed Balkan crisis of 1912–13 contributed to the advent of general war in numerous important respects. Most obviously, Serbia emerged from these events with both its prestige and its power enormously increased. It had added some million and a half people to its population, and could now mobilise an army of some 400,000 men. Conversely, as A.J.P. Taylor put it, 'the victory for Balkan nationalism was a disaster beyond remedy for the Habsburg monarchy'. Even with Serbia preoccupied, its foreign policy had appeared frozen into inactivity. This was partly due to the indecision of the new Foreign Minister, Count Berchtold, partly to Magyar distrust of actions that might create more Slav subjects for the Dual Monarchy, and partly to uncertainty as to Germany's attitude. By mid-1913, it was clear that the government of Austria-Hungary could not afford further retreat. When Serbian troops entered Albanian territory in October to 'mop up' partisan resistance, the Dual Monarchy issued an ultimatum, which foreshadowed that of 1914. On this occasion, Serbia yielded and withdrew its troops.

Political and popular attitudes among the leading powers

To what extent did this crisis make the leading European powers more willing to accept the prospect of war? There is certainly evidence of heightened tension at top political levels in Germany and France, and of increased military preparation. France, for instance, sought closer military ties with Russia, and showed less interest in restraining its major ally. When President Poincaré visited Russia in August 1912 he left his hosts in no doubt about France's attitude. Although their formal agreements only committed France to support Russia if it were attacked by Germany, Russia could expect French help in the event of a clash with Germany triggered by a confrontation with Austria-Hungary. In Germany the government remained reluctant initially to become involved in Balkan hostilities, but there were clear signs, nevertheless, of political unease and of military preparation to meet a future crisis. The government had already been attacked from all sides in the Reichstag (November 1911) when the compromise settlement over Morocco was debated. The next year and a half saw substantial increases in military estimates. In July 1913, the Reichstag sanctioned the addition of 130,000 men to the army in the biggest army estimate in German history. By October 1913, at the time of Vienna's ultimatum to Serbia over Albanian independence, the Kaiser was urging his ally to take a firm stance, and assuring it of

Leopold von Berchtold (1863–1942)
Entered Austro-Hungarian diplomatic service in 1893. Ambassador to Russia (1906). Succeeded Aehrenthal as Foreign Minister (1912). Co-operated with Conrad von Hötzendorf in issuing ultimatum to Serbia, underestimating the danger of Russian mobilisation. Dismissed from office in 1915.

unswerving German support. He informed Berchtold that month, in a fateful statement, that 'you can be certain that I stand behind you and am ready to draw the sword whenever your action makes it necessary. Whatever comes from Vienna is for me a command.'

Recent historians, however, have been at pains to point out that this does not necessarily mean that enthusiasm for war existed at more popular levels of society. In particular, Niall Ferguson provides a good deal of evidence (*The Pity of War*, 1998) to counteract the notion that popular support for militaristic policies was creating an irresistible impetus towards war. He emphasises, for example, that three consecutive general elections were won in Britain between 1906 and 1910 by a Liberal Party committed to expensive social reform. Similarly, the last pre-war elections in France and Germany brought considerable success for socialist parties officially committed to the cause of peace. In Germany, although much noise was made by such patriotic organisations as the Naval League, their combined membership amounted to little more than half a million Germans. In France, at the height of European tension, 236 deputies voted against a reform of the laws on military service, proposed by the government to increase the numbers recruited into the army. 'The evidence,' he concludes, 'is unequivocal: Europeans were not marching to war, but turning their backs on militarism.'

It is doubly tragic, therefore, that in diplomatic and military terms, by October 1913, many of the ingredients of the following year's catastrophe were present. Franco–Russian and Austro–German commitments were tighter than ever, the confidence and daring of Serbia were at a peak, and the prestige of Austria-Hungary and of Russia was at so low an ebb as to make them unable to tolerate any further blow. Only the attitudes of Great Britain and Italy remained uncertain.

> 1. Why was there a further political crisis in the Balkans in 1912–13?
>
> 2. Explain the reactions of the major European powers to the Balkan crisis in 1912–13.
>
> 3. In what respects was the second Balkan crisis in 1912–13 more dangerous for the general peace of Europe than the first Balkan crisis (1908–09) had been?

6.4 How did the July crisis of 1914 lead to general war in Europe?

Sarajevo and the response of Austria-Hungary

Archduke Franz Ferdinand (1863–1914)
Nephew of Franz Josef, and heir to the throne of Austria-Hungary from 1896. Inspector General of the army (1913). Assassinated at Sarajevo on 28 June 1914.

'Fifty years,' wrote Basil Liddell Hart, in *History of the First World War* (1972), 'were spent in the process of making Europe explosive. Five days were enough to detonate it.' On 28 June 1914, the final crisis was triggered by the assassination in the Bosnian town of Sarajevo of the Archduke Franz Ferdinand, nephew of the Austrian Emperor. His murderer was Gavrilo Princip, a member of a Serbian terrorist organisation known as the 'Black Hand'. Although it has proved impossible to establish any clear responsibility on the part of the Serbian government, it is clear that its intelligence chief, Colonel Dimitrievich, played a leading role in the conspiracy, and that its Prime Minister had some foreknowledge of the attempt. Ironically, as historian Norman Stone points out, in *The Eastern Front, 1914–17* (1973), the death of the Archduke removed one of the strongest influences for peace at court.

The opinion was now widespread that Serbian pretensions had to be checked. In this resolution the Dual Monarchy received backing from Berlin. Historians Fritz Fischer, Imanuel Geiss and others have interpreted this as showing the willingness, even the eagerness, of the German government to accept the consequences of general war. On the other hand, Germany could hardly accept the further humiliation of its only firm ally. Other authorities have produced evidence to indicate that Germany still hoped that the coming conflict might be confined to the Balkans. Nevertheless, Austria-Hungary was sufficiently encouraged to deliver an ultimatum to Serbia (23 July) framed in such extreme terms that it was almost impossible for Serbia to accept. Serbia's government was required, for instance, to suppress all anti-Austrian organisations and propaganda, and to dismiss any officials to whom the Vienna government might object.

The spread of the Balkan crisis

Within a week, Europe was at war. The first factor to determine this outcome was the reaction of Russia. Although Serbia's reaction to the ultimatum was conciliatory, it did not satisfy Austria-Hungary's demands, and it declared war on 28 July. For Russia to remain inactive would have stripped it of any influence in the Balkans and could have devalued it as an ally in the eyes of France. Thus Russia chose to mobilise its forces on its southern borders. Automatically, such action triggered the Austro–German alliance, and raised the question of German support for its ally.

The escalation of the crisis caused last-minute hesitations in Berlin, while the generals advised energetic action. Essentially, German military plans obliged it to act rapidly to deal with France before the Russian machine was fully operative. Germany thus took three fateful steps:

- On 31 July, it demanded the suspension of all Russian mobilisation.

- The following day, when mobilisation continued, Germany declared war.

- Lastly, it demanded from France a formal declaration of neutrality, and the surrender of the border fortresses of Toul and Verdun as guarantees.

Acceptance would have been incompatible with France's 'great power' status, and its inevitable refusal led to a further declaration of war by Germany (3 August).

Now German diplomacy centred upon attempts to keep Britain out of the war. Bethmann-Hollweg had already promised not to annex French territory and to restore the integrity of Belgium after the war. German military strategy, however, depended heavily upon the violation of Belgian neutrality for the purposes of the attack on France. When Germany invaded Belgium on 3 August, Britain's course was decided by its treaty obligations to Belgium, and the following day it, too, entered the war.

Why did the powers go to war?

Although the victors in 1918 were quick to formulate questions of 'war guilt', the outbreak of the conflict makes more sense if it is seen as a monstrous combination of miscalculations. The government of Austria-Hungary erred in believing that a clash with Serbia could be settled without wider complications. Russia's partial mobilisation on 30 July was undertaken without sufficient awareness of its effect upon German policy. In Berlin there was a whole series of misjudgements:

- the hope that an Austro–Serbian clash could be localised;

- the failure to appreciate that the invasion of Belgium would bring Britain into the war;

- the long-term failure to anticipate foreign reaction to the bullying tone of *Weltpolitik*.

- The further naive supposition that a brief and successful war might ease domestic difficulties was an error shared with Vienna and St Petersburg.

1. Describe the steps by which the murder of the Archduke Franz Ferdinand in Sarajevo led to general war between the European powers.

2. Are there any grounds for claiming that any one of the major European powers acted less responsibly in the 1914 crisis than the others?

The historian A.J.P. Taylor made an extremely important contribution to the understanding of events in 1914 when he argued that the conflict arose from feelings of weakness rather than feelings of strength. Russia and Austria-Hungary felt that compromise would destroy their credibility as major powers. France and Germany felt that valuable allies had to be supported lest they themselves be left in isolation. In the German army, too, the feeling predominated that war in 1914 was preferable to war in two or three years' time, when the Entente powers would be much stronger. Lastly, all the participants misjudged the nature of the conflict to which they were committing themselves. They anticipated campaigns as sharp and decisive as those of the Balkan Wars, or of the wars of 1859, 1866 or 1870. They anticipated no great strain upon society, and would have been horrified to think that four years of trench warfare, technological revolution and economic attrition were about to tear apart the fabric of European society.

6.5 Was Germany to blame for the outbreak of war in 1914?
A CASE STUDY IN HISTORICAL INTERPRETATION

History and politics in the inter-war years

Although 1918 marked the end of the military contest, it marked the beginning of a fierce war of words concerning the causes of the conflict, and the dealing out of 'war guilt'. Clause 231 of the peace treaty forced the defeated Germans to admit that they bore the moral responsibility for the bloodshed by virtue of their aggressive policies before 1914. If the politicians of the Weimar Republic were forced publicly to accept that interpretation, German historians were not. The analysis of German diplomatic archives began immediately, undertaken to prove German claims of innocence, and culminated in a 40-volume work entitled *The Grand Policy of the European Cabinets 1871–1914* (1922–27). The inter-war years also saw many interpretative works by German historians, such as H. von Delbrück's *The Peace of Versailles* (1930) and H. Oncken's *The German Reich and the Prehistory of the First World War* (1932). These stressed the validity of Germany's fear of encirclement, and sought to lay greater emphasis on French desires to regain Alsace-Lorraine, and Russian designs upon Constantinople.

In the course of the 1930s it became politically acceptable, and even desirable, to share the responsibility for the outbreak of war. The American historian Sidney Fay, in *The Origins of the World War* (1930), caught the mood of the time by interpreting the disaster as an unfortunate succession of accidents. Austria-Hungary started a crisis in the Balkans without anticipating that it would escalate as it did; Germany was then trapped by its close links to Austria-Hungary, which operated in much the same way as the links between France and Russia, to drag the states into the conflict. Even contemporary French writers, originally the firmest advocates of German war guilt, were forced to admit that although 'the immediate origins suffice to tilt the balance [of guilt] to the side of the Central Empires, … one does not discern in the other camp any miraculous will for peace' (J. Isaac, *A Historical Debate, 1914: The Problem of the Origins of the War*, published in 1933).

The Fischer thesis and its critics

The compromise widely accepted as orthodox by western historians for 30 years was challenged dramatically in the 1960s by the work of the German historian Fritz Fischer. In *Germany's Aims in the First World War* (1961), he shifted a great deal of responsibility for the outbreak of war back on to German shoulders, claiming that its leaders had deliberately accepted the risk of war for the furtherance of their political ambitions during the course of the July Crisis of 1914. Fischer later claimed, in *The War of Illusions* (1969), that German actions since 1911 proved a desire, a preparation and a provocation of war. Naturally, such an interpretation provoked great opposition in Germany. Gerhard Ritter, then completing his masterpiece on German militarism – *The Sword and the Sceptre* (1954–68) – led the counter-attack. Ritter accepted that it was sadly true that the civil authorities had steadily abdicated their responsibilities in the face of military pressures during the reign of Wilhelm II, but argued that this did not amount to premeditated aggression. Another of Fischer's critics was Egmont Zechlin. In *The Outbreak of War in 1914* and the *Problem of War Aims in International Policy* (1972), Zechlin argues that although Bethmann-Hollweg took a calculated, and ultimately disastrous, risk in 1914, his objectives were essentially defensive, aiming to break the diplomatic encirclement which he believed to be stifling Germany.

More recently, the Fischer thesis has been modified by Hartmut Pogge von Strandmann, in *Germany and the Coming of War* (1988), and by H.W. Koch, in *The Origins of the First World War: Great Power Rivalry and German War Aims* (1984). Strandmann seeks to modify the nature of German war guilt by stressing that the error of its leaders was that they anticipated a short war with limited human costs. Koch's emphasis has been upon Germany's fear of isolation, and upon the concern of its leaders with the consequences of staying out of the conflict.

Yet Fischer has received much influential support among German historians. For instance, Imanuel Geiss, in *German Foreign Policy, 1871–1914* (1976), presents a modified version of Fischer's interpretation which still heartily condemns the conduct of Germany's leaders. Geiss concludes that Germany's unconditional support for Austria-Hungary was the decisive factor in the July Crisis, not only encouraging politicians in Vienna to take violent action, but also convincing Russian and French leaders that their countries were at risk, and that they needed to defend themselves. The German action in 1914 was compatible with its previous foreign policy, and thus implies a considerable degree of responsibility for the outcome.

Beyond Germany, the most frequent criticism of the Fischer thesis has been that it considers German actions and responsibilities too much in isolation from those of the other combatants. Some historians have been eager to stress the irresponsible actions of other states, and indeed of groups whose mentalities were not peculiar to individual states. Some have focused attention upon the intricate system of alliances that connected the interests of the major powers and on the considerable influence that military commanders exercised over many European governments. In *The Struggle for Mastery in Europe* (1954), A.J.P. Taylor played down the importance of the system of alliances that existed in 1914, stressing how loose and informal much of it was. Indeed, so loose was the system that one state, Italy, could actually change sides after the outbreak of the war. On the other hand, Taylor laid great stress upon the role of military commanders who advocated war in 1914, because they believed that the balance of military power was temporarily in their favour, and who argued against delay because their plans for mobilisation operated to a strict timetable.

Of the other European states, Austria-Hungary and Serbia have been criticised most for their irresponsible behaviour in the course of the Balkan crisis. Following the lead of Sidney Fay in the 1930s, Gordon Martel in *The Origins of the First World War* (1987), Fritz Fellner in *1914: Decisions for War* (1995) and others have blamed Serbian and Austro-Hungarian nationalists for plunging recklessly into a 'Third Balkan War', which spilled over to engulf the rest of the continent.

It is interesting to note that some recent work has revised views on the Balkan crisis in two important respects. It suggests that Serbia was too greatly drained by earlier Balkan wars to plan actively for a third. At the same time, there is some documentary evidence that Austria-Hungary's undoubted enthusiasm for a Balkan struggle was focused firmly upon Serbia until it was deflected and re-routed by German enthusiasm for a wider confrontation with Russia. While alternatives certainly exist to placing the blame on the shoulders of the German leaders, the role that they played continues to be regarded as central to the events that precipitated the war.

Marxist historians and the guilt of capitalism

For Marxist historians, of course, the issue of German war guilt was largely irrelevant in explaining the outbreak of the First World War. The favoured Marxist interpretation was that put forward by Lenin himself in his essay, 'Imperialism, the Highest Form of Capitalism' (1916). Lenin's case was that the war was the inevitable result of the development of capitalism into the monopoly stage, wherein capitalists were bound to compete aggressively for limited resources and markets. European imperialism in the decades before 1914 was the result of the final stages of monopoly capitalism, because colonies represented new markets and new resources to these advanced capitalists. The First World War, in Lenin's view, had to be seen as a clash between states goaded into confrontation by the selfish interests of their capitalists.

Popular as such an interpretation remained for many years in left-wing circles, many objections have since been raised to it. Historian David Fieldhouse, in *The Colonial Empires* (1966), led the way in showing how small the extent of investment in the new colonies was and how Great Britain, for example, invested far more in the USA than in any new acquisition. Russia, too, remained far more popular with investors, especially French ones, than any African or Asian territory. Further objections were based upon emerging evidence that the major European powers were by no means locked into cut-throat competition with each other, as Lenin imagined. In particular, the French economic historian Raymond Poidevin showed, in *Economic and Financial Relations Between France and Germany from 1898 to 1914* (1969), strong links and substantial community of interest between the business communities of the rival belligerent states. Between 1893 and 1913, French exports to Germany doubled, while trade in the opposite direction trebled. More recently, the work of the American, Carl Stirkwerda, has indicated that such economic links occur between all of the European states that clashed in 1914–18. Raymond Poidevin's picture is one of politicians leading reluctant capitalists into confrontation, rather than the other way around. His categorical conclusion is that 'economic and financial questions are not at the root of Germany's declaration of war on France [in 1914].'

1. What different attitudes have historians taken over the issue of German 'war guilt'?

2. What are the main arguments against the proposition that Germany was responsible for the outbreak of war in 1914?

3. Why has the issue of responsibility for the First World War caused so much controversy among German historians?

6.6 What were the war aims of the respective powers at the outbreak of the conflict?

Only one of the great European powers that entered the war in August 1914 had any clear idea of what they hoped to gain by victory. Austria-Hungary desired to end the challenge of South Slav nationalism, while the other states entered the conflict primarily through fear of the consequences of neutrality. In all other cases, therefore, late 1914 presented the bizarre sight of combatants clumsily formulating war aims after the conflict had begun.

A propaganda poster produced in Germany in 1914 which pretends to show that Britain might launch an attack on Germany through Belgium. It shows how British troops might threaten the industries of the Rhineland on the tenth day after mobilisation.

What impact is the poster supposed to have upon German public opinion?

Germany and the 'September Programme'

German propaganda portrayed the war as an attempt to escape strangulation by the encirclement policy of jealous and hostile neighbours, and righteously proclaimed that Germany was 'not driven by the lust of conquest'. On 9 September 1914, however, under pressure from industrial and Pan-German interests, and from public opinion inflamed by the early success of German arms, the Chancellor signed the so-called 'September Programme'. This made it clear that the war aim of achieving 'security for the German Reich in west and east for all imaginable time' involved an unparalleled programme of annexations and expansion. Predictably, the 'September Programme' has provided historians who have considered Germany guilty of premeditated aggression in 1914 – such as Fritz Fischer – with their main weapon. Others have preferred to see the programme as a chauvinistic response to early German victories.

Under the Programme's proposals:

● Germany was to demand the fortress of Belfort, the ore fields of French Lorraine and possibly a strategic coastal strip from Dunkirk to Boulogne from France.

● In addition, France would have to pay an indemnity, and accept a disadvantageous commercial treaty.

- Belgium, by losing Liège, Verviers and possibly Antwerp, would become a German **satellite**.

- Luxembourg would become a German federal province.

No such specific details were outlined for the east, but the general principle of the eventual peace settlement was to push Russia back 'as far as possible from Germany's eastern frontier'. Germany's conception of security consisted, therefore, of domination of Central Europe (*Mitteleuropa*), with Austria-Hungary as a junior partner. Important controls would also be exercised over its western and eastern neighbours. If the war had not begun as a war of conquest, it became one in September 1914.

British, French and Russian war aims

On the Entente side, the allies were effectively fighting for their survival as major powers, but public opinion demanded the formulation of more appealing war aims than this. As the major threat to their status was the growth of German power, British and French war aims in particular came to concentrate upon the destruction of those forces which made Germany an 'international danger'. Propaganda demanded the elimination of Junker militarism, and of the power of the house of Hohenzollern as essentials for a stable peace, for a Europe 'safe for democracy'. It was not quite consistent with these aims that the provisions upon which Britain was most insistent were the elimination of the German navy and colonial empire. Both were less of a threat to 'democracy' than to British trading interests. The French equivalent was to demand the return of Alsace and Lorraine. It was only indirectly, and over the course of the next year, that the dismantling of the Habsburg Empire and the establishment in its place of independent **nation states**, also became an article of faith for the allies.

1. What were the major war aims outlined in Germany's 'September Programme'?

2. How convincing is the argument that the major European powers went to war in 1914, not because they had specific war aims, but because they feared diplomatic isolation?

Russia had little to gain by defeating Germany, except for more troublesome Polish subjects, and its official war aims soon came to concentrate upon the old attractions of the Dardanelles and Constantinople. In March–April 1915, Britain and France finally agreed that Russia should have these in the event of victory, as long as they were compensated by gains in Egypt and the Near East. In the event of an Entente victory, therefore, the Ottoman Empire, too, was doomed to disintegration.

6.7 Why did the war become static between 1914 and 1916?

The initial war of movement and the failure of the Schlieffen Plan

On both fronts, at the outset of the war, the combatants anticipated campaigns of movement with the accent on offensive strategies and rapid results. In the west, the French pinned their hopes upon 'Plan XVII'. This dictated a thrust into the Saarland and into Lorraine, with decisive encounters close to the battlefields of 1870, and won by the natural *élan* (dash) of the French soldier. The German High Command had chosen a different geographical location. Their 'Schlieffen Plan' proposed a bold sweep by seven-eighths of Germany's western armies through Belgium and Luxembourg to envelop the French forces, held in check by the remaining German troops. Victory was expected within about six weeks, after which the bulk of the German forces would be free to confront the threat from Russia.

The German plan had considerable weaknesses. It was liable to dangerous delays by the destruction of bridges and railways, not to mention by enemy action. Yet it was very nearly successful. The German offensive

Joseph Joffre (1852–1931)
Saw service in Tonkin, Sudan and Madagascar and was promoted to General (1902). Became Chief of French General Staff (1911). Commanded troops in northern France and played a major role in resisting the German offensive in 1914. Commander-in-Chief of French forces (1915). Resigned after Battle of the Somme (1916) but was made Marshal of France for his services to the French war effort.

commenced on 4 August, took the border fortress of Liège within two weeks, and entered Brussels on 20 August. Meanwhile, the French offensive ran into stubborn resistance in Lorraine and in the Ardennes and its troops began to retreat with heavy casualties. The British Expeditionary Force, after an initially successful delaying action at Mons (23–24 August), was also forced to fall back to avoid isolation. Now the German commanders departed from the original plan of Count von Schlieffen. To avoid creating a break in the German line, Generals Kluck and Moltke chose to swing east of Paris to finish off Joseph Joffre's retreating Frenchmen, instead of surrounding and capturing the French capital.

On 5–9 September, the invaders and Joffre's regrouped armies fought the Battle of the Marne. This western engagement had indeed determined the future shape of the war, although in a different sense than the combatants had intended. The allied victory ensured that the Schlieffen Plan was a failure, while the Germans' establishment of strong defensive positions along the river Aisne, to check their own retreat, virtually put an end to the 'war of movement' and established the future pattern of trench warfare and siege tactics. The 'war of movement' had one last phase, as both forces attempted outflanking movements to the west of their opponents. When, in mid-November, the rival forces reached the Channel coast, a line of trenches extended unbroken for 720 kilometres, from the sea to the Alps.

This stabilisation of the Western Front was also created by the unprecedented losses of 1914. Some sectors of the front units had lost up to 40% of their strength, and a little over 10% of the French officer corps had been killed. **Munitions** manufacturers, too, had not catered for a lengthy conflict, and stocks of shells had been halved. In the last weeks of 1914 both sides were drawing breath and preparing for a form of warfare that neither had experienced nor anticipated.

Munitions: Military equipment and supplies, especially bombs, shells and guns.

The search for allies

In the short term, both sides sought to strengthen their alliances by tempting neutrals into their 'camps'. The greatest uncertainties surrounded Italy, formally linked by the Triple Alliance to Germany and to Austria-Hungary, yet set against the latter by all the precedents of 19th-century history. Only the Entente could offer Italy the Habsburg territories

The initial enthusiasm for war is demonstrated by these students in the streets of Berlin, 1914. Young Germans such as these died in their thousands at Ypres just a few weeks later.

in the Tyrol and down the Adriatic coast that its nationalists demanded to complete the process of unification. Thus Italy finally sided with France, Britain and Russia in May 1915. Its war had little to do with the issues that convulsed the rest of Europe and much to do with the anti-Austrian tradition of the 19th century. Among the Balkan states, Russia's growing ambitions facilitated the task of the Dual Alliance powers, and Turkey (December 1914) and Bulgaria (September 1915) both declared war on the Entente. In its turn, Bulgaria's old rival, Romania, entered the war on the side of the Entente in August 1916, although it declared war only on Austria-Hungary.

Stalemate in 1915

Where strategy had failed to achieve a decisive breakthrough in 1914, the next two years saw the increasing use of new technology in an attempt to break the deadlock. In April 1915, near the Belgian town of Ypres, the Germans used poison gas for the first time on the Western Front. As anticipated, it caused panic and severe losses. It knocked the desired hole in the allied lines, but it also handicapped and delayed the subsequent German advance, and the line was closed up in time. Allied offensives in 1915 preferred the new technology of heavy artillery and prefaced their attacks with enormous bombardments using hundreds of thousands of shells. The subsequent assaults usually foundered upon a fully-prepared second line of defences, behind the original German trenches. Many historians have taken an extremely negative view of military tactics at this time, concluding that the western commanders launched attacks not from any real hope of victory, but to keep their troops in a state of alert.

The cost was enormous. The battles of Artois (May), Loos and Champagne (September) cost 135,000 French dead and killed 140,000 Germans. This contributed to a total for 1915 on the Western Front of 400,000 killed or captured, and over a million wounded. Survivors also suffered unprecedented hardships. A French officer's description of troops returning from the front conveys their suffering:

> 'Squads came on, their heads bowed; stricken, sad eyes appearing from beneath field caps; rusty, muddy rifles were held suspended by the sling. Caps and faces were coloured alike by the dry mud, and then covered by more mud. The men were now beyond speech; they no longer had strength even to complain; you could see in their eyes an abyss of grief, a petrification [change to stone] through dust and strain. These dumb faces proclaimed a martyrdom of hideous proportions.'

Verdun and the Somme

The year 1916 was dominated in the west by one enormous engagement, the most terrible of the war. The logic behind German strategy at the Battle of Verdun was that if France were militarily and economically weakened, almost to the limit of its endurance, then Britain in turn would find itself isolated and be forced to seek peace. To achieve this, a blow would be struck at the place of paramount importance. This would leave France the alternatives of withdrawal, with its disastrous effect on morale, or resistance, in which case German bombardment would bleed its resources white.

The bombardment began on 21 February 1916 and used some two million shells. The subsequent infantry advance captured 3 kilometres of ground in three days. Then General Pétain took command of Verdun to conduct one of the great defences of history. French units were rotated regularly so that none would be completely overwhelmed by the dreadful

---

Philippe Pétain (1856–1951)
Entered French army in 1876 and commanded an army corps at the outbreak of war in 1914. His successful defence of Verdun (1916) made him a national hero. In turn, he became Commander-in-Chief of French army (1917), Marshal of France (1918), Inspector General of Army (1929) and Minister of War (1934). Pétain became Prime Minister after French defeat (1940) and signed **armistice** with Germany. Head of state of 'Vichy' France (1942). Condemned to death for treason upon the liberation of France (1945), but his sentence was commuted to life imprisonment.

Armistice: Agreement between countries who are at war with one another to stop fighting for a time and to discuss ways of making a peaceful settlement.

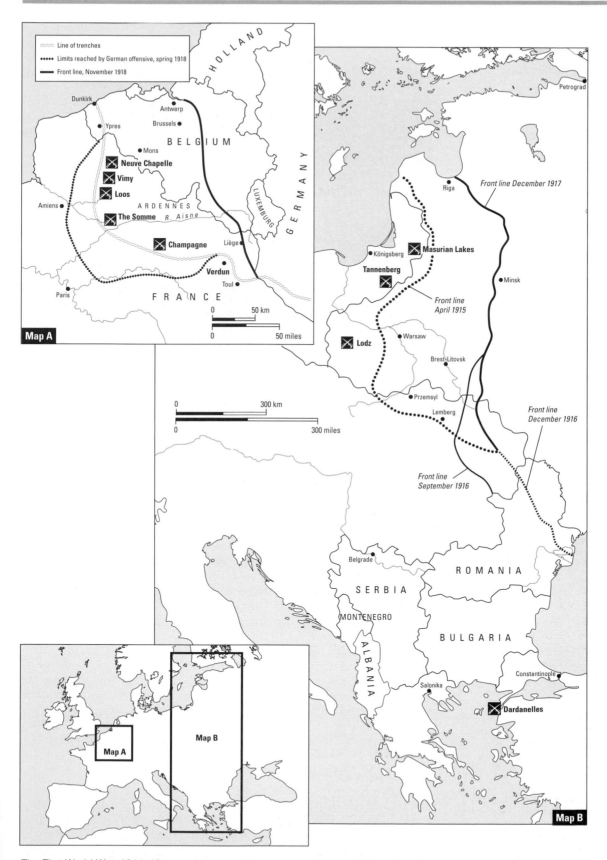

The First World War, 1914–18

The trenches as they became: a British trench during the Battle the Somme, 1916

conditions in which it fought. The road from Bar-le-Duc became the 'Sacred Road' (*La Voie Sacrée*), over which lorries passed at intervals of 14 seconds to supply the defences. In June, the Germans captured one of the foremost defences, Fort Vaux, and plans were prepared for evacuation, but German resources gave out first and they discontinued their offensive in mid-July. French counter-attacks in October and December regained virtually all their earlier losses.

The massive casualty list of 700,000 dead was evenly divided between the two sides, but it has been argued that the French suffered a further disadvantage in that the widespread experience of the horrors of this battle did much to breed the pacifism that affected France in the 1930s. According to the French historian Marc Ferro, in *The Great War, 1914–18* (1973), 'Troops coming up to relieve the soldiers were often overwhelmed at the horror of Verdun; they saw an implacable fate before them, of digging a grave to stay alive, and then supporting it with their corpses … The only certainty was death – for one, or other, or all.'

Further west, on the Somme, the allies launched their own massive offensive (July–November 1916) in part to deflect German resources from Verdun. Despite a week of preliminary bombardment, the failure of the offensive was evident within minutes of its launch. Failure to admit as much cost 600,000 casualties for no significant gain. Between them the two monumental failures of 1916 brought an end to the 'war of attrition' on the Western Front.

Why was no decisive outcome achieved on the other European fronts 1914–1916?

Russian defeats in 1914

The Russians, too, expected early successes, although less from rapid strategic thrusts than from the huge numbers of peasant soldiers that they could mobilise. On 17 August, far earlier than the authors of the Schlieffen Plan had envisaged, the Russian 'steamroller' entered German territory in East Prussia. Three days later, General Rennenkampf defeated a German

Paul von Hindenburg (1847–1934)
Prussian soldier from a traditional Junker background. Saw military service in Austro–Prussian (1866) and Franco–Prussian (1870) Wars, and retired in 1911. Recalled from retirement upon outbreak of war (1914) to take command, with Ludendorff, of German forces on the Eastern Front. Gained major victories at Tannenberg and at the Masurian Lakes. Promoted to Field Marshal (1916). Succeeded Friedrich Ebert as President of the Weimar Republic (1925) and, despite his mistrust of the Nazis, appointed Hitler as Chancellor in 1933.

Erich von Ludendorff (1865–1937)
Responsible for German mobilisation and deployment plans (1908) and for revision of the Schlieffen Plan. Shared command on the Eastern Front with Hindenburg (1916). Planned Spring Offensive (1918) and opposed application later that year for armistice terms. Convinced that Germany had been betrayed from within, he became associated with extreme right-wing politics, taking part in the Kapp *Putsch* (1920) and in Hitler's Beerhall *Putsch* (1923), and sitting in the Reichstag (1924–28) as a Nazi deputy.

force at Gumbinnen. The defeat merely brought on to the scene the two most successful German commanders of the war: Paul von Hindenburg and Erich von Ludendorff.

In the campaign of the next month, by which they sought to defend the Junker heartland of Prussia, they were helped by a variety of Russian shortcomings and errors. The Russian army had attacked before it was fully ready for the task in order to give maximum aid to the French, and the personal hostility between the Russian Generals Rennenkampf and Samsonov made co-operation between the two main attacking forces difficult. Furthermore, the generals allowed the two Russian armies to become separated by the 80-kilometre chain of the Masurian Lakes. As a result, Hindenburg and Ludendorff were able to tackle the two forces individually. Samsonov was defeated in the engagement christened the Battle of Tannenburg (26–29 August) in memory of, and in revenge for, the defeat of the Teutonic Knights by the Slavs in 1410. Less than two weeks later, Rennenkampf's army was similarly defeated at the Battle of the Masurian Lakes (8–9 September). In the Russian retreat, the Germans took approximately 130,000 prisoners.

A war of attrition in the east

These two great battles saved Prussia from Russian invasion and established Hindenburg as the major German folk-hero of the war. Their influence on the war in the east as a whole should not, however, be overestimated. Indeed, by forcing the withdrawal of German troops from the Western Front, the Russian offensive had made no small contribution to the defeat of the Schlieffen Plan. Further south, Russia secured some notable successes against its main rival, Austria-Hungary. Lemburg (Lvov), the fourth largest city in the Dual Monarchy, was captured in early September, an event which, in the words of the military historian John Keegan, in *The First World War* (1998), 'deprived the Austrian army of its best and bravest element, never to be replaced'.

Hesitant Russian leadership and substantial German intervention in support of the crumbling Habsburg forces then combined to produce two years of fluctuating fortunes on the main eastern fronts. The year 1915 was marked by a slow and costly rolling back of the Russian forces beyond their frontiers:

● The long German campaign in Poland, launched in October 1914, finally achieved its purpose with the capture of Warsaw (August 1915).

● A combined Austro–German offensive in the Carpathians (May 1915) recaptured most of Russia's gains of 1914 by late June.

● By the end of the year, the Russian lines had withdrawn some 450 kilometres, leaving behind a million dead and a further million prisoners.

The Brusilov Offensive

The following year, 1916, witnessed the greatest Russian successes of the war. Remarkably, neither its resources nor its morale had been crushed by the earlier reverses. Historian Norman Stone, in *The Eastern Front 1914–1917* (1975), emphasises the upswing in Russian military supplies and production by this point in the war, and J.N. Westwood stresses that, since 1812, retreat was not necessarily seen as a shameful or dispiriting factor in Russian military circles. Urged on by Russia's allies to relieve pressure on Verdun and on the Italian front, General Brusilov launched a massive offensive over a wide front in June 1916. Its initial success was startling. Three of the four Russian armies involved achieved an immediate breakthrough and within five days Brusilov had taken 70,000 prisoners. By early August however, lack of adequate resources, political jealousy at headquarters, and a further influx of German support for the wavering Austrians had all brought the 'Brusilov Offensive' to a halt.

Nevertheless, the 340,000 casualties inflicted upon Austria-Hungary, plus another 400,000 taken prisoner, were more than the Dual Monarchy could stand. The offensive, states historian A.J.P. Taylor, 'marked the moment when the armies of Austria-Hungary lost their fighting spirit. Unity, cohesion, loyalty vanished; and from this time Austria-Hungary was kept in the war by German power.' It also marked the last great effort of the Russians, which almost achieved its aim of eliminating Austria-Hungary from the conflict. Where victory might possibly have prolonged the life of the Russian monarchy, a further million casualties combined with mounting civilian hardships at home were to lead the Romanov dynasty into its final crisis.

The Central Powers in the Balkans

In the Balkans, meanwhile, the issue that had started the whole conflict was largely decided by late 1915. At first, Austria-Hungary's offensive foundered upon stubborn Serbian resistance and suicidal counter-attack. The invaders held the Serbian capital, Belgrade, for just two weeks in December 1914, and were then flung back with 100,000 casualties. Serbian losses were even higher, and its army was further ravaged by disease. In mid-1915, two factors combined to seal Serbia's fate. One was the German decision to intervene in the interests of maintaining safe communications with Turkey, and the second was the entry of Bulgaria into the war. The Serbian army was overwhelmed by a joint Austro–German–Bulgarian offensive in October 1915, and allied forces planning to come to its aid through Greek territory from Salonika encountered enormous geographical obstacles, as well as fierce political objections from the Greek government. The remnants of the Serbian army at least saved face by an epic retreat through Albania to the sea. From there they were evacuated to Greece to continue the struggle, but without success.

The entry of Romania into the war on the side of the Entente was a brief and unhappy episode. Badly equipped and poorly led, its army was in retreat within a month of its first campaign (August 1916). Romania's contribution effectively ended with the fall of its capital city, Bucharest, to German forces in early December.

The failure of the Gallipoli campaign

The most ambitious undertaking in this theatre of war was the assault upon the Gallipoli peninsula, to gain control of the Dardanelles (February–November 1915). It was motivated primarily by the deadlock on the Western Front, and was conceived as a combined operation by sea and land forces to capture Constantinople, to knock Turkey out of the war, and to re-open secure lines of communication with the hard-pressed Russians. The operation's prospects at the time of the initial naval bombardment of the Turkish defences (February 1915) were bright. The allies had the advantage of surprise, and the Turkish positions were weak. The allied campaign, however, was distinguished by 'short-sighted lethargy'. A landing in strength was not attempted until April, and in the ensuing months the allied cause suffered from lack of co-ordinated command, shortages of supplies, delays and elementary tactical errors. The loss of four allied battleships to Turkish mines further dampened the initial enthusiasm of the naval commanders.

When the operation was finally abandoned, in November, it had cost the allies 250,000 men, dead, wounded or captured. The campaign had served to convince most allied commanders that the war could only be settled on the Western Front.

The Austro–Italian front

Meanwhile, Italy's entry into the war produced a campaign of attrition, grim and fruitless even by the standards established in France. In answer to the Italian strategy of an attack along the line of the river Isonzo in the north-western corner of the country, Austro-Hungarian forces occupied a line of mountainous defensive positions. As the Italian historian P. Pieri noted, 'the river could not be crossed until the mountains had been seized, and the mountains could not be seized until the river had been crossed'. Thus, between June 1915 and August 1917, 11 separate battles of the Isonzo were fought, costing Italy nearly a third of its original army strength for minimal gains. Even as a diversion the Isonzo Front was of little value, tying down only a dozen Austrian divisions.

When a breakthrough finally came (October 1917) it was the Italians who fell back in disorder, handicapped by their own low morale and lack of ammunition, in the face of a combined Austro–German offensive at Caporetto. The Italian army had lost over 300,000 men, many miles of territory, and very nearly the war, before its forces were successfully regrouped on the line of the river Piave in November. But it was an exhausted Austrian army, pressed by allied victories in the Balkans, and disrupted by domestic upheavals, that was finally swept from Italian soil in October 1918 in the Battle of Vittorio Veneto.

To what extent was Britain able to maintain its naval supremacy in the war at sea?

Two decades of rising naval expenditure, and the development of fleets of fast, heavily armed **dreadnoughts**, had created the impression by 1914 that the disputes between Britain and Germany would be settled primarily by a major confrontation between their fleets. Ironically, the earliest naval events of the war made it clear that decisive roles would be played by cheaper and less glamorous weapons. On 22 September 1914 the German submarine 'U9' sank three British cruisers within minutes, and a month later the British battleship HMS 'Audacious' was sunk by a mine. It immediately became obvious that battle fleets could not after all range freely in search of each other.

In the early months of the war, German ships were mainly concerned with raiding missions against British and allied commerce on the high seas. The 'Emden' in the Indian Ocean and Admiral von Spee's cruiser squadron in the Pacific did much damage, the latter badly shaking British complacency by destroying a British force off the Chilean coast (1 November 1914). Eventually, the re-disposition of British resources won back the advantage. Von Spee's force was destroyed at the Battle of the Falkland Islands (December 1914) and the sinking of the 'Dresden' in March 1915 effectively ended the threat from German surface raiders.

The British navy enjoyed surface supremacy for the rest of the war – a fact of enormous strategic importance. It allowed 8.5 million troops to be mobilised from the Empire without a single loss at sea. It established and maintained the crippling blockade imposed upon Germany and facilitated the conquest of nearly all German colonies in the first year of the war. Ultimately, it made possible the convoy system that helped thwart German submarine warfare, and the transport of American men and equipment to play their decisive role in the European conflict.

The Battle of Jutland

Nevertheless, the war did produce two more threats to that British

---

1. **What problems were encountered by the Russian war effort on the Eastern Front between 1914 and 1916?**

2. **Why did Gallipoli and northern Italy become major theatres of war in 1915–16?**

3. **How much justification was there by the end of 1916 for the view of some military commanders that the war could only be decided on the Western Front?**

Dreadnoughts: A type of battleship, first launched by Britain in 1906, which was more heavily armed and armoured than previous types. Its launch helped to intensify the naval race between Germany and Britain.

Admiral Maximilian Graf von Spee (1861–1914)
Entered German navy in 1878, and served in colonies from 1887. Commanded North Sea Fleet (1908) and Far Eastern Squadron (1912). At the outbreak of war he defeated a British force at Coronel, but at the Battle of the Falkland Islands (December 1914), his flagship 'Scharnhorst' sank with all hands.

Admiral Reinhard Scheer (1863–1928)
Chief of Staff of the High Seas Fleet (1910). Scheer was an early advocate and strategist of submarine warfare. Commander of the High Seas Fleet (1916), and devised the strategy that culminated in the Battle of Jutland. Chief of Admiralty Staff (1918).

Capital ships: Warships (e.g. battleships) of the largest class.

Admiralty: British government department in charge of the navy.

1. *By what means did Germany attempt to damage or destroy British naval supremacy during the First World War?*

2. *How convincing is the argument that German attempts to challenge British naval supremacy were a complete failure?*

supremacy. The first was the Battle of Jutland (31 May 1916), the only major encounter in naval history between massed fleets of dreadnoughts. Fought in the North Sea, the battle resulted from the eagerness of the new German commander, Admiral Scheer, to tempt sections of the Grand Fleet out of their ports into the open sea where they might be attacked by superior German forces. The British ability to decipher German radio signals meant that Scheer had to undertake an engagement involving some 250 ships. The German fleet demonstrated superior gunnery and superior ship design. It lost two **capital ships**, nine lesser vessels and 2,500 men, compared with the three capital ships, 11 lesser vessels and 6,000 men lost by the British. Both sides claimed victory, both with some justification, but the fact remained that only the outright crippling of the British fleet would have transferred the strategic initiative to the Germans, and this they failed to achieve.

The German submarine campaign

Although the German surface fleet played no further role in the war, its submarines did. Even as the dreadnoughts were failing to impose a stranglehold on Britain, there was a dramatic rise in the amount of British shipping sunk by U-boat action. In February 1917, when Germany adopted unrestricted submarine warfare, Britain lost 464,000 tons of shipping. In April it lost 834,000 tons, and between February and June 1917 one ship in four dealing with British ports was destroyed. British corn supplies dwindled to the equivalent of six weeks' normal consumption and defeat seemed near.

The adoption of the system of escorted convoys, in the face of much opposition from the **Admiralty**, did not eliminate the submarine threat. In the first quarter of 1918 Britain still lost over a million tons of merchant shipping. The convoy system reduced losses, however, to a level that could be made good by new vessels leaving the shipyards. By the end of the war, the new counter-technology of mines, depth charges and other devices had destroyed half of the U-boat fleet. Considering, too, the role that German submarines played in bringing the USA into the conflict on the allied side, it becomes clear that their use, although an extremely dangerous tactic, was ultimately an unsuccessful one.

6.8 What impact did this prolonged war make upon the domestic populations of the combatants?

1914: the triumph of patriotism

L'union sacrée (French – sacred union): Term used to indicate that Frenchmen had forgotten their traditional political differences in order to unite in the 'sacred' wartime cause of serving the motherland.

Conscientious objection: Term used to describe the refusal by an individual to fight in the war on grounds of religious or moral belief. Although it was not illegal to be a 'conscientious objector' such people were often regarded as cowards by popular opinion, and were harshly treated.

Apart from the new brand of 'total' warfare waged at the front, the First World War was also remarkable for the fact that it was the first to have a substantial impact upon the civilian populations left at home. At first, there was little sign that this impact would be negative. The popularity of the conflict in all the participating countries was not in doubt. In France, earlier political differences were submerged in the 'sacred union' (*l'union sacrée*) for the defence of the country. Where a rate of **conscientious objection** of 13% had been feared by the security services, the actual level was only 1.5% of those summoned to the colours. Germans, similarly, spoke of the *Burgfriede*, the domestic peace that reigns in a besieged fortress. Speaking of mid-1915, the historian A.J.P. Taylor concluded that 'there was, as yet, hardly a flicker of discontent or discouragement in any belligerent country'.

The development of economic warfare

The first dents to appear in this universal optimism resulted from the rapid spread of economic warfare. Germany's geographical position made it most vulnerable to this form of attack, and its own merchant navy had virtually ceased to function by the end of 1914. Although imports continued to seep in through neutral neighbours, the value of German trade with the USA, for instance, fell from 68 million dollars in December 1914 to 10 million in January 1915.

Germany's recourse to submarine warfare later subjected Britain to similar difficulties, and the German occupation of northern France and of Poland deprived France and Russia, respectively, of important industrial resources. The entry of Turkey into the war aggravated Russia's problems, with domestic results that would eventually bring down the regime. Food supplies were also hit by the mobilisation of large numbers of men and horses as the war progressed. It has been estimated that in Germany agricultural production fell by 50%–70%, according to the individual region. The drop in Russia was 50% and in France it ranged between 30% and 50%. Germany was the first to introduce rationing, limiting supplies of bread, meat, potatoes and fats. Turkey, in particular, suffered an alarming rise in the death rate from diseases such as typhus.

Social change: the roles of the state and women

In several respects, the war resulted in the greater subjection of the citizen to central political authority. Germany was the first combatant to take measures to direct and to control resources and production, creating the War Materials Department (*Kriegsrohstoffabteilung*) in 1914. All combatant countries, however, soon experienced government pressure to push available labour into war industries. By the end of the war, these industries employed 76% of all industrial labour in Russia, and 64% in Italy.

A further notable result of the war was the substantial employment of female labour in order to release men for the forces. In France, by 1917, one in four war workers was female, and Joseph Joffre could claim that 'if the women in the war factories stopped for 20 minutes, we should lose the war'. In Britain, too, in A.J.P. Taylor's words, 'by the end of the war, it was no longer true that woman's place was in the home'.

The citizen also felt the influence of central authority in the unparalleled degree of propaganda and censorship. News of military failures, of heavy casualties, and of anything else that could contribute to 'defeatism' was progressively eliminated from publications.

Conscription: Making people in a particular country join the army, navy or air force.

The enormous losses of the early campaigns also made the citizens in most warring countries liable for the first time to military **conscription**. France introduced conscription at an early stage of the war, and lost men at such a rate that those scheduled for call-up in 1917 were called in December 1915. Even Britain, with its relatively modest contribution to the war on land, abandoned the principle of a volunteer army in January 1916.

The growth of war-weariness

For the first time, the civilian did not need to go to the front to become a casualty of war. The new and developing technology of the conflict produced several means of striking at the enemy's resources and population. Paris was shelled at regular intervals, at a range of 126 kilometres, by the massive gun christened by the Germans 'Long Max'. London, meanwhile, suffered its first air-raids. As part of the retaliation demanded by public opinion, British planes in the last year of the war inflicted 24 million marks' worth of damage on German factories and towns.

Eventually the strain of war, at the front and at home, broke down the enthusiasm of 1914. Isolated socialist and pacifist voices were raised against the war. September 1915 saw the publication of the Zimmerwald Manifesto by international socialists meeting in Switzerland. Even so, discontent was ultimately the result of price rises and declining living standards. Reliable figures are incomplete, but it is possible to state that in England in 1917 food prices were 70% higher than in 1914, while wages were only 18% up. The figures for France were 74% and 30% respectively, while those for Italy were 84% and 38%. (The social impact of the war upon Russia is described in detail in Chapter 7.) The contrast between the figures above and the substantial increases in the profits made by most branches of heavy industry began to trigger off militant action by 1917. The table below shows the initial fall in strike action at the outbreak of war, in contrast to the renewal of industrial unrest as the strains of three years of total war attacked the fabric of society.

1. In what ways did popular attitudes towards the First World War change between 1914 and 1917?

2. 'Although little changed at the front, the First World War transformed the domestic societies of the states that fought it.' Do you agree with this statement?

Number of strikes, 1913–18

	1913	1914	1915	1916	1917	1918
Russia	2,404	3,534	928	1,410	1,938	–
Britain	1,459	972	672	532	730	1,165
France	1,073	690	98	314	697	499
Germany	2,127	1,115	137	240	561	531

From Marc Ferro, *The Great War, 1914–18*, Routledge (1973)

6.9 What prospects did either side have for success in 1917?

The allies' failure to achieve a breakthrough

After the failure of the policy of attrition on the Western Front in 1916, allied commanders could devise no better plan than a return to the optimistic and unrealistic offensive tactics of 1914. Joffre's replacement at the head of the French forces, General Robert Nivelle, was another firm believer in the *élan* of the French infantryman, and was able to 'sell' the idea of a combined allied offensive to the British. However, as the Germans had withdrawn (March 1917) to prepared positions on the so-called Hindenburg and Siegfried lines, the 'Nivelle Offensive' of April was launched against the best defences that the Germans had occupied so far. Although some objectives were achieved, such as the Chemin des Dames and Vimy Ridge, the casualty list of 118,000 losses on the French side alone told a familiar story of wasted lives.

In May 1917, a disillusioned Nivelle was replaced by Philippe Pétain who, returning to the tactics successful at Verdun, declared himself committed to a waiting game: 'I am waiting for Americans and tanks.' For the rest of the year, British troops bore the brunt of the futile offensives on the Western Front. The Battle of Messines (June) produced some successes, including the spectacular use of mining operations to blow up German positions, but the Third Battle of Ypres, or Passchendaele (July–November), became a by-word for muddy deadlock. No significant advantage was secured, despite 324,000 casualties.

Only the Battle of Cambrai brought promise of an end to the stalemate. There, on 20 November 1917, a massed force of 381 British tanks broke through the German lines and achieved an advance of 8 kilometres.

Success was only partial. The infantry could not keep up with the advance, and there were not enough reserves. Thus German troops were able to repair the initial damage within ten days. Nevertheless, the world's first true tank action gave a foretaste of the new 'war of movement' that northern France would witness a generation later.

The entry of the USA into the war

If tanks did not fulfil Pétain's expectations, the year 1917 also witnessed a decisive increase in allied strength. The isolationism that had so far characterised America's attitude to the war was ultimately overcome by two German errors:

1 the decision to wage unlimited submarine warfare from February 1917, which inevitably involved attacks upon American ships and loss of American lives;

2 the dispatch of the so-called Zimmermann Telegram.

The Zimmermann Telegram

In March 1917, the German Secretary of State authorised his minister in Mexico to offer that country German support in an attack upon the USA, for which Mexico would regain those territories lost to its neighbour in the 19th century. Intercepted, the message had a predictable effect upon public opinion in the USA. Several authorities have stressed, however, the extent to which the USA was, in any case, committed to the allies by February 1917. American producers had deals to provide copper, cotton, wheat and other commodities, and its bankers had forwarded huge loans. Thus German submarines, and the threat of ultimate German victory, put substantial American interests at risk. The fall of the Tsar, in March 1917, also removed the ideological obstacle to American involvement. The war could now be portrayed as a conflict between democracy and German militarism. Having broken off relations with Germany on 2 February over the submarine issue, President Wilson declared war on 6 April.

Woodrow Wilson's Fourteen Points, published as an initial basis for peace in 1918

1. There should be no secret diplomacy between states. All international treaties should be openly negotiated, and all their terms should be published.
2. The use of the high seas should be freely available to all nations without restriction.
3. Economic barriers to international trade should be removed.
4. All states should agree to a reduction in armaments.
5. All states should work towards the dissolution of their colonial empires, and the independence of the territories that they had colonised.
6. German troops should evacuate all occupied Russian territory.
7. German troops should evacuate all occupied Belgian territory.
8. Alsace and Lorraine should be returned to France.
9. The frontiers of Italy should be readjusted in such a manner as takes account of the nationality of the inhabitants.
10. The nationalities governed by the Austro-Hungarian Empire should be allowed to determine their independent political futures.
11. German troops should evacuate all occupied territory in Romania, Serbia and Montenegro, and the independence of those states should be guaranteed.
12. The nationalities governed by the Ottoman Empire should be allowed to determine their independent political futures, and the Dardanelles should be opened permanently to international shipping.
13. An independent state of Poland should be created with access to the sea.
14. An international association of nations should be formed to safeguard peace and to guarantee the independence of all states, great and small.

American war aims: the Fourteen Points, January 1918

In moral terms, American intervention changed the nature of war. Without any threat to its security, and far removed from the territorial concerns of the European combatants, the USA approached the war as a moral crusade for the preservation of democracy. This was confirmed by President Woodrow Wilson's major statement on his country's war aims in his 'Fourteen Points' (8 January 1918). Some of his demands – for the evacuation of occupied Belgian and Russian territories, the restoration of Alsace-Lorraine to France, the establishment of self-government among the minority peoples of the Habsburg Empire – were fully consistent with earlier allied declarations. On the other hand, the calls for the abolition of secret diplomacy, for total freedom of the seas, for the abolition of all trade restrictions, for a general reduction in armaments, and for the 'absolute impartial adjustment of all colonial claims', were not at all what the allies had originally had in mind.

France and Italy hang on

1. What events, and what aims, brought the USA into the First World War?

2. How convincing is the argument that the western allies were on the verge of defeat by the end of 1917?

3. How different were American war aims in 1918 from those of the European powers at the start of the conflict?

Materially, this intervention was unlikely to make an immediate impact. Time was needed for the mobilisation of men and resources, and thus the American declaration was, in A.J.P. Taylor's phrase, 'a promissory note for the future, provided that the allies held on until it could be cashed'. Several factors in 1917 did indeed cast doubt upon the ability of America's partners to survive long enough to benefit from its assistance. On the Western Front, 1917 saw the French army shaken by a series of mutinies involving 54 divisions, mainly in protest against the murderous strategy of the commanders. Miraculously, Pétain was able to restore order before the Germans realised their opportunity. Some 23,000 soldiers were charged as a result, and over 430 sentenced to death, although it now seems that only 50–55 were executed.

Meanwhile the Austrian offensive at Caporetto threatened the continued existence of the Italian Front. Most serious of all, the aftermath of the Bolshevik Revolution in November saw the total withdrawal of Russia's forces from the conflict. Even at the end of 1917, it was far from certain that American involvement would decide the war in the allies' favour.

6.10 Why did the war effort of Germany and its allies collapse in 1918?

The German Spring offensive

The year 1918 opened with the dual prospect for Germany of immediate advantages, in the form of men and supplies transferred from the Eastern Front, but long-term disadvantage from the influx of American resources and the continued effects of the allied blockade. Ludendorff's strategy was thus to throw everything into a final 'Peace Offensive' (*Friedensturm*) to drive Britain and France out of the war. Three major offensives won the greatest German successes of the western conflict. In March, 35 divisions on the Somme made gains of about 65 kilometres against the British. In April, in Flanders, a breakthrough was achieved which for a time threatened allied control of the Channel ports. In May, on the river Aisne, the French line broke, and German forces once again reached the Marne within 80 kilometres of Paris.

The strategy had not, however, achieved the desired victory. Each advance, as it lost its drive, left German forces deep in a **salient**, around

Salient: Narrow area where an army has pushed its front line forward into enemy territory.

which the allies massed their growing forces. Meanwhile Germany struggled to replace its latest 800,000 casualties. Allied forces at last came under co-ordinated control with the appointment of General Foch in April as Commander-in-Chief of the Allied Armies in France. The last German offensive of the war came in July around Reims. It met stiff opposition and made no significant progress. Instead, the French counter-attack made a breakthrough, and Ludendorff's forces fell back to safer ground.

The allied breakthrough

The 8 August 1918 marked the beginning of the end for Germany. On what Ludendorff dubbed 'The Black Day', a combined allied offensive made the greatest gains achieved since the stabilisation of the front in 1914. A British tank attack east of Amiens, in particular, broke the German line and advanced some 9 kilometres. Yet the German resistance did not collapse then, nor during the next allied offensive in mid-September. Their morale, however, suffered a fatal blow. The loss of ground, combined with disappointment with the results of their own *Friedensturm*, 'shattered their faith in victory which, until that moment, carried the Germans forward. They no longer wanted to win. They wanted only to end the war.' (A.J.P. Taylor)

The collapse of Germany's system of alliances

For at least a year, war-weariness had affected the capitals of all the warring nations. The 'sacred union' in France had been strained to breaking point by the decision of the socialists to leave the cabinet in September 1917. As early as November 1916, the Emperor Karl, succeeding Franz Josef at the head of the Habsburg Empire, had made tentative peace proposals to the allies. While the rise to power of Georges Clemenceau in Paris (November 1917) had strengthened the fight against defeatism in France, morale in Germany and Austria continued to decline. By January 1918, the daily flour ration in Vienna had dropped to 165 grams, food trains from the east were plundered, and the number of desertions from the forces rose sharply.

In June the German Secretary of State, Richard von Kühlmann, publicly broached the subject of a compromise peace, but was disowned and forced from office by the military leaders. By early October, however, reverses on the Western Front and the surrender of Bulgaria (29 September) to the east, had changed their minds. Ludendorff acknowledged the need to withdraw from occupied territories, and to accept Social Democrats into the government in order to pacify the democrats among the allies. On 4 October, the new government led by the liberal Prince Max of Baden requested an armistice based upon the 'Fourteen Points'. On 20 October, Germany officially ended submarine warfare.

Meanwhile, although the war effort in the west was maintained, that in the east collapsed. Turkey signed an armistice in late October, broken by highly successful British campaigns in the Middle East. At the same time the Austro-Hungarian Empire quietly disintegrated, with the peaceful declaration of independent nationhood by the Czechs, the Yugoslavs and the Hungarians (31 October). Three days later, the remnants of the Habsburg armies requested an armistice. The sequence of events in Germany, too, made further resistance impossible. On 20 October, naval crews at Kiel began to mutiny in protest against orders to resume operations at sea. On 9 November 1918, a German Republic was proclaimed in Berlin by Social Democrats, and the Kaiser left his throne for exile in Holland.

1. **What events caused Germany to ask for an armistice in November 1918?**

2. **What were the consequences for Germany of the failure of its Spring Offensive in 1918?**

3. **'The allies won the First World War because the Americans arrived on time.' Do you agree with this statement?**

The threat of domestic revolution added urgency to the German government's quest for peace. Although horrified by the severity of the armistice terms dictated by the allies, the German delegation signed them at Compiègne, in northern France, on 11 November 1918.

- Germany was to hand over its fleet, and its vast stocks of war material.

- It was to evacuate all occupied territories on the west and to permit allied occupation of the left bank of the Rhine.

- It was to annul the peace treaties made with defeated Russia and Romania.

As a formal, impotent protest, the leader of the German delegation stated that 'a nation of 70 millions suffers, but does not die'. Ferdinand Foch remarked *'très bien'* ('very good'), and closed the interview that ended the First World War.

6.11 What was the impact of the First World War upon Europe?

The political and economic impact

It is hard to overstate the political impact of the First World War upon the 20th century. Although it left many problems still to be resolved, its impact upon the map of Europe was revolutionary. With the almost simultaneous collapse of three great empires – Germany, Russia and Austria-Hungary – the major points of reference in a century of European history vanished. The traditional balance of power was destroyed, and the peace settlement failed to put anything substantial in its place. In Russia, Tsarism was replaced by the most radical regime that modern Europe had witnessed, and that was to exercise a profound influence upon world history for the next 75 years. Now that the collapse of the Soviet Union has undermined the Marxist claim that the triumph of communism was inevitable, it becomes easier to appreciate the crucial role that the First World War played in causing the Russian Revolution. In addition, the Turkish Empire was seriously reduced, and a variety of new 'successor states' – Austria, Hungary, Czechoslovakia and, indirectly, Poland and Yugoslavia – emerged from the chaos of the war. Equally sensational was the war's impact upon the future of European politics. With the intervention by the USA, the whole role of Europe in the world was called in question. Although the truth took some time to sink in, Europe in effect ceased to be the centre of the world in 1918.

A by-product of these changes was, as historian Niall Ferguson emphasises in *The Pity of War* (1998), a major triumph of republicanism in Europe. 'When the strain of war began to tell it was the monarchy which was the first among the established institutions to lose legitimacy; so that the war led to a triumph of republicanism undreamt of even in the 1790s.' Where France, Switzerland and Portugal were the only European republics on the eve of war, post-war republics emerged in Germany, Russia, in each of the 'successor states' of the Austro-Hungarian Empire and, shortly afterwards, in Ireland. One might go further than that. In effect, the war destroyed forever the assumption that the traditional governing élites 'knew best' and that their economic and social predominance implied that they possessed some superior talent for government. It is scarcely surprising that the next two decades were dominated by radical political views of many different and conflicting natures. In terms of the conflict's impact upon the map and the political systems of Europe, it is fair to say that only in the 1990s did Europe really begin to escape from the direct consequences of its 'Great War'.

Politically, the First World War was also remarkable for what it did not achieve. Neither the victorious governments, nor those that had suffered defeat, saw in the disaster any real need to question the principles by which they governed. Britain and France, far from abandoning colonial expansionism, seized upon the defeat of Germany and Turkey to add to their overseas empires. Nationalism remained a powerful force in European politics, whether it was fuelled by triumph, or by a sense of injustice in defeat. US President Woodrow Wilson's suggestion of a radical new political morality, involving 'collective security', and the abandonment of militarism and colonialism, generally fell upon deaf ears.

Most important of all, perhaps, was the economic impact of the war. The total cost (listed below), of more than £34,000 million, represents the wreck of Europe's 19th-century economic development. As Niall Ferguson concludes, 'The war literally and metaphorically blew up the achievements of a century of economic advance.' Staggering as such figures are, they do not tell the whole story. If other factors are taken into account, such as the loss of trade during the war years, the loss of foreign investments, and subsequent losses caused by economic instability resulting from the war, a devastating picture emerges.

The cost of the First World War

	Dead (millions)	Financial cost (£ million)
British Empire	0.947	6,418
French Empire	1.400	5,200
Germany	1.800	8,300
Austria-Hungary	1.200	4,100
Russia	1.700	5,060
USA	0.116	2,600
Italy	0.650	2,400
Serbia	0.048	–

The human and emotional impact

The human and emotional cost of the war is more difficult to comprehend and to quantify. Mere statistics, powerful as they are, cannot do full justice to the impact of the 'Great War'. The numbers of the dead are laid out above, yet in many respects the survivors had greater social impact than the dead. The huge numbers of soldiers permanently disabled by their injuries constituted an enormous burden for each of the combatant states in the years ahead. Of 13 million Germans who served in the war, for instance, 2.7 million were permanently disabled and 800,000 were subsequently supported by state pensions. Of British war veterans, 41,000 lost a limb in the fighting.

It now appears that the dead constituted more of an emotional than a demographic problem. Although much was subsequently written about a lost generation, recent research appears to indicate that patterns of European population were not greatly changed by the war. The number of young men aged between 15 and 24 in England and Wales was greater in 1921 than it had been in 1911. Similarly, the proportion of the German population aged between 15 and 45 was greater in 1925 (23.5%) than it had been in 1910 (22.8%). One specific generation, nevertheless, had been hard hit. In France, for instance, the generation that would have flourished in the 1920s and 1930s – those aged between 20 and 40 in 1914 – had lost 20% of their number in the war, with a further 10% rendered incapable of long-term employment.

The emotional impact of the war remains difficult to evaluate, and it is hard to give more than a taste here of the complex issues involved. It is fashionable nowadays to emphasise the anti-war emotions contained in much post-war literature, such as the English war poets, Siegfried Sassoon and Wilfred Owen, or in Erich Maria Remarque's celebrated German novel, *All Quiet on the Western Front* (*Im Westen Nichts Neues*, 1928). Käthe Kollwitz's statues of 'The Grieving Parents' in the German war cemetery at Vladslo, in Belgium, also convey a powerful image of hopeless loss. Yet the neighbouring British cemeteries convey a very different message. They are serene and dignified, stressing that the sacrifice of the dead was a noble thing, and that 'their name liveth for evermore'.

Similarly, the literary works that we now consider to be representative of the post-war period were far outnumbered by works that stressed the comradeship and patriotism of war. One does not have to look deeply into Germany's post-war history to discover that the taste for militarism had not yet been exhausted. Neither material losses nor emotional damage, therefore, were sufficient to make this 'the war to end all wars'. Perhaps it is only later generations, which no longer feel the patriotism and hatreds of the time, who perceive the war entirely as wasteful and sterile.

1. In what respects did the combatants pay a high price for their participation in the First World War?

2. What, if anything, was changed in Europe by the First World War?

Source-based questions: Unrestricted submarine warfare

Study Sources 1–5 below and then answer questions (a) and (b) which follow:

SOURCE 1

(From a memorandum written by Field Marshal Falkenhayn to the Kaiser, December 1915)

Submarine warfare strikes at the enemy's most sensitive spot, because it aims at severing his overseas communications. If the definite promises of the naval authorities, that the unrestricted submarine war must force England to yield in the course of 1916, are realised, we must face the fact that the United States may take up a hostile attitude. She cannot intervene decisively in the war in time to make England fight on when that country sees the spectre of hunger rise up before her island. There is only one shadow over this encouraging picture of the future. We have to assume that the naval authorities are not making a mistake. We have no large store of experience to draw upon in this matter.

SOURCE 2

(Admiral Capelle, addressing the budgetary committee of the German Reichstag, January 1917)

They will not even come, because our submarines will sink them. Thus America from a military point of view means nothing, and again nothing, and for a third time nothing.

SOURCE 3

(From Gerard de Groot, The First World War, *published in 2001)*

On 22 December 1916, Admiral Henning von Höltzendorff, Chief of the Admiralty Staff, submitted a memo to the Chancellor in which he stated that 'The war demands a decision by Autumn 1917 if it is not to end disastrously for us.' Since Germany could not win a protracted war, the submarine seemed the only salvation. Civilian advisers, carefully studying British shipping tables and rates of consumption, calculated that if sinkings exceeded 600,000 tons per month for six months, British imports would reduce by 39%, a fatal level of loss. If the campaign was launched in February, defeat would come before the August harvest.

Source-based questions: Unrestricted submarine warfare

SOURCE 4

(From Niall Ferguson, The Pity of War, *published in 1998)*

The German gamble which has been subjected to most criticism was the gamble that unrestricted submarine warfare would defeat Britain before the United States could make an effective military contribution to the war. This policy was tried for a third time from 1 February 1917, when the Admiralty Staff promised that Britain would have to sue for peace 'within five months'. In fairness to the German naval planners, the U-boats initially exceeded the original target of sinking 600,000 tons a month; indeed, they bagged 841,118 tons in April. But their calculations were in every other respect wrong. They had underestimated (1) Britain's ability to expand her own wheat production; (2) the normal size of the American wheat crop; (3) the tonnage available to Britain. Incredibly, they had also over-estimated the number of submarines they themselves possessed or could possess.

SOURCE 5

(From Paul G. Halpern, A Naval History of World War I, *published in 1994)*

The convoy system was extended gradually. The initial emphasis was upon homebound vessels. These were the vessels carrying vital supplies, and the U-boats had also concentrated their attention upon them. In the disastrous month of April 1917, 18% of homeward bound vessels had been sunk, compared to only 7% of those outward bound. This changed after the introduction of convoys. The U-boat commanders now found convoys hard to find and difficult to attack. The presence of escorts worked against attack on the surface by gunfire, and with the convoy zigzagging it proved difficult to get into a favourable firing position.

Answer both questions (a) and (b).

(a) Using your own knowledge, and the evidence of Sources 3, 4 and 5, what do you consider to have been the main weaknesses of the German decision to use submarine warfare to decide the outcome of the First World War? [10 marks]

(b) From 1914 onwards, 'German conduct of the war consisted of a series of gambles, which ultimately led to disaster'. Using your own knowledge, and the evidence of all five sources, explain how far you agree with this claim.

[20 marks]

The Russian Revolutions, 1914–1924

Key Issues

- *What impact did the First World War have upon Russian politics and society?*
- *How did the Bolsheviks seize power in 1917?*
- *How did the Bolsheviks deal with the political and economic problems that beset them in 1918–1924?*

7.1 What was the impact of the First World War upon Russia?

7.2 What triggered the February/March Revolution of 1917?

7.3 Why was the Provisional Government unable to solve the problems that confronted it in 1917?

7.4 What factors made the Bolsheviks such an important political force in 1917?

7.5 How did the Bolsheviks establish their power in Russia in 1917–19?

7.6 Why did civil war break out in Russia in 1918?

7.7 How and why were the White forces defeated in the Russian Civil War?

7.8 Why did Lenin launch the New Economic Policy in 1921?

7.9 Did the Bolsheviks launch a cultural revolution in Russia between 1917 and 1924?

7.10 Historical interpretation: Was the Russian Revolution the inevitable outcome of class struggle?

Framework of Events

1914	(July) Germany and Austria-Hungary declare war on Russia (August) Russian advance halted in East Prussia
1915	German advance into Poland and the Baltic provinces. Nicholas II assumes direct command of Russian forces
1916	Brusilov Offensive makes gains against Austro-Hungarian forces
1917	(February/March) Strikes and army mutinies lead to abdication of Nicholas II. Formation of Provisional Government (April) Arrival of Lenin in Petrograd (August) Unsuccessful coup by General Kornilov (October/November) Bolshevik seizure of power
1918	(March) Treaty of Brest-Litovsk ends war with Germany. Beginning of foreign military intervention against the Bolsheviks (July) Murder of the Imperial family
1919	(July–October) Successful offensives by Red Army against White forces
1920	Conflict between Red Army and Polish forces (November) Final withdrawal of White forces
1921	(March) Kronstadt uprising. Introduction of New Economic Policy (April) Stalin elected General Secretary of Russian Communist Party (May) Conclusion of Treaty of Rapallo with Germany
1922	(May) Lenin suffers stroke
1923	Beginning of contest between Stalin and Trotsky for party leadership
1924	(January) Death of Lenin.

Overview

RUSSIA embarked upon the war against Germany and Austria-Hungary at a critical point in its history. To a greater extent than any of the other major combatants, Russia had faced daunting domestic problems in the course of the past decade. Industrialisation had given rise to urban poverty and unrest, and it remained unclear whether the reforms of Pyotr Stolypin had effectively pacified and stabilised the Russian peasantry, and broadened the basis of moderate conservative support for the Tsar's government. What is certain, however, is that Russia was as yet ill equipped to sustain a long war against so powerful an industrial state as Germany.

The duration of the First World War took all of the major combatants by surprise. Although all were greatly weakened by it, none suffered so severely as Russia. Heavy casualties and soaring food prices enhanced long-standing tensions in Russian society, and had a particular impact upon the industrial workers in the major cities. More important still was the succession of political errors committed by the Tsar and by other key members of the regime. The Tsar's decision to run the war as an autocrat, his refusal to co-operate with patriotic elements in the Duma and elsewhere, and his personal assumption of military responsibility all served to alienate elements which might otherwise have provided moderate conservative support for Nicholas. When the hardships of the war produced riots and strikes at the beginning of 1917, important elements in the army, in the Duma, and even within the Imperial family, could no longer see any reason to support a leader whose methods of government now appeared foolish and bankrupt. In many respects, the revolt of February/March 1917 was as spontaneous and leaderless as that of 1905. This time, however, there appeared to be an alternative form of government to that of the Tsar. Only 11 years after the formation of the Duma, some of its members sought to establish a government to fill the vacuum that Nicholas had left, substituting the legitimacy of popular election for the legitimacy of Divine Right. It was a remarkable step to take, as deserving of the title of 'revolution' as was the Bolshevik rising that followed later in the year.

The Provisional Government found itself in an impossible situation. In terms of the logic that had governed Russian politics before 1914, it had a degree of legitimacy, for its members represented several of the mainstream tendencies of Russian opposition politics. It had to deal, however, with a very different logic, born out of years of war, hunger and hardship. The Provisional Government failed because it could not reconcile the interests of its moderate members, and of its wartime allies, with the urgent demands of war-weary Russian troops, hungry Russian workers, and land-hungry peasants. Its failure was accelerated by the appearance on the scene of a new and powerful force, in the form of the Bolshevik Party. Its leader, Lenin, exploited the difficult circumstances of 1917 brilliantly, but ruthlessly. He promised the bulk of the population exactly what they desired: an immediate end to the war and a rapid resolution to the land question. By these promises, he had already formed a strong basis of support among Russian workers, before he cast aside electoral niceties and seized power by a daring *coup d'état* in October/November 1917.

By the early months of 1918, however, the Bolshevik coup appeared to be anything but a 'masterstroke'. Instead of calmly proceeding 'to build the socialist order', Lenin was confronted with a terrible array of obstacles to the maintenance of Bolshevik power. Instead of a universal revolution fuelled by the collapse of international capitalism, they faced resistance from a variety of Russian opponents, from liberals and radicals of rival tendencies, as well as Tsarists, often supported by foreign capitalist powers. It became necessary to introduce strict measures of recruitment and of procurement of food in order to be able to fight and to win a long civil war. Bolshevik success in this war resulted from the effectiveness of their organisation, and the committed support that they received from some portions of the population, as well as from the diversity of aims, the poor leadership and inadequate organisation of their 'White' opponents.

The years of civil war were of great importance in forming the nature of the communist state. On the most obvious level, these were the years in which the Bolsheviks imposed their authority over the greater part of the old Tsarist empire, and in which they eliminated most of their serious rivals. To do so, however, they had been forced to adopt many of the autocratic tools that Tsarist government had employed, and which socialist idealism had habitually rejected. A large, disciplined army was necessary to ensure military victory. An equally authoritarian and disciplined party structure, backed by ruthless political police, was necessary to ensure political discipline. Tight economic control was essential to feed the soldiers and workers, and to ensure that the new regime would not be subverted by its capitalist enemies. In international terms, the state was utterly isolated, surrounded by capitalist states that feared and mistrusted its ideology, and which had given the Soviet leadership, by their intervention in the civil war, good reason to expect further assaults in the future from the capitalist 'bloc'. By the time the civil war was won, pre-revolutionary communist theory had largely been discarded, and the foundations of the Stalinist state were clearly visible.

All this had been achieved at an appalling cost. The Russian economy had collapsed, with industrial production at the lowest level for decades, and millions starving as the agrarian economy failed even more spectacularly. Having eliminated so many elements of Tsarist Russia, the Bolsheviks continued to be threatened by one key element. They had to find an answer to the problem of the Russian peasantry, far less willing, now that the threat of the Whites had receded, to tolerate the demands of the Bolsheviks for the cheap sale or surrender of their crops. Incidents such as the Kronstadt rebellion (see page 208) made it clear that former supporters of the Bolsheviks, soldiers and urban workers, were equally alienated by the hardships that arose from this economic crisis. Under these pressures the Bolsheviks were forced to make concessions, and the last months of Lenin's life saw the introduction of the New Economic Policy.

The Russian calendar in 1917

In 1917 Russia was still using the Julian calendar, which originated in ancient Rome. In most of Europe this had been replaced by the Gregorian calendar, devised by Pope Gregory XIII in 1582. By 1917 the difference between the two calendars was approximately ten days. Thus the confusion as to whether the Russian Revolution is known as the 'October Revolution' (24–25 October) or the 'November Revolution' (7–8 November).

7.1 What was the impact of the First World War upon Russia?

What was the impact upon the Tsarist regime?

The initial popularity of the war

Despite grim forebodings in some informed circles, the declaration of war in 1914 was undoubtedly popular in Russia. Although the former Minister of the Interior, P.N. Durnovo, accurately warned that the main burden of fighting would fall on Russia, voices such as his were drowned out in the swell of popular enthusiasm. The immediate voting of war credits by the Duma (8 August), the plundering of the German embassy by patriotic students and the general acceptance of the government's ban on the sale of vodka, all bore witness to the readiness at first to suspend old hostilities in defence of 'Mother Russia'. Even the capital city was renamed, the Germanic sound of St Petersburg giving way to the Slav Petrograd. Briefly, the Tsar enjoyed more popularity than at any other point in his reign. For once he could pose convincingly as the personification of all the Russians. Yet within three years he was Tsar no more, his prestige worn away in a succession of failures and miscalculations. Three interrelating factors stand out as contributing to this last collapse of Tsarist prestige.

War and the autocracy

Firstly, the patriotic formation of such bodies as the Union of Zemstva, to provide medical facilities, and the Congress of Representatives of Industry and Trade (August 1914), to co-ordinate production, raised an old, thorny question. How far could representative bodies, and the latter included representatives of the workers, be allowed to influence the conduct of the war? The attitude of the government was clearly that the autocracy should exercise sole control. A matter of particular controversy was the formation of 'military zones' (July 1914), comprising most of Finland, Poland, the Baltic provinces, the Caucasus and Petrograd. Within them all civil authority was subjected to that of the military, and every obstacle was put in the way of would-be civilian participation. To many it seemed that political ideology was becoming more important than the effective prosecution of the war. This impression grew stronger in the course of 1915 and in June of that year the existing *zemstvo* and municipal organisations merged to form the All-Russian Union of Zemstva and Cities (*ZemGor*). Although they continued to be denied any active role in the conduct of the war, such bodies as *ZemGor* and the Duma acted as a focus for liberal discontent. The historian David Christian has even gone so far as to describe them as constituting 'the embryo of an alternative government'. The Tsar bitterly blamed 'disloyal' liberals for these tensions, but modern commentators are more inclined to blame the Tsar. 'The truth is,' states the historian Hugh Seton-Watson, 'that the insuperable obstacle was his dogmatic devotion to autocracy.'

Secondly, at this point came the decision of the Tsar to assume personal command as Commander-in-Chief of the armed forces (September 1915) and to take up residence at the front. However understandable in terms of royal duty and military morale, the decision directly identified the Tsar with all future military disasters. It left the government in Petrograd at the mercy of the Empress' infatuations and the schemes of political opportunists.

The role of Rasputin

Thirdly, the most famous, and perhaps the most damaging, of these factors was the increased influence over the Empress, and thus over government policy, of Grigori Rasputin. With the Tsar at the front, Rasputin became the main influence upon the deeply religious Empress.

Grigori Rasputin (1871–1916)
A Siberian *starets* or holy man, Rasputin had been known to the Imperial family since 1905. His influence over them dated from 1907 when it began to appear that he was able to control the haemophilia (a blood disease) from which the heir to the throne, Alexis, suffered. The means by which he did this have never been satisfactorily explained. There were damaging rumours of a sexual relationship between Tsarina Alexandra and Rasputin, though they were never proved. Rasputin's extravagant lifestyle and frequent bouts of drunkenness made him a public scandal. He was murdered in December 1916 by a young Russian noble.

Mikhail Rodzianko (1859–1924)
Of aristocratic and military background, he became a leading advocate of liberal reform of the autocracy. A leader of the Octobrists, he served as a member of the third and fourth Dumas and led the Duma from March 1911. Strongly advocated a constitutional monarchy in 1917.

1. What factors undermined the political credibility of the Russian government between 1914 and 1917?

2. In what ways was the Russian war effort in 1914–17 hindered by the autocratic nature of its government?

Treason: The crime of betraying your country, for example by helping its enemies or by trying to overthrow the government. Historically, treason was a crime punishable by death.

The view of contemporary opponents such as the prominent Duma politician Mikhail Rodzianko that Rasputin was the supreme evil influence on the government is not always accepted today. Some have seen him rather as the tool of self-seeking schemers. At any rate, contemporaries saw his advice to the Empress as the main force behind the 'ministerial leapfrog' that occupied the year beginning in September 1915. Some ministries had as many as three or four chiefs within the year, most of them nonentities. Rasputin's murder in December 1916 came too late. The damage to the government and its reputation was irreparable and many contemporaries, remembering the German origins of the Empress, could not avoid the suspicion of **treason**.

What was the impact upon the Russian people?

In the end, the collapse of the Romanov dynasty in Russia was not triggered by ideological arguments, but by the suffering imposed by the war upon the Russian people.

The organisation and equipment of the army

The most immediate hardships, of course, were borne by those actually serving in the armed forces. Although Russia only mobilised a little less than 9% of its population during the war, compared with about 20% in both Germany and France, the size of the Russian population meant that a substantial number experienced the horrors of the front. The Russian army totalled 5.3 million men after the initial mobilisation (Germany and France mobilised 3.8 million at this point), and a total of 15.3 million Russians had seen military service by the end of hostilities. Numbers, however, were the Russian soldier's only advantage. Compared to his opposite numbers in other armies he was worse armed, worse treated and worse led. Shortcomings of armament and tactics exposed in the war of 1904–05 were being treated, but had not been overcome by the outbreak of war in 1914. It was still not unusual in 1915 for Russian artillery to be limited to two or three shells a day, and after mobilisation in 1914 the infantry had only two rifles for every three soldiers. Men were sent into battle with instructions to help themselves to the weapons of fallen comrades. Such factors made casualty levels that were, in any case, horrendous all the harder to bear. By early 1917, Russia had lost 1.6 million dead, 3.9 million wounded and 2.4 million taken prisoner.

The impact upon the civilian population

The civilian population also had increasingly daunting problems to face. The year 1916 was a comparatively good one for military production, with rifle production doubled and that of heavy artillery quadrupled, but these advances were made at the expense of civilian needs. Locomotive production, for example, was halved between 1913 and 1916 with only 67 new engines completed in 1916. This, together with constant military interference with the railway network for strategic purposes, contributed to the semi-breakdown of communication and distribution systems that was the main cause of urban food shortages.

There were other factors, too. Conscription caused a scarcity of both

1. What hardships did the Russian people suffer as a result of the First World War?

2. How convincing is the argument that the sufferings imposed by the First World War were entirely responsible for the discontent felt by the Russian people in the years leading up to 1917?

men and horses on the larger country estates, and town populations increased as war industries demanded extra labour. Generally, though, there was enough food. It simply was not getting to those who needed it. Indeed, historian Norman Stone shows, in *The Eastern Front, 1914–1917* (1975), that military shortages, too, were due less to failures of production than to inefficient distribution. Fuel shortages were another consistent problem. After the early loss of the Polish coalfields, total coal production in Russia never reached the same level as was achieved in the last year of peace, and an increasing proportion of what fuel there was was channelled towards military uses. Food prices rose dramatically. On average – and the figures were actually higher for major urban areas such as Petrograd – the price of flour rose by 99% between 1913 and 1916, meat by 232%, butter by 124% and salt by 483%. Money wages, it is true, rose by 133% over the same period, but this figure has to be set against a drop in the value of the rouble to only 56% of its pre-war value.

7.2 What triggered the February/March Revolution of 1917?

The growth of liberal opposition

Paul Miliukov (1859–1943)
Liberal politician and historian. Exiled for his political views (1895), he returned after the 1905 revolution. Founder member of the Kadet Party. Member of Third and Fourth Dumas, and headed the 'Progressive Bloc' during the First World War. As Minister for Foreign Affairs in the Provisional Government, he advocated continuation of the war and was forced to resign. Lived in exile in France from 1920.

Abdication: The act by which a monarch gives up his/her throne, usually in favour of a named successor.

If the First World War does not fully explain the collapse of the Tsarist regime, it did act as an accelerator in the process of alienating the Russian people from their rulers. By August 1915, the combination of the Kadets, Octobrists and Progressists in the Duma into the so-called 'Progressive Bloc', demanding a government 'possessing the confidence of the public', indicated that the old wounds were open once more. The government's answer was to suspend the sittings of the Duma (15 September 1915). Between that date and January 1916, when the Duma re-assembled, the dispute centred upon the conduct of the ministers including the premier, Ivan Goremykin, the Foreign Minister, S.D. Sazonov, and the War Minister, A.A. Polivanov. By mid-November 1916, the liberal politicians in the Duma had decided upon a more uncompromising attitude towards the government and its failures. On 15 November the assembly heard a famous charge of official incompetence by Paul Miliukov. Questioning whether government policy represented 'stupidity or treason', he concluded that 'we have lost faith in the ability of this government to achieve victory'. By January 1917 some leading members had even prepared provisional plans to force Nicholas' **abdication** in favour of his son.

The collapse of civilian and military morale

If some commentators have stressed the role of the liberals in the final discrediting of the monarchy, there is wide agreement that neither they, nor any other organised political groups, bear responsibility for the events that finally brought it down. 'The collapse of the Romanov autocracy,' stated the American commentator William H. Chamberlin, 'was one of the most leaderless, spontaneous, anonymous revolutions of all time.'

The initiative came primarily from the Petrograd workers whose patience with the deprivations of war was nearing exhaustion as 1917 opened. In January, some 150,000 of them had demonstrated on the anniversary of Bloody Sunday, and 80,000 had demonstrated support for the re-opened Duma in February. International Women's Day (8 March) brought tens of thousands of women, exasperated by months of food shortages, on to the streets. The coincidence of this with a wage strike at the Putilov works raised the number of demonstrators on that day to a new 'high' of perhaps 240,000.

The decisive anti-Tsarist factor, however, was the armed forces. The major difference between the events of 1917 and those of 1905 lay in the attitude of the Petrograd garrison. The shooting of 40 demonstrators on 11 March broke the morale of many of the conscript soldiers, and regiment after regiment associated with, and then actively supported, the strikers. Even the dreaded Cossack regiments refused to obey their officers. By the end of 12 March, Petrograd was in the hands of a revolution without recognised leaders, at a cost of an estimated 1,300 civilian and military lives. 'Not one party,' wrote the socialist observer N.N. Sukhanov in 1955, 'was preparing for the great overturn.'

The abdication of the Tsar

In the task of filling the power vacuum in Petrograd the liberal members of the Duma had the advantage of being on the spot, but their attitude was highly ambiguous. They half obeyed the Tsar's order to disperse, by transforming themselves into a Provisional Committee (12 March). Most of those members who supported Rodzianko's advice to Nicholas to abdicate did so only in the hope of salvaging something of the monarchy by crowning a more popular, constitutional Tsar. That these men ended as the Provisional Government of a republic was largely due to the indecision and fatalism of the Tsar himself.

Having originally dismissed the Duma's pleas for last-ditch reforms as 'some nonsense from that fatty Rodzianko', Nicholas then toyed with the idea of a military assault upon his own capital. He was dissuaded by the pleas of his generals, notably Brusilov and Ruzsky, who wanted constitutional reform. However, Nicholas was unable to compromise his own autocracy, and agreed to abdicate (15 March). The following day his brother, the Grand Duke Michael, refused the crown, leaving Russia a republic after 304 years of Romanov rule.

1. Which political and social groups opposed the Tsar's government at the beginning of 1917?

2. Why did the Tsar's government collapse in February/March 1917?

7.3 Why was the Provisional Government unable to solve the problems that confronted it in 1917?

Georgi Lvov (1861–1925)
Aristocratic liberal whose earlier political involvement was with the *zemstvo* movement. President of the Provisional Government (1917). Sought co-operation with the Soviet and resigned (July 1917) when this proved impossible.

Trudoviks (Russian *'Trud'* – Labour): A non-Marxist socialist group, founded in April 1906 to participate in the First Duma. Its deputies were a mixture of peasant representatives and radical intellectuals.

Who were Russia's new leaders?

The new republic was in the hands of two powers tolerating, but scarcely supporting each other. The Provisional Committee of the Duma formed itself into a Provisional Government (15 March) containing the most notable Kadet and Octobrist leaders. Georgi Lvov was the first premier, with Paul Miliukov as Foreign Minister and Alexander Guchkov as Minister of the Interior. Its rival for influence was the Petrograd Soviet, formed on 12 March, after the model of 1905, by the spontaneous action of workers and soldiers. It was at first an unwieldy body of up to 3,000 members, not dominated by any party, but by individuals of various persuasions. Among its leading orators, Alexander Kerensky was a **Trudovik** member of the Duma, while N. Chkeidze and M.I. Skobelev were Mensheviks (see insert on page 195).

Lenin was later to accuse the Soviet of a 'voluntary surrender of state power to the bourgeoisie and its Provisional Government'. The charge is not strictly fair in that, while the Duma politicians took on the responsibility of government, the support of workers and of soldiers left the Soviet with most of the practical power. Such was its control over post, railway and telegraph services in Petrograd that virtually nothing could be done without its consent. Guchkov himself wrote that 'the Provisional Government possesses no real power and its orders are executed only as this is permitted by the Soviet of Workers' and Soldiers' Deputies.'

The Soviet's 'Order Number One' (14 March) decreed the establishment of soldiers' councils in each regiment of the armed forces, thus extending its influence to the military sector. From May 1917, the Soviet took part more directly in government when six Mensheviks and Trudoviks, including Skobelev (Minister of Labour) and Alexander Kerensky (Minister of War), became ministers in the Provisional Government. From July, Kerensky actually led the government as premier, but failed to bridge the gap of mistrust that separated the bourgeois body from that of the Petrograd workers, leading to an uneasy co-existence.

Alexander Kerensky (1881–1970)

Elected to the Fourth Duma as a Trudovik member, and opposed the voting of war credits. Successively Minister of Justice, War Minister and Prime Minister in the Provisional Government in 1917. Subsequently lived in exile in France and in the USA. By a remarkable coincidence he was born in the same town as Lenin, and his father was headmaster of the school that Lenin attended.

The land question

The first steps towards a policy that would be acceptable to both bodies were easily agreed. On its first day in office the Provisional Government decreed an eight-point programme that included a complete amnesty for all political prisoners, total political and religious freedom, and the promise of elections to a constituent assembly. Poland's right to independence was at last recognised (30 March) and capital punishment was abolished, even in the armed forces.

Thereafter, the problems of policy became more contentious. Two major tasks confronted the government, the more pressing of which was satisfying the peasants' age-old demand for land. Although the government quickly recognised their right to the great landed estates, an official policy of partition was impossible to implement without inviting mutiny and desertion by peasant soldiers 'trapped' at the front while their local estates were distributed among their neighbours. The peasants, however, were unwilling to wait. Thus disorder spread in the countryside as the peasants took the law into their own hands. The government received nearly 700 complaints about illegal attacks upon landed property in June 1917, and over 1,100 in July. It was the turn of the peasant now to pose as 'the autocrat of Russia'.

The maintenance of the war effort

Clearly, a solution to the land problem depended upon a solution to the second problem, that of the war in which Russia was engaged. The revolution raised the question of what war aims Russia should now pursue. The unanimous conviction of the Provisional Government was that the war should be pursued to a victorious conclusion. Miliukov, for one, saw no reason to abandon the original aims of annexations in eastern Europe and in the Turkish Empire, but was so far out of touch with popular opinion that he was forced to resign (15 May). The attitude of the Soviet was not for immediate peace either, for such a peace might merely put them at the mercy of a monarchist Germany. Instead, they rejected the 'policy of annexations' and refused 'to serve as an instrument of conquest and violence in the hands of kings, landowners and bankers'. Compromising between popular pressure and the need to honour obligations to Russia's allies, the Provisional Government accepted (8 April) the prime war aim of 'the establishment of a stable peace on the basis of the self-determination of nations'.

The collapse of the war effort, and the Kornilov Affair

The collapse of the war effort was the first major failure of the new government. Its July offensive in Galicia, aimed at proving the government's worth to allies and Russians alike, ended in the retreat of demoralised and under-equipped forces over a large area. In the same month came demands for the autonomy of the Ukraine, to which some ministers seemed ready to agree, while the left-wing 'July Rising' led by Bolshevik sympathisers from the Kronstadt naval base further illustrated the precariousness of the government's position.

In September, the threat came from the right. General Lavr Kornilov, appointed by the government to head the armed forces, marched on Petrograd. His main aim was probably to oust the Soviet which he saw as undermining military discipline, but his actions and pronouncements could be seen as attempting to impose a counter-revolutionary regime. His failure, largely due to the refusal of troops to obey his orders, left the prestige of the government at a new low ebb, and strengthened the hand of the Bolshevik extremists in the Soviet.

The attitude of historians to the events of June–September 1917 have been deeply influenced by their political sympathies. The role of the Bolshevik Party in the July Rising was played down by Soviet writers, who portrayed the events as spontaneous. Many western commentators, on the other hand, followed the line of historian Daniel Shub, in *Lenin* (1966), seeing the events as a planned 'coup' from which the Bolshevik leaders retreated at the last moment due to loss of nerve. More recently, Robert Service (*Lenin*, 2000) has directly contradicted this interpretation, asserting that the disturbances took Lenin by surprise, and that he played a leading role in restraining his Bolshevik followers. The truth of the Kornilov affair has been equally difficult to unravel. Most Soviet sources, and some non-Soviet writers, asserted that Kerensky was using Kornilov (who in Trotsky's phrase had 'the heart of a lion, but the brains of a lamb') for his own anti-Soviet ends. The charge has never been proven, and was strenuously denied in Kerensky's own writings.

What was Lenin's contribution to communist theory and organisation before 1917?

No individual made so radical and influential an impact upon the history of Russia between 1870 and 1991 as did Vladimir Ilyich Ulyanov, known as Lenin. The details of his early life appear below, but his impact as a revolutionary can be dated from 1902, when he published one of his most influential works, entitled *What is to be Done?* In it, Lenin rejected the arguments of previous Russian socialists who wished to limit themselves to legal economic activities, or who continued to place their faith in the peasantry as a revolutionary force. Instead, Lenin stressed the need for a

1. What policies did the Provisional Government adopt towards the problems of land ownership and the continuation of the war?

2. Why was the Provisional Government in Russia unable to consolidate and maintain its power in 1917?

3. How convincing is the claim that, by October 1917, 'the Provisional Government was politically bankrupt, having failed in all its main policy aims'?

Proletariat: The working classes. Increasingly, in the late 19th century and 20th century the term was applied specifically to working-class people in industrial, urban areas.

Vladimir Ilyich Lenin (1870–1924) Originally V.I. Ulyanov. Born in Simbirsk (later renamed Ulyanovsk in his honour), the son of a teacher and school inspector. The key event of his early life seems to have been the execution of his elder brother, Alexander, in 1887 for his involvement in an attempt to assassinate the Tsar. The event appears to have triggered latent radical tendencies in the younger Ulyanov, and

to have marked him as a radical both in his own mind and in the view of the authorities. The years between 1887 and 1900 – with their mixture of expulsion from university, practice as a radical lawyer, imprisonment in Siberia, and eventual flight to western Europe – present a picture familiar from the biographies of many contemporary Russian radicals. During the second phase of his political life, Lenin

distinguished himself as a prolific writer and publicist, explaining Marxist theory and laying down his strong views on how the future struggle of Russian socialism should be organised. The most important development of these years was perhaps the foundation, with Julius Martov in Germany (1900), of the journal *The Spark* (*Iskra*). In 1903 Lenin brought about a split in the Russian Social Democratic Labour Party, between the

Bolsheviks and the Mensheviks (see insert opposite). He spent much of the next years of his life in exile in western Europe. He returned to Petrograd following the February 1917 revolution and urged an immediate seizure of power by the **proletariat**. In October 1917, Lenin led the Bolshevik revolution, and became the head of the first Soviet government until his death.

'party of a new type'. He envisaged a disciplined and dedicated group of professional revolutionaries, which would act, in Lenin's famous phrase, as the 'vanguard of the proletariat'. By rejecting reliance upon the eventual good sense of workers and peasants, by rejecting the aid of well-meaning but amateurish intellectuals, and by rejecting terrorism, *What is to be Done?* represented a substantial break with the past traditions of the Russian left. Such an organisation, however, was unacceptable to many who wished for a broader, more popular basis to the party, and who distrusted Lenin's tendency towards autocratic leadership.

At the second congress of the Russian Social Democratic Workers' Party (**RSDRP**) in London in 1903, the party split into the 'Men of the Majority' (*Bolsheviki*), favouring the views of Lenin, and the 'Men of the Minority' (*Mensheviki*), favouring the more democratic alternative now championed by Julius Martov. The terms are misleading, as Lenin's group had actually been outvoted by the end of the congress, but the names coined by him stuck firmly to the factions whose differences further weakened the short-term effectiveness of the RSDRP.

On the eve of the First World War, Lenin enjoyed a dual reputation within the narrow circles that constituted Russian Marxism. In addition to being one of the outstanding theorists and **revisionists** of the movement, he was also a determined political **pragmatist**, wholly convinced of the correctness of his own interpretation of events, and largely intolerant of opposition from within the movement.

RSDRP: The initials of the Russian Social Democratic Workers' Party, the formal name of the Russian Communist Party.

Revisionists: Socialists whose actions or opinions differ from orthodox Marxist theory, and who are therefore considered to be wrong and dangerous by orthodox Marxists.

Pragmatist: Person who deal with problems, or thinks about problems, in a practical way rather than in a theoretical way.

Political groups in Russia 1917–1921

Octobrists: Russian Liberals who regarded the 1905 October Manifesto as the limit for constitutional change within Russia.

Constitutional Democrats (Kadets): Russian Liberals who regarded the 1905 October Manifesto as a step on the road to full parliamentary government for Russia.

Social Revolutionaries: A radical group who wanted to transfer land to the Russian peasantry.

Left Social Revolutionaries: Those social revolutionaries who were willing to form a coalition with the Bolsheviks from October/November 1917. They left the coalition following the Treaty of Brest-Litovsk and attempted to overthrow the Bolshevik government in 1918.

Bolsheviks (known as Communists from 1918): Lenin's party. (See also page 137.)

Mensheviks: Those members of the Russian Social Democrat Party which supported the Provisional Government and wanted to see the establishment of a liberal democratic republic before Russia eventually became a socialist country.

Tsarists: Those who wanted to see the return of monarchic government under a member of the Romanov family.

Greens: A political grouping associated with the Ukraine anarchist Nestor Makno. They opposed both the Bolsheviks and the Whites during the Russian Civil War.

Nationalists: Groups who wanted to see the creation of their own national state from the old Russian Empire. Included Georgians, Ukrainians and people from the Baltic lands (Latvia, Lithuania and Estonia). By 1922 several areas had left the old Russian Empire to form new, independent states, such as Latvia. Lenin attempted to deal with the 'nationalities' issue with the creation of the Union of Soviet Socialist Republics (USSR) in 1922. This created 'socialist republics' in the Ukraine, **Transcaucasia** and White Russia (modern Belarus) as well as Russia.

Transcaucasia: The collective term for the territories of the Russian Empire, such as Georgia, Armenia and Azerbaijan, that lay beyond the Caucasus Mountains.

1. On what issues did Bolsheviks and Mensheviks disagree?

2. In what ways did Lenin add to, or alter, orthodox Marxist teaching?

3. In what ways were the Bolsheviks different from the Russian radicals who had previously tried to overthrow the Tsarist regime?

Lenin addresses the crowd in Red Square, Moscow, on the first anniversary of the Revolution, October/November 1918.

7.4 What factors made the Bolsheviks such an important political force in 1917?

Bolshevik strengths and weaknesses in early 1917

The major turning point in the destiny of the revolution was Lenin's arrival in Petrograd (16 April). He found the Bolsheviks in Russia in a sad state. They numbered only 26,000 members, were in a minority in the Petrograd Soviet and were divided on the issue of co-operation with the Provisional Government. On the other hand, they had so far 'kept their hands clean' by avoiding identification with the failures of that administration. The fact that Lenin and his comrades had their passage from exile in Switzerland arranged for them by the German government was of ambiguous value. It naturally laid the Bolsheviks open to the charge of being German agents. Although Lenin was, of course, serving Germany's purpose by further disruption of the Russia war effort, the charge has not been taken seriously by historians in its literal sense. However, the allegation that the Bolsheviks subsequently received large sums of German money to further their cause might have better foundation. Daniel Shub, for example, has produced evidence of transactions which, if genuine, would have given the Bolsheviks a substantial economic advantage over their revolutionary rivals.

It may be, however, that the real strength of the Bolsheviks lay less in the fact that they transformed events in 1917, than that they reflected important forces within Russian politics. A number of western historians, working in the 1970s and 1980s (see also section 7.10), focused their attention more upon the rank and file of the revolutionary movement than upon its leaders. Studying the development of trade unions and of civil rights among the urban workers, and social and economic development among the peasantry, they reached the conclusion that these constituted the real revolutionary force within Russia in 1917. The Bolsheviks, in their view, enjoyed success at this time, not because they converted the workers to their views, or had superior resources, but because they represented most accurately the aspirations of 'progressive' workers. Such a view has several important implications for the interpretation of Russian history. In this view, the great strength of the Bolshevik Party in 1917 was that it was flexible and open, rather than hierarchical and authoritarian – a genuine party of radical workers and peasants.

Lenin's programme in 1917

A major advantage of the Bolsheviks was that, alone of the major participants in the events of 1917, they offered a political programme that was truly radical. The programme that Lenin pronounced upon his arrival, and published in *Pravda* in the so-called 'April Theses', was a complete rejection of the co-operation between the Soviet and the Provisional Government that was even advocated by a number of Bolsheviks. The ten points included:

Pravda (Russian – Truth): The official newspaper of the Russian Communist Party.

- an appeal for an immediate end to the war;

- total withdrawal of support from the government;

- socialisation of the economy;

- the transfer of all state power to the Soviets.

The slogan 'All power to the Soviets' was not necessarily an immediate demand, for the Bolsheviks were far from controlling these bodies. What was immediate was the need for Lenin to impose his will upon his own party, and for constant propaganda to win the support of those alienated by the delays and failures of the Provisional Government. Lenin's contribution to this propaganda was *The State and Revolution* (published in 1918) in which he set forth in the Russian context the Marxist doctrine of the need completely to dismember the bourgeois state before a proletarian society could be constructed. This form of persuasion was less effective than the simple slogans ('End the War', or 'Bread, Peace, Land') aimed at less sophisticated political thinkers. 'If the peasants had not read Lenin,' Trotsky observed, 'Lenin had clearly read the thoughts of the peasants.'

Strengthening the Bolshevik position

1. What new policies and tactics did Lenin propose when he arrived in Russia in 1917?

2. How would you explain the increase in support for the Bolsheviks in Russia in the course of 1917?

3. 'The Bolsheviks did not seize power; they simply picked it up.' How accurate is this assessment of the October/November Revolution in 1917?

Meanwhile the Bolsheviks generally accepted Lenin's policy of opposition to and separation from the Provisional Government. At the first Congress of Soviets in June, where only 10% of representatives of 305 Soviets were Bolshevik, Lenin unsuccessfully advocated a break with the government. In July, complicity in the Petrograd rising led to an open attack upon the Bolsheviks, and a government attempt to arrest leaders such as Lenin, Zinoviev and Kamenev. Bolshevik support grew in these months for both negative and positive reasons. Among the negative reasons were the collapse of the government's military offensive, the reaction of Petrograd workers to the Kornilov Affair, and the suspicion that Kerensky might be willing to abandon Petrograd to the advancing Germans. More positive were the Bolshevik promises to tackle the questions of land and of peace and the growing support for the party among Petrograd factory Soviets.

By August, the party had 200,000 members, produced 41 different newspapers, and had recruited a striking force of 10,000 'Red Guards' in the factories, whose workers were often, in Lenin's words, 'more Bolshevik than the Bolsheviks'. When the Petrograd Soviet was re-elected in September, the Bolsheviks held a majority of seats for the first time – a success repeated in Moscow and elsewhere.

7.5 How did the Bolsheviks establish their power in Russia in 1917–19?

The circumstances under which the Provisional Government lost power during the 'second revolution' of October/November 1917 were in direct contrast to those that had brought them to power. True, major social and economic problems persisted. Industrial production was badly disrupted. Some industrial plants closed, causing unemployment, and inflation quickly cancelled out any benefit that the workers may have gained in terms of higher wages. The army came closer to disintegration, demoralised by continuing failure and by Bolshevik propaganda. 'The soldiers,' recalled N. Sukhanov, 'flowed through the countryside from the rear and the front, recalling a great migration of peoples.' An estimated two million desertions took place in the course of 1917.

The October/November coup

Unlike the events of February/March 1917, those of October/November owed little to spontaneous discontent, and almost everything to the deliberate actions of a tightly-knit group of revolutionary leaders. By late September, Lenin had decided that the circumstances were right for the Bolsheviks to bid for power. The decision had nothing to do with the feelings of the people. 'We cannot be guided by the mood of the masses,' he wrote at the time, 'that is changeable and unaccountable. The masses have given their confidence to the Bolsheviks and ask from them not words, but deeds.' It took over a month for Lenin to convince the party as a whole, and even then such notable members as Grigori Zinoviev and Lev Kamenev (see Chapter 8) stood out against him. His arguments in favour of an immediate rebellion were based not only upon the fear of a 'second Kornilov affair', or of a surrender of Petrograd to the Germans, but especially upon the hopeful signs of unrest in the German forces. This encouraged him to hope for international working-class support for a communist coup.

It was also essential to have practical control before the meeting of the next Congress of Soviets, which might be more difficult still to convince of the merits of such an adventure. The weapon for rebellion also presented itself with the formation (26 October) of the Military Revolutionary Committee by the Soviet, pledged to protect Petrograd against the Germans. With 48 Bolsheviks among its 66 members, it was capable of being turned against other enemies.

The 'revolution' of 24–25 October/7–8 November was, in reality, an extremely skilful military *coup d'état* directed predominately by Trotsky. Key positions such as railway stations, telephone exchanges, banks and post offices were seized by 'Red Guards' with a distinct lack of opposition from their opponents. The body assembled at the Tauride Palace to discuss the formation of a Constituent Assembly was dismissed. Then late on 25 October/8 November the half-hearted defence of the Winter Palace, now the headquarters of the Provisional Government, was overcome. The second Congress of Soviets, meeting that same day in Petrograd, now had 390 Bolshevik representatives, only too eager to accept Lenin's *fait accompli*. For Kerensky, there was no immediate alternative to flight, while the Mensheviks and the Social Revolutionaries, with only 80 and 180 seats respectively in the Congress, had little choice but to accept Trotsky's dismissal: 'You have played out your role. Go where you belong: to the dust heap of history.'

What judgement should be made on the Provisional Government that fell after eight months in office? The programme and theory of the government were admirable, as the most liberal constitution that the continent

Fait accompli: (French – accomplished fact): A political fact or event that cannot be changed or modified, and thus must be accepted.

had yet seen had been created out of Europe's strictest autocracy. However, 1917 was a time for action on pressing problems, not for theory. Although noble in intent, the programme was ill-defined and poorly enforced. Kerensky, in his memoirs, lays most of the blame for this upon those who 'betrayed' the government, most notably Kornilov and his supporters. Others are inclined to blame Kerensky himself, for whom, in the words of the historian Donald Treadgold, 'oratory became a substitute for action'.

The extension of Bolshevik power

Lenin's first speech to the Congress of Soviets consisted of a simple statement: 'We shall now proceed to construct the socialist order.' As the historian D. Mitchell has pointed out, however, the business of ruling Russia was not so simple. 'The Bolsheviks had not captured a Ship of State, they had boarded a derelict.' The priority of the first Soviet government was, therefore, the extension and consolidation of Bolshevik power. In early November, the authority of the administration elected by the Congress extended little beyond Petrograd. Lenin was chairman of the Council of **People's Commissars**, Alexei Rykov Commissar of the Interior, and Leon Trotsky Commissar for Foreign Affairs. In some places, as in Moscow, Kiev, Kazan and Smolensk, Bolsheviks had to overcome stern armed resistance. November, nevertheless, saw 15 main provincial towns fall into their hands, followed by 13 in December and a further 15 in January 1918.

Within the territory that the Bolsheviks controlled the main constitutional opposition to them came from the election of the long-awaited Constituent Assembly, which gathered in Petrograd with 380 Social Revolutionary (SR) representatives as against only 168 Bolsheviks. Lenin, however, was in no mood for constitutional games, and the body was dispersed by force after less than two days. It was, declared Lenin, 'a complete and frank liquidation of the idea of democracy by the idea of dictatorship'.

The CHEKA and the Red Army

The Marxist concept of the 'dictatorship of the proletariat' also involved the formation of two armed forces to destroy the remnants of aristocratic and bourgeois power. A secret police force known as the 'Extraordinary Commission' (but generally known as the CHEKA, from its Russian initials) was formed. In contrast to the leniency of the Provisional Government, its aim was quite openly to combat 'counter-revolution' by means of terror. One of its leaders claimed, 'The CHEKA does not judge, it strikes.' Its chief was Felix Dzerzhinsky, but contemporary evidence clearly indicates the role played by Lenin himself in enforcing the policy of terror. In July 1918, he urged that 'the energy and mass nature of the terror must be encouraged' and, a month later, called for it to be extended even 'to execute and exterminate hundreds of prostitutes, drunken soldiers, former officers, etc'. The Imperial family, under arrest at Ekaterinburg, were the most famous victims (July 1918). The official figure for executions in 1918 is 6,300, but this must be regarded as a conservative estimate.

The Bolshevik regime, having undermined and dispersed an army upon which it could not depend, now set about the formation of an army of its own. The Red Army was formed in January 1918, open to all 'class-conscious' workers of 18 years of age or more. The bourgeoisie was banned from membership, but 50,000 former Tsarist officers were retained to train the new force. To oversee them and the force as a whole, political commissars were attached to each unit, responsible for **indoctrination** and

People's Commissars: Because the title of 'Minister' was discredited by its association with the Tsarist regime, ministers in the Soviet government officially bore the title 'People's Commissar'.

Alexei Rykov (1881–1938)
Joined the Bolsheviks in 1903, but mistrusted Lenin and supported plans for a coalition government in 1917. Commissar for the Interior (1917–18). Politburo member (1924–28). Opposed the leadership of Stalin, and was removed from office and eventually executed.

Felix Dzerzhinsky (1877–1926)
A dedicated Polish Bolshevik, Dzerzhinsky joined the Communist Party in Lithuania in 1895. Member of the Party's Central Committee (1917–26). Head of the CHEKA (December 1917). Commissar for Internal Affairs (March 1919). Member of the Politburo and Chairman of the Supreme Council of National Economy (1924).

Indoctrination: The teaching of a particular belief or attitude with the aim that those being taught will not accept any other belief or attitude.

1. *What tactics did the Bolsheviks use against their opponents within Russia in the course of 1917 and 1918?*

2. *Why did the Bolsheviks decide to seize power in November 1917?*

for ensuring that the army remained under Bolshevik control. The reforms made since February/March 1917 were systematically cancelled to ensure reliable discipline.

● The powers of the regimental councils were curtailed.

● The practice of electing officers was abolished.

● The death penalty for deserters was reintroduced.

By August 1919 the Red Army numbered 300,000, and by January 1920 it boasted over 5,000,000 members, under the supreme command of Leon Trotsky.

What were the bases of Bolshevik policy in the early stages of Communist power?

The first Soviet constitution

Meanwhile, the constitution of the state took shape. A series of decrees in February 1918 attacked the Church, separating it from the state and banning religious teaching in schools. Another series, between April and June, nationalised banks, mineral resources, industrial concerns and foreign trade, and made the inheritance of property illegal. A formal constitution became law on 10 July 1918. The state was given the name of the Russian Soviet Federated Socialist Republic (RSFSR). It proclaimed itself a classless society, with freedom of worship, no private ownership of property, and based upon the economic principle of 'He who does not work, neither shall he eat'. The electoral system was based upon the unit of the village and city soviets, culminating in the All-Russian Congress of Soviets, the supreme authority in the state. Election was by universal suffrage, with the exception of former members or agents of the Tsarist government, those who profited from the labour of others, those with unearned income, priests, lunatics and criminals.

Ending the problem of the war: the Treaty of Brest-Litovsk (March 1918)

In the first days of Soviet power, the Bolsheviks produced a 'Decree on Peace' and a 'Decree on Land', as their earlier propaganda had obliged them to do. The former called upon all participants in the war to begin immediate peace negotiations, while the latter abolished all landed ownership, but encouraged the peasantry to continue the process of carving up the great estates themselves. The achievement of such ideals was not, however, such an easy matter.

   The new regime formally opened peace negotiations with the Central Powers at Brest-Litovsk in late November, confident that the Bolshevik coup would trigger a general European revolution, thus ending the war. When, by early 1918, this had not materialised, and the impatient Germans had pushed deeper into Russian territory, Lenin was eventually able to convince his party that a separate peace was necessary. The Treaty of Brest-Litovsk was concluded on 3 March 1918. From a patriotic point of view, its terms were disastrous. Georgia, the Ukraine, Latvia, Lithuania and Poland came formally under German occupation. This meant that, of its pre-war resources, Russia lost 26% of its population, 32% of its arable land, 33% of its manufacturing industry, and 75% of its coal and iron resources. In explaining the decision of the Bolsheviks to make this sacrifice, it must be remembered that most of the lost territory was not actually under Bolshevik control in any case. Above all, the most pressing motive was that stated by Lenin himself in 1920: 'we gained a little time, and sacrificed a great deal of space for it'.

Economic policy: War Communism

The succession of events of which the Treaty of Brest-Litovsk was part soon demonstrated the inadequacy of edicts such as the 'Decree on Land' and the 'Decree on Workers' Control'. The piecemeal division of land by peasant committees and the direction of factories by workers' committees proved wholly unsatisfactory as Russia was stripped of huge agricultural and industrial resources while faced simultaneously with the likelihood of a large-scale civil conflict. It was soon evident to Lenin that the intended slow progress towards nationalisation of the 'commanding heights' of the economy, such as fuel, transport and banking, was insufficient. The formation of a Supreme Economic Council (*Vesenkha*) in December 1917 can be seen as the first step towards the policy established by the 'Decree on Nationalisation' (June 1918), and now known as 'War Communism'. The main features of War Communism were:

● strict centralised control of all forms of economic production and distribution;

● virtual outlawing of all private trade;

● near destruction of the money economy by the printing of vast quantities of bank notes.

In January 1918, there were 27 billion roubles' worth of notes in circulation, backed by only 1.3 million roubles in gold. Three years later, the figures were 1,168 billion and 0.07 million.

In the countryside the main evidence of the new policy was the large-scale requisitioning of grain in order to feed the towns. In June 1918, the government formed 'Committees of Poor Peasants' to control the richer peasants, or *kulaks*, but soon had to resort to confiscation of supplies by military force. All food distribution was centralised into the hands of a Commissariat of Food and a Commissariat of Agriculture. These divided the population into four categories, the food ration of each depending upon its contribution to the economy. The highest category had roughly one-seventh of the calories received by German workers at the height of the allied blockade, while the lowest had rations insufficient to prevent starvation.

The disillusioned peasantry turned, as before, to disorder. In 1918, 249 rural risings were recorded, and 99 in Bolshevik-controlled territory the following year. In the towns the main feature was the wholesale nationalisation, which extended by December 1920 to all enterprises employing ten or more people, a total of about 37,000 enterprises. This was accompanied by:

● the forced mobilisation of unemployed labour to serve essential strategic industries;

● the outlawing of strikes;

● a large-scale desertion of the towns in favour of the countryside where food seemed more easily available.

Petrograd, with a population of 2.5 million in 1917, had only 0.6 million inhabitants three years later.

Kulaks: Richer, semi-capitalist peasants. The term literally means a 'fist', as a sign of money-grabbing.

1. What policies did the Bolsheviks use to tackle the economic problems that faced them after their seizure of power in 1917?

2. Did the Bolsheviks gain more than they lost by the Treaty of Brest-Litovsk?

3. To what extent, by the end of 1918, had the Bolsheviks solved the problems that faced them when they initially came to power?

7.6 Why did civil war break out in Russia in 1918?

Anton Denikin (1872–1947)
After service in the Russo–Japanese war and the First World War, Denikin supported Kornilov's coup against the Provisional Government in 1917. After the Bolshevik seizure of power, he formed and commanded the White army in south-east Russia. Relatively successful in military terms, he was politically clumsy and failed to co-operate effectively with civilian bodies or with national minorities.

Lavr Kornilov (1870–1918)
Of Cossack origins, he served with distinction in the Russo–Japanese war and in the First World War. Appointed to command the Petrograd garrison (1917) by the Provisional Government, he later led an unsuccessful coup against that government. Commanded White forces in southern Russia until killed in action.

Cossacks: Peoples of southern USSR, noted from early times as horsemen.

Who were the Whites, and what did they stand for?

By early 1918, the events of the 'second revolution' had alienated large sections of the Russian population from the Bolshevik government, but without uniting the aims or motives of these opponents. Whereas the Reds fought in the Civil War for very specific aims and Marxist-Leninist principles, albeit with a strong degree of compulsion at times, the Whites formed no such grouping. Broadly, the White forces consisted of three main parts:

- those attached to other revolutionary groups, hostile to or rejected by the Bolsheviks;

- former officers of the Imperial army, usually resentful of the 'betrayal' at Brest-Litovsk;

- nationalist groups seeking independence for their particular minority.

The administration that established itself in the Don region of southern Russia early in 1918 illustrates this diversity. Its military leaders were Tsarist generals, such as Anton Denikin, Lavr Kornilov and P.N. Krasnov, who had also held office under the Provisional Government and now claimed to fight 'until the Provisional Government and order in the nation are restored'. The politicians who joined them, however, were a mixture of Kadets such as Paul Miliukov, and SRs such as V. Chernov. Other SRs concentrated their forces further north, along the Volga, where they established an administration based at Samara (June 1918). In the Don region, the nationalist element was represented by the **Cossacks**, whose local ambitions clashed fundamentally with such White slogans as Alexeyev's 'Russia One and Indivisible'.

What kind of a war did this make for? The traditional interpretation among Soviet historians was that the Bolsheviks fought an essentially defensive war. Controlling a central zone of about one million square miles, with a population of about 60 million, they beat off various attempts by 'White' forces to penetrate this territory. In his recent work on the civil war, however, Evan Mawdsley (*The Russian Civil War*, 1987) paints a different picture. He prefers to see the war as a series of expeditions launched by the Red Army in an attempt to extend their control to more remote areas of the former Russian Empire, with the initiative lying in most cases with the Bolsheviks.

The disintegration of the Russian Empire

With the collapse of traditional authority in the Russian state, several regions were quick to declare themselves independent. Thus republics were proclaimed in Ukraine and in Transcaucasia (November 1917) and in Finland (December 1917). With the collapse of the German war effort in the next year, Estonia, Latvia, Lithuania and Poland all pressed their own claims to independence. The Polish claim was especially complicated. Both the Soviet government and the victorious allies assembled at Versailles (France) recognised Poland's right to independence. It was not clear, however, whether its eastern borders were to be fixed by the so-called Curzon Line, drawn by the allies around the main areas of Polish-speaking populations, or by the historic borders of the old Polish kingdom as it had existed before partition in 1772. The difference was considerable, and involved a Polish claim to much of Lithuania, the Ukraine and Byelorussia. The dispute raised tensions between Poland and its new communist neighbour that were to culminate in war in 1920.

The role of the Czechoslovak Legion

The great catalyst of civil conflict in Russia was the successful 'revolt' of the Czechoslovak Legion. The Legion had been formed in 1917 from Czechs and Slovaks resident in Russia, and from prisoners of war. It was dedicated to the fight for independence from the crumbling Austro-Hungarian Empire. After Brest-Litovsk it had placed itself at the disposal of the French, and begun a long journey via Siberia and the USA to continue the fight on the Western Front. In May 1918, a confrontation with Hungarian prisoners at Cheliabinsk led local Soviet officials to attempt to disarm the Legion. Instead they themselves were seized, and when Trotsky ordered military retaliation, the well-organised and well-equipped Czechs proceeded to seize and occupy all the main towns along the Trans-Siberian railway in the regions of Cheliabinsk, Omsk and Irkutsk. Although the Legion had no specifically anti-Bolshevik aims, its resounding success against Soviet forces provided enormous encouragement for the White cause. By June, representatives of the SRs had combined with the Czechs to form a third centre of White administration at Omsk.

Why did foreign powers intervene in the Russian Civil War?

The motives that led Russia's former allies to intervene in its internal conflicts have been the subject of considerable controversy. The standard interpretation among Soviet historians naturally reflected the contemporary view expressed by Lenin, who portrayed the allied missions as a concerted attempt to suppress communism. Some western commentators have accepted this view. For example, E.H. Carr, in *A History of Soviet Russia, 1917–1929* (1966), described the allies' declared intention of reopening the world war in the east against Germany as 'a pretext'. He speaks of 'the fear and hatred felt by the western governments for the revolutionary regime'.

Historian John Bradley (*Civil War in Russia*, 1975) has pointed to a number of factors that contradict this interpretation. A plan by Marshal Foch for a co-ordinated anti-Bolshevik campaign (January 1919) was rejected by allied leaders at Versailles. In February 1919, the Americans in particular were proposing negotiations between the Reds and Whites at Prinkipo Island, near Istanbul. It is also true that Britain and the USA had come close, before Brest-Litovsk, to aiding the Red Army, at Trotsky's request, against the Germans.

There is much evidence that, in its early stages, allied intervention in the Russian conflict should be viewed in the context of the world war. The separate peace made by the Bolsheviks at Brest-Litovsk released huge German forces and resources for use on the Western Front. It thus became imperative for the western allies to restart the war in the east, or at least, to prevent Germany from making free use of the Russian, Polish and Ukrainian raw materials available to them under the terms of Brest-Litovsk. German success in the east also seemed to threaten large concentrations of allied stores supplied earlier to Russia. It is no coincidence that British forces landed first in Murmansk (March 1918), and that British and Japanese forces also concentrated on the distant port of Vladivostok (April 1918) which was far from the Bolshevik 'heartland', but where substantial allied stores were housed. Britain's seizure of Baku was also motivated by the desire to keep local oil resources out of hostile hands.

Allied motives after 1918

Even after the end of the First World War, the allies still had pressing reasons for intervention. The French, for instance, continued to have a pressing motive in the form of the vast sum of 16 billion francs invested in Tsarist Russia between 1887 and 1917, in enterprises now nationalised without compensation by the Soviet State. Britain and the USA had lesser investments to defend. Japan, after the hard-won gains of 1904–05, found the prospect opening up of substantial territorial gains in eastern Asia at Russia's expense. That they failed to realise these ambitions was primarily due to the presence of American troops in Siberia, more concerned with checking Japanese annexations in the east than with combating Bolshevism further west. Nevertheless, by late 1918, as many as 70,000 Japanese troops had occupied Vladivostok, northern Sakhalin and much of Siberia east of Lake Baikal. Only when the Third **Communist International ('*Comintern*')** began, in mid-1919, to proclaim the 'overthrow of capitalism, the establishment of the dictatorship of the proletariat and of the International Soviet republic' did intervention become overtly ideological. By then allied efforts in Russia had become negligible.

Communist International ('*Comintern*'): The body established in the early years of the 20th century to co-ordinate the activities of communist parties in different states.

The scale and the achievement of intervention

The scale and scope of the intervention were, in any case, strictly limited. At the end of 1918 there were only about 150,000 troops in northern Russia and these were affected by war-weariness after four years of European conflict. The USA sent only about 6,000 to the Siberian theatre of war, and then with strictly limited objectives. More important were the substantial sums of money and the large quantities of military stores made available to the Whites. Britain and France both allocated the equivalent of £20 million for this purpose, although the historian R. Luckett stresses, in *The White Generals* (1971), that corruption and inefficiency often meant that relatively little of this aid actually reached the front.

The success achieved by the intervention was even more limited. The number of troops involved was small, and only in the north, around Murmansk and Arkhangelsk, did foreign troops really predominate in the White war effort. Aims and motives were all too often at odds, as in Siberia, where the political views of Admiral Kolchak's regime were so undemocratic that the Americans refused all co-operation with him, and the French could only co-operate with the greatest difficulty. In all, the intervention probably gave far greater assistance to the Soviet authorities who could now draw a veil over domestic disagreements by claiming that they were defending Russia against foreign imperialism. At the conclusion of British involvement, Lord Curzon described it as 'a totally discredited affair and a complete failure'. The same judgement could probably extend to the allied intervention as a whole.

1. For what reasons did the various factions oppose the Bolsheviks from 1918 onwards?

2. How convincing is the argument that allied forces intervened in the Russian Civil War because their governments were ideologically opposed to the Bolsheviks?

3. 'The intervention of the allies in the Russian Civil War was ill-judged, incoherent and achieved nothing.' What evidence can be given in support of this statement?

7.7 How and why were the White forces defeated in the Russian Civil War?

The White armies

In the summer of 1918, the combination of forces ranged against the Soviet government seemed to many observers to be overwhelming. To the south, the Volunteer Army under Anton Denikin, with French and British support, had cleared the Don and Kuban regions of Bolsheviks, and threatened the food and fuel supplies to Soviet-controlled areas. To the east, the varied forces occupying Siberia and controlling the Trans-Siberian Railway had at last agreed (September 1918) to the formation of a coalition government, the Directory. To the north, White forces under the Tsarist general E.K. Miller, with British support, controlled the ports of Murmansk and Arkhangelsk. To the west lay the Germans and a variety of hostile nationalists. Even in Russia, less-organised opposition, especially among the peasants and the SRs, led to risings in some 25 towns and cities. There was a rash of assassination attempts that killed M.S. Uritsky, chief of the Petrograd CHEKA, and the German ambassador, and saw Lenin himself seriously wounded.

The defeat of Kolchak, Yudenich and Denikin

The first concern of the Soviet government was to tackle the opposition forces centred upon Omsk. Their eventual success owed as much to the shortcomings of their opponents as to the efforts of the Red Army itself. Certainly Trotsky's organisation and the military leadership of commanders such as Mikhail Frunze were important factors. The Whites, nevertheless, were disunited and quarrelsome. The internal dispute that brought down the Directory (November 1918) resulted in the elevation of Alexander Kolchak, formerly Admiral of the Black Sea Fleet and a staunch political conservative, to the title of 'Supreme Ruler of All the Russias'. His failure to establish satisfactory understandings with the SRs, the Czechs, or even with some of the allies, contributed to a steady retreat after reaching Perm and Ufa in March 1919. By June, Kolchak's force had been pushed back beyond the Urals, and Soviet forces captured Omsk itself in November. Kolchak suffered the indignity of being handed over to the Red Army by the commander of the local French forces, and was duly shot (7 February 1920).

In the south and west, similarly, White forces under Denikin and under Nikolai Yudenich initially made rapid progress. In two months (August–October 1919), Denikin's forces advanced from Odessa to within 400 kilometres of Moscow, while Yudenich came within 50 kilometres of Petrograd in mid-October. In both cases, retreat was as rapid as the advance had been. Stubborn defence, organised by Trotsky, thwarted Yudenich before a counter-attack drove him back into Estonia. Between October and December, Bolshevik forces pushed Denikin back until most of the Ukraine had been recaptured from the Whites. From April 1920, only the force in the Crimea under Peter Wrangel stood between the Red Army and victory. Wrangel was probably the most able of the White commanders, but he came on the scene too late. His army won some notable victories while the Red Army was distracted by the Poles, but in mid-November 1920 he, too, with 135,000 soldiers and civilians, evacuated the Crimea, the last stronghold of the White cause.

What were the causes and the extent of the Bolshevik success?

Contemporaries tended to assume that the forces ranged against the Red Army, often consisting of professional soldiers commanded by experienced officers, constituted a formidable obstacle to Bolshevik success. Soviet historians, too, liked the version of events that cast the Red Army as brave fighters against overwhelming odds. In reality, the Bolshevik success, like that of the Japanese in Korea in 1905, was not as surprising as it might seem at first. In the south and in the east the White armies fought on wide fronts, often in areas with poor communications. Although they occupied large geographical areas, this often gave them control over relatively small populations, and few areas of major industrial production.

Assessing the quality of leadership of the White forces, Evan Mawdsley has concluded that 'the Whites possessed military talent in abundance, but very limited capacity for state-building or for the rallying of popular support.' With the exception of Wrangel, none of the military leaders could sympathise with, or even understand the hopes and wishes of the

Mikhail Frunze (1885–1925)
Joined the Bolsheviks in 1904 and was active in the revolutionary events of 1905. Led communists in Byelorussia and Moscow in 1917. Commanded Red Army units in the Urals (11919), gaining successes against Kolchak, and defeated Wrangel in the Crimea (1920).

Alexander Kolchak (1873–1920)
After heroic service in the Russo–Japanese war and the First World War, Kolchak formed and commanded White forces in the Far East. He headed the Provisional All-Russian Government based in Omsk (1918), declaring himself 'Supreme Ruler'. Captured by Czech forces (1919), he was handed over to the Bolsheviks and executed.

Nikolai Yudenich (1862–1933)
A highly successful commander in the First World War, gaining notable victories against the Turks. Commanded White forces in north-western Russia (1919).

Peter Wrangel (1878–1928)
After cavalry service in the First World War, Wrangel commanded White forces in the Kuban and the Caucasus (1918–19), capturing Tsaritsyn. He served with Denikin and, after his defeat, organised the evacuation of White forces via the Crimea (1920). Probably the most able of the White commanders because he exercised strong discipline over his men and had an intelligent agrarian policy to appeal to the peasantry.

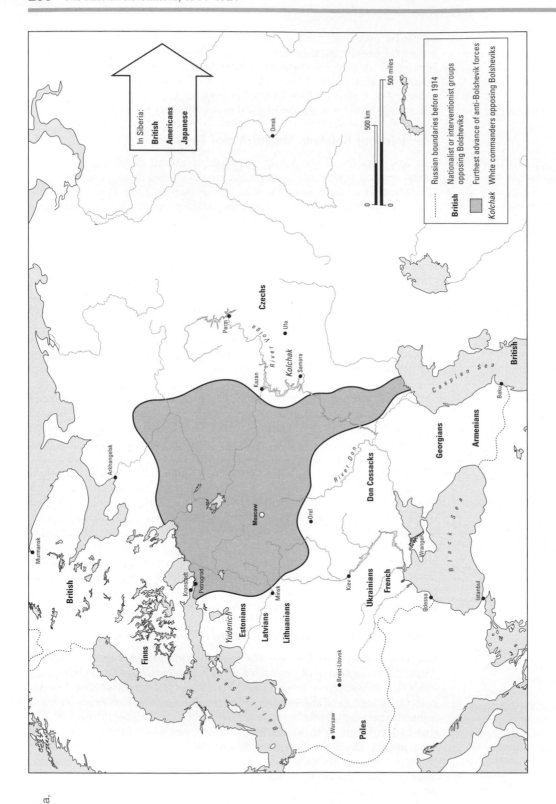

In Siberia:
British
Americans
Japanese

500 km
500 miles

Russian boundaries before 1914
Nationalist or interventionist groups opposing Bolsheviks
Furthest advance of anti-Bolshevik forces
British   White commanders opposing Bolsheviks
Kolchak

Omsk

Czechs

Perm

Ufa

Volga

River

Kolchak

Kazan

Samara

Caspian Sea

British

Baku

Arkhangelsk

Georgians

Armenians

River Don

Don Cossacks

Murmansk

British

Moscow

Orel

Black Sea

Wrangel

Kronstadt
Petrograd

Yudenich

Kiev

Ukrainians

French

Istanbul

Odessa

Finns

Estonians

Latvians

Lithuanians

Minsk

Baltic Sea

Brest-Litovsk

Warsaw

Poles

The Civil War in
European Russia,
1918–21

peasantry and the national minorities. These leaders became hopelessly identified with the restoration of the landlords and the old regime. In addition, the aims of the military leaders were sometimes at odds with those of the intervening allies. 'I think most of us were secretly in sympathy with the Bolsheviks,' wrote a British officer serving with Kolchak's forces, 'after our experiences with the corruption and cowardice of the other side.'

The political leaders who identified themselves with the White cause made almost no impact on policy or on international relations at all. 'They failed to recognise,' wrote the American historian, Anatole Mazour, 'that they were coping with a great revolution and not an isolated plot.'

The Communists, meanwhile, quite apart from the resources that they controlled, had the benefits of excellent leadership and coherent policy and propaganda. The historian Louis Fischer's description of Lenin as 'a one-man political-military staff' (*The Life of Lenin*, 1965) is inaccurate only insofar as it undervalues the dynamic role played by Trotsky. Appointed Commissar for War in March 1918, Trotsky made his main contribution to the revolution by his brilliant direction of the war on most of the major fronts. For all of these reasons, the traditional judgement about the likely outcome of the Russian Civil War has now been stood on its head, with the majority of historians echoing the judgement of Richard Pipes: 'the victory of the Red Army was a foregone conclusion.'

The only serious objection to Pipes' conclusion, perhaps, is that it does not apply evenly to all of the various theatres of war. In Poland, for instance, the Red Army had encountered a much more difficult opponent, an army of 740,000 men commanded by a government and leadership much more stable than those of the 'white' Russian regimes. In April 1920, Poland and Russia had finally resorted to arms to settle the question of the boundaries of the new Polish state. This was far more of a national war than an affair of Red versus White. It brought varying fortunes for the participants. In May 1920 the Poles, under Marshal Pilsudski, were in Kiev. Two months later the Red Army was within reach of Warsaw. Finally, by August 1920, with moral and material aid from the allies, Pilsudski's counter-attack had driven the Red Army almost back to Minsk. The Treaty of Riga (18 March 1921), like Brest-Litovsk, was accepted by Lenin because 'a bad peace seemed to me cheaper than the prolongation of the war'. It settled Russia's western borders until 1939 by granting Poland Galicia and parts of Byelorussia, and by confirming the independence of Estonia, Latvia and Lithuania.

1. *What elements are emphasised by the poster as those which Lenin was most concerned to defeat in 1920?*

2. *How accurate is the poster as a portrayal of Lenin's priorities in 1920?*

'Comrade Lenin sweeps away the world's dirt', a propaganda poster produced in 1920

1. *What were the main weaknesses of the White commanders during the Russian Civil War?*

2. *Was the weakness of the Whites the main cause of the Bolshevik victory in the Russian Civil War? Explain your answer fully.*

7.8 Why did Lenin launch the New Economic Policy in 1921?

The failure of War Communism

By 1921, social and economic life in Russia had been brought to its knees by a series of disasters. The rigours and miscalculations of War Communism combined with the damage caused by the civil war. The number of deaths directly caused by the war has been estimated by the historian Robert Conquest (*The Great Terror: a Reassessment*, 1990) as 'no more than a million', but the economic collapse that accompanied war had far more drastic effects. Urban industry declined disastrously. The Russian coal industry in 1921 produced 27% of its pre-war output, a large proportion compared with steel (5.5%), pig iron (2.5%) or copper (1.7%). **Inflation** had effectively destroyed the rouble (Russian currency), and some 90% of all wages were '**paid in kind**'. This was made worse by disastrous famines. Especially serious in the Ukraine and in other parts of southern Russia, the famines probably caused some five million deaths. Taking into account associated diseases, the casualty figure for the years 1917–21 may be as high as 9 million.

Inflation: A general increase in the prices of goods and services in a country.

'**Paid in kind**': Payment is provided in the form of goods, rather than in money.

The Kronstadt rebellion

Probably as serious, from Lenin's point of view, was the evidence of political discontent from within the Communists' own ranks. The most spectacular example of widespread refusal to tolerate any further the deprivations of wartime came with the revolt at the Kronstadt naval base (February/March 1921), originally a major source of Bolshevik support. The demands of the sailors included freedom of the press, elections by secret ballot, and the release of political prisoners. The rising was brutally suppressed like similar, lesser peasant risings, but it could not be ignored. 'It illuminated reality,' stated Lenin, 'like a flash of lightning', and perhaps contributed more than any other factor to the government's decision to pursue a New Economic Policy (NEP).

Lenin made it very clear that the NEP was another in the series of temporary compromises that communist theory had to make when confronted with adverse circumstances. 'Life has exposed our error,' he told the Party. 'There was a need of a series of transitional stages to Communism.' The NEP was thus a sort of economic Brest-Litovsk and, like that treaty, had to be imposed against fierce criticism from communist purists.

The nature of the NEP

The major features of the new policy were concerned with agriculture. Above all, the government decided to abandon the requisitioning of grain supplies from peasants and to demand instead a tax paid in food, set at a lower level. The peasant retained some of his surplus which he was now permitted to sell for private profit, and was thus likely to be encouraged to grow more. Although the land remained the property of the state, the peasant was free to hire labour, machinery, and so forth.

In industry, freedom of enterprise was restored in a host of small factories and workshops, while the state continued to control the 'dominating heights' of the economy, such as heavy industry, transport and foreign trade. In 1922, 88.5% of all enterprises were privately run, although the smallness of their scale is indicated by the fact that they employed only 12.4% of the workforce.

The third main feature of the NEP was the restoration of a stable soviet currency. In October 1922, the reconstituted State Bank introduced the reconstituted rouble, backed by precious metals and foreign currency. Early in 1923, savings banks were reopened.

The achievement of the NEP

The path of the NEP was not always smooth. Bad harvests and drought in 1921 cancelled out most of the benefits to be gained by the peasants. In 1923, they had to contend with the so-called 'scissors crisis' when declining food prices and the soaring price of industrial goods minimised their gain from free enterprise. The government had to defend itself, right up to the launching of collectivisation in 1928, against the charge that it was defending this 'state capitalism' as a preparation for a return to private capitalism.

Indeed, in 1923 it was true that 75% of Russian retail trade was being handled by the 'Nepmen', the private traders who flourished under the NEP. Thus one of the by-products of the NEP was the strengthening of party discipline to eliminate internal friction. Over 30% of the party's membership was expelled between 1921 and 1924, a precedent that was to have grave implications in the 1930s. Eventually the aims of the policy – the restoration of production and of economic stability – were largely achieved. The table shows that, in most major industries, production figures by 1926 had nearly regained their pre-war levels.

1. How useful is this data to a historian writing about Russian history in the period 1913–1926?

2. Does the data support the view that the NEP was a success? Explain your answer.

Russian economic indicators, 1913–1926

	Factory output (million new roubles)	Coal (million tons)	Electricity (million kW)	Steel (thousand tons)	Grain (million tons)
1913	10,251	29.0	1,945	4,231	80.1
1920	1,410	8.7	–	–	46.1
1921	2,004	8.9	520	183	37.6
1922	2,619	9.5	775	392	50.3
1923	4,005	13.7	1,146	709	56.6
1924	4,660	16.1	1,562	1,140	51.4
1925	7,739	18.1	2,925	2,135	72.5
1926	11,083	27.6	3,508	3,141	76.8

From Alec Nove, *An Economic History of the USSR* (1982)

The death of Lenin

1. What evidence was there in 1921 of the failure of the policy of War Communism?

2. What were the main features of the New Economic Policy?

3. Was the introduction of the NEP in 1921 a success for the Soviet government?

Lenin did not live to see this recovery completed. A series of strokes that began in May 1922 finally killed him in January 1924. His organisational genius and unique blend of determination and flexibility played a greater role than anything else in the creation of soviet power. Public reaction to his death, represented by the millions who filed past his embalmed body in Moscow's Red Square, showed that the Communists now had a saint to respect, like the Orthodox Church before them. However, Lenin's insistence upon party power and party discipline, and his initiation of the policy of terror as a political weapon, also made him the creator of those elements in Russian Communism that were to dominate its history in the 1930s.

Source-based questions: The role of Lenin

Study the following FOUR passages – A, B, C and D – about the role played by Lenin in the establishment of Communism in Russia, and answer BOTH of the sub-questions which follow.

SOURCE A

From History of the Communist Party of the Soviet Union (Bolsheviks), *published in the Soviet Union in 1938. This version portrays Lenin as the guiding genius of the Revolution.*

What would have happened to the Party, to our revolution, to Marxism, if Lenin had been overawed by the letter of Marxism and had not had the courage to replace one of the old propositions of Marxism, formulated by Engels, by the new proposition regarding the republic of Soviets, a proposition that corresponded to the new historical conditions? The Party would have groped in the dark, the Soviets would have been disorganised, we should not have had a Soviet power, and the Marxist theory would have suffered a severe setback. The proletariat would have lost, and the enemies of the proletariat would have won.

SOURCE B

From: Robert Service writing in Critical Companion to the Russian Revolution *(ed. Acton, Chernaiev and Rosenberg), published in 1997. This historian emphasises that a strong revolutionary tradition existed in Russia before Lenin came upon the scene.*

The influence of Lenin should not be exaggerated. Lenin did not invent most of the attitudes of Russian revolutionaries. They pre-dated him. The populist terrorists in the 1860s–1880s had developed many of them; and they were not entirely absent from certain trends in European nineteenth-century socialism and anarchism. Furthermore, several of the Russian Marxists did not need Lenin to resuscitate this tradition for them. It had not been Lenin but Plekhanov who had first pleaded the case for scientific, anti-sentimental and dictatorial policies. And several of Lenin's contemporaries – Trotsky comes immediately to mind – were developing the tradition at the same time as him. Lenin had the greatest but not the sole influence. Nor should we overstate the scope of Lenin's influence in other ways. It must always be taken into account that Lenin had little direct regular contact with Russia before April 1917. His influence was confined to what he could achieve by his journalism and his correspondence. Even in 1917 his contact with Bolsheviks and the rest of society was not uninterrupted. Arriving in Petrograd in early April, he fled again in early July and returned to a fitful, clandestine presence in the capital only in mid-October. No photographs of him were published, no film appeared. His appearances at mass meetings were rare.

SOURCE C

From Martin McCauley, The Soviet Union 1917–1991, *published in 1993. This historian argues that Lenin's leadership was exercised in conjunction with a number of other influential Bolsheviks.*

Lenin was the natural leader of the party, but he had to reaffirm his credentials repeatedly. Not by nature a dictator, he never sought to silence his critics by institutional means. He expected and accepted opposition from his colleagues. Every member of the Politburo during Lenin's active political life (up to 1922) disagreed with him on a major issue. How could it be otherwise with the party attempting to build a new society on Russian soil? However, this lack of consensus on many major issues imposed a heavy burden on the leader. Lenin, moreover, had very definite views on which policies should be adopted and implemented. Although factionalism was officially banned after March 1921 he was a master factionalist. If he was in a minority in the Politburo he did not submit, he fought on. Since the Politburo conferred enormous prestige and privilege, its members could cultivate their own constituencies. Zinoviev was party leader in Petrograd and president of the Comintern; Kamenev headed the Moscow party organisation; Trotsky was Commissar for War; Rykov was Lenin's deputy on *Sovnarkom*; Tomsky headed the trade unions, and there was also Stalin.

Source-based questions: The role of Lenin

SOURCE D

From: Richard Pipes, Russia under the Bolshevik Regime 1919–1924, *published in 1994. This historian believes that Lenin exercised a degree of control over the Bolsheviks that foreshadowed the regime of Stalin.*

In Soviet Russia, the personal dictatorship of Lenin over his party was camouflaged by such formulas as 'democratic centralism' and the custom of de-emphasising the role of individuals in favour of impersonal historic forces. It is nevertheless true that within a year after taking power, Lenin became the unchallenged boss of the Communist Party, around whom emerged a veritable personality cult. Lenin never tolerated a view that conflicted with his own, even if it happened to be that of the majority. By 1920 it was a violation of Party regulations, punishable by expulsion, to form 'factions', a 'faction' being any group that acted in concert against first Lenin's and then Stalin's will: Lenin and Stalin were immune to the charge of 'factionalism'.

(i) Compare Passages A and B on the importance of Lenin in the establishment of Russian communism.   [15 marks]

(ii) Using these four passages and your own knowledge, explain how and why historians disagree about the role that Lenin played in the foundation and development of communist government in Russia.   [30 marks]

Source-based questions: The Kronstadt Rebellion

Study the following source material and then answer the questions which follow.

SOURCE A

From The Russian Tragedy *by A. Berkman, published in 1922*

The 'triumph' of the Bolsheviks over Kronstadt held within itself the defeat of Bolshevism. It exposed the true character of the Communist dictatorship. The whole Bolshevik economic system was changed as a result of the Kronstadt events. This 'triumph' sounded the death knell of Bolshevism with its Party dictatorship, mad centralisation, CHEKA terrorism and bureaucratic castes. It demonstrated that the Bolshevik regime is unmitigated tyranny and reaction. Kronstadt was the first popular and entirely independent attempt at liberation from the yoke of State Socialism, an attempt made directly by the people, by the workers, soldiers and sailors themselves.

SOURCE B

Declaration made by the Kronstadt Temporary Revolutionary Committee, 8 March 1921

The glorious arms of labour's state – the sickle and hammer – have actually been replaced by the Communist authorities with the bayonet and barred window. With the aid of militarised trade unions they have bound the workers to their benches. To the protests of the peasants, expressed in spontaneous uprisings, and of the workers, who are compelled to strike by the circumstances of their life, they answer with mass executions and bloodthirstiness, in which they are not surpassed by the Tsarist generals.

Source-based questions: The Kronstadt Rebellion

SOURCE C

Trotsky's view of the Kronstadt Rebellion, stated in a letter written from exile in Mexico, August 1937.

The best, most self-sacrificing sailors were completely withdrawn from Kronstadt. What remained was the grey mass without political education and unprepared for revolutionary sacrifice. The country was starving. The Kronstadters demanded privileges. The uprising was dictated by the desire to get privileged food rations. The victory of this uprising could bring nothing but the victory of the counter-revolution, regardless of what the sailors had in their heads. But the ideas themselves were deeply reactionary. They reflected the hostility of the backward peasantry toward the worker, the hatred of the petty bourgeois for revolutionary discipline.

(a) Use Source A and your own knowledge.

Explain briefly what the author means in Source A by his statement that 'the whole Bolshevik economic system was changed as a result of the Kronstadt events'. [3 marks]

(b) Use Sources B and C and your own knowledge.

Explain how Source B differs from Source C in its interpretation of the motives behind the Kronstadt rebellion. [7 marks]

(c) Use Sources A, B and C and your own knowledge.

Explain the relative importance of the different forms of opposition that the Bolshevik government encountered in establishing its authority in Russia between the October Revolution in 1917 and the death of Lenin in 1924. [15 marks]

7.9 Did the Bolsheviks launch a cultural revolution in Russia between 1917 and 1924?

The period from 1917 to the end of the NEP experiment was one of unparalleled experimentation in Russian culture. Although a large number of artists and writers left the country at the outbreak of the revolution, those who remained revelled in the brief freedom from Tsarist censorship. They accepted the Soviet doctrine that they were now freer agents, released from the exploitation of bourgeois and aristocratic patrons.

The 'constructivists'

Immediately, the revolution raised new controversy, which was eventually resolved by the pressure of the state. Those artists who keenly supported the new regime, calling themselves 'constructivists', claimed that art should now serve an active social and political purpose. One of the greatest literary figures of the immediate post-revolutionary period was the poet Vladimir Mayakovsky, of whom T. Frankel has written, in *Revolution in Russia: Reassessment of 1917* (1992), 'his every effort was to unify art and life, to enlist art in the service of society'. His work in this period included slogans for political campaigns and posters as well as pro-Bolshevik poetry.

Theatre, too, rallied to the new atmosphere of revolution and liberation. The producer and designer Vsevolod Meyerhold teamed up with Mayakovsky and the artist Kasimir Malevich to produce the pageant 'Mystery Bouffe' (1918) which showed the proletariat defeating its exploiters. In 1920, Nikolai Yevreinov celebrated the third anniversary of the Revolution with a re-enactment of the storming of the Winter Palace,

employing a cast of 8,000, and founding the tradition of May Day parades in Red Square. The group that formed itself around the journal *Proletarian Culture* (*Proletkult*) also enjoyed brief success between 1918 and 1922 in their efforts to found new literary and cultural forms by, and for, workers.

The 'fellow travellers'

A more lasting achievement was made by that group of writers and artists in Russia characterised by Trotsky as the 'fellow travellers'. In general, these men and women were not communists, but were broadly in sympathy with the ideals of the revolution. They found much fascinating human material in the great events of the revolution and the civil war. Some of the leading writers were D.A. Furmanov (*Chapaev*), V.V. Ivanov (*Armoured Train No. 14–69*), and Mikhail Sholokhov (*Quiet Flows the Don*). Another, E.I. Zamyatin, produced a political satire, *We* (1920), in which he showed a regimented socialist society whose inhabitants were identified only by numbers: the forerunner both of Aldous Huxley's *Brave New World* and George Orwell's *1984*. In poetry, Sergei Yesenin rivalled Mayakovsky's popularity with work that was highly personal, almost mystical.

'The cinema,' Lenin declared in 1921, 'is for us the most important of all the arts.' Naturally, therefore, the new art form found itself constrained at first to serve largely propagandistic purposes. Nevertheless, in the greater freedom of the NEP period, the Soviet cinema produced more than its fair share of the art's early classics, notable examples being Sergei Eisenstein's 'Battleship Potemkin', A.P. Dovzhenko's 'The Land', and V.I. Pudovkin's 'Mother', a film version of Gorky's novel. Music produced only one immediate heir to the great Russian traditions in Dmitri Shostakovich. He produced his First Symphony in 1926, and the subtitles given to the next two, the 'October' and the 'May Day' symphonies (1927 and 1929), demonstrated the tightrope that he, too, had to walk between artistic expression and official disapproval.

The growth of state control over the arts

Surrealist: A term that fits both literature and painting, although Surrealist art has become better known. The Surrealist movement began in 1924. Surrealist paintings are of two main sorts: one where conventional techniques are used to depict a futuristic scene; the other is more inventive in technique.

The growth of collectivist policies under Stalin, however, also extended to the arts. Earlier means of artistic control employed during the civil war, such as the state's monopoly over publishing through the State Publishing Organisation (*Gosizdat*) were renewed. Also, new controls were introduced, such as the concentration of artists and writers into official unions. A policy aimed at constraining artists and writers strictly to serve the purposes of government policy saw the collapse of the best elements in the revived Russian culture. The artists Marc Chagall and Vasili Kandinsky had already chosen in the early 1920s to conduct their experiments in **Surrealist** painting in western Europe. Zamyatin followed them in 1931. In 1930 Mayakovsky, who had recently attacked the bureaucracy and narrow-mindedness of Soviet leadership in 'The Bedbug' (1929) and 'The Bathhouse' (1930), committed suicide. Even Maxim Gorky, the greatest of the Soviet writers, had protested against the 'disgraceful attitude' of the Soviet leaders 'towards the freedoms of speech and of person'. His own death in 1935 was surrounded by suspicious circumstances and rumours of poison.

1. In which areas of Russian culture did the Bolshevik revolution have its greatest impact?

2. To what extent were the arts in Russia turned to political purposes in the 15 years after 1917?

The period 1928–1953 was to be the age of 'Socialist Realism' in art, under which Soviet artists and writers were to concentrate upon subjects helpful to the building of a socialist society. Such subjects were defined by Basil Dmytryshyn as including 'contented cows, dedicated milkmaids, devoted pig breeders, vigilant party members, and young lovers arguing by the light of the moon about the problems of industrial production'.

7.10 Was the Russian Revolution the inevitable outcome of class struggle?
A CASE STUDY IN HISTORICAL INTERPRETATION

However much historians claim that it is objective and unbiased, their work is frequently influenced by their political views or by the political environment in which they live. Sometimes, their work does not even aim at objectivity, but is planned and executed to serve a political purpose. No series of events in modern history has been so open to distortion, or been written about with so much partisan enthusiasm, as the Russian revolutions.

Soviet interpretations of 1917

For most of the 20th century the events of 1917 formed the basis of one of the most powerful political systems on earth. For Soviet writers, therefore, interpretations of the Bolsheviks' success were far from being abstract academic arguments. Instead, they provided the entire justification of the society and the political system in which they lived and worked, and the 'correct' interpretation of the Russian Revolution was as important as any other issue of political doctrine within the USSR. As the politics of the Soviet Union shifted, so did the historical explanations of its origins, producing not one Marxist interpretation, but a succession of subtly different versions.

As early as 1918, the Bolsheviks were justifying their actions of the previous year, eager to show that the October/November coup was not merely a piece of political opportunism. In *The Russian Revolution to Brest-Litovsk* (1918), Trotsky argued that the Bolsheviks enjoyed a broad basis of support among the Russian workers, arising from their correct interpretation of the class struggle. This would have led them to power by legitimate, democratic means had it not been for the counter-revolutionary conspiracies of Kornilov, Kerensky and others. In the short term, therefore, the October coup was forced upon the Bolsheviks by their opponents. Such a view received enthusiastic support from the American socialist writer, John Reed, whose eye-witness account – *Ten Days That Shook the World* (1919) – remained for many years one of the most influential accounts of the October Revolution.

Once firmly established in power, however, the Soviet leadership changed its tune. The Bolsheviks were now pictured in a more dominant role, moulding and directing the Russian working classes, rather than responding to their democratic will. Trotsky and Iakovlev, in *On the Historical Significance of October* (1922), now portrayed the October coup as a political masterstroke, splendidly orchestrated by the Bolshevik leadership. This was in sharp contrast to the spontaneous and chaotic events of the February revolution. The distinction was between a party that truly understood the inevitable logic of class struggle, and groupings that attempted to pervert the course of history for their selfish ends. In their success the Bolsheviks had enjoyed two great advantages: their clear understanding of Marxist principles and their centralised, disciplined organisation. Such organisational and ideological strengths, of course, owed an enormous debt to the genius of Lenin.

In the same way the Stalinist era produced a further very different version of the same events as it became politically unacceptable to attribute important roles in the revolution to men whom Stalin had declared to be 'enemies of the people'. This process culminated, in 1939, in the publication of the official *Short Course of the History of the Russian Communist Party (Bolsheviks)*. This new interpretation either minimised or ignored the roles played by Stalin's political rivals. Stalin himself emerged as a key figure, at the right hand of Lenin himself. This official version also made one other important change, attributing a leading role to the Bolsheviks in the February revolution and therefore enhancing their role in the events of 1917 as a whole. Throughout the events of 1917, it was now claimed, the Bolsheviks followed the inevitable logic of class struggle, acting as 'a revolutionary party of the proletariat, a party free from opportunism and revolutionary in its attitude towards the bourgeoisie and its state power'.

Western interpretations of 1917

Meanwhile, outside the Soviet Union, several groups wrote about the Russian revolutions with distinctly different agendas. One agenda was that of socialist commentators unsympathetic to Bolshevism, who claimed that Lenin's actions in and after 1917 were premature. Economic development and the class struggle in Russia had not yet reached the stage where proletarian revolution was viable. The revolution was rushed into a socialist phase before a mature bourgeois phase had been attained, in direct defiance of Marxist principles. This view was strongly argued, for instance, by exiled Mensheviks such as Viktor Chernov (*The Great Russian Revolution*, 1936) and T. Dan (*The Origins of Bolshevism*, 1964). Such interpretations naturally placed less emphasis upon impersonal economic and social forces, or upon the theoretical correctness of the Bolshevik Party as a whole. Instead, they place Lenin at the centre of the events of 1917. The British historian E.H. Carr, in *A History of the Soviet Union, 1917–1929* (1966), represents that view in writing that 'the triumph of the party seemed almost exclusively due to Lenin's consistent success in stamping his personality upon it and leading his often reluctant colleagues in his train'. Few western writers have questioned the greatness of Lenin, but many have tempered their praise with an awareness of his role in the formation of subsequent communist dictatorship. Such an interpretation characterised the work of many American writers during the 'Cold War' period. It can be seen in the work of Daniel Shub (*Lenin: A Biography*, 1948), Adam Ulam (*Lenin and the Bolsheviks*, 1965) and Richard Pipes (*Revolutionary Russia*, 1968), all of whom see the revolution primarily as resulting from the cataclysmic disaster of the World War, brilliantly and cynically exploited by Lenin.

Such overall conclusions are very similar to those reached by those western historians who identified themselves with the 'liberal' school of interpretation. These writers see Russia's political history since the mid-19th century – through the emancipation of the serfs, the formation of the *zemstva*, and then of the Duma – as a promising progression towards liberal institutions. Those writers who have taken an optimistic view of Russia's economic development under Witte and Stolypin have also made an important contribution to this line of argument. This progress was then shattered by Russia's disastrous involvement in the First World War, which provided the extremists with their opportunity. In the beginning this view was put forward by disappointed Russian liberals, such as Paul Miliukov in *History of the Second Russian Revolution* (1921) and M. Florinski in *The End of the Russian Empire* (1931). The line was taken up later by Leonard Schapiro in *The Origins of Communist Autocracy* (1955) and by the English authority, Hugh Seton-Watson in *The Russian Empire, 1801–1917* (1967).

Western historical writing in the 'Cold War' era did produce, however, one school of thought which reached very different conclusions about the nature and origins of the Russian revolutions. This was developed in the 1970s and 1980s by historians who wished to study the revolution from 'below', rather than from the viewpoint of the leaders. These focused upon such issues as the development of trade unions and of civil rights among the urban workers, political developments within the armed forces, and social and economic development among the peasantry. Such work as that of Diane Koenker (*Moscow Workers and the 1917 Revolution*, 1981), Evan Mawdsley (*The Russian Revolution and the Baltic Fleet*, 1978), and Teodor Shanin (*The Awkward Class: Political Sociology of the Peasantry in a Developing Society, Russia 1910–1925*, 1972) returned working-class politics to the centre of events. The Bolsheviks, in their view, enjoyed success in 1917, not because they forced the workers into line, but because they represented most accurately the long-standing aspirations of such 'progressive' workers. Such a view has several important implications for the interpretation of Russian history. It portrays the Bolshevik Party in 1917 as flexible and open, rather than hierarchical and authoritarian, as a genuine party of radical workers and peasants, rather than a party dominated by intellectuals and émigrés. An associated conclusion would be that the Bolshevik Party, therefore, changed its nature in the years that followed, that it was the pressures of the civil war that made the party brutal and authoritarian.

The collapse of the Soviet Union in 1991 naturally had a very dramatic impact upon historical writing about the revolution. On a political level it undermined the orthodox Soviet interpretation of the revolution, and made it implausible to view the Bolshevik success in 1917 as part of a logical, world-wide progression towards communism. Conversely, it enabled 'Cold War' historians in the west to assume that they had been right all along, and that they had now won the argument. Such is certainly the spirit in which the conservative American historian Richard Pipes published *The Russian Revolution, 1899–1919* in 1990. Most important in the longer term, however, was the fact that the archives in Russia were no longer under strict government control, and that western historians may research in them more freely. Perhaps the most important work to result from these freer circumstances to date has been that of Orlando Figes (*A People's Tragedy: the Russian Revolution 1891–1924*, 1996). Figes takes a much less heroic view of these events, depicting a revolution that was really directed by no-one, neither by the Bolsheviks nor by abstract theories of class struggle. Instead, deeply rooted in Russia's past political and social history, it led to economic and social disaster in the early 1920s, and to an oppressive regime which alone could restore some form of order to Russia's chaotic society. Another leading researcher of recent years, Robert Service, also stresses the tensions that existed in an extremely complex society. In *A History of 20th Century Russia* (1997), he takes a more political approach than Figes. In emphasising, however, the range of social and ethnic tension that existed in Russia on the eve of war, and the inadequacy of the government's understanding of them, he too sees an increasing sense of chaos in Tsarist Russia. Revolution, in his conclusion, was the 'practically inevitable' outcome of such a situation. A decade of post-Soviet research, therefore, begins to suggest social and political tensions of a revolutionary nature, which were channelled and directed in the longer term by a highly organised and ruthless political party.

1. In what ways did Soviet historians differ at various times in their interpretation of the events of 1917?

2. Explain why the interpretations of the Russian revolutions has caused such debate and controversy between historians.

The USSR in the age of Stalin, 1924–1956

Key Issues

- *How did Stalin become dictator of the Soviet Union?*

- *To what extent, and by what means, did the Soviet Union emerge as a major industrial power in the 1930s?*

- *How secure was the Soviet Union from foreign attack by the end of the 1930s?*

- *How was Stalin's power re-affirmed after the Second World War?*

Framework of Events

1922	Stalin appointed General Secretary of Party's Central Committee. Lenin incapacitated by a stroke.
1924	Death of Lenin
1925	Dismissal of Trotsky as Commissar for War
1927	Procurement crisis
1928–32	First Five-Year Plan
1929	Beginning of agricultural collectivisation
1932–33	Major famine in the Ukraine
1933–37	Second Five-Year Plan
1934	Assassination of Sergei Kirov, and beginning of the political purges USSR admitted to League of Nations
1935	Beginning of 'Great Terror' Trials of Kamenev and Zinoviev
1936	Purge extended to the armed forces Trial of Marshal Tukhachevsky
1937–41	Third Five-Year Plan
1939	Nazi–Soviet Pact. Soviet forces occupy eastern Poland and the Baltic states.
1941	German attack on Soviet Union
1945	German surrender. Soviet occupation of much of eastern Europe. Fourth Five-Year Plan launched.
1953	Death of Stalin
1956	Khrushchev's 'Secret Speech'.

Overview

LENIN departed the political scene abruptly, leaving his successors a mixed inheritance. He had completed part of the task that the Bolsheviks had undertaken in 1917, for the regime had defeated its domestic enemies, and was firmly established in power. In terms of Soviet society and of the Soviet economy, however, he left an unfinished revolution, and a revolution in danger. The international revolt expected in the aftermath of the First World War had not materialised. Not only did the Soviet Union confront a hostile, capitalist world on its own, but it faced it with an economic system that lagged way behind those of the western powers. Levels of industrial production were generally lower than they had been before the war, and Russia's vast territories and resources were exploited inadequately, if at all. Perhaps the most pressing problem of all was that of securing from a suspicious and conservative peasantry a sufficient quantity of food to feed the industrial workers whose labour, in both ideological and practical terms, formed the foundation of the new Soviet society. Faced with such unforeseen problems, communist theorists proposed a variety of solutions, and Stalin's rise to power owed much to the fact that his solution was the most acceptable to a battered and war-weary society. It was his view that the Soviet Union should abandon any reliance upon foreign communists and international revolution, and should use its own substantial resources to achieve economic progress.

Stalin's system of government was characterised by two outstanding features. The first was the ruthless mobilisation of Russia's enormous economic resources in order to achieve industrial parity with the great capitalist economies. The second feature was the development of a powerful state system, capable of driving forward such a policy and of overcoming all opposition. By the end of the 1930s, the powers of the political police had expanded enormously and were backed by a system of prison and labour camps of unprecedented proportions. Stalin's pretence that he was using these powers against class enemies and the agents of foreign capitalism was largely untrue. Although the battle to compel the peasantry was real enough, more dangerous opposition came from within the Communist Party, and even from within the government itself. Stalin attacked this opposition by the crudest methods of power politics – in the 1920s to establish his leadership, and in the 1930s to consolidate his power and to drive forward his policies. Trumped-up and emotive charges were brought against his opponents, and they were eliminated from political life either by execution or distant imprisonment.

By the end of the 1930s, Stalin had achieved two goals. Firstly, he effectively created a new form of Soviet government, replacing the Bolsheviks who had followed Lenin in 1917 with a new brand of Soviet politician. From a younger generation, these men and women were usually from distinctly proletarian backgrounds, far removed from the intellectuals who had planned the early theories of Bolshevism and the 1917 revolution. More radical still, Stalin overrode the authority of the Party, and created an extremely powerful and remarkably successful system of personal rule. Secondly, he had turned the Soviet Union into a major industrial power, capable of surviving the enormous demands of the **'Great Patriotic War'**, and of emerging after 1945 as one of the two great world powers. On the other hand, a high price had been paid for these achievements. The social and humanitarian idealism that had accompanied the 1917 revolution

'Great Patriotic War': The name by which the Second World War is usually referred to in Russia. It helps to show how Stalin wished to present the conflict to the Soviet people, as a defence of the motherland, akin to the war of 1812, rather than as a part of a wider struggle.

had been abandoned. It had given way to new forms of political and economic brutality that eventually undermined the claims of the Soviet Union to provide a new and superior social pattern.

It was perhaps in the area of foreign policy that Stalin inherited the most complex and insoluble problems. When Stalin first established his authority in the Soviet Union it was already clear that Lenin's initial assumptions about foreign policy were naïve and inaccurate. The Russian Revolution did not trigger the collapse of world capitalism, and it would be necessary for the Soviet Union to define its stance towards its capitalist neighbours. Unfortunately, between the mid-1920s and the mid-1930s, Soviet politicians adopted two different and contradictory stances. Working through *Comintern*, some sought Soviet security through the promotion of communism within the capitalist states. At the same time, the Soviet Foreign Ministry sought orthodox diplomatic relations with many of the European states. Such relations assumed much greater importance in the 1930s, as powerful enemies began to emerge to the west and to the east of the Soviet Union, in Germany and in Japan. From the mid-1930s onwards, the Soviet Union conducted its foreign policy in an orthodox fashion, seeking allies against those forces that threatened its security. Yet its position among the European powers remained unorthodox. Conservative politicians in France, Britain and Eastern Europe could not trust a power that had recently supported the principle of international revolution. Nor could Stalin feel confident that these politicians would not in the end prefer Hitler's ideology to his own. In some cases, he had

Comintern: Shortened term for the (third) Communist International. Between 1919 and 1943 this was nominally the organisation responsible for the co-ordination of international communist activity.

The political structure of the Soviet Union in the mid-1920s

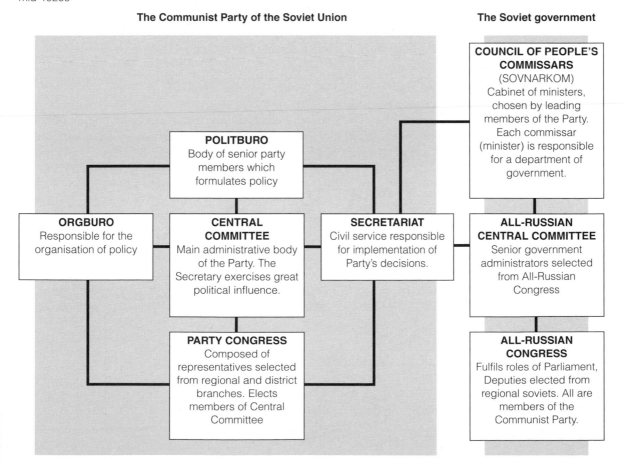

The Communist Party of the Soviet Union　　　　**The Soviet government**

POLITBURO
Body of senior party members which formulates policy

COUNCIL OF PEOPLE'S COMMISSARS
(SOVNARKOM)
Cabinet of ministers, chosen by leading members of the Party. Each commissar (minister) is responsible for a department of government.

ORGBURO
Responsible for the organisation of policy

CENTRAL COMMITTEE
Main administrative body of the Party. The Secretary exercises great political influence.

SECRETARIAT
Civil service responsible for implementation of Party's decisions.

ALL-RUSSIAN CENTRAL COMMITTEE
Senior government administrators selected from All-Russian Congress

PARTY CONGRESS
Composed of representatives selected from regional and district branches. Elects members of Central Committee

ALL-RUSSIAN CONGRESS
Fulfils roles of Parliament, Deputies elected from regional soviets. All are members of the Communist Party.

good grounds for his suspicions. Perhaps the best bet for the security of the Soviet Union was to imitate the capitalist powers and to do a deal with Hitler. That option, too, proved unsuccessful in the long run. When Nazi Germany repudiated the 1939 pact, and launched its attack upon the Soviet Union in 1941, Stalin was left in isolation, his foreign policy a failure in all important respects.

Desperate as the plight of the Soviet Union appeared in late 1941, the power of the state and the prestige of its leader were transformed in the course of the next four years. The cost to the Soviet Union of the Great Patriotic War was huge, and its human and material losses were by far the worst of any of the combatants. The fruits of victory, on the other hand, were immense: the USSR gained control over the territories and economies of most of the states of eastern Europe, and emerged as the greatest power on the European and Asian continents, matched in global terms only by the USA. Perhaps the greatest benefits went to Stalin himself. He emerged with his domestic power and reputation enhanced to the extent that he appeared as the infallible father of the state, without a domestic political rival.

In the last eight years of his life, Stalin used this vast power to restore and to consolidate the political and economic system that he had established in the 1930s. The reconstruction of the Soviet economy once again went hand in hand with the subordination of the peasantry to the requirements of the urban workers, and the imposition of political terror.

If such policies could be justified in the 1930s as necessary steps in the creation of a communist society, it does not seem that they were as readily accepted by Soviet politicians in the post-war years. Although they did not dare to oppose Stalin during his lifetime, they were very quick indeed to reform his system after his death. Reforms were quickly applied to the secret police and to the system of prison camps, and the Soviet economy moved in directions more favourable to the peasantry and to the production of consumer goods. In 1956, indeed, Nikita Khrushchev felt strong enough to condemn Stalin's methods and to abandon his 'cult of the personality'. Soviet foreign policy was to demonstrate in the next 15 years that some of Stalin's principles and priorities lived on. In terms of domestic policy, however, an era of ruthless economic planning and of political terror was indeed at an end.

A more cynical view of Soviet government. This cartoon, entitled 'The Stalin Constitution' shows Stalin occupying every position and playing every role. It was published by Russian exiles in 1936.

8.1 Who was Josef Stalin?

Political formation

Born Josef Djugashvili (21 January 1879), the future dictator of the Soviet Union was not Russian by birth. He came from the small town of Gori, in Georgia, and was the son of a shoemaker, and the grandson of serfs. As such, he was one of the few true proletarians in the leading ranks of the Bolshevik Party. The most significant features of his early life were the harshness and occasional brutality of his father and the unusual ambition and devotion of his mother, which secured for him the rare privilege of 11 years of education (1888–99). It is significant that the theological college in Tbilisi – that Djugashvili attended from 1894 until his expulsion five years later – had a history of student unrest and political disloyalty. 'I became a Marxist,' its most famous student later recalled, 'because of my social position, but also because of the harsh intolerance and discipline that crushed me so mercilessly at the seminary.'

Stalin's political stance seems to have developed steadily between 1898, when he joined a social democratic underground group in Tbilisi, and 1904 when he clearly identified himself with the Bolshevik faction of the communists. Unlike those of the intellectual Marxists in exile, Stalin's subsequent career followed a practical path of strike organisation, agitation and armed robberies for the benefit of party funds, interspersed with periods of imprisonment and Siberian exile. He used the name 'Koba' from 1902, and signed himself 'Stalin' ('man of steel') for the first time in 1913. The leading traits of his character – distrust, alertness, dissimulation, endurance and, above all, an intense sense of class hatred – can all be traced from his childhood and early career. For Stalin this hatred was never merely a matter of Marxist theory. The historian Isaac Deutscher wrote in *Stalin: A Political Biography* (1966), 'In Djugashvili, class hatred was not his second nature – it was his first.'

Stalin's reputation in local revolutionary circles expanded to a wider stage between 1905 (when he travelled abroad for the first time to attend a Bolshevik conference in Finland) and 1912 (when he was appointed by Lenin to the Central Committee of the party). Perhaps Lenin's choice was determined by his desire to shake up the assembly of theoretical Marxists with a rougher breed of revolutionary. In exile in Siberia at the beginning of 1917, Stalin quickly assumed a number of unobtrusive but influential roles in the revolution. He was editor of the Bolshevik journal *Pravda*, leader of the Petrograd Soviet, and temporary director of Bolshevik strategy until the return of the exiles from abroad. If not a familiar public figure, he was a man of substantial internal political influence, as the events of the next decade were to demonstrate.

1. What roles had Stalin played within the Bolshevik Party by the time it seized power in 1917?

2. In what ways was Stalin's background different from those of other leading Bolsheviks of 1917?

Josef Stalin (1879–1953)

Adopted name of Josef Djugashvili. Became a leading member of the Bolshevik Party in its early stages and was active in the October Revolution in 1917. Stalin became People's Commissar for Nationalities in the first Soviet government, and General Secretary of the Bolshevik Party's Central Committee (1922–53). After Lenin's death, he took over the leadership of the Soviet Union, and launched the Five-Year Plans for the industrialisation of the Soviet Union and the collectivisation of Soviet agriculture. Signed the Nazi–Soviet Pact (1939) but failed to prevent the German invasion of the Soviet Union two years later. Stalin provided strong leadership during the war years, and it was largely Soviet military strength which led to the collapse of the Nazi regime in 1945.

8.2 How did Stalin win the struggle to succeed Lenin as leader of the Soviet state?

Nikolai Bukharin (1888–1938)
Intellectual Bolshevik. Opposed Lenin over the Treaty of Brest-Litovsk (1918). Supported Stalin against Trotsky, but later opposed his policies on the planned economy and authoritarian government. Arrested and executed.

Grigori Zinoviev (1883–1936)
Joined Lenin in exile in 1903. Editor of *Pravda* and Chairman of *Comintern*. Supported Stalin against Trotsky, but subsequently switched allegiance. Dismissed from office and expelled from Party (1927). Arrested and executed.

Lev Kamenev (1883–1936)
Moderate Bolshevik who opposed Lenin's 'adventurism' in the course of 1917. Head of Moscow Soviet (1918–25). Dismissed from Politburo (1925) and subsequently from Party. Accused of Kirov's murder in 1936, and executed.

Politburo: Officially a sub-committee of the Central Committee of the Communist Party of the USSR responsible for the definition and execution of government policy. In effect, under Stalin, the main executive body of Soviet government.

Orgburo: The body designed by the Central Committee to oversee the organisation and resourcing of government policies.

The strokes that removed Lenin from active politics (26 May 1922), and which finally killed him (21 January 1924), destroyed the undisputed source of leadership in Russia. 'The impact of Lenin's illness on the Bolshevik leadership can hardly be exaggerated,' wrote Isaac Deutscher. 'The whole constellation ceased, almost at once, to shine with the reflected light of its master mind.'

The main candidates for the succession

There could be no adequate replacement for Lenin's genius, and the short-comings of the various candidates had already been aptly summarised in his Testament, composed during his last illness. Leon Trotsky, for all his great intellectual qualities, was guilty of a 'too far-reaching self-confidence and a disposition to be too much attracted by the purely administrative side of affairs'. Grigori Zinoviev and Lev Kamenev had shown a disturbing hesitancy in the months before the seizure of power in October 1917, and Nikolai Bukharin's grasp of theoretical Marxism was regarded as faulty. Josef Stalin, lastly, offset his great practical abilities with an excessive roughness, impatience and lack of caution and of consideration for his colleagues.

The main feature of the struggle for the succession during the last weeks of Lenin's life was the isolation of Trotsky from the other candidates. In part this was due to his personal arrogance, and in part because he never lived down the lateness of his conversion to Bolshevism. Furthermore, his achievements at the head of the Red Army were offset by the widespread fear that this military leader might turn against the Russian Revolution, as General Bonaparte had turned against the French Revolution (see *Europe 1760–1871*). The failure of his campaign between October 1923 and January 1924 for greater democracy in the upper reaches of the party stressed the narrowness of his support, and his absence through illness from Lenin's funeral badly undermined his credibility as a successor in the popular view.

On the other hand, the coalition that opposed him – Zinoviev, Kamenev and Stalin – exerted immense influence. Zinoviev dominated the party organisation in Petrograd (renamed Leningrad in honour of the dead leader in 1924), and was head of the *Comintern*. Kamenev exercised similar influence in Moscow. Stalin, while occupying the unglamorous post of Commissar for Nationalities, had spent the past years insinuating himself into a strong position in the party bureaucracy. Not only was he a member of the party's inner cabinet (**Politburo**) but, like Zinoviev and Kamenev, he was also prominent in the executive bureau (**Orgburo**) and in the Commissariat of Workers' and Peasants' Inspection, which was responsible for the elimination of economic inefficiency and corruption. Above all, since 1922, Stalin had held the post of general secretary of the party's Central Committee. This enabled him to exert considerable control over party membership. In terms of the range of political weapons available to him, no other Bolshevik was the rival of Stalin.

Stalin's control over the party machinery

In 1924 it was widely assumed that the death of Lenin would result in a collective leadership of the Soviet Union. The reasons for the steady decline of that form of political authority, and the emergence of Stalin's undisputed leadership, are complex. Neither the Stalinist explanation, that he offered the only correct analysis of the future course of the Soviet

Union, nor Trotsky's bitter reflection that Stalin rode to power on a wave of war-weariness and reaction, is fully satisfactory. In large part the phenomenon must be explained by Stalin's political skill, and by his shrewd handling of the weapons at his disposal.

Foremost among these was the party machinery over which he exercised such control, and which he could use to assign supporters of his opponents to remote posts, while admitting to high office those upon whose support he could rely. The promotion to the Central Committee of Anastas Mikoyan (1923) and Lazar Kaganovich (1924), and to the Politburo of Vyacheslav Molotov and Mikhail Kalinin (1926), marked the emergence of a new school of 'Stalinist' Bolsheviks. The appointment of Sergei Kirov as head of the party in Leningrad (1926), formerly Zinoviev's stronghold, and of Kliment Voroshilov in Trotsky's former military office (1925), marked the extension of this tactic to key political areas. At this crucial point in the struggle, the Stalinists also enjoyed the support of the 'Rightist' wing of the party, headed by Nikolai Bukharin, Mikhail Tomsky and Alexei Rykov.

Creating the cult of Lenin

Secondly, Stalin showed great skill, both in the creation of a cult of 'Leninism', and in the formation of his own image as 'the best, the staunchest, the truest comrade-in-arms of Lenin'. His stage-management of Lenin's funeral was, according to historian Isaac Deutscher, in *Stalin: A Political Biography* (1966), 'calculated to stir the mind of a primitive, semi-oriental people into a mood of exaltation for the new Leninist cult'. The effect was compounded by Stalin's foundation of the Lenin Institute (January 1924), and by a series of calculated lectures on 'The Foundations of Leninism' delivered at the Communist University in Moscow (April 1924). Given his late conversion to Bolshevism, Trotsky was at a particular disadvantage in terms of Leninist orthodoxy.

Stalin's third great advantage lay in the blameless simplicity of his former private and political life. His image as the uncomplicated and dedicated peasant, married to the daughter of an old Bolshevik (1918), contrasted favourably with those of his more sophisticated rivals. As Commissar for Nationalities, moreover, he could claim the successful merging of the national republics into the Union of Soviet Socialist Republics (1922) as one of the greatest achievements of the revolution to date.

Presidium: A permanent administrative committee, especially in communist countries.

Anastas Mikoyan (1895–1978)
Joined the Bolsheviks in 1915. Central Committee member (1923), and consistent supporter of Stalin. Member of Politburo (1935–52). Subsequently supported Khrushchev (see page 245) and remained leading 'elder statesman' in USSR to the time of his death.

Lazar Kaganovich (1893–1991)
Supporter of Stalin in the struggle for the succession to Lenin. Secretary of the Central Committee (1924–25 and 1928–29). Active in the implementation of forced collectivisation (1929 onwards), and as a 'trouble-shooter' in various Soviet ministries (1935 onwards). Dismissed by Khrushchev (1957) and sent to manage a cement factory.

Mikhail Kalinin (1875–1946)
Close associate of Lenin from 1913, and supporter of Stalin in succession struggle. Member of the Politburo (1925–46). Titular head of state (1938–46).

Sergei Kirov (1886–1934)
Bolshevik activist from 1904. Central Committee member (1923). Head of Party in Leningrad (1925). Member of the Politburo (1930). Secretary of Central Committee (1934). Assassinated 1 December 1934.

Kliment Voroshilov (1881–1970)
Bolshevik from 1903, and played military role in Civil War. Helped Dzerzhinsky to form CHEKA. Commissar for Defence (1934–41). Marshal of the Soviet Union (1935), and thus a leading figure in the Soviet war effort between 1940–45. Chairman of the **Presidium** of the Supreme Soviet (1953–60), but subsequently lost influence.

Lastly, Stalin benefited from a string of tactical errors by his most prominent opponents. Trotsky's attack upon such elements of Lenin's policy as the New Economic Policy, in his essays 'Lessons of October' (1924), was a miscalculation in the prevailing atmosphere of 'Lenin worship'. The refusal of both Trotsky and Zinoviev to publish Lenin's Testament, with its damaging verdict upon Stalin, saved Stalin from the most dangerous threat to his position. Indeed, the historian Roy Medvedev, in *On Stalin and Stalinism* (1983), has stressed that in the crucial early stages of the contest, 'Trotsky considered it beneath his dignity to engage actively in a struggle for power'. The belated union of Trotsky, Zinoviev and Kamenev (1926) in the so-called 'United Opposition' to Stalin, was unlikely to increase their credibility in the light of their mutual hostility a few months earlier.

It is important to remember how ill-equipped most members of the Politburo were to cope with a political opponent of Stalin's talents. As the historian Martin McCauley explains, in *Stalin and Stalinism* (1995), 'the Politburo opponents of Stalin had had little practical experience of politics before 1917. They had not mounted the party ladder step by step and had not had to claw their way up; 1917 made them, at a stroke, key political figures. They were singularly ill-equipped to recognise a party climber when they saw one.' From 1926 onwards, the position of this opposition became more and more hopeless. Isolated and outnumbered, Zinoviev lost his leadership of the Communist International, and all three leaders of the 'United Opposition' were voted off the Politburo by the end of the year. In October 1927, Trotsky and Zinoviev lost their places on the Central Committee, and were expelled altogether from the Party a month later, followed by 75 of their supporters. In January 1928, Trotsky began a period of internal exile in Soviet Asia, and was taking the first steps upon a road to banishment from the USSR that was only to end with his assassination in Mexico City in 1940.

> 1. Who were Stalin's rivals for the leadership of the USSR after the death of Lenin?
>
> 2. How convincing is the argument that Stalin's success in securing power in the 1920s owed more to the weaknesses and mistakes of his rivals than to his own strengths?

8.3 What were the main features of 'Stalinism'?

'Socialism in one country'

The leadership struggle of the late 1920s was certainly in part a clash of powerful personalities. Yet it was also a genuine dispute about the future path of Soviet Communism. The candidates, for instance, differed over the issue of democratic decision making within the party, over the pace at which the economic backwardness of the Soviet Union should be tackled, and over the roles allowed to independent merchants, manufacturers and peasants under the New Economic Policy. Above all, the dispute centred upon two alternative views of the future of Bolshevism.

Trotsky and his followers held fast to the theory of the 'permanency of revolution'. The revolution in Russia, they claimed, could not be regarded as an end in itself, but only as a vital link in the wider process of European and even world revolution. By its example, and with the continued assistance of the Soviet Union, the revolution would eventually lead to the general destruction of capitalism. Only then could the future of the Soviet system be secure. It was a view closely in accord with the expectations of Lenin right up to his death, but offered a prospect of further struggle that was profoundly unattractive after recent Russian sufferings. It was most discouraging in the light of recent socialist failures in Germany, Hungary and elsewhere.

Although Stalin seems to have subscribed to this view until late 1924, he then began to formulate an alternative usually known as the theory of 'socialism in one country'. By this he stressed that, despite the Soviet

Union's present state of ruin and exhaustion, its immense resources would be sufficient for the construction of a stable socialist society, without external aid. Within two years, 'Trotskyism' was being officially condemned as 'a lack of faith in the strength and capabilities of the Russian revolution and a negation and repudiation of Lenin's theory of proletarian revolution'. While Stalin left open the possibility of future Soviet participation in a wider revolution, he made consolidation of the Russian achievement an unalterable priority.

The appeal of 'socialism in one country'

By the last two years of the decade, Stalin's thesis had won complete dominance over that of Trotsky as the official view of the Soviet government. Some writers have explained this as the natural consequence of Stalin's political victory within the party. It is now, however, more usual to reverse this reasoning and to see Stalin's political supremacy as the result, rather than the cause, of the wide acceptance of the theory of 'socialism in one country'. The American historian S.F. Cohen argues strongly in *The Soviet Union since Stalin* (1980) that Stalin's rise depended in large part upon his acceptance by the 'influentials' within the Party, and that a majority of them supported him 'less because of his bureaucratic power than because they preferred his leadership and policies. To some extent their choice doubtless expressed their identification with the General Secretary as a forceful practical politician.'

Why was the principle so widely accepted? Firstly, however unorthodox it was in pure Leninist terms, it was hard to dispute the practical logic of Stalin's approach in the light of contemporary European developments. Secondly, it offered the prospect of a future that lay wholly in Soviet hands, and involved little dependence upon forces beyond Soviet control. Lastly, it offered to the Soviet people as a whole the prospect of relief from the enormous suffering and perpetual struggle of the decade 1914–24. There was probably much justification in Trotsky's later conviction that the unreadiness of the people to undertake a further era of struggle contributed largely to his defeat in the leadership contest.

The 'Stalinist' state

Important as this all-embracing strategy was, the control of Stalin and his supporters depended upon effective and ruthless implementation of their policies. By the end of the 1920s, a complex system of state machinery had been established for this purpose.

● *The constitution of 1924*

The theoretical heart of Soviet political organisation in 1928 was the constitution introduced in 1924. It confirmed the merger of the component national units of the old Empire into the Union of Soviet Socialist Republics (USSR), and left each republic with the theoretical right to leave the Union if its 'non-Russian working class' so wished. In reality, any such wish would invariably be treated as the counter-revolutionary agitation of nationalist, bourgeois elements. At the head of the constitutional structure stood the All-Russian Congress of Soviets, with its executive Central Committee, and its élite Presidium, in which all major decisions were made. Below stretched a hierarchy of Soviets – at republican, provincial, district and local levels. All adults had the right to vote, except those deprived of citizenship. That right extended only to the election of local soviet members who, in turn, selected members for each higher soviet. The system thus constituted a complex filter to test the orthodoxy of each aspiring politician.

● The Communist Party of the Soviet Union

The articles of the constitution veiled the three main driving forces behind Soviet politics. The first of these was the Communist Party of the Soviet Union (Bolshevik), membership of which was an essential qualification for every potential political candidate. It was a body that had undergone great changes since the heady days of 1917. By 1922 a series of purges had rid the party of any serious ideological diversity, eliminating the last traces of Menshevik or Social Revolutionary opinion. In the later 1920s two more changes took place. The party grew steadily in size, from 1.3 million members in early 1928 to 3.5 million in January 1933. It also changed its composition – becoming less of a party of the workers, who constituted 48.6% of membership in the 1930s, and more a party of a new, Soviet-educated **intelligentsia**.

● The political police

The constitution also failed to indicate the growing importance of the government agencies for internal security. The State Political Administration (GPU or OGPU) was the successor of the CHEKA, the first communist secret police. Until his death in 1926, it was headed by the CHEKA's founder, Felix Dzerzhinsky. Its duties were vaguely defined but, as the historian Leonard Schapiro notes, in *The Communist Party of the Soviet Union* (1970), 'in practice, it never lacked the power to do whatever it was required to do by the party'. In July 1934, the OGPU was merged into a wider body, the People's Commissariat of Internal Affairs (NKVD). Under the leadership of Genrikh Yagoda (1934–36), Nikolai Yezhov (1936–38) and Lavrenti Beria (1938–53), the NKVD was the main tool for the internal policy of the Soviet state. It supervised many of the most important and dangerous projects of the Five-Year Plans, including the Pechora railway and the White Sea ('Belamor') Ship Canal, played a central role in the purging of the Party, and controlled a labour force perhaps as large as 10 million in the state's prison camps.

● The army

Another element in the practical government of the USSR – the army – was also brought under close party control by the end of the 1920s. Trotsky's hopes of a citizen militia, under direct proletarian control, were killed off by the necessities of the Civil War. In 1925 Trotsky himself was replaced as Commissar for War by Mikhail Frunze. A series of reforms in 1924–25 placed the political supervision of the army firmly in the hands of the Party's Central Committee. This confirmed the system of dual command whereby the military commanders worked alongside political commissars who took precedence over them in all political decisions. By 1933, all senior commanders and 93% of divisional commanders were party members. The degree of authority enjoyed by the Party was illustrated in October 1925 when Frunze was ordered by his political superiors to undergo a medical operation from which he died. This authority was, of course, to be confirmed spectacularly during the course of the political purges of the 1930s.

Intelligentsia: The most educated people in a country or community, especially those interested in the arts, philosophy and politics.

---

1. In what ways did Stalin and Trotsky disagree about the path that should be taken by Russian Communism after 1924?

2. What were the main agencies by which the Soviet state was controlled in the early years of Stalin's power?

3. Why was the principle of 'socialism in one country' popular with Soviet politicians in the late 1920s?

Genrikh Yagoda (1891–1938)
Prominent member and leader of Soviet security police. Joined CHEKA in 1920, becoming deputy head of GPU (1924) and chief of NKVD (1934), in which capacity he was responsible for initiating the purges. Dismissed in 1936, and arrested and executed two years later.

Nikolai Yezhov (1895–1939)
Commissar for Internal Affairs (1936), and thus responsible for the most brutal stages of the purges. Dismissed and appointed Commissar for Water Transport (1938), but soon arrested and executed as a scapegoat for the excesses of the purges.

Lavrenti Beria (1899–1953)
Of Georgian origin. Commissar for Internal Affairs (1938) and thus responsible for state security, and head of KGB. Politburo member (1939). Prominent in the Soviet war effort, and in the post-war establishment of Soviet control over eastern Europe. Arrested and executed after the death of Stalin.

8.4 Why was the NEP abandoned in favour of a planned economy?

The most dramatic policy decision taken by the Stalinist establishment was the abandonment of Lenin's New Economic Policy, and of Bukharin's policy of 'the creep at a snail's pace' towards socialism. Apart from the obvious ideological hostility within the party to the NEP, it is also true that it had, by 1926, largely achieved its industrial purpose. The toleration of a degree of private economic activity had restored output in most major areas of the economy to pre-1914 levels, and the level of private trading outside agriculture dropped steadily from 42.5% of the total (1924–25) to 22.5% (1928). The alternative of rapid, forced industrial growth through centralised planning and control had been advanced by Trotsky, Kamenev and Zinoviev in the mid-1920s, but had been resisted by Stalin as too great a departure from Leninism. Predictably, he now changed his view and broke with his former 'rightist' allies. Tomsky's leadership of the Soviet Trade Unions, Bukharin's post at the head of the *Comintern*, and Rykov's chairmanship of the Council of Commissars (*Sovnarkom*), all passed to Stalinists in June 1929. The public admission by the 'rightists' that their views were faulty (November 1929) marks the beginning of Stalin's undisputed power in the USSR which was to last until his death in 1953.

Why did Stalin now change course so abruptly to embrace the policies of his conquered opponents?

Although this has sometimes been seen as a cynical expression of his new-found political security, it is more likely that Stalin's change of course was a pragmatic response to the risk of substantial food shortages resulting from the so-called '**procurement** crisis' of 1927–28. Despite the decline in private industrial trade, in 1928 the independent peasant continued to cultivate 97.3% of the farmland of the Soviet Union. The difficulty in procuring sufficient grain supplies for the industrial towns arose in part from the inefficiency of many small, private farms, but also from the peasants' reluctance to deliver grain at the artificially low prices offered by the state. The result was a shortfall of 2 million tons of grain by 1927. This was potentially disastrous in view of the role played by urban hunger in the events of 1917. Under such circumstances, the policy of 'socialism in one country' risked falling at the first hurdle thanks, it was felt, to the greed of the richer peasants, the *kulaks*.

Procurement: The act of obtaining something, such as supplies, for an army or other organisation.

What is the value of such a photograph as a historical source?

A 'spontaneous' demonstration by peasants against the *kulaks*, 1930. Their banner declares 'We demand collectivisation and the extermination of the *kulaks* as a class'.

The principle of the Five-Year Plans

1. *What were the main differences between the NEP and the policy of economic planning that Stalin introduced at the end of the 1920s?*

2. *Why did Stalin's government find it necessary in the late 1920s (a) to undertake a policy of rapid industrialisation and (b) to collectivise agriculture?*

The introduction of the first Five-Year Plan, to run from 1928 to 1933, committed the USSR to the path of planned and centralised economic policy. A second Five-Year Plan followed (1933–37), while a third (1937–42) was disrupted by the outbreak of war. The overall aim of these plans was to match and to overhaul the economies of the advanced capitalist states in the shortest possible time. 'We are fifty or a hundred years behind the advanced countries,' Stalin declared in 1931. 'We must make good this distance in ten years. Either we do it, or we shall be crushed.' In view of the fate that befell the USSR in 1941, the prediction proved to be uncannily accurate.

The main tool of the government in these tasks was the Central Planning Committee (*Gosplan*). In industry, the planned economy meant an expansion of output, an improvement of communications, and the discovery and exploitation of new resources – all carried out in accordance with predetermined production quotas. In agriculture it meant not only the forced grain procurements of 1928–29, but also a fundamental change in the agrarian life of the USSR. The way out of Russia's agrarian backwardness, Stalin declared to the party in December 1927, 'is to turn the small and scattered peasant farms into large united farms based upon cultivation of the land in common'. Although it was stressed that the party should proceed with caution, the statement spelled the end of the brief decade of liberation for the Russian peasant, and marked the beginning of the era of **collectivisation**.

8.5 What were the achievements of the planned economy?

Agriculture: the elimination of the kulaks

No branch of the Soviet economy was as sensationally affected by the policy of centralisation as agriculture. In the short term, the 'evils' of small-scale farming, inadequate equipment, and low proportions of the harvest reaching the market, were combated by rigorous and often brutal searches for, and confiscation of, grain stocks by local officials. In the longer term, under the Five-Year Plan, they were combated by the forcible collectivisation of peasant production. Some historians, such as Roy Medvedev, have

'Sacking grain', an oil painting by the Soviet artist Tatyana Yablonskaya

At roughly what date, and for what purpose, would this picture have been painted?

seen this as a 'war against the peasant', as a logical extension of Bolshevik class struggle, eliminating the last class grouping in the Soviet Union that still earned its living from the ownership of property. Others have preferred to view it as a 'war between peasants', in which the government's main weapon against the prosperous *kulaks*, just under a million of the total peasantry, was the jealousy of the seven million poor peasants (*Bedniaks*), those without livestock or modern implements of any kind.

With the aid of party officials, police and army, a class war was waged in the countryside between late 1928 and March 1930, involving the dispossession, deportation and often the murder of those designated as *kulaks*. By 1930, it was announced that 58% of peasant holdings were 'collectivised', although the term usually only meant that the land, livestock and equipment of the *kulaks* was handed over for communal use by the *Bedniaks*. The middle peasants (*Seredniaks*) were not only scared into the collectives by the fate of the *kulaks*, but left with no alternative form of livelihood.

In 1930, even Stalin seems to have taken fright at the 'pandemonium' reigning in rural Russia. By blaming local officials for over-zealousness, and authorising withdrawal from collectives, the government produced the sharp drop indicated in the table below. In reality, policy remained unchanged. The ruthless elimination of the private farmer continued until, in 1938, the Soviet Union boasted 242,000 collective farms. These farms subdivided into two basic types:

● The state farm (*Sovkhoz*) was entirely state property, on which peasants worked for wages.

● The collective farm (*Kolkhoz*) was a 'voluntary' co-operative, on which land and equipment were collectively owned by the peasantry. Until 1958, no collective farm possessed its own heavy machinery. Instead, they were served by 'machine tractor stations', whose state-owned machinery and state-controlled specialists were at the disposal of the peasantry.

Each *Kolkhoz* was committed to deliver a substantial proportion of its produce to the state, while on a *Sovkhoz* the produce was, in any case, state property.

Collectivisation

Year	Percentage of rural household collectivised
December 1928	1.7
October 1929	4.1
March 1930	58.0
September 1930	21.0
1931	52.7
1932	61.5
1933	65.6
1934	71.4
1935	83.2
1936	90.5

The cost of collectivisation

It is certain that, as the Soviet commentator Dmitri Volkogonov wrote in *Stalin, Triumph and Tragedy* (1991), 'Stalin's forced agrarian revolution condemned Soviet agriculture to decades of stagnation. The bloody experiment, costing millions of lives, brought the country no relief.' Destruction by rebellious peasants, the loss of *kulak* expertise, and the inexperience of many collective farm managers resulted in a sharp decline in many areas of production. Between 1928 and 1934 the cattle population of the USSR declined from 66.8 million to 33.5 million, the number of sheep and goats fell from 114.6 million to 36.5 million, and the number of horses from 34 million to 16.5 million. The historian David Christian notes in *Imperial and Soviet Russia: Power, Privilege and the Challenge of Modernity* (1997) that these policies 'condemned a whole generation of Russians to a meatless diet', but in many rural areas the overall impact was far more serious than that. Grain shortages, combined with continued forced procurements, led to catastrophic rural famine. This was especially severe in the Ukraine and northern Caucasus region, where successive census figures between 1933 and 1938 suggest a death toll of around five million people.

Only slowly, as a government confident of victory showed more tolerance towards small-scale private enterprise among the peasantry, did livestock populations and rural living standards rise. Not until 1940 did figures for grain production match those of 1914. What short-term gains there were from collectivisation were enjoyed by Soviet industry, which benefited from a flow of surplus peasant labour into more attractive factory occupations, and by industrial workers, who gained a reliable, if not always plentiful, supply of cheap grain. A crucial part of the basis of Soviet industrial power was thus laid, at the cost of the peasantry. Stalin himself would later privately compare this battle with the later struggle for survival against the Germans, and there are important similarities between the two. In both cases, the Soviet state paid an enormous and terrifying price, even if it achieved an outstanding victory. The proportion of the harvest procured to feed urban workers in 1940 was nearly twice that procured in 1929; 40% compared with 22%. Alone among Russian governments in the 19th and early 20th centuries, Stalin's regime had truly broken the will and resistance of the Russian peasantry and subjected it to the wider purposes of the state.

Industry: the first Five-Year Plan

The task of the first Five-Year Plan, commenced in 1928, was nothing less than to lay the foundations for the transformation of Soviet society into an industrial force comparable to the United States of America. Its main emphasis fell upon the production of energy and of construction materials: coal, oil, electricity, iron, steel and cement. The rate of increase envisaged, averaging an annual rate of 20%, was hugely unrealistic, and the declaration (31 December 1932) that the plan had been completed in four years, was a propaganda exercise. Detractors might point to significant shortfalls, as in steel production (where only 62% of the quota was completed), in iron (59%), in heavy metallurgy (67.7%) and in consumer goods (73.5%).

A friendlier observer might still conclude that the achievement of 1928–32 was substantial:

- Machinery output increased four times, oil production doubled and electrical output in 1932 was 250% of the 1928 figure.

- 17 new blast furnaces were completed and 20 others modernised.

- 15 new rolling mills came into operation, with 12 others reconstructed.

The plan also produced some notable 'show pieces', such as the new centres of iron and steel production at Magnitogorsk in the Urals, and Kuznetsk in central Siberia. Also there was the building of the Dnieprostroi Dam, the biggest in Europe. Stalin's own criticism of the Dnieprostroi project in the mid-1920s – that it was like a poor peasant spending money on a gramophone instead of buying a cow – remained true, but he was now far more appreciative of the propaganda value of such achievements.

The Five-Year Plans

	1927	1932	(goal)	1937	(goal)
Electricity (million kWh)	505	1,340	(2,200)	3,620	(3,800)
Coal (million tons)	35.4	64.3	(75)	128	(152.5)
Oil (million tons)	11.7	21.4	(22)	28.5	(46.8)
Iron ore (million tons)	5.7	12.1	(19)	?	?
Pig iron (million tons)	3.3	6.2	(10)	14.5	(16)
Steel (million tons)	4.0	5.9	(10.4)	17.7	(17)
Labour force (millions)	11.3	22.8	(15.8)	26.9	(28.9)

The second Five-Year Plan

The second Five-Year Plan, which ran its full course from 1933 to 1937, avoided some of the mistakes of the first. Its average annual target was a rather more reasonable 14% increase, and by virtue of a more experienced and better-trained workforce avoided at least some of the waste and poor quality of 1928–32. Priority continued to be given to heavy industry, but greater emphasis was now placed upon newer metallurgical resources, such as lead, zinc, nickel and tin. The second plan also concentrated more upon the improvement of Soviet communications. Railways were largely double-tracked, and this sphere of activity produced many of the plan's 'show pieces', such as the Moscow–Volga and Volga–Don Canals and the palatial Moscow Metro.

Before the end of the second Five-Year Plan, the deteriorating international situation called for more and more state investment to be diverted to rearmament and began to interfere with the projections of the planners. Whereas armaments had consumed only 3.4% of total expenditure in 1933, the figure had swollen to 16.1% in 1936, and in 1940, the third year of the third plan, accounted for 32.6% of government investment.

Nevertheless, there can be little doubt that the pre-war Five-Year Plans achieved their primary aims. By 1940, Soviet society and the Soviet economy had been transformed, especially in the following respects.

● Production of industrial goods was roughly 2.6 times greater than in 1928.

● Some key industrial sectors, such as iron, oil and electricity, had grown at an even faster rate.

● The size of the urban work force (32% of the total working population), relative to the peasantry (47%), had increased rapidly.

● The gross national product of the Soviet Union had increased by nearly 12% between 1928 and 1937, far more rapidly than those of Britain (2.5%), Germany (2.6%) or the USA (1.3%).

● Unemployment had dwindled from about 1.7 million in 1929 to virtually zero.

The plans may be criticised for lack of realism, for administrative inefficiency, and for the human cost they entailed, yet the goal of making the Soviet Union an industrial power was undoubtedly achieved.

1. In which main respects did Russian industry advance during the first and second Five-Year Plans?

2. How convincing is the argument that the collectivisation of agriculture was an 'ideological triumph, but an economic disaster'?

3. 'On balance, the first two Five-Year Plans were successful.' Do you agree with this statement?

8.6 What was the impact of Soviet economic policy upon the industrial workers?

The regimentation of industrial labour

Quite apart from the obvious deprivations suffered by much of the peasantry in the course of collectivisation, the Five-Year Plans also involved considerable sacrifice for many industrial workers. The initial stage of industrialisation rode roughshod over the individual freedom of the Soviet worker. The government's more ambitious projects might involve the mobilisation of labour to remote areas, working with inadequate equipment and without facilities and comforts of their own, closely supervised by NKVD 'shock brigades'. Unrealistic production quotas usually meant the neglect of safety precautions and the risk of prosecution as a 'saboteur' or 'wrecker', if the targets were not met.

The replacement of Tomsky by N.M. Shvernik as head of Soviet Trade Unions (June 1929) turned these bodies into virtual government departments unresponsive to the interests of the individual workers. Similarly, the worker found him or herself hedged in by a whole new body of Soviet law. Absenteeism from work without due cause became an offence punishable by loss of job, food rations and housing (November 1932). The internal passport system of Tsarist days was reintroduced (December 1932) to prevent the drift of labour from areas of greatest need. It must be doubtful whether the gradual and irregular introduction of such facilities as subsidised canteen meals and free medical attention fully offset these losses.

Prices and wages

Tremendous difficulties confront the historian who tries to make precise judgements about industrial standards of living in this period. The task, writes Alec Nove in *An Economic History of the USSR* (1969), 'is rendered almost impossible not only by the existence of rationing, price differences and shortages, but also queues, declines in quality and neglect of consumer requirements'. There can be little doubt, however, that the first years of collectivisation were accompanied by a wave of rises in food prices. In 1933 alone, official Soviet figures showed rises of 80% in the cost of bread and eggs, and of 55% in the cost of butter. Alec Nove is uncompromising in his description of the years 1928–33 as witnessing 'the most precipitous decline in living standards known in recorded history'.

Subsequent years saw a steady improvement in levels of wages and of consumer goods production. Nevertheless, western and Soviet research has agreed that 'real' wages in 1937 were not more than 85% of the 1928 level, an indication of how low the level was in 1933. Such statistics, of course, often hide more immediate problems. While the number of industrial workers doubled in 1927–32, the living space created for them increased by only 16%. Thus 'overcrowding, shared kitchens, frayed nerves, limited sanitation and poorly maintained buildings became a way of life for a whole generation of Soviet people' (Martin McCauley, *The Soviet Union 1917–1991*, 1993).

The worsening international situation after 1938 ended the temporary trend towards better living standards. Once again, the production of consumer goods was limited and government control over the workforce was tightened. Renewed labour legislation in 1940 lengthened the working week from five days to six, and made absenteeism, which came to include lateness for work by more than 20 minutes, a criminal offence punishable now by imprisonment.

'Stakhanovite' movement: This took its name from a Donbas miner, Alexei Stakhanov. In September 1935 he achieved the (probably contrived) feat of cutting 14 times his quota of coal. Such workers stood to gain rewards in many forms, such as higher salaries, access to better housing and to scarce consumer goods.

1. In what ways did the living conditions of workers in Soviet industry change as a result of the Five-Year Plans?

2. 'The Soviet state gained but the Soviet people lost as a consequence of the economic policies pursued by Stalin in the period 1928–1945.' Discuss this statement.

The Stakhanovites

For a select few, the industrial drive could bring recognition and rewards. The abandonment in 1931 of earlier attempts to level wages paved the way for the privileged treatment of the most skilled and productive workers. This culminated in the '**Stakhanovite**' movement. For the average worker the 'Stakhanovites' were the cause of greater government pressure for increased production. Thus government decrees of 1936, 1938 and 1939 all demanded the raising of shift production quotas by as much as 50%. In general, it was not until the later 1950s, when the scars of war had been partly erased, that the Soviet government ceased to sacrifice the interests of the individual workers to those of the state.

8.7 Why did Stalin carry out far-reaching political purges in the 1930s?

Precedents for the purges

Having initiated an economic transformation of revolutionary proportions, Stalin set about the transformation of the Soviet Communist Party by a series of murderous and far-reaching purges (1934–38). In seeking to establish his motives we must first realise that purges in themselves were common in Soviet government. In addition to the purges carried out during Lenin's lifetime, 116,000 members had been expelled from the party in April 1929 on charges of 'passivity', 'lack of discipline', or as 'alien elements'. They were followed by another 800,000 in 1933. The Five-Year Plan also brought '**show trials**' in its wake, such as the Shakhti trial (1928) in which bourgeois mining specialists and foreign technicians were accused of sabotage. It is with some justification, therefore, that some historians refer to Soviet government between the wars as the 'permanent purge'. The 'Great Purge', like London's 'Great Plague', was merely an extreme example of a well-known phenomenon. It was striking in its extent, and in that its victims were not Whites or *kulaks*, but respected Communists and comrades of Lenin himself.

'**Show trials**': Trials held by the government for political purposes. They serve, not to establish the guilt or innocence of the accused, but to convey a propaganda message to the public and to foreign observers.

Motives for the purges

Stalin's precise motivation is not easy to establish. The official contemporary claim, that the party was infiltrated by 'Trotskyites', 'Zinovievites' and 'Bukharinites' who were all agents of international capitalism, can no longer be taken seriously. Nor does the claim that Stalin sought scapegoats for domestic economic problems explain the eventual scale of the purges. The

Isvestya (Russian – 'News'): Daily newspaper founded in 1918 as the official organ of the Soviet government.

most important factor was probably the growth of opposition within the party to Stalin's ruthless and divisive policies, especially to the pace and consequences of collectivisation. Trotsky wrote from exile in March 1933 that 'within the party and beyond, the slogan "Down with Stalin" is heard more and more widely'. N.M. Riutin was more explicit in 1932: 'The rights of the Party have been usurped by a tiny gang of unprincipled political intriguers. Stalin and his clique are destroying the communist cause.'

Stalin's political opponents still retained some influence. Bukharin for instance was now editor of *Isvestya*. Without doubt the emergence of Sergei Kirov, head of the party organisation in Leningrad, seemed to many to offer a capable and popular alternative to Stalin. The fact that five members of the ten-man Politburo in 1934 (Kirov, Kossyar, Kuibyshev, Ordzhonikidze and Rudzutak) died in various circumstances in the years of the purge, suggests that resistance to Stalin may even have been widespread in the top ranks of government. Nikita Khrushchev was probably close to the truth when he stated in his 'Secret Speech' of 1956 that Stalin had committed his excesses to boost and guarantee his own security, the continuation of his supremacy, and the supremacy of his policies within the Soviet Union.

The murder of Kirov

The course of the Great Purge may be divided into three stages. The first stage can be dated from 1 December 1934, when the leader of the Leningrad administration, Sergei Kirov, was assassinated at his office. Historians remain uncertain as to whether or not Kirov died at Stalin's orders. Official Soviet sources successively blamed the crime on foreign capitalists, on Soviet 'rightists', and on Trotskyites, while many western writers conclude that Stalin was directly responsible for the murder of a potential rival. The historian Isaac Deutscher, on the other hand, suggests in *Stalin: a Political Biography* (1966) that Stalin may have been genuinely shocked by the event, but turned it to his own purposes – much as the German Nazis had recently exploited the lucky stroke of the Reichstag fire (see Chapter 10).

A feature of this first stage was that the senior ranks of the party remained untouched. The 14 men executed for Kirov's murder were all minor figures and, although Kamenev and Zinoviev were imprisoned for 'opposition', they were not directly accused of the assassination. Nevertheless, the deaths at this time of Politburo member Valerian Kuibyshev (1935) and of the writer Maxim Gorky (1936) have never been satisfactorily explained, and may mark the beginning of the elimination of those who opposed Stalin's chosen path. In retrospect, this early stage also saw the establishment of the machinery and personnel necessary for the succeeding waves of purges. By appointing Andrei Zhdanov in Kirov's place in Leningrad, by placing Nikita Khrushchev at the head of the party in Moscow, and by subjecting the law courts to the influence of Andrei Vyshinsky as Chief Procurator, Stalin ensured reliable implementation of his orders in several vital areas of the administration.

The second stage was triggered in August 1936 by the arrest and execution of Kamenev, Zinoviev and 14 others. They were charged with plotting terrorist activities, including the death of Kirov, on behalf of the 'Trotskyite-Zinovievite Counter-Revolutionary Bloc'. Their trials produced several features soon to become familiar, notably the confessions of the accused and the implication in those confessions of other prominent figures. Why did these men confess? The application of torture, and of threats to their families, undoubtedly explains much. It has also been argued that many of the victims of the purges saw their deaths as a last

Andrei Zhdanov (1896–1948) Bolshevik from 1915 and member of the Central Committee in 1930. Secretary of Central Committee (1934). Head of Party in Leningrad	(1934–44) after murder of Kirov. Politburo member (1939). Prominent in establishment of Cominform (1947). Died in mysterious circumstance (31 August 1948).	**Andrei Vyshinsky (1883–1954)** Jurist and diplomat. Despite his initial sympathy for the Mensheviks, Vyshinsky enjoyed a brilliant judicial career under Stalin.	Procurator of the RSFSR (1931–33); Procurator of the USSR (1935–39). Thus conducted many of the 'show trials' during the purges. Commissar for Internal Affairs (1949–52).

service to a party to which they had dedicated their lives, and which they genuinely believed to be under attack. 'The loyalty of these men to the idea of The Party', writes historian Leonard Schapiro, 'was in the last resort the main reason for Stalin's victory.' The same writer also stresses the number of accused who refused to confess, and who therefore met their fate under more obscure circumstances.

Nevertheless, Stalin's control of events was not yet complete, as was demonstrated by the acquittal (September 1936) of Bukharin and Rykov on charges arising out of the earlier trials. This acquittal is often seen as the trigger of the third and greatest wave of purges. Among its first victims was Yagoda, head of the NKVD. One of the first tasks of his successor, Yezhov, was the preparation of renewed charges of treason and espionage against Bukharin and Rykov. The fact that the Commander-in-Chief of the Red Army, Marshal Tukhachevsky, and several other senior officers, were also tried and shot (June 1937) for plotting with Japan and Germany, indicated that the armed forces too were about to be 'cleansed'.

The last series of 'show trials' ran into 1938, involving the condemnation of 21 prominent Bolsheviks including Bukharin and Rykov. These, however, were merely the tip of the iceberg of suspicion and implication that involved the friends, families and subordinates of the accused. Suspicion reached into every area of Soviet life. No reliable figures as to the extent of the purges are possible, of course. It is extremely unlikely that the total number of deaths can be estimated at less than hundreds of thousands, while the total population of the USSR's penal camps (prisons) by 1940 has sometimes been set as high as 10 million.

1. Who were the victims of Stalin's political purges?

2. What reasons were given at the time, and what explanations have been given by later historians, for the political purges that Stalin carried out in the 1930s?

3. In what ways did the nature of Stalin's purges change as the 1930s progressed?

Did the political purges of the 1930s strengthen or weaken Stalin's regime?

The establishment of a Stalinist élite
When the great tide of political persecution receded in 1938, ending with the execution of Yezhov and other NKVD functionaries, two major changes in Soviet government were noticeable. Firstly, the political position of Stalin himself was almost unchallengeable. All possible sources of opposition, in the party, in the armed forces, among economic and political theorists, had been crushed. 'Every man in the Politburo,' wrote Leonard Schapiro, 'was a tried and proved follower of the leader, who could be relied upon to support him through every twist and turn of policy. Below the Politburo nothing counted.'

Secondly, the Soviet Communist Party, which had borne the brunt of the purges, was transformed. It was not just a matter of personnel, a substitution of Zhdanov, Khrushchev, Voroshilov and Molotov for Zinoviev, Kamenev, Bukharin and Rykov. Stalin had effectively destroyed the revolutionary generation of Russian communists. Of the 139 Central Committee members in 1934, over 90 had been shot. Of 1,961 delegates to the 17th Party Congress in the same year, 1,108 were arrested in the purges.

Foreign communists living in Russia also suffered heavily. The

Capitalists: Supporters of the economic system of capitalism, which is based on the theory that possession of capital or money leads to the making of profits through the power of investment.

Fascists: Supporters of a highly nationalistic political ideology, aiming to overthrow democracy and set up a dictatorship. Central to such groups is the heroic leader and the extensive use of propaganda.

Imperialists: Supporters of the belief that one nation should take over other areas as colonies or dependent territories.

Renegade communists: Supporters of communism who abandon the political beliefs that they used to have, and accept opposing or different beliefs.

1. What were the results of Stalin's purges for the government of the USSR?

2. 'There was no purpose behind the political purges of the 1930s other than the consolidation of Stalin's personal authority.' To what extent to you agree with this statement?

Hungarian revolutionary leader Béla Kun was among the NVKD's victims. Of Lenin's Politburo, only Stalin and Trotsky remained alive, the latter under sentence of death passed in his absence. Stalin knew, as Isaac Deutscher has explained, 'that the older generation of revolutionaries would always look upon him as a falsifier of first truths, and usurper. He now appealed to the young generation which knew little or nothing about the pristine ideas of Bolshevism and was unwilling to be bothered about them.'

In short, a generation of officials replaced a generation of revolutionaries. One should not overlook the fact, however, that this new generation supported their leader with enthusiasm and affection. Stalin did not rule the Soviet Union in the last 15 years of his life through terror alone, but enjoyed, as the historian David Christian stresses, 'the support, in particular, of younger party members, industrial managers, and government and police officials who benefited from the changes of the 1930s'.

The impact of the purges upon Soviet security
Apart from the human cost, the whole security of the Soviet Union was nearly undermined as the price of this transformation. The Red Army, in particular, paid a terrible price for arousing Stalin's mistrust. Three marshals out of five, and 13 army commanders out of 15 died. Ninety per cent of all Soviet generals, 80% of all colonels, and an estimated 30,000 officers below the rank of colonel lost their posts and often their lives. The difficulties experienced in the 'Winter War' with Finland in 1939–40 may be traced directly to the loss of so much military expertise in the purges.

The foreign relations of the Soviet Union were also bound to be adversely affected. Foreign powers were offered the alternatives of viewing the Soviet Union as a state riddled with treason, if the charges against purge victims were accurate, or as a power led by a madman if the charges were false. Lastly, the less tangible legacy of the purges may be traced in the insularity and siege mentality that characterised Soviet society for the next two generations. Such responses were natural in a society led to believe that it was under assault from **capitalists**, **fascists**, **imperialists** and **renegade communists** alike. This legacy also survived for years in 'a grotesque fear of initiative and responsibility in all grades of the administration' (Deutscher). This was a direct result of the personal peril that accompanied any position of responsibility during the years of Stalin's purges.

8.8 Did Stalinism achieve a social revolution within the USSR?

Historian Isaac Deutscher writes that 'Stalin offered the people a mixed diet of terror and illusion.' Alongside the terror of the purges, Stalin created the illusion of a true dawn of socialism represented by the formulation of a new Soviet constitution in 1936. The theoretical basis of the document was the assumption that victory over the *kulaks* had ended the decade and a half of class struggle in Russia and that a truly socialist order had now been constructed.

Government and the rights of the individual

By comparison with its predecessor, the 'Stalin Constitution' extended the jurisdiction of the central, federal government. Moscow now exercised control, through All-Union ministries, over all important areas of administration, such as defence and foreign affairs. This left responsibility for such relatively minor matters as elementary education to the constituent republics. This dominance was confirmed by Moscow's overall control of the budget, and by the pervasive influence of the Party. The chief legislative body of the USSR continued to be the Supreme Soviet, whose Presidium continued to exercise all major executive functions of the state.

As a further indication of the end of class warfare, clergymen, former Tsarist officials, and other 'class enemies', now enjoyed full civil rights again. Among the rights now guaranteed to Soviet citizens were:

- freedom of speech

- freedom of the press

- the rights to work, to rest and leisure

- the right to education

- the right to maintenance in old age and in sickness.

The constitution stated quite clearly that these rights existed only if exercised 'in conformity with the interests of the working people and in order to strengthen the socialist system'.

Soviet educational achievements

Overall, the educational achievement of the Soviet government between the wars was impressive. The introduction of compulsory primary education (July 1930) resulted in the doubling of the Soviet Union's primary school population, from nine million to 18 million, between 1920 and 1933. Meanwhile, the number of secondary pupils rose from 0.5 million (1922) to 3.5 million (1933). In 1941, the total school population of the USSR was around 35 million. The greatest achievement was the victory over the traditional peasant curse of illiteracy. This afflicted 75% of the population in 1917, but was rare by the outbreak of the Second World War, by which time 70,000 public libraries had opened in the Soviet Union.

Who received this education?

The drive to educate children of working-class origin to the exclusion of others was abandoned in the early 1930s to meet the demands of the Five-Year Plan. The proportion of women in higher education rose sharply, and by 1940, 58% of all higher education places (40% in engineering and 46% in agriculture) were held by females. The nationalities of the USSR, on the other hand, were not evenly represented. In the course of the 1930s, Russians, Ukrainians and Jews accounted for 80% of all the places in higher education.

The family

As social stability became the government's priority, the family began to revert to its traditional role. As an institution it had been under severe pressure in the 1920s, from revolutionary notions such as free love, free divorce and legalised abortions. It was also under pressure from the efforts of such party organisations as the Communist League of Youth (*Komsomol*), to divert the allegiance of the young. A fall in the official birth rate and a rise in crime figures prompted an official change of course. Decrees, such as that which established parental responsibility for the misdemeanours of their children (May 1935), and that which made abortion illegal except upon medical grounds (June 1936), reinstated the family as the basis of society. The role of the mother was also traditionalised by a system of rewards for child bearing. A mother of five children received the 'medal of motherhood', while the mother of ten became a 'mother heroine'.

Komsomol: Shortened form of Russian words meaning 'Communist League of Youth'. Youth organisation founded in 1917 (although the name only dates from 1926) with the aim of preparing youth for active membership of the Soviet Communist Party.

Religion and the state

The most serious opposition to the Bolsheviks in their attempts to create a new society had come from established religions, especially from the Orthodox Church. Marxists could not easily tolerate a philosophy that stressed the importance of the next world at the expense of material conditions in this one. On the other hand, the creation of martyrs was counter-productive. It was assumed that religious belief, being a feature of the old society, would lose all purpose as the new society took shape. The Soviet compromise was thus to strip the churches of all material possessions and of all state power, but to enshrine in successive constitutions the right to freedom of worship, alongside the right to have no religious beliefs at all.

Thus, in 1918, Church and state were formally separated. This involved the confiscation of all Church property, but allowed congregations to lease back buildings from the state, and to maintain priests for their worship. In 1921 public religious instruction was declared illegal for all citizens under 18 years of age, and churchmen were deprived of civil rights as 'non-productive workers'. After an initial period of resistance, which saw the imprisonment of religious leaders for anti-communist utterances, and for refusal to surrender Church property, the Orthodox Church and most other religious communities settled into a period of uneasy co-existence with the Soviet regime. Undoubtedly, the political influence of the Orthodox Church was destroyed. There is much evidence to suggest, however, that its spiritual influence survived, diminished but unbroken. The Orthodox Church received its reward for its patience during the war years of 1941–45, when the need for national unity caused the government to restore some of its former autonomy.

> 1. In what areas of Soviet life had Stalin's regime brought about the most important changes by the end of the 1930s?
>
> 2. The 'Stalin Constitution' of 1936 suggested that all Soviet citizens were now equal in a classless society. How true was this?

8.9 What factors guided Soviet foreign policy between the two world wars?

The theory of Communist foreign policy

In the immediate aftermath of the October/November Revolution, many Soviet theorists did not anticipate any problems in the formulation of foreign policy. In their view the Russian revolution was the forerunner of the general collapse of capitalism, and heralded the end of international tensions and disputes, which were the product of capitalist rivalries. Instead, in the next three years they witnessed the traumas of civil war and of foreign intervention. To this was added the total failure of those Communists who, in Germany and in Hungary, attempted to follow the Russian example. By the conclusion of the peace treaties in Paris, Russia's international situation was precarious. It was isolated, surrounded by hostile powers, and in great economic difficulties. Thus, the central aim of Soviet foreign policy between the wars was simple and singular: it was survival.

Two principal routes to survival suggested themselves in the 1920s. For Trotsky, and for many others on the left of the Bolshevik Party, the favoured foreign policy was collaboration with foreign revolutionaries to undermine the strength of the capitalist regimes. The consolidation of Stalin's power, however, saw an irreversible drift away from this internationalism. In foreign, as in domestic, policies, Stalin saw the best hope for Soviet survival in the development of material strength. Where normal co-existence with capitalist states served Soviet interests, he was quite willing to accept it.

Communist foreign policy in practice, 1921–1929

The fact remained that the Soviet Union had no natural allies among the European powers, no states with whom it had an overall community of interests. They remained capitalist powers and, according to the historian George Kennan in *Soviet Foreign Policy, 1917–1941* (1978), 'the enmity Stalin bore towards the western bourgeois world was no less fierce than that of Lenin'. Thus, Soviet contacts with Britain and with France remained ambiguous. The declaration of G.V. Chicherin, Commissar for Foreign Affairs (October 1921), that Russia was willing to recognise and honour Tsarist debts to other powers, helped to counteract initial hostility. In the years that followed, the Soviet government secured several important benefits from the victorious powers. A trade agreement was secured with Britain in March 1921, and Britain, France and Italy officially recognised the Soviet regime in 1924. Mutual suspicion about long-term motives, however, made closer relations impossible. The incident of the so-called 'Zinoviev Letter', purporting to contain instructions to British agitators for political and economic disruption (October 1924), showed the fragility of Soviet credibility. Although it was never proved genuine, many conservatives remained convinced that Russia still harboured ambitions for international revolution. Indeed, between 1927 and 1929, all official relations between Britain and the Soviet Union were severed.

The Treaty of Rapallo

Superficially, the greatest successes for Soviet diplomacy were scored in dealings with Germany. In the short term, the signature of the Treaty of Rapallo (April 1922) seemed a triumph. The establishment of full diplomatic relations with Germany ended Soviet isolation and ensured that Germany would drop claims for the repayment of Tsarist debts. The military and economic advice gained from Germany was invaluable in the post-revolutionary chaos. In the longer term, however, the appearance of triumph was deceptive. The Treaty of Rapallo provided a sharp shock to the allies, and their assumption that it concealed a deeper relationship between Germany and the Soviet Union soured Soviet relations with the west until 1941. Furthermore, Rapallo was not an alliance, but merely an arrangement useful to two isolated and apprehensive states. Russian relations with Germany continued to seesaw for a decade afterwards. Germany's apparent integration into the Versailles 'system', through the Locarno Pact and the Dawes Plan (see Chapter 11), could be interpreted in Moscow as evidence of growing capitalist solidarity. Conversely, incidents such as the failed communist rising in Germany in October 1923 served to renew fears of revolutionary internationalism.

Stalin's reaction to Nazism

Although, in retrospect, the rise of Adolf Hitler was a turning point in Soviet–German relations, it does not seem that Stalin was immediately aware of the fact. Contemporary Japanese expansion in China probably made it unclear whether the greater threat to Soviet territory lay in the west or in the east. **Nazism**, in the view of Soviet theorists, was not a new phenomenon. It was the inevitable death agony of capitalism caused by the recent economic crisis. To seek allies among the capitalist powers against a purely capitalist threat would thus be absurd. It is not clear at what point Stalin changed his view of Nazism. Several commentators have attached great importance to the non-aggression pact between Germany and Poland in January 1934. This suggested that, whatever the nature of Nazism, it was making common cause with Russia's enemies to threaten the domestic security of the Soviet Union.

Nazism: Shortened form of the German *Nationalsozialist*. The National Socialist Party in Germany, led by Adolf Hilter from 1920 and in power 1933–45 (see Chapter 10). The ideology and practice of Nazism includes racist nationalism and state control of the economy.

League of Nations: Association of self-governing states and dominions created as part of the 1919 Peace Treaty, 'in order to promote international co-operation and to achieve international peace and security'. The USA did not join, and the association's failure to deal effectively with outbreaks in Japan, Italy and Germany in the 1930s meant that it has lost its relevance by the outbreak of the Second World War. It was subsequently replaced by the United Nations.

1. What different ideas did Soviet leaders put forward in the 1920s about preserving the security of the Soviet Union?

2. How serious was the foreign threat to the Soviet Union in the 1920s and 1930s?

3. In what ways, if any, was Soviet foreign policy changed by the rise of Nazism in the 1930s?

Certainly 1934 saw a major change in the tactics of Soviet diplomacy. Firstly, the Soviet Union showed great interest once more in understandings with western states. It concluded mutual assistance pacts with Czechoslovakia and France (May 1935). In the course of these negotiations the USSR also undertook to enter the **League of Nations** (September 1934). Such moves probably had the dual motive of scaring Hitler into a revision of aggressive plans and ensuring that, if he did start a conflict, it would be fought on several fronts, and not concentrated against the USSR.

Lastly, the nature of Moscow's advice to foreign communist parties changed radically. For a decade they had been consistently instructed that socialists and social democrats were capitalist allies and false friends. Now they were advised and instructed to form 'popular front' alliances with those parties, in order to present more effective opposition to the real enemy, Fascism.

There can be little doubt that by 1935 the Soviet government had clearly identified the threat posed by Nazism. They had not, however, identified any reliable ally against that threat. It is hard to resist the conclusion, from a more detailed narrative of Soviet diplomacy in the late 1930s (see Chapter 11), that Stalin sought international security without any real conviction that it could be found anywhere other than in the industrial and military strength of the Soviet Union itself.

8.10 By what means did the Soviet government re-establish political control and economic stability after the Second World War?

The enormous triumph of the Soviet Union in defeating the Nazi invaders was obviously achieved at a huge cost. Nevertheless, it left the Soviet government stronger than it had ever been before. The prestige of the regime, and especially the personal prestige of Stalin himself, was at an unprecedented level. In effect, there was no challenge within the Soviet Union to Stalin's authority, or to the policies that he put forward. In addition, the advance of Soviet troops deep into the states of eastern Europe broke the ring of hostile powers that had surrounded the Soviet Union before the war, and gave it greater territorial security than it had ever enjoyed hitherto. To many, this seemed to provide the perfect opportunity for the liberalisation of Soviet politics, now that the regime was no longer under such direct threat. Instead of devising new policies, however, Stalin reacted to this victory by implementing the old ones with renewed energy and determination. The years between 1945 and 1953 came to constitute what the historian Martin McCauley has called the period of 'High Stalinism'.

In general, historians have viewed these final years of Stalin's rule in one of two ways. Contemporary commentators, and many since, have seen this as the high point of his career, as a period of 'mature dictatorship' in which Stalin at last exercised the kind of power to which he had always aspired. More recently, others have seen these final years as the ultimate proof of

Stalin's failure. In pursuing the same policies as before the war, despite the strengths of his personal position, Stalin demonstrated the misconceptions upon which his government was based. He continued to be driven by the same mistrust, by the same neurotic fears of enemies at home and abroad, as had haunted him in the 1930s. Such commentators see this as the main explanation for the rapid abandonment of so much of the structure of Stalinism in the weeks and months immediately after his death. The historian Chris Ward, in *Stalin's Russia* (1993), paints just such a picture of the final years of Stalinism. 'This was no self-confident tyrant in charge of a smoothly functioning totalitarian machine, but a sick old man, unpredictable, dangerous, lied to by terrified subordinates [and] presiding over a ramshackle bureaucracy.'

How effectively did the Soviet Union overcome the economic damage of the war?

The greatest and most immediate challenge facing the Soviet government was to overcome the material and economic damage that the war had inflicted upon the Soviet Union. The scale of the task can hardly be overstated.

- 70,000 villages in the occupied regions of the Soviet Union had been completely destroyed.

- 17 million head of cattle had been lost.

- 65,000 kilometres of railway track had been destroyed.

- 50% of all urban living space available in the pre-war years had now ceased to exist.

- An estimated 25 million Soviet citizens were homeless.

Labour shortages, of course, were acute. An estimated nine million Soviet citizens had died in combat or in prisoner of war camps. Many, many more had died at the hands of the occupying forces, so many that the Soviet commentator Dmitri Volkogonov (*Stalin, Triumph and Tragedy*, 1991) has put the total Soviet death roll as high as 26 million. With combat losses taking such a heavy toll upon the male population, women constituted 47% of the Soviet labour force in 1950. On the other hand, military victory provided some compensations for these disadvantages. The creation of a block of client states in eastern Europe, for instance (see Chapter 13), not only provided territorial security, but also created enormous opportunities for economic plunder. Alone among the victorious powers, the Soviet Union demanded huge **reparation payments** from Germany, amounting to $10,000 million (at 1938 values), and collected much of this by stripping industrial installations in Germany to transfer the materials to the USSR. Similar tactics were applied in Hungary, Romania and Bulgaria. In addition, the domestic labour force was enhanced by the contribution of two million German prisoners of war.

Reparation payments: Payments made by a defeated state to compensate the victorious state(s) for damage or expenses caused by the war.

The challenge of reconstruction was confronted by the Fourth Five-Year Plan, running from 1946 to 1950. A further Five-Year Plan operated from 1951 to 1955 to consolidate the process of recovery. Naturally the priority of these plans was to rectify the damage suffered by the Soviet economy during the war years and, in industrial terms, the plans achieved an enormous degree of success. In all major areas of the industrial economy, 1940 levels of production had not only been restored by 1950, but had been surpassed by some margin.

- Steel production stood at 27.3 million tons, compared to 18.3 million.

- Oil production was 37.9 million tons, compared to 31.1 million.

- National income was 61% higher than the pre-war level.

- Industrial wages were nearly twice the 1940 level.

These impressive statistics did not extend to the agrarian economy. Indeed, in terms of Soviet agriculture, the Fourth Five-Year Plan has been viewed by some historians as a missed opportunity. Martin McCauley emphasises, for example, in *The Soviet Union 1917–1991* (1993), that in the atmosphere of post-war euphoria, the opportunity existed to relax some of the pressures that had been applied to the Russian peasantry to force them into collectivisation in the first place. There was no need to return to the 1930s. Nevertheless, the Soviet government after 1945 did largely maintain the policy of building high industrial productivity upon the hardship of the peasants. Much of this pressure was exerted in order to rebuild the system of collective farms ravaged by the war. A decree of September 1946 ordered the return to the collective system of large quantities of livestock and of land that had slipped out of the control of the collective farms during the disruption caused by the fighting. Machinery, of course, was also in short supply and, with the Plan's primary emphasis placed upon the reconstruction of industry, the grain harvest of 1946 was less than half that of 1940. Even by 1950, grain production had still not reached the levels achieved immediately before the war.

Agricultural recovery was further handicapped by the adoption of some bizarre biological theories. Radical Soviet biologists – of whom T.D. Lysenko and V.R. Vilyams were the most notable – rejected orthodox theories of genetics. They replaced them with theories of their own which seemed to be more in line with socialist ideology. This new 'agrobiology' was also in line with the government's preference for 'Russian' thinking, free from humiliating intellectual reliance upon the West. The problem was that the theories did not work. Despite dangerous falls in production levels, Lysenko's theories remained in fashion until the 1960s and were also employed in communist China where, between 1959 and 1961, they contributed to a catastrophic famine.

The re-establishment of political authoritarianism

Several factors combined to ensure that the domestic political atmosphere would be as tense as it had been immediately before the war. In the first place, the armed conflict with Germany quickly gave way to the diplomatic confrontation with the western powers that became known as the Cold War (see Chapter 13). Once again the Soviet government had reason to regard with suspicion anyone who had recently been in contact with foreign political influences. This was particularly tragic for those who had been taken prisoner, or who had been compelled to perform forced labour in Germany during the war. Instead of liberation and a welcome return to their homeland, many of these found that they were regarded with extreme suspicion. Many were marched straight from their POW camps into the labour camps of the NKVD and about two million prisoners of war, aware of the fate that awaited them, had to be forcibly returned to the Soviet Union by the British and Americans who had 'liberated' them in Germany.

In addition, Stalin was as determined as ever to eliminate any threats to his personal authority which may have survived the war, or which might actually have been generated by the war. One such threat emanated from the army, which had covered itself with glory in the course of the conflict. Many men and women had been admitted to the ranks of the Party solely on the basis of wartime acts of bravery, and the need was felt now to restore the ideological integrity that had been diluted by this policy. An average of 100,000 expulsions from the Party took place each year between 1945 and Stalin's death in 1953. A greater potential threat to Stalin's position was posed by some of the military commanders who had played the most prominent roles in achieving victory. Stalin quickly tackled the direct political influence of such men by dissolving (September 1945) the State Defence Committee, predominantly staffed by leading military figures. The greatest of them all, Marshal Zhukov, defender of Leningrad and victor of Stalingrad, was severely criticised for 'awarding himself the laurels of principal victor'. There is even some evidence that plans were made to bring trumped-up treason charges against him but, in a rare example of restraint, Stalin was content to reduce Zhukov to a less prestigious military position.

In the final years of Stalin's life, nevertheless, there were clear signs that he was planning a further round of political purges, similar to those of the 1930s. The death of Andrei Zhdanov, the Party chief in Leningrad, was closely followed by the mysterious 'Leningrad Affair'. In 1949, all five Party secretaries in Leningrad, along with many other local officials, were arrested and subsequently executed. Recalling that the purges of the 1930s had begun with the murder of the Party chief in Leningrad, some historians have speculated that Zhdanov himself may have been a victim of Stalin's habitual mistrust. Elsewhere many prominent and established 'Stalinists', such as Molotov, Mikoyan and Khrushchev, were removed from office, although they returned to positions of influence shortly afterwards. The most ominous signs came in early 1953, with the announcement in the Soviet press that a plot had been discovered within the **Kremlin** itself. It was announced that doctors within the Kremlin medical centre were plotting, in the pay of the western powers, to murder leading Soviet politicians. Indeed, they were already responsible for the deaths of two such leaders: Zhdanov (died in 1948) and A.S. Shcherbakov, who had died suddenly in 1945. A new purge seemed to be in the offing but, within days, Stalin himself was dead. Almost immediately, it was admitted by his successors that the so-called 'Doctors' Plot' was a fabrication.

More serious and practical problems faced the Soviet government in imposing its authority upon the territories that had been added to the USSR in eastern Europe. This was particularly true in the Baltic territories of Estonia, Latvia and Lithuania – independent states from 1918 to 1939 and then, after a very brief Soviet occupation, subjected to German occupation until 1944. Now designated as republics of the Soviet Union, these territories scarcely welcomed their new status. To overcome their reluctance, the Soviet government pursued policies that were far harsher than the policies of 'russification' undertaken by the Tsarist government here and elsewhere 50 years earlier (see Chapter 2). Over 200,000 inhabitants of the three former states were deported and imprisoned immediately for the roles that they had played during the German occupation, and another wave of deportations in 1949 removed a further 150,000. What amounted to a partisan war of resistance took place in the territories between 1945 and 1952, with casualties running into thousands. To replace those who were deported, and to correct the political balance, Russian immigration took place on a similar scale. 180,000 Russians were settled in Estonia (1944–47) and 400,000 in Latvia (1945–59). By 1953 the proportion of native Latvians in the population of the Soviet republic stood at a mere 60%.

Kremlin: Location of the Soviet central government in Moscow.

The control of Soviet culture

The third major feature of Soviet policy during these years is perhaps a little more difficult to understand. In the course of the war the Soviet Union had been involved to an unprecedented degree in the politics of western Europe and of the USA. Its leaders, its intellectuals, and even many of the ordinary soldiers had come into contact with westerners more closely than at any stage in the 1920s and 1930s. Rather than creating a bridge between the USSR and the West, however, Stalin was determined to reverse this process, and to ensure that his own vision of Soviet ideology and culture would not be polluted by ideas imported from the West. Those who appeared to favour such ideas were branded 'cosmopolitan', and the government launched an unswerving programme of 'anti-cosmopolitanism'.

A key figure in the enforcement of this policy was Andrei Zhdanov, an increasingly powerful figure after the war until his death in 1948. In the view of Zhdanov and his accomplices 'servility towards everything foreign' became a prime cultural, and therefore political, crime. Writers, musicians and artists were strongly discouraged from taking a favourable attitude towards western culture, and from implying that major figures in Russian culture owed any great debt to the culture of western Europe. Conversely, the official line insisted upon the superiority of Russian culture, and upon its independence from outside influences. Magazines were closed down because of their editorial policies, and the careers of writers were wrecked, notably that of the poet Anna Akhmatova. Even established masters of Soviet culture, loaded with awards in the 1930s, were brought to account. The greatest Russian film-maker of the era, Sergei Eisenstein, died in disgrace because of 'ignorance of historical facts' that he had demonstrated in the last part of his great film 'Ivan the Terrible'. World famous composers, such as Shostakovich and Prokofiev, were similarly criticised and penalised by the Soviet government.

More dangerous and disturbing was the fact that this climate of intellectual isolation also extended to industry and science. We have already seen some of the consequences of its operation in the field of biology and crop-science. Martin McCauley has summarised the intellectual atmosphere that existed in the Soviet Union at this time. 'It was suddenly found that Russians had discovered everything worth discovering. Anything their geniuses had not hit upon was not worth knowing or was simply false. Relativity theory, quantum mechanics, genetics were nothing more than pseudo-sciences.'

8.11 In what respects did Stalin's successors moderate his policies in the years immediately after his death?

On 1 March 1953, Stalin suffered a massive stroke and died four days later. His death, like that of Lenin 30 years earlier, gave rise to genuine public grief, and to genuine popular concern that the state could barely expect to survive without the influence of its great leader. Unlike the death of Lenin, however, it did not lead to the creation of a 'cult of Stalin', to attempts to enshrine the leader's policies as a lasting ideology. On the contrary, certain elements of the Stalinist system were under attack within days of his death. Not only was it immediately announced that there was no substance to the 'Doctors' Plot', but an amnesty was quickly declared for many non-political prisoners serving shorter sentences in the prison camps. Over one million were released, including many close relatives of leading Soviet politicians. Between 1953 and 1955, over 10,000 prisoners were also released from prison camps as the result of appeals against illegal convictions.

Georgi Malenkov (1902–1988)
Communist Party official from early 1920s, and member of the Central Committee from 1941. Prime Minister of the USSR (1953–55), siding eventually with Khrushchev against Beria, and advocating economic reform. Ousted from power in 1957, he was assigned to manage a hydroelectric station in Kazakhstan.

Nikita Khrushchev (1894–1971)
Made General Secretary of the Communist Party of Soviet Union on Stalin's death in 1953. In the following power struggle Khrushchev first ousted Malenkov and then Bulganin to become Soviet leader. He created the Warsaw Pact (1955). Denounced Stalin at 20th Party Congress in 1956. Responsible for creating crises over Berlin (1958–61) and Cuba (1962), both foreign policy failures. Khrushchev was ousted from power in 1964 over failure of domestic agricultural reforms and foreign policy failures.

The most striking change to the Stalinist system lay in the fact that, after his death, political power was no longer concentrated solely in the hands of one man. Stalin had named no specific successor, and on the face of it the Soviet Union was heading for a period of collective leadership. Among the prominent figures who seemed likely to exercise this leadership were Georgi Malenkov, Vyacheslav Molotov and Nikita Khrushchev, all close associates of Stalin over the years, but Lavrenti Beria appeared to occupy the most powerful position. As Minister of Internal Affairs he enjoyed control over the secret police, and had been a key figure in the enforcement of Stalin's will during the last 15 years of the dictator's life. Paradoxically, Beria's powerful position proved to be his undoing. So clear was the possibility that he might resurrect the methods and the authority of Stalin that other prominent figures were quick to ally against him. He was arrested at a meeting of the Party Presidium (26 June 1953), falsely accused of spying and shot shortly afterwards. The execution of a further 30 NKVD men between 1953 and 1956 effectively ensured the control of the Party over the secret police. This control was emphasised by placing the secret police under the control of a newly-formed Committee of State Security (KGB). The executions also marked the end of this form of blood-letting within the USSR.

The power struggle that resulted in the eclipse of Malenkov and the triumph of Khrushchev was more complex. In this Malenkov was handicapped by his initial alignment with Beria, while Khrushchev, like Stalin in the 1920s, benefited from his position within the Politburo and his office as Secretary of the Party's Central Committee. From this power base he was able, like Stalin before him, to place supporters – men like Leonid Brezhnev – in positions of influence. Malenkov's misjudgement in backing the 'Anti-Party Group', members of the government who wanted to limit the authority of the Party, played directly into the hands of Khrushchev. By 1957 the latter had emerged as the dominant figure in Soviet politics, and the political career of Malenkov was effectively at an end.

A further parallel with the 1920s lay in the fact that the power struggle centred around different visions of the economic future of the USSR. Both candidates envisaged measures that would ease the burdens of the working population, and improve Soviet standards of living. Malenkov's proposed 'New Course' placed an unparalleled emphasis upon the production of consumer goods. Well-intentioned, it nevertheless cost him the support of those in charge of, or dependent upon heavy industry, angry at the prospect of state funds being channelled away from traditional areas of industrial and military production. Khrushchev had a different strategy for the creation of higher living standards. His 'Virgin Lands' programme, launched in February 1954, envisaged a substantial increase in food supplies, not by placing further pressure upon the peasantry, but by exploiting vast areas of land that had never previously been used for agriculture. Between 1954 and 1956, young Party members and members of *Komsomol* helped to bring 36 million hectares of such land, equivalent to the total farmland of Canada, under cultivation. During this period, 300,000 people emigrated to areas of western Siberia, Kazakhstan and the Caucasus. At last agricultural production showed significant improvement: the grain harvest in 1956 stood at 125 million tons, compared with 82.5 million tons three years earlier. The policy also constituted a very important change in the balance of the Soviet economy, and a major departure from the practices of the Stalinist economy. As David Christian has written, 'the Soviet countryside ceased to be an exploited colony of the Soviet town. Instead, it became a massive recipient of investment resources and subsidies.'

A range of other reforms also indicated that the emphases of the Soviet economic and social systems were shifting. Tuition fees for higher education were abandoned, pensions were increased and housing was given higher priority in economic planning. The control of the Soviet economy was significantly decentralised, with much initiative removed from the ministries in Moscow and delegated to local officials.

What was the significance of Khrushchev's 'secret speech'?

The impression that the Soviet government was moving away from the precepts of Stalin was sensationally confirmed in February 1956. In a closed session of the 20th Party Congress Nikita Khrushchev delivered what has become known as his 'secret speech'. In it, he accused Stalin of excessive ruthlessness in his political purges, testified to the innocence of many of the victims, played down Stalin's role in the victory over Germany, and denounced the development by Stalin of a **'cult of the personality'**. Particularly fierce criticism was reserved for Stalin's decision to purge the military leadership on the eve of war, and for his ignorance of agricultural realities within the Soviet Union.

'**Cult of personality**': A term used to describe a form of political leadership in which the virtues and achievements (real or invented) of the leader are allowed to obscure the political principles on which the regime is based.

To what extent did this 'secret speech' mark the abandonment of Stalinism? Critics have produced several lines of argument to claim that the speech was in part a calculated and self-serving attempt by Khrushchev to aid and consolidate his own rise to power. They emphasise that his criticism was restricted to the period between 1934 and 1953, and thus made no reference to forced collectivisation and industrialisation. These elements, the bases of the current Soviet society, continued to be praised as great achievements. The criticisms were also carefully phrased to discredit the absurdities of Stalinism, without discrediting the current politicians who had been instrumental in them. Equally, in the context of foreign policy, events in Hungary and Czechoslovakia over the next 15 years were to prove that the Soviet government had not departed from the priorities laid down by Stalin in 1945.

It is equally possible, however, to take a much more positive view of Khrushchev's actions. The evidence that has emerged since the collapse of the Soviet Union makes it clear that in delivering the 'secret speech' Khrushchev took a courageous and highly controversial step, the risks far outweighing the potential, personal advantages. His colleagues were extremely wary of the possible consequences of this rejection of Stalin's authority, of the danger of public disorder and of the questions that might be raised about their own roles in the crimes of the 1930s and 1940s. Fearful of the possible reaction to the speech, they insisted that it should not be delivered in the normal course of the Party Congress. Nor is it clear that Khrushchev cemented his own political position by taking this gamble. Many remained uneasy about the step that he had taken. Not only did it generate a short-term crisis in his leadership in 1957, it also gave rise to resentments and suspicions that followed him right up to his fall from power in 1964.

Perhaps the speech was driven, therefore, less by personal ambition than by a genuine conviction that Soviet government had to change direction. We have seen earlier that a number of historians are now inclined to view the Stalinist system as sterile and inefficient in its final years, and to believe that many Soviet politicians recognised it as such. From this point of view, traumatic as it was, the 'secret speech' was a necessary rite of passage, a bold step from one phase of Soviet history to the next. It is also difficult to deny that the speech was important in terms of political morality, and that in this respect too it marked an important development in Soviet government. By specifically condemning the worst excesses of Stalin's domestic rule, the speech distanced the Party from those excesses, and did much to ensure that they would not happen again. Khrushchev later claimed this as his most important achievement. When he himself was ejected from office he commented, 'could anyone have ever dreamed of telling Stalin that he no longer pleased us and that he should retire? He would have made mincemeat of us. Now everything is different. Fear has disappeared, and a dialogue is carried on among equals.'

8.12 *To what extent were Stalin's policies a logical continuation of the work of Lenin?*
A CASE STUDY IN HISTORICAL INTERPRETATION

Totalitarian: A political system in which there is only one political party, and this party controls everything and does not allow any opposition parties.

Objective historical assessment of Stalin's work is relatively new. As recently as 1983, Martin McCauley, in *Stalin and Stalinism*, could still write that 'Stalin has left an indelible mark on Soviet development, and his shadow extends to the present day. The system of rule he evolved is essentially intact in the USSR.' So fundamental was Stalin's contribution to the construction of the Soviet Union, and to the superpower confrontation of the Cold War (see Chapter 13), that historical judgements were frequently influenced by the author's political standpoint.

This was never truer than in the Soviet Union itself during Stalin's period in power. Exercising complete control over a **totalitarian** regime, Stalin and his successors could ensure that his work was represented in whatever light was most desirable. It was essential to maintain Stalin's claims that he had been among the closest revolutionary colleagues of Lenin, and that he was now the right person to continue the ideology of Marx and Lenin. Such a claim conferred an enormous degree of political credibility and moral authority upon his policies and decisions. As early as 1924 Stalin published a short work entitled *The Foundations of Leninism*, in which he ascribed many of his own ideas, including the principle of 'socialism in one country', to Lenin. The re-writing of the history of the revolution was seriously underway by 1934, and culminated in 1939 with the publication of the *Short Course of the History of the Russian Communist Party (Bolsheviks)*, which remained the official version of the Party's and the revolution's history for the next two decades.

Upon Stalin's death in 1953, an important shift took place in the official Soviet view of the former leader. His successors in power were ready to condemn Stalin's methods, but not to reject the end-product of his work, nor to dissociate it from the work and aims of Lenin. Stalin, it was now declared, had pursued the same fundamental aims as the original Bolsheviks, although he had erred in the 1930s by allowing the 'cult of personality' to develop and by taking savage and unwarranted actions against other Communists in the purges. This compromise was summarised by Nikita Khrushchev in a speech in 1957.

> 'It is, of course, a bad thing that Stalin launched into deviations and mistakes, which harmed our cause. But even when he committed mistakes and allowed the laws to be broken, he did that with the full conviction that he was defending the gains of the Revolution, the cause of socialism.'

In the last years of Soviet power, however, the rejection of 'Stalinism' became more explicit. In 1988 and 1989 the government of Mikhail Gorbachev went so far as to overturn the legal verdicts against many of those condemned as traitors and criminals during Stalin's purges.

Historians writing in western Europe, or in the USA, were not under direct political pressure of this kind, but many were impressed by the

'**Determinist**': Used in the study of history to indicate the belief that historical events are broadly determined by forces that cannot be significantly changed by the actions of individuals. In particular, it is used to describe the Marxist view that historical events are predominantly determined by economic forces.

impetus, and sometimes by the achievements, of the Soviet revolution as a whole. It seemed undeniable, in the 1960s and 1970s, that Soviet leaders between the world wars had engineered one of the most monumental achievements of the 20th century. Besides, where these western writers adopted a '**determinist**' view of history, it was impossible to believe that the forces that created the revolution in Russia could have been deflected or re-routed to any significant extent by the will of one man. E.H. Carr, the most prolific English writer on Soviet history, certainly wrote with such assumptions in mind. In *A History of Soviet Russia and The Russian Revolution from Lenin to Stalin* (1979), he concentrated less upon the personal rule of Stalin, and more upon the dynamic impetus of the original revolution in Russia. Far from diverting those revolutionary forces, Carr concluded, Stalin was borne along by them, and to an extent they dictated the policies that he pursued and the outcome of those policies, just as they had done in Lenin's case. The biographer of Stalin, Isaac Deutscher, placed his subject in the context of even wider historical forces. Rather than concentrating directly upon the revolution, Deutscher emphasised the continuities in Russian social, economic and political development, seeing factors in these that explain the particular course taken by Soviet socialism. Lenin and Stalin both worked in a context in which there was no tradition of democratic decision making, and in which the rigid enforcement of the orders of central government constituted the norm.

David Lane, in *Leninism: a Sociological Interpretation* (1981), and Alec Nove, in *An Economic History of the USSR* (1969), are two more leading authorities who have examined Stalin's work in the context of wider trends in Russian history. Both placed their emphasis upon the agricultural and industrial backwardness of post-revolutionary Russia, which confronted the Bolsheviks with the alternatives of drastic action or ultimate political failure. In the long term, they conclude, the responses of Lenin and Stalin to these challenges differed only in practical detail, and not in their ideological priorities.

An alternative 'school' of thought, however, insisted that the future of Russian communism could have been secured by other means, without the enormous human cost that Stalin's policies entailed. Stalin's fiercest political rival, Leon Trotsky, can be regarded as the founder of this 'school'. In exile from the Soviet Union, and in such works as *The Revolution Betrayed* (1937), Trotsky portrayed Stalin as a political and intellectual mediocrity, whose whole career in power constituted a betrayal of the principles of Marx and Lenin. The essential features of the 'Stalinist' system – the building of the party bureaucracy, the development of personal leadership, the whole concept of 'Socialism in one country' – ran contrary to the ideological lines laid down by the founders of Communism. The man responsible for this perversion of the revolution was, in Trotsky's phrase, the 'gravedigger of the revolution'.

In the last years of the Soviet regime it became safer to express such views within the USSR, and a similar interpretation was put forward there by Roy Medvedev, in *On Stalin and Stalinism* (1979). An orthodox Leninist, Medvedev condemned Stalin as a perverter of Leninist principles, and as the man responsible for diverting the revolution from its correct course. In the west, criticism of this kind has been expressed in the work of historian Robert Conquest (*The Great Terror: a Re-assessment*, 1990). While Conquest is no Marxist, and has no cause to commend the work of Lenin, he clearly recognises the need for industrialisation and modernisation in Russia after Lenin's death. He is convinced, however, that these goals could have been achieved without the brutality and repression of the 1930s. Above all, Conquest argues that what Stalin achieved was an increase in Soviet power, rather than an improvement in the living standards and the quality of life of Soviet citizens, which were presumably the prime objectives of Lenin's original revolution. These, he emphasises, were little better in 1953 than they had been on the eve of the First World War.

With the collapse of the Soviet system, it is no longer easy to view Stalin's excesses as justifiable steps along the road to 'inevitable' socialism. At the same time, the cooling of political emotions makes it easier to carry out a more objective comparison of the aims and methods of Lenin and Stalin. For many commentators, 'Leninism' and 'Stalinism' have much in common. The difference between the two men lay not in their aims or even in their methods, but simply in the circumstances that prevailed during their times in power. Indeed, in many respects, Lenin had already started out on the path that Stalin trod. It was Lenin, after all, who founded the political police, and who carried out the first purges of Party members. During the brief period of War Communism, Lenin's hostility towards the peasants, as a counter-revolutionary force, could be said to anticipate that of Stalin during collectivisation. It is also possible to blame Lenin for many of the problems that Stalin inherited. His opportunism in seizing power in 1917 forced the Bolsheviks to build communism in a society that had nothing like the industrial basis that Marx had considered a pre-requisite of any successful socialist revolution. In addition, Lenin was fundamentally wrong in assuming that the First World War would precipitate 'sister' revolutions across Europe. Lenin's early death then left his successors to find solutions to these problems. It might be convincingly argued that Stalin's policies and methods derived directly, not from Lenin's vision and insight, but from his mistakes.

Nevertheless, the fact remains that the nature of the Soviet Communist Party changed enormously between the death of Lenin and the outbreak of the Second World War. Although Lenin defined the Party in a relatively narrow way, and gave it an authoritarian role, it was the Party that directed policy in the early days of the revolution. The machinery of the Party was so important that Stalin had to gain control of it before he could secure his own authority. Over the next 15 years, however, Stalin changed the nature and role of the Party significantly. The purges did not only eliminate individual communists, they eradicated a type of communist politician. Lenin's colleagues were essentially 'western' thinkers, following the ideology of a western European thinker, and assuming that their revolution would be shared with the workers of western Europe. Stalin replaced them with men who knew nothing of western Europe, who were inward looking, exclusively concerned with the growth of Russia, and actively distrustful of socialist movements elsewhere in Europe. At the very least, this was a strategy so distinct from any that Lenin considered that it could hardly be regarded as 'Leninism'. Staffed by such men, the Party played little more than a bureaucratic role, and was clearly subordinated to Stalin's personal will. In Martin McCauley's words, 'the leader took over from the Party and collective wisdom was concentrated in him. He, and not the Party, became the guide and inspirer of the masses.'

1. What different views have been put forward by historians about the degree of continuity that existed between the work of Lenin and that of Stalin?

2. Why have historians in the Soviet Union and in the West reached so many different conclusions about the work of Stalin?

Source-based questions: Stalin's purges

Study Sources 1 and 2 below and then answer questions (a) to (c) which follow.

SOURCE 1

(A statement by Yuri Pyatakov on the political trials held in 1935. A leading Bolshevik, Pyatakov was later executed during the purges)

One cannot find the words fully to express one's indignation and disgust. These people have lost the last semblance of humanity. They must be destroyed like carrion that is polluting the pure, bracing air of the land of the Soviets; dangerous carrion which may cause the death of our leaders, and has already caused the death of one of the best people in the land, that wonderful comrade and leader, S.M. Kirov. Many of us, including myself, by our complacency and lack of vigilance, unconsciously helped these bandits to commit their black deeds.

SOURCE 2

(A report on the purges, made by Stalin to the Central Committee of the Communist Party in 1937)

The espionage-diversionist work of the Trotskyite agents of the Japanese-German secret police was a complete surprise to some of our comrades. Our Party comrades have not noticed that Trotskyism has ceased to be the political tendency in the working class that it was seven or eight years ago. Trotskyism has become a frenzied and unprincipled band of wreckers, spies and murderers, acting upon instructions from intelligence service organs of foreign states.

(a) Study Sources 1 and 2.

What explanations do the authors of these Sources give for the political purges of the 1930s? [5 marks]

(b) In what ways did the scope of these political purges expand in the course of the 1930s? [7 marks]

(c) What were the major effects of the political purges of the 1930s upon the domestic politics and foreign policy of the Soviet Union? [18 marks]

Source-based questions: The peasantry in Russia and the Soviet Union

(a) Study Source A.

From this Source and your own knowledge, explain the reference to 'the dictatorship of the proletariat'. [20 marks]

(b) Study Sources A, B and C.

Compare the attitudes towards the Russian peasantry expressed in these sources. [40 marks]

(c) Study all of the Sources.

Using all of these Sources and your own knowledge, examine the judgement that 'the problems posed by the peasantry for the Soviet government between 1918 and 1932 were political rather than economic'. [60 marks]

SOURCE A

A Soviet official reports on peasant attitudes in the countryside

The peasant uprisings develop because of widespread dissatisfaction on the part of small property-owners in the countryside with the dictatorship of the proletariat, which directs at them the cutting edge of implacable compulsion. The Soviet regime is identified with flying visits by commissars. In the countryside the Soviet regime is still predominantly military-administrative rather than economic in character. In the eyes of the peasants it is tyrannical and is not a system that, before all else, organises and ministers to the countryside itself.

Report sent to Lenin by the head of the CHEKA in Tambov province (20 July 1921)

SOURCE B

Stalin comments upon the lack of participation by peasants in the Soviet regime.

Our Party's growth in the countryside is terribly slow. I do not mean to say that it ought to grow by leaps and bounds, but the percentage of the peasantry that we have in the Party is, after all, very insignificant. Our Party is a workers' party. But it is also clear that without an alliance with the peasantry the dictatorship of the proletariat is impossible, that the Party must have a certain percentage of the best people among the peasantry in its ranks.

From a speech by Stalin delivered in 1927

SOURCE C

Stalin outlines his plans to transform the mentality of the peasantry through their employment on collective farms.

A great deal of work has still to be done to remould the peasant collective farmer, to set right his individualistic mentality and to transform him into a real working member of a socialist society. And the more rapidly the collective farms are provided with machines, the more rapidly this will be achieved. The greatest importance of the collective farms lies precisely in that they represent the principal base for the employment of machinery and tractors in agriculture, that they constitute the principal base for remoulding the peasant, for changing his mentality in the spirit of socialism.

From Stalin's speech 'Concerning Questions of Agrarian Policy in the USSR', December 1929

SOURCE D

Two comments by industrial workers upon the way in which food shortages affect the fulfilment of the industrial Five-Year Plan

i) The building of socialism is not done by Bolsheviks alone. It should not be forgotten that many millions of workers are participating in the building of socialism. A horse can drag seventy-five poods [a Russian measurement of weight], but its owner has loaded it with a hundred poods, and in addition he's fed it poorly. No matter how much he uses the whip, it still won't be able to move the cart. This is also true of the working class. They've loaded it with socialist competition, shock work, overfulfilling the industrial and financial plan. And what does the worker live on? One hundred and fifty grams of salted mutton, and soup without any of the usual additives, neither carrots, beets, flour nor salt pork. Mere dishwater.

ii) The press trumpets 'Give us coal, steel, iron, and so on and so forth. Shame on those who fail to fulfil the industrial and financial plan.' I say the following: 'Dear newspaper trumpeters, come and visit us in the Donbas. We'll treat you to a bottle of hot water, instead of tea, a hunk not of bread but of something incomprehensible, boiled water without sugar, and then, dear friend, kindly go and mine the coal quota.'

Letters written to Pravda *by a worker in Tula, and by a coal-miner in the Donbas region, September 1930*

OCR unit 2582

Source-based questions: Stalin and the Revolution

Study the following source material and then answer the questions which follow.

SOURCE A

Adapted from Nikita Khrushchev's 'secret speech', February 1956

Comrades: we must abolish the cult of the individual decisively, once and for all. It is necessary to condemn and to eradicate in a Bolshevik manner the cult of the individual as alien to Marxism-Leninism, and to fight inexorably against all attempts to bring back this practice in one form or another. In this connection we will be forced to do much work in order to correct the widely spread erroneous views connected with the cult of the individual in the sphere of history, philosophy, economy and other sciences, as well as in literature and the fine arts. We must restore completely the Leninist principles of Soviet socialist democracy, expressed in the Constitution of the Soviet Union, to fight wilfulness of individuals abusing their power. The evil caused by acts violating revolutionary socialist legality which have accumulated over a long period as a result of the negative influence of the cult of the individual must be completely corrected.

SOURCE B

From a speech by Stalin on the Five-Year Plan, 1931

It is sometimes asked whether it is not possible to slow down the tempo of industrialisation somewhat. No comrades, it is not possible. The tempo must not be reduced. On the contrary, we must increase it as much as is within our powers and possibilities. This is dictated to us by our obligations to the workers and peasants of the USSR. To slacken the tempo would mean falling behind. And those who fall behind get beaten. Old Russia suffered continual beatings because of her backwardness. We are fifty or a hundred years behind the advanced countries. We must make good this distance in ten years. Either we do it, or we shall be crushed.

SOURCE C

Adapted from Stalin: Triumph and Tragedy, *by Dmitri Volkogonov, published in 1991*

Stalinism took the primacy of the state over society to absurd limits. It was a system that depended upon a vast and powerful bureaucracy at all levels, and within this environment of political absolutism, the leader's decisions were increasingly divorced from economic reality. Much of what happened in the Soviet Union did so because freedom had been disregarded and scorned. One of the main aims of the October Revolution had been freedom, and yet its victory did not free the people. The deepest corruption of the Stalinist system lay in removing man as such from the centre of society's goals, and in replacing him with the state as a machine which magnified one man only.

SOURCE D

From Stalin, A Political Biography, *by Isaac Deutscher, published in 1966*

In 1945 Stalin stood in the full blaze of popular recognition and gratitude. These feelings were spontaneous, genuine, not engineered by official propagandists. Overworked slogans about the 'achievements of the Stalinist era' now conveyed fresh meaning not only to young people, but to sceptics and malcontents of the older generation. The nation was willing to forgive Stalin even his misdeeds and to retain in its memory only his better efforts. This new appreciation of Stalin's role did not spring only from afterthoughts born in the flush of victory. The truth was that the war could not have been won without the intensive industrialisation of Russia, and of her eastern provinces in particular. Nor could it have been won without the collectivisation of large numbers of farms.

(a) Use Source A and your own knowledge.

Explain what the author of Source A means by 'the cult of the individual'.   [5 marks]

(b) Compare Sources C and D and use your own knowledge.

How do Sources C and D differ in the conclusions that they draw about the historical importance of Stalin's policies?   [10 marks]

(c) Use Sources A, B, C and D and your own knowledge.

How convincing is the argument that Stalin's period in power served mainly to strengthen the Soviet state and to increase its chances of survival?   [15 marks]

9 Italy, 1870–1943

Key Issues

- *How stable and powerful was the Italian state in the 40 years before 1914?*

- *How and why did Italy make the transition from democracy to Fascism in the 1920s?*

- *What was the impact of Fascist rule upon Italian politics and society between 1922 and 1943?*

Framework of Events

1870	Incorporation of Rome into the Kingdom of Italy
1878	Death of Victor Emmanuel II; succession of Umberto I
1881	Treaty of Bardo establishes French protectorate over Tunisia and excludes Italian interests
1882	Triple Alliance between Italy, Germany and Austria
1887	Renewal of Triple Alliance. Introduction of protective tariffs. Massacre of Italian troops at Dogali in Abyssinia
1889	Italy claims protectorate over Abyssinia by Treaty of Ucciali
1896	Major defeat of Italian troops by Abyssinian forces at Adowa. Italy renounces claims to Tunis
1898	Bread riots in Milan suppressed with considerable loss of life. Franco–Italian tariff war ended by commercial treaty
1900	Assassination of King Umberto
1904	General strike in Italy, with violent incidents in Milan. Subsequent elections return a conservative majority
1911	Italy declares war on Turkey and annexes Libya
1912	Introduction of new electoral law by Giolitti
1914	Outbreak of First World War, in which Italy is initially neutral
1915	Italy enters First World War as ally of Britain and France
1919	(March) Formation of first Fascist 'combat group' by Mussolini (September) Seizure of Fiume by D'Annunzio
1922	Fascist 'March on Rome'
1923	Acerbo electoral law. Italian invasion of Corfu
1924	Murder of the socialist deputy, Matteotti
1925	Inauguration of 'battle for grain'

1926	Government decrees given the power of laws. Creation of special tribunal for political crimes. Rocco Law on Fascist syndicates is passed
1929	Conclusion of Lateran Accords between Italian state and Catholic Church
1934	First meetings between Hitler and Mussolini in Venice
1935	Invasion of Abyssinia
1936	Establishment of Rome–Berlin 'Axis'
1938	Introduction of anti-Semitic legislation in Italy. Mussolini deflects European conflict by his intercession in the Munich Conference
1939	Italian invasion of Albania. Conclusion of 'Pact of Steel' with Germany
1940	Italian declaration of war on France and Britain
1943	(July) Mussolini resigns.

Overview

Risorgimento (Italian – 'Resurgence'): The name given to the movement for Italian liberation and unification in the 19th century. It was based upon the assumption that Italy was, in effect, recovering the predominance that it had enjoyed in the days of the Roman Empire.

Piedmont: The former Italian kingdom that had led the causes of Italian unification and resistance to Austrian rule in Italy in the mid-19th century. Piedmont was one of the prosperous northern regions of Italy.

Idealists: People whose beliefs and behaviour are based on ideals.

Camillo, Conte di Cavour (1810–1861)
The most influential politician of the *Risorgimento*. Minister of Agriculture (1850), Minister of Finance (1850) and Prime Minister (1852–61) of the Kingdom of Piedmont. Cavour did much to recruit French assistance for Piedmont in its struggle against Austria, and engineered the attachment of Sicily, Naples and the Central Duchies to the united Italian state.

ITALY in 1870 was Europe's youngest state, its unification only completed that year by the occupation of Rome. It had been brought together by a combination of forces, not always working towards the same goal. The greatest statesman of the *Risorgimento*, Camillo di Cavour, had been primarily concerned to consolidate and to expand the authority of the Kingdom of **Piedmont** in northern Italy and to eliminate the challenge that Austria posed to it in those parts. Others desired the creation of a united Italian state, but even these differed over the nature of that united state. **Idealists** such as Giuseppe Mazzini and Giuseppe Garibaldi worked for a radical state, directed by principles of popular sovereignty. Others were happy to accept the leadership of a conservative monarchy, and placed their trust in King Victor Emmanuel II of Piedmont. The two programmes came together in 1860 when, grasping the opportunity provided by the defeat of Austria in 1859, Garibaldi seized the southern territories of Sicily and Naples. Realising that the only alternatives now were to accept a radical southern republic, or to embrace the principle of full unification, Cavour spent the last months of his life ensuring that Piedmontese authority and Piedmontese institutions would predominate in the south. He ensured that it would not be swamped there by the radicalism of Garibaldi. As a result, Cavour's successors were faced with the complex problems of bringing modern nationhood and economic prosperity to a state whose superficial unity was based upon neither of these elements.

It is important to bear this background in mind when assessing the degree of success achieved by Italian governments between 1870 and 1943. Similarly, you are likely to gain an imperfect understanding of Italian Fascism if it is placed too much in the context of inter-war Europe, rather than that of pre-1914 Italy. Dominated by the administrations of Francesco Crispi and Giovanni Giolitti, Italian governments between 1870 and 1914 sought to modernise Italy by many of the conventional methods used by other European regimes at this time: industrialisation; foreign expansion; colonial policy. Giolitti seriously sought a broader, firmer base of parliamentary support as the basis of strength for his government.

The impact of the First World War upon Italy was similar to that upon other European states: serious economic consequences for a national economy that had been quite unprepared for such strains in 1914. The conduct of the war also did much to discredit the regime, and the political ideals that had led Italy into such a conflict. What was unusual in the case of Italy was that these ideals were parliamentary and liberal, and it is a measure of the shallowness of their roots that such ideals should have been submerged in Italy, when they survived in post-war France or Britain. In Italy, however, the ineffectiveness of parliamentary politicians was blamed, with some justification, for the conduct of the war, and for Italy's failure to achieve the territorial gains for which it had entered the war in the first place.

Here, as elsewhere in Europe, the threat of communism provided an added impetus towards the establishment of a political movement that offered a tempting mixture of economic security, social conservatism, and national self-fulfilment. It should not surprise us that Benito Mussolini's Fascist movement gained such a rapid and complete hold over the rival political forces. Parliamentary democracy was weak and unpopular in any case. The traditional ruling élites merely tolerated rather than valued it, and the Catholic Church had opposed it from the outset. The alliance of Catholicism with Fascism in 1929 guaranteed Mussolini's political victory within Italy.

The fact remained that Mussolini and the Fascists now had to tackle the same problems that had confronted the united Italian state throughout its existence. In terms of domestic policy, it might be argued that Mussolini was more successful than his predecessors in one respect. By direct and ruthless political methods, he put an end to the divisions and in-fighting that had marked Italian politics throughout the previous century. His great talent, perhaps his only talent, was the acquisition and advertisement of power. Most limiting factors – such as parliament, other political parties and the monarchy itself – were effectively eliminated as real forces in Italian politics. Unfortunately, it is not clear that the Fascist regime made effective use of the power that it seized. Flashy and dramatic policies were put forward for economic modernisation and for the peaceful regulation of class relations, but these appear to have made only limited progress by the end of the 1930s. At that point, of course, what gains had been made were swept away in the disastrous wreckage of Fascist foreign policy.

Before and after the establishment of Fascist government, consistent themes can be found in Italian foreign policy. Seeking to guarantee security within Europe, but also to extend the prestige of the young Italian state, Italian diplomats pursued three conflicting courses between the 1880s and the 1930s.

- The anti-Austrian theme had its origins in the *Risorgimento*, and in the subsequent demands of nationalists for further territorial gains at Austria's expense.

- The contradictory anti-French theme was also based upon territorial claims, to Nice, Savoy and Corsica, but also upon colonial rivalry in North Africa.

- The Italian desire for colonial expansion provided the third theme, which greatly complicated its relationships with the western democracies, both before and after the First World War.

The difficulties that Italian diplomats experienced in choosing between these courses of action were illustrated by the abandonment of the Triple Alliance and the decision in 1915 to enter the First World War on the side of Britain and France. They can be seen again in the 1930s as Mussolini sought expansion at the same time as protecting himself against the consequences of Nazi expansion. The weak response of his British and French allies to German aggression, their apparent betrayal of Italy over Abyssinia, and the growing impression that Hitler would emerge as the dominant force in Europe, encouraged Italy once more to attach itself to what appeared to be the stronger side. In all important respects this turned out to be a terrible and fateful miscalculation, and the war that followed destroyed the Italian Fascist state. In the event, it was the fall of Italian Fascism in 1943, rather than its establishment in the 1920s, that proved to be a turning point in Italian history.

Italy in 1870

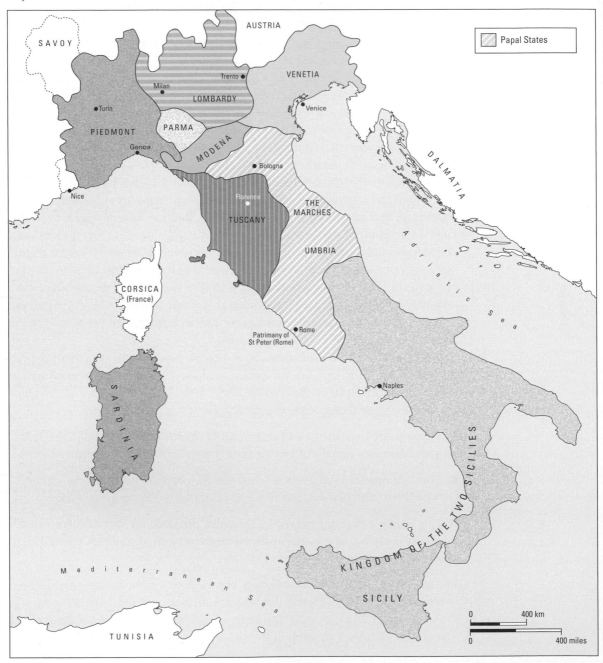

Italy's Prime Ministers, 1869–1943

J. Lanza	Dec. 1869 – July 1873
M. Minghetti	July 1873 – March 1876
A. Depretis	March 1876 – March 1878
B. Cairoli	March – Dec. 1878
A. Depretis	Dec. 1878 – July 1879
B. Cairoli	July 1879 – May 1881
A. Depretis	May 1881 – August 1887
F. Crispi	August 1887 – Feb. 1891
A. di Rudini	Feb. 1891 – May 1892
J. Giolitti	May–Dec. 1893
F. Crispi	Dec. 1893 – March 1896
A. di Rudini	March 1896 – June 1898
L. Pelloux	June 1898 – June 1900
G. Saracco	June 1900 – Feb. 1901
G. Zanardelli	Feb. 1901 – Nov. 1903
G. Giolitti	Nov. 1903 – March 1905
A. Fortis	March 1905 – Feb. 1906
S. de Sonnino	Feb.–May 1906
G. Giolitti	May 1906 – Dec. 1909
S. de Sonnino	Dec. 1909 – March 1910
L. Luzzatti	March 1910 – March 1911
G. Giolitti	March 1911 – March 1914
A. Salandra	March 1914 – June 1916
P. Boselli	June 1916 – Oct. 1917
V. Orlando	Oct. 1917 – June 1919
G. Giolitti	June 1919 – June 1920
L. Faeta	June 1920 – Feb. 1922
B. Mussolini	Feb. 1922 – July 1943

9.1 How strong was parliamentary government in Italy between 1871 and 1914?

The background and nature of Italian parliamentary government

Superficially, it might seem surprising that Fascism established itself so firmly in Italy, a state apparently founded throughout its 60 years' existence up to 1920 upon liberal parliamentary principles and upon the moderate concepts of constitutional monarchy. The fact becomes easier to understand when one analyses the historical background of Italian democracy, and appreciates the factors that distinguished it from other European varieties.

The Italian state and the Italian constitution at the end of the 19th century were direct results of the politics of the *Risorgimento*, the movement by which Italy was unified in the mid-century. Italy's constitution was, in effect, the limited constitution (*Il Statuto*) that had been granted in Piedmont in the course of the 1848 revolutions. Its strict qualifications, based upon property and upon literacy, limited the electorate in 1870 to 8% of adult males (2.2% of the total population). This left the Crown with extensive powers. The constitution specifically acknowledged the King as 'the supreme Head of State; he commands all the land and naval forces; he declares war, he makes treaties of peace, alliance, commerce, etc., informing parliament of them as soon as the interests and security of the State permit'. In support of the monarchy, the Italian army remained large and heavily financed, partly as a means of advertising Italy's 'great power' status, but also because of the high degree of internal unrest that characterised this stage of Italian history. A 'state of siege', involving martial law and the substitution of military courts for the normal civil courts, was declared on ten occasions between 1861 and 1922. 'Italy was not yet a peaceful enough country,' writes Martin Clark in *Modern Italy 1871–1982* (1984), 'to survive without periods of military law and military repression, [and] each military intervention lowered the prestige of the Crown and made national unity even more precarious.'

Parliamentary politics and 'Transformism'

In addition to, and perhaps as a result of, its limited powers, Italian parliamentary politics were characterised by a weak party system. Deputies represented the interests of their constituents, rather than the ideology of a

'**Transformism**' (*traformismo*): The practice first developed by Cavour of welding together large and unlikely coalitions in support of ministries. By granting favours to individuals or to the communities that they represented, ministers might 'transform' opponents into supporters and improve the prospects of their administration and of their legislative programmes.

Agostino Depretis (1813–1887)
A follower of Mazzini in his youth, Depretis later supported the form of Italian unity represented by Cavour and the Piedmontese monarchy. He entered the Italian parliament in 1873, and was Prime Minister on several occasions between 1876 and 1881. His administrations passed important reforms concerning education, taxation and the franchise, and engineered Italy's entry into the Triple Alliance (1882).

Francesco Crispi (1819–1901)
Active in revolt against the King of Naples in 1848, and subsequently in exile. A prominent member of Garibaldi's expedition to Sicily (1860) and an opponent of Piedmont's annexation of Sicily and Naples. He served as Minister of the Interior (1876 and 1877) and Prime Minister (1887–90, 1893–96). In foreign affairs his policy was pro-German, anti-French, and in favour of colonial expansion.

Giovanni Giolitti (1842–1928)
Minister of Finance under Crispi (1889–90). Minister of the Interior (1901–03). Prime Minister (1903–05, 1906–09, 1911–14). In his last years Giolitti was an opponent of Fascism, having failed to form an electoral alliance with Mussolini.

Syndicalists: Industrial workers belonging to the syndicalism movement which had as its objective the transfer of the means of production and distribution from their present owners to unions of workers for the benefit of the workers. The method generally favoured for this was the general strike.

---

political party, and were likely to lose their seats if they could not secure favours from ministers. Ministers had no firm basis of party loyalty to rely upon and were likely to lose office if they did not dispense favours to a sufficient number of deputies. Indeed, by 1892 Italy had experienced 28 different governments in its 32 years as a unified state. The result of such instability was '**Transformism**' (*traformismo*). The three longest-serving premiers of the period – Agostino Depretis, Francesco Crispi and Giovanni Giolitti – were all masters of the practice. Thus it eliminated true party spirit and ruled out any real clash of alternative party principles. It is easy to understand how parliamentary politics came to be regarded by many Italian observers as corrupt and self-interested, a far cry from the high principles that had motivated many of the heroes of the *Risorgimento*. All too often, it seemed, what was justified as a means to political stability became, in Denis Mack Smith's words, 'a common refuge where they laid aside their internal quarrels and joined in parcelling out power and jobbery'.

Although this form of administration had its legislative successes, Italy remained a country of enormous social and economic problems. In many respects Giolitti, in particular, was a worthy successor to Cavour, the greatest politician of the *Risorgimento*. Cavour had brought about substantial improvements in the economic prosperity of Piedmont, but he had often done so by political means that would have seemed extremely dubious in France or in Great Britain. Giolitti's administrations could also point to important successes, including a range of laws for agricultural improvement (1897–1906) and an important new electoral law (1912). The rate of illiteracy – one of Italy's most profound problems – was reduced to 11% in the north, although it remained as high as 90% in parts of southern Italy. Such was the cost of 'Transformism'.

Even relatively successful and stable ministries made little effort to reform the major problems of southern Italy – agricultural backwardness, the influence of the great landowners, the power of the Mafia in Sicily – largely because of the political difficulties that such policies would have entailed. The southern provinces remained backward and poverty-stricken, with 90% of Sicilian army recruits rejected as medically unfit. The sociologist L. Franchetti described in 1902 how 'peasant risings, which usually lead to bloodshed, are characteristic and normal events in the public life of the south', which was 'without any middle class, even without workers who are above the poverty level and possess a rudimentary education'.

It is worth noting that the problems of the south also had an impact upon the development of the more prosperous north. Illiterate and unskilled, the southern peasant was difficult to employ in any industrial capacity, and was highly unlikely to serve as a consumer of the north's industrial produce. The product of 'Transformism' was, in short, partial and unsatisfactory.

The enemies of Italian democracy

Beyond the inherent weaknesses of the Italian parliamentary system, two major groups regarded the liberal state with almost unrelieved hostility. One was the growing force of socialism, stimulated by the industrial growth of the north in the late 1880s and the early 1890s, and to a lesser extent by the poverty of agricultural workers. By the eve of the First World War, the socialists were capturing 25% of electoral votes. As an alternative to liberalism before the war it was weakened by its constant divisions, and by the preference of many of its leaders for reform rather than revolution. Its many offshoots, such as the anarchists, the **syndicalists** and the early Communist Party, represented a substantial force in opposition to the whole basis of parliamentary government.

Papacy: The position, power and authority of the Pope.

Boycott: Refusing to have any dealings with someone. The origins of the word 'boycott' lie in the nationalist agitation in Ireland in the late 1870s. During the depression of that time tenants were frequently evicted and the land taken over by others. Frequently, those who took over the land from evicted tenants were treated with hostility and given no help. This fate befell Captain Boycott in County Mayo.

'Irredentism': The view of Italian nationalists that, despite the achievements of the *Risorgimento*, certain Italian territories – such as Nice, Savoy, Dalmatia and Ilyria – remained 'unredeemed' (*irredenta*) from foreign control, and should be added to the united Italian state.

Gabriele D'Annunzio (1863–1938)
One of Italy's most prolific writers of the period, he turned to an active role in nationalist politics in the years before the First World War. He was a supporter of direct and heroic political action, in the tradition of Guiseppe Garibaldi (1807–1882). This culminated in his seizure of Fiume in the name of Italy (1919).

---

1. What were the main causes of political tension in Italy in the years between 1871 and 1914?

2. Why was it so difficult to establish a stable parliamentary democracy in Italy in the 40 years after unification?

Political tension was heightened in the 1890s by a bitter and protracted 'tariff war' with France. Protective tariffs adopted by France provoked Italian counter-measures, causing a reduction in Italian exports and ending many of the French loans that had recently helped to finance Italy's industrial expansion. Unemployment rose in northern industrial areas, and there were bread riots in Milan (May 1898). A railway strike in 1902 and a general strike in 1904 helped to increase the general sense of political tension. The plans of Luigi Pelloux's government in 1898 to introduce martial law and to govern by royal decree provided a foretaste of Fascist measures. The assassination of King Umberto in 1900 only added to the sense of crisis.

By this stage, however, socialism had over-played its hand, and the elections of 1904 saw a heavy defeat for the radical left. For much of the decade before the First World War, Italian governments underestimated this opposition from the left. Giolitti claimed in parliament that the socialists had 'put Marx in the attic' and believed that his new electoral law (1912) would provide a broad basis of support for his form of government. In effect, the law provided universal male suffrage for all over the age of 30, with the exception of illiterates who had avoided military service. He was wrong. At the national congress of the Italian socialist party in 1912, the radical left gained the upper hand. Among the younger generation of socialist leaders, such as Benito Mussolini, opposition to bourgeois parliamentary government became stronger than ever. The elections that took place in 1913 under the new electoral law left the foundations of Italian parliamentary government no more secure than they had ever been.

The second hostile force was the Catholic Church. On poor terms with Piedmont from the 1850s onwards, the Church's relations with united Italy were totally undermined by the Italian seizure of Rome in 1870. Deprived by the Franco–Prussian War of its main political allies – the French – the **Papacy** could do no more than protest and express hostility to all subsequent Italian governments. Until the turn of the century the Church instructed good Catholics to **boycott** elections, and scarcely any leading figure in national politics was a practising Catholic. When Pope Pius X officially relaxed this boycott in 1904, it was not out of any regard for the state, but from fear of the increasing influence of socialism. The Church, therefore, became the potential ally of the more conservative elements in the state. As such, it was equally likely to be an ally, active or passive, of the anti-Marxist forces that arose in the wake of the First World War.

In addition to these hostile elements, the government might also expect to encounter opposition from another source. In the years immediately before the First World War, parliamentary government increasingly came under attack from resurgent nationalism. Such emotions were fuelled by the conviction of many patriots that the work of unification remained incomplete. Such **'irredentism'** was provoked by failures in Italian colonial policy. The wounds caused by the defeat and humiliation at Adowa, in Abyssinia (1896), never really healed.

In the decade before 1914, Enrico Corradini stood at the head of a militant nationalist movement which roundly blamed the failures of Italian colonial and foreign policy upon the 'soft' influences of the parliamentary regime. He received influential support from one of Italy's most famous writers, Gabriele D'Annunzio, who advocated an assertive and chauvinistic foreign policy, preferably under a government with a single, all-powerful leader. The nationalist movement received great stimulus from the war of 1911–12 in which Italy secured Libya from Turkey, while the mismanagement and huge cost of the war went further to discredit the existing regime. The entry of Italy into the European war in 1915 naturally enhanced the influence of this movement to an extent unprecedented since the capture of Rome in 1870.

9.2 To what extent was the Italian economy modernised and strengthened between unification and the outbreak of the First World War?

The economic inheritance of the Kingdom of Italy

To a large extent, German unification was based upon previous economic growth and development, but this was not the case with Italy. The Italian economy in the 1870s remained predominantly agricultural, with more than 60% of the working population employed on the land. Wide variations existed between different regions in agricultural practice and in the prosperity that these produced, especially between the far north and the far south. The agrarian economy of the south continued to be dominated by the vast feudal estates of the nobility (*latifundia*). Often absent from their estates, these owners had little direct concern for productivity or innovation. Employment was seasonal, and poverty was the rule for most of the peasant labourers. Circumstances were usually more favourable in the more fertile north, yet even there productivity was low by the standards of western Europe. With some 40% of the crop consumed by the farmers themselves, even the domestic market was often insufficiently supplied. In industrial terms, too, Italy suffered from the limited nature of its resources. Italy's potential as an industrial and military power was limited by the fact that its iron and steel production was very low. Fuel supplies were limited, with coal still only 12% of Italy's imports in 1914. In the north, on the other hand, water power was abundant and permitted the development of electrical, chemical and textile production in the later years of the 19th century.

Political unification did not bring about any rapid improvement. The process of unification had resulted in an enormous government debt, and the first two decades of union coincided with an international economic slump. The northern regions benefited, to an extent, from their contact with the more prosperous economies of western Europe. The historian Martin Clark describes them as being brought 'into close and often brutal contact with the modern world'. However there was little prospect of greater investment or greater enterprise in the south. Successive governments intervened energetically, but with limited effect. Railway construction, in particular, was perceived as a priority. Historian S.B. Clough refers, in *The Economic History of Modern Italy* (1964), to 'an almost frantic effort on the part of the government to get railways built where they did not exist'. Important as these railways were, they were constructed a decade or more before any significant upturn took place in the Italian economy, and they cannot be regarded as a direct stimulus.

Steadily, too, the government abandoned the traditional free trade policies of the Cavour era. Major tariffs introduced in 1878 and 1887 transformed Italy into a protectionist state. 'Behind tariff walls,' Tom Kemp notes, in *Industrialisation in Nineteenth Century Europe* (1985), 'the state extended direct and indirect aid to the heavy industries which the nationalists associated with economic independence and political power.' Even so, by 1914, annual steel production was still less than a million tons, and coal production stood only at 11.5 million tons. Italian society in the decades after unification continued to demonstrate many of the familiar symptoms of widespread poverty. In 1881, over 38% of all Italian army conscripts were rejected on grounds of poor health, deformity or insufficient growth. Between 1884 and 1886, 50,000 deaths from cholera were recorded, 27,000 from typhoid in 1887, and 15,000 per year in the 1880s from malaria.

How important was industry in Italy by 1914?

Some historians have claimed that it was during the years 1896–1914 that Italy experienced its true economic revolution. The period saw the foundation of the *Banca d'Italia* (Bank of Italy) and a considerable upswing in industrial production, supported by improved economic conditions across Europe as a whole. Giolitti's governments hastened this process by increasing the number of government orders placed with Italian manufacturers, by taking Italian railways into government ownership, and by launching a further ambitious programme of railway building. In the 25 years before the outbreak of the First World War, national income rose by 50%, and industrial production rose to constitute 25% of total national output.

Italy also played an active part in the early development of the motor industry, particularly with the establishment of the Fiat company in 1899. The benefits of this development were felt exclusively in the north, where a triangle formed by Milan, Genoa and Turin possessed a substantial working population and a prosperous middle class. Strenuous government efforts in the decade before 1914 to encourage industrial development in the south foundered upon the familiar obstacles of unskilled labour, lack of local resources, and a backward system of communications.

A similar pattern is evident in Italian agriculture. With the introduction of protective tariffs, agricultural prices and production increased, from 3.6 million tons in the mid-1890s to 4.6 million in 1911–13, but these benefits were mainly limited to such northern regions as Piedmont, Lombardy and southern Veneto. In relative terms, the south slipped further behind, and served largely as a source of cheap labour. The relative inability of the Italian economy to absorb this labour was clearly demonstrated by the amount of emigration: by 1914, nearly 6 million Italians out of 41 million lived and worked abroad. It also seems that the economic growth evident around the turn of the century was running out of steam long before the coming of war in 1914. A rate of growth that had reached nearly 14% per year between 1896 and 1908 had declined to a mere 2% per year in the last years of peace.

By 1914 it was just possible to perceive Italy as a developed industrial power. Politically, especially in the foreign and colonial arenas, its leaders behaved as though it was already the equal of the other great powers. Yet Italy suffered from some distinct weaknesses. Its growth rate was uneven, and in decline by 1914. There was too great an emphasis upon heavy industry, and the inequality between the north and the south was as striking as ever. Poverty remained a serious and widespread problem. The Italian economy, like the economies of other states that had made a late start to the process of industrialisation – like that of Russia for instance – could be judged in two distinct ways in 1914. Some historians have stressed the progress that was made from unpromising origins. On the other hand, it was foolish to believe that Italy was truly the equal of the great industrial states of Europe, and that it could match them in such trials as the world war would provide. Many problems remained to be solved before Italy could play the role that its nationalist leaders designed and advocated for it.

1. In what respects had Italy modernised its industrial economy by 1914?

2. What evidence is there for and against the claim that Italy became a modern, industrialised state in the years between 1871 and 1914?

9.3 By what means and with what success did Italy seek great power status in the years 1870–1914?

In many respects the *Risorgimento* had proved to be a 'partial revolution'. The state that it produced was guaranteed neither security nor self-respect by a process of unification that had depended so heavily upon the actions of other European powers. The state of mind of Italian patriots in the early years of unity has been neatly summarised by Martin Clark: 'There was a general feeling of disillusionment in post-1870 Italy. Rome had been won, but ingloriously; the *Risorgimento* had succeeded, but after too many lost battles; Italy had a large army, but other Europeans did not take it seriously.'

Italian colonial ambitions

Italy's colonial policy in the late 19th century had much in common with that of France at the same period. Both were dictated by the realities of the country's status in European politics. Just as the alternative for France was 'revenge' against Germany, the call from Italian nationalists was for a continuation of unification, for a bid to gain such territories as the South Tyrol, Istria or Dalmatia, which still lay in Austrian hands. With the prospect of further French support declining, and with the consistent improvement in Austro–German relations, such an 'irredentist' policy was scarcely possible. Italian prestige would have to be sought elsewhere.

Italy's colonial ambitions centred upon Africa, and particularly upon territories in the north and east of that continent. Ten years of involvement in Abyssinia and Eritrea, however, brought little success. The occupation of the port of Massawa on the Red Sea (1885) was undermined by the massacre of 500 Italian troops at Dogali (1887). The succession of the Emperor Menelik (1888) seemed to bring a pro-Italian ruler to the Abyssinian throne, but Menelik's sympathy for Italian interests evaporated as those interests extended deeper into Abyssinia and as a protectorate was established over Eritrea. Although Italian politicians disagreed about the value of colonial policy, Crispi's administration clearly regarded colonial commitment as the best way to distract attention from internal political divisions. His decision to intensify campaigns in Abyssinia led to disaster and humiliation when an Italian force was heavily defeated by Menelik at Adowa (1 March 1896). It was the only example in the 19th century of an African state gaining a definitive victory over a would-be coloniser, and had a predictable impact upon nationalist feelings within Italy. The most direct political result was the resignation of Crispi.

Italy achieved only a little more success in North Africa. Attempts to establish influence over Tunisia, only a relatively short distance from Sicily, clashed directly with those of France. Lacking the diplomatic 'muscle' to compete effectively, Italy had acknowledged that region as part of the French 'sphere of influence' by 1881. There was some later compensation, however, in the form of an agreement (1902) whereby France and Italy recognised the respective interests of each state in Morocco and in Libya, nominally a Turkish possession. When France began to implement its claims to Morocco (1911), it was time for Italy to take similar action in Libya. Strong financial and nationalist interests were also at work in this initiative. At first, the Libyan campaign proved no easier than that in Abyssinia, but the outbreak of war in the Balkans put Turkey in an impossible position, and by the end of 1912 it had cut its losses, leaving Libya under Italian control.

Italy's European diplomacy

In terms of European diplomacy, Italy found itself in an ambiguous position, which guaranteed its security, but left it with little scope for the pursuit of European territorial ambitions. In the course of the *Risorgimento* the keystone of Piedmontese/Italian foreign policy had been friendship with Britain and France. After 1870, French friendship was of relatively little value in the light of France's weakness and isolation. Besides, many factors had arisen since 1859 to undermine the good relations between the states.

● The transfer of Nice and Savoy to France in 1860 was never fully accepted.

- French and Italian ambitions in the western Mediterranean were incompatible.

- It came as a great blow to Italian prestige when, in 1881, the French occupied Tunisia, where Italian settlers hugely outnumbered French.

Happily, Italy found itself courted by other powers. Good relations with the new and powerful German state had begun with military co-operation in 1866, and Bismarck proved eager to maintain those relations, not least as a means of guaranteeing the isolation of France. As Germany improved its relations with Austria, Italy found it easier to mend its own relations with that traditional enemy. This was the logic behind the Triple Alliance that was concluded between the three states in May 1882.

Yet Italian attitudes to the Triple Alliance remained ambiguous. Conservative politicians relished this identification with the monarchical governments of Germany and Austria, while nationalists regretted that the treaty made it harder to squeeze further territorial concessions out of Austria. Besides, Italy had relatively little need of the guarantees that the treaty provided against French aggression. With the resolution of Franco–Italian disputes over North Africa, and with the steady extension of Austrian influence in the Balkans, it became harder to see just what advantages Italy derived from the Triple Alliance. Although it remained the official basis of Italian diplomacy on the eve of the First World War, such factors had eroded Italy's enthusiasm and commitment. Thus, upon the outbreak of war in 1914, Italy not only refused to act upon the terms of the Triple Alliance, but concluded an agreement with France. Under its terms, Italy undertook to declare war on its allies in return for a guarantee that it would gain Trento, the South Tyrol, Trieste and Dalmatia at the end of the conflict. It was a remarkable piece of political opportunism and in the light of the military and diplomatic failures that followed (see Chapter 6), was likely to discredit the politicians who took such a gamble.

1. In what regions and for what reasons did Italy seek colonial possessions in the decades after 1914?

2. To what extent did Italian foreign policy between 1871 and 1914 achieve its objectives?

9.4 What factors contributed to the rise of Italian Fascism in the years after the First World War?

The birth of the Fascist movement

The immediate post-war period held considerable promise for an ambitious politician. The frustrations of the peace treaty, the economic difficulties that produced two million Italian unemployed by November 1919, and the subsequent disillusionment of many ex-servicemen, reduced the prestige of

Mussolini with Blackshirt leaders on the March of Rome, 28 October 1922

Benito Mussolini (1883–1945)

Born (29 July 1883) the son of a blacksmith, near Forli in the Romagna. Mussolini's hostility towards bourgeois society may be traced to his hard childhood, and to the enthusiastic, republican socialism of his father. In his turbulent, violent personality as a young man may be seen the beginnings of the vigorous, often incoherent, gestures that later characterised so much of Fascist policy. The young Mussolini was expelled four times from his various schools for indiscipline and violence. His biographer, Denis Mack Smith, has concluded that the innate streak of violence in his character was of as great importance in his development as any of the political philosophers by whom he later claimed to have been influenced.

Failing to find satisfaction or success in his brief career as a teacher, Mussolini was soon set upon the road of political agitation, organisation and journalism. His success as editor of a provincial socialist journal (1909–12) led to national recognition and appointment to the editorship of Italy's primary socialist newspaper *Avanti!* (Forward!) in November 1912. Some of the future bases of Fascism can be discerned in his views during this period.

Mussolini was expelled from the socialist movement in 1914 for advocating Italian intervention in the First World War. In 1919, he founded the Fascist Movement, which was backed by many landowners and industrialists and by the heads of the army and police. He became Prime Minister (October 1922) as head of a coalition government. In 1925, he assumed dictatorial powers, and banned all opposition parties. His Blackshirt followers (see photo) were the forerunners of Hitler's Brownshirts (see Chapter 10). During the Second World War Mussolini's prestige was destroyed by defeats in Africa and Greece, the allied invasion of Sicily and discontent at home. He was compelled to resign (July 1943) by his own Fascist Grand Council. Mussolini was freed from prison by German parachutists two months later and set up a Fascist government in north Italy. He and his mistress, Clara Petacci, were captured while heading for the Swiss border, and shot.

Fascio: A bundle of rods with an axe at its centre. It was a symbol of unity and strength.

Lictors: Officials in ancient Rome who accompanied and protected the magistrates of the city, and who bore the symbols of the magistrates' office.

the liberal regime to a new low ebb. It was under these circumstances, in March 1919, that Benito Mussolini formed the first 'combat group' (*Fascio di combattimento*) in Milan. The name of the group, and of the movement, was derived from the *fascio*, the insignia of the *lictors* of ancient Rome. Initially, the programme proposed by these 'Fascists' showed the continuing influence of left-wing politics, and especially of French syndicalism. They proposed:

● the abolition of the monarchy and the establishment of a republic;

● the decentralisation of government;

● the abolition of conscription;

● the closure of all banks and of the stock exchange;

● profit sharing and management participation by the workers;

● the seizure of Church lands.

For Mussolini, however, as Denis Mack Smith states, in *Mussolini* (1981), 'Fascism was not a system of immutable [unchanging] beliefs but a path to political power'. When the party only polled 4,795 votes in the Milan elections of November 1919, Fascist policy began a steady movement to the right.

Although the rise of Fascism in Italy had deeper and more complex causes than Benito Mussolini, his personality had a profound influence upon the form taken by the movement (see profile). Identified with the left wing of Italian socialism, Mussolini was a violent critic of parliamentary government, and of those socialists who sought parliamentary seats. His solutions to the social and economic problems of contemporary Italy were revolutionary, and he was vitriolic in his attacks upon socialists who sought change by moderate reform.

The outbreak of war brought about a radical change in Mussolini's political stance. By condemning Italian neutrality in a sensational editorial in *Avanti!* (18 October 1914), Mussolini not only flew in the face of accepted socialist policy, but effectively turned his back on the party for ever. His change of heart has been interpreted in a variety of fashions. His former socialist colleagues, in their sense of betrayal, brought charges of foreign bribery. Other critics have seen it as an acknowledgement that, with his recent election defeat in Forli (October 1913) and the collapse of the revolutionary 'Red Week' riots (June 1914), the political future of socialism seemed bleak. His biographer Christopher Hibbert has been more generous in his view (1962) that Mussolini was attracted to intervention in the war by the anticipation that it would bring nearer the revolutionary upheaval for which he hoped. Although Fascist historians later invented a number of heroic exploits for Mussolini, his military service seems to have been uneventful, apart from an injury received during a training exercise. When he returned to civilian life and journalism, the editorials of his new journal *Il Popolo d'Italia* (The Italian People) were distinguished by views easily recognisable as Fascism. Prominent among them were the demand that post-war Italy should be governed by those who had fought for the country, and the resentment that Italy should be cheated of such fruits of victory as Fiume (see below).

The nature of Fascist support

From 1920, Fascist policy stressed the twin themes of nationalism and anti-Bolshevism. Fervent support for D'Annunzio in his spectacular, illegal seizure of the city of Fiume for Italy (September 1919) seemed almost to annex him to the Fascist cause. Meanwhile, the anti-communist violence of the Fascist action squads (*Squadristi*) and the new party line in favour of free enterprise went a long way towards reassuring the middle classes. The change of direction was a substantial success. Big business was eager to subsidise this valuable anti-communist force, and substantial contributions from such sources as the Fiat motor company, the Pirelli tyre company and the Italian Banking Association put the Fascists on a firmer financial footing than most of their rivals. By late 1921 the party claimed 320,000 members, of whom 18,000 were landowners, 14,000 were small-scale traders, and 4,000 were industrialists. However, many of the party's members were peasants (36,000) or members of the urban working classes (23,000) seeking a refuge from what they saw as the twin evils of capitalism and socialism.

Squadristi: The paramilitary (see page 266) units used by the Fascist Party in Italy to terrorise political opponents.

The spectacular growth of this Fascist faction made it a natural candidate for a place in one of the government's 'Transformist' coalitions. Giolitti had already aided the growth of Fascism by turning a blind eye to the excesses of the *Squadristi* when, in May 1921, he accepted Mussolini's offer of an electoral pact. As part of a government alliance, the Fascists won 35 parliamentary seats in the elections of that year. This was a small start in a house of 535 seats, but it gave Mussolini and his fellow deputies a new authority, respectability and a valuable freedom from arrest.

What were Mussolini's tactics as leader of the Fascist movement?

It was neither probable nor desirable to many in the Fascist movement that they should come to power by these parliamentary means. Mussolini himself found his style of public speaking ill-suited to parliamentary debate, while other Fascist deputies showed their contempt for the institution by brandishing pistols in the chamber and assaulting socialist deputies.

In the event, the crisis in Italian politics continued to operate to the advantage of the Fascists. A general strike called by the socialists in August 1922 gave the *Squadristi* an opportunity to pose as the country's sole protection against the imminent 'red' threat. The strike, badly organised and ill led, collapsed within 24 hours, creating the impression that the nation had been saved while the liberal regime stood helplessly by. At the same time as formulating a plan for the seizure of strategic points in Milan and other major cities, and for a subsequent march on Rome, Mussolini sought to reassure influential sectors of Italian opinion of Fascism's regard for the monarchy and for economic liberalism.

The *coup d'état* began on 27 October 1922. In many cities, the active or passive support of local government guaranteed success, but it seemed unlikely that the 26,000 Fascists converging on Rome could succeed against the regular troops in their path. Success was, however, guaranteed by the surprising refusal of King Victor Emmanuel III to sign his Prime Minister's decree of martial law. Historians seeking to explain this fateful timidity have variously stressed the degree of pro-Fascist feeling in court circles, and the effect of veiled Fascist threats to replace the king with the Duke of Aosta. 'Temperamentally,' wrote Denis Mack Smith, the king 'was drawn to anyone who would take firm decisions and control domestic unrest.' Putting aside any doubts, Mussolini exploited his position of strength and had, by 29 October, received a royal summons to form a ministry as the youngest Prime Minister in Italian history.

The official historians of Fascism portrayed the events of October 1922 as a glorious national revolution. More recently, it has become fashionable to belittle the Fascist rising and to stress the surrender of the regime through panic, weakness or self-interest. The truth lies between the two extremes. The insurrection was, indeed, a bold stroke, a substantial risk by its leaders. It was carefully and intelligently prepared. On the other hand, it was resistible. Fascism owed its triumph ultimately, not to Fascists alone, but to the mass of conservatives, businessmen, army officers, traders and peasants who saw Mussolini as the alternative to anarchy.

By what means and with what success did the Fascist dictatorship establish its control over the Italian state?

The dismantling of parliamentarianism
It was never likely that the Fascist leadership would be content merely to capture the machinery of the liberal state. After an initially conciliatory attitude to other non-socialist parties, the first years in power were dedicated to the steady destruction of parliamentarianism in Italy. The success of the party's *Squadristi* in the early years of the movement was such that Mussolini now transformed them (December 1922) into an official **paramilitary** body called the Volunteer Militia for National Security. Their wholesale use of violence and intimidation was to be a prominent feature of Italian elections in the 1920s.

The new Prime Minister also had more subtle means at his disposal. A new electoral law was drafted by G. Acerbo (July 1923) which aimed to transform Fascism's minority status. It proposed that any party gaining more votes than any of its rivals, providing that it gained at least 25% of the total, would be entitled to two-thirds of the seats in the assembly. This, it was claimed, was in the interests of political stability. It should be noted that this law, like others in the early days of Mussolini's power, was passed with the help of liberal votes.

This form of parliamentary government limped on for five years, until a further electoral law (September 1928) decreed that the whole composition of parliament should be determined by the Fascist Grand Council, headed by Mussolini. This body would formulate a list of 400 nominees, which the electorate would be invited to accept or reject *en masse*. Given the means of intimidation in the government's hands, it is perhaps surprising that as many as 136,000 voters rejected the list in 1929. By 1934, however, the number of rejections had fallen to 15,000.

---

1. In what ways and for what reasons did Mussolini's political views become more right wing between 1910 and the early 1920s?

2. Which sections of the Italian population were most attracted to Fascism in the early 1920s, and for what reasons?

Paramilitary: An organisation which is similar to an army but is not the official army of the country. This term is often used to describe guerrilla outfits.

Matteotti's murder and the 'Aventine Secession'

*1. What steps did the
Fascists take in the
1920s to weaken the
authority of parliament
in the Italian political
system?*

*2. What events
transformed the
Fascists so rapidly
from an extreme
political faction to a
party of government?*

The Acerbo electoral law and the violence of the 1924 elections also began the decisive clash with the Fascist Party's major rivals, the socialists. A socialist deputy, Giacomo Matteotti, showed great courage in his open defiance and criticism of Fascist methods. This led to his kidnap and subsequent murder by Fascist thugs. Whether or not Mussolini had directly encouraged or ordered the crime, he clearly bore the moral responsibility for it, and his political position became extremely vulnerable. Two factors aided his survival. Once again, the political tactics of the socialists were naïve. Their reaction to the death of Matteotti was to leave parliament in protest. This action became known as the 'Aventine Secession', in remembrance of an incident in ancient Roman history. Their eloquent gesture merely left the Fascists in fuller control. Secondly, King Victor Emmanuel, the only man with the constitutional power to dismiss Mussolini, once again shirked a hard decision and accepted the argument of force.

Initially shaken by the Matteotti crisis, Mussolini now seemed to exploit the new-found strength of his position. The historian F.W. Deakin has stressed, in *The Brutal Friendship* (1962), the important role in this played by subordinates. Of special importance was the work of the new party secretary, Roberto Farinacci, in overhauling and centralising the party machinery for the tasks of national government. The first months of 1925 saw a miniature 'reign of terror' characterised by house searches, closures of hostile newspapers, harassment of political opponents and constant attacks upon freedom of association and of speech. In November, a plot against Mussolini's life by a former socialist deputy, Zaniboni, provided the pretext for the official suppression of the socialist party. A series of decrees to strengthen the powers of provincial Fascist officers, a formal decree (October 1926) banning all other political parties and the formation (September 1926) of a secret police force, the OVRA, completed the apparatus of political dictatorship.

9.5 Did the Fascist regime achieve a political revolution in Italy?

The years 1923–25 formed a period of ambiguous policy statements designed to attract the widest possible support, and of negative assaults upon existing institutions. Only slowly did the outline of a Fascist 'new order' emerge. In theory, this 'new order' owed much to the ideas of syndicalism put forward in the late 19th century by the French political thinker, Georges Sorel. In Italian hands, however, the theories of Sorel were changed significantly. From being a means towards the revolutionary overthrow of capitalism, the 'corporative' system in Italy posed as a solution to the problems of class warfare. It also served as a bridge between the factions of workers and employers in the interests of the fatherland.

What was corporativism?

The suppression of existing socialist and Catholic trade unions paved the way for the so-called Rocco Law of April 1926. This law, while outlawing both workers' strikes and employers' **lockouts**, gave legal recognition to the Fascist syndicates. Although these syndicates consisted exclusively either of workers or employers, the law provided for corporations, or 'central liaison organs', to mediate between the two. The actual implementation of this new order was extremely slow. Only in March 1930 was a National Council of Corporations created as an advisory body on the development of the system, and not until 1934 were the corporations actually set up. By 1936 there were 22 of them representing all the major branches of industrial, agricultural, artistic and professional life in Italy. Mussolini claimed to see in these corporations the logical successors to the parliament, which now had no reason to exist, he claimed, with the death of the multi-party system. Indeed, in 1938–39, the parliamentary system was abolished in name as well as in practice, and replaced by a **Chamber of Fasces and Corporations**.

In theory, therefore, the government of Italy moved towards a decentralised state in which the varying interests of workers and employers were directly represented through their corporations. In reality, in the words of the contemporary historian G. Salvemini, **corporativism** was 'an elaborate piece of imposing humbug'. For all their activity in an advisory capacity, the corporations had no role in the formulation of economic policy, which remained firmly in the government's hands. In each corporation, furthermore, the representatives of employers and workers were joined by officials of the Ministry of Corporations, whose task was to ensure that the government's view prevailed. The theory of decentralisation barely masked the reality of rigid Fascist control.

The distribution of power in the Fascist state

If corporativism did not dominate the Italian state under Fascist rule, then what did? As we have seen, much Fascist energy in the early years of power was poured into the task of disarming existing sources of influence such as the other political parties and parliament, the trade unions or the Church. The powers of the monarchy, already limited, were further restricted by measures that gave Mussolini the power to make laws by decree (January 1926), and deprived King Victor Emmanuel of the right to select the Prime Minister (December 1928). On a local level, elected mayors were replaced by nominated Fascist officials known as *podestà*. Even the local powers of the Fascist *Ras* found themselves subjected to central authority. They were unable to resist largely because their intense rivalry with each other made them so easy to isolate.

Apart from the corporations, the major new constitutional feature of the 1920s was the Fascist Grand Council. This was a body of 56 'hierarchs' (*gerarchi*), later reduced to 30, whose function as an organ of state came to include determining the succession both to the throne and to the office of Prime Minister. Even so, the powers defined for it by the laws of 1928–29 make it clear that the Grand Council, too, played only a secondary role. Its membership, times of meetings, even the agenda that it should discuss, all remained the firm prerogative of the *Duce*. In short, the end-product of the Fascist revolution was the personal dictatorship of Benito Mussolini. Two factors help to explain his success in this respect in the 1920s and 1930s. One is the comparative mediocrity of other leading Fascists. 'Most of them,' wrote Denis Mack Smith, 'were unintelligent, grasping, jealous and incompetent, and jockeyed for place by telling tales against their rivals.' Of the men closest to the *Duce* some, like Roberto Farinacci and Italo Balbo, were glorified street fighters, lacking Mussolini's political flair. Some, like Dino Grandi, were too submissive to provide firm opposition. Others, like the future Foreign Minister Galaezzo Ciano, had tied their own fate too closely to that of their leader to risk toppling him. Italian Fascism produced no Goering, no Himmler, and certainly no Röhm (see Chapter 10).

Mussolini's image and leadership

The second factor in Mussolini's favour was his own enormous talent for self-advertisement. He exploited his journalistic talents to the full, not only convincing many Italians that 'Mussolini is always right', but creating

---

Chamber of Fasces and Corporations: A pseudo-parliamentary system consisting of Fascist representatives drawn from administrative and industrial bodies.

Corporativism: System of government propounded by Benito Mussolini in which trade and professional organisations, or corporations, are the basis of society and political activity.

Ras: The local Fascist party leaders took their nickname from the semi-independent chieftains of Abyssinia.

Italo Balbo (1896–1940)
A leading Fascist from the early days of the movement, and an organiser with Mussolini of the 'March on Rome' (1922). Minister for Aviation and Governor of Libya (1933–40).

Dino Grandi (1895–1988)
Joined the Fascist Party in 1922. Foreign Minister (1929–32). Italian ambassador to London (1932–39) in which capacity he was effective in disarming British opposition to Italian foreign policy. As a member of the Fascist Grand Council, he engineered the dismissal of Mussolini in 1943.

Galaezzo Ciano (1903–1944)
Participated in the 'March on Rome' (1922), and rose to high office after marriage to Mussolini's daughter (1930). Minister of Press and Propaganda (1934); then Foreign Minister (1936). Although he played a large part in the formation of the Italian–German alliance, he was reluctant to enter the war. Sought an understanding with the allies from 1942, and was eventually tried and executed for treason.

an image, far from the truth, of a man who possessed all the talents. The controlled press portrayed him as an excellent violinist, fine horseman, daring pilot, bold war hero, and as an intellectual who had mastered all the major philosophies of the day and had found time to memorise whole sections of Dante's poems. This mastery of publicity – which made him a genius at the art of seizing power – goes far to explain the disappointing record of the Fascist government. Historian Denis Mack Smith has summarised Mussolini's failings as an administrator admirably. 'Mussolini's own mental processes never ceased to be governed by slogans and eight-column headlines. He preferred to argue and speechify rather than to penetrate behind words to reality and so never properly dissected a problem. Fascism, which affected to despise speeches and talk, was itself essentially rhetoric and blather.'

Relations between State and Church

One influential element in Italian life could not be subdued or suppressed by threats and violence. Relations between Fascism and the Catholic Church remained complex throughout the 1920s. While Mussolini and other Fascist leaders never lost their fierce anti-clericalism, and both groups remained divided over the question of the education and indoctrination of youth, in other respects they shared common ground. Ever the realist, Mussolini never seriously imagined that he could govern Italy successfully with Catholic opposition. The Papacy, for all its reservations, still saw Fascism as the only alternative to the godless doctrines of socialism.

Despite an interlude of tension in 1927, when the State dissolved the Catholic boy-scout movement, Church and State extended olive branches to each other. Gentile's education act (February 1923) restored the compulsory religious education that the liberal regime had abolished in **elementary schools**. The following year, the Pope did Fascism a service by withdrawing his support from the Catholic Popular Party, an electoral rival. Always too progressive for the tastes of Pope Pius XI, the Popular Party could not survive the blow, and Mussolini was left free of major parliamentary rivals.

Elementary schools: Where children are taught for the first six or eight years of their education.

These signs of mutual respect reached fruition with the signature of a batch of agreements known as the Lateran Accords (February 1929). For the Church, the Accords settled most of the outstanding conflicts between the Papacy and the Italian State. By creating the tiny state within Rome,

The Lateran Accords have the desired effect: schoolchildren greeting priests with the Fascist salute.

Absolutism: A political system in which one ruler or leader has complete power and authority over the country.

1. What was corporativism supposed to achieve in Italy, and to what extent did it do so?

2. What possible restraints were there in the Fascist State on the personal authority of Mussolini, and why were they not more effective?

3. What was achieved through the Lateran Accords of 1929 (a) for the Catholic Church and (b) for the Fascist State?

known as the Vatican City, the State restored some of the Papacy's temporal authority. Furthermore, it confirmed Catholicism as 'the only state religion', extended compulsory religious education to secondary schools and outlawed divorce. Lastly, the Papacy received financial compensation, amounting to some 1,750 million lire, for its losses since the Italian seizure of Rome in 1870. Mussolini's gains from the Accords were less tangible, but were perhaps greater. By linking his administration with the immense moral influence of the Church, he entered upon a period of unprecedented national popularity. The Lateran Accords thus represented the greatest political success of his career and the most lasting impact of Fascist government on modern Italy.

It should not be imagined that the agreements of 1929 represented a surrender by either party. Mussolini immediately reminded parliament that the Italian state 'is Catholic … but it is above all Fascist'. In 1931 a further crisis illustrated the lines beyond which neither side would step. In that year, Mussolini declared the disbanding of the youth and student groups affiliated to Catholic Action, an educational and moral organisation highly prized by Pius XI. In the face of a papal counter-attack, Mussolini replaced the dissolution order with lesser limitations on the groups' activities. The incident illustrated the limitations upon Fascist **absolutism** in Italy, the value of silent Catholic support to the government and, thereby, the shrewdness of the understanding reached in 1929.

9.6 What was the impact of Fascism upon Italian culture, society and the economy?

Education and the media

The control of education was considered essential by the Fascist regime. In the classroom, the 'fascistisation' of youth involved the strict control of textbooks and of curriculum, and the removal of teachers critical of Fascist principles. The primary purpose of the school was now to teach the young such Fascist virtues as manliness, patriotism and obedience. 'A child who asks "Why?",' declared a textbook approved for eight-year-olds, 'is like a bayonet made of milk. "You must obey because you must," said Mussolini, when explaining the reasons for obedience.'

Glorification of the *Duce* was, of course, another important educational element. Outside the school, Italy set a pattern for other authoritarian regimes by the law (April 1926) which introduced a system of compulsory youth organisation to coax the male child into the required Fascist path. From four to eight the boy would belong to the 'Sons of the She-Wolf' (*Figli della Lupa*), from eight to 14 to the *Balilla*, and to the age of 18 to the 'Vanguard' (*Avanguardisti*). From 1937, the best graduates of this system might join the 'Young Fascists' (*Giovani Fascisti*) until the age of 21. Whatever the political success of the system, the Fascist years marked no great advance in conventional educational areas. Illiteracy, which stood at 48.5% in 1901, had been reduced by the liberals to 30% by 1921, but still stood above 20% in 1931.

In common with the contemporary Soviet government, Fascist Italy demanded in theory that all aspects of the cultural life of the society should support and sustain the regime. For the first time in western

Europe, a government attempted to turn the communications machinery of a modern state to a co-ordinated political purpose. The press was steadily subjected to the party line by the suppression of political papers such as *Avanti!* and consistent pressure upon other editors and owners.

Fascism and sport

Sport, too, was highly prized by the regime, both as a breeder of Fascist virtues and as a source of nationalist propaganda. On a popular level, the *Dopolavoro* ('for the sake of labour') organisation was formed in May 1925. It hoped to provide for 'the healthy and profitable occupation of the workers' leisure hours', by means such as cheap holidays, libraries, lectures and theatrical entertainment. On a more élite level, several major sports were reorganised and centralised, and their international successes exploited by the state. In soccer, the 1934 World Cup competition was held in, and won by, Italy. It retained the trophy in 1938, to the great satisfaction of the Fascist regime. As boxing was naturally regarded by Mussolini as 'an essentially Fascist method of self-expression', the triumph of Primo Carnera (1933) in the World Heavyweight Championship was hailed as a further proof of Fascist virility.

The limits of cultural control

Like its ambiguous relationship with the Church, Fascism's failure to dominate Italian cultural life illustrates the limits of its absolutism. Although the movement had a considerable appeal in intellectual circles in its early days, this was partly dissipated by its later authoritarianism. The conductor, Arturo Toscanini, a Fascist candidate in 1919, left Italy for America in the 1920s. He was followed by the historian Gaetano Salvemini in 1925 and the physicist Enrico Fermi in 1938. Italy's greatest intellectual figure, the philosopher and historian Benedetto Croce, was an opponent of the regime from 1925, when he organised an anti-Fascist manifesto. Yet he not only remained in the country throughout Mussolini's years in power, but continued to produce liberal historical works, and to publish his liberal review *La Critica*. Although usually cited as an example of Fascist weakness, this might possibly be ascribed to Fascist tolerance of an influential rival, putting Croce in the same bracket as the Pope. Certainly, he would not have survived either in Nazi Germany or in Stalin's USSR.

A greater failure was the inability to found any true 'Fascist culture'. Although Nobel Prizes for literature went to Grazia Deledda (1926) and to Luigi Pirandello (1936), neither was truly a Fascist. Despite the much publicised foundation of the Royal Academy of Italy (October 1929), the literature and art encouraged by the regime remained conformist, old-fashioned and lifeless. Only in engineering and music did names of international repute, such as Pier Luigi Nervi and Ottorino Respighi, emerge during the two decades of Fascist Italy.

To what extent did the Italian economy benefit from the years of Fascist government?

The abandonment of liberal economics and the return to protectionism
Italian Fascism inherited a depressing range of economic problems, including a sizeable budget deficit and a total of 500,000 unemployed. Its most consistent success in tackling these was achieved in 1922–25 when, largely for reasons of political expediency, the Ministry of Finance was in the hands of the liberal economist, Alberto De Stefani. His measures included the abolition of price-fixing and of rent controls, and the reduction of government expenditure wherever possible. His achievements included a

1. By what means did the Fascist State seek to control educational and cultural activities in the Italy?

2. How justifiable is the claim that Mussolini was able to achieve a cultural revolution in Italy?

Mussolini delivers a speech, inaugurating work on the draining of the Pontine Marshes.

What characteristic features of Mussolini's style of government are evident in this photograph?

budget that was in surplus for the first time since 1918, and a reduction in the total of unemployed to only 122,000.

Mussolini's motives for departing from this policy, and for replacing De Stefani with the financier and industrialist Giuseppe Volpi, have been the subject of debate. To Marxist commentators – of whom the contemporary French journalist D. Guerin was an extreme example – the reversion to protectionism was proof that Mussolini was doing the bidding of Italian capitalism. Heavy import duties were imposed, for example, upon grain, sugar and milk. Denis Mack Smith, however, is adamant that 'Mussolini was no mere instrument of business and agrarian interests'. He does concede that 'his ignorance of economics and human nature left him an easy target for sharks who wanted protective duties or who extracted money from the state for quite impossible schemes of industrialisation'. An explanation consistent with other areas of Fascist policy is that Mussolini was influenced by considerations of political prestige. Certainly, the revaluation of the Italian currency the lire (August 1926) at 90 to the pound, gave it an artificial impression of strength. The immediate result of this swing to protection was that the Italian economy ran into difficulties long before the **Wall Street Crash**. The low exchange rate of the lire deterred tourist traffic and damaged trade in luxury commodities.

Wall Street Crash: Collapse of the American stock market which took place in October 1929. Nearly 13 million shares changed hands on the New York Stock Exchange on 24 October. Shock waves from the 'Crash' were felt all around the world. Many people lost a lot of money.

Autarky (or *autarchy*): Economic policy aiming at national self-sufficiency in terms of raw materials and other essential economic resources.

The battles for land, grain and births

By 1930 the government, tempted by the prospects of domestic prestige and foreign military adventures, had adopted the principle of *autarky*, that is of economic self-sufficiency. The policy bred some impressive successes, such as the five-fold increase in electricity production between 1917 and 1942, and the spectacular rise in motor production by 1941, when an estimated 34,000 cars were completed. In typically flashy Fascist fashion, however, the policy was constructed around three great national 'struggles'.

1. The 'battle for grain', officially started in 1925, was superficially successful. Production figures that had been steady at 40 million 'quintals' since 1870 rose to 60 million in 1930 and to 80 million by 1939. Some agricultural experts have pointed out that the official fixation with grain damaged other forms of agricultural output, and kept the relative cost of Italian grain production high.

2. The 'battle for land' was also marked by notable successes. Most famous of the land reclamation schemes was the draining of the Pontine Marshes near Rome to provide hundreds of thousands of acres of new farmland. Much of it, unfortunately, was lost again in 1943–45 due to the ravages and neglect of war. It is also well worth noting that Fascist attentions to southern Italy resulted in a more effective control of Mafia activities than was achieved before or since. In the same vein of public works, which combined public utility with political propaganda, was the construction of motorways (*autostrada*) between Italy's main urban centres, and the electrification of some 5,000 kilometres of Italy's railway system.

3. Least necessary, and least successful, of the Fascist 'struggles' was the 'battle for births'. Imagining that an increased population would provide proof of Italian virility and would support its claims for colonies, Mussolini demanded a rapid rise in the birth rate. Parents of large families were rewarded, while bachelors, with the exceptions of priests and maimed war veterans, were penalised by high taxes (1926). Abortion and contraception, of course, were outlawed. In this aim, so foolish in relation to Italy's limited resources, the *Duce* suffered bitter disappointment. Although the Italian population rose from 37.5 million (1921) to 44.4 million (1941), two different factors were primarily responsible. These were the fall in the death rate, and the restrictions placed upon immigration by the USA.

Did the Fascist regime bring about significant social and economic change?

Sanctions: Measures taken by countries to restrict or prohibit trade and official contact with a country that has broken international law.

The 'balance sheet' of the policy of *autarky* was not altogether negative. It produced some durable monuments, and served Italy well when the League of Nations imposed **sanctions** upon it in the course of the Abyssinian War. In terms of industrial growth, however, its narrow political motives made the period 1925–40 one of the most stagnant in Italy's economic history. In those years the annual growth in productivity was only 0.8%, compared with 3.8% in 1901–25 and 3.5% in 1940–52. Cut off from the mainstream of world economics, Italy suffered recession earlier than other European powers, yet drew little benefit from the steady world recovery of the mid-1930s.

The Fascist 'revolution' in Italy failed to transform the lives of the ordinary Italians as many of its early supporters had hoped. The 'battle for land', although a potent political symbol, fell far short of any substantial change in the pattern of land ownership in Italy. In 1930, the peasant smallholder made up 87.3% of the farming population, yet held only 13.2% of the farmland. The richest 0.5% of the landed population, on the other hand, still farmed 41.9% of the available land. No significant change occurred in these proportions in the next decade. Smallholders and small-scale businessmen alike found survival increasingly difficult, with an annual average of 7,000 small farms passing to the exchequer as a result of their owners' failure to pay land tax.

Naturally, the Fascist period was for most Italians one of stagnant or declining living standards. The task of penetrating and interpreting

Fascist statistics is a complex one, and researchers have differed in their conclusions. They have not disputed improvement or decline, but merely about the rate of decline. The historian Federico Chabod claims that the Italian farm labourer lost half, and in some cases more, of the real value of his wages. C. Vannutelli claims a drop in the average 'per capita' income of the Italians from 3,079 lire (1929) to 1,829 (1934). The figures have to be set against a falling cost of living and a subsequent rise of the 'per capita' income to return to the 1929 level by 1937.

Against this, one should also note the range of social benefits that the workers' syndicates secured, most of them late in the Fascist period. Sick pay was first introduced in 1928, followed ten years later by a 'package' comprising end-of-year bonuses, paid holidays and redundancy pay. Although it is possible that the lot of the worker in Fascist Italy may have been less severe than it has been painted, there is much to show that the years 1923–40 marked little improvement in the worker's life.

- The right to strike was abolished.

- The government's 'Charter of Labour' (1927) failed to guarantee a minimum wage.

- Unemployment rose from 110,000 (1926) to over a million (1933), before levelling off at around 700,000.

1. What problems did the Fascist government identify in the Italian economy, and how did it seek to solve them?

2. What aspects of Fascist economic policy, if any, may be judged to have been successful?

9.7 What was the influence of Italian Fascism upon right-wing politics elsewhere in Europe?

The conquering political idea of the inter-war years?

Considering the steady collapse of liberal democratic forms of government throughout Europe in the 1920s and 1930s, it would be tempting to see Mussolini as the founder of the conquering political idea of the era. By the end of the 1930s, authoritarian governments had been established in Germany, Spain, Portugal, Hungary, Austria, Romania, Yugoslavia and Poland. Even in France democracy was under severe strain. One should not exaggerate, however, the international influence of the Italian Fascist form of government which Mussolini himself had declared earlier in his career was 'not for export'.

Many apparent similarities between Fascism and these other movements result not from conscious imitation by the latter, but from common features in the movements' origins. Hungary, like Italy, received a strong nationalist impulse from the supposed injustices of the peace treaties, and the short-lived socialist regime of Béla Kun (1919) which left an even stronger anti-communist feeling than the one which had helped Mussolini to power. The threatening closeness of the Soviet Union also stimulated anti-Marxist passions in Hungary, Poland, Finland and Romania alike.

The extent of Italian influence on the European right

When Italian Fascism did directly influence its 'sister' movements, it was in the one area where Mussolini showed true mastery – in the tactics of the seizure and consolidation of power. There can be little doubt of the direct influence upon Hitler of the Fascist use of salutes, uniforms and rallies as means of fascinating the public, and of the use of organised violence to terrorise one's enemies. In Germany, however, these tactics remained means to other ends, whereas in Italy they too often appeared as ends in themselves. Much later, Adolf Hitler remained fond of referring to

Mussolini as 'his only friend', and of claiming that it was the Italian's example that had given him the initial courage to pursue his own political ambitions. In Hitler's consolidation of power many elements, such as the suppression of the press and of the trade unions, had close parallels in Italy. Throughout Europe, especially where Fascist movements struggled to achieve power, the rituals and trappings of Italian Fascism were imitated in Oswald Mosley's British Union of Fascists, among the French *Cagoulards*, and in the Romanian Iron Guards.

Direct imitations of Italian ideology or methods of government are, however, harder to detect. Corporativism appeared in the right-wing programmes of Antonio Salazar in Portugal and of Engelbert Dollfuss in Austria, while the Italian 'Charter of Labour' (1927) found echoes in Spanish 'Falangist' policy and in Portugal. Neither had any parallel in the Nazi movement. The French *Cagoulards* and the Austrian *Heimwehr* were rare in having direct contact with the Italian government. In many cases, it is easier to pick out direct contrasts with Italian Fascism. The Catholicism that Mussolini tolerated because he could not defeat it was a central factor in the **authoritarianism** of Dollfuss in Austria and of the *Falange Espanol*. The Orthodox Church played an equally strong role in the thoughts of Codreanu, creator of the Romanian Iron Guard movement. Where Italian Fascism had made, in effect, a prisoner of the monarchy, the Spanish dictator Primo de Rivera was mainly motivated by an unswerving loyalty to the Crown. Totalitarianism, to which Mussolini aspired, but which only Hitler perfected, was not seriously sought by Primo de Rivera, by Dollfuss, or by Pilsudski in Poland. Their opponents continued to operate in public, albeit often under difficult conditions. In short, it is as easy to overestimate the international influence of Italian Fascism, as it is to exaggerate the united nature of right-wing politics in inter-war Europe. As Elizabeth Wiskemann remarked, in *Fascism in Italy* (1969), 'Italian Fascism was not the conquering creed of the 20th century', but merely in some superficial respects 'led a political fashion for two decades'.

Authoritarianism: Political system favouring or enforcing obedience to the authority of the state, to the detriment of personal liberty.

Falange Espanol ('Spanish Phalanx'): A nationalist and élitist group founded (October 1933) by José Antonio Primo de Rivera. It was influenced by the tactics of the Nazis.

1. In what respects, if any, did Italian Fascism truly influence other right-wing movements in Europe in the 1920s and the 1930s?

2. How convincing is the argument that Fascism in the 1920s and 1930s should be seen as a consistent and coherent European movement?

The influence of Nazism upon Italian Fascism

By the late 1930s, there was increasing evidence that Fascism itself was coming strongly under the influence of more dynamic forces. Several of the means by which Mussolini sought to revive his regime appeared to be reflections of German practices, although he strongly denied it. The Ministry of Popular Culture (*Minculpop*), set up in June 1937, played much the same role as Josef Goebbels' Propaganda Ministry (see Chapter 10). Above all, the range of anti-semitic legislation which successively forbade foreign Jews to enter Italy (September 1938), and banned Italian Jews from public, academic and party posts (November 1938), seemed absurd in a country with so little previous history of anti-semitism. It could only be seen as an imitation by Mussolini of his more forceful partner. Such a trivial matter as the introduction of the 'goosestep' into the Italian army, under the new title of the 'Roman step' (*Passo Romano*), convinced many of the extent to which 'Fascism in Italy lost its character and became a poor imitation of German National Socialism' (Elizabeth Wiskemann).

9.8 What were the aims of Fascist foreign policy 1922–1934?

The bases of foreign policy

Although the details of Fascist Italy's international dealings are to be found elsewhere (see Chapter 11), it is apt to consider here the broader principles that shaped those dealings. Foreign policy played a leading role in the government of Fascist Italy. Not only did the aggressive poses struck by Mussolini and his followers make it essential to pursue a 'dynamic' policy, but there were many in Italy in the 1930s who believed that the government used foreign affairs as a convenient distraction from the stagnation of domestic policies. A leader who declared, as Mussolini did, that 'it is a crime not to be strong', was committed to seek national prestige wherever possible. Italian foreign policy, however, provides no parallel to the programme of *Mein Kampf*. Many historians have concluded that Fascist policy was unclear, based simply upon seeking advantages wherever they could be found. Those who see more consistent purpose in Fascist foreign policy have usually agreed with the contemporary English statesman, Lord Halifax, who saw in Mussolini's aims 'the classic Italian role of balancing between Germany and the western powers'.

Relations with Britain, France and Germany, 1922–1934

Certainly, Mussolini carefully pointed out to parliament upon coming to office (November 1922) that, although Italy had no intention of abandoning its wartime allies, it did not accept the peace treaties as permanent or perfect. It would not hesitate to seek revision 'if their absurdity becomes evident'. Neither France nor Britain was a 'natural' ally for Fascist Italy. Both were liberal democracies, often highly critical of Mussolini's domestic policies and methods. Also, both had interests in the Mediterranean which, Mussolini told the Italians in the style of the Roman Empire, was *Mare Nostrum* ('Our Sea'). Between Italy and France, the old territorial claims to Corsica, Nice and Savoy (lost in the days of Italy's weakness) still rankled. The years of the Ruhr occupation, of economic crises and the consolidation of the Soviet Union were no time, however, to desert such apparently powerful allies.

Italian relations with Germany remained even more ambiguous. The rise of Nazism excited two conflicting emotions in Mussolini. On the one hand, he was enormously pleased at the triumph of 'his' doctrines in so powerful a state. For many years, he badly underestimated the German leader. 'In politics,' he told an associate in the early 1930s, 'it is undeniable that I am more intelligent than Hitler.' On the other hand, the prospect of resurgent German nationalism creating a 'Greater Germany' on Italy's borders horrified Mussolini.

Austria provided one of the keys to Italy's alignment in the 1930s. By 1922, Italy's traditional enemy had been reduced to the status of a weak 'buffer' state between Italy and Germany. Its territory in the South Tyrol had been ceded to Italy and the Fascist government had pursued a brutal policy of 'Italianisation'. It forbade the use of German, and changed place names and personal names in what now had to be referred to as the '*Alto Adige*'.

The prospect that Austria might become a province of a dynamic German state, committed to rule over all German territories, was the greatest problem facing Italian diplomats in 1925–35. The protection of Italy's frontier on the Brenner Pass was Mussolini's main motive in his co-operation with France and Britain in the Locarno Pacts and in the subsequent Four-Power Pact and Stresa agreement (see Chapter 11). By way of unilateral action, Mussolini sought to prop up Austria by subsidising, from 1930, the anti-Nazi *Heimwehr* militia. He also concluded the Rome Protocols (March 1934), an agreement to promote trade between Italy, Hungary and Austria.

Italian ambitions in the Balkans and in Africa

Meanwhile, Italy was unwilling to accept the international repose envisaged by the peace treaties and the League of Nations. It sought to improve its influence and status in traditional areas of involvement. The first of these was on the east coast of the Adriatic. In 1923 Mussolini defied the League of Nations by an invasion of the Greek island of Corfu to exact compensation for the murder of Italians engaged on League business. The eventual withdrawal from Corfu was followed by more permanent gains. Agreement with Yugoslavia (January 1924) allowed Italy to acquire Fiume, designated a 'free city' by the peace treaties. In November 1926, a pact with Albania tied that state to close economic dependence upon Italy. By the time of the treaty with Hungary (April 1927), supplying arms and aid to the chief revisionist state in eastern Europe, Mussolini had become, in the words of Elizabeth Wiskemann, 'the chief anti-democratic conspirator of Europe'. Also, he had established a strong position as patron of the minor states of eastern Europe.

The second area of ambition was Africa. Mussolini's main justification was that imperialism provided relief for Italy's problems of overpopulation. The historian Denis Mack Smith has dismissed this as bogus, preferring to see African expansion as a means of rivalling the Mediterranean influence of Britain and France. Thus, much of the 1920s saw a brutal colonial war in Libya, and a systematic build-up of arms and resources in Somalia. The latter policy betrayed the plans that Mussolini was nursing even then for his major colonial project, the acquisition of Abyssinia (see Chapter 11).

The failure of Fascist foreign policy

Aggrandisement: The act of making oneself or one's country larger and/or more powerful.

Superficially, the confused and hesitant nature of western diplomacy in the 1930s seemed to offer great hopes for this policy of opportunistic **aggrandisement**. That it ultimately brought disaster was due to three main factors.

1. *In what areas did Fascist Italy seek to extend its power and influence?*

2. *To what extent is it accurate to regard Nazi Germany as a 'natural ally' for Italy in the 1930s?*

3. *Why did Fascist Italy move away from Britain and France, and towards Nazi Germany, in the course of the 1930s?*

1. From 1932, Mussolini was in personal control of foreign policy, free from the restraints of traditional diplomats, and frequently the prisoner of his own rhetoric. He had dismissed Dino Grandi as Foreign Minister, first taking over the duties himself, and then transferring them to his submissive son-in-law, Count Ciano.

2. Mussolini badly underestimated Adolf Hitler and, by his own destabilisation of European politics, helped to further the projects of the man who was ultimately to destroy Fascist Italy.

3. For all his warlike slogans, Mussolini totally failed to provide Italy with the means to fight and to win a modern war although he was head of the armed forces by 1932.

When the Versailles peace settlement finally collapsed in 1939, writes Denis Mack Smith in *Mussolini's Roman Empire*, 'the prosaic truth turned out to be that only ten divisions were ready to fight and these were under strength, with antiquated and inadequate equipment'. The air force, which Mussolini boasted would 'darken the sky', was described by a contemporary aviation expert as 'irremediably out of date'.

9.9 How justifiable was Italy's intervention in war in 1915 and in 1940?
A CASE STUDY IN HISTORICAL INTERPRETATION

Twice in the first half of the 20th century – in 1914 and in 1939–40 – Italy found itself on the fringes of an international crisis that threatened Europe with general war. In both cases it chose to intervene, with drastic consequences. From the viewpoint of a British or a French commentator, the two decisions may at first seem very different. One appears as the brave decision of a democratic government to side with other democratic regimes, and the other as a piece of cynical opportunism on the part of a Fascist dictator out to share in the spoils of an immoral war. Viewed in a broader context, however, it may appear that the logic behind the two decisions was similar and that they demonstrate the continuity that existed in Italian history between the creation of the united state and the fall of Mussolini.

Historians have largely turned away from the traditional left-wing interpretation that Italy went to war in 1914 at the suggestion of its capitalists, and particularly of armament manufacturers. The socialist writer, Guiliano Procacci (*History of the Italian People*, 1970) points out that there is little evidence for this. He adds that, as American industrialists demonstrated, it was often more profitable to remain neutral and thus to sell weapons to both sides. Most recent writers have viewed the decision as a diplomatic one, based upon considerations of security and of possible territorial gain. Martin Clark, in *Modern Italy 1871–1982* (1984), concludes that the decision was relatively sound. Austria had already breached the terms of the Triple Alliance by failing to consult its ally over its actions in the crisis of 1914. Italy was justified, therefore, in standing aloof as the crisis unravelled. Yet neutrality involved risks of its own, and it was dangerous to abandon one set of allies without cultivating another. The prospect of siding with the Entente powers seemed much more attractive by the end of 1914, for the French victory on the Marne had thwarted German hopes for a rapid victory, and perhaps their hopes of any victory at all. An Entente victory, of course, held the promise of territorial losses for Austria, and subsequent gains for Italy.

Historians C.J. Lowe and F. Marzari, in *Italian Foreign Policy 1870–1940* (1975), lay the emphasis slightly differently, stressing that Italy regarded Britain as the major factor. If Britain remained neutral, then Italian participation on the side of Germany and Austria-Hungary remained viable. If Britain fought against those states, however, its naval power in the Mediterranean made it impossible for Italy to contemplate opposition. Just as they had done in the great wars of the *Risorgimento*, Italy attempted to persuade Austria to surrender territory as the price of neutrality, rather than as the prize for military victory. Only when Austria refused did the Italian government conclude its agreement with Britain and France.

A more sinister interpretation of these events is that Italy entered the war through one of the most blatant examples of that 'secret diplomacy' which the US President Woodrow Wilson condemned so roundly in 1919. This interpretation continues to emphasise the motive of territorial gain, but makes intervention the responsibility of a narrow, élite group of Italian politicians. It claims that the Prime Minister, Sidney de Sonnino, and the Foreign Minister, Antonio Salandra, guarded their secrets so closely that parliament was not consulted, and even the army commanders remained ignorant of government policy until war was almost upon them. Where other states may have been able to blame patriotic agitation and widespread **jingoism** for their involvement in the disasters of the war, many sectors of Italian society showed a distinct lack of enthusiasm. Italian historian A. Monticone, in *Da Giolitti a Salandra* (1969), concluded that 'Salandra, when signing the Pact of London, was fully aware that he was acting against the great majority of the Italian people.' Three hundred parliamentary deputies protested, industrialists feared that their supplies of raw materials would dry up and the veteran Italian statesman Giovanni Giolitti expressed the opinion that 'the people in the government deserve to be shot'.

In the 1930s, Mussolini's government responded to the increasing instability of Europe by reversing this diplomatic process. Working at first with Italy's First World War allies, Britain and France, he later cultivated

Jingoism: Fanatical and unreasonable belief in the superiority of your country, especially when it involves support for a war against another country.

close relations with Germany, culminating in military intervention on Hitler's side in 1940. In Martin Clark's view, Mussolini was playing the same diplomatic game as his predecessors. Having gained little from friendship with the liberal democracies, either in terms of security or territory (see Chapter 11), Italy drifted towards Germany in part to wring concessions from the British and the French, and to resurrect the alliance of the early 1930s with specific gains for Italy. It might even be claimed that, with considerable prestige won at Munich as the saviour of European peace, and with the annexation of Albania in 1939, the policy had its successes. Lowe and Mazari view Mussolini's growing friendship with Hitler as a relatively responsible and sensible policy. Given the consistent hostility with which Italian policy was now viewed by London and Paris, 'Rome could not help but reflect that Germany was her only reliable friend. If the choice facing Italy was either isolation or alliance with the Reich, the alliance always carried with it the possibility – or the illusion – of exercising restraint on Germany's dynamism.'

Why, though, did Italy sign the Pact of Steel in 1939, committing itself to military support for Germany? It has been argued that, even then, Mussolini sought short-term Italian gains from the crisis, rather than an all-out war for which Italy was scarcely prepared. 'His policy in 1938–39,' Martin Clark writes, 'was essentially still that of manoeuvring for advantage among the contending powers, meanwhile hoping that a European war could be avoided.' Lowe and Marzari suggest that Mussolini certainly saw it as an 'alliance with the strong', and thus as a guarantee of Italian security, but was greatly reassured in 1939 by the assumption that it would be at least three years before any hostilities would begin. 'That such a war-free period was crucial to his policy,' Lowe and Marzari have concluded, 'cannot be doubted.'

Mussolini's biographer, Denis Mack Smith (*Mussolini*, 1981), takes a more negative view of Mussolini's actions in 1939. His account is of irresponsible and heavy-handed **war-mongering**. Mussolini, he claims, was fully aware of Hitler's plans over Poland when he signed the Pact of Steel, and simply hoped to use the destabilisation that Hitler's attack on Poland would cause to further his own ambitions in the Balkans and in the Mediterranean. Worse still, these plans were unrealistic and unclear. 'He thought once again of taking Tunisia or Algeria, and the chiefs of staff were told to have plans ready for an attack on Yugoslavia and Greece. These were hardly the actions of someone dedicated to the cause of peace, as he later claimed, nor did they have much contact with reality.' Mack Smith is severely critical of Mussolini's diplomacy, and of his political realism in the months leading up to the war. Mussolini was out of his depth at this stage. He was prone to put propaganda in the place of serious preparation, and approached the crisis with armed forces that he knew to be inadequate for a prolonged modern war. This was not the first time, however, that Italy had found itself in this position. Mussolini's misconceptions about the war that he was undertaking in 1940 were therefore not unlike those of Italy's leaders when they approached war in 1914.

When war suddenly flared up in 1939, as in 1914, the first Italian response was to stand aloof from the conflict, and to pursue a policy of non-belligerence. Yet to shirk the German alliance now, after years of Mussolini's rhetoric about territorial revision and decadent democracies, would place the Fascist regime in an impossible and embarrassing position. As had happened in 1914, the crisis advanced at a faster rate than Italian policy had anticipated. Mussolini, like Sonnino and Salandra in 1914, based his decision upon events in northern France. Where the French had won a great victory in 1914, they collapsed utterly in 1940. Mussolini's final decision to go to war was motivated by the assumption

War-mongering: Encouraging people to expect war or trying to get a war started.

1. *What different interpretations have been provided by historians of Italy's decisions to go to war (a) in 1915 and (b) in 1940?*

2. *What arguments are there for and against the claim that in 1915 and in 1940 alike, it was broadly in Italy's best interests to go to war?*

that German victories in northern France in 1940 were decisive. It was the worst of many miscalculations.

Overall, the fact remains that the fateful decisions of 1915 and 1940 were made without any serious reference to ideology. Both were informed by the traditional realities of Italian foreign policy. As ever, Italy lacked the resources to initiate or to steer European diplomacy. On the other hand, it remained sufficiently attractive as an ally to be courted by the major powers, and to anticipate substantial rewards for its support. Such a policy, in the years of the *Risorgimento*, formed one of the bases for Italian unification. In 1914–18, the same policy achieved mixed results. Italy found itself on the winning side, but appeared to be cheated of the rewards that it had been promised. In 1940–45, the policy was attempted for the third time. This time, Italy's leader had seriously miscalculated the nature of the conflict in which he sought to participate, with fatal consequences for regime and leader alike.

9.10 What was the impact upon Mussolini's political authority of Italy's participation in the Second World War?

What was the military and economic impact of the war upon Italy?

Mussolini's decision to join the war in 1940 was a calculated gamble. He anticipated a short campaign, directed primarily against France, and resulting in cheap, but significant, territorial gains. At first, everything went according to plan, for France had surrendered within two weeks of Italy's intervention. Elsewhere – in North Africa, in the Balkans, and subsequently in Russia – the fighting continued. Italy had made absolutely no preparation for such campaigns, and for all Mussolini's warlike propaganda, its forces were ill-equipped to sustain them. The campaign that Mussolini launched against Greece (October 1940) ended in disaster as the Greeks drove Italian forces back into Albania, and the loss of five warships at the Battle of Cape Matapan (March 1941) ensured that naval supremacy in the Mediterranean would lie with the British. By the summer of the same year, nearly 400,000 Italian soldiers had surrendered to the British in North Africa. Despite German aid, Italy had lost all its African possessions by the beginning of 1943. In each of these theatres of war, the Italian campaigns had been chaotic, with adequate equipment for only 35 of the 75 divisions that the army put in the field. As he held the offices of Minister of War, Minister of the Navy and Minister of the Air Force, as well as the rank of Supreme Commander, Mussolini's personal responsibility was direct and undeniable.

Just as the Italian armed forces were unable to meet the requirements of a modern, technological war, so the Italian economy lacked the means to adapt. Above all, Italy suffered in this respect from its lack of raw materials and energy resources. Hydro-electric power could not easily be increased to meet wartime demands, oil resources in Libya had not yet been detected, and steel production actually declined in the course of the war, leaving Italy largely dependent upon hand-outs from its German allies. To make matters worse, Italian industrial centres were systematically bombed by the allies from the autumn of 1942 onwards. In many combatant states, the war effort provided a stimulus to industrial production; in Italy it went some way towards wiping out the limited progress that had already been made. 'Northern Italy,' Martin Clark concludes, 'was one of the few places where aerial bombing proved effective in the Second World War. It disrupted production, it shattered morale, and it forced thousands of people to flee from the cities.' Inevitably, low levels of wartime production were accompanied by a virtual breakdown in the production of consumer goods. The recruitment of thousands of peasant soldiers also had a severe impact upon levels of food production.

What was the political response to military failure?

Under such circumstances, the pretence and propaganda of the Fascist party and its leaders quickly crumbled. Indeed, Mussolini himself delivered none of his characteristic public addresses after mid-1940. Local officials in Sicily began to ignore government directives, and Italian control of newly acquired territories in the Balkans crumbled in the face of powerful resistance movements. From 1940 onwards, the Germans actually began to govern the South Tyrol (*Alto Adige*) as part of their own territory. A major strike in Turin (March 1943) provided the first evidence that anti-Fascist political groups within Italy were beginning to exploit the economic and social chaos. Liberals, socialists, Communists and Catholics all began to produce their own anti-war propaganda, and their own versions of Italy's best escape route from this disaster.

Despite the post-war claims of such groups, however, it was not their activity that ultimately undermined the Fascist regime. Like many of the leaders who fell from power in the course of the 20th century, Mussolini was ousted because he lost the support of the élite groups that had initially supported him. Army officers, aristocrats and church leaders were deeply involved in the conspiracies that began to form in 1942–43. Mussolini's decision to sack a large proportion of his **Cabinet** in February 1943 ensured that a number of prominent Fascists also turned against him. By that time, Ciano and other prominent members of the Italian establishment had been in contact with the allies for several months, attempting to negotiate a safe and honourable withdrawal from the war. The central, co-ordinating figure was King Victor Emmanuel III himself, equally concerned to limit the harm done to his country, and to ensure the future of his dynasty.

The final crisis of the Fascist government was precipitated by military events in July 1943, when allied troops landed in Sicily, quickly occupying the island, and when allied aircraft bombed Rome for the first time. Under these conditions the Fascist Grand Council met (24 July 1943), itself a rare event, and voted to end Mussolini's personal dictatorship and to return supreme political authority to the King. The following day, Victor Emmanuel dismissed and arrested Mussolini, and appointed Marshal Badoglio in his place.

As it had risen from obscurity as a consequence of one world war, the Fascist regime now collapsed because of its failure in a second conflict. In the longer term, and like all other aspects of Italy's wartime activities, this coup failed in all respects. While Marshal Badoglio hesitantly negotiated an armistice with the allies, German forces anticipated Italian intentions, entered the country and seized strategic points including the capital itself. This ensured that the worst aspects of Italy's involvement in the Second World War were still to come. For a further year the population and **infrastructure** of the state suffered terrible damage as Italy became a major battlefield between Germany and the allies. Mussolini's political career was also resurrected briefly, in humiliating fashion, as he was snatched from captivity by German commandos and installed as the 'puppet ruler' of a Fascist republic in northern Italy (1943–45). There he finally met his death at the hands of Communist resistance fighters in the final days of the war.

Cabinet: Group of the most senior and powerful ministers in a government who meet to discuss and decide policies.

Infrastructure: The basic structure on which a country, society or organisation is built, such as the facilities, services and equipment that are needed for it to function properly.

Source-based questions: Mussolini's foreign policy, 1936–1940

SOURCE A

The German ambassador to Rome reports a conversation with Mussolini in January 1936.

Mussolini received me this afternoon. He thought that it would now be possible to achieve a fundamental improvement in German–Italian relations and to dispose of the only dispute, namely, the Austrian problem. Since we had always declared that we did not wish to infringe Austria's independence, the simplest method would be for Berlin and Vienna to settle their relations on the basis of Austrian independence, e.g. in the form of a treaty of friendship with a non-aggression pact, which would in practice bring Austria into Germany's wake. If Austria, as a formally quite independent state, were thus in practice to become a German satellite, he would have no objection.

From a report by the German ambassador to the German Foreign Office, 7 January 1936.

SOURCE B

The Italian Foreign Minister comments upon Mussolini's aims in foreign policy in 1938

It seems to me that there is not much hope of a *rapprochement* [coming together] with France. The *Duce*, in my usual interview with him, traced the lines that our future policy will have to follow. 'Objectives: Djibouti, at least to the extent of joint rule and neutralisation; Tunisia, with a more or less similar regime; Corsica, Italian and never gallicised, to be ruled directly; the frontier to be pushed back to the River Var. I am not interested in Savoy, which is neither historically nor geographically Italian. This is the general pattern of our claims. I do not specify one or five or ten years. The timing will be settled by events, but we must never lose sight of this goal.'

From the Diary of Count Ciano, Italian Foreign Minister, 8 November 1938

SOURCE C

The Italian Foreign Minister comments upon Mussolini's decision not to go to war in 1939

The *Duce* is calm. He has already decided not to intervene, and the struggle that has agitated his spirits during these last weeks has ceased. He telephones personally to Attolico [the Italian ambassador in Berlin] urging him to entreat Hitler to send him a telegram releasing him from the obligations of the alliance. He does not want to seem untrustworthy in the eyes of the German people, nor in the eyes of the Italian people, who, to tell the truth, do not show too many scruples, blinded as they are by anti-German hatred.

From the Diary of Count Ciano, Italian Foreign Minister, 1 September 1939

SOURCE D

The Italian Foreign Minister comments upon Mussolini's decision to go to war in 1940

Mussolini begins to talk as follows: 'Some months ago I said that the allies had lost the victory. Today I tell you that they have lost the war. We Italians are already sufficiently dishonoured. Any delay is inconceivable. We have no time to lose. Within a month I shall declare war. I shall attack France and Britain from the air and from the sea.' Today, for the first time, I did not answer. Unfortunately I can do nothing to hold the *Duce* back. He has decided to act, and act he will. He believes in German success and in the rapidity of this success.

From the Diary of Count Ciano, Italian Foreign Minister, 13 May 1940

(a) Study Source A.

From this source and from your own knowledge, explain the reference to 'the Austrian problem'.
[20 marks]

(b) Study Sources C and D.

To what extent do these sources indicate that Mussolini's foreign policy underwent a fundamental change in the years 1939 and 1940?
[40 marks]

(c) Study all of the sources.

From these sources, and from your own knowledge, how far would you agree with the claim that 'Mussolini's foreign policy in the 1930s had no consistent principles or aims'?
[60 marks]

Source-based questions: The style and substance of Italian Fascism

Study sources 1–5 below and then answer questions (a) and (b) which follow.

SOURCE 1

(From Nicholas Doumanis, Italy: Inventing the Nation, *published in 2001)*

It was the war experience itself, and especially the crisis precipitated by the debacle at Caporetto, that converted many Italians into fully-fledged nationalists. Especially important in galvanising mass support for right-wing nationalism were the 'unpatriotic', disruptive activities of the Left and the Liberal regime's failure to keep the home front in order. Much of bourgeois Italy was therefore attracted to the nationalist rhetoric of the Fascist movement, which outwardly sought to distinguish itself from the Liberal order by conducting a decisive and violent campaign against the Left.

Fascism was principally committed to creating a great nation out of a feeble one, and nationalism was the fundamental basis of its beliefs. The Fascists did not offer a clear political programme, for among their ranks one could find monarchists and republicans, as well as revolutionaries and conservatives, but if anything can be salvaged from their obtuse rhetoric and muddled theories, it was the absolute moral primacy of the nation. It was nationalism that bound this motley cohort together. For the Fascists 'Italia' demanded precedence over class and religion, even family and monarchy. Their challenge was to transmit that passionate fervour for 'Italia' to every Italian regardless of class or gender. As Roberto Farinacci, one of the more radical leaders of the early period once asserted, 'In Italy no one can be an anti-Fascist because an anti-Fascist cannot be an Italian.' The Fascists hoped that they would establish their political legitimacy with a simple rendition of national culture and identity.

SOURCE 2

(From Denis Mack Smith, Mussolini, *published in 1981)*

Mussolini was anxious for the public to think of him as an immensely hard worker, whose working day might last 18 or 19 hours. It was he who suggested to journalists that they might like to spread stories of his industriousness. This legend, like so many others, was false. His staff sometimes had orders to leave a light in his office at night to give the impression that he was working late. He was, in fact, a heavy sleeper who liked going to bed early and staying there for nine hours, not being disturbed even in emergencies. Mussolini was no idler, but the stories of his extraordinary industry and efficiency were exaggerated. He tried to persuade people that he kept up an average of 25 meetings a day throughout the year and that in seven years he had transacted 1,887,112 items of business. This last figure invites suspicion by its characteristic precision and works out at nearly 100 items each hour over a sixty-hour week. Moreover he said that he found time each day for some sporting activity and, each evening, for playing his precious collection of violins. The dramatist Pirandello interpreted Mussolini as being essentially an actor pretending to be the person Italians wanted him to be.

SOURCE 3

(From Martin Clark, Modern Italy 1871–1982, *published in 1984)*

Yet the new political system was not simply the old regime in more authoritarian form. The loss of certain traditional liberties – a free press, free speech, free association – was not trivial, and certainly hurt many members of Italy's former élite: the respectable Liberal anti-Fascists and the Freemasons were the great losers of 1925–26. The price may have been worth paying if it secured law and order, political stability and the maintenance of privilege, but it was still a high price. Moreover, Mussolini was always setting up new institutions and adopting new policies – the battles for wheat and for births, the corporations and the labour tribunals, the youth movements and the Dopolavoro. Many existing state institutions were left largely unchanged, but that is not necessarily proof of continuity of policy. The Fascist government was always innovating, always invading new areas of society and indeed new areas of the world.

Edexcel Unit 6

Source-based questions: The style and substance of Italian Fascism

SOURCE 4

(From Mussolini's first speech as Prime Minister to the Italian Parliament, November 1922)

Before attaining this position I was asked on all sides for a programme. Alas! It is not programmes that are lacking in Italy; it is the men and the willingness to apply the programmes. All the problems of Italian life, all of them I say, have been solved on paper. What is lacking is the will to translate them into fact. Today the Government represents this firm and decisive will.

SOURCE 5

(From a tract on Fascist beliefs, written by Mussolini in 1934)

The Fascist State is not indifferent to religious phenomena in general, nor does it maintain an attitude of indifference to Roman Catholicism, the special positive religion of the Italians. The Fascist State sees in religion one of the deepest of spiritual manifestations, and for this reason it not only respects religion, but defends and protects it. The Fascist State does not seek, as did Bolshevism, to erase God from the soul of man. Fascism respects the God of monks, saints and heroes, and it also respects God as conceived by the innocent and primitive heart of the people.

Answer both questions (a) and (b).

(a) Using your own knowledge, and the evidence of Sources 1, 2 and 5, what do you consider to have been the main appeal of Fascism to Italians in the 1920s? [10 marks]

(b) 'For all its claims to be a radical movement, Italian Fascism was mainly a change in political style, and created few significant changes in the social and economic life of Italians.' Using your own knowledge, and the evidence of all five sources, explain how far you agree with this interpretation. [20 marks]

Germany, 1918–1945

Key Issues

- *How stable was the Weimar Republic in the 1920s?*

- *Why was Hitler able to establish such a powerful dictatorship in Germany in the course of the 1930s?*

- *What were the effects of the Nazi dictatorship upon German politics and society?*

Framework of Events

1918	(November) Abdication of Kaiser Wilhelm II. Armistice signed to end First World War
1919	(February) Friedrich Ebert elected President of the German Republic
	(July) Adoption of Weimar constitution. Spartacist rising
1920	(March) Failure of Kapp *Putsch*
1921	(May) Germany agrees to pay reparations demanded by allies
1922	(April) Treaty of Rapallo between Germany and Russia
1923	(January) Occupation of the Ruhr by French and Belgian troops
	(August) Appointment of Gustav Stresemann as Chancellor
	(November) Failure of Hitler's Beerhall *Putsch*. Introduction of *Rentenmark* as German currency
1924	(September) Introduction of Dawes Plan

1924	(April) Election of Paul von Hindenburg as President of German Republic
	(December) Signature of Locarno Treaties
1926	(September) Germany admitted to League of Nations
1929	(February) Germany accepts Kellogg–Briand Pact
	(October) Collapse of American Stock Market
1930	(March) Brüning becomes German Chancellor
	(September) Nazis win 107 seats in Reichstag elections
1931	(June) Hoover moratorium on reparation payments
1932	(April) Hitler wins 13 million votes in presidential election, but is defeated by Hindenburg
	(June) Von Papen becomes Chancellor
	(July) Nazis win 230 seats in Reichstag elections
	(December) Von Schleicher becomes Chancellor
1933	(January) Hitler appointed German Chancellor
	(February) Reichstag fire
	(March) Enabling Law grants Hitler emergency powers
	(April) National boycott of Jewish businesses
	(October) German withdrawal from League of Nations
1934	(January) German–Polish non-aggression pact
	(June) Purge of SA leaders in 'Night of the Long Knives'
	(August) Death of President Hindenburg; Hitler assumes title of *Führer*
1935	(January) Plebiscite authorises return of Saarland to Germany
	(September) Nuremberg Race Laws against Jews
1936	(March) German remilitarisation of Rhineland
	(August) Introduction of compulsory military service
	(October) Introduction of economic Four-Year Plan
1938	(March) German *Anschluss* with Austria
	(October) German occupation of Sudetenland
	(November) 'Crystal Night' (*Kristalnacht*) anti-Jewish pogrom
1939	(March) Germany renounces non-aggression pact with Poland
	(May) Conclusion of 'Pact of Steel' with Italy
	(August) Conclusion of pact with Soviet Union
	(September) German invasion of Poland. Britain and France declare war on Germany
1941	(September) Removal of teachers considered disloyal to Nazis
	(December) 'Rationalisation Decree'
1942	(May) Start of bomber raids on German cities
1944	(July) Attempt to assassinate Hitler.

Overview

THE Weimar Republic was not simply an artificial regime brought into existence by the peculiar circumstances that prevailed in 1918. In part, it had its roots in a tradition of German social democracy that can be traced back, through the Bismarckian period, to the 1848 revolutions and beyond. This tradition, committed to constitutional government and to the rule of law, had attracted sufficient support in the pre-war years to make the Social Democrats the largest party in the Reichstag (German parliament). The Social Democrats were hurried into power in 1918, not by the due process of parliamentary election, and certainly not by significant long-term shifts in social and economic structures. Instead the change was precipitated by the catastrophe that overtook the German war effort in that year. At that point, finding themselves at a military disadvantage from which there seemed to be no escape, the German generals sued for peace in the full expectation that the terms would reflect the even nature of the long conflict. As a means to that end, they entered into an unlikely alliance with Social Democrat politicians, and abandoned the Kaiser who had seemed hitherto to provide the best guarantee of their interests. When much harsher peace terms were put to them, they had no choice but to accept them, given the military situation on the Western Front and the political instability at home.

After such promising parliamentary progress in peacetime, therefore, German social democracy was catapulted into power with three substantial handicaps. One, of course, was its share of responsibility for the harsh peace terms imposed upon Germany by the Treaty of Versailles. Another was that social democracy had to compete in the years after 1918 with other powerful political traditions and with new political forces. Even if the German army had been defeated, and that certainly was not the case on the Eastern Front, German conservatism and German nationalism remained strong and influential. From the east, too, came the influence of the Russian Revolution to make German Communism a far stronger force than it had ever been in the pre-war years. The third handicap was of a more practical nature, for this new government was obliged to meet the enormous economic demands imposed upon it by the victorious allies.

However, the Weimar Republic survived in spite of, and perhaps because of, these circumstances. It survived the challenge of political extremism in the years immediately after the war because conservative elements, such as the army, were willing to support it against the 'greater evil' of Communism. It survived the economic chaos of 1923 for two main reasons. In part its image was enhanced by the patriotic stance that it was able to strike when French forces occupied the Ruhr. It was also of the greatest importance that the subsequent collapse of the German currency convinced the United States of America that they should participate actively in a more moderate enforcement of the peace terms. It was possible to believe, in the later 1920s, that the German Republic was edging towards normality.

A second catastrophe – the collapse of the American stock market in 1929 – undermined the Republic's position altogether. The very nature of the crisis ensured that Germany would receive no further assistance from the powerful capitalist economies that had come to its aid in 1923. In the early 1930s, moreover, social democracy faced a new threat from the right wing of German politics. After their failure to seize power by naked violence in the early 1920s, the National Socialists (Nazis) had reinvented themselves as a parliamentary party with a manifesto that embraced the whole range of German political discontent. In these catastrophic economic circumstances, their appeal as a new and radical force proved irresistible to many German voters and, ultimately, to Germany's political hierarchy.

Adolf Hitler came to office with an insane vision of Germany's political future, but with a remarkable talent as a pragmatic politician. The circumstances under which the Nazis came to power imposed two priorities upon them. One was the elimination of rival political forces in what was still, in 1933, a constitutional state; the other was the solution of the enormous social and economic problems that had played such a major role in the Nazis' success. Both of these goals had been achieved to a large degree by 1937 by ruthless and single-minded means. Many historians doubt the long-term viability of the Nazi economy by this date, and some have recently begun to question whether Nazism had indeed overcome

Germany after the Treaty of
Versailles

all differences of political opinion within Germany. Nevertheless, it is clear that
the Nazi regime was turning in the late 1930s towards the fulfilment of its wider
ideological aims. Whether Nazi anti-semitism, the revision of the Versailles
Treaty, and the pursuit of territorial expansion in eastern Europe followed a
master plan, or whether Hitler improvised such policies as circumstances
allowed, these were clearly among the priorities of German politics in the late
1930s. They led German policy into a wider arena. If they were not the sole
causes of the world conflict that developed between 1939 and 1941, they
contributed enormously to the destruction of the German state and to a dramatic
redirection of German history in the second half of the 20th century.

10.1 How true is it that the Weimar Republic was brought into being by, and represented, democratic interests in Germany?

The political forces within the Republic

Republican government in Germany was born (9 November 1918) under
the most unfavourable circumstances. Quite apart from the imminent
collapse of the war effort, and the abdication of the Kaiser, the fleet was in
mutiny at Kiel and at Wilhelmshaven. Soldiers' and workers' councils had
appeared in Berlin, Cologne and Munich, where a Bavarian Republic had
been declared. The name by which the German republic is commonly
known derived from the fact that the dangerous condition of the capital in
1919 obliged the newly elected National Assembly to meet in the small
provincial town of Weimar. The early failure of successive emergency

Friedrich Ebert (1871–1925)
SPD deputy in the Reichstag (1912). Party leader (1913). President of the German Republic (1919–25).

General Wilhelm Groener (1867–1939)
Military commander and politician. Succeeded Erich von Ludendorff as head of General Staff (1918). Subsequently Minister of Transport (1920–23) and Minster of Defence (1928–32) under the German Republic.

Proportional representation: System of voting in which each political party is represented in the parliament in proportion to the number of people who vote for it in the election.

governments, the desire of many conservatives to present a liberal front to the allies, and the radical nature of much anti-government agitation, all placed the Social Democratic Party (SPD) at the forefront of events. The shape of the Weimar Republic was to be determined by the state and by the aims of that party.

The German socialist movement was deeply divided. An Independent Social Democratic Party (USPD) had broken away from the SPD (April 1917), and a more extreme Communist Party (KPD) had been formed in November 1918. While the Communists supported the seizure of power and the implementation of radical programmes, the SPD followed the lead of its chief, Friedrich Ebert, in preferring peaceful, democratic change through an elected assembly. The non-revolutionary nature of Ebert's government was confirmed on the first day of the Republic's life, when he accepted the offer from General Groener of army assistance against the forces of the left. His decision undoubtedly strengthened his government by alliance with such a traditional and respected force. Groener possibly saved Germany from the intervention of allied troops. Naturally, however, the decision drew fierce criticism from the left. This was increased in the next few weeks when army units, aided by a newly formed Volunteer Corps (*Freikorps*), bloodily suppressed a Communist ('Spartacist') rising in Berlin (January 1919) and dispersed the 'Soviet' that had briefly held power in Munich (April 1919). Thus, while the Republic came to power across the corpses of some of its enemies, it owed that passage to a force that was merely a temporary ally. In the light of subsequent events, it was ominous that Groener had made no promise to protect the Republic from the forces of the right.

The Weimar constitution

The elections to the National Assembly (January 1919) placed the SPD at the head of the poll, but without an overall majority. It was thus obliged to enter a coalition with the Centre Party and the Democratic Party (DDP), which was to characterise the fragmented nature of political life in the Weimar Republic. The constitution drafted by the Assembly (July 1919) nevertheless represented a considerable democratic advance since 1914. It named the Reichstag as the sovereign authority of the state, and decreed that it should be elected every four years by **proportional representation**, by all men and women over the age of 21. The President, elected every seven years, was subject to the authority of the Reichstag, although he also possessed special powers for use in an emergency. A further outstanding break from the principles of the Bismarckian constitution concerned the powers of the upper house (*Reichsrat*). This continued to represent the interests of the component parts of the federal state, but was now subservient in all respects to the Reichstag. These component parts, instead of existing as sovereign kingdoms or duchies, were now designated merely as provinces (*Länder*).

A vigorous historical debate has surrounded the events of 1918–19 and their significance. For historian A.J. Nicholls they represented a true democratic advance for Germany (*Weimar and the Rise of Hitler*, 1968), bringing peace and a more genuinely representative system in place of the parliamentary 'charades' of

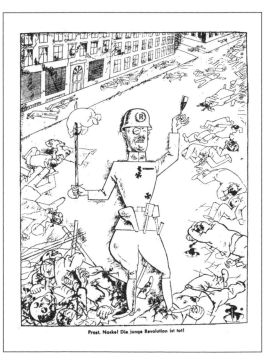

Prost. Noskel Die junge Revolution ist tot!

A satire by artist George Grosz on the conservative triumph in the early years of the Weimar Republic. The caption reads: 'Cheers. Noske! The Young Revolution is Dead.'

1. What reasons led to the formation of a republican government, under Social Democrat leadership, in Germany in 1918?

2. To what extent was a democratic form of government established in Germany 1918–19?

Bismarck's time. Yet to Gordon Craig (*Germany 1866–1945*, 1978) these events constituted an 'aborted revolution' which failed to change basic political attitudes and prejudices, and which thus condemned the republic to failure in the long run. John Hiden has compromised between the two positions, seeing the 1919 constitution, like the events that gave birth to it, as 'a synthesis between progressive political and social ideas and the desire to protect traditional institutions'.

10.2 What forces in Germany opposed the Weimar Republic and for what reasons?

Social democracy: A kind of socialism in which people are allowed a relatively large amount of freedom.

As imminent defeat in war brought the Republic into being, so its most pressing task was the conclusion of peace. In this task its freedom of action was almost nil. Advised by the military chiefs that continuation of hostilities was impossible, and forced to accept the allies' terms as the only alternative to invasion, the Weimar Republic nevertheless inherited a legacy of bitterness and resentment at its actions. German hopes that peace would be based upon Woodrow Wilson's 'Fourteen Points' (see Chapter 6), and that the replacement of the Kaiser by **social democracy** would incline the allies to leniency, proved misplaced. The terms that the republican ministers Müller and Bell finally accepted caused resentment. Among the causes of resentment were the following:

- Germany would not be accepted into the League of Nations.

- Germany lost eastern territories to states that could not pretend to have defeated it.

- Future German industry would pass the fruits of its labour to foreign capitalists in the form of reparations.

Worse, it was claimed that the German armies had not been beaten by the allies at all, but betrayed by the secret enemy at home – the socialist and the Jew. The myth of the 'Stab in the Back' (*Dolchstoss*) was born.

Despite the widespread feeling that 'the true basis of the Republic is not the Weimar Constitution but the Treaty of Versailles', it is not fair to imagine that the regime was doomed by the circumstances of its birth. For all its losses, republican Germany still had potentially the strongest economy in Europe, and its recovery was rapid. The political demoralisation caused by Versailles was a more serious problem, for it not only guaranteed a constant right-wing opposition to the Republic, but also undermined the initial enthusiasm of more moderate patriots for the regime. The future of the Weimar Republic, therefore, depended upon surviving long enough for such passions to cool.

Opponents on the left

The acceptance of the Weimar constitution in the Reichstag, by 262 votes to 75, and the success of the more moderate political parties in the elections of 1919, should not obscure the hostility that existed in Germany to the new

Ernst Thälmann (1886–1944)
Originally active in the trade union movement and in the Social Democratic Party, Thälmann joined the German Communist Party in 1924. Party Secretary, and twice party candidate in presidential elections. Arrested by the Nazis (1933), and died in Buchenwald concentration camp.

Gregor Strasser (1892–1934)
Joined the Nazi Party in 1920 and took part in the Beerhall *Putsch* (1923). Favoured the left-wing elements of National Socialist doctrine and opposed Hitler's alliances with 'big business'. Strasser resigned his party office in protest in 1932, and was murdered during the 'Night of the Long Knives'. His brother Otto (1897–1974), also prominent on the left wing of the movement, left the Nazi Party in 1930, and fled into exile in Canada.

Völkisch: German adjective used to describe a policy or idea based upon the principle of race. The *völkisch* groups laid their stress upon the concept of race (*Volk*), preaching the superiority of German racial characteristics and culture, and the need to protect them against alien influences, especially the harmful influence of the Jews.

Putschism: Violent insurrection. *Putsch* is a German word indicating the violent seizure of power by a group or party. It is the equivalent of the French *coup d'état*.

Stormtroopers: Small groups of well-armed foot soldiers. The *Sturmabteilung* (SA or Brownshirts) was a paramilitary force in Germany in the early 1930s. It was an organisation of about 4.5 million men who fought street battles against their opponents.

regime. The election result, as the left-wing commentator E. Troeltsch explained it, was not really a vote of confidence, for 'this democracy was in essence an anti-revolutionary system, dedicated to the maintenance of order and opposed to the dictatorship of the proletariat'. On the left extreme of the Republic's enemies stood the KPD, separated from the regime by a gulf of bitterness formed during the risings of 1919, and by the brutal murders of Communist leaders Karl Liebknecht and Rosa Luxemburg by *Freikorps* men. By December 1920, when its decision to join the International (the International Organisation of Communist and Socialist Parties) attracted many converts from the USPD, the KPD could boast a membership of 400,000 with 33 daily newspapers at its disposal. Although closely tied to a pro-Moscow policy by the leadership of Ernst Thälmann (1925–33), the party pursued a cautious policy, preferring to consolidate its strength, membership and influence steadily, rather than undertaking further adventures of the sort that had failed in 1919. Its achievement was, however, unimpressive. It failed to win any great influence among the trade unions, and alienated many potential supporters by its pro-Soviet stance. Nevertheless, the hostility between communists and social democrats continued into the next decade and helps to explain the failure of the left in Germany to resist the rise of Nazism.

Opponents on the right

A more daunting array of political opponents lay to the right of the Republic. The nationalists, grouped especially around the German National People's Party (DNVP) represented the brand of conservatism that desired a return to the principles and institutions of Wilhelmine Germany. The DNVP had influential support in the civil service, within the legal system, among industrialists, and in the churches. Indeed, the hostility of the legal system towards the Republic was clearly shown in the lenient sentences passed against right-wing terrorists and rebels. The nationalist threat to the regime was, nevertheless, limited by several factors. The leadership of the DNVP was divided over the issue of co-operation with the republican regime, and the whole emphasis of the party's policies was upon principles partly compromised by the defeat of the old Germany in the First World War.

In the course of the later 1920s, the nationalists began to surrender the leadership of the right-wing opposition to the National Socialist German Workers' Party (NSDAP or 'Nazis'), the most successful of the *völkisch* groups that appeared on the right of German politics. Founded in 1919 by Anton Drexler, but soon dominated by the brilliant orator Adolf Hitler, the Nazis came close to ruin in their early life by placing their trust in a policy of *putschism*. This resulted in public discredit and in the imprisonment of their leaders. Although the subsequent change of tactics – whereby the NSDAP now sought power by parliamentary means – led to poor results, the party had hidden strengths. Its local organisation, although uneven, was especially strong in Bavaria. Elsewhere it employed some notable local leaders, such as Gregor Strasser and Julius Streicher, who ensured tight local discipline.

It also deployed a powerful paramilitary force, the **stormtroopers** (*Sturmabteilung* or SA), which proved more than a match for its Communist rivals in the street violence that scarred the political life of the Weimar Republic. Lastly, its broad policy appealed to the resentments of defeated Germans, both 'national' and 'socialist'. Although this policy had little success in the years of republican prosperity, it promised to serve the party well should Germany once more fall upon hard times.

It is open to dispute whether the German Army (*Reichswehr*), in its

1. **What reasons did German nationalists and German communists have to feel that they had been betrayed by the Weimar Republic?**

2. **To what extent do you agree with the claim that 'the greatest handicap of the Weimar Republic lay in the fact that it had accepted the terms of the Versailles Treaty'?**

reduced, post-Versailles form, should be numbered among the Republic's enemies. Although it had done a great deal to enable the Weimar government to survive its first weeks, there was much in the principles of the traditional officer class, which still drew 21% of its membership from the nobility, that was at odds with the philosophy of the social-democratic Republic. The view of Hans von Seeckt (Chief of Army Command 1920–26) was that the *Reichswehr* should be an apolitical body, preserving its traditional values above the hurly-burly of party rivalry. Comparison between *Reichswehr* action in 1919, and its refusal to act against army veterans in *Freikorps* units during the Kapp *Putsch*, clearly showed that its attitude towards the government was merely lukewarm. In the words of John Hiden, in *The Weimar Republic* (1974), it 'would tolerate the Republic for the time being in its own interests'.

10.3 Why were the years 1920–1923 a period of crisis for the Weimar Republic?

The Kapp Putsch (1920) and the Beerhall Putsch (1923)

In its first months the Weimar Republic fought for its life against the hostility of the left, surviving by virtue of its temporary allies. In the next four years, however, there was much to maintain the sense of crisis and bitterness. The publication in April 1921 of the magnitude of Germany's reparation payments to the allies, combined with Matthias Erzberger's plans to strengthen the national economy by taxes upon war profits and inherited wealth to create enormous resentment on the right. This merged with existing nationalist hostility to subject the Republic to increasing right-wing violence. During these stages of the Republic's life, wrote historian Gordon Craig, 'its normal state was crisis'.

The first of these violent assaults was the Kapp *Putsch* (March 1920). Although this attempted coup was a symptom of wider right-wing discontent, the immediate trigger was the government's attempts to disband a *Freikorps* unit under Captain Ehrhardt at the request of the allies. Ominously, the *Reichswehr* took up a neutral stance, claiming that 'obviously there can be no talk of letting *Reichswehr* fight against *Reichswehr*'. Wolfgang Kapp's plans were frustrated instead by Berlin workers and civil servants who refused the orders of the rebels and denied them transport facilities and publicity. Unfortunately, this action was not repeated in later moments of republican peril.

Meanwhile, Germany experienced political violence and assassination unparalleled in its history. The most spectacular examples were the murders of Matthias Erzberger (August 1921) and of Walter Rathenau (June 1922). The final drama of this period of right-wing pressure was played out in Munich in November 1923, when Hitler and some Nazi followers attempted to exploit a clash between the reactionary government of Bavaria and the federal authorities. Their aim was a 'March on Berlin' after the style of Mussolini's recent 'March on Rome' (see Chapter 9). Police action reduced the so-called 'Beerhall *Putsch*' to a fiasco. Taken out of context the activities of Kapp and Hitler appear to pose little threat to the Weimar Republic. Nevertheless, the lenient sentences passed on the

Matthias Erzberger (1875–1921)
Reichstag deputy (1903) and leader of the Centre Party. Favourable to a peace settlement from 1916, he was a member of the delegation that signed the armistice in 1918. Foreign Minister in the German Republic, he was assassinated by nationalists.

Walter Rathenau (1867–1922)
President of the AEG electrical company, and director (1915) of Germany's war economy. Foreign Minister of the German Republic (1922) and signatory of the Treaty of Rapallo, he was assassinated by nationalists.

Value of the Reichsmark against the dollar

July 1914	4.2
July 1919	14.0
July 1920	39.5
July 1921	76.7
July 1922	493.2
Jan. 1923	1 7,972.0
July 1923	353,412.0
Aug. 1923	4,620,455.0
Sept. 1923	98,860,000.0
Oct. 1923	25,260,208,000.0
15 Nov. 1923	4,200,000,000,000.0

Source: Gordon Craig, *Germany 1866–1945*

1. What evidence was there of political and economic instability in Germany in the years 1919–23?

2. What were the main causes of the inflation that struck Germany in 1923, and upon whom did it have the greatest impact?

offenders – five years' imprisonment for Hitler and no punishment for any of Ehrhardt's *Freikorps* men – made clear the sympathy for their cause in high places. The Reichstag elections held in June 1920 added further indications of the ascendancy of the right.

Inflation

By the time of Hitler's *Putsch*, the Republic had also to confront a more serious threat from an international source. The reasons for, and the course of, the Franco-Belgian occupation of the Ruhr in January 1923 are described in Chapter 11. Here we have to consider the domestic effects of that action upon Germany. The most sensational of these was the acceleration of the decline of the *Reichsmark* (German currency) that had been in progress since the war. The initial blame lay, not with the French invasion, but with the crippling cost of the war, the pressure of reparation demands, and the Republic's misguided policy of printing money to meet budget deficits. As the table shows, the decline now raced out of control. Apart from its role in the origins of inflation, the government bore some responsibility for not checking it at an early stage. 'Cheap money' had its attractions for industrialists who now found plant and wages cheap, and for landowners whose mortgages were easier to pay off. Some enormous fortunes, such as that of the industrialist Hugo Stinnes, were forged out of this financial chaos. Inflation, on the other hand, had no consolations for the small saver or investor whose carefully accumulated sums and guaranteed interest became worthless in a matter of days.

The collapse of the value of pensions and savings ruined many, and the number of recipients of public relief in 1923 was three times that in 1913. 'Millions of Germans,' wrote Gordon Craig in *Germany 1866–1945* (1981), 'who had passively accepted the transition from Empire to Republic suffered deprivations that shattered their faith in the democratic process and left them cynical and alienated.' As a further ominous by-product many trade unions, unable in the crisis to protect their members' interests, suffered a sharp drop in their rolls and in their political influence.

10.4 In what respects did the years 1924–1929 constitute 'the golden age of the Weimar Republic'?

Stable political leadership: Gustav Stresemann and Paul von Hindenburg

The Weimar Republic not only survived, but launched upon the most successful period of its life, a period when long-term survival at last seemed possible. Two factors contributed greatly to this recovery. For the first time, the Republic had leaders who commanded respect, for the fall of Chancellor Cuno (August 1923) brought into office the major political

Gustav Stresemann (1879–1929) His political apprenticeship had been served in nationalist and militarist circles but, despite his initial sympathy with the Kapp rebels in 1920, he was shocked by the growth of political violence and instability in Germany. Stresemann became a republican and was both Chancellor (1923) and Foreign Minister (1923–29) of the Weimar Republic. Achievements: reducing war reparations paid by Germany after the Treaty of Versailles; negotiating Locarno Treaties (1925); and negotiating Germany's entry into League of Nations. Won the 1926 Nobel Peace Prize with Aristide Briand.

Chancellors of Weimar Germany 1919–1933

Paul Scheidemann	1919 (Feb. – June)	W. Marx	1923–1924
G. Bauer	1919–1920	Hans Luther	1925–1926
H. Müller	1920 (March– June)	H. Müller	1929–1930
C. Fehrenbach	1920–1921	Heinrich Brüning	1930–1932
Joseph Wirth	1921–1922	Franz von Papen	1932 (May–Nov.)
Wilhelm Cuno	1922–1923	Kurt von Schleicher	1932–1933
Gustav Stresemann	1923 (August–Nov.)	Adolf Hitler	1933–

figure of the Republic, Gustav Stresemann. Stresemann became republican because he was horrified by the more radical alternatives. His political background, nevertheless, was that of an orthodox conservative, and made him acceptable to many people who could barely tolerate his predecessors. Although Chancellor for only three months, he continued to exert a profound influence upon German politics from the Foreign Ministry until his death in 1929.

Shortly after the emergence of Stresemann, the death of Friedrich Ebert (February 1925) brought to the presidency of the Republic the wartime hero Field Marshal Paul von Hindenburg, a man of impeccable patriotic credentials. His election was largely an expression of nostalgia for the stability and strength of the 'old' Germany. 'The truth is,' Stresemann testified, 'that Germans want no president in a top hat. He must wear a uniform and plenty of decorations.' Hindenburg, however, wore both his uniform and his office with tact, and effectively defended the Republic from the worst barbs of its right-wing opponents.

The second vital factor in the recovery of the Republic was the desire of the wartime allies to prevent the collapse or political disintegration of Germany. Foreign co-operation was central to the regime's new lease of life.

The establishment of financial stability

Reparations: Payments made by a defeated state to compensate the victorious state(s) for damage or expenses caused by the war.

The first achievements of the revived Republic were the rescue of the German currency and the regulation of **reparations**. At the end of 1923, thanks to the work of Hans Luther at the Ministry of Finance, the discredited *Reichsmark* was replaced by the so-called '*Rentenmark*'. In the absence of sufficient gold reserves, the new currency was backed in theory by Germany's agricultural and industrial resources. It was a new, largely fictitious, form of security, which relied heavily upon foreign goodwill for its general acceptance. There was enough of this goodwill, however, not only to support the stabilisation of the currency, but also to regulate the question of Germany's reparation payments through the formulation of the Dawes Plan (see Chapter 11) in 1924. Outwardly, the German economy presented a picture in the later 1920s of stability and prosperity. The emergence of giant industrial combines such as I.G. Farben and United Steelworks (*Vereinigte Stahlwerke*) in 1926 seemed to testify to the renewed dynamism of German heavy industry. In 1927, overall production figures at last matched those of 1913.

The achievement of domestic political stability

Financial stability was accompanied by a greater degree of political stability. Apart from the acceptability of Stresemann and Hindenburg, the economic recovery blunted nationalist opposition to the Republic by appeasing the industrialists who played a substantial role in the DNVP. The armed forces, too, seemed to be on better terms with the Republic after the resignation of von Seeckt (October 1926) as commander of the *Wehrmacht*. After the appointment of General Groener (December 1927) as Defence Minister, 1928–29 provided two pieces of electoral comfort for the government. The Reichstag elections in May 1928 provided the worst results for a decade for the parties of the political extremes. Between them the DNVP (14.2%), the NSDAP (2.6%) and the KPD (10.6%) secured less than 30% of the popular vote. In December 1929 a **referendum** took place, forced by a coalition of nationalists and Nazis, trying to condemn the Young Plan and proposing treason charges against the government for doing deals with foreign interests. Only 13.8% of the votes cast agreed with this interpretation of government policy.

Referendum (or plebiscite): A form of political consultation in which the electorate is asked for its response to a specific measure proposed by the government.

Why, and with what success, did Weimar Germany adopt a 'policy of fulfilment' in foreign affairs?

'For most Germans,' writes John Hiden in *The Weimar Republic* (1974), 'foreign policy meant an unremitting effort to revise the terms of the Treaty of Versailles.' Successive German governments sought to remedy the dangerous diplomatic isolation that resulted from defeat, and to restore the degree of national independence lost to the allies and to their occupation agencies. The first method they used was the simple tactic of sullen obstruction.

● The clauses of the treaty directed against the Kaiser and other alleged war criminals were never effectively enforced.

● The disbanding of paramilitary organisations was slow and unreliable.

● The clauses relating to disarmament were implemented only under constant allied supervision.

Such a policy could not be successful for long against opponents with both the determination and the means to enforce the treaty terms. German policy thus changed under the chancellorship of Joseph Wirth (May 1921–November 1922) to one of 'fulfilment' (*Erfüllungspolitik*). This apparent co-operation with the allies was one of the greatest causes of bitterness among the right-wing opponents of the regime. It played a direct role in stirring the political violence of the period.

It was, nevertheless, a sensible and realistic policy. It was designed to encourage future allied leniency towards Germany, and its introduction coincided with a successful solution to the problem of diplomatic isolation. The conclusion of the Treaty of Rapallo with the Soviet Union in April 1922 created investment opportunities for Germany. It also greatly improved the prospects of evading the military restrictions imposed at Versailles. However, it may also be argued that it did a great deal, in combination with the chaos caused by French occupation of the Ruhr, to frighten the western allies into taking a more reasonable attitude towards Germany.

The greatest successes of *Erfüllungspolitik* were achieved whilst Gustav Stresemann controlled the Foreign Ministry. He combined the broad principles of 'fulfilment' with an attempt to lay foundations for the revision of the peace treaties. Stresemann was portrayed by liberal historians as a 'good European', eager to put co-operation in the place of confrontation, while historians of the Marxist left saw him as a capitalist reaching an accommodation with the other western powers for essentially anti-Soviet reasons. The publication of his official papers indicated that Stresemann was neither of these things. His primary aim was to rid Germany of foreign restraints, and to regain full sovereignty and freedom of political action. Thus the Locarno Pact of 1925 guaranteed Germany's western borders against further incursions, without committing Germany to acceptance of the hated territorial settlement in the east. It also paved the way for Germany's acceptance into the international community of the League of Nations. The agreement of the Dawes Plan in 1924 and the Young Plan in 1929 were classic examples of this policy of 'fulfilment' (see Chapter 11). They reduced Germany's total reparations debt, and gained foreign recognition of its difficulties in paying it off at all.

Steadily, from January 1926, Germany began to reap the fruits of this policy. In that month, British withdrawal from Cologne marked the first major reduction of the occupying forces. This was followed in January 1927 by the withdrawal from Germany of the Inter-Allied Control Commission, the major 'watchdog' of the Versailles terms. Before the fall of the Republic, the evacuation of foreign troops was completed by the French withdrawal (August 1929). Within two years, the continuation of reparation payments had been dealt a near fatal blow by Chancellor Brüning's successful application to the USA for a '**moratorium**' (June 1931). No area of policy under the Weimar Republic could claim to rival the success of its foreign policy. Its tragedy was that the government failed consistently to convince the political extremists of the constructive good sense of that policy. When the international economic crisis undermined the Republic, its foreign policy of restrained national reassertion was to be one of the first casualties of its collapse.

Moratorium: A legally authorised delay in the performance of a legal duty or obligation. From the Latin *mora* – delay.

Was the Republic secure at the end of the 1920s?

For all these shifts in policy, and for all the improvements that had taken place in its status and stability, the Weimar Republic still had its weaknesses. It seemed to be winning the public relations battle as the end of the 1920s approached, but it had established few durable institutions to sustain it in time of crisis. The lukewarm toleration of the regime shown by the *Reichswehr* was not widely imitated by the civil service, the universities or the schools. The historian K.S. Pinson describes in detail the atmosphere of German education in the 1920s.

Political parties in Weimar Germany

DNVP (the German National People's Party): a conservative, nationalist party that was opposed to the creation of German democracy. Wanted a return to the authoritarian type of government under Wilhelm II. Supported the large-scale landowners of eastern Germany. Wanted protective tariffs against imported food-stuffs. Developed from the Fatherland Front and the Conservative Party of the last years of the Kaiser's reign.

DVP (the German People's Party): Weimar equivalent of the National Liberal Party of Bismarck's and Wilhelm II's Germany. Represented the interests of 'big business'. Most prominent politician was Gustav Stresemann.

Zentrum (the Centre Party): represented the interests of the Catholic Church in Germany. Linked with the BVP (Bavarian People's Party) which represented Catholic interests in Bavaria.

DDP (the German Democratic Party): supported German democracy. Weimar equivalent of the Progressive Liberal Party of Bismarck's and Wilhelm II's Germany. Supported by the middle class. Electoral support declined rapidly from 1920.

SPD (the Social Democratic Party): the largest party in Germany for most of the Weimar period. Represented the interests of the German working class. It had existed since 1875 and supported the creation of a socialist state through democratic means.

KPD (the Communist Party): formed in 1920 from the Spartacists and elements of the Independent Social Democratic Party. Wanted to create a communist state. Opposed to democracy. Main rival for working-class support of the SPD.

NSDAP (the National Socialist German Workers' Party, or Nazi Party): Hitler's party. Wanted to overthrow Weimar democracy and the Treaty of Versailles. Initially planned to achieve this through revolution. After 1925 Hitler attempted to achieve power through the ballot box and intimidation by the SA stormtroopers. Largest party in the Reichstag by 1932 but never gained more than one-third of the votes before January 1933.

1. In what respects were domestic politics in Germany more stable between 1924 and 1929 than they had been in the previous five years?

2. How convincing is the claim that 'the Weimar Republic was on the verge of success until undermined by the international economic crisis of 1929'?

3. Did the foreign policy of the Weimar Republic serve Germany's best interests?

'The essential control of both lower and higher education remained in the hands of those who had nothing but contempt for the Republic and who therefore made no effort to prepare the German youth for republican citizenship. Not a single school text in Weimar Germany presented the true story of German defeat in 1918. Germany geography texts still inculcated in the minds of the young the definition that Germany was a country surrounded on all sides by enemies.'

Nor had the Republic developed a system of parliamentary parties strong enough to give stability to its democracy. The classic Weimar coalition parties – the Social Democrats, the Democratic Party and the Centre Party – remained divided on many points of economic, political and religious doctrine. Their lack of cohesion in the face of the rise of a popular anti-democratic movement would play a major role in the disasters of the early 1930s.

Lastly, for all the appearance of superficial prosperity, the basis of the German economy was unsound. Industrial investment and government expenses were not adequately financed from German capital or German profits. More than a third of all capital invested in Germany in the late 1920s came from foreign loans. Imports between 1924 and 1930 were always greater than exports. The total deficit of the German budget over these years amounted to nearly 1.3 billion *Reichsmarks*. It is impossible to deny that in the years 1924–29 the Weimar Republic was progressing and was achieving some signs of permanency. In that limited period, however, normality was never quite achieved, and when it appeared close it proved only a brief interlude between two disasters.

10.5 Why was the Weimar Republic unable to survive the crisis generated by the Wall Street Crash?

The economic impact of the crash upon Germany

Stresemann had warned in 1928, 'Germany is dancing on a volcano. If the short-term credits are called in a large section of our economy would collapse.' Indeed, within days of Stresemann's premature death (3 October 1929), the slump in the Wall Street stock market (24 October 1929) triggered off just such a phenomenon. Germany's foreign capital, which had stood at 5 billion marks in 1928, dropped by half in 1929, and shrank to a mere 700 million marks in 1930. Loans began to be called in and bankruptcies multiplied. With the government consistently reluctant to set off renewed inflation, the crisis manifested itself primarily as massive unemployment. The problem had haunted Germany since the recovery of 1925, with 2 million out of work in the winter of 1925–26 and 1.5 million jobless a year later. The rise towards the disastrous figures of the Depression began in the summer of 1928. In mid-1929, 1.5 million were unemployed and in the following year the figures soared out of control. Three million were affected in the winter of 1929–30, 5 million by the end of the following summer and 6 million in January 1932.

The political impact of the crash upon Germany

Extremism: The behaviour or beliefs of people who wish to bring about political or social change by doing things that other people consider too severe or disruptive, often using violence.

The main political result of the economic slump was a substantial revival of **extremism**. As the table on page 298 indicates, the elections of 1930–32 were marked by a dramatic growth of influence for those parties that offered extreme solutions to the contemporary distress. The KPD achieved greater support than it had ever had before, but above all it was the Nazis that benefited from the economic tragedy.

Elections to the Reichstag, 1919–1932

	Jan. 1919	June 1920	May 1924	Dec. 1924	May 1928	Sept. 1930	July 1932	Nov. 1932
NSDAP	–	–	32	14	12	107	230	196
DNVP	44	71	95	103	73	41	37	52
DVP	19	65	45	51	45	30	7	11
Centre	91	85	81	88	78	87	98	90
DDP	75	39	28	32	25	20	4	2
SPD	165	102	100	131	153	143	133	121
USPD	22	84	–	–	–	–	–	–
KPD	–	4	62	45	54	77	89	100

There can be no doubt that the economic crisis played a major role in the increasing popularity of the NSDAP. For example, the research of historian Martin Broszat, in *The Hitler State* (1981), has established that, of all the working class recruits joining the Nazi Party in 1930–33, some 55% were unemployed. Nevertheless, there was nothing inevitable about the Nazi advent to power. They never represented a majority in the Reichstag and their electoral fortunes were in decline by late 1932. Their triumph resulted from the degeneration and miscalculations of republican politics in the years of economic crisis.

Brüning's administration

Heinrich Brüning (1885–1970)
A leading figure in German Catholic politics, prominent in the Centre Party (becoming its leader in 1929). Brüning was a social, political and economic conservative, a war veteran, and hostile to the principles of social democracy. Appointed Chancellor (1930), and Foreign Minister (1931). Resigned both offices in 1932, and lived in exile in the USA.

The resignation of Chancellor Müller's cabinet (March 1930) – the Republic's last Social Democrat administration – marked the end of majority government in Germany. As the political parties of the centre continued to place sectional interests before national needs, the effective government of the state fell into the hands of President Hindenburg and advisors such as General Groener and General von Schleicher. Their primary aim was less the protection of democracy and parliamentary government than the formation of a more authoritative and authoritarian government to face the economic crisis. Their first choice as Chancellor, Heinrich Brüning, had admirable qualifications for the office. He sought to cement his administration with some foreign success, such as the suspension of reparation payments, and he tackled Germany's domestic crisis by orthodox, deflationary economic tactics. Reductions in social services and in unemployment benefits, at the time when they were needed most, were unlikely to rally wide support, and they led to Brüning's damaging reputation as the 'Hunger Chancellor'. They also drove many of the unemployed into the ranks of the paramilitary organisations. Meanwhile, military expenditure and subsidies to the *Junker* farmers were maintained.

Brüning's greatest political error, however, was the dissolution of the Reichstag (July 1930) in search of a secure majority. Instead, at a time of mounting crisis, he found the political extremism and the violence of the streets translated into Reichstag seats. Continued failure to curb economic depression, and to achieve ministerial stability, finally encouraged the President to replace Brüning with Franz von Papen in May 1932. This was the move which, according to the liberal historian Erich Eyck, 'killed not only the German Republic, but the peace of Europe'.

**Franz von Papen
(1879–1969)**
Member of the Centre
Party and deputy in the
Prussian *Landtag*
(1923–32). Chancellor of
the German Republic
(1932). Narrowly escaped

assassination during the
'Night of the Long Knives'.
Tried at Nuremberg for his
role in assisting the Nazis
to power, but acquitted.

**Kurt von Schleicher
(1882–1934)**
After active service in the
Imperial German Army, he
became a senior officer in
the *Reichswehr* (1919–29).
Appointed Defence
Minister in von Papen's

government (1932), he
then served briefly as
Chancellor. Unable to
reach agreement with
Hitler, Schleicher resigned
(1933), and was murdered
during the 'Night of the
Long Knives' (1934).

Papen, Schleicher and the advent of the Nazis

Franz von Papen's responsibility for the advent of the Nazis was great. In June, he lifted the ban that Brüning had placed upon the *Sturmabteilung*. In July, he used the resultant street violence, and the spate of deaths in clashes between Nazis and Communists, as the pretext to dismiss the Social Democrat provincial government in Prussia, one of the last strongholds of democratic government in Germany. Like Brüning before him, his decision to hold new elections (July 1932) played into the hands of the Nazis with their increasing support. Papen's efforts to establish an electoral alliance with Hitler as the junior partner were frustrated, both by Hitler's refusal to accept any office less than that of Chancellor, and by the aged President's personal and social dislike of Hitler. With Papen's resignation, the President had only one alternative to Hitler himself. When Kurt von Schleicher failed in his brief chancellorship (December 1932 – January 1933) to split the Nazi leadership by negotiating with Gregor Strasser, Hindenburg at last accepted Adolf Hitler as the only alternative to political chaos and possible civil war.

Hitler thus became Chancellor on 30 January 1933, with a cabinet of three Nazis and ten conservatives, the latter representing the vain hope of the traditional German right that they might still use the dynamic force of Nazism for their own purposes. A seven-hour torchlight parade by the SA in the streets of Berlin formed the funeral celebrations of the Weimar Republic.

1. What was the economic and political impact of the Wall Street Crash upon Germany?

2. How did the economic crisis of 1929 help to bring Hitler and the Nazis to power in Germany?

3. Why did the Weimar Republic survive the crisis of 1923, but not that which began in 1929?

10.6 What was the contribution of Adolf Hitler to the rise of Nazism?

Adolf Hitler (1889–1945)

Judaism: Religion of the Jewish people, which is based on the Old Testament of the Bible and the Talmud (book of laws and traditions).

Born in the small Austrian town of Braunau am Inn (20 April 1889), Hitler was the son of a customs official already well into middle age. Academically and socially, the young Hitler was a failure. His inability to gain admission to the Academy of Fine Arts in Vienna (1907) formed the prelude to 'five years of misery and woe', living by odd jobs and occasional artistic work. Hitler's 'Greater German' nationalism was already formed, and he later claimed that it was in Vienna that he first formulated the intense hatred of Jews and **Judaism** that was thereafter a central feature of his political beliefs. Convinced of the decadence of the Austro-Hungarian Empire, and of the invincibility of the racially purer German Reich, Hitler evaded Austrian conscription in 1914 to serve in a Bavarian regiment. After a creditable military career at the Western Front, he was stunned by the sudden collapse of the German war effort in November 1918. For him, there could be no other explanation than that all patriotic Germans had been vilely betrayed by the socialists, Marxists and Jews prominent in the November 'revolution' and in the subsequent Weimar Republic. In subsequent years, Hitler propagated the myth of the 'stab in the back', not only because of its propaganda value, but also because he was personally convinced of its truth. His natural place thereafter was in the ranks of the extreme nationalist opposition to the Republic. In September 1917 he joined the German Workers' Party which shortly afterwards changed its name to the National Socialist German Workers' Party (NSDAP). By July 1921 Hitler was its chairman.

Hitler as orator and publicist

Hitler's tenure of power in Germany lasted only 12 years. His tenure of real international power was shorter by half. Yet the fact that his is undoubtedly the best known face, and his the best documented political career of the century, bears witness to the extraordinary impact of the man. Hitler's primary qualification for a political career was his extraordinary talent as an orator. In part, this was based upon careful study of all the elements of public speaking, and brilliant mastery of the tactics of dogmatic assertion, sarcasm and emotional appeal. As W. Carr wrote in *History of Germany, 1815–1985* (1987), 'a Hitler speech was superb theatre. Hitler was his own script writer, choreographer and actor-manager all rolled into one.'

His success was not wholly explained, however, by contrived effects, but was largely due to the intense sincerity of his nationalistic feelings, and by his ability to communicate with the outrage and frustration of millions of Germans. A contemporary, Otto Strasser, described the effect of a speech as follows.

'He enters a hall. He sniffs the air. For a moment he gropes, feels his way, senses the atmosphere. Suddenly he bursts forth. His words go like an arrow to their target; he touches every private wound on the raw, liberating the mass unconscious, expressing its innermost aspirations, telling it what it most wants to hear.'

1. What was the impact of Germany's defeat in the First World War upon Adolf Hitler's political thinking?

2. To what extent do Hitler's personal talents explain the rise and the appeal of Nazism in the late 1920s and the early 1930s?

Such skills were more than adequate for one who saw himself at first only as a 'drummer' preparing the way for a greater leader, a John the Baptist, smoothing the way for Germany's true saviour. The stage at which he came to believe in himself as that saviour is unclear; perhaps as he reformulated his political views after the failure of the Munich *Putsch* of 1923. The years after 1923 saw the emergence of Hitler as unchallenged party leader.

Hitler achieved and fulfilled this role in an unorthodox fashion, for his were not the usual talents of political organiser and administrator. He was lazy, and often bored by practical detail. Administrative inefficiency, however, was outweighed by a remarkable political instinct, an unconquerable will power and self-confidence, total ruthlessness, and a talent for winning the dogged devotion of individuals. It is quite possible that Hitler cultivated his disinterest in detail and practicalities to maintain party unity, and to present the image that he maintained so well as the man of destiny, far above the petty wrangling that corrupted mundane politics (see also section 10.15). These were the talents that transformed Adolf Hitler from the 'nobody of Vienna' into the most dynamic and fateful figure in German history.

10.7 What were the main political and social doctrines of National Socialism?

The ancestry of Nazism

The intellectual roots of Nazism must be sought in a variety of locations. Many commentators, especially in the years immediately after the Second

World War, interpreted Nazism as a movement that grew naturally from the authoritarianism and nationalism of earlier German history (see Chapter 3). It is hardly surprising that many German historians, such as Gerhard Ritter in *The Historical Foundations of the Rise of National Socialism* (1955), favoured a different view of Nazism. They saw it, not as the product of German history, but as the product of the unprecedented social and economic pressures upon Europe in the 1920s and 1930s. Another prominent German authority, Karl Bracher, in *The German Dictatorship* (1978), may be closest to the truth when he combines the two schools of thought. 'Past research has made clear that an examination of the roots of National Socialism must be conducted simultaneously on two levels; the German and the overall European.'

Essentially a distillation of resentments and fears, Nazism was a rag-bag of elements borrowed from most of the major political tendencies of the last century. From Germany alone it borrowed the conservative **Realpolitik** of Bismarck, the nationalism of Johann Fichte and the godless humanism of Friedrich Nietzsche. Its racial theories leaned heavily upon those of the Comte de Gobineau (*Essay on the Inequality of the Human Races*, 1855) and of Houston Stewart Chamberlain (*Foundations of the Nineteenth Century*, 1899). Both men had argued from the lunatic fringes of **Darwinism** that the key to human development lay in the inevitable triumph of the **Aryan races** over 'lesser varieties of mankind'. From further afield, and more recently, came the practical examples provided by Italian Fascism, with its attractive trappings and its bold seizure of national power. Also there was the ruthless example of Stalin in his consolidation of power in the Soviet Union. Although he was distanced from Stalin's political aims, Hitler could only feel the greatest respect for Stalin's coldly logical methods. 'Stalin and I,' he was to declare, 'are the only ones who see the future.'

The philosophy of Mein Kampf

Some semblance of cohesion and consistency was given to this variety of influences by the initial programme of the National Socialist Party (February 1920) which predated Hitler's dominance over the party and, more importantly, by Hitler's own political testament *My Struggle* (*Mein Kampf*). This was written during his imprisonment after the failure of the 1923 coup, and published in 1925. A rambling and highly personal work, *Mein Kampf* provided no precise manifesto for future government, but made clear the essential principles upon which the Nazis and their leader intended to proceed.

Central to Hitler's argument was the conviction that the only true basis of the state was not that of class interest (an invention of Marxism and Judaism) or of community or economic interest, but that of race. It was thus the primary duty of the German state to unite within its borders all those of common racial origin, and to eliminate alien elements that might weaken or corrupt the ethnic community (*Volksgemeinschaft*). In the case of Germany, this meant the elimination of the influence of the Jews. In Hitler's view their international conspiracy bore the responsibility for all Germany's recent ills. Subsequently, the major duty of the state would be the provision of adequate resources and 'living space' (*Lebensraum*) for the population that dwelt by right within its boundaries. As the preservation of its people was the reason for the state's existence, it was not only permissible, but positively desirable, for the state to acquire this *Lebensraum* by struggle against neighbouring races. Nor did Hitler attempt to dodge the implications of this doctrine in the specific case of Germany. 'History proves', he declared in *Mein Kampf*, 'that the German people owes its existence solely to its determination to fight in the east and to obtain land

Realpolitik: Policy that is based upon real, practical considerations, rather than upon abstract principles or ideals.

Darwinism: The views of Charles Darwin (1809–1882), the great British biologist, who defined the principles of evolution among animal species. Some political and social commentators believed that similar laws of development applied to the human race as well, and that some races were thus more highly developed than others. Such views are usually referred to as 'Social Darwinism'.

Aryan races: Term used by racists to indicate those Nordic and Anglo-Saxon races which the Nazis supposed to be superior to others.

Lebensraum (German – 'living space'): That foreign territory which, in the view of extreme German nationalists, had to be seized for the proper future maintenance of the German race.

by military conquest. Land in Europe is only to be gained at the expense of Russia.'

Political authority: the **Führerprinzip**

To provide the dynamism and the unity of purpose necessary for the achievement of such a visionary programme, Nazism defined the 'leader principle' (*Führerprinzip*). Thereby, each level of Nazi organisation was committed to unquestioning obedience to its chief, with ultimate allegiance owed to the man at the apex of the pyramid of command, the *Führer*. This gave the appearance of consistency to a divided movement and ensured Hitler's personal authority. It also appealed to millions of Germans for whom representative democracy seemed a short road to economic ruin and to national humiliation. This principle allowed the Nazis to pose not merely as the latest candidates for party political power, but as the appointed guardians of the destiny of the whole German nation.

The socialist element in Nazism

For all this, there was still considerable disagreement within the Nazi ranks in 1933 about what the party's priorities should be. To such men as the brothers Otto and Gregor Strasser, and to many of the ex-soldiers who filled the ranks of the SA, the socialist element was central to National Socialism. The priority of the movement should be to overturn the great capitalist enterprises that had made such a contribution to the economic hardships of the past decade. 'We are enemies,' Gregor Strasser wrote, 'deadly enemies, of the present-day capitalist economy with its exploitation of the economically weak, with its unjust wage system, with its immoral evaluation of the individual according to property.' To Hitler such doctrine was divisive, and alienated forces without which German national greatness could scarcely be restored. For him, it remained essential to concentrate upon such vague and emotive concepts as 'Fatherland', *'Volk'*, 'loyalty' and 'sacrifice'.

Nazism, like Fascism in Italy, retained an element of negative cohesion in its prime targets of hate. The Versailles Treaty, the Weimar Republic, parliamentary liberalism in general, Marxism, and Judaism, were all condemned. They were the objects that united the Nazi movement in 1933.

To whom did Nazism appeal and for what reasons?

An analysis of 4,800 party members in 1923 showed 60% of them originated from the lower middle, or skilled working classes. These were men who had established some small stake in the world and feared that social and economic chaos would drag them back to the bottom of the ladder. Shopkeepers and tradesmen (14%), clerks and minor officials (17%), skilled craftsmen (20%) and specialist workers (9%), were prominent on party lists. It is not difficult to understand why both party membership and electoral support stagnated during the relative stability of 1924–29, to be regenerated by renewed economic crisis in the wake of the Wall Street Crash (see Chapter 11). In 1928, the party had 40,000 members, received about 1.03 million votes, and won 12 Reichstag seats. Between 1931 and 1932, those figures rose to 800,000, 16.5 million, and 230 respectively. The motives of these new followers were probably similar to those that moved Albert Speer after his first exposure to Hitler's oratory in 1931.

'Here it seemed to me was hope. Here were new ideals, a new understanding, new tasks. The perils of communism could be checked, Hitler persuaded us, and instead of hopeless unemployment, Germany

Führer (German – leader): Name for the person in charge of the Nazi organisation, namely Adolf Hitler. An essential feature of Nazism. 'The *Führer*,' wrote Nazi theorist Ernst Huber in 1933, 'is the bearer of the people's will; he is independent of all groups, associations, and interests. In his will the will of the people is realised.'

'Volk': Term meaning 'the people': should usually be understood in a racial sense, rather than in a class sense. It designates those who are united by their German blood, rather than the common people of Germany.

1. What were the main racial theories and beliefs of the Nazi Party when it came to power in 1933?

2. What was the relative importance of nationalism and socialism in the doctrines of the Nazi Party?

could move towards economic recovery. It must have been during these months that my mother saw an SA parade in the streets of Heidelberg. The sight of discipline in a time of chaos, the impression of energy in an atmosphere of universal hopelessness, seems to have won her over too.'

Two major modifications to this pattern of lower middle-class support had occurred in the years 1930–33. The first was the emergence of the Nazis as the prime representatives of nationalist politics. This arose from the so-called Harzberg Agreement (October 1930) with the Nationalist Party, based upon a common anti-republican campaign in opposition especially to the Young Plan. The co-operation of such nationalist figures as the industrialist Alfred Hugenberg, Hjalmar Schacht (head of the Reichsbank) and Franz Seldte (head of the *Stahlhelm* veterans' organisation) extended Nazi influence into spheres where it could scarcely have hoped to penetrate before. The second modification was the party's remarkably successful campaign to win peasant support, and to infiltrate existing agrarian organisations. H. Gies has shown, in *Nazism and the Third Reich* (1972), that the Nazi share of the rural vote rose from 22.6% (1930) to 52.4% (1933), while their share of the urban vote never rose higher than 39.6% (1933).

> 1. Identify the main groups that supported Hitler in Germany in 1933.
>
> 2. Explain the popularity of the Nazis in Germany in 1933.

10.8 How was Nazi power consolidated after 1933?

The Reichstag fire and the Enabling Act

Hermann Goering (1893–1946)
Joined the Nazi Party (1922) after distinguished war service as a pilot. President of the Reichstag (1932–45). Minister President of Prussia and Minister for Aviation (1933–45). Commander-in-Chief of the *Luftwaffe* (1934–45). Responsible for the Four-Year Plan (1936–45). Convicted and condemned at Nuremberg, he committed suicide before execution.

Despite their popular pose as a revolutionary party, the Nazis had come to power by constitutional means. Nevertheless, the years after 1933 witnessed a Nazi takeover of the machinery of the German state that was little short of revolutionary. Like Mussolini in 1923, Hitler was never likely to be satisfied with power limited by a constitution and by the presence in the state of parties and interests potentially hostile to his own. At first, his tactics for strengthening his position centred upon the Reichstag election to be held in March. He prepared for this with a massive propaganda campaign that stressed the continuity between Nazism and other forms of German conservatism, and by practical measures such as Hermann Goering's rapid extension of Nazi control over the police and civil service in Prussia. The result still left the Nazis with the direct support of only 43.9% of the population, but by then a whole new range of possibilities had opened up for Hitler.

The fire that destroyed the Reichstag building (27 February 1933) provided such a convenient crisis for the Nazis that it was supposed for many years that their agents had started it. It now seems that van der Lubbe, the Dutch Communist who was accused of the crime, really did commit it. The government may merely have exploited the happy coincidence. This powerful illustration of the 'Communist threat', upon which Nazi propaganda had long insisted, went a long way to ensuring public acceptance in the arrest of Communist deputies and in the passage of two measures central to the collapse of German democracy. The arrests themselves strengthened Hitler's position in the Reichstag. The Decree for the Protection of People and State (28 February) suspended the essential freedoms of the individual, giving the state unprecedented rights of search, arrest and censorship. The Enabling Law (23 March), which only the SPD opposed, transferred full legislative and executive power to the Chancellor (Hitler) for a period of four years. Undoubtedly, German democracy was destroyed by Hitler, but he was abetted in the crime by so-called democrats who lacked the determination to keep liberty alive.

Gleichschaltung

Long before the expiry of that four-year period, Hitler had destroyed or neutralised all those groups and institutions in a position to impose limits upon his power. This policy was referred to by the term *Gleichschaltung* (co-ordination). In some cases, the weapon used was the naked exercise of state or party power. By the Law against the New Formation of Parties, the KPD and the SPD were formally outlawed and their property seized, and all other political parties, except the Nazis, were declared illegal. By accepting this law such well-established organisations as the Catholic Centre Party effectively dissolved themselves and accepted Nazi dictatorship. In January 1934, Hitler abolished the provincial assemblies of the *Länder*. In their places he put Nazi governors (*Reichstatthalter*), and made Germany a centralised, unitary state for the first time.

Other institutions weakened their positions by attempts to compromise with the new government. The socialist trade unions had already guaranteed their non-intervention in political questions. They had also accepted the supervision of a Nazi *Reichskommissar* when, on 2 May 1933, stormtroopers occupied their offices throughout Germany, dissolved them, and began the enrolment of all labour into a German Labour Front. Other institutions lost their independence by a process of subtle infiltration. The Prussian civil service was brought under firmer control by the dismissal of nearly 30% of its officers on racial grounds or on grounds of 'incompetence'. The legal and academic professions became subject to Nazi 'fronts' or 'academies' outside which there was little hope of practice or of professional advancement.

Winning over other conservative elements in German politics

Three major elements in German society were too powerful to be directly coerced, and perhaps bear more guilt for the accommodations that they reached with Hitler. The support of German industry for Hitler had got seriously underway in 1928–29. His disciplining of the Strasser 'wing' of the party, and his subsequent alliance with the conservative Nationalist Party had convinced its leaders that the Nazis were not, as the contemporary joke had it, 'like a beefsteak, brown on the outside but red in the middle'. At this early stage, substantial financial contributions to the party were made by a variety of banking and mining interests, headed by the steel magnate Fritz Thyssen. Hitler's consistent policies of anti-socialist legislation and subsequent rearmament earned much wider support in these areas in the years immediately after his seizure of power.

The Catholic Church, too, was quick to seek an arrangement with the new regime, which now found it convenient to play down its essentially anti-Christian nature. A Concordat (July 1933) was concluded with the Nazi state in an attempt to preserve the Church's educational influence and similar privileges. In this agreement the Church authorities undertook to dissuade Catholic priests from political activity, and did much to hasten the collapse of the Centre Party. Unlike the Lateran Accords concluded with Mussolini (see Chapter 9), the Concordat represented almost complete surrender to the new political leadership. Certain elements in the Lutheran Church, by agreeing to the formation of a Reich Church (*Reichskirche*), surrendered in similarly abject fashion. In this case, however, a breakaway Confessional Church managed to survive as a symbol of Christian opposition to Nazism.

Like the major industrialists, the German army (*Reichswehr*) shared a community of interest with the Nazi *Führer*. Its commanders had little objection to his declared nationalist aims, while the realisation of those aims seemed unlikely without heavy industry to produce weapons and without soldiers to use them. Although elements of suspicion remained, the army accepted the promises that had been made to it in February and March 1933 as to its future role. While this gave Hitler the support of the army, he had to wait longer for any substantial element of direct control. The death of President Hindenburg (August 1934) not only made possible the combination of the offices of President and Chancellor in the new office of '*Führer* and Chancellor', but also gave Hitler the chance to revise his relationship with the army. By imposing a new oath of allegiance upon all ranks (August 1934), he ensured their commitment directly to 'the *Führer* of the German *Reich* and People, Adolf Hitler'. The later dismissal of the War Minister, General von Blomberg (January 1938), over the scandal of his marriage to a former prostitute, and of the Army Commander-in-Chief, General von Fritsch (February 1938), over trumped-up charges of homosexuality, reinforced Hitler's control over the army at a time of increasing foreign commitment.

The Night of the Long Knives

Ernst Röhm (1887–1934)
Leader of the Nazi Brownshirts (SA). On the pretext of an intended SA *Putsch* by the Brownshirts, the Nazis had several hundred of them killed, including Röhm. The event is known as the 'Night of the Long Knives' (29–30 June 1934).

For all these successes in 'co-ordinating' influential elements in the state into the Nazi system, Hitler could not feel wholly secure by the beginning of 1934. Ironically, the greatest surviving threat to him and to his policies came from within the Nazis' own ranks. The paramilitary SA had been formed in the early days of the movement to provide physical protection for Nazi meetings and to disrupt those of their opponents. Its attraction for former soldiers, as well as for hooligans, was enormous, and by late 1933 its numbers had swollen to some 2.5 million men. To its leader, Ernst Röhm, it represented the central weapon of the Nazi Revolution, the German equivalent of Trotsky's Red Army. It would guarantee the radical transformation of German society and, by taking over the functions of the *Reichswehr*, would guarantee the Nazification of the state. To Hitler, the SA was an embarrassing legacy of the years of struggle. It had fulfilled its street-fighting purpose and served now only to scare industrialists and conservative army officers by its radical posturing. Besides, with the SA under his command, Röhm stood as the only man in the Nazi Party realistically able to challenge the power of Hitler.

There has been much dispute among historians over the process by which Hitler reached the decision to eliminate the threat of the SA. Joachim Fest (*Hitler*, 1973), and Martin Broszat (*The Hitler State*, 1981) picture Hitler upon a deliberate collision course with Röhm since the beginning of 1934. Alan Bullock argued that Hitler would have been willing to delay, had it not been for mounting pressure from the *Reichswehr*. Another important factor was the ill-health of President Hindenburg, which made it imperative for Hitler to enjoy full *Reichswehr* support when the opportunity arose for him to take over the dead President's functions. In any case, the decision had been taken by late June when Hitler unleashed the purge known since as the 'Night of the Long Knives' (29–30 June 1934). A pretext was provided by a series of bogus SA 'revolts' in Berlin and Munich, staged by Himmler, Goering and their agents.

Schutzstaffel (SS – 'protection squad'): Paramilitary force, originally recruited as Hilter's protection squad. Subsequently entrusted with many of the main policy tasks of the Nazi regime.

The estimates of the numbers murdered by SS (*Schutzstaffel*) squads, with material support from the *Reichswehr*, range from a low of 77 to a high of 401. The bulk of these were SA men, including Röhm himself, shot in prison without trial. The opportunity to settle diverse scores with old rivals was too good to miss. The dead also included General von Kahr, who had deserted Hitler in the 1923 *Putsch*, Gregor Strasser, who had long opposed him within the party, and a number of other non-Nazi political figures.

The 'Night of the Long Knives' was Hitler's most spectacular, and probably his most successful, piece of *Realpolitik*. For all the initial shock

1. **What obstacles were there to Hitler's overall political control of Germany when he came to power in 1933?**

2. **How true is the claim that Hitler had complete control over German domestic politics by the end of 1934?**

that it caused, it had eliminated the threat from the left of the party and removed important conservative interests outside the party. Less than three weeks after the event, 38,000,000 Germans gave their tacit support by accepting in a plebiscite vote Hitler's assumption of the office of '*Führer* and Chancellor'.

 Source-based questions: The political role of the SA

SOURCE 1

Ernst Röhm, writing in June 1933, outlines his views of the role of the SA.

A tremendous victory has been won. But not absolute victory! The new state did not have to disown the bearers of the will to revolution as the November men had to do. In the new Germany the disciplined brown storm battalions stand side by side with the armed forces.

But not as part of them. The *Reichswehr* has its own undisputed task: it is committed to defend the borders of the Reich. The police have to keep down the lawbreakers. Beside these stand the SA and the SS as the third power factor of the new state with special tasks, for they are the foundation pillars of the coming National Socialist State. They will not tolerate the German revolution going to sleep or being betrayed at the halfway stage by non-combatants.

If the bourgeois simpletons think that the 'national' revolution has already lasted too long, whether they like it or not, we will continue our struggle with them; if they are unwilling, without them; and if necessary, against them.

(a) Study Source 1.

What do we learn from Source 1 about the role that Röhm believed the SA should play within the Nazi state? [5 marks]

(b) **How did Hitler deal with the threat that Röhm and the SA posed to his own vision of Nazi policy?** [7 marks]

(c) **What reasons did some elements in German politics and society have for rejecting the message put forward by Röhm, and yet still supporting the Nazi Party?** [18 marks]

10.9 How did the Nazi state impose its authority?

Centralised authority, or a confusion of administrations?

In theory, the power structure of the Nazi state was extremely simple. The far-reaching process of *Gleichschaltung* had transformed Germany into a state dominated by its single political party. 'The party,' declared Hitler in mid-1933, 'has now become the state', and that principle was legally enshrined in the Law to Ensure the Unity of Party and State (December 1933). Behind the authority of the party lay, in principle, the authority of one man. Thus, in 1939, the Nazi theorist Ernst Huber could define the basis of the Nazi constitution as follows: 'we must speak, not of state power, but of *Führer* power, if we want to describe political power in the national Reich correctly. The *Führer* power is not hemmed in by conditions and controls, and jealously guarded individual rights, but is free and independent, exclusive and without restriction.'

In reality, the smoothly functioning Nazi state was never much more than a myth, for government consisted largely of a jostling for influence between the old ministerial hierarchies and a variety of party bodies that sought to supervise or to control them. In several cases, ministers who were Nazis only in the sense of collaboration, such as Schwerin von Krosigk at the Ministry of Finance and Hjalmar Schacht at the Ministry of Economics, were highly successful in preserving the traditions of their departments. On the other hand, the Minister of the Interior, Wilhelm Frick, a Nazi himself, ultimately failed to prevent the infiltration of his department by the Party Chancellery under Martin Bormann. The Foreign Office found itself in competition with the Nazi Bureau for Foreign Affairs, headed by Alfred Rosenberg, and with the specialist agencies headed by Joachim von Ribbentrop, before he himself became Foreign Minister in 1938. The pattern of 'dualism, struggles over competence, and duplication of function' was repeated at local government level between local administrators and Nazi provincial chiefs (*Gauleiters* – see page 372). In all cases, a high price was paid in terms of administrative efficiency.

Some have claimed that this confusion arose from Hitler's great failings, his boredom with administrative detail, and his preference for wider questions, especially in foreign affairs. It is also quite possible that Hitler saw the departmental in-fighting as a deliberate means of maintaining his personal power, being the great arbiter in any such dispute. He was satisfied

Martin Bormann (1900–1945?)
Joined the Nazi Party in 1925. Deputy to Rudolf Hess (1933–41). Personal secretary to Hitler (1941–45). Assumed to have died during the last days of the war although his body was never identified.

Alfred Rosenberg (1893–1946)
Joined the Nazis in 1919, and became one of their leading theoreticians. Editor of the Nazi newspaper *Völkische Beobachter* (1921). Head of the party's office for foreign affairs. Minister for the occupied territories (1941–45). Condemned at the Nuremberg Trials and executed.

Joachim von Ribbentrop (1893–1946)
A late convert to membership of the Nazi Party (1932). Adviser to Hitler on foreign affairs. Ambassador to London (1936–38); Foreign Minister (1938–45).

Condemned to death at Nuremberg and executed.

Joseph Goebbels (1897–1945)
Joined the Nazi Party in 1922, and originally identified himself with its left wing. *Gauleiter* of Berlin and Minister for Information and Propaganda (1933–45). Responsible for directing the 'total war' effort (1942–45). Committed suicide during the last days of the war.

Heinrich Himmler (1900–1945)
Took part in the Beerhall *Putsch* (1923). Head of the SS (1929–45); Head of the Gestapo (1934–45); *Reichsführer SS* and Chief of German Police (1936–45); *Reichskommissar* for the Consolidation of the German People (1939–45); Minister of the Interior (1943–45). Committed suicide when captured by the allies.

with a system that enabled him to block any initiative or individual unacceptable to him.

The roles of propaganda and terror

The Nazi state had two great cohesive agents, both directly responsible to the *Führer*. One of these was the Ministry of Propaganda under the guidance of Joseph Goebbels. This reached new heights of sophistication through more complex and powerful media than had been available a generation earlier. The second body was the SS, with its secret police offshoot, the 'Gestapo' (*Geheime Staatspolizei*: Secret State Police).

Founded in 1925, but transformed four years later with the appointment of Himmler as its commander, the SS differed from the SA in several important respects. Whereas the SA was a mass organisation, relying upon force of numbers for its effect, the SS was an élite force, under Hitler's direct control. As such, its role extended rapidly once the Nazis were in power. From 1932 it dominated the party's intelligence work, from 1934 it had effective control of the nation's police system, and under the emergency laws of 1933, the SS controlled the concentration camps which sprang up to receive political opponents of the Nazi regime.

If there ever was such a thing as a Nazi state, it was primarily an organism for ensuring the maintenance of power, and the SS was at its centre. Surveying the general incoherence of Nazi administration, historian Gordon Craig concludes that 'the force that prevented the regime from dissolving into chaos was terror, and its instrument was the SS'. The activities of the SS therefore expanded further as war increased the need for cohesion in Nazi policy after 1939. Its members dominated the administration of the occupied territories. Its military wing, the '*Waffen SS*', sought to exert more and more influence over military affairs, resurrecting the threat that the army appeared to have conquered in the 'Night of the Long Knives'.

There is no doubt that this power was hugely effective in the negative sense of destroying opposition. What it succeeded in creating now remains to be seen.

1. By what means did Hitler and the Nazi Party maintain their authority over Germany between 1933 and 1939?

2. How important was the element of terror and intimidation in the maintenance of Nazi authority in Germany in the 1930s?

3. What evidence is there to support the claim that the administration of the Nazi state was confused and incoherent?

10.10 How radical were the economic changes that the Nazis brought about in Germany?

Whatever the effects of terror and propaganda, the Nazi regime depended for its survival upon the solution of the economic problems that had caused so many voters to turn to the party in 1929–32. Yet at no time, as Karl Bracher writes in *The German Dictatorship* (1978), 'did National Socialism develop a consistent economic or social theory'. In place of such a theory, Nazism had a set of fixed and sometimes contradictory commitments. Within the context of those commitments its economic achievements were considerable.

● **The drive for full employment** Firstly, to maintain popular sympathy and industrial support, an expansion of industrial activity and a dramatic reduction of unemployment were necessary. Without departing from the essential principles followed by Papen and Schleicher, the government poured money into public works. The most spectacular example of this was the construction of 7,000 kilometres of motorway (*Autobahn*). Aided by the recruitment of many of the unemployed into the Reich Labour Service, the unemployment figures fell from nearly 6 million to 2.5 million within 18 months of the Nazis' advent to power. With the subsequent expansion of heavy industry to meet the needs of rearmament, and the reintroduction of military conscription (1935), the Nazis could claim almost complete success by 1939, when unemployment figures stood at less than 200,000.

● **Nazism and the 'little man'** The second range of commitments was met with less consistency and with less obvious success. A complex programme of legislation was introduced to preserve the German peasantry from the twin curses of rising industrial prices and falling prices for their agricultural produce. All peasant debts, totalling 12 billion *Reichsmarks*, were suspended between March and October 1933, and many imported foodstuffs were subjected to higher tariffs. The Hereditary Farm Law (October 1933) gave the small-scale farmer security of tenure by forbidding the sale, confiscation, division or mortgaging of any farm of between 7.5 and 10 hectares, owned by farmers of Aryan blood. While this ensured the permanence of the peasant food producer – the very foundation of the German race in the view of many Nazi theorists – the law militated against the development of larger farming units and new farming methods. Ultimately, it worked against the self-sufficiency that was a major economic aim of the Nazi state. By 1936 the price of many basic foodstuffs had increased by up to 50% since the Nazis came to power.

The urban equivalent of the peasant, the small-scale trader or business man, gained still less from the regime that he had helped to bring to power. A number of laws – such as the Law for the Protection of the Retail Trade (May 1933) which was designed to protect the trader against the influence of the larger concerns – were far outweighed by the continued advance of 'big business'. This can be shown by the 1,500 new **cartel** arrangements between mid-1933 and the end of 1936. Whereas only 40% of German production was in the hands of monopolists in 1933, the proportion had grown to 70% by 1937.

Cartel: Economic arrangement whereby major manufacturers agree to share markets, rather than to compete for them. The aim is usually to fix prices for the benefit of the manufacturers and to guarantee levels of sales and profits.

Nazism and 'big business'

Ultimately the regime would support the larger enterprises, given that its long-term priorities were rearmament and self-sufficiency in all strategic products. This was perhaps the only economic goal towards which Nazi Germany moved with any consistency in the 1930s. The first phase of the policy was supervised by Hjalmar Schacht as President of the Reichsbank (from May 1933) and Minister of Economics (from June 1934). His major achievement was to limit the drain of Germany's foreign exchange by paying foreign debts in *Reichsmarks*. He also concluded a series of trade agreements, notably with Balkan and South American states, whereby Germany paid for its purchases in *Reichsmarks*, which thus encouraged its trade partners to purchase German goods in return. Schacht's great weakness, from the Nazi point of view, was his financial orthodoxy. His reluctance to spend more than Germany was earning threatened to put the brake on the process of rearmament. It became necessary to devise machinery for this task, which was directly under the control of the *Führer*. Thus, in August 1936, the Four-Year Plan was announced, and its direction was entrusted to Hermann Goering, a man of no economic talent, but with impeccable Nazi credentials. The primary aim of the Four-Year Plan was to achieve self-sufficiency in strategic industrial and agricultural products, either by increasing production or by developing synthetic substitutes. The plan had its important 'showpiece' successes, such as the Hermann Goering Steelworks erected at Watenstedt-Salzgitter. It established a complicated system of controls over prices, and the distribution of raw materials, but in some important respects – in fuel, rubber and light metals – Germany remained well short of self-sufficiency in 1939.

Conclusions

By most orthodox economic criteria, the economy of Nazi Germany was chaotic. Its reserves of foreign currency remained low, and its balance of payments remained dramatically in deficit. Karl Bracher and other historians have painted a picture of the ruination of the economy by Nazi exploitation. On the other hand, B.H. Klein (*Germany's Economic Preparations for War*, 1959) denies that preparation for war totally dominated German economic activity, stressing that production of consumer goods rose steadily right up to the eve of war in 1939. Certainly, by a mixture of Schacht's clever financing and 'windfalls' such as the confiscation of Jewish property and the seizure of Austrian assets after the *Anschluss* (see Chapter 11), the economy produced impressive results.

The German economy under the Nazis

	Unemployed (million)	Coal (million tons)	Iron ore (million tons)	Pig iron (million tons)	Steel (million tons)	Arms budget (billion RM)
1932	6.042 (January) 5.392 (July)	118.6	2.6	6.1	8.2	1.9
1935	2.974 (January) 1.754 (July)	143.0	6.0	12.8	16.2	6.0
1938	1.052 (January) 0.218 (July)	186.4	12.4	18.1	21.9	17.2

1. Which sections of the German population benefited from Nazi economic policies in the 1930s?

2. Is there any justification for the claim that the Nazis brought about an economic revolution in Germany in the 1930s?

From the 1930s, Marxist historians were eager to portray the Nazi regime as a political 'front' working in effect for Germany's capitalists, and essentially serving their economic interests. According to this interpretation, the suppression of trade unions and the expansion of heavy industrial output were among the 'tasks allotted by finance capital to its Fascism' (D. Eichholtz, 1969). More recent writers on the political left, however, have been forced to accept that it was Nazi ideology, rather than capitalist interests, that held the upper hand in this relationship. T.W. Mason, for instance (*Nazism and the Third Reich*, 1972), has shown convincingly that, although there was a degree of co-operation between industry and Nazism up to 1936, thereafter all major decisions were taken with the regime's political objectives in view. Often these decisions involved consequences of which the business community heartily disapproved, as in the case of attacks upon Jewish financial and industrial institutions. The decline of Hjalmar Schacht's influence, culminating in his resignation from the Reichsbank (January 1939), typifies the dominance of Nazism in its grim alliance with capitalism. Historian Karl Bracher has supported these views in his conclusion that 'the basic principle of National Socialist economic policy was to use the traditional capitalist structure with its competent economic bureaucracy to move towards its prime objective: acceleration of rearmament'.

10.11 Did the Nazis bring about social and cultural revolutions in Germany?

Promise of radical social change probably ranked only a little lower than the prospect of economic recovery and national resurgence as a vote winner for the Nazis in 1929–32. In the event, hopes of a 'social revolution' were frustrated. The dominant classes continued in most cases to exercise their social and economic functions, and the Nazi advocates of radical change were eliminated. What change there was served not as a revolutionary end in itself, but as a means towards the broader Nazi aims of the consolidation of power and the preparation of the nation for war.

The living standards of the German worker

The emptiness of Nazi promises of a 'social revolution' should not lead one to suppose that German workers gained nothing from their industrial co-operation with Nazi strategy. Many contemporary commentators, such as R.A. Brady (1937) and F. Neumann (1942), stressed the class nature of the Third Reich and saw it primarily as a middle-class mechanism for the exploitation of the working class. More recent authorities, such as D. Schönbaum, in *Hitler's Social Revolution* (1967), have indicated instead the solid benefits that many German workers received during this period. Although they lost important rights, such as that of union representation, it may be that they were awarded prosperity as a consolation prize for the loss of political freedom. Their greatest gain was, of course, employment. Arguments about the wage levels of the Third Reich are theoretical in view of the fact that 6 million workers were not receiving a salary of any sort in 1932. In any case, there is evidence that although average wages remained around the 1932 levels, skilled workers and workers in strategic industries such as metallurgy, engineering and building benefited markedly from Nazi industrial expansion with wage increases of up to 30%. Production and sales figures for consumer goods in the immediate pre-war years suggest a distinct rise in the standard of living.

Nor should the activities of the 'Strength through Joy' (*Kraft durch Freude*) programme, for all their propaganda content, be dismissed solely as 'window dressing'. In 1938 alone, 180,000 Germans enjoyed holiday cruises under its auspices, while 10 million took holidays of one kind or another. Its activities also extended to evening classes, and a large variety of cultural and sporting activities.

Yet material rewards were often offset by declining conditions of employment. Above all, the German worker frequently put in far longer hours than any of his or her counterparts in western Europe or the USA. The industrial demands of the regime made 10% increases in hours commonplace, with rises of 25% in some specialised areas of employment. The national average working week lasted 49 hours in 1939, rising to 52 by 1943, with an increase of 150% in the number of industrial accidents in 1933–39, and a 200% increase in occupational diseases. Remarkably, such increases appear to have been broadly accepted by the majority of German workers, whether motivated by material gain or by patriotism. Whatever the motive, we have to accept the verdict of the historian Richard Grunberger: 'the working class that Karl Marx had seen as being in the van of the proletarian revolution significantly extended the lifespan of the Third Reich by exertions that came very close to giving it victory'.

The subsidiary role of women in Nazi society

A significant feature of Nazi society in the 1930s was its reactionary view of the place of women. The duties of women were defined by the party's propaganda in the slogan 'Children, Church, Kitchen' (*Kinder, Kirche, Küche*). Every effort was made to eliminate them from leading roles in political and economic life. To an extent this was an ideological aim, based upon the mystical Nazi regard for the breeding and rearing of a pure race. As Richard Grunberger also observes, 'women basked in Nazi esteem between marriage and menopause'. The policy also had a practical purpose, in that the removal of women from the competition for jobs made the full employment of the male population easier. Thus by 1936 only 37 of Germany's 7,000 university teachers were women, while married women were banned by law from the legal and medical professions, from the civil service, and from higher office in the Nazi party. Interest-free loans were made available to newlyweds who undertook that the wife would not seek employment outside the home.

The birth rate did indeed rise, from 1,200,000 births in 1934, to 1,410,000 in 1939. While the Nazis claimed this as a success for their methods, however, it remains quite likely that the increase may simply have arisen from the improving economic circumstances in contemporary Germany. In the Nazi attitude to women, as in other areas of Nazi policy, the necessities of politics came eventually to triumph over ideology. The industrial expansion of the Four-Year Plan once more made female employment unavoidable. Although professional posts remained closed to them, women once more constituted 33% of the total German workforce by 1939.

The rejection of Weimar culture

With the advent of the Nazis to power, one of the most exciting, experimental periods in Germany's cultural history gave way to one of the most stagnant. The 1920s had witnessed a period of unparalleled innovation and experiment in German art. In the aftermath of the collapse of the 'old' Germany, many of the cultural values of that 'old' society were challenged and re-interpreted. The dramatic work and production of Bertholt Brecht, the music of Kurt Weill, and the architecture of the Bauhaus movement are some examples of the inventiveness of 'Weimar' culture. It was immediately evident that artistic freedom played little part in Nazi philosophy and that cultural activity, like all other social and economic functions, was to be 'co-ordinated' to the needs of the regime. This view was summarised by Goebbels (December 1934), with the judgement that art 'remains free within its own laws of development but it is bound to the moral, social and national principles of the state'.

As in all other areas of activity, the Nazis quickly devised complex machinery to implement this 'co-ordination'. The Reich Chamber of Culture (*Reichskulturkammer* – September 1933), under the presidency of Goebbels, was the central body outside which no 'maker of culture' could legally practise his or her craft. Political undesirables and non-Aryans were automatically excluded. Cruder tactics were necessary to deal with the works of art already executed. 'Exhibitions of Shameful Art' (*Schandausstellungen*) were held, notably in Karlsruhe (1933) and in Munich (1937), with the works of **expressionists**, **cubists** and other modern movements prominent. The destruction of rejected books and paintings by fire was widespread. In Berlin in 1939, over 1,000 paintings and 3,700 drawings by modern artists were destroyed. The result of this was to rip the heart out of German art, literature and music. The list of those who abandoned their country to work abroad includes novelists and playwrights such as Thomas and Heinrich Mann, Stefan Zweig and Bertholt Brecht, the painter Oskar Kokoschka, and masters of the new art of cinema, Josef Sternberg and Fritz Lang.

1. In what ways were German workers affected by Nazi economic and social policies in the 1930s?

2. Is it justifiable to claim that the Nazi policies improved the living standards of many Germans in the 1930s?

Expressionists: Artists who use a style known as 'expressionism', in which reality is distorted in order to express their own emotions or inner visions.

Cubists: Artists who use the first abstract style of the 20th century in which objects, landscapes and people are represented as many-sided solids.

The characteristics of Nazi art

Official taste in the Third Reich had three main distinguishing features.

Internationalism: The response to cultural stimuli from abroad that had characterised the art of the Weimar period.

Philistinism: The act of being a 'Philistine', a person who has no feeling for art, or whose artistic taste is vulgar.

1. The first was the rejection of **internationalism**.

2. In its place, it demanded a stress upon, and a glorification of, those values that Nazism preached in other areas of policy.

3. It was frequently dominated by a conservatism, often a **philistinism**, that reflected the intellectual mediocrity of many of Germany's new leaders.

As historian Gordon Craig puts it, most of the products of this cultural 'revolution' were 'of a quality so inferior as to be embarrassing. What passed for Nazi art, when it was not a mere disguise for propaganda, was a reflection of the aesthetic ideals of a culturally retarded lower middle class, full of moral attitudinising and mock heroics and sentimentality and emphasis upon the German soul and the sacredness of the soil.' In literature one might refer to the books of Werner Beumelburg, a specialist in glorifying the spiritual experience of war, or of Hans Blunck, with his emphasis upon Nordic legend. In sculpture, Arno Breker's gigantic evocations of Teutonic manhood found particular favour with the *Führer* himself. Musical taste was dominated by the German 'giants' of the classical past, Ludwig van Beethoven and Amadeus Mozart, and by the German epics of Richard Wagner.

Hitler, on holiday in Austria, signing postcards for two girls. A daily procession of visitors climbed the mountain to march past the 'Führer'.

Propaganda and the cinema

In one discipline alone the products of the Third Reich rose above mediocrity. Although the film industry constituted in Goebbels' view 'one of the most modern and scientific methods of influencing the masses', he used it sparingly and intelligently. The most famous films of the era, such as *Hitler Youth Quex* (1933), *The Jew Süss* (1940), and *Ohm Krüger* (1941), an exposé of British atrocities during the Boer War, all had clear political points to make. Yet these were subtly conveyed, and the films did have artistic merit. The most famous of contemporary German directors, Leni Riefenstahl, showed in her major works, *The Triumph of the Will* (1935), portraying the 1934 Nazi party rally at Nuremberg, and Olympia (1937), on the Berlin Olympic Games, that an obvious propaganda message could be conveyed with flair and originality.

Nazism and education

The theme of mediocrity is evident once more in German education under Nazism. The creation of a centralised Reich Education Ministry (May 1934) involved no major change in the structure of the educational system, but led to a radical revision of syllabuses. Great stress was now laid upon history, biology and German as the media by which the philosophy of Nazism could best be put across, while the stress upon physical fitness and development raised the gym teacher to a higher level of prestige than he or she had ever previously enjoyed.

University teaching, too, was subject to adjustments, such as the dismissal of 'unreliable' teachers, and the banning of such 'Jewish' theses as Einstein's Theory of Relativity. Between 1933 and 1938 45% of all university posts changed hands. As Nazi agencies competed with established

1. What features were the Nazis most eager to introduce into German art and culture in the 1930s?

2. What purposes were art and education supposed to serve in Nazi society?

bodies in other spheres, so too in education. Youth organisations sought to ensure the indoctrination of the young, to the great detriment of academic standards. From December 1936 it was compulsory for boys to serve in the *Jungvolk* organisation, paralleled by the *Jungmädel* organisation for girls, between the ages of 10–14. Thereafter, the boys graduated to the 'Hitler Youth' (*Hitlerjugend*) and the girls to the 'German Girls' League' (*Bund Deutsche Mädchen*) until the age of 18.

10.12 By what stages and with what effect did Nazi Germany develop its policy of anti-semitism?

The motives behind Nazi anti-semitism

Many of the domestic ideological poses struck by Nazism before it achieved power were eventually sacrificed to the practicalities of power politics. This was not the case with anti-semitism. Some writers have tried to see in Nazi anti-semitism a tool for the achievement of other aims, as, in historian A.J.P. Taylor's phrase, 'a showy substitute for social change' (*The Course of German History*, 1961). Yet the consistency of Nazi policy, even when it appeared ill-advised in terms of foreign relations or of the economy, can leave us in little doubt that hatred of Jews was central to Hitler's beliefs. 'The Jews,' wrote the historian Lucy Dawidowicz in *The War Against the Jews, 1933–45* (1979), 'inhabited Hitler's mind. He believed that they were the source of all evil, misfortune and tragedy.' Such views appealed to a long tradition of German anti-semitism deriving from economic envy of Jewish commercial success. To this was added intellectual opposition to such 'modern' notions as parliamentary government and liberalism, through which some Jews had reached political and social emancipation in recent decades.

This is not to say that Nazi anti-semites had any clear idea in 1933 as to how they would tackle the Jewish 'menace'. Their reasoning dictated that Jews should be excluded from positions of social and political influence. Thus a series of laws (April 1933) banned them from the civil service, the universities and from journalism. Popular emotion led to outbreaks of violence against Jewish businesses, to the horror of more orthodox nationalists, fearful of foreign reaction and of the breakdown of law and order. For economic reasons, however, Jewish activity in stockbroking and banking remained unimpaired until 1937.

Towards a 'Jew-free' state, 1935–1939

From 1935, with increasing domestic security and greater foreign success, the confidence of the Nazis grew. The Nuremberg Laws (September 1935) and the National Law of Citizenship (November 1935) outlawed all marital and sexual contact between Jews and Aryans. Jews were stripped of their nationality by the stipulation that only Aryan blood entitled one to membership of the German nation. In August 1936, Hitler dictated the principle that the whole Jewish community would be held responsible for the misdeeds of any of its members. The most spectacular application of this principle came on the night of 9–10 November 1938 (*Kristalnacht*). In a major pogrom following the murder of a German diplomat by a Jewish

'Kristalnacht': Jewish shops damaged and plundered, November 1938

student in Paris, 7,000 Jewish businesses were attacked, about 100 Jews were murdered, and thousands more were beaten and intimidated. *'Kristalnacht'* marked a significant step from legal and economic pressure upon the Jewish community, to naked violence.

Subsequently, Nazi policy escalated to include the removal of Jews from the economy and, if possible, from the country itself. The 'Decree on Eliminating Jews from German Economic Life' (November 1938) made it illegal for them to work in sales, services, crafts or management. In January 1939, a Reich Central Office for Jewish Emigration was established to arrange for the expulsion of those with adequate funds and with somewhere to go.

The start of the war in 1939 left the majority of Germany's 500,000 Jews stranded without livelihood or political rights in a country that disowned them. Hitler's apparent conviction that foreign opposition to Germany was part of an international Jewish plot left them in an even more perilous position. 'If the international Jewish financiers in and outside Europe,' he told the Reichstag in January 1939, 'should succeed in plunging the nations into a world war, then the result will be the annihilation of the Jewish race in Europe.' For once Hitler was true to his propaganda, and the war years were to witness the formulation at last of a 'final solution' to the 'Jewish problem' (see Chapter 12).

1. What steps did the Nazis government take between 1933 and 1939 to make Germany a 'Jew-free' state?

2. How convincing is the claim that 'the solution of the "Jewish Question" was the most important aim that the Nazi regime set itself in the 1930s'?

10.13 To what extent was Nazi authority resisted within Germany?

A relatively recent trend in historical research on the Third Reich has concentrated upon German resistance and opposition to the Nazi regime. Like many such trends it can be traced to the political interests and motives of the societies in which it takes place. Many writers in Germany, and elsewhere in the west, were concerned to counter the notion of Germany's collective guilt for the crimes of Nazism, and to hasten the political reintegration of West Germany through membership of the European Economic Community. In the German Democratic Republic (East Germany), meanwhile, the emphasis was laid, for obvious political reasons, upon the role played by German Communists in resisting Nazism, thus enhancing their claims to power in the post-war years.

Such research has demonstrated that a significant degree of dissatisfaction and discontent survived in Germany against Nazi rule, especially after the outbreak of war. The historian Ian Kershaw notes in *The Nazi Dictatorship* (1993) that 'the extent of disillusionment and discontent in almost all sections of the population, rooted in the socio-economic experience of daily life, is remarkable'. The extensive research by Martin Broszat into Bavaria under the Nazis (*Bavaria at the time of the Nazis, 1977–83*) also exposed a significant degree of everyday defiance arising from irritation and anger at the regime. He cites, in particular, 'refusal to give the "Heil Hitler" greeting; insistence upon hanging out the church flag instead of the swastika banner; public criticism of anti-church measures by Catholic priests'.

Recent writers have also shown great interest in the anti-social and anti-establishment movements that existed among German youth in the war years, in direct contrast to the Hitler Youth and other Nazi movements. The so-called 'Edelweiss Pirates', with their various sub-groups, developed socio-political activities so unacceptable to the Nazis that they sometimes received the death penalty. The 'Swing Movement' had a more cultural emphasis, although its emphasis upon American and British jazz music and dance made it equally unacceptable to the regime. One may draw two kinds of conclusion from such examples. The relatively comforting conclusion that the Nazi ideal of totalitarian authority was not fully achieved must be set against the fact that opposition of this kind could have little impact upon the policies and the overall control of the Nazi regime. In no way can such opponents claim to have reduced the capacity of the Nazis to pursue policies of aggressive war and of **genocide**.

Genocide: The deliberate murder of a whole community or race.

Political and religious opposition

There is plenty of evidence of resistance in areas of German politics and society, which were better placed to obstruct Nazi intentions. Unfortunately, it is equally evident that the Nazis dealt ruthlessly with such opposition and, in most cases, rendered it powerless. This dual conclusion is borne out by the estimated figures relating to the fate of members of SPD and the KPD after the two parties were declared illegal. It has been estimated that 150,000 of their supporters were imprisoned, while 40,000 went into exile and 12,000 were convicted of high treason by Nazi courts.

As the policies of the regime became more radical, the Catholic Church also expressed a degree of opposition. In particular, the papal **encyclical** *Mit brennender Sorge*, issued in 1937, protested that by embarking upon a programme of **euthanasia** the Nazis had broken important provisions of the Concordat concluded in 1933. By the outbreak of war, however, some 400 Catholic priests had been sent to concentration camps, illustrating once again that moral objections could do little to deflect the Nazis from their purposes. The brave personal opposition of such pastors (clergymen) as Martin Niemöller and Dietrich Bonhoeffer cannot hide the fact that Protestant opposition as a whole tended to be less focused, as the Protestant faith was more fragmented in Germany.

Encyclical: A papal letter, circulated to bishops of the Church, or to those in one particular country.

Euthanasia: The act of killing those who are considered too ill, handicapped or old to be able to contribute profitably to society.

It may be true that, as historian Gerhard Ritter wrote in *The Sword and the Sceptre* (1972), 'the majority of educated Germans were very distrustful of the Hitler propaganda. Very many felt at the time of Hitler's victory that his political system was foreign to them.' Nevertheless, the German conservative élite, and the army in particular, gave valuable support to the Nazis in the early stages of their rise to power. Signs of alienation began to appear much later, as Nazi policies became more radical, and in particular as military defeat became increasingly likely. The attempt by army officers

Internecine: Mutually destructive, or involving conflict within a specific group or nation.

1. What elements within the German population resisted Nazi authority after 1933?

2. Were German opponents of Nazi authority able to do anything after 1933 that significantly hindered the power of Hitler's government?

to assassinate Hitler at Rastenburg, in July 1944, shows how serious such opposition had become. On the other hand, the subsequent arrest and execution of many leading officers and high-ranking civilians shows that, even on the brink of defeat, the Nazi regime retained the power to deal ruthlessly and effectively with its domestic opponents.

In short, the study of German opposition to Hitler has thrown up many examples of personal bravery, but has provided little evidence to suggest that it threatened the policies of the Third Reich in any significant way. Ian Kershaw's judgement, in *The Nazi Dictatorship: Problems and Perspectives in Interpretation* (1993), provides an apt summary.

'The ineffectiveness and failure of German resistance to Nazism had its roots in the strife-torn political climate of the Weimar Republic. The **internecine** conflict on the left, the enthusiasm of the conservative right to act as gravediggers to the Republic, and the massive popular readiness to embrace authoritarianism, explain divisions within, and lack of popular support for, resistance during the dictatorship.'

10.14 What were the main aims and methods of Nazi foreign policy?

Did Nazi foreign policy depart from the traditional aims of German foreign policy?

For Hitler and for many in his party it is probable that foreign affairs represented the true purpose of the Third Reich. The domestic transformation of the first years of Nazi power was primarily carried out to fit Germany for the performance of its international tasks. 'Before conquering the external enemy,' Hitler had written in *Mein Kampf*, 'the enemy at home would have to be eliminated.' It has nevertheless become a matter of some controversy whether the foreign policy of Nazi Germany really did represent a radical change of direction, or whether Hitler merely continued well-established traditions of German power politics. The latter view was put forward by a number of distinguished German historians, such as Friedrich Meinecke and Andreas Hillgruber, and received the most enthusiastic support in Britain from A.J.P. Taylor. 'In one sphere alone,' writes Taylor of Hitler, 'he changed nothing. His foreign policy was that of his predecessors, of the professional diplomats at the Foreign Ministry, and indeed of virtually all Germans.' For this school of thought, the terms imposed upon Russia in the Treaty of Brest-Litovsk in 1917 provide strong evidence of Germany's eastern ambitions long before the advent of Hitler.

On the other hand, many contemporaries, as well as more recent writers, saw in Hitler, in his racial doctrines, and in his professions in *Mein Kampf*, a new and more dangerous force. 'This is not a man of the past,' declared the French ambassador in 1933, 'and his objective is not to restore, purely and simply, the state of things in 1914.'

The aims laid down in *Mein Kampf* and elsewhere – whether or not they should be regarded as a premeditated and serious programme for Nazi foreign policy – in fact constitute a combination of familiar projects and new twists. Firstly, Hitler stated the necessity to overturn the Versailles settlement, with which any diplomat of the Weimar Republic would have agreed. He aimed to destroy the inequalities of Germany's position on armaments and reparations, and to regain those portions of its population separated from the Reich by the peace terms. Secondly, Hitler was determined to unite

Hitler's foreign policy 1935–39

The map legend:

① Plebiscite to join Germany 1935
② Czech territory given to Germany by Munich agreement Sept. 1938 (Sudetenland)
③ Czech territory taken by Poland Sept. 1938
④ Slovak territory to Hungary Nov. 1938
⑤ Annexed by Germany 1938 (*Anschluss*)
⑥ Occupied by Hungary March 1939
⑦ Annexation of Memel March 1939
⑧ German satellite state of Slovakia from March 1939
⑨ Annexed by Germany, March 1939

with the Reich those Germans who had previously not been part of it: his fellow Austrians, for example, or the Sudetenlanders. This was a deliberate departure from Bismarck's 'Little Germany' in favour of the *Grossdeutschland* that Bismarck had feared and rejected. Thirdly, this *Grossdeutschland* would require 'living space' (*Lebensraum*) to provide agricultural and industrial resources for its population. This was a dangerous and explosive combination of Wilhelmine expansion and newer racial determinism.

The natural enemies of Nazi Germany

The implications of such a programme for Germany's future foreign relations were clear. For Hitler, Russia was the natural enemy, with its combination of inferior Slavic culture, detested Bolshevism, and he thought, Jewish-dominated government. France, too, although a declining power, would be a certain opponent for the future. It was the staunchest supporter of the hated Versailles system, was patron and protector of several of the detested eastern European states, and would have to be dealt with to avoid once more running the risk of war on two fronts. Britain, an essentially maritime and colonial power, and Italy, Fascist and with primarily Mediterranean interests, were not natural enemies of Germany. At an early stage in his career, Hitler envisaged fundamental departures both from Nazi ideology and from traditional German policies, to ensure the cooperation of Britain and Italy in his general plans. In the case of Britain he showed himself willing to renounce the lost German colonies, subject of so much propaganda after 1919; in the case of Italy, he refrained from claiming the Germans of the South Tyrol as subjects of *Grossdeutschland*.

By what methods did Nazi Germany pursue its aims in foreign policy?

For all the dispute over the originality of Germany's international aims during the Nazi period, there is general agreement about the flexibility with which those aims were pursued. The diplomatic methods of the Nazi era fall broadly into two sections.

1. The first three years from 1933 formed a period of caution, dictated by domestic weakness and by widespread foreign distrust. Germany successfully avoided commitments to such international bodies as the League of Nations and the Disarmament Conference, which might have compromised its future freedom of action. Instead it made headway with the disruption of the French system of eastern European alliances, while consistently reassuring foreign opinion as to its peaceful intentions. Through that period, too, ran the theme of rearmament. The reintroduction of conscription (1935), the agreement with Great Britain over the reconstruction of the German Navy (1935), and the steady rebuilding of an air force (*Luftwaffe*) that already boasted 2,000 aircraft by late 1934, all illustrate this theme.

2. The years 1936–37 undoubtedly witnessed a switch to the offensive, whether this was inspired by greater domestic security or by weaknesses in the diplomacy of Hitler's opponents. The introduction of the Four-Year Plan prepared the way in material terms, and the so-called 'Hossbach Conference' (November 1937) is often seen as the significant moment in the development of Nazi expansionism. There, in a meeting with the heads of the armed forces and of the Foreign Ministry, the subject of which is known to us through the minutes recorded by Colonel Hossbach, Hitler defined the immediate principles of his policy. Repeating the principle of *Lebensraum*, he noted that Germany's present military superiority over its rivals could not be expected to last beyond 1943–45. Thereafter, the **obsolescence** of German material, and the re-equipment of other armed forces would narrow the gap. Therefore, the minutes report, 'it was his unalterable resolve to solve Germany's problem of space at the latest by 1943–45'. Although the timetable retained some flexibility, the subsequent expansion of armament production, and the removal of such 'doubters' as von Blomberg, Schacht and Neurath from office, clearly indicate that the threats made to the future peace of Europe were not idle.

Obsolescence: The state of being no longer needed or no longer desirable because something newer or more efficient has been invented.

1. What arguments have historians used to demonstrate whether or not the Nazis departed from the traditional aims of German foreign policy?

2. 'What was new about German foreign policy in the 1930s was not so much its aims as the methods by which they were pursued.' How far would you agree with this statement?

10.15 Who was really in control of the Third Reich?
A CASE STUDY IN HISTORICAL INTERPRETATION

The immediate aftermath of the Second World War produced two dominant interpretations of the Third Reich and of the forces that motivated it.

As is often the case with historical interpretation so soon after the event, both served broader political purposes. To Soviet historians, and to those in the west who favoured a Marxist interpretation of history, the issue of political control in the Third Reich was perfectly clear. The history of Nazi Germany, like all other history, was a story of class struggle. In the Marxist view, Nazism had to be seen as the last resort of embattled and besieged capitalism in the aftermath of the Russian Revolution and of the Great Depression. German capitalists and property owners had funded and supported the Nazis in order to protect themselves from the threat of the working classes. Even before the war, historians such as R.A. Brady, in *The Spirit and Structure of German Fascism* (1937), had put forward the view of Nazism as a mass middle-class movement confronting and defeating a mass working-class enemy. They had no doubt that it was capitalism that was in control of the Third Reich.

Such a view receives less support today. Although no-one would question that capitalists – especially those with a stake in the armaments industry – gained enormous benefits from their support of Nazism, it is widely held that the political and racial aims of Nazism usually took precedence over orthodox economic considerations whenever the two clashed. Thus orthodox financiers were pushed aside when they raised objections to elements of the Nazi rearmament programme in the late 1930s. It is also hard to see any motives behind the 'final solution' other than the imperative of Nazi racial theory.

The dominant interpretation among western historians at this time was that which laid its emphasis primarily upon the personality and priorities of Adolf Hitler himself. Alan Bullock's classic work, *Hitler: A Study in Tyranny* (1962), was the first comprehensive biography of Hitler. It placed him firmly at the centre of the political history of the Third Reich. Bullock further developed this view in *Hitler and Stalin: Parallel Lives* (1991). After exhaustive work among captured German archives, Alan Bullock was confidently able to conclude that 'the evidence leaves no doubt that no other man played a role in the Nazi revolution or in the history of the Third Reich remotely comparable with that of Adolf Hitler'. The American historian, Norman Rich, in *Hitler's War Aims* (1974), supported that interpretation with even greater emphasis: 'The point cannot be stressed too strongly: Hitler was master in the Third Reich.'

In recent years a number of leading historians of the Third Reich have considered it necessary to revise this view of Hitler. It has not seriously been questioned that Hitler's role in the formulation of Nazi policy and in the projection and promotion of the Nazi cause was of fundamental importance. In these respects he was indeed the key figure in the Nazi movement. Once the Nazis were firmly established in government, however, historians find little evidence to suggest that Hitler dictated the details of government or closely directed the implementation of policy. On the contrary, there is much to suggest that his lifestyle and work habits became much too casual and erratic for him to do so effectively. Albert Speer reported that Hitler 'rose late in the morning [and] from the subsequent dinner onwards he more or less wasted his time until the early hours of the evening. His rare appointments in the afternoon were imperilled by his passion for looking at building plans.' Ian Kershaw, in *The Nazi Dictatorship* (1993), extends this chaotic picture of Hitler's style of government to the war years. He claims that the German war effort was frequently handicapped by Hitler's 'eccentric working hours, his aversion to putting anything down on paper, his lengthy absences from Berlin, his inaccessibility even for important ministers, his impatience with the complexities of intricate problems, and his tendency to seize impulsively upon random strands of information or half-baked judgements from cronies and court favourites'.

Power vacuum: A region in which no state exercises sufficient power to be able to play the dominant political role.

Sicherheitsdienst (SD): The Security Service in Nazi Germany.

Such a view of Hitler has led historians to several different interpretations of the government of the Third Reich in its latter stages. One is that certain institutions within the Nazi state did indeed have the strength and coherence to step into this **power vacuum**. The formal institutions of the state were quite unable to fulfil such a role. The Reichstag after 1934 performed merely formal functions, and the cabinet rarely met. A much more powerful influence was exerted within the state by the complex of police forces constituted by the SS, the Gestapo and the *Sicherheitsdienst* (SD). Certainly as the war progressed, the authority and control exercised by these forces expanded considerably. The establishment of the *Waffen SS* extended their influence over the armed forces, and their take-over of the concentration camps not only ousted the SA from those functions, but also presented the SS with substantial economic and political resources. The SS also enjoyed a degree of control in the occupied territories.

Other historians consider that this is to exaggerate the freedom of action that these police institutions enjoyed. They point to the fact that important Nazi leaders, such as Goering and Bormann, stood outside this police coalition and actively opposed its influence. Local research on the war years has also suggested that, under the pressure of the war, the Gestapo became less and less effective. They were increasingly dependent upon denunciations from members of the public. Such arguments lead logically to the conclusion that the Reich suffered a crisis of leadership from the late 1930s onwards, and that the inconsistency and contradiction in Nazi government arose entirely from the *Führer's* weaknesses. Martin Broszat's view of German government from the late 1930s onwards, in *The Hitler State* (1981), is that it consisted of 'a shambles of constantly shifting power-bases and warring factions'. Hitler's role in this scenario was largely that of the symbolic leader whose prestige made it important for any given faction to obtain his sanction for their initiative.

1. **In what different ways have historians interpreted the issue of Hitler's personal authority within the Nazi party?**

2. **What arguments are there for and against the claim that Nazi Germany suffered from a 'crisis of leadership' in the late 1930s and the early 1940s?**

Other commentators have accepted Hitler's limitations as a working head of state, but have still given him a major role in the functioning of Nazi government. Karl Bracher, in *The German Dictatorship* (1978), is the most prominent of those who have interpreted Hitler's style of government as a deliberate ploy, designed to 'divide and rule', to set his subordinates at odds with each other, and thereby to assure himself of the final decision. A variation on this is the so-called 'intentionalist' argument put forward by such authorities as Andreas Hillgruber (*Hitler's Strategie: Politik und Kriegsführung*, 1965) and Klaus Hildebrand (*The Foreign Policy of the Third Reich*, 1973). This argument claims that Hitler's influence over Nazism was so great that his 'intentions' – his essential vision of Nazi aims and priorities – continued to act as the major influence upon the conduct of Nazi government. Even if the timing and detail of policy were not necessarily devised by the *Führer*, the fundamental vision and authority that lay behind them were still his.

10.16 What was the impact of the Second World War upon civilian life in Germany?

How was Germany governed during the war years?

In general, the Second World War served to aggravate the divisions and confusions that existed before 1939 in the government of the Third Reich. One of the most striking features of wartime government was the steady withdrawal of Adolf Hitler, for so long the public inspiration of the Nazi movement, from the public eye. From November 1941 he assumed direct responsibility for all military operations, and was only rarely seen in public after that date. Such important matters as war production and law and order were left in the hands of the various agencies that competed for influence in Nazi Germany.

In particular, the SS under Heinrich Himmler and the Party Chancellery under Martin Bormann extended their influence, at the expense of the traditional ministries of the state. The SS played an increasingly important role in the economic organisation of the state, largely through the creation of an extensive group of companies involved in war production (*Deutsche Wirtschaftsbetriebe*). It also became involved in a complex range of strategic economic activities, including mining, armament manufacture and the production of foodstuff. In addition, the SS had at its disposal the enormous slave-labour resources of the concentration camps. It has been suggested by Alan Milward, a leading expert on the economic history of the war, that in building this economic 'empire' Himmler envisaged such a degree of control over the German economy as would ultimately undermine conventional German capitalism. At the same time, control over the Gestapo and the security service (SD) gave Himmler an unrivalled degree of influence within German society. The rapid expansion of the *Waffen SS* also extended this influence into the heart of the German army.

Although Martin Bormann could not seriously rival so extensive an 'empire', he had the advantage of working in close proximity to the *Führer* himself. Between 1943, when he was appointed as Hitler's personal secretary, and 1945, he was able to ensure that the Party Chancellery steadily eliminated the influence of the Reichs Chancellery, the body by which government business had traditionally been forwarded to the head of state. The influence of traditional administrative bodies was steadily eroded. Local administration, for instance, came increasingly under the control of the Party as the powers of the *Gauleiters* were extended. Appointed Reich Defence Commissioners (September 1939), they assumed responsibility for military matters within their *Gau*, and in 1943 were given overall control of all local civil administration. From September 1944, the *Gauleiters* were also responsible for the activities of the **Volkssturm**. Similarly, education, the judiciary and the civil service came under even tighter Party control. Wartime measures provided for the removal of teachers who were considered to be insufficiently loyal to the party (September 1941) and for a purge of leading officials in the Ministry of Justice (April 1942).

Volkssturm: A party militia established to form a last line of resistance against invading allied forces.

How effective was the German economy during the war years?

Traditionally, historians have assumed that in 1939 the Nazi state envisaged a war made up of short, sharp conflicts, interspersed with periods of temporary peace in which the economy could recover and consolidate. Only in 1942, when it became clear that the Reich was locked into a more profound conflict, did this '*Blitzkrieg* mentality' give way to a state of 'total war', in which the economic resources of the state were exploited to the full. Such an interpretation was challenged by Richard Overy, in *War and the German Economy: a Reinterpretation* (1982). In his view, Germany's leaders had been anticipating a prolonged state of 'total war' since the mid-1930s, and the German economy had been geared to meet such demands since the establishment of the Four-Year Plan in 1936. The German economy was better prepared for the pressure of prolonged warfare than historians have usually imagined. Nevertheless, the government was taken by surprise by the Franco–British declaration of war in 1939, and became involved in an extensive conflict earlier than expected.

It was for this reason, Richard Overy argues, that the German war economy quickly encountered serious difficulties. Also, its organisation was confused and inefficient. Gordon Craig adds, in *Germany 1866–1945* (1978), that the Nazi government remembered very clearly the collapse of civilian morale in the last years of the First World War, and did not wish to risk a similar collapse by mobilising the economy too rigorously in 1940. Overy's reinterpretation identified a range of problems that included shortage of raw materials, shortage of manpower, and characteristic disputes about the control and the priorities of production. The provision of more workers was one of the major achievements of the German war economy. It was brought about by three distinct strategies.

- One was the comprehensive redeployment of the existing German workforce, which meant that by 1943 61% of all German labour was employed in war production, compared with 21% in 1939.

- The second was an enormous increase in the female workforce, amounting to half the female population by the beginning of 1944.

- Lastly, as is noted in Chapter 12, the Nazi authorities in occupied territories were able to recruit or to conscript enormous numbers of foreign workers (a total of 8 million by 1944) to aid war production in the Reich.

Greater problems existed over the co-ordination of resources and production. These were addressed by Hitler's 'Rationalisation Decree' (December 1941), which sought to streamline war production and to restructure control of the economy. The architects of this restructuring were Fritz Todt, who was appointed Minister for Armaments and Munitions in March 1940, and Albert Speer who succeeded him upon his death in February 1942. Its main institution was the Central Planning Board set up in April 1942. Speer's memoirs (*Inside the Third Reich*, 1970) make it clear that, while his personal friendship with Hitler was of great value, and endowed the minister with considerable authority, his efforts were still liable to be resisted at every turn by other vested interests, such as those of the *Gauleiters* or of the SS.

How much did Todt and Speer achieve?

It could be argued that Todt and Speer were remarkably successful in maintaining high levels of war production under the most difficult circumstances (see Chapter 12). The statistics for military production between 1942 and 1944 are impressive, with weapon production trebled despite the fact that the funds allocated to such production only increased by 50%. Even so, statistics suggest that the German economy was under enormous stress from 1943 onwards. In that year allied bombing forced the diversion of two million men and 50,000 pieces of artillery into anti-aircraft service. By the following year, according to Speer himself, aircraft production was 31% below target, and tank production 35% below. In the final year of the war, it has been estimated, absenteeism in German factories ran at a daily average of 25%, due to illness, stress and the dislocation caused by enemy action.

What was the impact of war upon the civilian population?

The war placed a considerable strain upon the German population from the outset. Strict rationing came into force at the start of the war, and between 1939 and 1941 German workers were considerably less well fed than their British counterparts. Consumption declined by 25%, compared with only 12% in Britain. Research suggests that German civilians derived little benefit from the additional food resources that were made available by German military victories, the vast bulk of them being directed towards

'White Rose' movement: A group of students, in which Hans and Sophie Scholl were prominent, which organised a protest at Munich University in February 1943 against Nazi atrocities. Convicted of distributing anti-state literature, the Scholls and some of their associates were hanged.

Assassination attempt on Hitler: Claus von Stauffenberg was the central figure in the most notable wartime attempt to assassinate Hitler. High-ranking army officers planted a bomb at military headquarters in East Prussia on 20 July 1944. Showing their hand, on the assumption that Hitler had been killed, the conspirators were easily identified, arrested and executed.

Morgenthau Plan: A plan devised between 1943 and 1945 by Henry Morgenthau, Secretary to the US Treasury, for the organisation of the German economy at the end of the war. His intention was that defeated Germany should be divided once more into a number of minor states, that the industrial bases of these states should be dismantled, and that their economies should be primarily agricultural.

1. In what different ways did the Nazi Party further extend its influence over German political and economic life in the years 1939–45?

2. By what means did the German economy meet the demands of 'total war'?

3. How much justification is there for the claim that 'the Nazi government organised its war effort efficiently and met the demands of total war with considerable success'?

military consumption. Other commodities, such as clothing, also became more difficult to obtain as production was geared increasingly towards the requirements of the war effort. As early as 1941, 40% of all textile output and 44% of all manufactured clothing was earmarked for use by the armed forces.

The civilian population within the Reich remained relatively sheltered from enemy action until 1942. In that year, the British and American air forces abandoned their policy of avoiding areas of heavy civilian population. The first of a series of 'thousand bomber raids' was launched against Cologne in May 1942, and in August of the following year another such raid killed 40,000 civilians in Hamburg. From mid-1944, Germany's enemies enjoyed almost total aerial superiority, and the vulnerability of German towns to devastating aerial attack became ever greater. The final official statistics for the damage caused to Germany by aerial bombardment alone are staggering. In the years immediately after the war, the Federal Statistical Office in Wiesbaden established that 593,000 German civilians had been killed by this means, and that 3,370,000 buildings had been destroyed, including 600,000 in Berlin alone.

Under such circumstances it is surprising that the German population maintained its will to resist. Morale was clearly documented through the regular reports produced throughout the war years by the SD. These indicated considerable enthusiasm in the first year or so, followed by (in Goebbels' phrase) 'a light depression' by the end of 1940. Within two years, once the USA had entered the war and the *Wehrmacht* had encountered disaster at Stalingrad, the reports indicate a decline in optimism that was never to be reversed. Certainly these years did produce some opposition to the Nazi regime. Sometimes this was motivated by humanitarian principles, as was the case with the students who constituted the **'White Rose' movement** in Munich in 1943. Sometimes it was motivated by conservative disillusion at the course of the war, as demonstrated by the officers who supported the **assassination attempt on Hitler** the following year. Indeed, the number of Germans held in concentration camps rose dramatically in the later stages of the war, from 100,000 in 1942 to 500,000 in the final year of the conflict.

Generally, however, there is much evidence to suggest that Nazi propaganda had been so effective that public confidence in Hitler's leadership remained high, even when Germany was on the verge of defeat. Historians have agreed no explanation of this, but have drawn attention to a range of factors. Goebbels worked incessantly in the Ministry of Propaganda. He pursued clever tactics in stressing to Germans what the consequences of defeat might be: pillage and rape at the hands of vengeful and barbaric Russians, for instance; or the destruction of the nation's industrial wealth by the terms of the **Morgenthau Plan**. Public faith in Hitler's personal infallibility also remained high until the very last stages of the war. Albert Speer's anecdote from the last weeks of the war probably captured a mood that was relatively familiar.

'In Westphalia, in March 1945, I stood unrecognised in a farmyard talking to the farmers. The faith in Hitler that had been hammered into their minds all these years was still strong. Hitler could never lose the war, they declared. Even among members of the government I still encountered this naïve faith in deliberately withheld secret weapons that at the last moment would annihilate an enemy recklessly advancing into the country.'

Source-based questions: Conformity and resistance in Nazi Germany

SOURCE 1

From Joachim Fest, Hitler, *published in 1974*

The peculiar babble of voices presumably speaking for the German opposition, should make it clear that it was not a bloc. To treat it as if it were a single concept is inaccurate; it was a loose assemblage of many groups objectively and personally antagonistic and united only in antipathy for the regime. Three of these groups emerge with somewhat sharper contours. (1) The Kreisau Circle, called after Count Helmut James von Moltke's Silesian estate. This was chiefly a discussion group of high-minded friends imbued with ideas both of Christianity and socialist reform. (2) Then there was the group of conservative and nationalist notables gathered around Carl Goerdeler, the former mayor of Leipzig, and General Ludwig Beck, the former army chief of staff. These men, not yet understanding the meaning of Hitler's policies, were still claiming a leading role for a Greater Germany within Europe. So strong was their leaning towards an authoritarian state, that they have been called a continuation of the anti-democratic opposition in the Weimar Republic. (3) Finally, there was a group of younger military men such as von Stauffenberg, with no pronounced ideological affiliations, although for the most part they sought ties with the Left.

In terms of background, a strikingly large number of the conspirators belonged to the Old Prussian nobility. There were also members of the clergy, the academic professions, and high-ranking civil servants. On the whole, those oppositionists who were now beginning to urge action were people originally from the conservative or liberal camp, with a sprinkling of Social Democrats. The Left was still suffering from the effects of the persecution, but it too, with characteristic ideological rigidity, feared any alliance with army officers as a 'pact with the devil'. Among the many participants in the opposition there was, significantly, not a single representative of the Weimar Republic; that republic did not survive even in the Resistance. But members of the lower middle class were also conspicuously absent, and also businessmen. The latter remained fixated upon the traditional German alliance between industrial interests and power politics. Business always came to heel when the state whistled.

SOURCE 2

From T.W. Mason, Worker Opposition in National Socialist Germany, *published in 1981*

I would like to start by drawing a distinction between the political resistance of the working class under National Socialism and that which I want to call Worker opposition.

To political resistance belong only the politically conscious actions of members of persecuted organisations, which strove to weaken or overthrow the dictatorship in the name of social democracy, communism or trade unionism. That is to say, political activity which was characterised by a rejection and challenging of National Socialism based on political principle. But this heroic, tragic battle in the underground in no way exhausts the role of the working class in the Third Reich. Alongside the dogged propaganda work of the illegal groups, from 1936 onwards, economic class conflict was revived once more in industry on a broad front. What is more this battle about the fundamental economic interests of the working class does not even seem to have been organised in any way. It expressed itself in spontaneous walkouts, in collective pressure on employers and on National Socialist institutions, in go-slows, staying off work, taking sick leave, etc.

This refusal of the working classes to subordinate itself fully to the National Socialist system of dictatorship can be called opposition: it made use of the contradictions within the capitalist economic order and of the dictatorship, and sharpened these contradictions. This distinction between 'Opposition' and 'Resistance' is based upon the actual historical experiences of the working class, which are of central importance for an analysis of this entire theme, for the factual separation of the illegal resistance groups from their class was a decisive success of the state-political terror in the Third Reich.

Source-based questions: Conformity and resistance in Nazi Germany

SOURCE 3

From Ian Kershaw, The Nazi Dictatorship, *published in 1993*

As institutions the Churches offered something less than fundamental resistance to Nazism. Their considerable efforts and energies in opposing Nazi interference with traditional practices were not matched by equally vigorous denunciation of Nazi inhumanity and barbarism – with the notable exception of [Cardinal] Galen's open attack on the 'euthanasia' programme in August 1941. In defence of humanitarian rights and civil liberties, the response of both churches was muted.

The detestation of Nazism was overwhelming within the Catholic Church and grew more extensive within the Evangelical Church. But defiant opposition in the sphere of the 'Church struggle' was compatible in both major denominations with approval of key areas of the regime's policies, above all where Nazism blended into 'mainstream' national aspirations: support for 'patriotic' foreign policy and war aims; obedience towards state authority (except where it was regarded as contravening divine law); approval for the destruction of 'atheistic' Marxism; and readiness to accept discrimination against Jews. In all of these areas the Churches as institutions felt on uncertain ground – a reflection of the fact that popular backing could not be guaranteed, and that such issues fell outside what was regarded as the legitimate sphere of Church opposition, which was correspondingly limited, fragmented and largely individual.

SOURCE 4

Statement issued by Catholic Bishops in Bavaria, December 1936

After the deplorable fight carried on by Communists, Free Thinkers and Freemasons against Christianity, we welcomed with gratitude the National Socialist profession of positive Christianity. Our *Führer* in a most impressive speech acknowledged the importance to the state of the two Christian Churches and promised them his protection.

Notwithstanding the Concordat of July 1933, there has developed an ever-growing struggle against the Papacy. Catholic organisations and societies were promised protection for their continued existence. In reality, their continuation has gradually become impossible. The clergy are regularly insulted in speeches, writings, broadcasts and cartoons, yet the perpetrators go unpunished.

It is not our intention to renounce the present form of government or its policy. The *Führer* can be certain that we will give all our moral support to his struggle against Bolshevism, but we do ask that our Church is permitted to enjoy her God-given rights and freedoms.

SOURCE 5

Part of a report secretly compiled by the underground organisation of the SPD, Autumn 1936

Although the anti-Bolshevik agitation is making a deep and powerful impact, the National Socialist mood has not penetrated very deeply. However, Hitler has understood how to appeal to nationalist instincts and emotional needs, which were already there. He stands outside the line of fire and criticism of the Government, whereas Goebbels is almost universally loathed, even among Nazis. The reduction in unemployment, and the drive it shows in its foreign policy are the big points in favour of Hitler's policy. He knows how to handle the popular mood and continually to win over the masses. No previous Reich Chancellor had understood anything of that.

Answer both questions (a) and (b).

(a) Using your own knowledge and the evidence of Sources 1, 3 and 4, what do you consider to have been the main reasons for which German conservatives entered into opposition to the Nazi regime in the period 1933–45? [10 marks]

(b) Using your own knowledge and the evidence of all five sources, how far do you agree with the judgement that 'Nazism failed to convince many Germans of its ideology, yet was never seriously threatened after 1933 by political or social opposition from within Germany'? [20 marks]

Source-based questions: The condition of the workers in the Third Reich

Study the four sources and then answer ALL of the sub-questions.

(a) Study Source C.

From the Source and your own knowledge, explain the reference to 'the time of inflation'.
[20 marks]

(b) Study Sources A and B.

Compare the judgements expressed in these Sources on the social projects launched by the Nazi state. *[40 marks]*

(c) Study all of the Sources.

Using all of these Sources and your own knowledge, explain how far you agree with the judgement that the German working classes derived no genuine benefits from Nazi rule in Germany between 1933 and 1939. *[60 marks]*

SOURCE A

A Nazi writer explains how the 'Strength Through Joy' movement represents the beginnings of a new society

The comradely experience of work and the equally comradely experience of leisure time belong together. In them lies the idea of social life itself. The 'Strength Through Joy' land and sea trips mean far more than social travel in the normal sense: their value lies neither in the type of transport nor in the destination of the journey, but solely in the community experience. It is the great experience of nature which provides the best prerequisite for comradeship, so that one can say that these trips undertaken together represent the beginnings of a transformation of social life. A new type of culture is in the process of being born.

Willi Müller, Social Life in the New Germany, published in Berlin in 1938

SOURCE B

Opponents of the Nazis argue that their social projects have hidden motives

For a large number of Germans the announcement of the People's Car came as a pleasant surprise. For a long time the Volkswagen was a big talking point among all classes of the population. With the Volkswagen the leadership of the Third Reich has killed several birds with one stone. In the first place, it removes for a period of several years money from the German consumer

which he would otherwise spend on goods that cannot be supplied. Secondly, and this is the most important thing, they have achieved a clever diversionary tactic in the sphere of domestic politics. This car obsession, which has been cleverly induced by the Propaganda Ministry, keeps the masses from becoming preoccupied with a depressing situation.

A report by underground SPD agents from the Rhineland, April 1939

SOURCE C

The Deputy Führer explains why German workers should accept wage-restraint

The *Führer* has repeatedly stated that under the present circumstances wage increases must lead to price increases. This in turn will lead to the endless vicious circle familiar to the German people from the time of inflation. Wage increases, therefore, can only be damaging rather than beneficial to the general public and to the individual, and so must be avoided at all costs. The fact that the economic position of large sections of our people is not what we would want it to be is the fault of the political, economic and trade union leadership of the post-war years. One must not overlook the importance of the fact that the virtual elimination of unemployment at the present time is due solely to the *Führer* and his movement.

A speech by Rudolf Hess, October 1937

SOURCE D

An official Nazi report gives details of working conditions in the revitalised German economy

The discrepancy between the available labour force and the number of orders has in general led to a considerable increase in the number of hours worked. Fifty-eight to 65 hours a week are no longer exceptional. And some factories continue overtime, even when there is a reduction in orders, because they are afraid of losing workers. The extraordinary demands made upon the German workers, particularly during the period of tension [caused by the crisis over Czechoslovakia], have on the whole been met without any difficulties. Thus the Reich Trustee of Labour for the Saar–Palatinate region reports that it is not uncommon for railway workers, for example, to work up to 16 hours a day.

Report of the Reich Trustees of Labour, Autumn 1938

The Twenty Years' Truce: international relations, 1919–1939

11.1 What forces shaped the terms of the Treaty of Versailles?

11.2 Why was the Versailles settlement unsatisfactory?

11.3 How effective was the League of Nations?

11.4 To what extent had international relations been stabilised by 1929?

11.5 What was the impact of the Wall Street Crash upon international relations?

11.6 Why was it not possible to form a European alliance against Hitler between 1933 and 1935?

11.7 In what respects had Hitler changed the Versailles settlement by 1938?

11.8 Why did war break out in 1939?

11.9 Historical interpretation: Did Hitler plan the outbreak of war in 1939?

Key Issues

- What were the strengths and weaknesses of the peace settlement drawn up at the end of the First World War?

- How realistic were the prospects of lasting peace in Europe in the 1920s?

- Why did the Versailles peace settlement collapse so spectacularly in the course of the 1930s?

Framework of Events

1919	(June) Signature of Treaty of Versailles
	(September) Signature of Treaty of St Germain
1920	Establishment of League of Nations
1922	Treaty of Rapallo between Germany and USSR
1923	French occupation of the Ruhr
1924	Introduction of Dawes Plan
1925	Locarno treaties
1926	Germany admitted to League of Nations
1928	Signature of Kellogg–Briand Pact
1929	Introduction of Young Plan
	(October) Collapse of US stock market, the 'Wall Street Crash'
1931	Hoover moratorium on German reparation payments. Japanese invasion of Manchuria
1932	Lausanne conference on reparation payments
1933	(January) Adolf Hitler appointed Chancellor of Germany
	(July) Four Power Pact between Britain, France, Italy and Germany
1934	German–Polish non-aggression pact
1935	Saar returned to Germany. Germany introduces military conscription. Stresa agreement
	(October) Italian invasion of Abyssinia
1936	(March) German remilitarisation of the Rhineland
	(July) Outbreak of civil war in Spain
	(November) Anti-Comintern pact between Germany and Japan
1937	Japan–China War begins with Japanese invasion of northern China. Italy joins Anti-Comintern pact and withdraws from League of Nations
1938	(March) German occupation of Austria
	(October) Munich Conference, followed by German occupation of Sudetenland

1939	(March) German occupation of Bohemia and Moravia in Czechoslovakia
	(May) 'Pact of Steel' between Germany and Italy
	(August) 'Ribbentrop–Molotov' pact between Germany and USSR
	(September) German invasion of Poland. Declaration of Second World War by Britain and France on Germany.

Overview

IN November 1918, the powers that had fought the First World War emerged into a world quite unlike that which they had fought to protect. The degree of potential instability that existed in the aftermath of the First World War was without precedent in recent European history. The Austro-Hungarian Empire had collapsed, to be replaced by a collection of smaller states, more viable in terms of national identity than in terms of military strength or of defensible borders. The Russian Empire had not only given way to a collection of new states, but also to a new political, social and economic system that declared itself hostile to all others in Europe. The United States of America, whose intervention in the war had been decisive, withdrew immediately into **isolationism**. Britain and France, who had lacked the means and the desire to direct European affairs in 1914, were certainly in no position to do so five years later. Between 1919 and the mid-1930s Europe was essentially a power vacuum.

Isolationism: A policy by which a state (e.g. the USA in the early 1930s) pursues its own domestic interests in isolation from the wider considerations of international politics.

The 1920s can be seen, in retrospect, as a 'false start' to attempts to solve the terrible problems created, or left unsolved, by the First World War. The victorious allies approached the problem of political reconstruction in Europe with two assumptions that proved to be false:

1. that they had won a clear-cut victory;

2. that the ground was now clear for a just and enlightened re-ordering of European politics.

The perception that Germany had been defeated may have been partly true in the military sense (although Germany had clearly defeated Russia on the Eastern Front), but it was distinctly false in terms of its economic potential, and in terms of the political ideas that had driven its recent expansion. Even in the 1920s the assumptions of the allies were undermined by the bitter resentment felt by Germany at the terms of the peace treaty, and at the presumption of German 'war guilt' upon which the treaty rested. This contributed directly to the second problem, that of how the hated peace treaty could be enforced. Neither of the alternative strategies employed by the allies – to force the terms upon Germany, or to persuade the Germans into grudging acceptance – proved altogether successful. A third strategy – of employing the resources of American capitalism to fund German, and thereby European stability – seemed to show distinct promise in the years 1924–29. When that option was wrecked by the collapse of the American stock market, the major powers of Europe found themselves plunged back into a political world dominated by national self-interest and the rule of military force.

In the aftermath of the Second World War it was broadly acceptable to attribute all the tragedies and failures of the past decades to the evil expansionism of the Nazi regime. More recently, however, some historians have placed greater emphasis upon

Disarmament: The act of reducing the number of weapons that a country has.

Unilateral: Countries make decisions without waiting for agreement from other countries.

Maginot Line: A line of military fortifications along the eastern and north-eastern borders of France, to defend against invasion. It was named after André Maginot, French politician (1877–1932).

Vichy government: The term used to describe the regime that governed the 'free' zone of France during the early part of the Nazi occupation. It took its name from the spa town of Vichy, in which it established its headquarters. It was largely dependent upon German goodwill, and was overthrown when German forces occupied the 'free' zone in 1943.

the context in which that regime operated, and upon the opportunities that it was able to exploit. They have become increasingly aware of the complexity of the problems posed for the western European powers by the economic collapse of 1929. Their understandable preoccupation with their domestic economies made them sympathetic to programmes of **disarmament**. In the cases of several powers, notably Britain and France, independence movements within their Asian colonies, and the willingness of Japan to exploit these movements, seemed to pose a threat to their interests as serious as that posed by the resurgence of Germany. At the same time, the destabilisation of western capitalism renewed fears about the intentions of Soviet Russia. It is of the greatest importance that, with the establishment and consolidation of the Soviet Union, Europe had to take into account a force that threatened not only the existing balance of power, but all existing social and economic structures. It is only with hindsight that we can identify Nazism as the major challenge that those powers faced in the 1930s.

It is no wonder that the states of Europe employed a number of strategies to deflect the German threat, as alternatives to confrontation. The most familiar and traditional of these was the formation of alliances that might deter Germany from aggressive action. By 1937, however, it appeared that none of the western European powers really had the stomach for the task. Besides, some states seemed to pursue this strategy at the same time as they made **unilateral** arrangements for their own security. It was hard to believe in France, for instance, as an international peacekeeper, as it retreated behind the barrier of the **Maginot Line** (see map on page 371). The second strategy was to appease Germany, to offer concessions in the hope that this would satisfy its revisionist demands and encourage it to act once again as a responsible member of the international community. In many respects it was an honourable and justifiable policy, but its effect was largely to convince Hitler that he had a free hand in Europe. A third strategy was to recognise Nazi Germany as the dominant European power of the future, and to align one's state with Hitler. Italy had taken this course voluntarily by 1938. France followed a similar course in 1940, under the **Vichy government**, forced into it by the discovery to its cost that the other methods did not work. Neither Italy nor France enjoyed much success in deflecting Hitler from the course that he had chosen.

11.1 *What forces shaped the terms of the Treaty of Versailles?*

November 1918 brought an armistice rather than a definitive peace. Some of its terms – such as the withdrawal of German forces beyond the Rhine, and the internment of its fleet – made it a foregone conclusion that Germany would be unable to restart hostilities. In effect, the leaders of the four main allied powers – France, Britain, the USA and Italy – were concerned during their six months of deliberation (13 January – 28 June 1919) with the preparation of the terms for peace that would be dictated to the representatives of Germany when at last they were allowed to appear in France. Rarely has the preparation of peace been attended by such high hopes and rarely has the feeling been so quickly apparent that the outcome of negotiations had fallen far short of initial expectations. 'We arrived,' wrote the British historian and diplomat Harold Nicolson, in *Peacemaking, 1919* (1967), 'determined that a peace of justice and wisdom should be negotiated: we left it conscious that the treaties imposed upon our enemies were neither wise nor just.' Others saw the price that Europe would pay for the shortcomings of the peace. 'This is not peace,' Ferdinand Foch is reported to have exclaimed when he heard the terms, 'it is a truce for 20 years.'

The political pressures

The first problem that handicapped the leaders of the allied powers in their search for a lasting peace was that they were not always free agents. The British Prime Minister, David Lloyd George, was in the process of fighting a general election in which popular anger produced such emotive slogans as 'Hang the Kaiser' and 'Squeeze the German lemon until the pips squeak'. In France, President Georges Clemenceau had to contend with anger and anxiety that the losses of the war should never be repeated. The priorities of the delegates also differed. French policy was dominated by an overwhelming desire for future security, for the achievement of which almost no imposition upon the German aggressor would be too great. Britain's view was moderated by a number of considerations. The **scuttling** of the German fleet at Scapa Flow (31 June 1919) guaranteed its own national security. At the same time, its traditional concern with the balance of power on the continent made Britain wary of weakening Germany excessively, especially as it became ever clearer that the Soviet regime in Russia was there to stay.

It was always likely that both sets of vested interests would be overridden by the concerns of the American President, Woodrow Wilson. He hoped to replace the outdated and corrupt criteria of European diplomacy with a lasting and just peace, based upon the satisfaction of justifiable national claims. He hoped for 'a peace without victory', a settlement that would not be dominated by selfish demands by the victors. Wilson was the central figure of the peace conference, partly because the USA alone had the manpower and financial resources to continue the struggle if necessary, and partly because of the enormous popularity that he enjoyed as 'the prophet of peace'. He could not, however, expect to impose his views upon the hard-bitten statesmen of Europe.

The desire to punish Germany

The 440 clauses that constituted the peace treaty with Germany were concerned with four major issues.

- At the heart of the treaty lay the contention that Germany bore the main burden of guilt for the outbreak of the 'Great War'. Clause 231 was a key element in the treaty, forcing Germany to acknowledge this guilt and responsibility. Without this 'war guilt clause' there would have been little moral justification for the other impositions upon Germany, and it is little surprise that this was a prime focus for German resentment in the inter-war years.

- Secondly, although the Treaty of Versailles made allowance for eventual general disarmament, Germany was to be disarmed immediately. As its armed forces were in future to cater only for the defence of its own territory, they were restricted to an army of 96,000 men and 4,000 officers, all serving for a period of 12 years. This was to prevent the build-up of experienced reserves. These armed forces were forbidden the use of any purely offensive weapons – tanks, heavy artillery, powered aircraft, submarines and capital warships.

- The boundaries of the German state were also adjusted to satisfy the demands of neighbouring nationalities. In the west, Alsace-Lorraine

---

Scuttling: The act whereby naval commanders order the sinking of their own ships. This is usually done to prevent them from falling into enemy hands.

David Lloyd George (1863–1945)
Leader of the Liberal Party. Chancellor of the Exchequer in Britain (1908–12). An energetic supporter of the British war effort, he was made Minister of Munitions (1915) and Prime Minister (1916–22).

Woodrow Wilson (1856–1924)
Leading Democrat politician. President of Princeton University (1902–10); Governor of New Jersey (1911–13). He was elected President of the USA in 1913 and in 1916. In 1920 he won the Nobel Peace Prize, but was forced to retire from politics through illness.

Territorial changes, 1919–24

returned to France and the small regions of Eupen and Malmedy became Belgian territory. Ideally, France would have wished to make greater inroads for its future security, either to advance its own border to the Rhine, or to create an independent and neutral state in the Rhineland. Both plans were opposed by Britain and America on ideological and rational grounds, and France had to be satisfied with a three-point settlement. The Rhineland was temporarily occupied by allied forces, all German forces were permanently banned from the Rhineland, and Britain and America promised their future aid in maintaining this settlement. To the north and east, Germany suffered further losses. North Schleswig once more became Danish territory, and territory in Posen and West Prussia was transferred to Poland, notably the infamous 'Polish corridor' giving the new state access to the sea. At the end of the 'corridor', the distinctly German city of Danzig became a 'free city' with Poland granted the use of its port facilities, its only access to the sea.

● Germany's 'war guilt' also provided justification for the allied demand for reparations. This was not the first time that victors in European

Tomas Masaryk (1850–1937)
Advocate of Czech
independence during the First
World War. Elected President of
Czechoslovakia in 1920, 1927
and 1934, before retiring
through ill health in 1935.

Edvard Beneš (1884–1948)
After working with Masaryk in
the cause of Czech
independence, Beneš served
as Foreign Minister of
Czechoslovakia (1918–35).
President of the Republic
(1935–39). Leader of the
Czech government in exile
(1941–45). Briefly president of
liberated Czechoslovakia until
ousted by communists in 1948.

1. What steps did the victorious allies take in the Treaty of Versailles to limit the future power of Germany?

2. How effectively did the terms of the Treaty of Versailles to serve the interests of Britain and France?

wars had claimed material compensation from the conquered, but the scale of the demands, like the scale of the war, was unprecedented. The allies proposed to charge Germany for the material damage done to them during the hostilities, a very considerable figure in the case of France. They also proposed to charge future expenses on such items as pensions for their widows and war wounded. This last item alone constituted nearly half the total bill of £6,600 million which was handed to the Germans by the Inter-Allied Reparations Commission when the task of estimation was eventually completed (May 1921).

Dismantling the Austro–Hungarian Empire

Although the peace settlement with Germany naturally dominated the attention of European statesmen, it was accompanied by a collection of other treaties made with Germany's former allies:

- with Austria at St Germain en Laye

- with Hungary at Trianon

- with Turkey at Sevres

- with Bulgaria at Neuilly.

The disappearance of the Habsburg Empire, that dominant feature of central Europe for five centuries, was central to these treaties. In its place stood the German state of Austria, specially forbidden by the treaties to unite with its fellow Germans to the north, and a number of new states. Yugoslavia, Czechoslovakia and Poland represented the fulfilment of national aspirations that had rumbled on throughout the 19th century. In the cases of Yugoslavia and Czechoslovakia the delegates around Paris had been able to do little but accept the actions of such national leaders as Tomas Masaryk and Edvard Beneš, who had seized their opportunities with the collapse of the Austro–Hungarian war effort. Hungary, after a century of increasing national fulfilment, now found itself stripped of Croatia, Slovenia, Slovakia and Ruthenia by these new states. Its resentment of these losses was to be a significant factor in the politics of central and eastern Europe over the next two decades.

11.2 Why was the Versailles settlement unsatisfactory?

The peace settlement of 1919 was unsuccessful. The historian A.J.P. Taylor's blunt judgement, in *The Origins of the Second World War* (1961), that 'the Second World War was, in large part, a repeat performance of the first' conveys clearly the extent to which the problems of 1919 were left unresolved. In part, its failure may be attributed to the enormous complexity of the problems facing the delegates. In 1815, at Vienna, European statesmen needed to regulate the territories of one state, Napoleonic France. In 1919, at Versailles, it was the empires of Germany, Turkey, Austria-Hungary and Russia – a large proportion of the European landmass – that lay in ruins. Several other distinct weaknesses in the final drafts of the treaties can also be identified.

German resentment

The main problem that was to haunt Europe for the next two and a half decades was German resentment of the terms imposed upon them. Although on the verge of military defeat in November 1918, German troops were still on foreign soil, and their representatives had approached the allies confident that a settlement would be offered based upon Wilson's 'Fourteen Points' (see Chapter 10).

Instead Germans found themselves presented with a dictated peace which stripped the Reich of 25,000 square miles (64,750 square kilometres) of territory and 7,000,000 inhabitants, about 13% and 10% of its respective totals. They found that, in many cases, Germany was treated according to principles quite different from those that governed the settlements with other states. Nationality was the proclaimed principle behind most territorial settlements, yet union between Germany and the German-speakers of Austria was specifically forbidden. Germany was disarmed and stripped of its colonies, while the victors retained their weapons and in some cases actually added to their colonial empires. Yet, although Germany was treated as a defeated power, it retained the means to become a great force in the world once more. It was not partitioned, as it was eventually to be in 1945, and it retained nearly 90% of its economic resources. Germany was deprived of its weapons, but retained the potential to produce modern replacements at a later date. As early as 1925, Germany's production of steel, for instance, was twice that of Great Britain. Its relative position in the European balance of power had hardly suffered from the collapse of the Russian and Austrian empires, that left a collection of relatively weak '**successor states**' on its eastern borders.

'**Successor states**': Those states that filled the vacuum left by the collapse of the Habsburg Empire in the aftermath of the First World War.

The disintegration of the wartime allied alliance

In 1918 the allied alliance that had fought the war was already in the process of disintegration. By 1920 it was in ruins. Firstly, the great power of Russia, a key factor in the considerations of 1914, was completely excluded from the deliberations of 1919. The 1917 Bolshevik revolution removed Russia temporarily from the diplomatic scene, but its eventual success, and its brief imitations in Hungary (March 1919) and Bavaria (April 1919), profoundly shocked the governing classes of Europe. As a result of the revolution, the attitudes of these classes towards Germany often became ambiguous. With Germany defeated, might not Communist Russia now be seen as the major threat to Europe's stability and security? If a relatively strong, conservative Germany were not preserved as a bulwark in central Europe, what would prevent the westward flow of the Communist tide? By mid-1919 it was clear that the USA would not fulfil this role, for it had turned its back on Europe as abruptly as it had intervened in the first place. The considerable prestige of President Wilson at Versailles had hidden the true weakness of its domestic position. Involvement in Europe had never been universally popular in the USA, and the prospect of a permanent peacekeeping role there was quite unacceptable to many American politicians. Accordingly, the Senate refused to ratify the treaties that Wilson had negotiated (November 1919). A year later, Wilson's party was out of power, and America was once again on the path of isolationism. In short, the implementation of the peace treaty had to be undertaken from 1919 without the participation of either of the powers that were to decide Europe's fate in 1939–45.

Keynes and the controversy over reparations

There has been little historical dispute about the importance of German resentment or the problems of enforcement in the failure of the Versailles settlement. The same cannot be said for the third area of objection that was raised to the peace terms. In an influential work, *The Economic Consequences of the Peace* (1920), the English economist J.M. Keynes denounced what he saw as the folly of the treaty's reparation clauses. By putting such intolerable pressure on the German economy, he concluded, the allies threatened the

John Maynard Keynes (1883–1946)
British economist; a fierce opponent of the allies' reparations policy at Versailles. Keynes proposed (1936) new theories on economic thinking and employment policy. He was an important figure in the organisation of international monetary arrangements in 1945.

Demagogues: Political leaders who try to win support by appealing to people's emotions rather than using rational arguments.

1. *What features of the Versailles Treaty were most resented by Germany? Give reasons for your answer.*

2. *Why did the peace settlement with Germany prove so difficult to enforce in the years after 1918?*

stability of the whole European economy of which it was part. 'This treaty,' he argued, 'ignores the economic solidarity of Europe, and by aiming at the economic life of Germany, it threatens the health and prosperity of the allies themselves.' Although influential in Britain and in the USA, Keynes' arguments aroused great opposition in France, the country most in need of reparations. There, they were most effectively answered by E. Mantoux, in *The Economic Consequences of Mr Keynes* (1944). The central part of Mantoux's argument was that the productivity of German industry during the 1930s, especially armaments manufacture, showed that the levels of reparations set in 1921 were, after all, within Germany's capacity.

Was the Versailles settlement doomed from the outset?

Mantoux's work is part of a substantial literature, written largely since the end of the Second World War, that has modified the earlier condemnation of the Versailles treaty. Where Winston Churchill saw 'a turbulent collision of embarrassed **demagogues**', where Keynes saw profound economic ignorance, and where Harold Nicolson saw a sad failure to stick to original high ideals, more recent writers have often cited extenuating circumstances. The French historian, Maurice Baumont, in *The Origins of the Second World War* (1978), has stressed that the shortcomings that survived the peace conference should not blind us to the fact that 'as a whole the treaties righted age-old wrongs', especially with regard to the subject nationalities of central Europe. The English historian Anthony Adamthwaite, in *The Making of the Second World War* (1977), has claimed that the main fault in 1919 lay, not with the terms of the treaties, but with the hopes that preceded them, so high that they were bound to be disappointed. 'No peace settlement could have fulfilled the millennial hopes of a new heaven and a new earth. It was the destruction of these Utopian hopes that provoked the denunciations of the settlement.' In addition to these criticisms, it is also possible to argue that the main problem with the treaty lay not in its terms but in the subsequent failure to enforce it effectively.

11.3 How effective was the League of Nations?

What was the purpose of the League?

The League of Nations was a central element in Woodrow Wilson's ideas on the establishment and maintenance of European and world peace. He believed in the concept of an international organisation able to rise above the selfish motives and the misunderstandings that, in his view, were the root causes of international conflict. In general, the idea was greeted with enthusiasm by the nations represented at the Versailles peace conference. Two distinct schools of thought developed as to the form it should take. France took the realistic view that such a body could only be influential if equipped with sufficient armed force to enforce its decisions. This was opposed by Great Britain, uneasy at the idea of an international armed force possibly under French command, and by other states who baulked at the idea of portions of their own forces coming under international control. Above all, President Wilson refused to allow his 'brain child' to become simply another weapon of traditional power politics, or one with which the victors could torment the defeated. Thus, the body whose Covenant, or constitution, was written specifically into each of the peace treaties, and which met for the first time in Geneva in December 1920, was primarily a forum to which nations in dispute could bring their problems for advice and settlement.

How was the League intended to work?

The Covenant of the League of Nations defined four main aims for the organisation:

● to prevent future wars by the peaceful settlement of international disputes;

● to promote disarmament;

● to supervise the **mandated territories** referred to it by the peace treaties, such as the former German colonies and the Saarland;

● to promote general international co-operation by its various organisations for social and economic work.

Its powers and the obligations of its members in these tasks were also clearly defined. Members in dispute with one another were obliged to refer their differences to one of three processes provided by the League:

● to the Permanent Court of International Justice;

● to **arbitration**;

● to enquiry by the Council of the League, its executive committee.

Failure to do so, or failure to take reasonable account of the resulting decisions, rendered offending members liable to **sanctions**. The allies had been so impressed by the effect of economic **embargoes** employed against Germany in the war that economic sanctions were chosen as the League's main weapon. The possibility of military sanctions was admitted, but their extent was left undefined, and they could only ever be applied if a member state agreed to put its own forces at the disposal of the League. In its 20-year life, the League never once sought to apply military sanctions.

Forty-two states originally subscribed to these terms, but there were some notable absentees. The USA, because of the Senate's refusal to ratify the peace terms, never became a member of the organisation inspired by

Mandated territories: Areas placed under the supervision of the League of Nations at the end of the First World War.

Arbitration: The judging of a dispute between nations or states by someone not involved, whose decision both sides agree to accept.

Sanctions: Measures taken by countries to restrict or prohibit trade and official contact with a country that has broken international law.

Embargoes: A non-violent form of political action in which pressure is placed upon a state by banning trade with that state.

The major institutions of the League of Nations

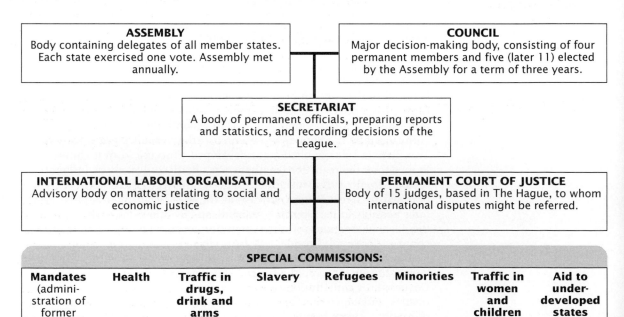

ASSEMBLY Body containing delegates of all member states. Each state exercised one vote. Assembly met annually.	**COUNCIL** Major decision-making body, consisting of four permanent members and five (later 11) elected by the Assembly for a term of three years.

SECRETARIAT
A body of permanent officials, preparing reports and statistics, and recording decisions of the League.

INTERNATIONAL LABOUR ORGANISATION Advisory body on matters relating to social and economic justice	**PERMANENT COURT OF JUSTICE** Body of 15 judges, based in The Hague, to whom international disputes might be referred.

SPECIAL COMMISSIONS:

Mandates (administration of former colonies)	Health	Traffic in drugs, drink and arms	Slavery	Refugees	Minorities	Traffic in women and children	Aid to under-developed states

their President. Soviet Russia did not become a member until 1934, the year after Japan left the League. Germany was a member only between 1926–33, its initial absence confirming the impression that the League stood in essence for the preservation of the 'status quo' established in 1919. None of the powers dissatisfied with either the terms or the principles of the peace settlement could happily accept or further the aims of the League of Nations.

What did the League achieve and what did it fail to achieve?

The League was not a total failure. When states accepted its mediatory functions it could and did reach notable settlements, as over the Åland Islands claimed by Sweden and Finland (1921), and in border disputes between Greece and Bulgaria (1924) and between Hungary and Yugoslavia (1934). When European statesmen such as Ramsay MacDonald, Gustav Stresemann and Aristide Briand worked with it in the late 1920s, it seemed to stand at the centre of European diplomacy. Its international bodies, such as the Health Organisation and the Advisory Committee on Traffic in Women and Children, still function today (as the World Health Organisation and UNICEF). It failed in its primary task, to prevent further war, due to the fact that the League represented a new concept of international relations in a world where most major powers were content to stick to the old selfish methods of force and *Realpolitik*.

In the major confrontations of the inter-war period the League failed, not because it could not find common ground between disputing parties, but because it was totally ignored by one or more of those parties. The League was bypassed in the case of Polish seizure of the town of Vilna (1920), Japanese aggression in Manchuria (1931), Italian attacks on Abyssinia (1935) and all of Hitler's expansionist moves. It had no means in its Covenant to prevent that. Two contemporary verdicts illustrate the League's weakness in the face of selfish acts of aggression. In all the cases just mentioned the judgement of Lord David Cecil held good, that 'the League of Nations has not been tried and found wanting; it has been found inconvenient and not tried'. Prominent among those who found the 'peace-mongering' of the League inconvenient was Benito Mussolini. He fully appreciated that, especially in the 1930s, the machinery of the League appealed only to those nations too weak to look after their own interests. 'The League is all right,' he declared, 'when sparrows quarrel. It fails when eagles fall out.'

Ramsay MacDonald (1866–1937)
Born in Scotland, son of a labourer. Joined the Independent Labour Party (1894) and became first secretary of the new Labour Party (1900). MacDonald was elected to Parliament in 1904. Leader of the Labour Party (1911–14 and 1923–31). Prime Minister in 1924 (Britain's first Labour Prime Minister) and in 1929–35. He left the Labour Party to form a national government with backing from both Liberal and Conservative parties. He resigned the premiership in 1935.

1. By what means did the League of Nations hope to preserve peace in the post-war world?

2. How much justification is there for the statement that 'the League of Nations failed because its aims were neither popular nor achievable'?

11.4 To what extent had international relations been stabilised by 1929?

Continuing confrontation: why did France invade the Ruhr in 1923?

In the years immediately after the conclusion of peace, it was France that faced the biggest problems over the enforcement of the treaty. For France, the questions of reparation payments, of post-war reconstruction and of German economic potential were not questions of morality or of theory, but of national survival. By 1920, however, the bases of French security proposed at Versailles lay in ruins. America had withdrawn from European involvement, Britain showed little interest in continuing the co-operation of wartime, and domestic developments in Germany offered little prospect of its willing acceptance of the settlement. Most serious for France's recovery and prosperity, Germany showed increasing reluctance to maintain its reparation payments. By the Wiesbaden Accords (October 1921),

France agreed to help German payments by accepting a proportion in raw materials and industrial produce, rather than in cash, but in the next year, these payments in kind had also slipped steadily into arrears.

Faced with the choice of using conciliation or confrontation to exact its due from Germany, public and political opinion in France inclined more and more toward the latter solution. This tendency was strengthened by the appointment of Raymond Poincaré as Prime Minister (January 1922).

The crisis in French–German relations erupted in November 1922 when Germany requested a suspension of its payments for up to four years in the face of domestic economic difficulties. It was Germany's third such request in three years and strongly suggested that the whole question of enforcing the Versailles settlement was at stake. It was this vital issue, rather than the trivial pretext of non-delivery of a batch of telegraph poles, that prompted France, with support from Italy and Belgium, to send troops across the Rhine into the industrial heartland of the Ruhr (January 1923). Protesting, with justification, that the invasion of its sovereign territory was against the terms of the peace treaty, the German government of Chancellor Cuno appealed with great success for a policy of **passive resistance** in the Ruhr. In February 1923, coal production there fell to 2.5 million tons, where 90 million had been mined in 1922. Three iron-smelting furnaces operated in March, where 70 had worked the previous year. Occasional terrorist attacks on troops and military action against German demonstrators raised the overall tension.

To overcome the effects of strikes and passive resistance, Poincaré appealed, with equal success, for unemployed Frenchmen and Belgians to operate mines, furnaces and railways in the Ruhr. Faced with the success of this ploy, with the total collapse of the German currency, and with the ominous spread of separatist movements in Germany, the government conceded defeat. Although it never became official French governmental policy, commanders in the Ruhr certainly showed some sympathy to political movements that proposed the establishment of an independent Rhineland state. With a united Germany at risk, Gustav Stresemann replaced Cuno as Chancellor in August 1923 and decreed the end of passive resistance within a month.

Was French intervention in the Ruhr successful?

What had Poincaré achieved in the Ruhr? Economically, he seemed to have triumphed, with France guaranteed 21% of the region's production up to December 1923 and 27% thereafter. Against this, Poincaré had reinforced the mistrust and apprehension among his former allies at the French threat to the balance of power, and had made difficult, if not impossible, any future co-operation between France and Germany. 'France,' wrote the Italian minister Count Sforza, 'has committed the supreme error of polarising against her the hostility of all the patriotic elements in the Reich.' The economic gains, important as they were, were largely invalidated by France's subsequent political isolation. In his own country, Poincaré came under attack, from the left wing for high-handed action in the interests of French capitalists, and from the right for withdrawing when the chance existed finally to break the unity and economic backbone of Germany. In terms of its political consequences it must be considered highly doubtful whether the Ruhr gamble was worth the cost.

Economic stabilisation: the Dawes Plan

At least France learned its lesson from the Ruhr adventure. The hostility of the British and American reaction, the dramatic decline in the franc (from 70 to the pound in 1922 to 240 to the pound in 1926), and the defeat of

---

Raymond Poincaré (1856–1934)
A hard-headed politician, a native of Lorraine who remembered Germany's past offences towards his home region, and was determined that Germany should not escape its due punishment. Member of the French Assembly from 1887. Finance Minister (1894–95). Prime Minister (1912–13). President of the Republic (1913–20), Foreign Minister (1922–24).

Passive resistance: A form of political resistance based upon peaceful actions (e.g. strike action), as opposed to acts of violence.

the National Bloc in the 1924 elections, all brought home the point that France could not safely rely upon unilateral action. The agreement between France, Britain and the USA (November 1923) to replace the reparations question upon an international footing, represented not only French misgivings, but British and American fears as to where unilateral action might lead in the future.

The result of this decision was the formation of the commission, chaired by the American economist Charles Dawes, which produced in April 1924 the so-called 'Dawes Plan' for the future regulation of redemption payments. By the Dawes Plan, which was to operate for five years, reparation payments would be guaranteed by two mortgages, one on Germany's railways, and the other on certain German industries, supplemented by deductions from certain German taxes. An American 'General Reparations Agent', Parker Gilbert, was to be installed in Germany to supervise payments. The amounts to be paid by Germany were substantially reduced, but this was outweighed in the French view by the facts that much of its post-war reconstruction was nearing completion, and that the plan once more involved its wartime allies in the collection of reparations. Thus, France accepted the Dawes Plan.

The five years of the Plan's operation have been described as the 'Golden Age' of reparations, with the allies receiving payments, in cash and in kind, with greater regularity than before. It was, however, a temporary measure, and was still accompanied by German complaints both at the level of payments and because no definite date had been fixed for their end. From the allied point of view, the plan also failed to provide any link between German payments and their own repayment of war debts to the USA.

The Young Plan (1929)

The Young Plan (June 1929), which was proposed to succeed the Dawes Plan, set out to tackle these questions. Although it further reduced the total to be paid by Germany, it linked French and British debts to the level of German payments, and set 1988 as the final year of reparation payments. It also continued American commitment and involvement in this vital area of European politics.

In both the Dawes Plan and the Young Plan the fatal weakness was that they were largely dependent upon the huge sums of foreign capital, two-thirds of it American, that were being invested in Germany in the late 1920s to stimulate and sustain its industries. J.M. Keynes had already written in 1926 that the duration of these arrangements was 'in the hands of the American capitalist'. Within three years, the great crisis of American capitalism was finally to wreck these hopeful prospects of economic reconciliation.

Diplomatic stabilisation: the Locarno Pact (1925)

For the German government, the primary objective of their agreement to the reparations plans was to clear their territory of foreign troops and to guard against their return. The first aim was only partially achieved. Although French and Belgian troops had withdrawn from the Ruhr by August 1925, allied troops remained in other Rhineland cities, such as Cologne, under the direct terms of the peace treaty. To complete the process, and to guard against the dangers of separatism in the Rhineland, Stresemann approached the allies with the boldest proposal of his political career and one that was by no means universally popular in Germany. At a meeting in Locarno, in Switzerland (February 1925), he proposed a voluntary German guarantee of its western borders. For France and Belgium, this meant that Germany freely gave up its claims to Alsace and

Lorraine and to Eupen and Malmedy. For Germany, it meant that France would no longer be able to use the weapon of invasion, or harbour hopes of an independent Rhineland state – factors that also made the proposals highly acceptable to Britain.

There were, however, shortcomings in the 'package' from the French viewpoint. Would Germany similarly acknowledge its eastern frontiers? Would it acknowledge the peace treaties as a whole? Italy, also party to the proposals, was equally keen that Stresemann should acknowledge Germany's southern border with Austria. The German government would not go so far, and the Locarno Pact agreed by Germany, France, Britain, Italy and Belgium (October 1925), apart from guaranteeing the current western borders of Germany, merely recognised France's treaty commitments to Poland and Czechoslovakia. These were commitments, however, that France would now find very hard to carry out without violating Germany's western frontiers.

The 'Briand–Kellogg' Pact (1928)

It must be understood that the French government accepted the Locarno terms, not because it misunderstood their implications, but because it had undertaken a significant change in its foreign policy. France had now deliberately abandoned attempts to control Germany in favour of attempts to draw Germany into international undertakings guaranteed by other powers. Locarno has to be seen as part of that programme. Germany's entry into the League of Nations (September 1926) was another essential element in the same programme. So, too was the 'Briand–Kellogg' Pact (August 1928) whereby the French Foreign Minister (Aristide Briand) and the American Secretary of State (William Kellogg) agreed to 'the renunciation of war as an instrument of national policy'. Of the 64 states invited to subscribe to this agreement, 62 did so. Brazil and Argentina were the exceptions. Although it has been widely attacked for its apparent naïvety, the pact was interpreted at the time as an important commitment to peace by the world's leading powers.

Conclusion

By the summer of 1929, when a conference at The Hague reached agreement on the evacuation of the Rhineland, five years earlier than envisaged at Versailles, the policy of reconciliation seemed largely vindicated and its future prospects inspired confidence. Locarno and German membership of the League of Nations seemed to create political stability in Europe; the Dawes Plan and its successor seemed to prove that reparations could be paid on a regular basis; the consultative spirit of the League of Nations seemed to be accepted by all major powers. The disintegration of this reassuring 'scenario' was abrupt. In July, the retirement of Poincaré removed the major source of stability in French politics. On 3 October, Stresemann died of a heart attack, aged 51, and exactly three weeks later, on 'Black Thursday', share values on the Wall Street Stock Market went into a disastrous decline. The 'Great Depression' had begun.

1. Explain the means by which France sought to deflect the threat of German recovery in the 1920s.

2. In what respects, and for what reasons, were international relations in Europe more stable in 1929 than they had been in 1923?

3. Why did the crisis in the American economy in 1929 make it so much more difficult to maintain the peace settlement in Europe?

11.5 What was the impact of the Wall Street Crash upon international relations?

The political impact of economic depression

The large-scale withdrawal of American capital from European investment, and the general fall in prices of industrial and agricultural goods, had serious implications for international relations. Any spirit of international co-operation that may have been emerging gave way to a desperate sense of 'every man for himself'. Nation after nation, for example, abandoned the **Gold Standard**, and most states hurriedly enclosed themselves behind tariff barriers in an attempt to minimise the domestic effects of the crisis.

By 1931, only France, Italy and Poland of the major European states continued to base their currencies upon gold. We saw in Chapter 10 that the economic crisis played a direct role in the rise of the Nazi Party to power in Germany between 1930 and 1933. Quite apart from aiding the spread of Fascism and self-interested nationalism, the Depression also prepared the ground for international appeasement of those forces. As Britain, America and other states slowly recovered, they sought safety in economic retrenchment and carefully balanced budgets. There seemed no room, at a time of careful housekeeping, for heavy arms expenditure, and the expense of another war was unthinkable. Besides, as the domestic affairs of France and Spain showed, the apparent failure of existing regimes to cope with the ills of capitalism caused many people to think of Bolshevism or of Fascism as an alternative. France, Spain, Belgium and even Britain were not immune from the forces that had engendered Nazism in Germany.

The Hoover Moratorium and the end of reparations

A direct casualty of the economic catastrophe was the Young Plan for reparation payments. In October 1930, German representatives had approached the US President Herbert Hoover, as the peace treaty entitled them to do, to request a suspension (or 'moratorium') of reparation payments in the light of increasing economic difficulties. The resultant Hoover Moratorium covered all inter-state debts from mid-1931 to mid-1932. By December 1931, however, it was clear that Europe was not experiencing the 'relatively short depression' for which a moratorium was designed. In that month the powers involved with the Young Plan met in Basle (Switzerland) to consider the reparations question. They concluded that 'an adjustment of all inter-governmental debts is the only lasting measure which is capable of restoring economic stability and true peace'. The Lausanne Conference (June 1932) agreed that reparations should be ended by a lump-sum payment of 3,000 million marks, relieving Germany of 90% of its outstanding debt. To the anger of the USA, its European debtors insisted that their war-debt repayments should also end. That anger was heightened when the French Assembly vetoed the government's proposal to make one final debt repayment to America. Thus, the financial clauses of the Treaty of Versailles ceased to exist. If France had gained on an economic level, its diplomatic account was left badly in debit by renewed isolation from the USA. The final lump-sum payment by Germany, incidentally, was never made.

The failure of disarmament

The principle of international disarmament was the second major casualty of the early 1930s. By the terms of the Versailles Treaty, in

Gold Standard: The convention whereby the value of a state's national currency is based upon the amount of gold held by that state. Abandoning the Gold Standard means that the state may issue a larger quantity of paper money than it would otherwise do.

theory, the disarmament of Germany was merely a preliminary to a general disarmament. Not until 1926, however, did a 'Preparatory Commission' meet in Geneva, and not until February 1932 did the conference finally gather there to begin deliberation. On the surface, the prospects seemed bright, for the renunciation of expensive armaments made good sense at a time of economic recession. France, consistently one of the most positive members of the conference, explored three different routes to the goal.

1. The original plan was that each nation should submit its major offensive weapons, planes, capital ships and heavy artillery to the control of the League of Nations, in order to provide a force to oppose aggression. It was, in short, a revival of the 1919 idea of a 'League with Teeth', and fell foul of the same objections about the infringement of national sovereignty. In the face of division among the wartime allies, Germany played its 'trump' card, demanded equal treatment with the allies on the question of armaments, and withdrew from the conference.

2. An agreement without Germany was so pointless that France effectively conceded the radical idea of German equality in its new 'Constructive Plan' (November 1932). This combined the idea of a League of Nations force with the maintenance of national defensive militias, and Germany's would be as large as that of any other state. The principle of German equality was also acknowledged within 'a system which would comprise security for all nations'. Germany returned to the conference but, with Italy, showed little interest in the 'Constructive Plan'.

3. After the failure of a British plan to establish a common limit of 200,000 men on the forces of France, Germany, Italy and Poland, the third French plan came close to success (June 1933). It proposed an eight-year period, during the latter half of which the continental armies would conform to the figures suggested by the British. With Britain, France, Italy and the USA in agreement, and Germany in danger of becoming trapped, Adolf Hitler withdrew finally from the conference (October 1933). Within five days he turned his back on international co-operation completely by quitting the League of Nations.

> 1. In what ways did the Wall Street Crash cause European states to change their political and economic policies?
>
> 2. Why was it so difficult after 1930 for states to agree (a) on the regulation of reparations and war debts (b) on disarmament?

11.6 Why was it not possible to form a European alliance against Hitler between 1933 and 1935?

The role of Mussolini

Collective security: A form of international security based upon the collective undertakings and co-operation of a large number of states, rather than reliance upon one's own military and economic resources, or upon those of the world's greatest powers.

The collapse of two essential parts of the **collective security** envisaged at Versailles caused the major powers of Western Europe to turn to the alternative form of security already explored with some success at Locarno. This form of security was provided by traditional pacts and alliances. The initiative this time came primarily from Mussolini who, in separate conversations with British and French ministers (March 1933), proposed the idea of a joint undertaking by Italy, France, Germany and Britain to take no unilateral action that might disturb the peace of Europe.

The motives of the four powers in following up the suggestion were various. Britain, in the words of the then Foreign Secretary, Sir John Simon, saw Italy as 'the key to European peace', and was willing to work with it to maintain a traditional balance of power. France shared these motives to an extent, although opinion there was by no means united as to the value of such a pact. Hitler, so soon after coming to power, was happy to take any step that reassured European opinion while he tackled domestic problems. Only in the case of Italy has there been real disagreement among historians. Those who have regarded Mussolini as cynical have seen his proposals as a means of separating France from its allies in eastern Europe, where Italy of course had ambitions, and perhaps from Britain. Others have regarded Mussolini as genuinely perturbed by the resurgence of Germany. They saw his proposals in 1933 as a genuine attempt to appease Hitler, by recognising Germany's great power status, while restricting its freedom of action by international guarantees.

The Four Power Pact between Britain, France, Italy and Germany

This pact, concluded in July 1933, committed the contracting states to co-operation for a period of ten years to preserve the peace of Europe. On the other hand, as a further step away from the Versailles settlement, it acknowledged the principle of 'reasonable revision' of the peace treaties. In fact, the pact was a 'dead letter' almost as soon as it was agreed. In October Hitler felt confident enough to leave the Disarmament Conference and the League of Nations. Within 18 months (March 1935) he had reintroduced conscription in Germany, which said little for his desire to co-operate with his neighbours. In the light of these events, the Four Power Pact was never ratified by the other powers. Its effects were wholly negative, providing a nasty shock for the eastern European states, who now found themselves excluded from the 'great power club'. The Soviet Union's reaction was to enter negotiations with France for a mutual assistance pact, possibly with a view to splitting this new capitalist bloc. Poland, apparently let down by France, reacted differently and concluded a non-aggression pact with Germany in January 1934.

The Stresa Front, 1935

Italy, France and Britain did not yet despair of combined action to preserve their security. Contacts between Mussolini and France's pro-Italian Foreign Minister, Pierre Laval, were fuelled by an attempted Nazi 'coup' in Austria (July 1934). This resulted in a set of Rome Agreements (January 1935) in which the parties seemed to have reached an understanding on European security and Italian colonial ambitions. With Britain drawn in once more, the Stresa Conference (April 1935) produced a three-sided agreement to oppose 'by all practical means, any unilateral repudiation of treaties, which may endanger the peace of Europe'. In theory, this 'Stresa Front', formed by the leaders of the three powers, was an imposing structure. In reality, it had a number of weaknesses. Far from preparing to fight Hitler, all the members hoped that the very existence of the 'Stresa Front' might discourage the German dictator from risking dangerous adventures. Mussolini, although his concern at Germany's rise was genuine, specifically desired this agreement to gain such European security as would enable him to pursue Italy's 'imperial destiny'. The reaction of his Stresa partners to his colonial policy was shortly to put this final attempt at great power equilibrium to the test.

Italy's invasion and conquest of Abyssinia

In October 1935 Italian forces began the pursuit of Mussolini's colonial plans by an open assault upon the East African state of Abyssinia (modern-day Ethiopia). The long-term motives for this attack reached back to the 19th century when Italy had marked out this region as its sphere of influence in the general 'scramble for Africa', and had suffered the humiliation of defeat at the hands of Abyssinian tribesmen at Adowa (1896). Not only did national pride demand some compensation for Adowa, but the aggressive nature of Italian Fascism demanded, in Mussolini's words, 'war for war's sake, since Fascism needs the glory of victory'. Besides, since Britain and France showed no signs of reducing their empires, was not Italy entitled to equal colonial status? Evidence suggests that Mussolini had determined his course by 1932. The precise timing of his attack, however, was dictated by various factors: by the rate of military preparation, and especially by Mussolini's conviction that his agreement with France and Britain at Stresa had ensured that Hitler would take no revisionist initiatives while his back was turned.

The new phase of Italian policy opened with a border incident at Wal-Wal (November 1934) and proceeded with a steady and obvious build-up of arms in Italian Somalia and Eritrea. On 2 October 1935, Italian troops invaded Abyssinia on the pretext that they were 'restoring order in a vast country left in the most atrocious slavery and the most primitive conditions of existence'. When local geography and the courage of the local tribesmen caused temporary embarrassment, Mussolini poured in huge resources: 400,000 men and the full weight of modern weaponry, aerial bombardment and the use of poison gas. The flight of the Abyssinian Emperor, Haile Selassie, and the capture of his capital, Addis Ababa, confirmed Italy's victory in May 1936.

What were the diplomatic implications of the Italian invasion?
The implications of the conquest of Abyssinia were not confined to East Africa. Abyssinia, despite its vague boundaries and semi-feudal government,

---

Haile Selassie (1892–1975)
Designated heir to the Empress of Abyssinia (1917). Abolished slavery in Abyssinia (1924). Emperor of Abyssinia (1930). Deposed by an army coup in 1974.

Italian invasion of Abyssinia, 1935–36

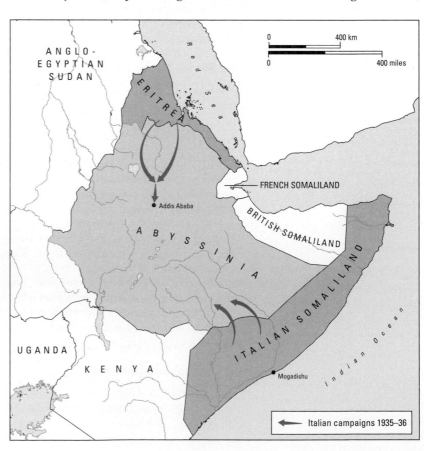

had been admitted to the League of Nations in 1923. It now demanded that the League apply the prescribed economic sanctions against the aggressor. Britain and France thus found themselves committed, with differing degrees of enthusiasm, to a boycott of all Italian goods and to a ban on exports of arms, rubber, and metal ore to Italy. The attempts of their foreign ministers, Samuel Hoare and Pierre Laval, to buy off either Mussolini or Haile Selassie ended in embarrassing failure. Worse still, their apparent 'double game' of applying sanctions and negotiating at the same time behind the back of the League of Nations effectively discredited both the League and the Stresa Front.

Furthermore, the sanctions were largely ineffective. The vital commodity of oil was not among the prohibited items and, in any case, non-members such as Germany, Japan and the USA were not committed to sanctions. Although Mussolini's whole policy over Stresa and Abyssinia was one of calculated deception, it seems likely that he was genuinely shocked by the imposition of economic sanctions. His assumption that Laval had granted him a 'free hand' by the Rome Agreements seemed confirmed by British and French silence at Stresa on the Abyssinian question, despite the contemporary build-up of Italian forces in Africa. Surely this had indicated their consent. To Mussolini, a League of Nations that allowed the Japanese to escape unpunished for their aggression in China, and then turned on Italy, was a 'front of conservation, of selfishness, and of hypocrisy'. Whatever their limitations, the 1935 agreements between France, Italy and Britain perished not necessarily because of Mussolini's deviousness, but because of the extraordinary confusion of British and French foreign policy.

Mussolini and Italian isolation

The key feature of European diplomatic relationships, and a major factor in the collapse of the balance of power in Europe after 1935, was the movement of Italy out of the orbit of London and Paris and into that of Berlin. Superficially appealing as the attraction of one Fascist dictatorship for another may have been, the coming together of Italy and Germany had little to do with ideology. According to the French commentator Maurice Baumont, Mussolini 'wanted to be on the side of power, the only decisive attraction for him'. In this context of power politics, he had drawn four lessons from the events of 1935–37.

1. It had become clear that the statesmen of Britain and France, and even less those of the League of Nations from which Italy withdrew in November 1937, had neither the will nor the means to check the resurgence of Germany.

2. It was evident that Italy could not pursue its interests in Abyssinia and in Spain and, at the same time, guard its security in central Europe.

3. Involvement in Spain had badly weakened Italy's international position. It had shown up weaknesses in its army, absorbed half of its foreign currency reserves, and established a gulf between Mussolini and the democracies without guaranteeing any gain or support from General Franco.

4. Perhaps most important of all, just as he became disgusted at the weakness of the western powers, so Mussolini was at once seduced and horrified by the power of Germany. After a relatively unsuccessful visit to Rome in 1934, Hitler had spared no effort to demonstrate German military strength when Mussolini came to Berlin (September 1937).

A Soviet view of western politics in 1936. The infant Hitler is protected by France, Britain, 'Wall Street' and the 'Ruhr magnates'.

How justified was this interpretation?

The Spanish Civil War

Civil War broke out in Spain in July 1936, when 'Nationalist' forces under General Franco attempted to launch a coup to overthrow the existing Republican government. This was the culmination of several years of tension, arising from the fall of the Spanish monarchy (1931) and the implementation of socialist and anti-Catholic reforms by the Republic that replaced it. Franco and the Nationalists enjoyed a distinct military superiority, but the conflict was complicated and prolonged by the fact that many foreign observers saw the war as part of a wider struggle between socialism and fascism. On the one hand, this led to the intervention of the 'international brigades', bodies of left-wing volunteers who travelled to Spain to fight for the Republic. On the other hand, both Hitler and Mussolini saw advantages in supporting Franco. Hitler limited himself to undercover intervention, sending 'volunteer' forces, such as the famous 'Condor Legion' to Spain to try out the new weapons with which German forces were being re-armed. Mussolini, however, committed substantial forces from the Italian regular army to the struggle, as part of his stance as the driving force behind right-wing politics in Europe. Britain and France remained strictly neutral in the conflict, while the Soviet Union only sent material aid to the Republicans under the strictest secrecy. This combination of factors confirmed the superiority of the Nationalists, and their victory was sealed by the fall of Madrid in March 1939.

The development of the German–Italian alliance

This alliance had its origins in the 'October Protocols' signed by Count Ciano in Berlin in 1936. They contained little more than vague

1. What were the main aims of Italian foreign policy between 1933 and 1936?

2. Why did Italy, France and Britain form pacts with each other in 1933–34 and why had these agreements fallen apart by 1936?

3. In what respects might the Italian invasion of Abyssinia be seen as a turning point in European international relations in the 1930s?

anti-Bolshevik phrases, but gave the relationship the name by which it is known to history, by declaring that the Berlin–Rome line was now 'an axis around which can revolve all those European states with a will to collaboration and peace'. In November 1937, shortly after Mussolini's fateful visit to Germany, this 'Axis' took on wider implications when Italy subscribed to the Anti-Comintern Pact, originally concluded between Germany and Japan (November 1936) to present a united front against Bolshevism.

The *Anschluss* of March 1938, and Italy's meek acceptance of it, indicated the extent to which Italian policy was already subject to that of Germany. Within two months, Hitler began to pressurise the Italian government to accept a full military alliance. Mussolini's initial reluctance to commit himself was worn down by May 1939, when he allowed Ciano to conclude the alliance known as the 'Pact of Steel'. This committed both sides to help each other in the event of one of them becoming 'involved in warlike complications'. The terms made no pretence to be merely defensive. The Pact of Steel constituted a triumph for Hitler in his re-orientation of European diplomacy, and completed Mussolini's loss of control over his own policy. 'In point of fact,' as Elizabeth Wiskemann has written, by underwriting all future German schemes, 'Mussolini gave Hitler *carte blanche* [complete freedom of action] to attack Poland and to plunge into the Second World War.'

11.7 In what respects had Hitler changed the Versailles settlement by 1938?

The remilitarisation of the Rhineland, 1936

The Abyssinian crisis preoccupied European statesmen for eight months (October 1935–May 1936), during which time Hitler struck his first blow at the territorial clauses of the Treaty of Versailles. On 7 March 1936, he ordered a force of 22,000 men into the Rhineland in direct defiance of those treaty terms that declared it a demilitarised zone. As pretext, he claimed that the French pact with the Soviet Union had breached the Locarno understanding. A more realistic explanation of his timing would, of course, take into account Italy's involvement in Abyssinia and the resultant weakening of the Stresa Front. Europe was taken by surprise, not by the fact of remilitarisation, but by the method. Diplomats had expected Hitler to negotiate; instead he took swift, decisive action, and offered negotiations afterwards – a method soon to become familiar. The operation succeeded through a combination of Hitler's boldness and French miscalculation. France's military leaders estimated that up to 295,000 German troops were available to Hitler and that their intervention would lead to a major conflict. Its political leaders thus concluded that they could intervene only with British aid, which was not forthcoming. It is now known that the German forces were under direct orders to withdraw if they met resistance. In Britain and France alike much public opinion felt that confrontation with Germany and Italy at the same time was folly, and that French friendship with the Soviet Union was unwise. In short, Hitler's move did not cause widespread popular outrage because, in the words of the French historian Maurice Baumont, 'a blow had been aimed, not at French territory, but only at the Treaty of Versailles, in which no one believed any longer'.

The results of the remilitarisation

The implications of the remilitarisation were substantial and complex. In combination with the Abyssinian affair, it seemed to show that the western powers were as unwilling as the League of Nations was unable to act against unilateral revision of the treaties. The effect on France's strategic position was disastrous. Hitler's action provided further disillusionment for nations such as Poland and Czechoslovakia, and the rapid fortification of Germany's frontiers now made it extremely difficult for France to fulfil its eastern pacts by attacks against Germany in the west. French reluctance to act alone also provided proof that it had become the junior partner in its relationship with Britain. Lastly, Hitler's bold gamble, like that of Mussolini in Abyssinia, was invaluable in strengthening his prestige and authority at home, especially in military circles. If Abyssinia destroyed the League of Nations, the remilitarisation of the Rhineland destroyed Locarno, and the way was thus open to the disaster of 1939.

Why did Anschluss *not take place before 1938?*

The question of union (*Anschluss*) between Austria and the German Reich was nearly a century old when Hitler came to power. It had its roots in the 19th-century contest for German leadership, seemingly settled by the triumph of Bismarck's Prussia and his careful exclusion of Austria from the German state. The loss of Austria's non-German territories in 1919, and the rise of Hitler, raised the question anew. At the beginning of the 1930s the long-established factors of language, and the memory of centuries during which Vienna had been the chief of the German cities, combined with the more modern consideration that many Austrians would undoubtedly be economically better off as part of a greater state. All were factors in favour of *Anschluss*.

The main factors against *Anschluss* were the desire of many Austrians to remain independent, still resenting the ascendancy of Berlin over Vienna, and the implacable hostility of the Versailles allies, especially of France and Italy. The project for a customs union between Germany and Austria (March 1931) had been undermined by French suspicion. 'They must take us for asses,' wrote the French politician, Édouard Herriot, 'if they think that we are able to forget that the political union of Germany was reached by way of a customs union.' The mismanaged coup by Austrian Nazis, with the knowledge of Hitler (July 1934), which ended in the murder of the Austrian Chancellor, Engelbert Dollfuss, foundered upon the prompt action of Mussolini who mobilised the Italian army on the Austrian frontier.

Why was Anschluss *possible in 1938?*

By the end of 1937 the situation had changed. French inactivity over the advance of German troops to its frontiers did not suggest that it would act energetically over Austria. Indeed, British and French diplomats, beset with domestic problems, had even indicated to their German counterparts that they had 'no objection to a marked extension of German influence in Austria obtained through evolutionary means'. Most significant was the changed attitude of Italy. Deeply committed to intervention in the Spanish Civil War, Mussolini was impressed by the shows of military power staged for him in Germany and had already begun his drift into Hitler's wake. Count Ciano, his son-in-law and Foreign Minister, expressed the hopelessness of Italy's position over Austrian independence: 'What in fact could we do? Start a war with Germany? At the first shot we fired every Austrian, without exception, would fall in behind the Germans against us.'

These developments might suggest that Hitler deliberately set out to absorb Austria in 1938. Indeed, the very first page of *Mein Kampf* made clear his attachment to the principle of German–Austrian unity. In *The Origins of the Second World War* (1961), however, A.J.P. Taylor set out a convincing argument to suggest that this was not the case. Although Hitler had hoped to be able to deal first with the question of the Sudetenland (see below), the argument runs, his hand was forced by two factors. The first of these was the continuing agitation by Austrian Nazis led by Arthur Seyss-Inquart, and the second was the rash decision of the new Austrian Chancellor, Kurt von Schuschnigg, to confront Hitler and force him to disown the agitators.

If Schuschnigg and Seyss-Inquart caused the crisis, Hitler nevertheless acted to exploit it, partly in the interests of *Anschluss,* but partly to distract attention from contemporary domestic disagreements. In a violent interview at Berchtesgaten (12 February 1938), Hitler accused Schuschnigg of racial treason, and demanded that Seyss-Inquart be admitted to the Austrian government. Although Schuschnigg accepted this demand, he attempted to defend his position by holding a referendum on the question of union with Germany. Unable to risk an anti-German vote, Hitler's hand was now forced. Successively, the German government demanded the postponement of the referendum, the replacement of Schuschnigg by Seyss-Inquart, and finally threatened military intervention. On 11 March, the Austrian Nazi leader, having formed a 'provisional government' of doubtful legality, requested the dispatch of German troops 'to restore order and save Austria from chaos'. Even so, it is doubtful whether Hitler envisaged more than a 'puppet' government under Seyss-Inquart. On 13 March, encouraged by the enthusiastic reception from Austrian crowds at Linz, and by Mussolini's meek acceptance of the principle of *Anschluss,* Hitler proclaimed the formal union of his native Austria with the German Reich.

What was the impact of Anschluss?

The *Anschluss* marked a clear escalation in Nazi policy as it involved the actual obliteration of an independent state set up by the peace treaties. Still, Hitler's action did not excite united European condemnation. The approval registered in the referendums Hitler now held (99.08% in Germany and 99.75% in Austria) was obviously in part the result of pressure and fear, but it probably also had a sound basis in pan-German feeling. 'In Austria,' claimed Hermann Goering at Nuremberg in 1945, 'we were not met with rifle shots and bombs; only one thing was thrown at us, flowers.' The British government merely made a formal protest. There was no French government. Camille Chautemps had resigned four days earlier and Leon Blum had yet to take office. Once again, rapid and risky action had reaped a rich reward. Hitler's confidence in such action was now to put the peace of Europe in increasing danger.

Czechoslovakia and the Sudetenland

If Hitler was serious in his desires either to unite all Germans in a single Reich, or to expand the territories of that Reich eastwards, the state of Czechoslovakia constituted a substantial obstacle in his path. It possessed a mountainous and easily defensible frontier with Germany, an army of 34 divisions well supplied by the Skoda arms factories at Pilsen, and enjoyed membership of a diplomatic system comprising France, Britain, Poland and the Soviet Union.

It also had its weaknesses. Czechoslovakia was, for instance, a state of minority groups. Apart from the uneasy union of Czechs and Slovaks at the heart of the state, Hungarians, Poles and Ukrainians had been placed under the authority of Prague to give the new creation territorial and

Sudetenland: An irregular ribbon of territory around the northern, western and southern periphery of Bohemia and Moravia.

Konrad Henlein (1898–1945)
Founder of the Sudeten German Party (1933). After the Nazi seizure of the Sudetenland, Henlein served as the senior Nazi official there until 1945.

1. By what stages did Hitler destroy the Versailles settlement between 1936 and 1938?

2. Why did Britain and France do so little between 1936 and 1938 to prevent Germany undermining the Versailles settlement?

economic viability. In fact, 35% of the population was neither Czech nor Slovak. The greatest of these minorities were the Germans of the **Sudetenland**. Spread through these regions were 3.25 million Germans, resentful that they no longer enjoyed the privileges that had been theirs under Habsburg rule. They were regarded with suspicion by the Czech government. Furthermore, the events of the mid-1930s isolated Czechoslovakia and increased its vulnerability. It had no border with friendly states such as France and the Soviet Union, could expect no help from Italy, as Austria had received none and, after the *Anschluss*, had a southern border with the enlarged Reich devoid of any natural defences.

As with Austria, Hitler did not so much cause a crisis over Czechoslovakia, as exploit one that was already developing. A key factor was the Sudeten Party, formed in 1935 by Konrad Henlein. Its political demands had grown by the time of Henlein's 'Karlsbad Programme' (April 1938) from a claim for equal treatment with the Czechs to a demand for full independence from Czechoslovakia. Still confident of French and British backing, the Czech President, Edvard Beneš, was happy to confront the Sudeten Germans. Hitler, more confident than ever after his Austrian successes, had no objection to confrontation. He was aided by a new turn in British and French policy.

11.8 Why did war break out in 1939?

What was the significance of the Munich conference for the policy of appeasement?

Neville Chamberlain (1869–1940)
British Conservative politician. Chancellor of the Exchequer (1923–24, 1931–37) and Prime Minister (1937–40). Chamberlain is particularly associated with the re-establishment of economic stability after the 'Great Depression' and with the policy of appeasement.

Edouard Daladier (1884–1970)
French radical politician. Prime Minister of France (1933, 1934). Minister of Defence (1936–38). Held the two offices combined between 1938 and 1940.

For at least two years up to 1938, the governments of Britain and France had inclined increasingly towards a policy of appeasement. That is to say that they were increasingly willing to make concessions to Germany, in the hope that Hitler's ambitions would be satisfied without the disaster of a military confrontation. It was in this spirit that they approached the question of the Sudetenland. Britain and France were committed by the second half of 1938 to a policy of persuading Beneš to grant Sudeten German demands. They were convinced by the events in Austria and by rumours of German troop movements (May 1938) that, if Hitler was determined to support Henlein, the choice lay between Czech concessions and a general war. Henlein's policy, however, and that of Hitler, was to 'demand so much that we never can be satisfied'. Thus, when the Czech President conceded the principal demands of the Sudeten Germans, their leaders started unsuccessful risings in Karlsbad, Eger and other centres (13 September) to sustain the tension. The danger that Hitler would intervene as he had in Austria broke the British and French nerve. Their respective premiers, Neville Chamberlain and Edouard Daladier, plunged into direct negotiations with Hitler, and Hitler correspondingly raised the stakes. At Berchtesgaten (15 September) and at Bad Godesberg (22 September), Chamberlain heard Hitler's demands escalate through direct German annexation of the Sudetenland, to immediate military occupation.

The meeting in Munich, September 1938. In the front, from the left, Neville Chamberlain, Edouard Daladier, Adolf Hitler and Benito Mussolini.

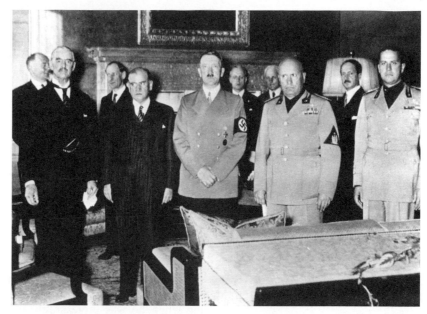

Six days later, Hitler agreed to a conference between himself, Chamberlain and Daladier, to be held in Munich with Mussolini as mediator. It has been suggested either that Hitler had become aware of the lack of enthusiasm in Germany for a military solution, or that he was disturbed by Mussolini's reluctance to give military support, or simply that he knew that his shaken opponents were willing now to allow him the bulk of his demands. Certainly the Munich Conference (29–30 September 1938) granted Hitler far more than he had been demanding a few weeks earlier. It was agreed between the powers that, although Germany would receive all Czech territory where Germans were in a majority, the transfer would be by stages, and under international supervision. In none of these negotiations was the Czech government consulted or allowed to participate. It was simply presented with the alternatives of acceptance or single combat with Germany.

Both morally and practically, the implications of the Munich agreement were enormous. The allies, especially the French with their direct treaty obligations, had betrayed Czechoslovakia. Although Britain, France, Italy and Germany all formally guaranteed its remaining territory, the state was in fact doomed by its losses. It no longer had a defensible frontier, it had lost 70% of its iron and steel resources, and the Skoda works. In addition, the Sudeten success provided great encouragement to other separatists. Hungary and Poland both revived claims to Czech territory, and the cause of Slovak separatism took on a new lease of life. In March 1939, having failed to cause the collapse of Czechoslovakia by the Sudeten crisis, Hitler was to cause a new crisis over the Slovak demands, and to force the Czechs to accept a German 'protectorate' over Bohemia and Moravia, while Hungary, Poland and the Slovaks achieved their desires. Czechoslovakia, therefore, like Poland in the past, died of partition. The tremendous popular relief at the avoidance of war was short-lived, and certainly did not survive Hitler's seizure of Prague in March. Despite the weakness displayed at Munich, and the loss of Czechoslovakia's 34 divisions to their cause, the subsequent military co-ordination between Britain and France, and their renewal of guarantees to Poland, Greece and Romania (March–April 1939) strongly suggested that the next crisis would be confronted with greater resolution.

The Soviet Union and the western allies

An undoubted casualty of the Munich surrender was the relationship between the western democracies and the Soviet Union. The relationship had suffered from mutual suspicion for a decade; suspicion on the Soviet side that the British and French secretly preferred German resurgence to the existence of a stable Soviet regime; suspicion in London and Paris either that Stalin still favoured the international spread of communism, or that his vicious domestic purges (see Chapter 8) had destroyed the USSR's viability as an ally. The Munich agreement, made without any reference to the Soviet Union, showed at best that the diplomacy of the western powers was incapable of checking German ambitions, and at worst represented a tacit agreement to Germany's quest for 'living space' in eastern Europe. Either way, the Soviet Union could no longer trust its security to Paris and London.

The German–Soviet pact (August 1939)

The first Soviet overtures for a more positive relationship with Nazi Germany came in May 1938, when the new ambassador to Berlin, A. Meretalov, received instructions to press for better commercial relations. At a time when he was increasingly preoccupied with the problem of Czechoslovakia, Hitler reacted favourably to anything that might separate the Soviet Union from his immediate enemies. In July, the governments reached an oral agreement on the ending of their hostile press campaigns. With the allied abandonment of Czechoslovakia, the Soviet government began to knock harder on Germany's door. The replacement of Maxim Litvinov as Commissar for Foreign Affairs by Vyacheslav Molotov (May 1939) was invested with great significance by foreign observers. Molotov, as a member of the Politburo, had the necessary power to engineer major policy changes, whereas Litvinov had been an advocate of collective security, and was furthermore a Jew. Nevertheless, it was widely agreed that Stalin at this stage was merely keeping open his option of choosing between Germany and the western democracies. In mid-August, when British–French–Soviet military negotiations in Moscow collapsed over the reluctance of Poland to allow Soviet troops to cross its territory in the event of an attack on Germany, Stalin and his advisors drew the conclusion that they had one remaining option for their national security.

Hitler responded far more rapidly and favourably than the allies had, for his short-term purposes were also served by a change of policy. With his sights now set on Poland, and with Britain and France renewing their pledges to the Poles, it was an urgent priority to ensure that his ambitions would not encounter Soviet opposition. This, and Stalin's desire for greater security for the Soviet frontiers, resulted in the startling agreement reached after only one day's negotiation in Moscow between Molotov and the German Foreign Minister, Joachim von Ribbentrop (23 August 1939).

The terms of the German–Soviet pact

To the outside world, the Ribbentrop–Molotov Pact took the form of a non-aggression treaty lasting ten years. Secretly, however, it divided the territories between the German and Soviet borders into 'spheres of influence'. Germany's comprised Poland, west of the rivers Narew, Vistula and San, and part of Lithuania. The Soviet zone comprised the rest of Poland and Lithuania, and the states of Estonia, Latvia and Finland. Germany expressed its disinterest in the Balkans and recognised Russia's interest in the Romanian territory of Bessarabia. Hitler, in short, received tacit Soviet approval to fulfil his designs on Danzig and the Polish 'corridor'. In return, Stalin not only triumphantly reversed the losses suffered by Russia during the Revolution and Civil War 20 years earlier, but seemed to have won a breathing space in terms both of time and of territory. With the Soviet occupation of their sphere of influence between June and August 1940, the amount of territory between a future invader and the vital centres of Leningrad and Moscow was increased by 300 kilometres.

To western commentators, this was seen as one of the most cynical treaties in world history, a complete reversal of the ideologies of both states. As the historian A.J.P. Taylor commented, however, 'it is difficult to see what other course Soviet Russia could have followed' in the light of western indifference. It was difficult, too, to see why their part in the destruction of Poland was worse than that of the allies in the destruction of Czechoslovakia. Doubtless both Hitler and Stalin believed that the pact ensured that the Polish question could now be solved without general war. In the event, by giving Hitler the confidence to attack Poland, without diverting Britain and France from their renewed guarantees, Stalin's signature made war in Europe inevitable.

The issue of Danzig

In the German view, the collapse of Czechoslovakia left one major element of the Versailles Treaty standing in eastern Europe. Hostility between Germans and Poles had a far longer history than the life of the post-war Polish state, but the treaty had created a new focus of hostility in the form of the 'free city' of Danzig. Even more resentment, perhaps, was caused by the 'corridor' of territory transferred in 1919 from Germany to Poland to connect Danzig with the Polish heartland. Although the treaty gave the Poles complete control of Danzig's docks, its customs duties, its railway system and foreign relations, Danzig was undeniably a German city. It was inhabited by 400,000 Germans and without a name in Polish until 'Gdansk' was invented in 1919. Similarly, the 'corridor' contained the homes of one million Germans. It was not a settlement that the majority of Germans were willing to tolerate freely.

The dual threat to Poland

Despite gaining its independence in the aftermath of the Russian Revolution, Poland was trapped between an unforgiving Germany to the west and a resentful Russia to the east. Polish apprehension was heightened in the 1920s by the Russo–German agreement at Rapallo and by the failure of the Locarno Pact to guarantee Germany's eastern borders. Thus Poland sought security through its own armed forces and through treaties with France.

By the mid-1930s, however, Poland's international position had been greatly complicated by the rise of Hitler, the bankruptcy of French policy towards eastern Europe, and the entry of the Soviet Union into the diplomatic arena. In general, under the direction of General Beck between 1932 and 1939, the Polish foreign ministry proceeded upon the assumption that the Soviet Union posed the greater threat to Poland. 'With the Germans,' he reputedly declared, 'we risk losing our liberty. With the Russians we lose our souls.' From this line of thought sprang the Polish–German non-aggression pact of 1934 and the persistent refusal to allow passage to Soviet troops across Polish territory in the event of war. Furthermore, overestimation of his nation's strength led Beck into the cynical policy whereby Poland participated in the partition of Czechoslovakia, gaining the region of Teschen (March 1939) and staking an unsuccessful claim to Slovakia.

Throughout this period Danzig, its local government in the hands of the local Nazi party since May 1933, remained a thorn in Polish–German relations. After the completion of his destruction of Czechoslovakia, the signs accumulated that Hitler intended next to turn his attentions towards Poland. As with Austria and Czechoslovakia, his initial policy was that of a war of nerves. In April 1939, Hitler not only renounced Germany's non-aggression pact with Poland, but renewed German claims to Danzig. In May, the 'Pact of Steel' agreement committed Italy to follow Hitler's path, and by August he was assured that the Soviet Union would not stand in his way. Meanwhile, the German press conducted a campaign of accusations concerning alleged persecution of Poland's German minority. Surely, under these circumstances, Britain and France would not risk themselves on Poland's behalf?

The crisis of August–September 1939

1. What did Hitler wish to gain in 1938–39 (a) from Czechoslovakia and (b) from Poland?

2. Why did Britain and France abandon their policy of appeasement after the Munich Conference?

3. What grounds are there for claiming that 'the Nazi–Soviet Pact of 1939 made European war inevitable'?

The last week of August 1939 was occupied by Anglo–French efforts to persuade Poland to sacrifice Danzig. This time, however, the situation differed in important respects from that at Munich the previous year. Poland, aware that surrender had not saved Czechoslovakia, refused now to compromise its national sovereignty. The two democratic governments, although eager to avoid war, refused to repeat their Munich performances. Perhaps they were encouraged by increasing evidence of Mussolini's reluctance to commit himself to war. Perhaps, as A.J.P. Taylor stressed, the political conservatives of Britain and France, rather than being terrified by the Russo–German agreement, became more hostile to Hitler now that he no longer posed as a defence against Communism. Maybe Chamberlain and Daladier recognised the futility of their Munich policy. General war, in the event, resulted from the conviction of both sides that the other was bluffing. 'The men I met at Munich,' Hitler declared to his generals, 'are not the kind to start another world war.'

So, on 1 September, German troops invaded Poland on the false pretext of Polish border violations. Only two days later did Britain and France issue separate ultimatums for German withdrawal, perhaps encouraging Hitler by their delay. Nevertheless, upon the expiry of the ultimatums, both powers declared war on Germany, ending the 'Twenty Years' Truce'.

11.9 Did Hitler plan the outbreak of war in 1939?
A CASE STUDY IN HISTORICAL INTERPRETATION

For some years after the conclusion of the Second World War this would not have appeared to be a controversial issue. Although a great deal was written about the war's origins, there was little historical objectivity in these accounts. Such documents as those edited by E.L. Woodward and Rohan Butler (*Documents on British Foreign Policy*, 1946 onwards) tended to present a favourable view of allied policy, and to confirm the validity of the charges made against German leaders at the Nuremberg war crimes trials. E.M. Robertson, in *The Origins of the Second World War* (1971), characterised this lack of objectivity when he described such historians as 'intelligence NCOs [non-commissioned officers] in plain clothes'. The conclusions reached during these decades were consistent and predictable. While the majority of states worked for peace, war had been started by a German government dedicated to the principle of overturning the Versailles settlement and fulfilling the racial claims of its leader. The historian T.D. Williams, commenting in 1958 on the work of Sir Lewis Namier (*In the Nazi Era*, 1952) stated that 'he has proved that Hitler wanted war. Nobody would, on the whole, now contest this fact.'

Hossbach Memorandum: A memo written by Colonel Hossbach in November 1937 to summarise the content of a meeting between Hitler and leading military commanders. Its content suggests that at this stage Hitler was making long-term preparations for war.

Demiurge: An independent creative force, or decisive power.

In 1961, however, in *The Origins of the Second World War*, A.J.P. Taylor did contest the fact. Refusing to see in *Mein Kampf* anything more than the daydreaming of a frustrated revolutionary, Taylor stressed the continuity between Hitler's foreign policy aims and those of earlier German politicians. He also dismissed the notion of a German master plan for conquest and viewed Hitler's policy in 1938–39 primarily as a skilful exploitation of openings offered to him by the errors and hesitations of British, French and Italian leaders. Although Hitler undoubtedly wanted to change the map of Europe, Taylor concluded, he did not necessarily seek war. War in 1939 did not result from Hitler's long-term determination to begin one, but from his short-term miscalculation of allied reaction to the Polish crisis.

Many writers accepted that Taylor had shed important light on some of the individual crises that preceded the Second World War, but his overall thesis provoked widespread controversy. Many prominent historians refused to accept that major pieces of evidence, such as Hitler's statements in *Mein Kampf* and in the **Hossbach Memorandum**, could simply be set aside. Hugh Trevor-Roper argued strongly that Hitler considered himself not merely a practical politician, but 'a thinker, a practical philosopher, the **demiurge** of a new age of history'. Some leading German historians, such as Andreas Hillgruber and Klaus Hildebrand, in *The Foreign Policy of the Third Reich* (1973), put forward the view that Hitler's long-term plans stretched beyond domination of eastern Europe, and aimed ultimately at world domination. They envisage Hitler pursuing these massive goals by a series of distinct stages, the first of which certainly involved aggression in eastern Europe in the early 1940s at the latest. Other authorities, such as Alan Milward in *The German War Economy* (1965), stressed that Taylor's preoccupation with diplomacy blinded him to the steady economic and social progress towards a war footing made since 1933.

The most important outcome of the Taylor controversy was that historians were now forced to consider other factors that contributed to the outbreak of war in 1939. Above all, he had drawn attention to the encouragement that Hitler derived from the hesitant and timid policies of other European states, such as Britain and France. Is it possible to claim that the policy of appeasement made a serious contribution to the collapse of the peace? The policy has, indeed, been widely criticised since the war, especially for such immoral aspects as the abandonment of Czechoslovakia in 1938.

Recent writers have argued, however, that it is unsatisfactory to view the policy of appeasement merely as a show of weakness and indecision, and that to see it in this way is to be wise after the event. In particular, Richard Overy in *The Origins of the Second World War* (1987) and *The Inter-War Crisis, 1919–1939* (1994) has insisted that the policy was formulated in just the same way as any other foreign policy, in order to defend the particular vested interests of the states concerned. 'British diplomacy', he wrote, 'was based on a global strategy of which the German question formed a part, and until 1935 a subordinate part.' With extensive imperial interests in Asia, which needed to be defended against the threat of Japanese expansion and aggression, it is unsurprising that the government showed reluctance to confront Hitler over his attitude to eastern Europe. While France was more directly threatened by German resurgence, it too had imperial interests to defend. It had also suffered so grievously in the First World War that its politicians could scarcely be blamed for wishing to avert a second conflict. Instead of dismissing appeasement as a bankrupt and cowardly policy, it might be more useful to conclude that it was part of an unfortunate but unavoidable conjunction of events. The 1930s found the leading powers of western Europe preoccupied with economic recovery and with the defence of imperial interests at the very moment when Hitler began to threaten the peace of Europe.

Important as the controversy over the Taylor thesis is in terms of detail, it is still possible to find agreement on the broad causes of the outbreak of war in 1939. The responsibility of expansionist elements in German policy has not seriously been questioned, and the less the outbreak is attributed directly to the 'evil genius' of Hitler himself, the more the historian is bound to concentrate on the continuous theme of expansion in recent German history and thought. This theme occupies the attention of the American journalist William Shirer in *Rise and Fall of the Third Reich* (1962). Returning to Hitler's aims and motives in the late 1930s, a sound compromise has been established by Alan Bullock (*Hitler: A Study in Tyranny*, 1962 and *Hitler and Stalin: Parallel Lives*, 1991) and by Donald Watt (*How War Came*, 1989). On the question of a Nazi master plan for aggression and aggrandisement, Alan Bullock concludes that 'Hitler's foreign policy combined consistency of aim with complete opportunism in methods and tactics'. The weakness of his opponents dictated the timing, but not the initial conception of Hitler's policy. On the specific problem of the outbreak of hostilities in 1939, Donald Watt resolves the question 'Did Hitler want war?' with the plausible conclusion that he did indeed desire an armed clash with Poland, and certainly envisaged a subsequent war of conquest against the USSR. Where the element of miscalculation and accident occurred was that he had not expected the violent destruction of Poland to involve him in a general European war with Britain and France, and did not foresee the eventual involvement of the USA in a global conflict.

1. What different interpretations have historians made of Hitler's conduct of German foreign policy in the late 1930s?

2. In what different ways have historians viewed the policy of appeasement since the publication of A.J.P. Taylor's controversial work in 1961?

Source-based questions: The policy of appeasement

Study the following FOUR passages – A, B, C and D – and answer both of the sub-questions which follow.

SOURCE A

From a memorandum written by Neville Chamberlain in November 1937. Chamberlain accepts the need to make concessions to Germany in order to preserve the peace of Europe.

The German visit was from my point of view a great success, because it achieved its object, that of creating an atmosphere in which it is possible to discuss with Germany the practical questions involved in a European settlement. Both Hitler and Goering said separately, and emphatically, that they had no desire or intention of making war, and I think that we may take this as correct, at least for the present. Of course, they want to dominate eastern Europe; they want as close a union with Austria as they can get without incorporating her in the Reich, and they want much the same things for the Sudeten Germans as

we did for the *Uitlanders* [the name given by the Boers to British settlers in South Africa] in the Transvaal.

SOURCE B

From R.J. Overy, The Origins of the Second World War, *published in 1987. This historian argues that the policy of appeasement made good sense in the context of previous British foreign policy.*

The word that British statesmen chose to describe their response was 'appeasement'. It was an unfortunate choice, for it came to imply a weak and fearful policy of concession to potential aggressors. In fact appeasement was far more than that. It was more or less consistent with the main lines of British foreign policy going back into the 19th century. By appeasement was meant a policy of adjustment and accommodation of conflicting interests broadly to conform with Britain's unique position in world affairs. It involved no preconceived plan of action, but rested upon a number of political and moral assumptions about the virtue of compromise and peaceableness. It involved using the instruments of British power – trading and financial strength, and a wealth of diplomatic experience – to their fullest advantage. But it also implied that there were limits to British policy beyond which other powers should not be permitted to go.

SOURCE C

From A.J.P. Taylor, The Origins of the Second World War, *published in 1961. Taylor argues that the policy of appeasement served positively to encourage Hitler in his expansionist plans.*

It did not occur to Chamberlain that Great Britain and France were unable to oppose German demands; rather he assumed that Germany, and Hitler in particular, would be grateful for concessions willingly made – concessions which, if Hitler failed to respond with equal good will, could also be withdrawn. On 19 November 1937 Halifax [the British Foreign Secretary] met Hitler at Berchtesgaden. Halifax said all that Hitler expected to hear. He praised Nazi Germany 'as the bulwark of Europe against Bolshevism'; he sympathised with past German grievances. England would not seek to maintain the existing settlement in central Europe. There was a condition attached: the changes must come without a general war. This was exactly what Hitler wanted himself. Halifax's remarks were an invitation to Hitler to promote German nationalist agitation in Danzig, Czechoslovakia and Austria; an assurance too that this agitation would not be opposed from without. All these remarks strengthened Hitler's conviction that he would meet little opposition from Great Britain and France.

SOURCE D

From Anthony Adamthwaite, France and the Coming of the Second World War, *published in 1977. This historian argues that French foreign policy in the 1930s was based essentially upon feelings of weakness.*

Timidity was the dominant characteristic of [French] political leadership. At the critical moments – in March 1936 and September 1938 – ministers shrank from any suggestion of constraining Germany by force. This timidity had three main causes. Firstly, there was the caution of the military chiefs. Early in 1936 before the Rhineland coup, Marshal Gamelin considered that France could not fight Germany with any certainty of victory. Secondly, French public opinion was deeply divided on social and economic issues and the lack of national unity prevented a forceful reposte to German initiatives. Thirdly, from September 1935 onwards, military and political leaders were convinced that France could not contemplate war with Germany unless assured of active British help. British assistance was judged essential for the protection of French shipping and supplies in the Mediterranean.

(a) **Compare Passages B and D on the motives that lay behind policies of appeasement in Britain and France.** [15 marks]

(b) **Using these four passages and your own knowledge, evaluate the claim that the policy of appeasement deserves a large proportion of the blame for the outbreak of the Second World War.** [30 marks]

Source-based questions: The end of the Twenty Years' Truce

Study the two sources and answer the questions which follow.

SOURCE 1

Hitler in conference with his military commanders, 23 May 1939

Living space proportionate to the greatness of the state is fundamental to every power. One can do without it for a time, but sooner or later the problem will have to be solved by hook or by crook. The alternatives are rise or decline. It is not Danzig that is at stake. For us it is a matter of expanding our living space in the east and making food supplies secure and also solving the problem of the Baltic States. No other opening can be seen in Europe. There is therefore no question of sparing Poland and we are left with the decision to attack Poland at the first suitable opportunity.

SOURCE 2

Minutes of a speech by Hitler to his military commanders, 27 August 1939

The following special reasons strengthen my resolve. There is no actual rearmament in England, just propaganda. The construction programme for the Navy for 1938 has not yet been fulfilled. Little has been done on land. England will only be able to send a maximum of three divisions to the continent. A little has been done for the Air Force, but it is only a beginning. France lacks men due to the decline in the birth rate. Little has been done for rearmament. The artillery is antiquated. France does not want to enter upon this adventure. The enemy had another hope, that Russia would become our enemy after the conquest of Poland. The enemy did not count upon my great power of resolution. Our enemies are little worms. I saw them at Munich.

(a) Study Sources 1 and 2.

What reasons does Hitler give for his decision to attack Poland? [5 marks]

(b) What steps had Hitler already taken before 1939 to revise the terms of the Versailles Treaty? [7 marks]

(c) Were diplomatic attempts to preserve European peace in the 1930s doomed to failure? Explain your answer. [18 marks]

Edexcel Unit 3

The Second World War

Key Issues

● *Why did the Second World War expand into a global conflict?*

● *What economic and racial policies did the Nazis pursue in the territories that they occupied?*

● *Why did the resistance of the Axis powers collapse in 1944–1945?*

Framework of Events

1939	(September) German invasion of Poland. Britain and France declare war on Germany
	(November) Beginning of 'Winter War' between USSR and Finland
1940	Russian annexation of Baltic states
	(April) German invasion of Norway and Denmark
	(May) German invasion of Holland, Belgium and France
	(June) Dunkirk evacuation and fall of France
	(July–September) Battle of Britain
1941	(March) 'Lend–Lease' agreement between Britain and USA
	(June) Germany launches 'Operation Barbarossa', the invasion of the USSR
	(September) Britain and USA sign 'Atlantic Charter'
	(December) Japanese attack upon Pearl Harbor. American entry into war
1942	(August) German assault on Stalingrad
	(October) German defeat in North Africa at El Alamein
1943	(January) German defeat at Stalingrad
	(July) German defeat at Kursk. Allied invasion of Italy. Mussolini falls from power
1944	(June) British and American forces launch D-Day landings in Normandy. Fall of Rome to allied forces
1945	(January) Fall of Warsaw to Soviet troops
	(February) Allied conference at Yalta. Allied forces cross the Rhine
	(April) Russian forces enter Berlin
	(May) Unconditional surrender of German forces
	(August) Atomic bombs dropped on Hiroshima and Nagasaki
	(September) Unconditional surrender of Japanese forces. Allied conference at Potsdam.

Overview

ALTHOUGH the Second World War was different in many respects from the war of 1914–18, it too began with a misconception. Hitler did not anticipate a global conflict of long duration, but had planned a series of limited, rapid campaigns that would achieve strictly defined objectives in a manner that would not stretch German economic resources. The first of these crushed Poland in a matter of weeks (September 1939) and another, the following year, destroyed French resistance almost as rapidly. Subsequently, however, Hitler's calculations began to go wrong. Britain did not immediately give in once its French ally had been defeated, nor did Hitler's third *Blitzkrieg*, launched from the air, succeed in bringing it to its knees. Instead, Britain gained material assistance from the United States of America and, within a year, could count the USA as a direct ally after Japanese aggression had brought them into the war. Nevertheless, Hitler's political and racial beliefs led him to believe that his next projected offensive, against the Soviet Union, must also succeed.

Blitzkrieg (German – 'lightning war'): A form of warfare in which victory is won by rapid, devastating and decisive offensives, rather than by protracted campaigns.

Germany owed its impressive successes in 1939–41 to the fact that its military commanders had perfected this art of *Blitzkrieg*. They had appreciated before any of their contemporaries the impact of large tank forces, supported from the air by superior forces of rapid fighter planes and dive-bombers. When this strategy failed a second time, however, and the Soviet Union survived the massive blow struck against it, it became clear that the Second World War would actually be decided in the same manner as the first. It would be won by those who possessed the greatest industrial resources and who could bring them most effectively to bear. By 1942 Hitler and his allies were involved in a great struggle that stretched from one end of Europe to the other, from the Channel coast to the Caspian Sea. It was linked with another struggle on the other side of the globe, for Japan's leaders had also miscalculated, underestimating America's aerial and naval power, failing similarly to achieve a quick 'knock-out' blow, and becoming locked in a desperate battle for survival in the Pacific. Britain's colonial interests in Canada, Australasia, South Africa and India drew those regions, too, into what was now a truly global war.

In effect, by the end of 1942, this was a war that Germany and its allies could not win. Germany in particular, however, adapted its war effort impressively in an attempt to stave off defeat. This involved the mobilisation of Germany's domestic economy to meet the demands of 'total war', and only from 1942 did the Nazis realise the country's potential for making war. It also meant the most ruthless exploitation of the resources available to Germany in the territories that it had occupied. Enormous efforts were made to seize material resources and to mobilise foreign labour to work in German industry, either by force or by more subtle inducements. One of the most remarkable features of this stage of the war was the willingness with which some elements within the occupied states, especially in western Europe, co-operated and collaborated with the invaders. This ruthless exploitation also stimulated resistance to the Germans, and in eastern Europe in particular, this put further obstacles in the path of Germany's war effort. At the same time, the Nazi leadership placed additional obstacles in its own path by judging that the time was now ripe for a 'final solution' to the 'problem' of Europe's Jewish population. Even as the war was being lost, human resources, transport and the like were being used for ferrying Jews to the concentration camps where genocide was to take place.

Great though the scope of the war was by 1942, its focus was the German campaign against the Soviet Union, and the decisive battles of the whole world war were those fought around Moscow, Leningrad and Stalingrad. There, once the invaders had lost the element of surprise, their forces were steadily ground down by the geography and climate of the region, and by the vast resources that the Soviet Union could mobilise. In the meantime, the American economy attained the highest levels of industrial production that the world had ever witnessed, and its military resources were steadily concentrated in Britain and in North Africa. In the course of 1944 Germany found itself fighting on three fronts. Whereas the First World War ended without a single foreign soldier on German soil, the Second World War drew to a close with the wholesale destruction of German cities, with Soviet troops in the heart of Berlin, and with the arrest and condemnation of many of Germany's political leaders. The year 1945 marked the most comprehensive military and political defeat that any modern state had ever experienced.

Six years of bitter conflict had serious implications for the political and economic balance of Europe and of the world at large. To say that they brought about the destruction of the German state, the downfall of the political regimes of several other European states, the end of Europe's international supremacy, and a new political balance between two world superpowers, is only to list some of the war's results. Some historians argue that the two world wars must be viewed together, the second completing some of the unfinished business of the first. Looked at in this way it might be possible to conclude that the extreme nationalist movements of the 1920s and the 1930s were only makeshift expedients to fill the gaps left by the collapse of the aristocratic empires of pre-1914 Europe. The defeat of such movements left supremacy in Europe to be disputed between the liberal democracies that were already well developed by 1914, and the vast socialist power of the Soviet Union that had achieved such apparent permanency under the rule of Joseph Stalin.

12.1 Why was the German war effort so successful in 1939–1940?

Military and tactical superiority

Wehrmacht: German armed forces other than *Waffen SS.*

The table on page 362 gives some indication of the relative strengths of the major European powers in 1939, yet such figures do not tell the whole story. As the lessons of the 1914–18 war should have taught, the importance of the 'big battalions' was now outweighed by technical and tactical superiority. In these respects, German leadership was indisputable. Under the influence of such commanders as Heinz Guderian and Erwin Rommel, the *Wehrmacht* had adopted the principles of mechanised warfare – of rapid thrusts against a slow-moving enemy to cut its lines of supply and of retreat – far more

| **Heinz Guderian (1888–1954)** An important pre-war theorist of tank warfare; one of the architects of the German *Panzer* divisions. | Commanded *Panzer* forces in Poland (1939), France and Russia (1940). Inspector General of tanks (1943). Chief of Staff of the *Wehrmacht* (1944). | **Erwin Rommel (1891–1944)** Commander of the Afrika Korps (1941–43). Commander of German forces in northern Italy | (1943). Commander of forces in France (1943–44). Implicated in the army plot to assassinate Hitler, Rommel was arrested and committed suicide. |

effectively than Germany's opponents. Germany enjoyed a distinct advantage in the areas vital to this 'lightning war', in the design and deployment of its tanks and the use of aerial support. It had turned its enforced disarmament of 1919 to its advantage, building modern weapons while its opponents laboured under the weight of obsolete equipment. The modern planes of the *Luftwaffe* were faster and more manoeuvrable than anything possessed by the French or the Poles.

Also, although Germany's 3,200 tanks did not represent a numerical superiority, models such as the PkwIII and the PkwIV were superior to their counterparts. The *Wehrmacht* also used these new weapons more effectively. Despite the entreaties in the early 1930s of a young tank officer, Colonel Charles de Gaulle, French military commanders continued to think of the tank as a form of mechanised horse, supporting the all-important infantry advances. Neither they nor their allies appreciated the value of the weapon used in massed formations. Their plans and their armies proceeded at the pace of the foot soldier in a military world dominated by the internal combustion engine. Most ominous of all for the allies' immediate prospects in the autumn of 1939 was the weakness of the Polish armed forces, largely unchanged since their successes against the Russians 20 years before.

The military balance of power in Europe, 1939

	Army divisions	No. of aircraft	Capital ships	Submarines
Germany	125	4,210	5	65
Italy	73	1,531	4	104
USSR	125	3,361	3	18
France	86	1,234	7	78
Great Britain	4	1,750	15	57
Poland	40	500	–	–

Source: A. Adamthwaite, *The Making of the Second World War* (1977)

Action in the east, inaction in the west

The historian A.J.P. Taylor wrote that 'although Hitler blundered in supposing that the two western powers would not go to war at all, his expectation that they would not go to war seriously turned out to be correct.' Poland received no material support from its allies and the tactics of all three powers contrasted starkly with those of the invaders. Poland became the first victim of the *Blitzkrieg* perfected by the German forces. Pitching armoured columns and overwhelming aerial superiority against an army that continued to trust in the mobility of large cavalry forces, the *Wehrmacht* made rapid progress eastwards, encircling the defending forces in a **pincer movement**. On 17 September the fate of Poland was sealed when Soviet forces began their occupation of its eastern regions. Within ten days the German and Soviet forces had reached the line agreed in the Ribbentrop–Molotov Pact (see Chapter 11), and the Polish state ceased to exist.

In the west, meanwhile, a different kind of war was being waged. The contemporary military historian, Sir Basil Liddell Hart, believed that the allies, with 86 French divisions alone, could have taken effective action against the 42 divisions that guarded the German frontier, without tanks, aircraft or substantial supplies. Yet nothing positive was done. This was largely due to the outmoded thinking of the French commanders, still

Pincer movement: Splitting your forces and moving them round either side of the enemy.

wedded to the defensive strategy of the previous war. It was also due to the hesitation of political leaders who had still not overcome the appeasement mentality of the last decade. Thus, when allied bombers did fly over German industrial towns, they dropped propaganda leaflets rather than bombs. This curious state of suspended hostility was christened the 'phoney war'. To the Germans it became the 'sitting-down war' (*Sitzkrieg*) in ironic contrast to the more effective tactics of the Eastern Front.

Illogically, the attention of allied strategists during this 'phoney war' turned towards Scandinavia. There, in the mines of Sweden and Norway, lay the source of 51% of Germany's supplies of iron ore. This might explain the allies' attempts to entice Norway and Sweden into the war on their side. However, with the opening of the Soviet Union's 'Winter War' with Finland (November 1939–March 1940), it is hard to resist the conclusion that the allied governments continued to be as much concerned with the Soviet threat as with that posed by Germany. Similarly, French actions in the Middle East against Hitler's Caspian oil supplies were as much anti-Soviet in conception as anti-German. In both cases, allied action proved hesitant and half-hearted. While they debated the mining of neutral Norwegian waters to prevent the passage of ore to Germany, Hitler ordered the extension of operations to Scandinavia to safeguard his supplies. The invasion of Denmark (April 1940), necessary for the purposes of communication, was an immediate success, but the simultaneous assault on Norway encountered stiffer resistance. By the end of June, however, all allied forces had been forced to withdraw, leaving Norway in German hands.

The fall of France

The 'phoney war' ended abruptly on 10 May 1940 with the launching of the German offensive into France and the **Low Countries**. Despite the months that had been available for preparation, the defending forces were taken largely unaware, not only by the speed and power of the German attack, but also by its strategy. Expecting an offensive like that of 1914, based upon a drive through central Belgium, allied strategists envisaged an advance into Belgium to check the enemy's right wing short of the French frontier while the rest of his forces dashed themselves against the defences of the Maginot Line. Indeed, until January 1940, Belgium had played a leading role in *Wehrmacht* plans. Only then had a daring new strategy been introduced. German commanders were aware that the allies regarded the hilly, wooded region of the Ardennes, beyond the flank of the Maginot Line, as virtually impassable, and that it was thus only lightly defended. General von Manstein therefore proposed an armoured attack across the river Meuse, into this weakest sector of the allied line.

In the event, the German offensive combined both strategies. For the first ten days Holland and Belgium suffered heavy aerial bombardment and assault by infantry, artillery and airborne troops. In particular, the bombing of Rotterdam, where nearly 1,000 civilians died within a few minutes, was unprecedented in European experience and created a deep psychological impression. The Dutch government surrendered on 15 May. British and French forces were drawn into Belgium to check the German advance and were threatened with encirclement when (12 May) a massive armoured force under General von Kleist broke through the Ardennes and breached the French line near Sedan. This breakthrough effectively decided the outcome of the battle for France. Faced with the alternatives of evacuation or annihilation, the British forces, with some 10,000 French troops, retreated to the Channel at Dunkirk. Here, by a combination of heroism, good fortune and puzzling German tactics, they were transported back to

Low Countries: The region forming the Kingdoms of Holland and Belgium, and the grand duchy of Luxembourg.

Ewald von Kleist (1881–1954)
Commanded German forces in the Caucasus, the Crimea and the Ukraine (1942–43). Relieved of his command by Hitler after ordering retreat on the Eastern Front. Died in captivity in the Soviet Union.

'The withdrawal from Dunkirk',
June 1940, by Charles Cundall

Britain by a fleet of 860 assorted vessels hastily assembled for the task
(26 May – 4 June). The operation owed much, perhaps everything, to
Hitler's curious decision to hold back tanks and aircraft that could have
destroyed the allied forces and their rescuers on the beaches. Variously
explained as a temporary loss of nerve, or as evidence of a continuing hope
that Britain would still conclude a separate peace, Hitler's decision allowed
an escape which, in subsequent British propaganda, did something to
obscure the magnitude of the allied defeat.

The new French line, along the rivers Aisne and Somme, broke three
days later, and the government abandoned Paris for the safety of the south
(9 June). Any remaining hope of national survival vanished the following
day when Mussolini judged the moment ripe for Italy, too, to declare war
on France. From their retreat near Bordeaux the French government, now
led by the hero of the First World War, Marshal Philippe Pétain, rejected
the option of flight to Africa and requested Germany's terms for an
armistice. In 46 days of fighting, France had lost 84,000 men dead,
120,000 injured and 1,500,000 taken prisoner. Considering the extent of
this defeat the terms dictated at Rethondes (21 June), in the same railway
carriage used for the German surrender in 1918, were moderate.

● With the exception of strategic areas in the north and along the
  Atlantic coast, French officials retained responsibility for civil
  administration.

● The French government retained complete sovereignty over the
  southern 40% of the country free from German military occupation.

● No territory was earmarked for annexation by Germany, although Italy
  claimed the return of Nice and Savoy.

● France kept control of its fleet and of its Empire.

Mohacs in 1526: Victory in the Battle of Mohacs allowed Turkish forces under Sultan Suleiman the Magnificent to overrun and destroy the Kingdom of Hungary. This seemed to contemporaries to represent the collapse of the outer defences of Christendom.

1. What were the main reasons for the rapid victory gained by German forces on the Western Front in 1940?

2. To what extent were Hitler's successes in 1939 and 1940 due to the weaknesses and mistakes of Germany's opponents?

• The fact remained, as the future would show, that with total military domination, Hitler could take what he did not now claim whenever he felt the need.

What were the causes and significance of the French defeat?

The astonishing collapse of France had many causes. Among these the confused foreign policy of the last two decades, the deep domestic divisions of recent years, and the extraordinary incompetence of commanders who neglected air power, mechanised forces and modern communications, are prominent. Although the transformation of this European conflict into a true world war was eventually to reverse the outcome of 1940, the significance of the German victory in purely European terms must not be underestimated. A nation that had held the first place in the affairs of the continent for three centuries had been rendered impotent within five weeks, and the rise of German power, checked at great cost in 1918, seemed after all to have reached its logical conclusion. The historians Peter Calvocoressi and Guy Wint, in *Total War* (1970), have summarised the impact of these events in his judgement that 'the fall of France opened an abyss of uncertainty for the whole continent and shook the imagination as perhaps nothing had shaken it since the victory of the Turks at **Mohacs in 1526**'.

12.2 How and why did the conflict expand in 1940–1942?

Winston Churchill (1874–1965)
British politician in Parliament from 1900 (as a Liberal until 1923). He held a number of ministerial offices, including First Lord of the Admiralty (1911–15) and Chancellor of the Exchequer (1924–29). Absent from the Cabinet in the 1930s, he returned in September 1939 to lead a coalition government (1940–45). Typifying resistance to the threat of Germany, he was also successful in forging the alliance with the USA and the USSR that led to Germany's unconditional surrender in 1945. Prime Minister again 1951–55. Churchill received the Nobel Prize for Literature (1945) and was made Knight of the Garter (1953).

This stage of the European conflict could scarcely have continued, let alone expanded, had not some basis survived for resistance against Nazi Germany. At first, the collapse of France seemed likely to end the war in western Europe. Britain's chances of continuing the struggle seemed hopeless. Its land forces, although extricated from Dunkirk, had lost most of their equipment, and the defence of 3,000 kilometres of coastline posed enormous problems. Yet, stiffened by the extraordinary leadership and resolution of the new Prime Minister, Winston Churchill, Britain did not sue for peace. Instead, Churchill announced his determination that 'we shall fight on the beaches, we shall fight on the landing grounds, we shall fight in the hills; we shall never surrender'. Hitler's response to this decision seems to have been conditioned by three factors.

1. Although it is unlikely that Britain could have resisted an invasion, no definite plans had been prepared for one, so sure was the German High Command that the fall of France would end the western campaign.

2. Hitler professed a persistent reluctance to treat a 'Germanic' civilisation in the same way that he had treated the Poles.

3. If Britain still needed to be prodded towards peace, the commander of the *Luftwaffe*, Hermann Goering, was determined that his forces should be allowed to demonstrate their effectiveness.

The Battle of Britain

Unlike the Battle of France, the Battle of Britain took the form of a concentrated aerial attack, firstly upon Britain's airfields, to gain total air supremacy, and then upon London and other centres to break the resistance of the civilian population. Neither effort was successful. The numerical superiority of the *Luftwaffe* – about 1,200 bombers and 1,000 fighters to some 900 British fighters – was offset by several other factors. The relatively light German bombers such as the Heinkel 111 and the Dornier 215 were vulnerable without substantial fighter support, and the range of such fighters as the Messerschmitt 109E was only sufficient to give them a few minutes of combat over British targets. On the British side, the Spitfire and Hurricane fighters were formidable weapons – fast, manoeuvrable, heavily armed, and with the advantage of fighting over their own territory. The rapid development of radar and its establishment along the southern and eastern coasts of Britain provided valuable early warning of the German bombers' approach.

Thus, in the main phase of the engagement (early August–late September 1940), the *Luftwaffe* lost over 1,100 aircraft, against a British loss of 650. Hitler, half-hearted in his campaign from the outset, and impatient to turn against his 'real' enemy in the east, suspended the plan for invasion on 17 September, and reduced *Luftwaffe* operations over Britain at the end of the month. Although the struggle was decided as much by German errors and miscalculations as by British strengths, the Battle of Britain represented a first checking of Germany's triumphant military progress, and the beginning of that over-stretching of its military resources that was to be its downfall.

The Mediterranean and the Balkans

In mid-1940, the conflict was a strictly limited one, tightly confined to areas of western and northern Europe. The failure of Germany in that summer to eliminate British opposition began a process of proliferation that transformed this into a truly global war. Firstly, after the failure of aerial warfare, the Atlantic Ocean became the major theatre of Anglo–German conflict. The German navy sought, with submarines, surface raiders and mines, to cut British supply lines. Secondly, the entry of Italy into the war inevitably spread the conflict to those areas that Mussolini considered to be his sphere of influence: the Balkans, the Mediterranean, and North Africa.

Two factors led to German involvement in these regions. The failure of Italian forces to sustain their offensive against Greece (October 1940) and the British decision to send aid to the Greeks seriously threatened interests that Germany had carefully built up in that region. By a mixture of bullying and diplomacy, Hitler had ensured that Hungary, Romania and Yugoslavia would remain sympathetic to German ambitions in eastern Europe, the source of valuable strategic supplies and potential assembly areas for anti-Soviet forces.

Axis: The name given to the alliance between Germany, Italy and Japan during the Second World War.

The hope that General Franco might repay his debt from the Spanish Civil War by supporting **Axis** interests in the Mediterranean had collapsed by the end of 1940. In a series of discussions in October and November the Spanish leader made it clear that his priority was domestic consolidation and reconstruction. Thus, with Italian forces checked in Greece and later in North Africa, and with the pro-German government of Yugoslavia overthrown by a *coup d'état* (March 1941), Hitler found himself forced into large-scale intervention. The military campaign was successful, with Greece cleared of hostile troops by late April and the island of Crete captured in May. Yet the commitment of 28 divisions to the Balkans and of several mechanised divisions to North Africa forced a postponement of the planned Russian offensive and the establishment of a costly and lasting 'sideshow' for the Germans.

The entry of the United States of America

Of far greater significance was the gradual involvement of the United States of America in the conflict. American isolationism, re-established by

> **Francisco Franco (1892–1975)**
> He was a general at 41. Commandant of the Military Academy at Saragossa, closed as part of the Republican Army reforms. After the Popular Front's victory of 1936 Franco was regarded as a threat to the Republic and was sent to the Canary Islands. From there he flew to Morocco and was soon the leader of the Nationalists. He was dictator ('El Caudillo') of Spain until his death.

Franklin D. Roosevelt (1882–1945)
Democrat senator for New York State (1910); Secretary for the Navy (1910); Governor of New York (1929); President of the USA (1932–45). In peacetime, his greatest achievements were those connected with the New Deal, to restore economic prosperity after the Great Depression. Roosevelt's foreign policy moved steadily away from isolationism, and he showed great sympathy for British resistance to Nazi Germany. The Japanese attack upon Pearl Harbor finally gave him the opportunity to lead the USA into the war.

the Senate's refusal to ratify the Versailles Treaty, and confirmed by three Neutrality Acts (1935, 1936, 1937), was only slowly eroded by the influence of Churchill's close personal relationship with President Franklin D. Roosevelt. Public opinion in the USA also took time to realise that world events were beginning to pose a direct threat to American interests. The fall of France, for instance, presented the prospect of an Atlantic Ocean dominated by hostile fleets at the same time as Japanese influence spread in the Pacific Ocean. The Battle of the Atlantic, with its extensive German submarine action, not only confirmed this prospect, but posed a definite danger to American shipping. By September 1940, there was sufficient support in the USA for the 'Destroyer Deal', which transferred 50 older ships into British hands. This was followed by the more important 'Lend–Lease' agreement (March 1941), by which purchase of war materials from American companies was financed by the American government regardless of Britain's current dollar reserves. By late 1941, largely due to the influence of Roosevelt himself, the USA had taken up an ambiguous position – clearly sympathetic to Germany's opponents, but not openly committed to war.

This position changed dramatically on 7 December 1941 with the Japanese air attack upon the American Pacific fleet at Pearl Harbor. The American declaration of war upon Japan was followed almost immediately (11 December) by Hitler's declaration of war upon the USA. Many have since followed the historian Alan Bullock in regarding this declaration as 'the greatest single mistake of his career'. On the other hand, some have interpreted Hitler's declaration of war as a simple acceptance of American hostility to Germany. Where Hitler certainly did commit a serious error was in grossly underestimating the strength of his new enemy. Applying his racial views to the USA, he refused to believe that a country 'half Judaised and the other half negrified' could effectively challenge Germany. Only slowly, in the phrase of historian Michael Burleigh (*The Third Reich: A New History*, 2000) did Hitler realise 'the creative, economic, intellectual and military potentialities he had stirred against himself, like a man surprised at the effects of poking a stick into a large beehive.'

The invasion of the USSR

The most far-reaching escalation of the European conflict came with Hitler's decision to launch his attack upon the Soviet Union. Although increasingly committed to secondary theatres of war, he would not postpone this major element in his policy beyond June 1941. The assault was dictated by long-term hostility to Bolshevism and by theories of *Lebensraum*, but there were also logical, short-term factors that determined its timing. An attack now upon the Soviet Union would leave Britain with no prospect of future support in Europe, and would leave Japan without any distraction in its impending confrontation with the USA. Besides, Hitler was convinced that his successes in eastern Europe would, sooner or later, cause Stalin to take action to redress the balance. It made no sense to delay until the Soviet Army had time to fortify the territories occupied in 1939. On 22 June 121 divisions of the *Wehrmacht*, with massive aerial support, were launched across the frontier. Dismissing his generals' insistence upon a direct assault on Moscow, Hitler made the Soviet capital only one of three objectives for his army. An attack upon Leningrad would secure his Baltic flank with Finnish aid, while a thrust into the Ukraine would secure valuable industrial and agricultural resources.

1. What factors enabled Britain to avoid invasion and defeat by Germany in 1940?

2. Why had Hitler decided by 1941 to go to war with both the USA and the Soviet Union?

12.3 Why did the German offensive against the Soviet Union fail?

At the time of the German offensive the Red Army had more men, more tanks, and more aircraft, yet the invaders enjoyed several advantages. They had the element of surprise, for Soviet propaganda had allowed no word to escape of worsening German–Soviet relations. They attacked an army which, although it had learned much from the difficult war with Finland a year earlier, had not yet had time to implement the necessary improvements in command and materials. The Red Army, uncertain which enemy posed the greater threat, still divided its forces between its frontier with the Germans and that in the east with Japan. Thus, the initial success of the German offensive was staggering. Soviet resistance was brave, but it lacked the co-ordination to contain the enemy advance for any period. In the north, Leningrad found itself surrounded and besieged by September. In the south, a Soviet force of 600,000 was surrounded and the key Ukrainian city of Kiev fell in the same month. By mid-October the *Wehrmacht* had pushed over 650 kilometres into central Russia and was within 80 kilometres of the Soviet capital. Soviet losses were huge; some three million men and 18,000 tanks in three months. Ominously, German casualties – some 750,000 of them – were also far higher than in any previous campaign.

Soviet recovery and resistance

Great as German successes were, none of the objectives of the invasion had been completely secured by the beginning of the autumn, and there were signs that the tide was turning. The first factor in the Soviet recovery was the weather. Heavy rain in October blocked the German advance with seas of mud, and heavy frosts in November exposed them to all the horrors of a winter campaign in Russia. Frostbite claimed 100,000 victims. Aircraft, tanks, lorries and guns could not operate for want of antifreeze, and men were reduced to stuffing their uniforms with paper to keep out temperatures as low as 40 degrees below freezing.

The German forces also encountered astonishing resistance from military and civilians alike. Although reinforced by fear of retribution from their own side from the NKVD (see Chapter 8), this resistance came mainly from patriotism, as a reaction to ill-advised German behaviour in the territories they occupied, and from an awareness of the nature of the German threat. In his first wartime address to the nation, Stalin played upon this awareness in his declaration that the enemy was 'out to seize our lands watered by the sweat of our brows, to seize our grain and oil, secured by the labour of our hands, to restore the rule of the landlords'.

It is also possible to argue that German resources were less suited to their task than is often supposed. In *The German Economy at War* (1965), historian Alan Milward is highly critical of German preparation for this vast undertaking. If the Nazi economy was deliberately geared for war, Milward argued, it was geared inadequately. Just as Hitler failed to defeat Britain because he had not built an air force adequate for the task, so he failed against the Soviet Union because he had not built a sufficient tank force. His failure to secure a quick victory in the east then forced him to strike at the resources of southern Russia where his army, insufficiently mobile for the task that he had set it, encountered its decisive defeat.

Leningrad and Stalingrad

Siege: A military operation in which an army tries to capture a town by surrounding it and preventing food or help from reaching the people inside.

In the north, German plans were narrowly frustrated. Of the seven Soviet cities awarded the title 'Hero City' after the war, none deserved it more than Leningrad. The **siege**, a product of Hitler's determination to destroy the cradle of Bolshevism, lasted from September 1941 to January 1944.

Georgi Zhukov (1896–1974) Commanded the Red Army in actions against the Japanese in the Far East (1939). Chief of Soviet General Staff	(1941). Commanded forces in the defence of Leningrad (1941), the defence of Stalingrad (1942), the campaigns in the Ukraine (1943–44), and the	invasion of Germany (1944–45). Zhukov was the first commander of Soviet occupation forces in Germany.

1. What were the consequences of Hitler's decision to attack the Soviet Union in 1941?

2. How would you explain (a) the initial weakness of the Soviet response to the German invasion and (b) the later success of Soviet resistance?

3. Why was the German war effort so much more successful in 1939–41 than in 1942–43?

Desperately short of food and precariously supplied by routes built over the ice of Lake Ladoga and by rail routes open to constant German attack, the inhabitants suffered constant bombardment and the threat of starvation. It is possible that the total casualty figures for the siege may have been as high as 1.5 million, most of them civilians. That Leningrad never fell was due to the heroism of the inhabitants, and to the shrewd defensive organisation of Marshal Georgi Zhukov. It also owed much to the eventual need of the *Wehrmacht* to divert substantial resources of men and material to the south-west of the USSR.

The key theatre of the European war in 1942 lay in Stalingrad. Given the industrial potential of the world's largest state and the failure of the 1941 campaign to crush its resistance, time was against Hitler. It was essential that Germany should complete the conquest of the oil-rich regions between the Black Sea and the Caspian as quickly as possible. In a fateful strategic decision, Hitler resolved to divide his southern forces between a drive against the Caucasian oilfields to the south and an assault upon the important communications centre of Stalingrad, on the Volga river, to the east. The personal links between Stalin and the city that bore his name gave the ensuing battle special significance for both sides. From September 1942 until January 1943, the streets, houses and factories of the city were the scene of constant and bitter fighting. This continued until the German Sixth Army, surrounded since November, but forbidden to retreat by Hitler, finally submitted. The battle cost the Germans 70,000 casualties, over 100,000 prisoners and vast quantities of guns and vehicles. The Soviet victory forced the retreat of those German forces further south that now faced the danger of being cut off. Worst of all, the invincible reputation of the *Wehrmacht* and the impetus of two years of *Blitzkrieg* campaigns in the east also died.

12.4 In what respects had the challenges facing Nazi Germany changed by the end of 1942?

This was now a transformed war, in which Germany and its allies no longer faced an Anglo–French alliance, but a coalition that included the world's two largest states. The balance of industrial and economic forces would now only admit one eventual outcome.

The Soviet war effort

Kremlin: Location of the Soviet central government in Moscow.

The Soviet Union brought to the conflict enormous industrial resources and a centralised political authority uniquely capable of mobilising and directing them. In the **Kremlin**, some of the government's firmest pre-war principles were now revised in the interests of national unity. The Orthodox Church was rehabilitated, and the privileges of higher military ranks were restored to ensure the army's undivided loyalty in the struggle. Industrially, on the other hand, the Soviet Union had lost much in the early months of the war, including some 60% of its coal and iron production and as much as 25% of its workforce.

The process of industrial re-organisation had already begun before the war, when the third Five-Year Plan had established many new industrial concentrations in the Ural mountains and in Siberia. These plants were beyond the reach of German attacks. Now they were supplemented at remarkable speed by the transfer of factories from the vulnerable western regions. In 1942 1,360 factories moved eastwards, and 2,250 new units of production arose there between 1942 and 1944. The astonishing nature of this achievement is conveyed by this description by the historian Peter Calvocoressi:

> 'At the new sites wooden structures were thrown up to house machinery, but there was often neither time nor materials to build houses for the workers. They slept on the floor by their machines. Mortality was high, output poor. The wonder is that they were not worse.'

Eventually, results were outstanding in regions old and new. The Moscow coalfield, reduced to an output of 590 tons per day in January 1942, was back to its pre-war norm of 35,000 tons per day by the following October. The trans-Ural regions, at their peak, were producing at 2.5 times the rate of the whole of Soviet industry in 1940. Russian military production overhauled that of Germany to reach a peak of 30,000 tanks and 40,000 aircraft in 1943.

The contribution of the United States of America

A glance at the industrial capacity of the USA suffices to show the vital role that nation played in the outcome of the Second World War. American increases in armament production in the war years were amazing – from 6,000 aircraft in 1940 to 96,000 in 1945, from under a thousand tanks in 1940 to 21,000 in 1943. Much of this went to fight the war in the Pacific, but the American contribution to the European theatre of war remained invaluable. On D-Day (6 June 1944) the British army operated 3,300 Sherman tanks and 86,000 American motor vehicles. Some 20% of the Royal Air Force's strength in 1943–45 was also made up of American planes. The USSR benefited from 'Lend–Lease' agreements (October 1941 and June 1942), similar to that negotiated with Britain. These agreements provided 2,000 tanks and 1,300 planes by mid-1942, at the height of the Soviet crisis.

British war production

Empire and Dominions: Although countries such as Australia, Canada, New Zealand and South Africa had become self-governing Dominions (legally independent in all internal and external matters, though economic and other ties remained), Britain still had a large Empire. Almost all the Dominions joined Britain to fight during the Second World War.

Although Great Britain could not match these figures, its contribution was considerable. Like the Soviet Union, Britain had won time to mobilise its resources and it did so effectively. From four divisions ready for combat in 1939, it could count on 60 by mid-1941, 20 of them from the **Empire and Dominions**. Domestic resources were also fully exploited. In 1940–42 British aircraft production was actually higher than that of Germany, and by the time Germany regained the lead in 1944, American and Soviet production had already put the issue of industrial supremacy beyond doubt.

The German war effort from 1942

Fritz Todt (1891–1942)
Inspector of German Highways (1932–42). Founder and Head of the Organisation Todt, and in charge of construction projects under the Four-Year Plan (1938–42). Minister for Armaments and Munitions (1940–42), until his death in a plane crash.

Against these overwhelming forces, the German economy performed miracles, but laboured under a variety of obstacles. It had never been geared for a long war, only for the production of materials for *Blitzkrieg*, and Germany needed to undergo a miniature 'industrial revolution' to meet its new crisis. Central figures in this process were Fritz Todt, Minister of Armaments and Munitions until his death in February 1942, and his

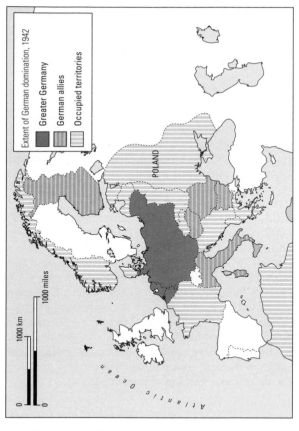

Extent of German domination, 1942
- Greater Germany
- German allies
- Occupied territories

POLAND

1000 km · 1000 miles

Atlantic Ocean

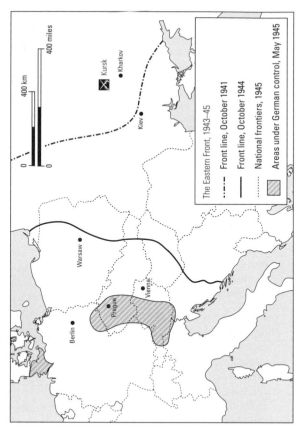

The Eastern Front, 1943–45
- Front line, October 1941
- Front line, October 1944
- National frontiers, 1945
- Areas under German control, May 1945

Kursk · Kharkov · Kiev · Warsaw · Vienna · Prague · Berlin

400 km · 400 miles

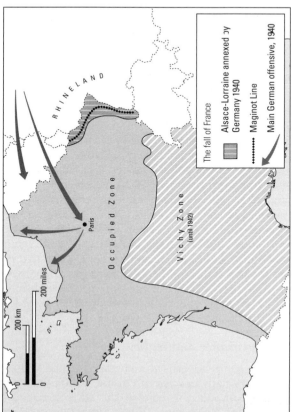

The fall of France
- Alsace-Lorraine annexed by Germany 1940
- Maginot Line
- Main German offensive, 1940

RHINELAND

Occupied Zone

Vichy Zone (until 1942)

Paris

200 km · 200 miles

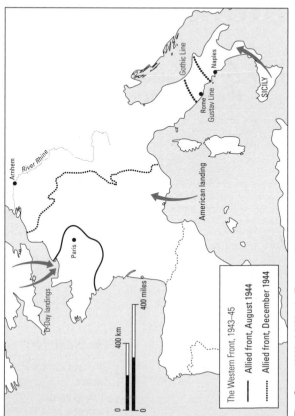

The Western Front, 1943–45
- Allied front, August 1944
- Allied front, December 1944

Gothic Line · Rome · Gustav Line · Naples · SICILY

Arnhem · River Rhine · American landing · Paris · D-Day landings

400 km · 400 miles

The Second World War in Europe, 1939–45

Albert Speer	Munitions (1942–45).	of information on the
(1905–1981)	Speer was tried at	government of Nazi
Architect, who directed	Nuremberg and	Germany.
many of Hitler's projects	imprisoned. The	
for the redevelopment of	memoirs that he wrote	
Berlin. Minister for	whilst in Spandau Prison	
Armaments and	are an important source	

Gauleiters: Senior Nazi officials, responsible for the administration of a *Gau* (province of the Reich).

1. **What disadvantages did Nazi Germany suffer from 1942 onwards in terms of the production of military material?**

2. **How convincing is the argument that Germany had the capacity to win the Second World War had it not been for the entry of the USA into the conflict?**

successor, Albert Speer. As a relatively civilised and realistic figure surrounded by Nazi extremists, Speer has since received lenient treatment both from the Nuremberg judges and, until recently, from historians. His role in equipping Germany to fight the war in 1942–45 was of great importance. Aircraft production reached a peak of 25,285 in 1944, as against 3,744 in 1940. The rebuilding of factories to protect them from air raids was so effective that 5,000 new aircraft were produced in the first four months of 1945 even as the allies were over-running Germany.

Speer could not, however, overcome Germany's severe political and geographical disadvantages. It was subjected to bombing from two sides while American and Siberian factories lay beyond the reach of its own aircraft. There was no central authority in Germany to co-ordinate production. While Hitler specialised in oratory, Speer had frequently to struggle against the influence of Goering, the chiefs of various state agencies, and the local jealousies of the *Gauleiters*, over questions of policy and resources. In the latter stages of the war, resources such as the coal and iron of the Ruhr and of Silesia shrank as allied forces advanced.

12.5 By what methods and with what success did Nazi Germany govern the territories that it conquered?

'Puppet' governments: Governments which appear, and pretend, to be independent, but which are in fact controlled by a foreign government (i.e. someone else is 'pulling the strings').

For four years, Nazi Germany dominated the mainland of Europe more completely than it had ever been dominated before. In the west, in France, Norway and Denmark, 'puppet' governments were installed, checked at every turn by German military commanders and representatives of the security forces, to ensure that German interests were served. **'Puppet' governments** also operated in the Balkans, Greece, Yugoslavia and Romania. In eastern Europe, where the 'inferior' Slavs could not be afforded even this limited freedom, direct German government was the rule. Poland was placed under the arbitrary authority of a German Governor-General (Hans Frank), and Bohemia and Moravia under that of a protector (first Constantine von Neurath, then Reinhard Heydrich, then Wilhelm Frick). The territories of Ostland and the Ukraine, created from captured Soviet territory, came under the authority of the *Reichsminister* for the East, the fanatical Nazi theorist, Alfred Rosenberg.

The Nazi 'New Order': appearance and reality

The 'new order' that these regimes advertised and imposed had a dual nature. In Nazi propaganda, especially in western Europe, it took the form of a gigantic union of European states to combat the alien menace of Judaism and its political offshoot, Bolshevism. It was a highly successful interpretation which found a living expression in the many international units, such as the French 'Legion of Volunteers Against Bolshevism' and the Belgian 'Flemish Legion', recruited in occupied countries to join the *Wehrmacht* on the Eastern Front.

In reality, the 'new order' took the form of a plundering of European resources for the exclusive benefit of Germany. This could be explained as a necessity imposed by the continuing war, but in large part it arose from the long-term plans of Nazi theorists. Hitler's aims in the Soviet Union were not merely to defeat its communist leadership, but to 'Germanise the country by the settlement of Germans and treat the natives as **redskins**'. Germany would provide the industrial heartland of this new Europe, and would in turn be fed by the less developed, largely agricultural territories that surrounded it.

Occupation administrations were assigned two main tasks: the economic exploitation of the conquered territories in the interests of the war effort, and the breaking of local political and intellectual structures. The first function was dominated by two central figures, Hermann Goering, as Commissioner of the Five-Year Plan, and Fritz Sauckel, the official responsible for the supply of labour to German industries. It took a number of forms, including the exploitation of local resources, such as the coal deposits of Silesia, the adaptation of local plant to German requirements, the transfer of some of that plant to German factories, and the recruitment of foreign labour for service in Germany. In the west, this last task was often tackled by subtle enticements, such as the promise of higher wages or the placing of obstacles in the way of local employment, but in eastern Europe physical force was the norm. Seven million foreign workers had been transferred to German factories by 1944, not more than 200,000 of them as volunteers, and foreign resources in the same year supplied some 20%–25% of the rations consumed by German civilians.

Although the system was effective in terms of quantity, it had its drawbacks. Forced labour was bound to be unreliable, especially in more skilled jobs, and the system provided tremendous problems for a transport network also committed to supplying troops on several fronts. As the historian Norman Rich points out, in *Hitler's War Aims* (1974), the two tasks of the occupation administrations frequently clashed with each other, when the military advantages of a friendly local population were sacrificed to the economic and ideological demands for suppression and exploitation.

Terror was a standard feature of the 'new order'. Sometimes it was deliberately applied as a matter of policy, as by the special SS squads (*Einsatzgruppen*) whose specific task in some eastern areas was to purge undesirable groups. The 33,000 Jews murdered at Babi Yar in the Ukraine (September 1941) were some of the victims of these groups. Sometimes atrocities were a means of reprisal following local opposition or resistance. Proclaiming that 'wars are not won by the methods of the Salvation Army', Hitler fully approved of General Keitel's 'Night and Mist' (*Nacht und Nebel*) order (December 1941) which prescribed death as the automatic punishment for any act of sabotage or resistance, and advised **summary execution**. Most occupied territories suffered some example of the German tactic of destroying whole communities, often at random, as reprisals for attacks upon German personnel. The deaths of nearly 200 innocent civilians at Lidice in Czechoslovakia (May 1942) and of 642 at Oradour sur Glane in France (July 1944) are the most notorious examples. To this list could be added Palmiry (near Warsaw), Televaag (Norway), Boves (Italy) and Putten (Netherlands).

'Redskins': A derogatory term used in America to refer to native Americans. In other words, Hitler planned to place the native populations in these areas upon 'reservations', as Americans had done with 'Red Indians', while German immigrants enjoyed the best resources.

Fritz Sauckel (1894–1946)
An adherent to Nazism, Sauckel held high administrative office within the movement from an early date. He was party chief in Thuringia from 1927, and subsequently administered that province as *Gauleiter* (see opposite) and as Governor (*Reichstatthalter*) 1933–45. In March 1942, Sauckel was given overall responsibility for the recruitment of foreign labour to serve the German economy. For his role in the exploitation of forced labour, he was tried at Nuremberg and executed.

Summary execution: Execution carried out on the spot, without any legal process.

How and why did politicians in the occupied territories collaborate with the Nazis?

Resistance to this Nazi 'new order', especially in the first two years of the war, remained the prerogative of a brave, but small, minority. The apparent finality of the German victories up to the end of 1941 made it seem that the main problem of the conquered was how to live with the conquerors. In general, as the historian Norman Rich concludes, 'the response of the European peoples to Nazi dominion reflects an instinct of people everywhere to cling to life and to seek physical and economic security for themselves and their families'.

Collaboration was especially evident in France where Pierre Laval, Foreign Minister from October 1940 and Prime Minister from April 1942, showed particular enthusiasm for co-operation with Germany. Although this made him the special butt of allied propaganda and led to his execution in 1945, Laval's fault was an inability to appreciate the international extent of the conflict, rather than any true sympathy with Nazi aims. Laval's motives were, indeed, simple. They were to save France from the fate of Poland, from dismemberment and disintegration. To do this it was necessary to co-operate with the new masters of Europe. Others had more positive motives, springing from an actual sympathy with the aims of Nazism, sometimes anti-semitic, sometimes anti-British, often anti-Communist. Thirdly, many collaborated simply because the Germans were the winners, with the money, the resources, business contracts and influence that people still sought in war as in peace.

France provided a rare example of an established government, staffed by credible, pre-war politicians, collaborating enthusiastically with the Germans. Yet western Europe provided many other examples of 'puppet' administrations and national Fascist bodies willing to co-operate for opportunist or ideological reasons. The Netherlands had a Nazi party, under A.A. Mussert, which claimed a membership of 50,000 during the war. Belgium had its Flemish nationalists under Staf de Clercq, who saw collaboration with the Germans as a means of breaking the power of the French-speaking **Walloons**. Not to be outdone, the Walloons produced enthusiastic collaborators of their own, in the form of the Rexist movement, led by Leon Degrelle. In Norway, the government of Vidkun Quisling, whose name gave a new word to the English language to describe such collaborators, enthusiastically supported the ideology of Nazism, but generally failed to convince the Norwegian people of its value. In all of these cases, the relationship with Germany ended in frustration as it became clear that Hitler sought, not ideological support, but unconditional domination.

Collaboration in eastern Europe

If open collaboration was rarer in eastern Europe, it was because Nazi theory generally forbade co-operation with the 'sub-human' Slavs. Some such co-operation, however, still existed. Even in the USSR racial minorities such as Tartars and Chechens sought German aid against Soviet oppression, and a Russian Liberation Army under General A.A. Vlasov numbered 50,000 men by the end of the war. Similarly, the anti-communist attitudes of Dmitri Mihailovic and his Chetnik force, and of Ante Pavelic in Yugoslavia offered possibilities for the German and Italian occupiers, which were generally thrown away because of the brutal and callous attitudes of Nazism towards the Slavs.

What did collaboration achieve?

The benefits of collaboration varied from case to case. In France, Laval's

---

Collaboration: The act of working with the enemy army or government which has taken control of your country by force. The collaborators give help to the enemy.

Walloons: The term used to describe the French-speaking natives of the Walloon provinces of Belgium.

Vidkun Quisling (1887–1945)
Leader from 1933 of the Norwegian Fascist Party. He aided the Nazis invasion of Norway in 1940 by delaying mobilisation of troops and by urging non-resistance. Quisling was made premier by Hitler (1942), but was arrested and shot as a traitor by the Norwegians three years later. His name (Quisling) became a generic term in the English language for a traitor who aids an occupying force.

Milice: A French paramilitary force that combated the resistance and attempted to maintain domestic stability in the last years of the occupation.

1. What were the main aims of the Nazi 'new order' (a) as portrayed in German propaganda and (b) in reality?

2. How effectively was the German war effort served by the Nazi authorities in the occupied territories?

3. Who benefited most from policies of collaboration, the Nazis or the populations of the territories that they occupied?

policy bore little fruit. It did not greatly hasten the return of prisoners-of-war, did not prevent a 50% rise in the mortality rate due largely to cases of malnutrition, and did not save France from total occupation when German interests demanded it (November 1942). On the other hand, it served the Germans well:

- 37% of all German materials and finances from foreign sources came from France, and tanks and army trucks rolled off the production lines of Renault and Berliet.

- 45,000 Frenchmen joined the *Milice*.

Elsewhere, the results were sometimes better. Slovakia was spared a German occupation by the co-operation of Joseph Tiso's government, while Admiral Horthy ensured that Hungary escaped lightly. Denmark succeeded in preserving its monarchy, part of its army, and even most of its Jews, all 7,000 of whom were smuggled into neutral Sweden. In short, it was sometimes possible after the war to justify collaboration in terms of short-term local successes. In the wider context of Nazi inhumanity, the policy was always much harder to justify.

12.6 Why did the Nazis pursue a 'Final Solution to the Jewish Question' in the war years?

'Final Solution' (*Endlösung*): This was the euphemism (polite expression) employed in German administration to describe the strategy of mass genocide by which German Jews and those in territories under German occupation would be systematically murdered in concentration camps or elsewhere. The implementation of this strategy is now more commonly referred to as 'the Holocaust'.

The prelude to the 'final solution'

The unprecedented domination that the Nazis enjoyed over the continent of Europe also provided them with the opportunity to implement the obsessive anti-semitism that was a prominent principle of their movement. Like his foreign policy, Hitler's anti-semitism was a mixture of unswerving principle and uncertain means. For all his hostility towards them, Hitler had little clear idea in 1939 what he intended to do with the Jews. The most likely official plan was that which called for the shipment of European Jews to the island of Madagascar in the Indian Ocean, which would be demanded from France for that purpose after that nation's defeat. The first two years of warfare, however, caused the rethinking of this plan. Firstly, although France was defeated, the continuing hostility of Britain made regular sea access to Madagascar difficult. Secondly, the fall of Poland enlarged the Jewish 'problem' dramatically. Whereas the Reich in 1939 had a Jewish population of about 357,000, the large number of Polish Jews meant that there were ten times that number in the Greater Reich in 1940. Between the invasion of Poland and that of the Soviet Union, concentration camps – not exclusively for Jews, but also for Poles, communists, gypsies, and others – were established in Poland at Auschwitz, Chelmno, Treblinka, Sobibor and Belsen. Even so, it was not until 1941, when continued Soviet resistance ruled out the interim plan of dumping the Jews in Siberia, that it was officially resolved that the 'final solution to the Jewish question' was to consist of wholesale and systematic extermination.

The scale of the 'final solution'

Between 1941 and 1944, technological refinements – such as the special Cyclon-B gas and specially designed ovens for incineration – allowed the 'final solution' to proceed with awful efficiency. Chelmno, with 1,000 victims a day in late 1941, was outrun by Treblinka, which managed up to 6,000 a day at its peak, while Auschwitz was responsible for the murder of some three million people in the course of three years.

The German government declared in November 1943, although it was not entirely correct, that there were no Jews left in the Greater Reich. By the end of the war, 50% of Belgian Jews, 66% of Romanian Jews and 75% of the Dutch community were dead. The best records for the protection of Jews were those of Denmark and of France, although in the latter case the government only preserved the lives of French Jews by assisting the capture and deportation of those who were not French citizens. Lucy Dawidowicz, in *The War Against the Jews, 1933–1945* (1990), has settled upon a figure of 5.93 million as the final toll of Jewish victims, estimating that it embraces 67% of occupied Europe's pre-war Jewish population. Nor should it be forgotten that some three million non-Jews, mainly Slavs and political opponents of Nazism, also died in extermination camps. These camps were responsible for the destruction, in the most horrible circumstances, of some 7.5 million human lives. Such is the monument to the 'new order' of Nazism.

The 'final solution' in the context of the war

1. What was Hitler's 'final solution' to the 'Jewish problem'?

2. How effective was the Nazis' implementation of the 'final solution'?

The insane intensity of this anti-semitism is illustrated by the fact that, while locked in an increasingly unsuccessful war, the German government still saw fit to devote substantial resources of manpower, communications and technology to this horrible task. In the midst of the eastern campaigns in 1942, trainloads of Jews from France, Belgium and the Netherlands were being shipped the length of Europe to the eastern camps. In 1943 and 1944, the SS was still expanding its programme to deal with Greek and Hungarian Jews. Only in October 1944, with the Red Army threatening to overrun the camps, did Himmler give the order for them to cease their dreadful routine.

12.7 Did the resistance movements in occupied Europe play any significant role in the defeat of Nazi Germany?
A CASE STUDY IN HISTORICAL INTERPRETATION

The German victories in the early stages of the war seemed to be so definitive that resistance to the Nazi 'new order' appeared useless. Only a small, but highly honourable minority chose to resist. Writing of the French resistance movements after 1941, in *France 1940–55* (1957), Alexander Werth identified simple national pride as the basis of other motives:

> 'they resisted because it was a matter of ordinary self respect to do so. They were unwilling to accept that while London was "taking it", or that while the Red Army was fighting the Battle of Stalingrad, France was doing nothing.'

Secondly, the brutality of German policy in the occupied territories convinced many of the need for resistance. This was especially true in the eastern territories, where the recruitment of forced labour made resistance the surer means towards survival. In France, too, it was the recruitment of labour that drove many young men into the countryside, where their groups took their names from the shrub-like bushes (*maquis*) that gave them shelter.

The entry into the war of the Soviet Union also stimulated resistance, setting the Communist parties of the occupied countries, previously nonplussed by the Russo–German Pact of 1939, in opposition to the invaders. In September 1941, General Keitel, as Chief of Staff, ordered that all acts of resistance or sabotage should be ascribed to Communists and that batches of alleged Communists should be executed as reprisals. Communists thus had little to lose by active resistance.

How effective was this resistance?

In many countries at the end of the war, national commentators attached great importance to the role that resistance had played in the defeat of Nazism. The official history of the French resistance movements ran to four volumes, and the title of the relevant volume in Henri Amouroux's comprehensive history of the occupation (*History of the French under the Occupation*, 1979), 'The People Awake', summarises the image that such writers wished to convey. Historians surveying the part played by resistance movements in the allied victory as a whole have generally been less impressed. Alan Milward, in *The German Economy at War* (1965), puts forward the view that in no case did a resistance movement seriously defeat German military intentions. The crushing of the Warsaw Rising (August 1944) and the heavy losses of the French resistance at Vercors (June 1944) showed the relative impotence of resistance forces when not backed by allied troops. The assassination of Reinhard Heydrich, 'Protector' of Bohemia and Moravia, was paid for with 1,500 Czech lives and the destruction of the villages of Lidice and Lezaky. The price exacted by the Germans in reprisals leads Alan Milward to his conclusion that resistance 'seems to have been seldom effective, sometimes stultifying, frequently dangerous, and almost always too costly'. Referring to France in particular, the historian John Keegan in *The Battle for History: Re-fighting the Second World War* (1995) reaches similar conclusions, stating that the resistance movement was 'a nuisance rather than an impediment to German operations'.

The impact of resistance must, in any case, be measured against the benefits that the occupiers gained from economic collaboration. Of all French exports, 82% went to Germany in 1943, and 84% of all Dutch exports. The expansion of the German army in the years of 'total war' would have been impossible without the industrial labour that was recruited from the occupied states. By 1944, this amounted to seven million workers, roughly 20% of the total labour force within Germany. In 1944, 10% of the French adult male population between 18 and 50 years of age was thus employed in Germany. It is impossible to resist the conclusion, therefore, that the support that the German war effort gained from the occupied territories of western Europe far outweighed any damage that the resistance movements could do to it.

It is important, however, to distinguish between the slight effect of resistance in western Europe, and the very different role that it played in eastern Europe. There, in John Keegan's words, 'it caused the occupiers considerable trouble, ranging in scale from chronic insecurity to outright civil war'. Although this can be explained in large part by the savage racial attitudes that the Nazis adopted towards local populations in the east, Keegan also links it to historical traditions of peasant opposition to national governments and, in the Balkans, to long traditions of local opposition to Turkish rule. In Greece and in Yugoslavia, resistance amounted effectively to lesser wars within the greater war. In Yugoslavia,

Partisan movement: An official organisation, made up of armed fighters, that is formed in a country occupied by enemy soldiers. The intention of the movement is to disrupt the occupying force as much as possible, usually by fighting.

Tito's **partisan movement** fought not only against the Germans, but equally against domestic elements, such as Bosnian Muslims, who viewed German occupation as a means of escaping Serbian domination. Thus the struggle against the Germans and their supporters effectively made Yugoslavia ungovernable, but at an enormous price. The war years probably claimed as many as 1.6 million lives, about 10% of the pre-war population. Similarly, in the Soviet Union, partisan groups played an important role in areas under German occupation. By mid-1942 there were an estimated 150,000 partisan fighters operating behind German lines in the Soviet Union, disrupting communications and tying down large numbers of regular troops.

In both western and eastern Europe, resistance groups achieved their greatest military impact when the German war effort was weakening and they could co-operate directly with advancing allied forces. In the west, resistance actions delayed and weakened important German units moving to combat the Normandy landings. The French FFI (*Forces Françaises de l'Interieur*) also played a significant role in the liberation of several French cities and in the final thrust into Germany. Sixty thousand Czech partisans fought with the Soviet Army, and local partisan forces played a major part in the liberation of Belgrade, and of many of the cities of northern Italy.

If it is difficult to argue that local resistance fighters changed the course of the war in general, it is possible to detect cases in which local initiatives did much to obstruct specific elements of Nazi policy. A prime example is that of Denmark. Overall, that country was controlled quite comfortably by the Nazis, and its political life showed a remarkable degree of continuity. When the occupying authorities attempted to implement the 'final solution', however, it received no co-operation from the Danes. In *The Rescue of the Danish Jews: Moral Courage under Stress* (1987), historian Leo Goldberger has shown how the entire Danish Jewish community was smuggled to safety in neutral Sweden. In the military context of the war, the Norwegian resistance also made an extremely important contribution through its co-operation with British intelligence agents to deny Germany the supplies that it needed to advance its atomic programme.

Most forms of non-violent resistance were of largely local significance. Norway provided a fine example of passive resistance when its bishops and high court judges resigned *en masse*. The dissemination of war news and propaganda was another important, but more dangerous, function. In Belgium alone some 300 illegal journals were published, and over 1,000 such papers appeared in France between 1940 and 1944. Belgium was also the centre of a complex network of groups specialising in the sheltering of allied airmen shot down over Europe, and in smuggling them back to home bases. Similar networks in Poland and in Czechoslovakia did valuable work by providing intelligence on German troop movements to allied forces. Considering such examples as these, the historian M.R.D. Foot in *Resistance* (1978) draws the important conclusion that 'the greatest good that resistance did lay in the hearts of the people who took part in it'. The greatest contribution of resistance lay not so much in what it achieved during the war, as in the contribution that it made after the war to the re-establishment of national self-confidence and self-respect. This was particularly true in France, where the traumatic shock of defeat and occupation had been devastating, and where its scars still exist.

1. What different conclusions have historians drawn about the importance of resistance movements during the Second World War?

2. In what respects, and for what reasons, have historians disagreed about the importance of resistance movements in the history of the Second World War as a whole?

Source-based questions: Collaboration in France during the Second World War

Study the following source material and then answer the questions which follow.

SOURCE A

From Marshal Pétain's radio broadcast to the French people, 30 October 1940. Pétain was the leader of the Vichy government in France 1940–42.

It is with honour and to maintain ten centuries of French unity within the context of the new European order that I enter today upon the path of collaboration. This collaboration must be sincere. It must involve patient and confident effort. The present armistice is not a peace settlement. France is bound by many obligations with regard to her conqueror, but at least she retains her sovereignty.

SOURCE B

From a speech by Pierre Laval, Prime Minister of the Vichy government, 22 June 1942

My desire is to re-establish normal and trusting relations with Germany and with Italy. A new Europe will inevitably arise from this war, and I wish for a German victory because, without it, Bolshevism will establish itself everywhere. When I say that this policy is the only one that can ensure the status of France and guarantee her development in the peace to come, you must believe me and follow me. This war is a revolution from which a new world will spring. A younger Republic, stronger and more humane, will be born.

SOURCE C

Adolf Hitler explains to Mussolini his policy towards France, 18 June 1940.

As far as the case of France is concerned, the main point is to ensure that a French government continues to function on French soil. This will be much preferable to the situation that would arise if the French government refused to accept German terms, and fled abroad, to London, to continue the war. Apart from the problems that would arise with regard to the administration of the occupied territory, an understanding with the French government would be equally advantageous because of the French fleet. If that fleet were placed at the disposition of the British, in some categories of ships, British naval strength would be doubled.

(a) Use Source A and your own knowledge.

Explain briefly why Pétain refers to a 'new order' in European affairs. [3 marks]

(b) Use Sources A and B and your own knowledge.

Explain how the motives for collaboration with Germany expressed in Source B differ from those expressed in Source A. [7 marks]

(c) Use Sources A, B and C and your own knowledge.

How far does your knowledge of wartime collaboration, and the evidence contained in these sources, support the view that the Nazi regime always gained more from collaboration than the governments that collaborated with it? [15 marks]

Source-based questions: The Holocaust

Study the following four passages and answer both of the sub-questions which follow.

SOURCE A

An order signed by Herman Goering and dispatched to senior SS officers in July 1941

To supplement the task that was assigned to you on 24 January 1939, which dealt with the solution of the Jewish problem by emigration and evacuation in the most suitable way: I hereby charge you with making all necessary preparations with regard to organisational, technical and material matters for bringing about a complete solution of the Jewish question within the German sphere of influence in Europe. Whatever other government agencies are involved, these are to co-operate with you. I request you further to send me, in the near future, an overall plan covering the organisational, technical and material measures necessary for the accomplishment of the final solution of the Jewish question, which we desire.

SOURCE B

From Martin Broszat, The Hitler State, *published in 1981. This historian argues that the 'Final Solution' was an escalation of earlier German anti-semitic policies, and separate from them.*

The criminal mass destruction of the Jews must not be seen simply as the continuation of the legal discrimination against the Jews after 1933. Procedurally this was in fact a break with former practices and in that respect had a different quality. All the same, the previous laws and decrees which step by step had further discriminated against the Jews in Germany, had subjected them to emergency laws and had condemned them to a social ghetto, paved the way for the 'Final Solution'.

SOURCE C

From Lucy Dawidowicz, The War against the Jews 1933–45, *published in 1975. This historian argues that violent anti-semitism was always central to Nazi policy and that the 'Final Solution' was its logical culmination.*

Anti-semitism was the core of Hitler's system of beliefs and the central motivation of his policies. He believed himself to be the saviour who would bring redemption to the German people through the annihilation of the Jews, the people who embodied, in his eyes, the Satanic hosts. From the moment he made his entrance upon the historical stage until his death in a Berlin bunker, the sense of messianic mission never departed from him, nor could any appeal to reason deflect him from pursuing his murderous purpose.

SOURCE D

From David Goldhagen, Hitler's Willing Executioners, *published in 1996. This historian argues that the Holocaust was always the intended outcome of Hitler's anti-semitic philosophy, and that it was only delayed because Germany lacked the practical means to implement it.*

The genocide was the outgrowth not of Hitler's moods, not of local initiatives, not of the impersonal hand of structural obstacles, but of Hitler's idea to eliminate all Jewish power, an idea that was broadly shared in Germany. Rarely has a national leader so openly, frequently and emphatically announced an apocalyptic intention – in this case, to destroy Jewish power and even the Jews themselves – and made good on his promise. It is almost inexplicable that interpreters today could construe Hitler's oft stated intention to destroy the Jews to have been meant but metaphorically, or to have been but meaningless verbiage. The will to kill the Jews was not infused into Hitler and his followers by external conditions. Racial anti-semitism was the motive force of the eliminationist programme, pushing it to its logical genocidal conclusion once German military prowess succeeded in creating appropriate conditions.

(a) Compare the conclusions reached in passages B and D about the degree of continuity that existed in Nazi anti-semitic policy.   [15 marks]

(b) Using these four passages and your own knowledge, explain how and why historians disagree about the development of the Final Solution in Nazi anti-semitic policy.   [30 marks]

12.8 Why did the Axis collapse in 1944–1945?

The assault on Italy and the collapse of the Fascist government

The clearance of German and Italian troops from North Africa by combined British and American forces by May 1943 left the southern flank of Fascist Europe exposed. The daunting task of renewing the offensive against 'Fortress Europe' began (10 July 1943) with an allied assault upon Sicily, at the southern tip of Italy. It was not strongly resisted by the Axis forces and within six weeks the island was in allied hands. The decision to proceed from Sicily to the Italian mainland was unpopular with Stalin, who preferred an attack upon German forces in France, to relieve pressure upon the Soviet Union. However, it was based upon sound strategic sense. Italy was clearly the weakest point of the Axis, and by its elimination from the war the Mediterranean could be secured, and bases could be won for a future assault upon Germany.

The capture of Sicily caused the final crisis for the Italian Fascist government and transformed Italy's position in the war. Having joined Hitler's war effort when success seemed certain, Mussolini now faced an invasion of Italian territory, deprived of the services of 200,000 troops killed or captured in North Africa, and of a further million committed to distant theatres of war. Resistance to the allies could only be maintained by turning the country over to the Germans, clearly a terrible price to pay, and a rejection of all that Fascist nationalism stood for. Mussolini's failure to extricate himself from the disastrous German alliance caused the collapse of his political position which was wrecked by strikes and demonstrations, by the withdrawal of the support of the Fascist Grand Council (24 July 1943), and by his dismissal as Prime Minister by the King (25 July). Briefly, the Fascist government survived under the leadership of Marshal Badoglio. He had two primary aims: to maintain the credibility of Fascism, and to lead Italy into the allied camp without substantial German reprisals. On both counts he failed. While anti-Fascist partisan forces reduced parts of Italy to a state of civil war, and Italian forces disintegrated in the confusion, the German High Command took the decision to defend as much of the country as possible from the allied forces now on the mainland (9 September 1943).

Defending first the Gustav Line, midway between Naples and Rome, then the Gothic Line 190 kilometres further north, the *Wehrmacht* ensured that the allies would have to fight for every metre of Italian soil. Mussolini, sensationally rescued from imprisonment and installed as head of the 'Italian Social Republic' in the north, found himself reduced to the 'puppet' status of many of Germany's would-be allies. It was perhaps the logical outcome of his 'savage friendship' with Hitler. Rome was not occupied by the allies until 4 June 1944, and German troops continued to resist in Milan and other northern cities long after allied troops had crossed the Rhine.

The price paid by the allies for the 18 months of warfare in Italy was high, but for Italy itself that period constituted the final disaster of Fascism. A further 100,000 Italians died in military action, and bombing raids caused great damage to the cultural heritage of the nation. The destruction of the Benedictine monastery of Monte Cassino was only the worst example of many. Inflation and the **cost-of-living index** soared, the latter from a base of 100 in 1938 to 5,313 in October 1947. On top of this came political collapse. Badoglio's government disintegrated in June 1944 and King Victor Emmanuel III abdicated in May 1946. Forty-three days later a referendum in favour of a republic ended 85 years of Italian monarchy. Mussolini did not live to see all this. Captured by partisans as

Cost-of-living index: A list of the prices charged for goods and services. It is updated on a regular basis and shows how much prices are rising or falling.

he tried to flee into Switzerland, he was shot without trial, and his body hanged from a meat hook in a Milan square (28–29 April 1945).

The Western Front

By the beginning of 1944 British and American commanders were able to concentrate men and materials for their greatest undertaking, the re-invasion of France. The technical difficulties facing 'Operation Overlord' were enormous, including the laying of oil pipelines across the Channel, and the designing of artificial 'Mulberry' harbours to provide anchorages for subsequent supply ships. German hopes of resisting the invasion depended entirely on checking it on the landing beaches. That the High Command failed to do so owed much to the element of surprise, for they had judged an invasion more likely in the region of Calais, rather than in Normandy, and much to the enormous air superiority of the allies.

On D-Day (6 July 1944), the allies began to land 326,000 men along an 80-kilometre stretch of beach. Within a month, a million men had landed, suffering only 9,000 fatal casualties. Stiff German resistance around Caen and Falaise could not be sustained after a further American landing in the south (15 August). The collapse of German control in France was subsequently rapid. Paris was liberated, appropriately by Free French forces, on 24 August. Brussels and Antwerp were freed in the first week of September. By the onset of autumn, German forces were manning the defences of the Siegfried Line on their own frontiers.

The German war effort, however, was not quite exhausted. Contemporary historian Sir Basil Liddell Hart has stressed the decision of the allies to demand unconditional surrender, and the importance of this decision in encouraging last-ditch German resistance. In the last days of 1944 the *Wehrmacht* enjoyed its last successes on the Western Front. It defeated an allied attempt to outflank the Siegfried Line at Arnhem (17–24 September), and temporarily regained ground in the Ardennes by the counter-attack known as the 'Battle of the Bulge' (16 December 1944 – 13 January 1945). The first months of 1945, however, saw its steady disintegration. The *Wehrmacht* had to make good its losses by the conscription of raw teenagers, fuel supplies were on the brink of exhaustion, and the *Luftwaffe* had finally lost the struggle for air supremacy. Brilliant new weapons, such as the Messerschmitt 262 jet fighter and the V1 and V2 rockets, came too late to save the Reich.

The last stages of the German collapse

The surviving German units proved quite insufficient to prevent an allied crossing of the Rhine (7–23 March 1945). Thereafter the main cities of Germany fell regularly to the advancing allied forces until advanced American units made contact with the Soviet army at Torgau in Saxony (25 April 1945). Hitler's vision of a defeated Germany destroying itself in a Wagnerian 'Twilight of the Gods' came to nothing. Civilian morale was severely strained by the 'Thousand Bomber' raids on Dresden (13–14 February). Also the planned yard-by-yard resistance of the German 'Home Guard' (*Volkssturm*) failed to materialise, and local and central officials at last showed open defiance of Hitler's will by disobeying orders to destroy strategic buildings and important industrial plant.

1. Even if it were not dated, what elements in the cartoon indicate that it was published in the latter stages of the war?

2. Why would the Soviet government have been unlikely to publish this form of anti-German propaganda in 1941 or 1942?

A Soviet cartoon published in 1944. The original caption read: 'The general from the Eastern Front seeks orders, and the Führer deliberates.'

The Eastern Front

The rapid allied successes in the west owed much to the heavy German commitment on the Russian front. There, the campaigns of 1943 continued to be fought deep into Soviet territory, but with the Soviet army steadily developing numerical and technical superiority. A German counter-attack at Kharkov (February 1943) achieved considerable success, but could not be sustained, and an attempt to drive back Soviet forces at Kursk (July 1943) was thwarted in the biggest tank battle of the war. In the south, the Soviet army's own counter-attacks after the Battle of Kursk drove the German forces back to the river Dnieper and cut off those units occupying the Crimea.

In 1944 it was the turn of the northern units of the *Wehrmacht* to feel the weight of the Soviet offensive. In 1943 they had held a defensive line from Orel to Leningrad relatively comfortably, an illustration of the error of Hitler's offensive strategy in the south. Now, a series of massive Soviet campaigns finally broke the encirclement of Leningrad (January 1944), re-occupied Minsk in White Russia (July), and drove into Poland and the Baltic territories (August), capturing 30 German divisions in the process. Then offensives in the south cleared Soviet soil of German troops and caused the surrender of Germany's Romanian (August) and Bulgarian (September) allies.

The Soviet thrust into Germany

In the east, as in the west, the beginning of 1945 saw allied troops poised for the final thrust into the Greater German Reich. Although more heavily manned and equipped on the Eastern Front, Germany was similarly in no shape to resist. Hitler himself was now ravaged by nervous disease. As historian Alan Bullock describes him, in *Hitler: A Study in Tyranny* (1962), 'his orders became wilder and more contradictory, his demands more impossible, his decisions more arbitrary. His answer to every proposal was: no withdrawal.' In addition, Hitler had shattered his own High Command, dismissing such able generals as Erich von Manstein and Gerd von Rundstedt for their failures to carry out impossible tasks. Gunther von Kluge and Erwin Rommel had both committed suicide when their roles in a plot to murder Hitler and set the war upon a sounder footing (July 1944) were discovered.

The final assault, by four armies on a front from the Baltic to the Carpathian mountains, made rapid progress. In March, Soviet forces crossed the Oder river, driving beyond Berlin to ensure that it was their forces, and not those of their allies, that occupied the German capital. Although he has been criticised for it since, the commander of the western forces, General Eisenhower, kept strictly to the spheres of influence agreed by the political leaders and there was no race for Berlin.

The week from 30 April to 7 May 1945 witnessed the last days of the Third Reich. Raging against the incompetence of his generals, and repeating his doctrines of anti-semitism and of the German need for *Lebensraum*, Hitler killed himself on 30 April and had his body burned to ensure that it could not be treated as that of Mussolini had been. On 7 May, after several unsuccessful attempts to negotiate separate peace treaties and so to divide the allies, the German government ended the war in Europe by surrendering unconditionally to the combined allied forces.

1. What were the main military blows that the allies struck at German control of mainland Europe between 1943 and 1945?

2. To what extent do you agree with the claim that 'the success of the D-Day landings was the crucial factor in the defeat of Germany'?

12.9 What plans had the allies made for a peace settlement?

Although Germany and its allies entered the war with complex but quite well defined aims, its opponents, especially Britain and the Soviet Union, fought originally for no other reason than that war was forced upon them by German aggression. At first, their war aims were simple and largely negative; to survive, and to destroy Nazism as a means to survival.

Only in 1942 did it become practical to consider in detail the settlement that the allies should pursue in the event of their victory. In the diplomatic discussions that followed, three main European issues were at stake:

● the treatment of Germany after its defeat

● the fate of eastern European states

● the means of ensuring future stability.

General principles 'for common action to preserve peace and resist aggression in the post-war period' had been laid down in an Anglo–Russian treaty of May 1942, and by British agreements with America. Only in November 1943 did the allied leaders, Churchill, Roosevelt and Stalin, meet at Teheran in Iran, to define details. Although the Teheran meeting was preoccupied with military strategy against Germany, it contained the seeds of the post-war settlement and gave early indications of Soviet ambitions. Roosevelt suggested that post-war Germany be divided into five sectors, with its industrial heartlands of the Ruhr, the Saar, Hamburg and the Kiel Canal placed under international control. Stalin, determined that the Soviet Union would no longer be threatened by the instability of its immediate European neighbours, produced a 'shopping list'. This list stipulated future Soviet influence in East Prussia, and in most of those territories gained as a result of the 1939 pact with Germany.

The next meeting of the allied leaders was over a year later, at Yalta in the Crimea (4 February 1945). By then, German resistance was on the verge of collapse, and much of eastern Europe was in the hands of the Soviet Army. Roosevelt and Churchill have since incurred criticism for their apparent acquiescence in the establishment of a substantial Soviet sphere of influence, but practical circumstances left them with little choice. Only by force could eastern Europe be wrested from Soviet control, and even then it seems unlikely that forceful tactics could have succeeded.

Thus, Stalin emerged from Yalta with confirmation of his dominance in Romania, Bulgaria, Hungary and Poland. There was to be a lesser degree of Soviet influence in Yugoslavia, and none in Greece, because the Mediterranean location of those states made them as much subject to Anglo–American sea power as to Soviet land power. In return for this agreement, to which the Soviet Union stuck closely, Stalin agreed wholesale to American proposals for a four-zone occupation of Germany, with a zone allocated to the French, and for the establishment of a **United Nations organisation**. The last great **tripartite** meeting, at Potsdam (July 1945), was mainly concerned with the detailed implementation of the Yalta agreements.

The broad concept of a 'world organisation' to replace the League of Nations had arisen at Teheran, and at a separate meeting of foreign ministers in Moscow (November 1943). Its specific format was thrashed out at an inter-allied conference at Dumbarton Oaks, Washington, in August–October 1944. Among other decisions, it was agreed that the major powers sitting permanently on the central council of the organisation could employ a veto over any measure that displeased them. Between April and June 1945 delegates of 50 nations met in San Francisco to draft what has become the United Nations Charter. The decision that the seat of the United Nations Organisation should be in New York was perhaps symbolic of the fact that Europe was no longer the focal point of world politics.

United Nations organisation: Formed after the Second World War. It tries to encourage international peace, co-operation and friendship.

Tripartite: Discussions or agreements involving three people, three groups or three countries.

12.10 What were the immediate consequences of the conflict?

What was the cost of the war?

The impact of the Second World War upon the next generation of Europeans was two-fold: unparalleled physical and economic destruction, and revolutionary political change. The table below, including non-European powers for purposes of comparison, shows the enormous cost of the war.

The human losses of the USSR alone in 1941–45 were equal to the total casualty toll of the First World War, and German losses were double those of the earlier conflict. The nature of the warfare in the Second World War meant that British and French losses were lighter than in 1914–18, but the devastation of those areas that saw the bulk of the fighting exceeded all precedents. Again, the Soviet Union and Germany suffered most. In the USSR between half and three-quarters of all living quarters in the theatre of war were destroyed. In addition to its casualties, Europe faced the problem between 1939 and 1947 of some 16 million refugees rendered homeless by the fighting.

What was the political impact upon Europe?

Although the war made no such impact upon the map of Europe as the Napoleonic Wars and the First World War had done, its effect upon the political balance of the continent was revolutionary. Fascism and Nazism, proclaimed by Mussolini and Hitler as the dominant doctrines of the next millennium, vanished and have made no significant reappearance. Even more remarkable was that Germany, the central feature of the last century of European history, also vanished. When, eventually, two states emerged from the post-war chaos, both were closely tied to one of the two power blocs that now dominated world politics. The dominance that Germany had long aspired to and had briefly enjoyed now passed to the Soviet Union. Although not dominating the eastern European states in the same fashion as Germany had done, its military and economic superiority over the socialist republics that arose with Soviet assistance in Czechoslovakia, Poland, Hungary, Bulgaria and Romania, survived intact for over 40 years with only two serious challenges. Although Yugoslavia avoided such direct influence from Moscow, its socialist philosophy affiliated it to this formidable eastern bloc.

Indeed, the Soviet Union could claim to have emerged from the war, not only as the main European power, but perhaps as the only European power of world stature. European global dominance was one of the major casualties of the last great European war. The intercontinental empires of Britain, France, Italy, Belgium and the Netherlands were

Why did the USSR lose so many soldiers and Poland so many civilians during the Second World War?

Costs of the Second World War

	Probable military casualties	Probable civilian casualties	Probable cost (£ million)
USSR	13,600,000	7,700,000	23,253
Germany	3,480,000	3,890,000	53,084
Japan	1,700,000	360,000	10,317
Great Britain	452,000	60,000	12,446
Italy	330,000	85,000	5,267
USA	295,000	–	62,560
France	250,000	360,000	27,818
Poland	120,000	5,300,000	not known

racked with difficulties before 1939. The defeats of these powers, or the vast economic strain of their eventual victories, meant that the post-war history of their empires was one of steady liquidation. As a result, the whole nature of political confrontation in the world changed. It no longer centred around the economic and political ambitions of a few European states, but around the different conceptions of human freedom and democracy represented by the two great world powers – one created by refugees from Europe, the other as much Asian as European in its culture and history.

The war also contributed to the emergence of the other superpower. The enormous impact of the United States of America upon the war was matched by the impact of the war upon the USA. In 1940 a large proportion of America's economic potential remained unused, and the war played a crucial role in unleashing the full power of the world's greatest industrial economy. The nature of the confrontation between these two great powers was determined by another major product of the Second World War. The nuclear arms race dated from the dropping by the USA of the first atomic bomb on the Japanese city of Hiroshima (6 August 1945), the culmination of the increasing sophistication of weaponry during the war. In this, as in many other respects, a new era of European and world history began in 1945.

What changes did the Second World War bring about in the balance of political power in Europe?

Europe and the Cold War, 1945–1991

Key Issues

● *To what extent was the Cold War a global rather than a European problem?*

● *How did the division between East and West affect Europe during the Cold War?*

● *Why did the Cold War come to an end in 1991?*

Framework of Events

1945	(February) Yalta Conference between USSR, USA and Britain
	(May) Germany surrenders
	(July/August) Potsdam Conferences between USSR, USA and Britain
	(August) Nuclear attacks on Hiroshima and Nagasaki
1946	Churchill's Iron Curtain Speech
	Kennan's Long Telegram
1947	Truman Doctrine
	Marshall Plan
	USA takes over from Britain in Greece and Turkey
1948	Czechoslovak coup
	Berlin Airlift Crisis
1949	End of Berlin airlift; formation of West Germany and East Germany
	Creation of NATO
	USSR explodes 'A' bomb
1950	Korean War begins
1953	Stalin dies
	Ceasefire in Korea
1955	Austrian State Treaty
	West Germany joins NATO
	Warsaw Pact formed
1956	20th Party Congress of CPSU denounces Stalin
	Hungarian Uprising
	Poznan Rising in Poland
1958	Berlin Crisis begins
1961	Berlin Wall Crisis
1968	Prague Spring in Czechoslovakia
	Warsaw Pact invasion of Czechoslovakia
1972	*Détente* between USA and USSR
	SALT I treaty
1975	Helsinki Agreement
1978	John Paul II becomes Pope
1979	SALT II treaty
	Pope visits Poland

1980	Solidarity movement begins in Poland
1981	Martial Law in Poland
1985	Mikhail Gorbachev becomes Soviet leader
1988	INF Treaty between USSR and USA
1989	Velvet Revolution in Czechoslovakia
	Political change in Poland
	Berlin Wall comes down
1990	Ceauçescu overthrown in Romania
	East and West Germany unite into one country
1991	Anti-Gorbachev communist takeover prevented
	Gorbachev replaced by Boris Yeltsin
	Soviet Union collapses.

US Presidents 1945–1991

1945–1953	Harry S. Truman
1953–1961	Dwight D. Eisenhower
1961–1963	John F. Kennedy
1963–1969	Lyndon B. Johnson
1969–1974	Richard M. Nixon
1974–1977	Gerald R. Ford
1977–1981	James E.Carter
1981–1989	Ronald W. Reagan
1989–1993	George H. Bush

Chancellors of West Germany, 1949–1998

1949–1963	Konrad Adenauer (Christian Democrat)
1963–1966	Ludwig Erhard (Christian Democrat)
1966–1969	Kurt Kiesinger (Christian Democrat)
1969–1974	Willi Brandt (Social Democrat)
1974–1982	Helmut Schmidt (Social Democrat)
1982–1998	Helmut Kohl (Christian Democrat)

Soviet leaders 1945–1991

1945–1953	Joseph Stalin
1953–1955	Georgi Malenkov
1955–1958	Nikolai Bulganin and Nikita Khrushchev
1958–1964	Nikita Khrushchev
1964–1968	Alexander Kosygin and Leonid Brezhnev
1968–1982	Leonid Brezhnev
1982–1984	Yuri Andropov
1984–1985	Konstantin Chernenko
1985–1991	Mikhail Gorbachev

Dresden in ruins, 1945

Overview

Bi-polar: Division of the world into two major power blocs.

FOR nearly 45 years after the Second World War Europe was divided by the Cold War. In the **bi-polar** world of the two superpowers, the USSR and the USA, Europe was one of the most important areas of political and military tension.

The Cold War describes the period of tension between the USSR and the USA. It began in 1945, although tension between the two powers had existed since the Bolshevik Revolution of 1917. The Cold War involved conflict short of direct war between the two superpowers. It saw both sides constantly prepared for war. This situation was supported by a propaganda war where each side adopted a strong ideological position. The USA regarded itself as leader of the Free World against godless Communism. The USSR was the leader of the socialist world against a capitalist system that exploited the world. Spying and **economic warfare** were part of the conflict. The Cold War was not limited to Europe. Following the Communist victory in the Chinese Civil War, in 1949, it spread to Asia. The two most serious military conflicts during the Cold War occurred in Asia: the Korean War 1950–53 and the Vietnam War 1946–75. Furthermore, both the USA and the USSR attempted to 'win over' the newly independent countries of Africa and Asia. This involved conflicts in the Middle East and Africa.

Economic warfare: Using trade and the world economy to undermine the opposition. It could involve placing tariffs (taxes) on opponents' goods, banning trade with, or buying goods from, the opposition.

Why a Cold War developed between two wartime allies is still a matter of historical debate. However, in the years 1945–49 Europe was divided between the two sides. By 1949 Europe was clearly divided into communist and non-communist sectors. In eastern Europe the USSR established communist regimes which owed allegiance to Moscow. Throughout the period 1949–1980, the USSR faced challenges to its control of eastern Europe. This ranged from anti-communist riots in East Berlin (1953) to full-scale revolution in Hungary (1956). By 1989 opposition to communist control of eastern Europe was so widespread that all the Soviet **satellite states** disappeared in a matter of months.

Satellite states: Countries which are under the influence of a larger and more powerful neighbouring country.

The Cold War's front line was Germany. Since 1945 Germany had been divided into military zones of occupation. Throughout the period Germany remained under military occupation. Within Germany Berlin epitomised the conflict between East and West. In 1961 all-out nuclear war seemed possible as a result of the erection of the Berlin Wall. Up to 1989 the border between East and West Germany remained one of the most heavily defended in the world.

The Cold War ended during the late 1980s for a variety of reasons: the failure of the Soviet economy to match the armaments spending of the USA; the succession of Mikhail Gorbachev to the Soviet leadership. His twin policies of *Glasnost* (openness) and *Perestroika* (restructuring) undermined Soviet political control in Eastern Europe.

With remarkable suddenness the Iron Curtain which had divided Europe for over a generation had disappeared by the end of December 1989. Two years later communist rule came to an end in the USSR.

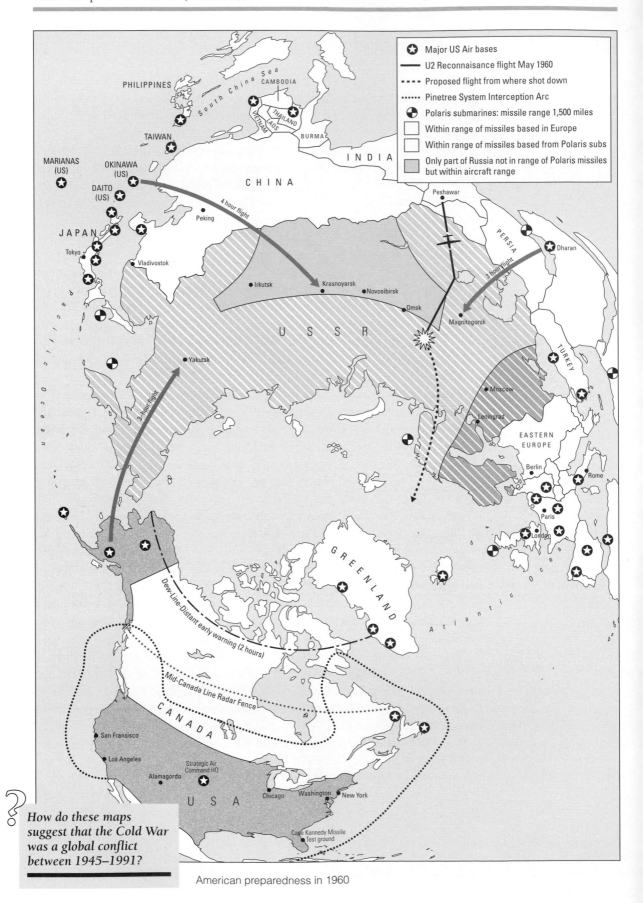

Legend

- ★ Major US Air bases
- —— U2 Reconnaisance flight May 1960
- - - - Proposed flight from where shot down
- ····· Pinetree System Interception Arc
- ◉ Polaris submarines: missile range 1,500 miles
- ☐ Within range of missiles based in Europe
- ☐ Within range of missiles based from Polaris subs
- ▨ Only part of Russia not in range of Polaris missiles but within aircraft range

Map labels: PHILIPPINES, South China Sea, CAMBODIA, VIETNAM, THAILAND, LAOS, BURMA, TAIWAN, INDIA, MARIANAS (US), OKINAWA (US), Peshawar, DAITO (US), CHINA, PERSIA, JAPAN, Peking, Dharan, Tokyo, Vladivostok, Irkutsk, Krasnoyarsk, Novosibirsk, Omsk, Magnitogorsk, U S S R, TURKEY, Yakutsk, Moscow, Leningrad, EASTERN EUROPE, Berlin, Rome, Paris, London, GREENLAND, Pacific Ocean, Atlantic Ocean, Dew-Line-Distant early warning (2 hours), Mid-Canada Line Radar Fence, CANADA, San Fransisco, Los Angeles, Strategic Air Command HQ, Alamagordo, Chicago, Washington, New York, U S A, Cape Kennedy Missile Test ground, 4 hour flight, 3-hour flight, 3 hour flight

How do these maps suggest that the Cold War was a global conflict between 1945–1991?

American preparedness in 1960

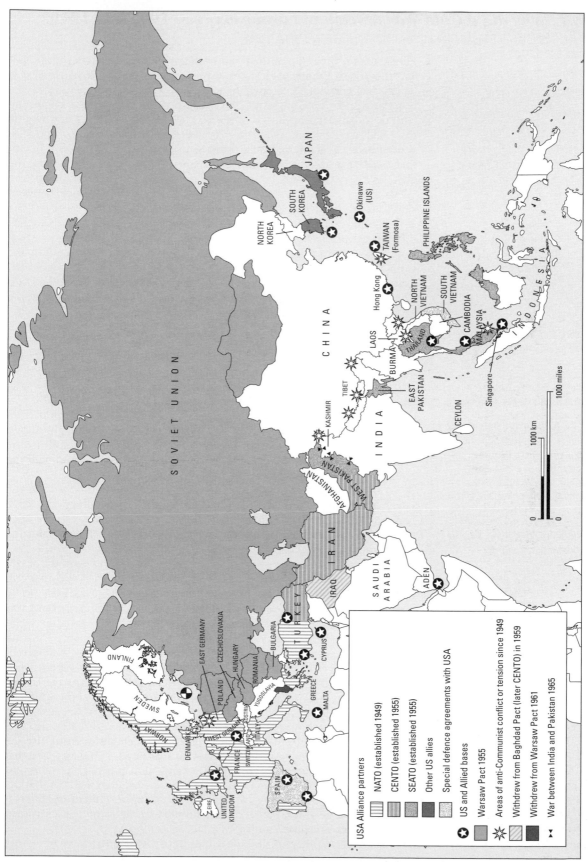

European and Asian alliances 1949–1965

USA Alliance partners
- NATO (established 1949)
- CENTO (established 1955)
- SEATO (established 1955)
- Other US allies
- Special defence agreements with USA

- US and Allied bases
- Warsaw Pact 1955
- Areas of anti-Communist conflict or tension since 1949
- Withdrew from Baghdad Pact (later CENTO) in 1959
- Withdrew from Warsaw Pact 1961
- War between India and Pakistan 1965

SOVIET UNION
FINLAND
SWEDEN
NORWAY
DENMARK
UNITED KINGDOM
EIRE
WEST GERMANY
EAST GERMANY
POLAND
CZECHOSLOVAKIA
HUNGARY
ROMANIA
BULGARIA
YUGOSLAVIA
AUSTRIA
SWITZERLAND
FRANCE
ITALY
SPAIN
GREECE
MALTA
TURKEY
CYPRUS
IRAQ
IRAN
AFGHANISTAN
WEST PAKISTAN
EAST PAKISTAN
SAUDI ARABIA
ADEN
INDIA
KASHMIR
TIBET
CEYLON
CHINA
NORTH KOREA
SOUTH KOREA
JAPAN
Okinawa (US)
TAIWAN (Formosa)
PHILIPPINE ISLANDS
Hong Kong
NORTH VIETNAM
SOUTH VIETNAM
LAOS
CAMBODIA
THAILAND
BURMA
MALAYSIA
Singapore
INDONESIA

1000 km
1000 miles

13.1 Why did a Cold War develop in Europe between 1945 and 1949?
A CASE STUDY IN HISTORICAL INTERPRETATION

Ever since the break-up of the Grand Alliance between the USA, the USSR and the British Empire took place at the end of the Second World War, a debate has taken place among historians to explain the creation of the bi-polar world. Some historians have regarded the Cold War as beginning with the Bolshevik Revolution in Russia (1917). This created a new regime that had as its programme the conversion of the whole world to communism. The international dimension of Soviet Communism meant that it was seen as a threat to non-communist states such as Britain and the USA. As a result, hostility between East and West had occurred long before 1945. In fact, the Grand Alliance was a 'marriage of convenience' between states, which had been mutually hostile to each other before 1941.

This interpretation of events places great emphasis on the ideological differences between the Soviet communist system and the western capitalist system. Both sides highlighted this difference throughout the Cold War. The USSR saw itself as the defender of the world's exploited classes against 'Big Business' in western capitalist countries like the USA. The USA, in turn, saw itself as the defender of the 'Free World' against the international ambitions of a communist dictatorship.

However, rather than seeing the origins of the Cold War as a clash of different ideologies some historians have highlighted other factors. One of these is the Soviet desire for security. By 1945 the USSR had suffered considerable human and material damage. Around 27 million Soviet citizens had died in the Second World War. In addition, a large part of the western USSR had suffered economic devastation. From 1945 Stalin was determined to prevent any further invasions of the Soviet Union from Europe. He therefore aimed to create Soviet-style regimes in neighbouring countries which would be natural allies of the USSR. As a result, in the years 1945–49 the USSR helped to establish communist regimes in all the countries under its sphere of influence in eastern Europe.

To support this, Stalin did little to support the communist side in the Greek Civil War (1945–49). He also did little to encourage the large communist parties that existed in France and Italy. Stalin is seen as a practical politician interested in protecting the USSR rather than someone who wanted to spread communism throughout Europe and the world.

Both these views have one thing in common. They both regard the Soviet Union as the main cause of the Cold War. However, from the 1960s, a group of western historians began to regard the USA as being at least partly responsible for the origins of the Cold War. This interpretation of events was given support by President Truman's recollection of the years after 1945, which were made in a series of memoirs (published in 1955–56). Truman's views were supported in *Present at the Creation* by Truman's Secretary of State, Dean Acheson. However, this 'orthodox' view was still supported in 1979 when Vojtech Mastny, in *Russia's Road to the Cold War*, saw the USSR's attempt to gain more influence in Europe as the main cause of the conflict.

American and western policy makers took this view because they interpreted Soviet actions in post-war Europe as threatening and provocative. In addition, in 1946, 'The Long Telegram' from the US ambassador in the USSR, George Kennan, to Washington DC suggested that the only way to prevent the growth of Soviet Union was openly to prevent further Soviet aggression. This view reinforced the belief in the USA that the Second World War in Europe was caused by the **appeasement** of Hitler. It became the basis of the policy of **containment** in the form of the Truman Doctrine, announced in March 1947.

The belief that the Soviet Union and, in particular, Stalin, were mainly

Harry S. Truman (1894–1972)
US President (1945–53). Possessed little knowledge of foreign affairs when he became president on Franklin Roosevelt's death in 1945. Truman was responsible for taking a hard line against Communism. He supported Churchill's **Iron Curtain speech**. It was President Truman who introduced containment policy. He stood up to the USSR over Berlin in 1948–49 but was accused by opponents of losing China to Communism by 1949.

Iron Curtain speech: Speech made by Winston Churchill at Fulton, Missouri, in 1946. It increased tension with the USSR by claiming that the eastern half of Europe was under tyranny (see opposite).

Appeasement: A policy of making concessions to a potentially hostile power in order to secure peace. Example: the 1938 Munich settlement, under which the German-speaking part of Czechoslovakia (the Sudetenland) was transferred to Hitler's Germany.

Containment: US policy for much of the Cold War. Put forward by President Truman in April 1947 as the Truman Doctrine. The aim of the policy was to limit the spread of world communism.

responsible for the breakdown of the Grand Alliance was challenged by a group of historians who offered a historical explanation different from the accepted, or orthodox, view. Known as 'revisionist historians', they believed that the USA was partly to blame for the post-1945 Cold War. In 1959 William Appleman, in *Tragedy of American Diplomacy*, was one of the first historians to claim that the USA, not the USSR, was to blame for the Cold War.

This view became popular in the 1960s as opposition to US involvement in the Vietnam War began to grow. This war ruined the USA's reputation as the defender of freedom and the opponent of **tyranny**. Two notable studies were *From Yalta to Vietnam* by David Horowitz (1967) and *The Rise to Globalism: a study of US foreign policy from 1938–1970* by Stephen Ambrose (1971).

The USA was responsible for causing the breakdown of the Grand Alliance for several reasons:

Tyranny: Cruel and unjust rule by a person or small group of people who have absolute power over everyone else in their country.

● During the presidency of Franklin D. Roosevelt, relations between the USA and USSR were kept on a reasonably friendly level. This was shown at the Yalta Conference of February 1945. However, this relationship changed when Roosevelt died in April 1945. His successor was Harry Truman. Truman had very little knowledge of foreign affairs. He also had an abrasive and direct style when dealing with representatives of the Soviet government such as Molotov, the

---

The start of the Cold War 1945–1949: who was responsible?

1945
4–12 February: Yalta Summit Conference takes place in the Crimea, in southern USSR. Stalin, Roosevelt and Churchill discuss the post-war political organisation of Europe. Roosevelt and Churchill are suspicious of Soviet plans for eastern Europe. In particular, they are concerned about the political future of Poland.

12 April: Roosevelt dies and is replaced by Vice-President Truman.

23 April: Truman confronts Molotov, Soviet Foreign Minister, over Soviet plans for eastern Europe.

17 July–2 August: Britain, the USA and USSR meet at Potsdam, Germany, in which the post-war borders of Europe are finalised. Germany and Austria are divided into four military zones of occupation. Truman informs Stalin that the USA possesses a new powerful weapon (he means the atomic bomb).

August: USA explodes 'A' bombs at Hiroshima and Nagasaki.

11 September–2 October: London Conference between USA, USSR, Britain, China and France. Major disagreements take place with USSR.

1946
5 March: Churchill makes 'Iron Curtain' speech in Fulton, Missouri, with Truman present. He criticises increased Communist controls over Soviet-occupied eastern Europe.

5 June: US plan for the control of atomic weapons (the Baruch Plan) openly criticised by USSR who dislike US monopoly over nuclear weapons technology.

10 September: Communists start civil war in Greece.

2 December: Bizonia created by joining US and British zones in Germany. USSR suspicious that the western Allies are trying to reunite Germany.

1947
12 March: Truman Doctrine announced in US Congress. US pledge aid to Greece and Turkey in their attempts to resist communism. Truman Doctrine aims to 'contain' the spread of communism in Europe and Asia.

5 June: European Recovery or Marshall Plan launched. USA to give massive economic aid to Europe. $13.2 billion given in aid.

10 July: the USSR forces Czechoslovakia and Poland to reject Marshall Aid.

1948
19–25 February: Communists take over Czechoslovakia. Means all eastern Europe (Romania, Albania, Bulgaria, Poland, Hungary) have communist-controlled governments.

24 June: USSR blocks all land routes to west Berlin. Start of Berlin airlift. Major confrontation between USSR and the western powers.

1949
22 January: Chinese Communists capture Beijing and are victorious in Chinese Civil War.

4 April: creation of North Atlantic Treaty Organisation (NATO) to defend Europe against Communist aggression.

8 May: creation of West Germany from US, British and French zones of occupation.

12 May: USSR ends blockade of West Berlin.

30 May: USSR sets up state of East Germany.

29 August: USSR successfully explodes an atomic bomb. The US atomic monopoly ends.

21 September: People's Republic of China created.

Marshall Aid: Proposed by US Secretary of State, George Marshall in June 1947. It was produced because of US concern about growing support for communism in Europe and fear that Europe would not recover as a trading partner. The aid was offered to all European states, including the USSR. Although Czechoslovakia originally applied for aid they were forced to withdraw under Soviet pressure. Between 1947 and 1952, $17 billion were given in aid.

Atomic diplomacy: The use of the threat of atomic weapons to force other nations to stop doing something, or to threaten them into submission. Example: in 1946, Truman threatened Stalin with nuclear weapons to force the Soviet military withdrawal from northern Iran.

Comecom: Council for Mutual Economic Aid (1949–91). Mainly a Soviet reaction to the Marshall Plan, it was dominated by the USSR. However, attempts were made to broaden its work. In 1971, a Complex Programme was introduced, leading to joint economic projects between states. In 1972, an investment bank was created. However, Comecon was partially undermined by Romania's desire to be more independent. Later it was broadened to include other communist states, such as Cuba who joined in 1972 and Vietnam in 1978.

1. In what ways have historians differed in their views of which country was most responsible for the outbreak of the Cold War after 1945?

2. Why, do you think, historians have differed in their interpretations of who was responsible for the Cold War?

3. On the basis of the information in this section, who do you think was most responsible for the Cold War, the USA or USSR? Explain your answer.

Soviet Foreign Minister. As a result, Truman must take personal responsibility for the breakdown in US–Soviet relations.

● There were important economic advantages for the USA in starting a cold war. US policymakers feared another economic depression once the Second World War was over. To prevent this from taking place the US government hoped to keep high levels of military and government expenditure. As a result, the USSR was portrayed as aggressive and threatening. To prevent the spread of Communism to western Europe, the US government launched the European Recovery Programme in 1947. Known as **Marshall Aid**, billions of US dollars were used to bring economic recovery to western Europe as the best means of limiting communist influence. Truman was responsible for creating the military-industrial complex where big business in the USA supported the conflict with the USSR in order to keep high levels of military spending.

● The USA contributed to the start of the Cold War because of Truman's use of **atomic diplomacy**. Some revisionist historians, such as Gar Alperovitz in *Atomic Diplomacy* (1965), believe that the use of atomic weapons against Japan was to display American military power to the Soviet Union.

However, other views have played down US policy in causing the Cold War. Historians such as John Lewis Gaddis, in *The United States and the Origins of the Cold War, 1941–1947*, believe the USA did not follow a consistent policy after 1945. Instead, the USA had to adjust to a rapidly changing European scene. This was due to a number of reasons:

● The weakness of Britain and France after 1945 forced the USA into taking a more active role in European affairs. France was economically exhausted and badly damaged by 1945. Although Britain tried to play an active role in European affairs after 1945, by 1947 it was clear that Britain was too weak. The British decision to stop aiding Greece and Turkey in that year demonstrates this point.

● The economic weakness of Europe after 1945 also forced a US response. The European Recovery, or Marshall Plan, of 1947–48 can be seen as a real attempt by the USA to help post-war reconstruction. It was offered to all European states including the USSR. Fortunately for the USA, the USSR refused to accept aid and also forced its eastern European satellite states to refuse. In its place the USSR established **Comecon**.

As mentioned by historian Derrick Murphy in 'The Cold War 1945–1949' in *Modern History Review*:

'It seems clear that some form of tension between the USA and USSR would have sprung up following the end of the Second World War. The two new superpowers were competing for influence in a new international order. Germany and Japan had been defeated and had suffered considerable economic damage. France and Italy had also suffered economically. The British Empire was in rapid decline as a world power.'

However, it was the speed of the collapse of the wartime Grand Alliance which shocked contemporaries and has captured the interests of historians. Roosevelt's untimely death, and his replacement by Truman, helped to speed up the collapse of the Alliance. The crude means used in creating Soviet regimes in Eastern Europe gave rise to much suspicion in the West. In the end, the creation of mutual suspicions, bolstered by fierce ideological rivalry, gave the Cold War its intensity and its potential for future military conflict.

13.2 How did the USSR establish control over eastern Europe 1945–1949?

An important cause of the Cold War was the way in which the USSR established communist control over eastern Europe from the end of the Second World War until 1949. To critics of the USSR this was evidence that Stalin had broken the agreements he had made at Yalta. It helped President Truman to ensure that his Doctrine became the basis of US foreign policy from March 1947. It also helped the Truman administration to get the Marshall Plan accepted by Congress.

Although eastern Europe had been 'liberated' by the Soviet Army, it did not have a strong tradition of support for Communism. Much of the area was agricultural. What little industry that had existed was all but destroyed by 1945. What had not been destroyed was usually removed to the Soviet Union as reparations. In particular, this was true of East Germany.

In two areas local communists did play an important role in creating communist regimes. In Yugoslavia Joseph Broz, known as 'Tito', led the Yugoslav resistance to the Nazis during the war. In Albania local communists overthrew King Zog to create a communist state in 1945.

Also parts of eastern Europe were taken over by the USSR. These were the former states of Latvia, Lithuania and Estonia. It also included the eastern part of Poland, Ruthenia (from Czechoslovakia) and Moldovia from Romania. Communist regimes were not established immediately on the arrival of the Soviet army. It took until February 1948 for a communist government to be established in Czechoslovakia.

So how did the USSR establish Soviet-style regimes in eastern Europe?

Poland

Before the end of the Second World War, Stalin had already laid the groundwork for the creation of a communist regime. In 1940 most of the officers of the Polish Army, captured by the Soviet army, had been murdered in captivity. In the summer of 1944 the Warsaw Uprising by anti-communist Poles was not supported by the Soviet Army. As a result, the Polish 'Home Army' was badly defeated by the Nazis. Once the Soviet Army had entered eastern Poland, in 1944, a pro-Communist regime was established at Lublin.

In June 1945, a government containing socialists, communists, Catholics and peasants was formed under the socialist Osobka. Under his government, the new boundaries of Poland were implemented. A major cause in the move towards communist control came from the unlikely quarter of the leader of the Peasant Party, Stanislaw Mikolajczyk. The Peasant Party performed well in a referendum held in June 1946. However, Mikolajczyk's demand for a large share in government and his conservative views forced the socialists into close partnership with the communists (Polish United Workers' Party). Eventually, these two groups merged and in January 1947 'rigged' the election to ensure a communist victory which then established a one-party state.

Romania

Romania had been a close ally of Nazi Germany during the Second World War. In August 1944, King Michael was successful in removing the pro-Nazi government. However, a communist-controlled government was achieved through a variety of means. Firstly, like Poland, communists were encouraged to join a government of national unity with non-communist parties known as the National Democratic Bloc government. Secondly,

Josef Broz, alias Tito (1892–1980)

Communist leader in Yugoslavia from 1937. During the Second World War Tito led the communist partisan army against the German, Italian and Croat and Serb nationalists. He was able to form a Yugoslav communist government in 1945, after liberating his own country from German control. A dispute with Stalin led to Yugoslavia's expulsion from Cominform (see page 397) in 1948. After that date, Tito led independent, neutral communist Yugoslavia until his death. Yugoslavia became a leading state in the non-aligned movement of countries not linked to NATO or the Soviet bloc.

encouraged by Moscow, the Romanian communists, under Gherghiu-Dej, took part in demonstrations to disrupt the government, beginning in January 1945. Finally, in March 1945, the Soviet Army intervened. It disarmed the Romanian army in the capital, Bucharest, and forced the King to appoint a government dominated by the communists under Groza.

Eventually, by November 1946, the communist and socialist parties had merged and dominated Romanian politics. In the elections of that month, they gained 80% of the vote. The communists provided opposition to traditional political parties which had been associated with military defeat. They also supported economic and social reform.

Hungary

Like Romania, Hungary had also been an ally of Hitler. In a predominantly rural country, the Smallholders' Party was popular after the war. They received 50% of the vote in the November 1945 election. However, as in Poland and Romania, the communists joined forces with the socialists offering a radical electoral package of social and economic reform in a country experiencing major economic crisis. In addition, the communists made sure they controlled the Ministry of the Interior. They used this control to good effect in 1947 by arresting the leader of the Smallholders' Party, Kovacs, for 'offences against the State'. The Prime Minister, Imre Nagy, was forced to resign. In a general election, in August 1947, the communists and their allies made sure they would win a large share of the vote (45%). By June 1948 the socialists had merged with the communist-dominated Hungarian Workers' Party.

Czechoslovakia

Of all the countries in Soviet-occupied Europe only Czechoslovakia had a pre-war tradition of democracy. During the latter stages of the Second World War, communist partisans had participated in the Slovak National Uprising. Czechoslovakia was also an industrialised state with a large working class. Therefore, unlike other Eastern Europe states, its Communist Party had sizeable support.

As in other eastern European countries, a multi-party government of national unity was formed at the end of the war. The Prime Minister, from May 1946, was Klement Gottwald. He allowed the communists to control the police and armed forces. In 1947 he was forced, by pressure from the USSR, to reject Marshall Aid.

However, the move towards communist control, like Poland, was forced by non-communists who wanted the President Edvard Beneš to follow a non-communist policy. To achieve this, all non-communist members of the government resigned in February 1948. Instead, the communists were able to portray this act as an attempt to create a reactionary, conservative government. Beneš supported the communists who had created 'action committees' to oppose a possible conservative government.

East Germany

At the end of the war Germany was divided into four military zones of occupation. The Soviet zone became East Germany (The German Democratic Republic) in 1949. It could be argued that the creation of a communist regime in East Germany was a direct result of actions by Britain and the USA. In their attempt to bring economic recovery to Germany, they had merged their zones, in 1946, to form **Bizonia**. By 1948 the three non-Soviet zones had created a new currency, the Deutschmark.

Stalin's response made matters worse. The Berlin Airlift Crisis of 1948–49 provided positive proof for the Truman Doctrine. It also portrayed the USSR as aggressive and threatening. The failure to force the western allies to abandon West Berlin was a major Soviet failure. It led

---

Imre Nagy (1896–1958)
A Hungarian Communist who criticised Stalin's political and economic policies. He was Prime Minister of Hungary (1953–55), following Stalin's death. He tried to introduce more liberal reforms but was replaced by Matyos Rakosi in 1955. In the Hungarian Uprising (October 1956), Nagy was returned to power. He supported Hungary's withdrawal from the Warsaw Pact (see page 399). Captured by Soviet troops and executed in 1958.

Bizonia: Name for the two military zones of Germany merged by the USA and Britain in 1946.

NATO: Stands for North Atlantic Treaty Organisation.

Cominform: Communist Information Bureau (1947–56). It was created as part of the Soviet response to Marshall Aid, an attempt to unite all communist parties in one organisation in order to co-ordinate political activity. It was seen by the West as a new version of Comintern (Communist International) which had been dissolved by Stalin in 1943. The aim of Cominform was to spread communist ideas. It was limited to communist parties in Europe, such as the Eastern bloc and France and Italy. Cominform remained the main organisation for co-operation between Eastern bloc countries until Khrushchev dissolved it in 1956. He hoped this move could lead to better relations with Tito's Yugoslavia which had been expelled from the organisation in 1948.

1. *What common features were there in the establishment of communist governments in eastern Europe after 1945?*

2. *How easy was it for the USSR to impose communist government in eastern Europe after 1945?*

directly to the creation of both **NATO** and West Germany. In retaliation, the Soviets created a Soviet-style regime in their German zone.

Summary

Soviet policy towards eastern Europe did not follow a carefully worked out plan. Stalin wanted friendly governments in these states for security reasons. However, there were some common features. In each of the states, communists joined forces with other parties to form governments of national unity. They used this position to gain control of the security system of each state. They were also aided by major political miscalculations by their opponents, most noticeably in Poland and Czechoslovakia.

Apart from Czechoslovakia, none of these states had traditions of democratic government. The dictatorship by the Communists merely replaced a tradition of dictatorship by other political groups. However, the Soviet Union did establish two institutions which helped bring some unity to Eastern Europe:

● **Cominform** helped bring co-ordination to most of the communist-controlled governments of eastern Europe. It led to a split between the USSR and the Communist government of Yugoslavia under Tito. The Yugoslav leader wanted to adopt a political line that was independent from Moscow. This split meant that although Yugoslavia remained communist-controlled it adopted a neutral position in foreign policy during the Cold War.

● Comecon was an economic organisation that aimed to bring all the eastern European economies into closer union with the USSR.

By the end of 1949 the pattern of political and economic development of eastern Europe was established. Communist government, based on the Soviet model, was created in all the states. Close links and guidance from Moscow were the norm. In addition, the economies of Eastern Europe now looked to the USSR rather than to the west as its main market. The 'Iron Curtain', which Churchill described in 1946, was now fully in place.

13.3 Why was Germany a central issue during the Cold War?

The tearing down of the Berlin Wall in 1989 was the symbolic end of the Cold War. From 1945 the position of Germany within Europe was a central issue. This was due to several reasons.

● When Germany was defeated, the Great Powers (the USSR, Britain and the USA) met at Potsdam, near Berlin, to decide on the future of Germany. As a result of the two Potsdam conferences, Germany and Austria were divided into four military zones of occupation. The USSR, the USA, Britain and France each controlled a zone. In addition, the two capital cities – Berlin and Vienna – were divided into four military zones. Through accident of geography both capital cities were within the Soviet zone of occupation. Therefore, the three western powers (Britain, the USA and France) could only have access to their zones by crossing Soviet-controlled territory. The problems caused by these arrangements increased tension between East and West.

● Secondly, although the allies met at the end of the war to consider the organisation of the post-war world, no formal peace treaty was signed. As a result, the futures of Germany and Austria were not decided.

Throughout the post-1945 period attempts were made to deal with the German and Austrian problems. The Austrian State Treaty of 1955 solved the latter. The four occupying powers agreed to leave Austria. As a result, Austria became a democratic but neutral state.

What impact did the Berlin Airlift Crisis (1948–1949) have on the Cold War?

The first major international crisis involving Germany came in 1948. In response to western attempts to create a single economic zone from their military zones, Stalin ordered the land blockade of West Berlin. Stalin's actions were prompted by the belief that the West wanted to reunite and remilitarise Germany. As a result, Soviet actions could be seen as defensive and based on security concerns. However, the West regarded Soviet action as aggressive and expansionist.

The Berlin Airlift Crisis greatly increased East–West tension. It led directly to the formation, in 1949, of two German states:

● West Germany, or the German Federal Republic, was pro-western and democratic.

● East Germany, or the German Democratic Republic, became a communist state.

The Berlin Airlift

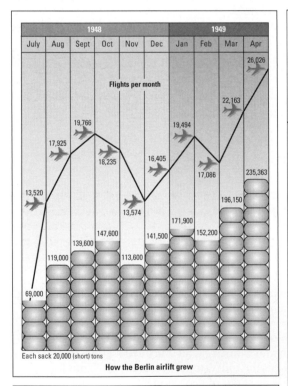

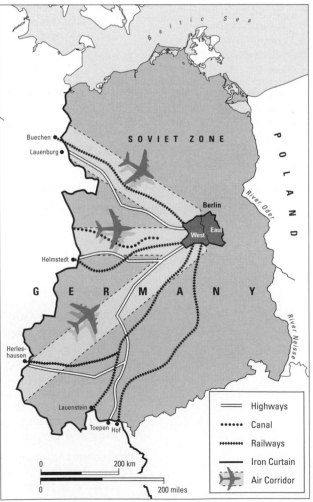

Airlifts statistics, 28 June 1948 – 11 May 1949			
	USAF	RAF	Civil
Flights to Berlin and back	131,378	49,733	13,879
Miles flown	69,257,475	18,205,284	4,866,093
Tonnage flown in (short tons)	1,214,339	281,727	87,619

Unfortunately, West Berlin was technically not part of this new West German state. It remained as three western military zones well within East Germany.

The crisis stands out as one of the major tests for the US foreign policy explained by President Truman to the US Congress in March 1947. This was the policy of containment.

Why was German re-armament a major issue in the early 1950s?

During the first half of the 1950s, German re-armament was a central issue in the European part of the Cold War. With the outbreak of the Korean War, US forces had to be spread across the globe in their attempt to contain the spread of communism. In addition, from 1953, the new US President, Dwight Eisenhower, planned to reduce the US **conventional forces**. The idea that West Germany would have a powerful armed force was viewed with suspicion by the USSR and France. Both nations had been the victims of German armed might during the first half of the century.

The French solution to the issue of German re-armament was the Pleven Plan, named after the French Prime Minister. In 1951, Rene Pleven suggested that West Germany should only have an armed force as part of a European army. In May 1952, as part of this process, the European Defence Community (EDC) was created involving West Germany, Italy, France, Belgium, Luxembourg and Holland.

The EDC failed to develop into a European army. This was due, in part, to opposition within France. More importantly, it was linked to a threatened withdrawal of US troops from Europe. In May 1955, with the French bowing to American pressure, West Germany became a member of NATO.

The USSR was bitterly opposed to German re-armament. They believed it broke the Potsdam Agreement of 1945. In 1955 the new Soviet leadership of Nikita Khrushchev and Nikolai Bulganin reacted to German re-armament by creating the **Warsaw Pact**, a military alliance of Eastern Bloc countries. From 1955 Europe was divided into two hostile military alliances, similar to the position before the First World War.

How serious was the issue of Berlin in the Cold War between 1958 and 1961?

The German question turned into one of the most serious crises in the Cold War. At issue was the status of Berlin. The Soviet leader created the crisis in 1958 by threatening to hand over the Soviet military zone in Berlin to East Germany. However, the crisis reached its height in 1961 with the building of the Berlin Wall.

Berlin was a key issue in East–West relations for several reasons. Firstly, West Berlin was a western military outpost well within the Communist bloc. Secondly, Berlin was the only gap in the 'Iron Curtain' where free travel between East and West could take place.

Ever since 1949 large numbers of East Germans had fled to the West through this 'gap'. By 1961 the East German state's existence was becoming undermined by this development. In the first six months of 1961 around 100,000 fled to West Berlin. In August alone 30,000 fled from East to West. In order to save East Germany and close the last gap in the Iron Curtain, the Warsaw Pact countries decided on 3 August to erect the Berlin Wall. On 12–13 August a temporary barrier was built, and eventually the Wall itself. The crisis was seen at the time as a major confrontation between East and West. On 26 October 1961, Soviet and US tanks collided briefly with each other, at Checkpoint Charlie. The erection of the wall closed the last gap in the Iron Curtain and stopped the flood of refugees from East Germany. It also confirmed the division of Germany into two states. Even

Conventional forces: Armed forces which did not use nuclear, biological or chemical weapons.

Dwight Eisenhower (1890–1969)
US President 1953–61. Supported New Look foreign policy that aimed to roll back the advance of Communism. However, this foreign policy was a little different to Truman's 'containment' policy. Eisenhower did nothing to aid the Hungarians in 1956. His presidency is also associated with the idea of 'brinkmanship' where Secretary of State John F. Dulles threatened the use of nuclear war as a diplomatic weapon.

Warsaw Pact: The military alliance of eastern bloc states created in 1955. It was created one week after West Germany was allowed to join NATO.

Central Europe 1955

though the USSR tried to interfere with convoys travelling from the West to Berlin in 1962 and 1963, it also confirmed the permanence of the western military presence in West Berlin. As the historian John W. Mason states in *The Cold War 1945 to 1991* (1996):

> 'The Wall solved the refugee problem at a stroke, but at the same time it became a symbol all over the world of repression in the Soviet sphere. Khrushchev withdrew his threat to make a separate peace treaty with East Germany and the Berlin crisis came to an end. He had failed to dislodge the West from Berlin and had come under fierce criticism from China for capitulating [giving in] to the capitalist powers.'

What message does each photograph give of the Berlin Wall?

(Left) Berlin Wall, 7 September 1962. East German policemen lift the body of Peter Fechter, who was shot down while trying to escape to the West.
(Right) Celebrations at the Berlin Wall after unification, 1989.

Détente: Relaxation of tension between countries; also characterised by increased economic co-operation and cultural exchanges, such as tours of the West by Soviet athletes and ballet companies.

SALT (Strategic Arms Limitation Treaty): The aim was to limit the increase in nuclear weapons. The first treaty, SALT I, was aimed at preventing the development of ABMs (Anti-Ballistic Missile systems).

How did the German question affect the creation of détente between East and West after 1962?

During the remainder of the 1960s, the main areas of confrontation in the Cold War were outside Europe. The most serious crisis occurred in October 1962 over Cuba. Later in the decade, conflict was centred on Vietnam. By the early 1970s a new era of the Cold War began: *détente*, a relaxation of tension between the two superpowers. This was highlighted in May 1972 when President Richard Nixon of the USA and Leonid Brezhnev of the USSR signed the **SALT** I treaty. This was the first major international treaty that attempted to limit the increase in strategic (nuclear) weapons.

Leonid Brezhnev (1906–1982)		
In 1964 he helped overthrow Khrushchev. Then became joint leader with Kosygin until 1967. Responsible for	Brezhnev Doctrine of 1968 and *détente* with the West from 1971. Economic policies at home led to lack of economic growth. Final years affected by Soviet	decision to invade Afghanistan that led to New Cold War.

Ostpolitik (German – 'Eastern policy'): German policy towards eastern Europe, associated mainly with the Federal Republic of Germany's cultivation of good relations with the German Democratic Republic and the rest of the Communist bloc in the 1960s.

> ### Willi Brandt (1913–1992)
> Adopted name of Karl Herbert Frahm, a German socialist politician. As mayor of West Berlin (1957–66), Brandt became internationally known during the Berlin Wall crisis. Federal chancellor (premier) of West Germany (1969–74). Played a key role in the remoulding of the Social Democratic Party (SPD). He was awarded the Nobel Peace Prize in 1971.

Non-proliferation treaty: To prevent the spread of nuclear weapons to new countries.

'Oder–Neisse Line': Border between East Germany and Poland in 1945. The rivers Oder and Neisse formed a natural barrier (see map on page 400).

Solidarity: Independent trade union movement in Poland.

INF (Intermediate Range Nuclear Forces): These were nuclear weapons based in and aimed at other parts of Europe. In the USSR these took the form of the mobile SS20 missile. The USA countered by basing Pershing I and II and Lance missiles in Germany and Cruise missiles in Britain.

During this period, West German leaders embarked on a new foreign policy which aimed to relax tension between the two German states: *Ostpolitik*. This led, eventually, to the Basic Treaty (December 1972). The main force behind *Ostpolitik* was the West German Social Democrat Willi Brandt.

Brandt's decision to increase links between the two Germanies was developed separately from the US desire to improve relations with the USSR. At times Brandt's plans were kept from the USA. As the historian Simon J. Ball notes in *The Cold War 1947 to 1991* (1998) '*détente* and *Ostpolitik* had quite different roots in different perceived national interest'. However, at no time did Brandt wish to cause a rift between West Germany and the rest of NATO. Nevertheless, Brandt wanted to ease East–West tension in central Europe mainly because Germany would be the main battlefield in any conflict. By the mid-1960s the two Germanies were host to large armed forces of both NATO and the Warsaw Pact. By improving relations with the East, Brandt hoped to create a '*Mitteleuropa*' (Middle Europe) area.

The Basic Treaty with East Germany was preceded by treaties, in 1970, with the USSR and Poland. In the Moscow Treaty with the USSR, West Germany promised to sign a nuclear **non-proliferation treaty** and would support the idea of a European security conference. In the Warsaw Treaty with Poland, Brandt accepted the '**Oder–Neisse Line**' as the permanent frontier between Poland and East Germany. This confirmed the acquisition by Poland of a large area of the former German state in 1945.

The 1972 Basic Treaty accepted the division of Germany into two states. However, it did not rule out the possibility of future unification. The treaty also allowed for closer economic links. The USSR supported the treaty because it gave international recognition to East Germany. It eventually led to both East and West Germany joining the United Nations (September 1973).

Brandt's *Ostpolitik* may have had different origins to *détente* but it helped to relax international tension in central Europe. Both policies led to the Helsinki Accords of August 1975. This was the high-water mark of *détente* in Europe. Thirty-five countries, including the two Germanies, signed these accords. The agreements included acceptance that all European borders were inviolable (permanent). They also suggested greater economic co-operation between East and West. Finally, the Accords required the signatories to respect human rights across Europe. This proved to be the most controversial aspect of the Accords and one which the Eastern bloc countries were criticised by the West for not implementing.

Why did Germany become the centre of a new crisis between East and West between 1979 and 1985?

The end of the 1970s saw a major deterioration in relations between East and West. In December 1979 the USSR invaded Afghanistan. In retaliation, the US Senate refused to ratify the SALT II treaty that had been negotiated by President Jimmy Carter. Carter then refused to allow US athletes to compete in the 1980 Moscow Olympic Games. In Eastern Europe martial law was declared in Poland (1981), as part of a campaign to suppress the independent trade union movement, **Solidarity**.

Germany and Europe, in general, became a centre for this increased conflict over the issue of nuclear weapons. By the late 1970s the main issue in the nuclear conflict between East and West were **INF (Intermediate Range Nuclear Forces)**. The deployment of these new nuclear weapons by the USA caused considerable protests in western Europe. A women's camp

Mikhail Gorbachev (1931–)
Soviet President (1985–91). Was a member of the Politburo from 1980. As general secretary of the Communist Party (CPSU) 1985–91 and president of the Supreme Soviet 1988–91, he introduced liberal reforms at home (*perestroika* and *glasnost*), proposed the introduction of multi-party democracy, and attempted to halt the arms race abroad. Nobel Peace Prize winner in 1990.

Ronald Reagan (1911–)
US President (1981–89). Republican with strong anti-communist views. He described the USSR as an 'evil empire'. During the 1980s he launched the biggest peacetime military build-up in US history. Reagan was a supporter of the Star Wars initiative. However, from 1985 he negotiated with Soviet leader Gorbachev towards reducing nuclear arsenals in START (strategic arms reduction talks).

'Strategic Defence Initiative': The US plan to develop satellite-based laser weapons which could destroy Soviet ICBMs (intercontinental ballistic missiles) in the outer atmosphere.

1. In what ways was Germany the centre of Cold War confrontation in Europe 1945–1989?

2. Why did disputes over Germany not lead to war between the USA and the USSR between 1945 and 1989?

3. 'In the period 1945–1989 Germans had virtually no control over their own affairs.' Assess the validity of this statement.

of anti-nuclear protesters was created at RAF Greenham Common, in the UK, against the deployment of Cruise missiles.

These developments increased tension with the USSR. This occurred for several reasons. Between 1979 and 1985 the USSR faced a major leadership crisis. Leonid Brezhnev was an ageing and ill leader by 1980. After his death, in 1982, he was followed, in succession, by Yuri Andropov and Konstantin Chernenko, both elderly and ill. Not until 1985 was the USSR led by a relatively young, dynamic leader, Mikhail Gorbachev.

Secondly, from 1981, the USA was led by Ronald Reagan. During his presidency he greatly increased military spending. In particular, he launched his 'Star Wars' or **'Strategic Defence Initiative'** (SDI) in March 1983. This initiative, if successfully introduced, would have made Soviet nuclear missiles ineffective.

The combination of these factors meant that Germany again became the centre of renewed military conflict between the USA and the USSR. Fortunately, the SDI proposal was never implemented and both Gorbachev and Reagan began, in 1985, to negotiate seriously about the reduction of nuclear weapons – and with them, international tension.

Summary

Throughout most of the Cold War in Europe, Germany was a major issue. This was due both to the legacy of the Second World War and to Germany's geographical location in the centre. The division of Germany into two states was a major symbol of the division of the world between East and West. When the Berlin Wall was finally torn down, in 1989, it was seen as the beginning of the end of the Cold War in Europe.

13.4 Why was it difficult for the USSR to maintain control of eastern Europe between 1949 and 1989?

By 1949 the Cold War division of Europe had occurred. The Iron Curtain had divided the continent into two distinct political and economic systems. In the East, the USSR dominated the region militarily. It had also imposed on the eastern European states a communist form of government and a communist economic system. Both looked to Moscow for leadership and guidance. As a result, Stalin had achieved one of his major post-war aims in Europe: he had created a security zone of friendly, dependent states on his western frontier.

However, in spite of the USSR's overwhelming military might, control of eastern Europe proved to be a problem for Soviet leaders. In the period 1949–81 the USSR faced a series of crises which tried either to change or remove Soviet influence in eastern Europe. Eventually, by 1989, Soviet control of eastern Europe disappeared almost overnight. In most countries this was achieved without bloodshed. Only in Romania was violent revolution part of this change.

What problems did the USSR face in trying to maintain control over eastern Europe?

Nationalism

One major problem faced by the USSR throughout this period was the issue of **nationalism**. In inter-war Europe (1919–39) Communism had never achieved majority support in any country outside the USSR. Even before 1948 the issue of nationalism and national independence had affected Soviet control. In mid-1948, Communist Yugoslavia was expelled from Cominform. From 1948 to the 1990s, Yugoslavia remained a communist state independent of the USSR. Under Tito, the Yugoslavs adopted a neutral position in the Cold War. Only after Tito's death (1980), did national tensions within Yugoslavia become a destabilising influence. These led eventually to the disintegration of Yugoslavia in the 1990s.

Nationalism: The desire of individual racial groups to form their own state.

Nationalism also affected Soviet control in other countries. In Poland resentment against Soviet control centred on two episodes in the Second World War.

- In 1943, the bodies of thousands of Polish army officers were uncovered by the Germans at Katyn in the USSR. The USSR was accused of the massacre.

- In 1944, the Soviet Army failed to aid the Polish Home Army in the Warsaw Uprising.

In Czechoslovakia resentment centred on the communist-led take-over of February 1948 which saw the murder or suicide of the Czech Foreign Minister, Jan Masaryk. In Hungary, which had fought as Hitler's ally on the Eastern Front (1941–44), the desire to re-assert national independence was also an issue.

Even within the Soviet Union national feeling had the potential to disrupt the state. By 1945 the USSR had absorbed formerly independent states such as Latvia, Lithuania and Estonia. Nationalist groups also existed in Georgia and the Ukraine.

Economic hardship

Unlike the rest of Europe, the Eastern bloc did not benefit from the billions of dollars in American aid under the European Recovery or Marshall Plan. The area had also suffered considerable economic damage as a result of the Second World War. The USSR had lost 27 million dead and Poland 25% of its population (6 million). In addition, large parts of eastern Europe had always been based on agriculture, with limited industry.

The introduction of Soviet-style central economic planning and collectivised agriculture (see Chapter 8) meant that eastern Europe followed a completely different economic course to the western world. Shortages of food and raw material, and the lack of economic freedom were important causes of resentment. The contrast between East and West was most apparent in Berlin. Before 1961, East Berliners could travel freely to West Berlin. The attraction of greater wealth and political freedom resulted in 2.7 million East Germans fleeing to West Berlin by the time the Berlin Wall was erected.

Lack of political and religious freedom

Like the USSR under Stalin, a Stalinist political system was established in all Eastern bloc states by 1949. Except for Czechoslovakia, eastern Europe did not have a strong tradition of democracy. A desire for a relaxation in

Atheism: The belief that there is no God.

Wladyslaw Gomulka (1905–1982)
Polish Communist. Came to power following Poznan Uprising of 1956 by posing as a Polish nationalist. He brought agricultural collectivisation to an end. In turn, he was ousted from power after strikes in 1970 following failure of his economic policies to bring improvements to the standard of living. He was replaced by Edouard Gierek.

the rigid control of the Communist Party was always apparent in almost every Eastern bloc state. This was most noticeable in the relations between communist governments and the Roman Catholic Church. Communist control over education and its support for **atheism** meant that conflict was inevitable. Catholic support for anti-communist groups occurred in Hungary, in 1956, with Cardinal Mindsentzy. It was most significant in Poland, the most Catholic of Eastern bloc states. The Catholic Church supported the free trade union movement, Solidarity. In 1978 the Catholic Church in the Eastern bloc received a considerable boost with the election of Cardinal Karol Wojtyla of Poland as Pope John Paul II. This led to a resurgence in Polish Catholicism which helped undermine communist rule.

How serious were the crises which faced the USSR in eastern Europe after 1949?

Hungary and Poland, 1956
Soviet control over eastern Europe was affected by political change within the Soviet Union, and relations between the USSR and the West. The combination of these two developments helped to undermine Soviet control in 1956.

Following Stalin's death in March 1953, a power struggle ensued. By 1955 Nikita Khrushchev emerged as the new Soviet leader. In 1956, at the 20th Party Congress of the Communist Party of the Soviet Union, Khrushchev denounced Stalin. The new Soviet leader criticised the barbarity of Stalin's rule and the growth of what Khrushchev called 'the cult of personality'. A new, less repressive regime was to be developed within the USSR.

On the international stage, relations between East and West seemed to be improving in 1955. In that year the USSR and the western powers signed the Austrian State Treaty. Soviet forces left eastern Austria. Austria was declared a united, neutral state. Hopes were high that this treaty would be followed by a similar one on Germany.

Partly as a result of these developments Soviet control faced major challenges in Poland and Hungary. In Poland on 28 June 1956, Polish workers began a series of political strikes aimed against Soviet-type rule and poor working conditions. Although the 'Poznan Rising' was put down by the Polish Army it did lead to a change in government. Wladyslaw Gomulka was recalled as Communist Party leader because of his close association with Polish nationalism.

More serious for the USSR was the Hungarian Uprising of October/ November. A popular movement developed which clashed with Soviet military forces in Budapest. This resulted in four days of street fighting at the end of October. The result was the creation of a multi-party government and the decision by Hungary to leave the Warsaw Pact. The Soviet reaction was to invade Hungary and quell the uprising by force. In the ensuing fighting, 3,000 Hungarians were killed and 200,000 fled the country.

Considerable controversy surrounds the actions of Hungarian communist Imre Nagy. To many Hungarians, he was a patriot who wanted to relax Soviet control. Like several other eastern European communists in the period, he believed that the Soviet Union would allow greater political freedom within their zone of influence. The Soviet Union executed Nagy for his part in the Uprising.

Developments in Poland and Hungary had several common characteristics. The relaxation of Stalinist control in the USSR led to demands for greater political freedom elsewhere. Both states also faced economic

Suez Crisis: Occurred following the decision by President Nasser of Egypt to nationalise the Suez Canal. The British and French, in league with the Israelis, invaded Egypt to take control of the canal. Britain and France were forced into a humiliating withdrawal because of Soviet and American opposition.

Alexander Dubček (1921–)
Czechoslovak leader who tried to introduce liberal reforms in the 'Prague Spring' of 1968. Overthrown by Warsaw Pact invasion; demoted to ambassador to Turkey in 1969; and then expelled from Communist Party (1970). Dubček re-emerged as a national figure during the Velvet Revolution of November 1989 when he became president of the Czechoslovak parliament.

Brezhnev Doctrine: The western name given to the policy put forward by the Soviet leader in 1968, Leonid Brezhnev, claiming that the USSR had the right to intervene in any communist state (i.e. any country in the 'Eastern bloc' where 'socialism' was under threat. This policy was abandoned by Gorbachev when he withdrew from Afghanistan.

Iranian Revolution in 1979: The Shah (Emperor) of Iran was overthrown in a revolution led by fundamentalist (extreme) Muslims. He was replaced by the religious leader, the Ayatollah Khomeini.

hardships that caused resentment. Finally, in neither state did the western powers wish to intervene. President Eisenhower (1953–61) had stated that his 'New Look' foreign policy planned to roll back communist influence around the world. However, the USA did not aid the Poles or the Hungarians. Britain and France did not intervene either. This was, in part, due to their military dependence on the USA through NATO. It was also due to their involvement in the **Suez Crisis** in October/November 1956.

Czechoslovakia, 1968

The 'Prague Spring' of 1968 was a major attempt by an Eastern bloc country to introduce a new liberal version of communist rule under the leadership of Alexander Dubček. In some ways Dubček's views were similar to those of Imre Nagy in Hungary in 1955–56. In the Action Programme of 10 April 1968 Dubček wanted to build 'a new profoundly democratic model of Czechoslovak socialism conforming to Czechoslovak conditions'. He wanted to broaden the basis of communist rule by including other organisations such as the trade unions. In this sense he was trying to recreate the National Front of 1945.

The rise of Dubček, and support for his ideas, had a number of causes. According to the historians G. and N. Swain, in *Eastern Europe since 1945* (1993), the liberals within the Slovak Communist Party had gradually increased their influence since the 12th Party Congress of the Czechoslovak Communist Party in December 1962, when Stalinism was denounced.

The increasing influence of liberal communists was combined with a decline in support for the Czech President Antonin Novotny because of major failings in the economy during the 1960s. This led to the abandonment of the five-year economic plan in 1962.

Dubček's liberal communism led to the creation of political groups outside the Communist Party, such as the Social Democrats in June 1968. Unlike the Hungarians in 1956, the Czechoslovaks made no attempt to leave the Warsaw Pact. Indeed, Czech leaders had agreed with the USSR by 1 August 1968 to suppress the Social Democrats and had re-affirmed Czechoslovakia's support for the Warsaw Pact and Comecon. Nevertheless, Warsaw Pact forces invaded Czechoslovakia on the night of 20–21 August. Unlike Hungary in 1956, they faced no armed resistance.

The Warsaw Pact invasion reinforced the Cold War split in Europe. Before the invasion, President Johnson had informed the Soviet leader Brezhnev that the USA would not intervene if the USSR took military action. The invasion also acted as an example of the **Brezhnev Doctrine**. As the historian S.J. Ball states in *The Cold War 1947 to 1991* (1998), 'there was a fear among (Soviet) Politburo members that the reformist spirit might affect the Ukraine and thus spread to the Soviet Union itself'.

Poland, 1980–1981

By 1980 the USA and the USSR entered a new, tense phase of the Cold War brought on by the Soviet invasion of Afghanistan and the issue of INF in Europe. This period also saw a major economic crisis affecting eastern Europe. There was a major oil crisis in 1973 and another following the **Iranian Revolution in 1979**. The poor economic performance of the Polish economy was made worse by a large international debt. In 1980–81 the USSR had to give Poland $3 billion in western currency to avoid economic collapse.

The economic crisis forced the Polish government to increase the prices of basic foodstuffs. This acted as the catalyst for a number of strikes which began at the Lenin shipyard in the northern port of Gdansk (formally Danzig). The strikes eventually developed into an independent trade

Lech Waleşa (1943–)
As an electrician in Lenin shipyard, Gdansk, Waleşa became leader of Solidarity, the free trade union movement in Poland, in 1980. A powerful orator and clever negotiator, he became well known worldwide due to intense media coverage of Polish affairs. Waleşa was placed under 'house arrest' in December 1981 when **martial law** was introduced. He was awarded the Nobel Peace Prize in 1983 and had a private audience with the Polish Pope John Paul II in the Vatican. Waleşa was elected President of Poland in 1990 but was defeated in the 1995 presidential election.

Martial law: Military law when applied to civilians. Normal civil rights are suspended, allowing the government to arrest individuals and detain them without trial. Suspects could be tried by military court (without a jury) and given the death penalty if found guilty.

union movement called Solidarity. Led by a shipyard electrician, Lech Waleşa, Solidarity had the support of political liberals and the Catholic Church, as well as disgruntled workers.

The Solidarity movement did have some success. Its rise led to the fall of Polish Communist leader Edouard Gierek. The union was recognised formally by Gierek's successor, Kania, in November 1980. Lech Waleşa was hailed as a leader of a democratic movement fighting depression.

However, as in Hungary and Czechoslovakia, an independent organisation such as Solidarity threatened Soviet control. Instead of a Soviet military invasion the Polish Prime Minister, General Jaruzelski, introduced **martial law** in December 1981 and banned Solidarity. Waleşa was placed under 'house arrest' for a year.

The collapse of Soviet influence in eastern Europe, 1989

The fall of all the communist regimes of eastern Europe within the space of a year and with little bloodshed was one of the more remarkable events of 20th-century Europe. It had some similarity to the Year of Revolutions of 1848. Unlike 1848, the revolutions of 1989 were successful.

Like the unrest that affected Poland and Hungary in 1956, the revolutions of 1989 had their origins within the USSR. The appointment of Mikhail Gorbachev as Soviet leader in 1985 began a process that was to lead directly to the events of 1989. His attempts to modernise the USSR led to the call for *glasnost* (openness) and *perestroika* (restructuring).

Gorbachev's new programme was the result of poor economic growth in the USSR and with it Soviet difficulties in keeping up with the USA in the arms race (see tables). However, the lessening of central political and economic control undermined the authority of the Communist Party in the USSR and in the Eastern bloc. Economic problems were not limited to the USSR. By 1989 Poland still had a foreign debt of $40 billion. Other Eastern bloc countries faced similar problems.

Within the space of a few short months in 1989, Jaruzelski in Poland began talks with Solidarity, Hungary opened its borders with the West and finally the Berlin Wall was opened.

How does the data contained here help to explain why the USSR faced financial problems caused by military spending?

Strategic bombers

	1956	1960	1965	1970	1975	1979
USA	560	550	630	405	330	316
USSR	60	175	200	190	140	140

Inter-continental ballistic missiles (ICBMs)

	1960	1962	1966	1968	1970	1972	1974	1979
USA	295	835	900	1,054	1,054	1,054	1,054	1,054
USSR	75	200	300	800	1,300	1,527	1,587	1,398

Submarine-launched ballistic missiles (SLBMs)

	1962	1965	1968	1972	1975	1979
USA	145	500	656	656	656	656
USSR	45	125	130	497	740	989

The main reason why the revolutions of 1989 succeeded was the unwillingness of the Soviet Union to implement the Brezhnev Doctrine. By 1989 the USSR was no longer in a position to put down widespread unrest in eastern Europe. The Soviet involvement in Afghanistan (1979–1989) had a similar impact on the USSR as the Vietnam War had

> ### Political revolution in eastern Europe, 1989
>
> 11 January: Hungary legalises independent political parties.
> 6 February: open discussion between Polish Communist Party and Solidarity.
> 15 February: Soviet forces complete withdrawal from Afghanistan.
> 25 April: Soviet Army begins withdrawal from Hungary.
> 4 June: Solidarity achieve success in Polish elections.
> 24 August: end of Communist rule in Poland. Tadeusz Mazowiecki becomes Prime Minister.
> 10 September: Hungarian government allows thousands of East German 'holidaymakers' to cross the border into Austria.
> 1 October: Thousands of East Germans allowed to leave for West through West German embassies in Warsaw and Prague.
> 18 October: East German leader Erich Honecker resigns; replaced by Egon Krenz.
> 10 November: Berlin Wall opened.
> November: Bulgarian Communist leader Topol Zhivkov overthrown.
> 17–27 November: Velvet Revolution in Czechoslovakia. Communism overthrown.
> 21 December: Armed revolution begins in Romania.
> 25 December: Romanian Communist leader Nicolae Ceauçescu executed.
> 28 December: Prague Spring leader Alexander Dubček elected leader of Czech parliament.

1. What problems did the USSR face in trying to keep control over eastern Europe from 1949 to 1989?

2. Why was the USSR able to keep control over eastern Europe between 1949 and 1989?

3. To what extent was nationalism the cause of anti-Soviet feeling in eastern Europe between 1949 and 1989?

on the USA. The political and economic crisis within the Soviet Union forced it to relinquish control over eastern Europe.

The revolution of 1989 also reflected another aspect of the Cold War. Throughout the Cold War period western propaganda claimed that communism had little support in eastern Europe. It was maintained only through Soviet military might. The events of 1989 seem to confirm that view.

13.5 Why did the Cold War come to an end in 1991?

According to the historian Martin McCauley in *Russia, America and the Cold War 1949 to 1991* (1998): 'The Cold War came to an end because it was impossible for two powers to divide and rule the world. The will power had drained away. The burden was so great that the Soviet Union buckled and then disintegrated. By 1991 the United States was no longer able to intervene at will and was immensely relieved when the need to do so, the communist threat, melted away.'

Another historian, Simon Ball, in *The Cold War 1947 to 1991* (1998), takes a similar view. He states that 'there is little doubt that the Cold War came to an end as a result of Soviet economic failure. This failure led in turn to a failure of nerve amongst the Soviet governing élite.'

Both historians point to the fact that by the late 1980s the USSR was no longer in a position to maintain the military forces necessary for superpower status. Few western observers were able to predict the rapid collapse of Soviet power in eastern Europe in 1989 and the end of the USSR in 1991. However, the *Economist* journal, in the 1980s, described the USSR as 'Upper Volta [now Burkina Faso] with missiles'. This suggested that the Soviet economy was of Third World standard. Also, Richard Perle, national security adviser to Ronald Reagan, had predicted in 1991 that any increase in the arms race between the superpowers would eventually lead to the bankruptcy of the Soviet Union.

Boris Yeltsin (1931–)
Communist reformer and
subsequently President of the
Russian Federation. In 1985 he
became communist mayor of
Moscow as part of
Gorbachev's plans to liberalise
Soviet politics. Yeltsin was
expelled from the Politburo
(Cabinet) in October 1987 as
part of a reaction against
Gorbachev's liberal reforms. In
1991, though, he was a major
figure in stopping traditional
communist take-over. He
replaced Gorbachev as leader
of the Russian state (December
1991). Twice elected President
of the Russian Federation. His
second term was badly
affected by his ill health. He
stood down in January 2000.

*1. What was the main
reason for the end of
the Cold War in 1991?
Explain your answer.*

*2. To what extent was
Mikhail Gorbachev
responsible for the end
of the Cold War?*

*3. Using information in
this chapter, was the
collapse of Soviet
control in eastern
Europe, and the USSR
itself, inevitable?*

Gorbachev's attempts to modernise the USSR were too little too late. The origins of the USSR's failure to control eastern Europe could be traced back to the years of stagnation in economic development under Brezhnev. In *Rise and Fall of the Great Powers* (1989), the historian Paul Kennedy states that a common cause of great power decline was over-commitment of military forces. Although a great Eurasian power, the Soviet Union simply did not possess the economic power to sustain a global conflict against the USA. Support for regimes such as Cuba, Angola, Vietnam and eastern Europe proved too demanding. The Soviet invasion of Afghanistan and a protracted war in that country lasting ten years was one military burden too many for the state.

Once Soviet military power weakened, the disruptive forces of nationalism took hold. The desire for national independence undermined Soviet influence in eastern Europe. It also undermined the USSR from within. By 1990 the Baltic states of Latvia, Lithuania and Estonia all sought independence from the USSR. In the Caucasus region, Georgia, Azerbaijan and Armenia followed suit. By 1991 the old USSR had fragmented into 15 separate states.

The failure of Gorbachev's attempts to modernise the USSR through *glasnost* and *perestroika* produced a backlash. Traditional communist leaders, such as Yegor Ligachev, had opposed Gorbachev's policies from the start. By August 1991 opposition within the Communist Party of the Soviet Union had become so great that an attempt was made to 'turn the clock back' by staging a take-over of the Soviet government. Soviet troops were sent to Moscow. Gorbachev and his family were placed under 'house arrest' while on holiday in the Crimea. The attempted coup failed completely. The soldiers mingled with civilians. Former Moscow mayor Boris Yeltsin persuaded the soldiers to lay down their arms. The USSR, like so many Eastern bloc countries in 1989, faced a peaceful revolution in government. The traditional communists were disgraced, Gorbachev was discredited. By the end of 1991 Yeltsin had replaced Gorbachev as leader. The USSR was replaced with the Commonwealth of Independent States made up of 11 of the former 15 republics of the USSR. In turn, this confederation collapsed leaving the Russian Federation merely one of 15 new independent states.

Source-based questions: Gorbachev and the Cold War

Study Sources 1–5 and answer questions (a) and (b) which follow.

SOURCE 1

(From The Cold War 1945–1991 *by John Mason, Routledge, 1996 pages 64–65)*

The accession of Gorbachev to power in March 1985 marked the beginning of the end of the cold war – indeed, he set out deliberately to end it. Arms control lay at the heart of the search for a political accommodation with the United States. Gorbachev and Reagan met in four summit meetings between 1985 and 1988 and transformed the chilly relationship between their countries into one of trust and conciliation by the end of the decade.

At their first summit meeting in Geneva in November 1985 no concrete results were achieved, but the two leaders agreed that 'a nuclear war cannot be won and must not be fought'. This statement represented a significant shift in Soviet thinking and pointed to the possibility that the Soviet Union might consider reducing its ICBM force. But Soviet opposition to SDI proved to be the main stumbling block to any practical agreement in arms control.

The second summit meeting between Reagan and Gorbachev was held at a reputedly haunted house in Reykjavik, Iceland, in October 1986. It was to prove the most bizarre meeting in the history of nuclear diplomacy. Contrary to each country's expectations, the agenda at Reykjavik turned out to be not arms control, not even arms reduction, but the most implausible theme of the nuclear age – complete disarmament. In the final session Reagan called for the elimination of all ballistic missiles within ten years. Gorbachev insisted that US research on SDI must be confined to the 'laboratory'. Reagan would make no concessions over SDI and the summit ended in failure.

SOURCE 2

(From Russia, America and the Cold War 1949–1991 *by Martin McCauley, 1998)*

The Geneva Summit (of 1985) was a watershed in relations. Gorbachev's attitude to Reagan was that he was more than a conservative, he was a political dinosaur. The American President reciprocated by viewing the Soviet Union as

(Burkina Faso) with missiles, but potentially a threat to the free world. He despised everything about communism. Reagan's dislike of Russia and Russians was abstract – he had never visited the country. However, the few Russians he had met, such as Dobrynin and Gromyko, he liked. Geneva was regarded as a success by both sides. The personal chemistry worked. One of the reasons for this was that Gorbachev noticed that Regan did not like detail. Reagan was keen to get across the message that a nuclear war could not be won, so should not be fought. The Russian proposed that the two superpowers should issue a statement that neither would be the first to launch a nuclear war. The US objected to this as it precluded an American nuclear response to a Soviet conventional invasion of western Europe. The compromise reached was to agree to prevent any war between them, whether nuclear or conventional.

SOURCE 3

(From Mikhail Gorbachev: Memoirs, *1996, commenting on the USSR's new foreign policy of 1986)*

We realised it was vitally necessary to correct the distorted ideas we had about other nations. These misconceptions had made us oppose the rest of the world for many decades, which had negative effects on our economy.

We understand that in today's world of mutual interdependence, progress is unthinkable for any society which is fenced off from the world by impenetrable state frontiers and ideological barriers. A country can develop its full potential by interacting with other societies, yet without giving up its own identity.

We realised that we could not ensure our country's security without reckoning with the interests of other countries, and that, in our nuclear age, you could not build a safe security system based solely on military means. This prompted us to propose an entirely new concept of global security, which included all aspects of international relations.

SOURCE 4

(From The Cold War *by Hugh Higgins, 1993)*

In 1985 global military expenditure was $940 billion (more than the entire income of the poorer half of the world). The two superpowers

Edexcel

Source-based questions: Gorbachev and the Cold War

were each devoting over $250 billion annually to defence. Their leaders were hard-pressed to find ways of carrying through the three essential functions of maintaining military security, satisfying the socio-economic needs of their citizens and ensuring sustaining economic growth.

SOURCE 5

(From a meeting of the Soviet Politburo (cabinet) on 22 October 1986. From Judgement in Moscow: A Dissident in the Kremlin Archives *by Vladimir Boukovsky, 1995)*

Gorbachev: We have to alter our views on the measures connected to the latest hostile behaviour of the American administration. The turn of events in Reykjavik reveals that our 'friends' in the USA lack any positive programme and are doing everything to increase pressure on us. And ... with extreme brutality, and are conducting themselves like true bandits.

We have to keep on applying pressure on the American administration by explaining our

positions to the public and demonstrate that the responsibility for the failure to agree on the limitation and liquidation of nuclear armaments rests fairly and squarely with the Americans.

Answer both questions (a) and (b).

(a) Using your own knowledge and the evidence in Sources, 1, 2 and 4 what do you consider to be the main reasons for the ending of the Cold War between the USA and USSR in the years 1985–1989?   *[10 marks]*

(b) 'The Cold War in Europe came to an end mainly because of the efforts of Mikhail Gorbachev.'

Using your own knowledge and the evidence from all five sources, explain how far you agree with this interpretation.   *[20 marks]*

The development of western Europe, 1945–1991

Key Issues

● How was western Europe able to recover so quickly from the damage caused by the Second World War?

● Why did economic integration advance so quickly in western Europe in the years after the Second World War?

● To what extent did western Europe advance towards political unity in the second half of the 20th century?

14.1 What was the condition of western Europe at the end of the Second World War?

14.2 Historical interpretation: To what extent was the Marshall Plan responsible for the economic recovery of western Europe up to 1955?

14.3 What were the main issues in the domestic politics of West Germany, 1950–1991?

14.4 What were the major domestic issues within French politics, 1945–1991?

14.5 By what means and with what success did Italy overcome its domestic political problems in the years 1945–1991?

14.6 Why was there so strong a movement towards economic integration in western Europe in the years after 1950?

14.7 Why did political integration take place more slowly than economic integration in this post-war period?

Framework of Events

1944	Liberation of France and establishment of Fourth Republic
1945	(May) Unconditional surrender of Germany ends Second World War in Europe
	Establishment of a republic in Italy
1947	(February) Signature of peace treaties with Italy, Finland, Hungary, Bulgaria and Romania
	(March) Establishment of Benelux customs union. Formulation and introduction of the Marshall Plan
1948	(March) Signature of Treaty of Brussels
	(April) Establishment of OEEC
1949	(April) Establishment of NATO
	(May) Signature of Statute of Council of Europe. Establishment of German Federal Republic (BRD) and German Democratic Republic (DDR)
1950	(May) Publication of Schuman Plan for European economic integration
1951	(April) Establishment of ECSC
1954	French forces defeated at Dien Bien Phu in Vietnam. Start of FLN revolt in Algeria
1955	German Federal Republic becomes sovereign state
1956	Substantial failure of British and French foreign policy in Suez Crisis
1957	(March) Treaty of Rome establishes the EEC
1958	Establishment of Fifth Republic in France
1960	(April) Unsuccessful army revolt in Algeria
1961	(May) Establishment of European Free Trade Association (EFTA)
1962	Establishment of Algerian independence
1963	(October) Resignation of Adenauer as West German Chancellor
1967	Combination of EEC, ECSC and Euratom to form European Community (EC)

1968	Major outbreaks of student and industrial unrest in France and West Germany
1969	Retirement of de Gaulle
	(October) Willi Brandt elected as West German Chancellor
1973	Admission of Britain, Eire and Denmark into EC. Beginning of middle-eastern oil crisis
1979	Introduction of European Monetary System (EMS)
1981	Admission of Greece into European Community
1986	Admission of Spain and Portugal into European Community
1991	Treaty of European Union at Maastricht. European Community becomes European Union (EU).

The names of the two German states

The official name of the state formed from the three western zones of occupation was *Die Bundesrepublik Deutschland* (BRD), usually translated as the German Federal Republic (FRG). The formal name of the state established by the Soviet Union in its zone was *Die Deutsche Demokratische Republik* (DDR), or German Democratic Republic (GDR). The word 'democratic' was obviously used in the socialist, rather than in the liberal, parliamentary sense. The situation was further complicated by the fact that neither state was recognised diplomatically by the supporters of the other. It was thus often convenient simply to refer to them informally as West Germany and East Germany. To avoid confusion, these terms are the ones used here to distinguish the two states.

Overview

THE year 1945 saw the end of the second continental war to have devastated Europe in the course of 30 years. In 1919, at the end of the First World War, the response of many of the states of western Europe was to return, as far as possible, to the norms of pre-war politics. Britain and France showed little enthusiasm for the 'new morality' that US President Woodrow Wilson hoped to inject into European politics. Instead, they sought to retain the great power status which had led them into the war in the first place. In Germany a new regime came to power, but the events of the next 20 years provided little evidence of an enlightened approach to power politics. By 1945 it was painfully obvious that these traditional norms were no longer viable. The economies of the states of western Europe were in ruins, devastated by occupation and bombing, or by the extraordinary efforts that had been necessary to ensure victory. In the east of the continent the Versailles structure of 'successor states' had proved itself inadequate by 1939, and had now been replaced by a political 'bloc' under the control of the Soviet Union.

The importance of 1945 was that it brought about awareness in western Europe that a radical new approach was necessary if the security and prosperity of that part of the continent were to be restored. Charles de Gaulle was right to claim in a speech of 1960 that Europe had only three choices:

● to be dominated by the Soviet Union

- to be dependent upon the United States of America,

- or to make its own way towards prosperity and security.

Few favoured the first of these options. The second course was of enormous importance in the early years of peace, when the Marshall Plan and the establishment of NATO solved the most pressing of western Europe's problems. It was the third option, however, that dominated western European history in the second half of the 20th century.

In the years that followed, western European statesmen pursued the principle of integration on three main levels. Some laid their emphasis upon the establishment of lasting economic prosperity, and others upon measures to guarantee military security. Some pursued the ideal of such long-term political integration as would eliminate nationalism and national self-interest as disruptive elements in European politics. Progress in one of these areas was far more rapid and single-minded than in the others. The years that followed proved that national self-interest was not yet dead, and that several European countries were not yet able to perceive themselves primarily as part of a larger European unit. True political integration in the second half of the 20th century was a slow process – some way short of completion as the century drew to a close.

Most progress was made in the field of economic integration. A series of bold and radical economic decisions – to pool production in certain key areas of heavy industry, to establish international authorities with the power to oversee this common production, and to establish huge free trade areas – transformed the economic life of western Europe. At the basis of these developments lay a radical political decision that the future of France and Germany depended upon reconciliation and co-operation, rather than upon the confrontation and hostility that had characterised their relations during the past 80 years. Not all of the states in western Europe had the freedom or the will power to re-orientate their recent history in this way. The growth of this European Union, therefore, was a slow process, extending over 30 years or more to date. By the end of the 20th century, however, only two western European states lay outside the union, and the prospects were improving for the extension of the union into eastern Europe.

Consistent as the process of western European integration was in the second half of the 20th century, it would be wrong to generalise about it and to portray it as the only theme within western European history during this period. Many of the states of western Europe experienced difficulties and traumas in these years, either arising from their earlier history, or as part of wider, international currents.

Decolonisation: Giving back to countries that were formerly colonies their political independence.

Charles de Gaulle (1890–1970)

After active service in the First World War, during which he was captured at Verdun (1916), de Gaulle became a prominent member of the French General Staff. He was an advocate of motorised warfare and the use of tanks, which he promoted in his book *Towards a Professional Army* (1934). Upon the defeat of France in 1940, he went into exile in London, where he established the French resistance. Backed by the western allies, he took charge of the Provisional Government (1945), but soon resigned in protest against political instability. A symbol of conservative stability in retirement, de Gaulle returned to politics to serve as President of the Republic (1958–69). During this period he re-orientated French politics by favouring **decolonisation**, and advancing France's role within the EEC. He resigned in 1969 in the aftermath of student and industrial unrest.

France was forced to come to terms with the termination of its imperial history, and nearly 20 years of French politics were dominated by the painful processes of decolonisation. In Germany the issues raised by the post-war division of the state were not resolved until the collapse of the Soviet 'bloc', and even then the process of re-unification posed particular difficulties. Most western European states felt the impact of the wave of discontent among students and industrial workers that was set off by factors such as the war in Vietnam in the late 1960s. In the last years of the 20th century, nevertheless, it certainly appeared that many of the initial objectives of the pioneers of western European integration had been achieved. The terrible damage of the Second World War had been repaired, a high degree of material prosperity had been attained, and no conflict had occurred in that part of the continent since 1945. In those important respects, the history of western Europe in the second half of the century contrasts very starkly indeed with that of the previous 50 years.

14.1 What was the condition of western Europe at the end of the Second World War?

The re-establishment of national boundaries in western Europe

The approach to the establishment of a lasting peace in 1945 was profoundly different from that taken in 1918. It is easy to forget, therefore, that in some respects the peacemakers had to face similar problems. For instance, treaties had to be drawn up to restore and revise boundaries destroyed during the war. One important difference lay in the fact that in 1945 Germany had surrendered unconditionally and played no role whatsoever in the treaties that ended the war. No recognised German government existed at the end of the war, and thus no treaty was signed with it. Without consultation, Germany suffered some predictable and serious losses.

● Alsace and Lorraine were restored to France.

● The Saarland was once again removed from direct German control, and its permanent future left open to future negotiation. The French hope that it might eventually become an independent state was frustrated by a plebiscite (referendum) in 1957 in which the region voted to become a West German province.

● Germany suffered significant losses in the east, where its boundaries were fixed along the line of the Oder and Neisse rivers (see page 398).

● Germany was divided into four zones of allied occupation, and eventually into two autonomous self-governing states.

In the course of 1946, however, treaties were negotiated with Germany's allies – with Italy, Bulgaria, Romania, Hungary and Finland – and were signed in February 1947. The consequences of these treaties for the settlement of eastern Europe were far-reaching and, like the changes to Germany's eastern borders, were dealt with in Chapter 13. In terms simply of western Europe, nevertheless, some important changes were made. Italy alone:

● restored annexed territories in Savoy and Corsica to France;

● surrendered Trieste, which became an international city under the control of the United Nations;

- returned the Dodecanese Islands to Greece;

- abandoned colonial territories in Abyssinia, Libya and Somalia;

- had limits set upon its armed forces;

- paid indemnities to Abyssinia, Albania, Greece, Yugoslavia and the USSR.

The other western European state that required the most careful and complex post-war regulation was Austria. Ending the war as part of the greater German Reich, Austria was also divided into four zones of military occupation. It was only after the death of Stalin that foreign forces were withdrawn to allow the resumption of normal political life. Austria was then reconstituted as an independent state, with the boundaries that had existed before *Anschluss* in 1938, and with the conditions that it should not reunite with Germany, and that it should remain neutral, on the same basis as neighbouring Switzerland.

The physical and human damage

The redrawing of national boundaries was a relatively simple matter, compared with the huge task of repairing the physical and human damage caused by the war. Such problems, of course, were far more serious than those faced in 1919, given the nature of the warfare and the nature of German policy in the regions that they had occupied. It is not easy to produce detailed evidence of the physical damage in Europe, because the same fighting and bombing that caused the damage also made it difficult, if not impossible, to keep detailed records. There can be no doubt, however, that the scale was enormous. Centres of civilian population had been bombed on an unprecedented scale. Several major German towns – such as Hamburg, Cologne and Dresden – had been rendered virtually uninhabitable, and Berlin had been further wrecked by the street fighting that preceded its capture by the Russian Army. In the Netherlands, Rotterdam was still in ruins as a result of German bombing in 1940. Several French cities, such as Caen and Le Havre, had suffered damage in the course of their liberation. Britain and France lost nearly 10% of their total housing stock in the war, Belgium lost nearly twice that proportion, and the figures for German losses were far higher.

Communications had also been damaged. No western European state faced such severe problems as the Soviet Union, where the fighting had destroyed an estimated 65,000 kilometres of railway track. However, every combatant state had experienced the strategic destruction of bridges, roads and railways. Italy claimed to have lost 50% of the **rolling stock** on its railways in the course of the fighting. Apart from the cost of repairing such damage, the destruction also presented enormous problems for the resumption of European trade. In terms of maritime trade alone, for example, Germany's merchant fleet had been reduced between 1939 and 1947 from 4,500 vessels to 700, that of Italy from 3,400 ships to 700, while the merchant marine of France had been roughly halved. Although Great Britain had avoided invasion and defeat, its economy had suffered irreversible damage in more subtle respects. It was, as the historian John Keegan describes it in *The Battle for History* (1997), 'a strategic victor but a net economic loser'.

During the period in 1940–41 when it stood alone against Germany, Great Britain had been forced to liquidate many of its foreign holdings in order to acquire vital raw materials. The process had wiped out the position that it held in 1939 of being one of the world's richest holders of foreign investments. Instead, it was left deeply indebted, in the form of war loans, to the USA.

Rolling stock: The engines, carriages and wagons used on a railway.

In the long term it was evident that these problems would be more difficult to solve because the war had loosened or dissolved the links of many European states with their colonial markets in Africa and Asia. Although the great crises of decolonisation still lay some years in the future, the world war had done much to rupture the traditional trading links of Britain and France and, to a lesser extent of the Netherlands. British exports to India, for example, stood at £34 million in 1934, but were less than half that sum at the end of the war.

Humanitarian problems: Difficulties associated with the welfare of people. The aim of humanitarianism is to improve life for people and to lessen their pain and suffering.

Refugees: People who are forced to leave their country because there is a war or because of their political or religious beliefs.

Gross national product: The total value at current prices of the annual flow of goods and services becoming available to a country for consumption and maintaining or adding to its material wealth.

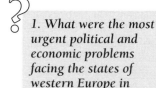

1. What were the most urgent political and economic problems facing the states of western Europe in 1945?

2. In what respects were the problems of reconstruction in western Europe in 1945 more difficult than those which had been faced in 1918?

Europe also faced **humanitarian problems** on a scale vastly greater than those which followed the First World War. The technology of the Second World War, together with the German schemes for the movement of labour forces and racial groups, had caused a displacement of population on a vast scale. In addition to the foreign labour conscripts, who now returned from Germany, to the concentration camp survivors and homeless victims of bombing, Germany suffered a vast influx of **refugees**. Many came from Germany's eastern territories, fleeing from the Russian advance. Meanwhile, large numbers of ethnic Germans were expelled from Hungary, Czechoslovakia and Yugoslavia so that these reconstituted states would not suffer again the problems caused by German minorities in the 1930s. The historian A.W. Purdue notes, in *A Companion to Modern European History 1871–1945* (1997), one of the great contrasts between peacemaking at the end of the two world wars: 'whereas Versailles had attempted to fit frontiers to peoples, now people were moved to fit frontiers'. It has been estimated that a total of about 50 million people were displaced from their homes in the course of the war, a figure roughly equal to the total number of deaths in the conflict. Probably about 20 million of these were homeless at the end of the war, and the work of the United Nations Relief and Rehabilitation Agency (UNRRA), to locate, register and re-house them all, continued for many years.

The terrible economic plight of Europe is put further into perspective if we consider the stimulus that the American economy received from the war. In 1940, 8.7 million American workers were unemployed. Four years later, not only had all been drawn back into work, but a further 10 million jobs had been created in American industry. Other statistics tell the same story of awesome industrial advance. The **gross national product** of the USA rose in the same period from $88 billion to $135 billion, output of manufactured goods increased by 300% and the productive capacity of the economy rose by 50%. This double process, of European destruction and American expansion, left the future of post-war Europe, in the short term at least, in the hands of the USA.

14.2 To what extent was the Marshall Plan responsible for the economic recovery of western Europe up to 1955?

A CASE STUDY IN HISTORICAL INTERPRETATION

Why was the Marshall Plan necessary?

The peculiar combination of circumstances at the end of the Second World War made economic recovery and a return to prosperity a particularly urgent requirement. Material damage and the problem of refugees were far more serious than at the end of the First World War. There also appeared to be serious political dangers in delay. Communism had already advanced over half of the continent and fears were well grounded that it might also threaten the western half if living standards remained low. The resurgence of right-wing extremism, too, was a prospect that could not be discounted in the event of prolonged economic depression.

Yet a range of practical obstacles stood in the way of rapid economic reconstruction. Even where effective wartime industries had been established, their conversion of peacetime production was a complex and expensive undertaking that most states could not afford. These states also faced problems of transport (damaged or disrupted by the war) and severe shortages of fuel for the factories and of food for the workers. In the case of Germany, economic life in many of the major cities had collapsed, and had been replaced by primitive systems of barter.

The first response of many western European states was to establish programmes of economic measures designed to hasten recovery. Farmers were offered generous subsidies to boost food production, extensive housing programmes were launched, and detailed provisions were made for social welfare. In Belgium in 1946, and in West Germany in 1948, far-reaching reform of the currency was undertaken.

Nevertheless, it was clear that the states of western Europe would take many years to recover by their own unaided efforts. The government of the USA was convinced from the closing years of the war that it could not risk the dangers involved in such a slow recovery, and that it would have to play a positive role. In addition to the political dangers already referred to, America's peacetime economy desperately needed stable European markets for its own goods and services. Negotiations in 1944 led to the establishment of two bodies intended to finance rapid recovery, the International Monetary Fund and the World Bank for Reconstruction and Development, now the World Bank.

The most significant development for western Europe, however, was the birth of the so-called 'Marshall Plan' in 1947. The brainchild of George C. Marshall, the project arose in large part from American fears that the recovery of the European economies was too slow. If the European economies were not placed upon a firmer footing, they might become dependent upon a constant flow of American economic aid. To avoid such a long-term drain upon American resources, the US government judged that it was preferable to inject enormous sums into the European economies in the short term. Britain and France took up the initiative with enthusiasm and convened a conference in Paris at which 16 European states indicated their willingness to participate in what was now designated as the European Recovery Programme (ERP). Nevertheless, the American plan was only partially successful. The broader proposal of a European customs union was rejected at this stage, and the suspicions of the Soviet Union ensured that the ERP would never be implemented in eastern Europe.

Did the Marshall Plan rescue the western European economies?

The simple statistics of sums received by individual western European states are set out here.

The wider issue of the overall impact of the Marshall Plan has caused greater controversy. The orthodox view of the plan's effect is that it provided

George C. Marshall (1880–1959)

During a distinguished military career, Marshall fought in France in the First World War, was adjutant to General Pershing (1919–24), and served as a major military advisor to President Roosevelt during the Second World War. He was appointed US Secretary of State in 1947, in which capacity he was the major force behind the European Recovery Programme (ERP). After retiring from politics in 1949, Marshall returned to office as Defence Secretary (1950–51) during the Korean War.

Sums allocated (in millions of dollars) to individual states by the ERP April 1948 – June 1951

Austria	560.8	Greece	515.1
Belgium and Luxembourg	546.6	Italy	1,297.3
Denmark	256.9	Netherlands	977.7
France	2,401.0	West Germany	1,297.3
Great Britain	2,713.6		

Total Marshall Plan allocation	**11,664.7**

'the crucial impetus for western European recovery, saving western Europe from the clutches of Soviet imperialism' (Till Geiger in *Western Europe: Economic and Social Change since 1945*, 1999). Yet some historians have questioned whether western Europe really needed to be saved. The immediate trigger of the Marshall Plan was the dip in European production during the severe winter of 1946–47, after a promising recovery immediately after the war. It is clear that Marshall saw this dip as a serious problem. However, the leading historian of the wartime and post-war economies has judged this to be an artificial crisis. Alan Milward, in *The Reconstruction of Western Europe, 1945–1951* (1984), considers that the European states might have contained the problem comfortably by cutting back on their spending of dollars. This, of course, would have been a severe blow to American exports, and Milward's argument is that the European states exaggerated the crisis by spending their dollar reserves freely. In part this was because they feared the possible political consequences of **austerity**, but also because they were confident that such a step would heighten American anxieties, and would lead to a comprehensive programme of American investment in European recovery.

There is thus some disagreement about the exact nature of American motives behind the Marshall Plan. In some quarters it has been interpreted primarily as a defensive measure, to defend the west against the threat of communism, which would advance with the advance of poverty. Elsewhere this danger has been minimised, and the vast American loans have been seen mainly as an aggressive American move to preserve their position at the head of a world capitalist 'bloc'. Such a view was put forward by commentators in the Soviet Union, and by many socialist writers in the west. Seen in this light, Till Geiger argues, 'the ERP might be interpreted as a gift in exchange for which the western European governments accepted American economic leadership'.

It is important to note, however, that American producers were not the only ones to benefit from the Marshall Plan. With more hard currency at their disposal, western European countries were also able to buy more from one another. The ERP was, therefore, a major factor in the post-war recovery of trade between the states of western Europe.

How great was the impact of the Marshall Plan upon individual European economies?

Whatever the direct impact of the Marshall Plan, the economic recovery of western Europe took place at a remarkable rate over the next few years. Nowhere was progress more spectacular than in West Germany, where it was popularly declared to amount to an 'economic miracle' (*Wirtschaftswunder*). Perhaps in some respects the German recovery was not as surprising as it might at first appear. Despite the devastation of the war, West Germany derived a number of distinct advantages from the circumstances of the late 1940s. For instance, in its demilitarised condition the Federal Republic itself did not have to spend any of its resources on armaments, a factor that was a significant drain on the other developed economies. In the broader context of German history it is also important to appreciate that the war had relieved West Germany of one of the most pressing difficulties experienced by the old Reich. With the destruction of the Junker class in eastern Germany, and the incorporation of their estates into the German Democratic Republic, the state no longer had to balance conflicting agricultural and industrial demands. To an extent the years of post-war reconstruction represented the economic triumph of the Ruhr industrialists within the German economy. The steelworks of the Ruhr also received a substantial boost from the outbreak of the Korean War, and the demand that it created for steel with

Austerity: Living cheaply or in poverty. The term was used after the Second World War to indicate the need to accept a low standard of living, and such disadvantages as food rationing, as the state recovered from the effects of war.

which to build weapons. In addition, West Germany enjoyed unusually good labour relations, a strong consensus in favour of the government's reconstruction policies, and an unfailing supply of labour, boosted by refugees from the east. Finally, the creation of the European Coal and Steel Community (ECSC) in 1951 also extended the 'domestic' market available to the producers of heavy industrial resources. On balance, although American funds played their role in West Germany's *Wirtschaftswunder*, it is likely that these other circumstances would have allowed the new state to make very rapid progress towards economic prosperity.

The importance of Marshall Plan funds for the regeneration of the French economy was much greater. The prospects for French recovery in 1945–47 were bleak. Resources were in short supply, labour relations were undermined by strong Communist influence within the trade unions, and inflation constituted a chronic problem. When Jean Monnet was appointed in 1946 to head the new Planning Commissariat (*Commisariat General du Plan*), he had much work to do. The resultant 'Monnet Plan' played a major role in France's response to its economic plight. As a comprehensive plan for the modernisation of the French economy, it was responsible for substantial improvements in farming methods and for the recovery of coal, electricity, steel and cement production as the bases for future French economic progress. It is difficult to determine how such progress at such a pace would have been possible had the introduction of the Monnet Plan not coincided with the arrival of massive financial aid in the shape of the Marshall Plan.

Similar conclusions may be drawn in Italy and in the **Benelux** countries. Italian war damage was far greater than that suffered by France, and the return to normality was hampered by the refusal of strong Communist and socialist groups to accept the simple restoration of capitalist production, and by the mistrust of central planning that arose from Mussolini's days in power. Italy, therefore, produced no equivalent to the Monnet Plan. Although it was aided by such factors as the discovery of natural gas resources in the Po Valley, Italian economic recovery would have been utterly impossible without the funds received from the USA. In Belgium and in the Netherlands, although less damage had been done by the war, there was also little scope for industrial modernisation and expansion. The Belgian coal industry was old-fashioned, and with limited domestic markets, both Belgium and the Netherlands suffered badly from the damage done to wider European markets. The Dutch economy had also suffered from the loss of colonial possessions in the Far East to the Japanese. Belgium, in fact, was very late in making any application for funds under the Marshall Plan, and received relatively little. Indirectly, however, these Benelux states were major beneficiaries of the recovery in European trade that was stimulated by the American funds.

Taken overall, the industrial achievement of western Europe in the first decade of peace was impressive. German and Italian industrial production in 1956 was more than double what it had been in 1937, the last year of normal, peacetime production. Although Britain and France had not advanced so rapidly, their overall production figures were still 50% higher than they had been in 1937. The table opposite provides statistical details of many of these favourable economic trends.

Benelux: A 'shorthand' term used to describe collectively Belgium, the Netherlands and Luxembourg. The term derives from the first letters of each country's name.

Jean Monnet (1888–1979)
French economist who served as Secretary General of the League of Nations (1919–23). Between 1923 and 1938, Monnet was involved with many important international economic projects, including re-organisation of the Polish economy and of the railways of China. He was an advocate and organiser of the combined Anglo-French war effort in 1940. Monnet collaborated with Robert Schuman in the production of the original project for the establishment of the ECSC and of the wider European economic union. President of the High Authority of the ECSC (1952–55). He founded the Committee for the United States of Europe in 1955.

1. What was the purpose of the European Recovery Programme?

2. What arguments are there for and against the claim that the Marshall Plan saved western Europe from economic collapse?

Economic performance in western European states, 1950–75

Output of coal and lignite (in million metric tons)

	1939	1946	1950	1955	1960	
Britain	233	240	220	225	197	*Production figures declined in the 1970s with the declining use of fossil fuels.*
France	47	39.8	53	57	58	
West Germany	351*	96.5	188	223	240	
Belgium	29	25.6	27	30	22	

Output of pig iron (in million metric tons)

	1930	1950	1975
Britain	6.3	9.8	12.1
France	10.1	7.8	22.4
West Germany	9.7*	9.5	30.1
Belgium	3.4	3.7	9.1
Italy	0.5	0.5	11.3

Output of steel (in million metric tons)

	1940	1950	1960	1975
Britain	13.4	16.6	24.7	20.2
France	4.4	8.7	17.3	27.0
West Germany	19.0*	12.1	30.1	40.4
Belgium	1.9	3.8	7.1	11.6
Italy	1.0	2.4	8.2	21.8

* pre-war German figures refer to the united Reich

Source: based upon figures in *The Longman Handbook of Modern European History 1763–1995* (edited by Chris Cook and John Stevenson, 1996)

To what extent do the statistics suggest that membership of the European Economic Community acted as a major stimulus to industrial production in western Europe in the 30 years after the end of the Second World War?

14.3 What were the main issues in the domestic politics of West Germany, 1950–1991?

The creation of the German Federal Republic

In one sense, domestic policy was a luxury that the new West German state could barely afford in the years that immediately followed the Second World War. To an extent unparalleled in the 19th and 20th centuries, Germany had lost control of its own affairs, and was at the mercy of the powers that had defeated it in 1945. In the three western zones of occupation, the most urgent priority was the establishment of a government sufficiently democratic to remain acceptable to the western allies and sufficiently stable to address the region's appalling economic problems. In the longer term, German politicians remained acutely aware of the division of the country into western and Soviet 'blocs', and could not wholly ignore the question of the future relationship between these 'blocs'. For many years, of course, this was an issue so closely connected with the Cold War interests of the superpowers that German politicians were allowed little initiative in the matter.

By 1948, it was already clear that the western allies were willing to accept the construction of an autonomous German state in the zones under their control. In that year, negotiations between the allied authorities and representatives of the German provinces (*Länder*) in the allied zones produced a set of constitutional proposals that were approved by referendum

**Konrad Adenauer
(1876–1967)**

After a legal career, Adenauer became Mayor of Cologne in 1917. In that position, he organised civil resistance to the French occupation of the Rhineland but, as a member of the Catholic Centre Party, was forced from office by the Nazis (1933). Founder and President of the Christian Democratic Union (CDU) in 1945, and elected first Chancellor of the West German state in 1949. Remaining Chancellor until 1963, Adenauer was a major architect of West Germany's political re-integration, of improved relation with France, and of the European Economic Community.

in 1949. These proposals sought to guard against the re-emergence of any new dictatorship by reducing the role of the President, by banning anti-democratic political parties, and by combining proportional representation with the election of constituency representatives. The elections that took place for the first West German Parliament (*Bundestag*) in August 1949 made it clear that two main figures would dominate the domestic politics of the new state. These were Konrad Adenauer, leader of the conservative Christian Democrats (CDU) and Kurt Schumacher, at the head of the revived Social Democrats (SPD). In a close fight, the CDU won 139 seats to the SPD's 131, and Adenauer became the first Federal Chancellor of the German Federal Republic (*Bundesrepublik Deutschland* – BRD), governing in coalition with the Free Democrats (FDP).

The economic problems that confronted Adenauer upon his election were enormous. Two million workers in the BRD were unemployed, and the state had to accommodate some 12 million refugees from what had been the eastern territories of the Reich. In addition, in the light of the rapid progress that was made towards integration and rehabilitation, it is easy to forget the level of mistrust that the new West German state still encountered in its relations with neighbouring states and with the occupation authorities. There was little that Adenauer could do under the prevailing circumstances to improve links with the eastern part of Germany, nor did he believe that he needed to be particularly active in this respect. In his view, the construction of a stable and prosperous society in West Germany would automatically create a magnet towards which East Germans would be drawn.

The achievement of social and political stability

The most striking feature of the development of West Germany from 1951 was its rapid economic growth. This growth naturally played an important role in ensuring the social and political stability of the new state. It is important, however, not to underestimate the potential in the devastated West German state for political instability and disruption, and it required a programme of government measures to defuse these threats. Increased industrial production, for instance, had to be accompanied by the establishment of stable and successful labour relations. A new Works Constitution Law (1952) extended worker participation in industrial management through the use of workers' consultative councils. It did much to ensure that West German workers would not respond to communist propaganda from East Germany.

Other pressing social issues were also tackled with considerable success. New housing was provided for 430,000 West Germans by 1952, and for 4 million by 1957. Social stability and recovery from the material losses of wartime were also greatly accelerated by the Equalisation of Burdens Act (1952). This made provision for more prosperous citizens, those least affected by the impact of the war, to contribute funds from which compensation could be paid to refugees and those who had lost most during the war. This took the form of a 50% tax (levied at 1948 values), payable over a period of 30 years.

Political stability was also enhanced by the consolidation of the CDU vote, and by the steady improvement in relations between Adenauer's government and the allied authorities. West Germany was recognised by the western allies as a sovereign state in May 1955, and its admission into NATO marked an important step forward in its integration into the inter-national community. In particular, this step raised the question of the re-establishment of a German army, a problem that was tackled by careful assurances that the new force would remain under the control of civilian politicians, and of the *Bundestag*.

By 1961 West Germany had made enormous social and economic progress, although it was becoming clear that the political ascendancy of Konrad Adenauer was drawing to a close. He was now 81 years old, and his position was increasingly challenged by the regenerated SPD under the leadership of Willi Brandt, Mayor of West Berlin. Adenauer's personal prestige was also damaged by his muted response to the construction of the Berlin Wall, and subsequently by his clumsy handling of a dispute with the magazine *Der Spiegel*. His attempts to prevent the publication of sensitive material by arresting the editors raised bitter and unwelcome memories of earlier German authoritarianism.

Historians have questioned how much of the old Germany lived on in Adenauer's state, or whether he had indeed created a new Germany. It was certainly possible to discern some strong elements of continuity, notably in the civil service and in the teaching profession, and propagandists in East Germany found it easy to 'expose' personalities in the west with a Nazi past. On the other hand, there was evidence that certain political and social attitudes had undergone a significant change. By the 1960s there was a distinct consensus in favour of European integration, and West German reservations on such subjects as re-armament and membership of NATO suggested strongly that German militarism was a thing of the past.

Why was there a period of instability in West German domestic politics in the 1960s and 1970s?

The CDU retained power as part of a conservative coalition until 1969, but the late 1960s were troubled years. Economic growth slowed, causing a relative 'slump' in the West German economy, and the lack of government interest in social reform created a degree of opposition and tension. On one level this was apparent in the electoral success of the SPD, which brought Willi Brandt to power in 1969. It was more spectacularly apparent in the wave of student revolt that swept West Germany, and other parts of Europe, in the late 1960s and the decade that followed. In part, this resulted from the unease of the younger generation of West Germans at the state's links with its past. Trials of Nazi war criminals in 1963–65 had raised serious issues between the generations, and the conservatism of the 'Great Coalition' throughout the 1960s raised fears that Germany might be reverting to bad old ways.

Outrage at the war in Vietnam, and familiar complaints about old-fashioned teaching and poor conditions in the universities completed a dangerous mixture. The spark was provided, in April 1968, by a right-wing attempt to assassinate Rudi Dutschke, one of the most prominent leaders of the radical students. The majority of West German cities were affected by the wave of student riots, while a more serious threat emerged in the development of **urban terrorism**. In particular, the Red Army Faction, otherwise known as the **Baader–Meinhof Gang**, under-took a campaign of arson and murder aimed to undermine the state and the capitalist economy.

One important response to this unrest was the extensive programme of social reform launched by Willi Brandt during his chancellorship. Pensions were increased, health insurance was extended, student grants were increased and made more widely available, the power of workers' councils was increased, and extensive measures were introduced to combat inequalities between the sexes. After a narrow electoral victory in 1969, Brandt won a more convincing victory in 1972, but soon found himself under considerable pressure within his party from Helmut Schmidt, who replaced him as Federal Chancellor in 1974. Helmut Schmidt faced many difficulties both in his leadership of the SPD and of

Urban terrorism: Violence (bombing, kidnapping etc.) in towns and cities in order to achieve political aims or to force a government to do something.

Baader–Meinhof Gang: Other name for the Red Army faction in West Germany in the 1960s and 1970s. Took the name 'Baader–Meinhof Gang' from its most prominent members, Andreas Baader and Ulrike Meinhof. Undertook a campaign of arson and murder aimed at undermining the state and the capitalist economy. Although Baader and Meinhof were arrested in 1972, this form of terrorism remained a major problem for the West German government until 1977. Then, with the failure of an aircraft hijacking designed to secure their releases, the leaders committed suicide in prison.

Helmut Schmidt (1918–)
German socialist politician, member of the Social Democratic Party. Elected to the *Bundestag* (federal parliament) in 1953. Interior Minister for Hamburg (1961–65); Defence Minister (1969–72) and Finance Minister (1972–74). Schmidt became Federal Chancellor (prime minister) on Willi Brandt's resignation in 1984. As Chancellor, Schmidt introduced social reforms and continued the policy of *Ostpolitik*. With French president Giscard d'Estaing, he started annual world and European economic summits.

Helmut Kohl (1930–)
German socialist politician, leader of the Christian Democratic Union. Federal Chancellor (prime minister) 1982–90. Oversaw the reunification of Germany in 1990. A dramatic fall in his popularity followed his miscalculation of the true costs of re-unification and effects on German economy. Managed to hang on and achieve a fourth electoral victory in 1994.

West Germany in the 1970s, notably the demands for radical reform from the left wing of his own party, and the opposition of many politicians to *Ostpolitik* (see below). He resisted such challenges with great success, to emerge with as much influence and prestige as a European politician as Adenauer had enjoyed 15 years earlier. In domestic politics, nevertheless, he continued to face considerable opposition over such issues as the deployment of NATO missiles on West German soil. The formation of a German Green Party in 1980 also provided a serious competitor for the SPD in its attempts to win left-wing and environmentalist votes. Schmidt retained power through a coalition with the FDP until September 1982, when his former allies transferred their support once again to the CDU in a deal that brought Helmut Kohl to office as Federal Chancellor.

'Ostpolitik'

The most important consequence of Willi Brandt's election as Federal Chancellor (prime minister) in 1969 was a radical change in West Germany's approach to the problem of its relationship with communist East Germany. For Brandt it was no longer sufficient to wait until the growing prosperity of the west finally pulled East Germany into its orbit. Such factors as the construction of the Berlin Wall in 1961 gave the division an air of permanence, and it therefore became all the more urgent that a formal relationship should be forged between the two halves of the German people. Willi Brandt had already taken some steps in this direction during his time as Mayor of Berlin, negotiating a Christmas 'truce' in 1963 during which Berliners might cross the wall to visit relatives. As Chancellor, he now launched a comprehensive 'eastern policy' (*Ostpolitik*).

The key to the success of this *Ostpolitik* lay in the hands of the Soviet Union, the political masters of East Germany, and a state which did not formally recognise the existence of West Germany. Brandt's most important achievement, therefore, was to negotiate a series of agreements which regulated West Germany's relations with the USSR and with other states within the Eastern 'bloc'.

- The Moscow Treaty (August 1970) by which West Germany recognised the western borders of Poland, thereby renouncing territory that had been transferred from Germany to Poland after the war. This agreement also provided for both German states to become members of the United Nations.

- The Warsaw Treaty (December 1970), by which West Germany and Poland recognised the 'Oder–Neisse line' as Poland's western border, and made arrangements for remaining Germans within Poland to emigrate to West Germany.

- The Prague Treaty (December 1973), by which West Germany recognised the post-war borders of Czechoslovakia.

- The Berlin Agreement (September 1971), by which the USSR recognised Berlin's links with West Germany and agreed to greater freedom of communication between West Berlin and the rest of the state.

These international agreements cleared away the diplomatic obstacles to bilateral agreements between the two German states. In 1972, the two German republics at last recognised each other as independent states, and made a series of agreements to promote communications and travel from one state to the other.

Eventually, in the 1990s, the two German states were to be reunited, not as a direct result of this policy, but as part of the general collapse of Soviet

1. What were the most urgent political and economic problems facing the government of the new West German state in 1949?

2. What was Ostpolitik *and what did it achieve?*

power in eastern Europe. Nevertheless, one must conclude that *Ostpolitik* was a major success for the government of West Germany. Its original stated objective was to 'ease the painful consequences of the division of our fatherland' and it achieved a great deal in this respect, with a substantial increase in phone calls and visits between the two states. It had a wider impact, however, especially in terms of the enormous loans that West Germany subsequently made to East Germany. The biggest of these was the loan of 1.95 billion Deutschmarks arranged in 1983–84. This caused many commentators to judge that, in effect, the East German state became financially dependent upon West Germany and that in this important respect *Ostpolitik* was drawing the two states very close to reunion.

14.4 What were the major domestic issues within French politics, 1945–1991?

What divisions and tensions existed within French politics at the end of the war?

Great efforts were made in 1944–45 by both French and allied politicians to create the illusion that France was in effect one of the victorious powers, emerging from the trials of war to resume its place among the major powers of Europe. The reality was very different, and French politics in the late 1940s had a good deal in common with the politics of West Germany. At best, its recent past could be interpreted as an era of division, of internal crisis, that had turned one Frenchman against another, and rendered the state liable to invasion and destruction in 1940. At worst, it had to be acknowledged that the right wing of French politics had been guilty of a high degree of collaboration with Nazi Germany (see Chapter 12), making a significant contribution to the German war effort and co-operating enthusiastically with German anti-semitic policies. The era of peace even began with France's own miniature version of the war-crimes trials that were taking place in Germany. Pierre Laval, the former Prime Minister, and Joseph Darnand, leader of the right-wing *Milice*, were among those convicted of treason and executed in 1945. A total of 125,000 prosecutions for collaboration in the first year of peace led to 40,000 similar convictions. The former head of state, Philippe Pétain, was also condemned to death for treason but, in view of his advanced age, the sentence was changed to life imprisonment.

Yet the wounds within French society were now too deep to be healed so easily. Resentment and hatred between those who had been involved in the resistance movements and those who had collaborated introduced new and complex divisions, very different from the old political divisions of the Third Republic in that they cut across the traditional lines of class interest. Even among those who had resisted the German occupation there were profound and potentially dangerous political divisions. The French Communists claimed to have lost 75,000 combatants in the course of the war, and naturally believed that these 'martyrs' conferred some legitimacy upon their claims to be the major post-war party of government.

Such a form of government was completely unacceptable to Charles de Gaulle, who had spent the war in London as head of the 'Free French' forces. He carefully established his own claims to power. In London, he claimed his had been the official French government in exile, and it had been his forces that had liberated Paris 'with the help of their British and American allies'. Such claims, though clearly absurd, did much to restore

French self-respect at the end of the most traumatic period in the nation's recent history. De Gaulle's greatest strength lay in the fact that, however ambiguous his relations were with the Americans and the British, his conservative politics were much more acceptable to the wartime allies than those of the activists within the resistance movements.

Why did the years 1945–1958 form such a period of instability in French politics?

It will be hard to understand French politics in the first decade or so of peace without recognising that de Gaulle's position, apparently so commanding, was actually largely artificial. It concealed a political culture of great diversity and with deep divisions. Although elected head of a Provisional Government in November 1945, he quickly found himself forced to make distasteful bargains with the Communists in order to form a government. Deeply unwilling to do so, he resigned in January 1946, laying the foundations for more than a decade of governmental instability.

If de Gaulle had retired because he anticipated a return to the divided and unstable party politics of the pre-war period, the next decade was to prove him right. Of the three main parties in contemporary French politics – the Communists (PCF), the socialists and the conservative Popular Republicans (MRP) – none could ever command a majority or anything close to one. Similarly, any form of close, workable coalition was undermined by mistrust between communists and socialists, and by fundamental political differences between communists and the MRP. A more sinister element was added in the mid-1950s by the emergence of a populist politician, Pierre Poujade, whose nationalist, pro-colonial and **xenophobic** mixture of policies recalled some of the more dangerous right-wing figures of the 1930s. The situation was complicated further by de Gaulle's decision to found the RPF (*Rassemblement du peuple Française* – a 'movement', he insisted, and not a political party) whose insistence upon national unity won much support away from the parties of the right. The confusion that this produced may be gauged from the fact that 22 different ministries were formed under the Fourth Republic between 1946 and 1958, and from the coining of a new term to describe the state of contemporary French politics: immobilism ('the politics of no change').

Contemporaries tended to dismiss the Fourth Republic as a failure, and there is evidence to support that judgement. The regime failed to establish stable, parliamentary government, and its foreign policy beyond Europe was disastrous. Inflation remained a consistent problem.

More recent historians have tended to treat it more kindly, pointing out that it initiated the important policy of reconciliation with Germany, and that in many respects its economic policy, in particular the 'Monnet Plan', laid some important bases for the economic successes of the Fifth Republic. In the last days of the Fourth Republic prosperity was growing, and French industrial output in 1956 was 87% higher than in 1938 (the last year of peace before the Second World War). Yet the political reputation of the regime was unable to withstand a succession of foreign crises and failures. The loss of Vietnam and humiliation over the Suez Crisis were bad enough, but the eruption of a more serious crisis in Algeria was more than the Republic could stand.

Decolonisation and the loss of Algeria

The first 20 years of peace formed a period of considerable success in France's relations with its European neighbours, but of disaster in its foreign policy beyond Europe. Although the Second World War had a considerable impact upon its overseas possessions, France still ended it in

Xenophobic: Showing a fear or extremely strong dislike of people from other countries.

principle as a colonial power. While it was clear that France would now have to redefine its relations with its overseas territories, it was hard for French politicians to contemplate the dissolution of the colonial empire. In the context of France's wartime defeat and occupation, these colonial possessions were its main claim to be considered a major power.

The original plan was to redefine colonial relationships by the creation of a French Union, in which the different territories would be linked to France in different ways, depending upon their earlier histories. Some would be protectorates (Tunisia and Morocco), some colonies (most of the West African territories), and some would be designated 'associate states' (Vietnam, Cambodia, Laos). Sovereignty would lie with the President of the Republic, and real power would continue to be exercised by the government in Paris.

Almost immediately the project suffered a major blow from the opposition of the movement for Vietnamese independence, the Viet Minh, under the leadership of Ho Chi Minh. Having already resisted the Japanese with some success, the Viet Minh turned their attention to the French from 1946 onwards, eventually gaining a crushing victory at Dien Bien Phu in May 1954. The defeat swung French public opinion decisively against this distant war, and convinced the government to abandon the defence of its Indo-Chinese possessions. The withdrawal marked a significant break with France's past, and ended a serious drain upon national finance, which had undermined attempts to regenerate the French economy.

It was one thing to abandon Vietnam, to grant autonomy to Tunisia (1956), or to begin negotiations for the independence of Morocco. It was a different matter altogether to contemplate the independence of Algeria. Not only had Algeria been a French possession for over a century, but it contained over a million French settlers. It was regarded administratively as part of the French state. Algiers, Oran and Constantine were designated as *départements* with equal status to those on the French mainland. Nevertheless, the European settlers enjoyed much greater political rights than the eight million native, Moslem Algerians. Discontent showed itself in the formation of a National Liberation Front (FLN) and an increasingly violent guerrilla campaign against the French. By 1957, France was deploying 400,000 troops to maintain its control of Algeria.

Départements: Largest local government units in France.

Riots in the streets of Algiers, 1960.

The violence in Algeria also had a devastating effect upon domestic politics within France. Not only did the military presence impose an enormous strain upon the economy, but successive governments were faced with fierce opposition, on the one hand from conservatives hostile to any suggestion of surrendering Algeria and, on the other, from left-wingers protesting at the violence with which French authority was maintained. These trends led in May 1958 to the eruption of 'Operation Resurrection', a coup launched by French settlers and army units in Algeria, aimed at preventing the hand-over of the country to the FLN.

Charles de Gaulle and the re-orientation of French politics

The revolt, and the support that it enjoyed at high political and military levels within France, finally demonstrated the impotence of the Fourth Republic. Its most important implication for French domestic politics was the emergence of Charles de Gaulle from retirement to 'save' the Republic. This he did on his own terms, insisting upon a new constitution (which effectively established the Fifth Republic), throwing a new political party (the UNR) into parliamentary elections with great success, and gaining 78% of the votes in the first presidential elections of the new Republic. The most notable feature of the new constitution was the greater power that it granted to the President. The President was now elected for a term of seven years, was entitled to appoint and to dismiss the Prime Minister, and had the power to dissolve parliament. In addition, the government could, in extraordinary circumstances and for a short time, govern by decree.

Beginning his presidency as a firm supporter of 'French Algeria', de Gaulle steadily realised the difficulties of this course, and moved towards a more flexible position. In September 1959 he accepted the principle of self-determination for Algeria, and did much to influence the outcome of a referendum (July 1961) which confirmed that course of action. A further army revolt against the principle of Algerian independence held many dangers, including attempts to assassinate de Gaulle, but by now the army rebels had lost the support of the French people as a whole. Agreement was reached in the course of 1962 with Algerian nationalist leaders, and the new state was recognised as independent in July of that year. In the meantime, in 1960, de Gaulle had also recognised the independence of all French colonies in West Africa. In effect, he was undertaking a major re-orientation of French policy, turning his back upon traditional, 19th-century areas of French greatness, and establishing the important principle that France's future role lay in Europe.

Nevertheless, it is important to realise that in some respects, de Gaulle's vision was still rooted in the past. 'France,' he declared, 'is not really herself unless in the front rank. France cannot be France without greatness.' Such a claim revealed the impact that French humiliation in 1940 had made upon de Gaulle, as upon many Frenchmen, and the extent to which his European policy was much more an attempt to carve out a new niche for France, than to achieve real European integration. The 1960s provided several illustrations of these priorities. De Gaulle's insistence that France should not be drawn into the American sphere of influence was reflected in his rejection of British membership of the European Economic Community (EEC) and in French withdrawal from its military commitments to NATO (1966). In parallel to this last measure, France developed its own military 'strike force' (*force de frappe*), exploding its first atomic weapon in 1960, and steadily developing an independent nuclear capability in the decades that followed. As we shall see later, de Gaulle remained insistent that France should enjoy special privileges within the

EEC, and that a bilateral relationship between France and West Germany should lie at the heart of this European co-operation.

The student revolt of 1968

In the long term it is evident that de Gaulle changed the direction of French history and provided a new international role for the country. This was less clearly appreciated by many of his contemporaries, and the President was probably the most notable casualty of the wave of student revolt and economic discontent that swept Europe at the end of the 1960s. In each case common, international factors combined with specific, domestic stimuli. In France, a substantial role was played by student protests within the universities at conservative teaching and at poor working and living conditions. These protests increased rapidly in May 1968 as university authorities called in police to disperse demonstrations and as trade unions called a general strike in support of the students.

In the last days of May, with the French Communist Party planning major demonstrations, with the government mobilising troops, and with de Gaulle mysteriously vanishing from the political scene for several days, the Republic seemed to be on the verge of collapse. In general terms, the situation was retrieved more easily in France than elsewhere, and the 'events of May' produced none of the prolonged urban terrorism witnessed in West Germany or in Italy. Encouraged by conservative counter-demonstrations, de Gaulle returned to the political scene and called a general election in which the 'Gaullists' made major gains. When he subsequently held a referendum to confirm his personal popularity (April 1969), the ploy misfired badly. With 53% of the electorate voting against him, de Gaulle retired from French politics for the last time.

French politics after de Gaulle

French conservatism learned a number of valuable lessons from the events that had destroyed de Gaulle. His successor, Georges Pompidou (1969–74), addressed some of the causes of the unrest directly by creating 43 new universities and by granting the trade unions the right to representation in the running of industrial companies. At the same time, he abandoned de Gaulle's European policy by accepting the principle of increased membership of the European Community, and supporting Britain's application for membership.

Under the presidency of Valéry Giscard d'Estaing (1974–81), France began to encounter new problems. Giscard responded at first to the middle-eastern oil crisis with an expensive and unsuccessful search for offshore oil resources. The next solution to the problem was large-scale investment in the French nuclear industry, which provided an independent source of energy at the cost of widespread protest from environmentalists. French society also changed in other respects, for this period witnessed the lowering of the voting age to 18, the legalisation of abortion, the liberalisation of divorce laws and the introduction of a **capital gains tax** on the most wealthy.

Two decades of considerable conservative continuity ended in 1981 with the electoral victory of François Mitterrand's Socialist–Communist coalition. It was the first time since 1936 that France had been governed by these political groupings, although the Communists left the alliance in 1984. The impact upon French politics and economics was mixed. An extensive programme of nationalisation brought the electricity and telecommunications industries, and several major banks, into public ownership. In addition, the death penalty was abolished. On the other hand, the budget deficit rose considerably and the rate of inflation stood at 14% in 1982. A

Georges Pompidou (1911–1974) After an early career in teaching, he entered politics in de Gaulle's cabinet in 1945. Served as Director General of the Rothschild Bank (1956–62) during de Gaulle's absence from French politics, but returned to office with his political chief in 1958. Prime Minister (1962), losing office in the course of the political disruption of 1968. Upon de Gaulle's retirement from politics, Pompidou was elected President of the Republic in 1969.

Capital gains tax: A tax by the government on an increase in capital value. The argument goes that since a person's individual purchasing power and standard of living in a given period depends not only on their income but also on any possible increase in the value of any capital they own, tax should be levied not only on income but also on capital gains.

François Mitterand (1916–1996)
French socialist politician. He had ministerial posts in 11 governments (1947–58), and formed the French Socialist Party (PS) in 1971. He was President of France from 1981 to 1995. Introduced proportional representation (see page 289) in 1985. From 1982, his administrations combined economic orthodoxy with social reform. Defeated Jacques Chirac in May 1988 to secure a second term in office as president. Towards the end of this presidency his failing health weakened his hold on power.

?

1. What factors brought Charles de Gaulle to power in France (a) in 1945 and (b) in 1958?

2. Why was the question of Algerian independence such a divisive one in French politics in the 1950s and 1960s?

3. In what respects might it be claimed that Charles de Gaulle provided France with a new political direction in Europe and in the world?

relatively high level of unemployment was one of the factors that fuelled racial tension, often aimed at North African immigrants, and the extremist National Front, led by Jean-Marie Le Pen, became an alarming feature of French politics in the 1980s. From 1986 onwards, when elections returned a substantial number of conservatives to parliament, Mitterand found himself in the awkward position of working with a conservative Prime Minister, Jacques Chirac. It was an uncomfortable arrangement that did much to end the impetus of socialist reform.

Towards the end of Mitterand's presidency, there were some signs that France's post-war history was coming full circle. Revelations about the President's early career indicated that, despite his activity in the Resistance in the closing stages of the Second World War, he had been involved in right-wing organisations in the 1930s, and had protected prominent wartime collaborators in recent years, including some suspected of war-crimes. At the time of his death, Mitterand was viewed in many quarters as an opportunist, who had swum with the tide in order to further his own career. Once again, in the 1980s, the ghosts of France's wartime experience returned to haunt contemporary politics.

14.5 By what means and with what success did Italy overcome its domestic political problems in the years 1945–1991?

How effectively were Italian politics re-stabilised in the post-war years?

In 1945 Italy, like Germany, had to rebuild national politics upon the ruins of an extremist regime destroyed by the war. Political forces within Italy, however, had played a large part in the destruction of Mussolini's Fascist government. It had been severely damaged by the resistance of Italian left-wing forces, communists and socialists, and finally dislodged by traditional conservative elements within Italian politics. King Victor Emmanuel III, Marshal Badoglio and their allies hoped to be able to negotiate with the allies, to preserve their own influence in post-war politics, and to deflect the influence of the communists. In these aims, they were largely unsuccessful. Seriously compromised by his earlier dealings with Mussolini, Victor Emmanuel was forced to abdicate, and the monarchy was rejected altogether by a referendum in 1945 that made Italy a republic.

Yet the parties of the left were also unable to make a decisive impact in the elections that took place in 1946. Suspicions of their links with the Soviet Union combined with the hostility of the Catholic Church to limit the Italian Communist Party to 19% of the vote. The socialists did only a little better. Most successful were the conservative Christian Democrats, whose leader, Alcide de Gasperi, served as Prime Minister (1945–53). The constitution of the new republic borrowed much from the pre-Fascist state, although it dropped the anti-clerical stance of early Italian liberalism and retained the Concordat that Mussolini had made with the Catholic Church. Thus equipped, the Christian Democrats were to dominate Italian government until the 1990s.

Nevertheless, with its electoral support fluctuating between 38% (1963) and 48% (1948) of the votes, the Christian Democrats never achieved an overall majority, and always governed as part of a coalition. This has given Italian politics a reputation for instability. Such an impression is supported by the fact that between 1945 and 1970 the country had a total of 28 governments and 12 prime ministers. On the other hand, these governments were formed largely from the same 'pool' of experienced politicians, and the changes consisted mainly of these politicians switching places and replacing one another. Change, therefore, did not necessarily entail inexperience or discontinuity. In this respect, contemporary Italian politics had settled into a familiar path. The historian Martin Clark's description of it in *Modern Italy, 1871–1982* (1984), as 'the politics of compromise and patronage, of temporary deals and temporary governments', should remind us very strongly of the 'Transformism' that characterised Italian politics in the decades immediately after unification (see Chapter 9).

The most serious sources of instability in the 1960s and 1970s were found outside parliamentary politics. As elsewhere in Europe, issues of student discontent played a large role in disturbances in 1968–69, although in Italy the situation was complicated by such issues as the conservatism of the Catholic Church and a limited revival of Fascism. Italy, like Germany, was seriously affected by a wave of urban terrorism, and this remained a serious political problem throughout the 1970s and into the 1980s. **Neo-Fascist groups** undoubtedly made a contribution to this terrorism, but the left-wing Red Brigade (founded in 1971) was the major force in the campaign of violence. The worst outrages of this period were the explosion that killed 16 people outside the Bank of Agriculture in Milan (December 1969) and the bomb attack on Bologna railway station in August 1980. The greatest political sensation was caused by the kidnap and murder (1978) of Aldo Moro, former Prime Minister and prominent member of the Christian Democrats. These last two events had a decisive impact upon public opinion, and the campaign of terror declined in the early 1980s as it became increasingly clear that it was counter-productive.

A further challenge to political stability in post-war Italy was mounted by organised crime. It was one of the great ironies of the defeat of Fascism from 1943 that the **Mafia**, which had been effectively confronted by Mussolini's government, was steadily reintroduced into Italy through contact with the American forces of occupation. For much of this period official efforts to deal with the problem were characterised by failure or by incompetence, and scandals erupted at regular intervals. Top Italian politicians were accused of links with the Mafia, and the leader of the government's special anti-Mafia unit, General Dalla Chiesa, was murdered. A law passed in 1965 to expel known *mafiosi* from Sicily, the traditional home of the organisation, proved to be a serious mistake, spreading Mafia activity to other parts of Italy. The government's greatest success against organised crime in the post-war period was achieved in 1987, when a special court in Palermo convicted and imprisoned more than 450 *mafiosi*. Important as this breakthrough was, subsequent bomb attacks and revenge killings suggested that the problem had not been eliminated.

How successful was Italy's post-war economic recovery?

With the exception of Germany, Italy suffered more extensive damage from the fighting in the Second World War than any other part of

Neo-Fascist groups: Groups copying the beliefs and ideology of the Fascists from an earlier era.

Mafia: Secret criminal organisation that was founded in Sicily and organises many illegal activities in Europe and the USA. Members of the Mafia are known as the *mafiosi*.

western Europe. The damage done to the economy of Italy was very serious indeed. Agricultural production in 1945 stood only at one-third of the level achieved in 1938, and industrial production was lower still. Yet Italy made rapid progress in the first years of peace, benefiting from the relatively low level of damage to industrial plant in the north of the country, and from a substantial injection of financial aid under the Marshall Plan. The discovery of natural gas deposits in the Po Valley was also of great importance, providing the country for the first time with a cheap source of energy.

In general, economic thinking reacted against the kind of central planning that Mussolini had employed, and was dominated by a 'free market' mentality. As a result, the stark division between the fortunes of northern and southern Italy (see Chapter 9) soon became evident once more. In the north of the country, industrial growth was so impressive that commentators wrote of Italy's own 'economic miracle'. Industrial production in the mid-1950s ran at more than twice the pre-war level, and by 1954 real wages were five times higher than at the end of the war. Italian industry recorded an average annual growth rate of 6% throughout the 1950s, with companies like Fiat and Olivetti developing into major enterprises on a world scale. Italy came to challenge France as the leader of the world's fashion and design industries. Membership of the European Community provided a stimulus to Italian industry, so much so that by 1980, Italy was ranked seventh among the leading industrial economies of the world.

Yet in the early stages of this recovery, many familiar problems persisted. Five million Italian adults were still illiterate in 1951, four million were unemployed in 1954, and much of the rural proletariat remained too poor to provide much of a market for industrial goods. The attempts of the governing Christian Democrats to tackle these problems met with limited success. Income tax was introduced in Italy for the first time, but conservative vested interests resisted any significant degree of land reform in the south. The issue of land reform became particularly urgent in the 1960s, aggravated by a population increase of over 9% and large-scale migration from the south to industrial cities of the north. Once again, little was achieved, and the tensions between northerners and southerners in the industrial cities became a significant feature of Italian politics, along with the economic problems of the south.

> 1. What factors made the Christian Democrats so successful in post-war Italian politics?
>
> 2. What arguments are there for and against the claim that Italy experienced an 'economic miracle' in the years after the Second World War?

14.6 Why was there so strong a movement towards economic integration in western Europe in the years after 1950?

The 'Six':
France
West Germany
Italy
Belgium
Holland
Luxembourg

Why was economic integration originally restricted to the 'Six'?

The second half of the 20th century saw a steady process by which western European states abandoned the independent pursuit of policy aims and to a large extent co-ordinated their economic and political interests. For such steps to be contemplated in the late 1940s and the early 1950s, required remarkable changes in traditional political thinking. It was more urgent, and therefore easier, for some states to make these changes than for others. Two states in particular, France and West Germany, had good reason to search for a new political beginning. For West Germany, integration offered the best route towards its two most urgent goals, political rehabilitation and economic recovery. For France, 70 years of confrontation with Germany had recently culminated in disaster and collapse. Co-operation offered not only a rapid route to economic recovery, but also a long-term alternative to political confrontation with its neighbour. In both cases it is also important to remember that, in the disturbed circumstances of the Cold War, the prospect of the spread of Communism in the midst of a shattered economy was very real.

Four other western European states had also been closely involved in, and seriously damaged by, the war; Italy, Belgium, the Netherlands and Luxembourg. For these states, economic integration offered wider markets for their goods than they could possibly have hoped for under other circumstances, as well as a degree of political security that was highly desirable in the light of recent events.

For these states economic integration sprang directly from the experience of their recent history. Other western European states found themselves in very different positions. Britain had not lost the war, and had not been invaded. Less uncertain in any case about its future security, Britain found further reassurance in its close political relationship with the USA, and in its close economic ties with the **Commonwealth**. The imperatives that drove many of the states of continental Europe did not apply to Britain. Spain and Portugal, meanwhile, were left in an unhappy and isolated position by the allied victory in 1945. While the power of Hitler and Mussolini had been destroyed, the right-wing regimes of Franco and Salazar survived for many years, distanced from the parliamentary democracy upon which western European integration was founded, and embarrassed by their former friendly relations with the defeated dictators. Sweden and Switzerland, meanwhile, could not contemplate a more active European role without abandoning long traditions of political neutrality, which seemed as important as ever in the tense atmosphere of the Cold War.

The first agencies for economic co-operation

Desirable as such integration was, it was not clear for some years what form it would take. When Winston Churchill proposed the formation of a Council of Europe in 1946, what he had in mind primarily was a form of political co-operation. This might have provided a united front against communism, and perhaps formed a basis for an alliance to balance the post-war superpowers of the USA and the USSR. In general, such political and military co-operation was less attractive to the states of western Europe than what came to be referred to as 'functional co-operation'. This was understood as practical co-operation in such areas as heavy industrial production.

The first projects for European co-operation thus occurred in these economic areas. April 1948 saw the establishment of the Organisation for European Economic Cooperation (OEEC), set up to promote trade within Europe between economies stimulated by the funds of the Marshall Plan. This was followed in 1950 by the European Payments Union (EPU) and by the Benelux Economic Union. The purpose of the EPU was to enable the transfer of European currencies, and thus to overcome problems that might arise from temporary difficulties that states experience with their **balance of payments**. The Benelux Economic Union instituted a high degree of free trade between Belgium, the Netherlands and Luxembourg. None of these organisations, however, was in any real sense a '**supranational**' body. They were simply economic agreements between sovereign states of a kind relatively common in recent European history.

The ECSC and the beginnings of supranational economic control

It was in this respect that the establishment of the European Coal and Steel Community (ECSC) in 1951 was a truly radical departure. The brainchild of Jean Monnet, French civil servant, and of Robert Schuman, the French

Commonwealth: An association of states comprising Britain and most of its former colonies and dominions. South African statesman Jan Smuts suggested its name. The 'British Commonwealth of Nations' was established in 1931. After the Second World War the name was modified to 'British Commonwealth', and the 'British' is frequently dropped.

Balance of payments: The equation between the sums spent and the sums earned by a state in its international trade, or in the trading of its currency.

Supranational: Giving up national sovereignty to the authority of an international body.

Robert Schuman (1886–1963)

A native of Luxembourg, he was active in French parliamentary politics from 1919, serving as Secretary of State for Refugees in 1940. He was Minister of Finance (1946–47), Prime Minister (1947–48) and Foreign Minister (1948–53). Schuman was involved in the adoption of the Marshall Plan (1948) and, with Jean Monnet, in the establishment of the ECSC (1951). Later, he was Minister of Justice (1955–56) and President of the European Parliament (1958).

Paul-Henri Spaak (1899–1972)

Entering Belgian parliamentary politics in 1932, he became Minister of Transport (1935) and Foreign Minister (1936). After the war he held office as Prime Minister (1946–49) and again as Foreign Minister. An enthusiastic champion of European co-operation, he later served as President of the Council of Europe (1949–51) and of the ECSC (1952–54). Spaak was Secretary General of NATO (1957–61).

Euratom: A political body to co-ordinate the development of nuclear energy within western Europe.

Foreign Minister, the project combined economic and political objectives. By combining coal and steel production in France and in West Germany, it aimed to stimulate economic recovery and growth in both states. By placing the process under the control of a genuinely supranational body, the High Authority, the project sought to ensure that German industrial recovery would not generate the same political dangers as it had in the 1930s. For reasons that were both pragmatic and symbolic, the common production of coal and steel would centre upon the Lorraine and Ruhr Valleys, so often in the past the focus of political differences between the two states.

The proposal by Monnet and Schuman was an immediate success. West Germany embraced the opportunity for an end to its own isolation with great enthusiasm, the USA welcomed so large a step towards European recovery, and Italy and the Benelux countries quickly appreciated the advantages that they would gain from membership. On the other hand, Britain and several other European states drew back from the prospect of placing such important economic resources under supranational control. In the years that followed, it soon became clear that such reluctance had been unwise: between 1951 and 1956 steel production within the ECSC increased by 50%, and overall industrial expansion took place at roughly twice the rate experienced in Britain. Over the same period trade between the six members of the ECSC increased by nearly 200%.

The immediate success of the ECSC was one of the factors that stimulated projects for further economic integration between the member states. It must be stressed, however, that external political factors also had considerable influence upon the timing of such moves. The Suez Crisis of 1956 was of particular significance, demonstrating to France and to Great Britain that European states could no longer expect to act against the interests and without the support of the superpowers. When, in the same year, the Soviet Union outraged public opinion in the west by its brutal suppression of the reformist government in Hungary, it was clear once more that there was simply no way in which the individual European states could back their protests with effective action. In political, as well as in economic terms the time seemed ripe to consider common structures.

The establishment of Euratom and of the EEC

Plans originating in the Benelux countries, with the Belgian Foreign Minister Paul-Henri Spaak and his Dutch counterpart Johan Beyen, culminated in the signature by 'the Six' of two treaties in 1957. The first of these set up Euratom, under a supranational High Authority similar to that which regulated the ECSC. The cheap energy that Euratom might produce for industrial use seemed especially attractive at a time when oil supplies were threatened by developments in the Middle East, and in particular by the Suez Crisis.

At the same time, the 'Six' committed themselves, by signing the Treaty of Rome, to the establishment of a general common market between them. The immediate aim of this European Economic Community (EEC) was to set up a customs union, with free and equal economic competition between its six members.

● No tariff barriers were to exist between the member states.

● Common tariffs were to be adopted for trade with states that were not members of the EEC.

● The members were to adopt a common stance in trade negotiations with other states.

● There would be free movement of labour within the community.

President de Gaulle rejects Britain's attempt to join the European Economic Community in 1967.

In the longer term, the six members committed themselves in principle to the formulation of common policies on defence, social reform and foreign relations. The establishment of the EEC was not without its problems, and the format that was finally established in 1957 owed much to the willingness of the West German Chancellor to make concessions in order to maintain good Franco–German relations. In particular, a greater degree of national freedom of action was permitted than had originally been planned. The Common Agricultural Policy (CAP) adopted by the community was designed with the interests of French farmers in mind. The version of the CAP eventually adopted in 1964 provided a system of protection and subsidy for producers, aimed at developing the agricultural industries within the member states, and at avoiding the food shortages that had occurred in the immediate post-war years. It established common prices for agricultural goods, generally set above the level of world prices, which naturally encouraged a high level of production.

On the other hand, the policy resulted in relatively high food prices within the member states, and in substantial surpluses of produce that could not be consumed within the community. These surpluses were often 'dumped' upon other markets, to the detriment of local producers.

The major institutions of the EEC, as established by the Treaty of Rome, make it clear that the original members sought the benefits of economic co-operation without really embracing the principle of 'supranationality'. The primary decision-making body, the Council of Ministers, was an organ by which the representatives of the individual governments, usually the Foreign Ministers, could consult, rather than one which overrode such sectional interests. The European Commission, meanwhile, proposed and policed common legislation, but did so primarily as a form of 'civil service', rather than as a governing body. A European Parliament was also established but, in its original form, it had no legislative authority. Only the European Court of Justice, established to enforce EEC law, was effectively able to override national law and government.

Why did membership of the EEC expand from 1970 onwards?

In purely economic terms, the EEC was an enormous and immediate success. All tariff barriers within the community had been removed by 1968, two years earlier than had been envisaged by the Treaty of Rome. Between 1957 and 1962 production within the member states increased by 27%, while that of the USA rose by only 18%, and that of Great Britain by 14%. Trade between member states over the same period rose by an enormous 170%.

What of the European states that had kept their distance from the EEC? Equally alert to the benefits of free trade, but hostile to the prospect of wider political integration, seven such states quickly set up an alternative economic union. Meeting in Stockholm in 1959, Britain, Switzerland, Austria, Denmark, Norway and Sweden established the European Free Trade Association (EFTA). Portugal quickly joined this group, and Finland became an associate member in 1961. EFTA, like the EEC, was a success. Trade between member countries increased by 71% in the first year of the life of the organisation, but the fact remained that the total population of the member states of EFTA was only half that of the members of the EEC. Besides, national economies of states within the EEC continued to perform better than the economies of EFTA members. The gross national product of the former in 1965 was 88% greater than it had been in 1953, while that of EFTA members had only increased by 54%. Clearly the benefits of membership did not adequately compensate for non-membership of the EEC.

Meanwhile some of the most formidable obstacles to the expansion of the European Community began to be eliminated. Although the Treaty of Rome had specifically catered for the future expansion of the EEC, such expansion had been vigorously opposed by Charles de Gaulle, whose conception of the European Community was that it should serve as an alternative basis for France's role as a major power. As a result, he disliked the idea of expansion, and was particularly suspicious of Britain's application for membership, in view of its continuing links with its former Empire, and its close political relationship with the USA. It had long been an important element of France's post-war foreign policy that it should establish its independence from the political and cultural influence of the USA. When de Gaulle was forced from power in 1969, however, such objections were dropped. His successor, Georges Pompidou, made it clear that no objections would be raised to new applications for membership.

Britain's application already had a long history, having first been put forward and rejected in 1962, and then again in 1967. It was the third application, in 1970, which proved successful. Denmark and the Republic of Ireland also entered the community under the terms of the treaty finalised in 1972. Norway's application for membership was approved at the same time, although its electorate rejected the opportunity in a referendum held in November 1972. In one important respect, this enlargement of the community took place at a bad moment. It was followed almost immediately by a recession caused primarily by the increase in oil prices, and the community did not receive the stimulus that had been expected from such expansion.

Although further expansion had been anticipated, with the establishment of special trading relations with Spain and Portugal (1970–72), it took nearly a decade for further recruitment to take place. Thereafter, expansion proceeded rapidly. The membership of Greece (1981), and of Spain and Portugal (1986), was based upon the re-establishment of stable democratic government in those states. By this stage the 12 members of the community contained a population of 345 million out of Europe's total (excluding the USSR) of 500 million. The inclusion of Finland, Sweden and Austria in 1995 effectively completed the recruitment of the major western European economies. At that point only Switzerland, with its long tradition of neutrality, and Norway, who once again rejected membership by referendum in 1992, remained outside the European Union.

By a separate set of processes, other regions, not all of them European, were admitted to associate membership status. This process had begun as early as 1963, when the Yaoundé Convention had granted associate status to former French and Belgian colonies. By the two Lomé Conventions (1975 and 1979) the same status was extended to most states in Africa, the Caribbean and the Pacific. Similarly, an agreement was drawn up with countries of southern Europe, who were permitted free trade with the EC in industrial, but not in agricultural, commodities.

1. What factors encouraged greater economic integration between western European states in the late 1940s and the 1950s?

2. In what respects were economic organisations such as the ECSC, Euratom and the EEC different from the agencies for economic co-operation that had preceded them?

3. Why did membership of the European Community remain static in the 1960s, but expand in later decades?

14.7 Why did political integration take place more slowly than economic integration in this post-war period?

European defence and the formation of NATO

In the immediate aftermath of the war, plans for political co-operation and integration within Europe took two very different forms. One was the relatively idealistic view of a United States of Europe, which would replace national rivalry and egoism with co-operation and common interest. The other was founded upon the more pragmatic considerations of military security, in the face of either a resurgence of German militarism or of Soviet aggression. The Pact of Brussels, between Britain, France and the Benelux countries (March 1947), was a traditional security pact drawn up with the specific aim of resisting 'a renewal by Germany of aggressive policy'. To a large extent it was immediately rendered obsolete by two American interventions. One of these was the Marshall Plan, and the other was the establishment of NATO. The USA had as great an interest in the security of western Europe as in its economic recovery, and American proposals for a military alliance were accepted with enthusiasm.

The North Atlantic Treaty Organisation (NATO), set up in April 1949, linked ten European states (Britain, France, Belgium, the Netherlands, Luxembourg, Italy, Denmark, Norway, Iceland and Portugal) with the USA and Canada, and continued for the rest of the century to form the basis for the defence of the western world. The combined impact of these interventions was that European security, at this stage by far the most important issue in international co-operation, was effectively guaranteed by the USA.

The very effectiveness of NATO removed much of the urgency behind plans for the political integration of western Europe. Thus, although further European initiatives for military integration were proposed, they came to nothing. The most detailed of these initiatives was the project proposed in 1950 by the French Premier René Pleven for a European Defence Community (EDC). Above all, the Pleven Plan addressed the problem of West German rearmament by integrating German troops into a common European force under the control of a minister of defence, a council of ministers and an assembly. Apart from channelling German rearmament in a manner compatible with European security, this also aimed to release Europe from strict reliance upon the USA.

In general, Pleven's scheme was too visionary. French reservations about German rearmament combined with British unwillingness to abandon the power of the USA for an unknown quantity, to doom the EDC to failure. The project finally collapsed in 1954. An attempt was also made to expand the Pact of Brussels by including Italy and West Germany in a Western European Union (WEU). Although this project was revived in the 1980s, it was designed to operate strictly through co-operation between national governments, and involved no supranational control of armed forces. In the event, the problem of a safe format for West German rearmament was largely resolved when that state was admitted to membership of NATO in 1954.

What were the main obstacles to political integration in the 1960s and 1970s?

If Britain stood as a major obstacle to political integration in the 1950s, that role was played in the 1960s by Charles de Gaulle. Although in many respects he was an enthusiastic supporter of the EEC, he saw the Community primarily as a vehicle for the restoration of France's status as a major power, rather than as a stepping stone to a European federation. His three foreign policy preoccupations illustrate this position clearly. He resisted American influence over European affairs, withdrawing France from the military arm of NATO and vetoing British membership of the EEC largely because of Britain's links with the USA. In his relations with Germany he preferred simple bilateral agreements between the two countries, such as the treaty of 1963, to broader co-operation within the EEC. He also defended French interests within the EEC vigorously, even causing a major crisis in 1965 by his insistence that France should be able to veto agricultural policies agreed by the other member states if they were

Crisis over oil prices (1973): As a response to the Arab–Israeli War of 1983, the major oil-producing Arab states raised the price of their oil in order to put pressure upon the western states to reduce their support for Israel. These rises naturally increased the production costs of western European industries, and had severe economic and social implications.

against French interests. His tactics succeeded when, by the Luxembourg Agreement (1966), it was decided that such measures should only be introduced with the unanimous agreement of the six member states. At roughly the same time, West German foreign policy was following its own particular path with the development of Willi Brandt's *Ostpolitik*. Although the EEC continued to thrive in economic terms, it appeared that the principle of supranational, political integration was rapidly receding.

De Gaulle's fall from power removed obstacles to the expansion of EEC membership. That expansion, however, tended to hinder political integration, as the community became preoccupied with the economic integration of its new members. At the same time, the Arab–Israeli War of 1973 set off a **crisis over oil prices**, during which member states sought to protect their own economic interests by unilateral action. France, for example, made its own deal with Saudi Arabia over oil supplies, while Britain approached Iran. This period of economic uncertainty and preoccupation within the European Community was further complicated by the Iran–Iraq War (1979–80), and by the increasing challenge mounted by Asian economies with faster growth rates than those in western Europe. Such steps help to illustrate the fact that, although member states have co-ordinated their foreign policies, this has only taken place on specific occasions and over specific issues. The EC applied common sanctions against Rhodesia (1975) after its unilateral declaration of independence, and against the USSR (1981) in protest against its policy towards Poland. The Community also pursued a common policy in 1975 in the course of the Helsinki Conference on Security and Co-operation. On the other hand, the member states could not agree upon a common response to Israeli action against the Lebanon, or on a common attitude towards Argentina's invasion of the Falkland Islands.

The movement towards monetary union

Nevertheless, the 1970s also saw the beginning of a further phase of European integration which, if not specifically political, tended to carry economic integration some way beyond its original objectives. Whereas the main feature of the EEC had been originally to dismantle barriers to trade, the emphasis was now upon the construction of common monetary institutions. Initial plans for European Monetary Union (EMU), launched in the early 1970s, failed because of the need of member states to revalue their currencies for their own purposes. This problem was made particularly acute by the crisis in oil prices. Formation of the European Monetary System (EMS) in March 1979 allowed for wider fluctuation in the value of national currencies, and introduced for the first time a common European Currency Unit (ECU). A more direct move towards the establishment of common political institutions took place in 1979, when the European Parliament was reformed by the introduction of direct elections of delegates to the assembly.

At the end of the period covered by this book important measures were being proposed within the European Community that promised at last to provide a real impetus towards greater unity. The major event in these developments was the preparation of the Treaty of European Union, which was signed at Maastricht in December 1991. As a preliminary to this treaty, the states of the EC had agreed to a Single Market Programme (SMP), which listed some 300 measures that required before the effective implementation of a single European market was possible. Primarily, these involved establishing complete freedom of movement of capital, goods, people and services within the community.

1. What were the main obstacles to political integration between the states of western Europe between 1950 and 1971?

2. To what extent would you agree with the claim that, up to 1991, European leaders had shown no real interest in the political union between their states?

The debate within the member states generated by the Maastricht Treaty clearly illustrated contemporary attitudes toward the issue of political integration. On the one hand, the treaty established an enhanced European Union, with monetary union between the member states as a clearly defined goal. On the other hand, many states continued to express reservations about the perceived surrender of national sovereignty. Close-fought referendums took place in France and in Denmark (1992–93) before those countries ratified the agreement. Such issues as foreign policy, defence policy and the administration of justice remained beyond the scope of the treaty. Unity in such respects as these remains the major challenge facing the European Union at the opening of the 21st century.

? Source-based questions: The development of European integration

Study the four sources on the establishment of European economic unity, and then answer all of the sub-questions.

(a) Study Source C.

From this Source and your own knowledge, explain the statement that 'at Rome they have created two communities'.   [20 marks]

(b) Study Sources A and D.

How similar are the reasons put forward by the authors of these Sources for European integration?   [40 marks]

(c) Study all of the Sources.

Using all of these Sources and your own knowledge, assess the view that 'projects for European integration up to 1960 were more concerned to avoid the mistakes of the past than to fulfil any new vision of a united Europe'.   [60 marks]

SOURCE A

A British statesman explains the necessity for European co-operation in the years immediately after the Second World War

I am now going to say something that will astonish you. The first step in the re-creation of the European family must be a partnership between France and Germany. In this way only can France recover the usual leadership of Europe. There can be no revival of Europe without a spiritually great France and a spiritually great Germany. The structure of the United States of Europe, if well and truly built, will be such as to make the material strength of a single state less important. Great Britain, the British Commonwealth of Nations, mighty America and, I trust, Soviet Russia must be the friends and sponsors of the new Europe and must champion its right to live and shine.

From a speech by Winston Churchill delivered in Zurich, September 1946.

OCR unit 2582

SOURCE B

One of the main architects of European economic co-operation explains the aims of his policy.

Europe will not be created all at once, nor will it be constructed as a whole. It is essential for the coming together of the European nations that the political opposition of France and Germany should be eliminated: the action that is taken must touch France and Germany above all others. With that goal in mind, the French government immediately proposes to take action on a specific, but decisive issue. The French government proposes to place the combined coal and steel production of France and Germany under the control of a common High Authority of an organisation in which other European states will be free to participate. Production in common of coal and steel will ensure the establishment of common bases of economic development, the first stage in a European federation.

Part of the speech by Robert Schuman, in which he introduced the Schuman Plan for European economic integration, May 1950

SOURCE C

A French left-wing deputy criticises the limited nature of the Treaty of Rome.

They speak to us of 'Europe', but that isn't what this is about. It is true that at Rome they have created two communities: a political community and an atomic community. Yet you know full well that there is nothing 'European' about them except the name. From the outset you exclude all the countries of eastern Europe, which are as European as the others, and the majority of other countries. Six European countries out of 27. Perhaps that is a success, but it is a limited one. It is true that this would cause only slight harm, easily put right, if there was the slightest hope that any of the 21 excluded countries might integrate themselves into the organisation that has been constructed. But you know that this is an illusion. The United Kingdom, 50% of whose trade is with the countries of the Commonwealth, obviously cannot join your organisation.

Speech by Pierre Cot in the French parliament, July 1957

SOURCE D

The French President outlines his vision for the future expansion of the European Economic Community.

The first idea is that western Europe should organise itself in such a way as to attract others and to create a balance to those two mammoth powers, the United States and Russia. As long as our countries remain separated they are an easy prey for the Russians, unless they are protected by the Americans. They therefore have the choice between becoming Russian colonies or American protectorates. We can begin with these five or six countries which form the kernel of Europe, but we must undertake nothing which blocks the path of other countries; Spain, Portugal, Britain, if she manages to separate herself from the Commonwealth and from the United States, one day Scandinavia and why not Poland and the other satellites if, one day, the Iron Curtain should ever be lifted.

From a policy statement by Charles de Gaulle, January 1960

Further Reading

CHAPTER 2   The consolidation of Russian conservatism, 1855–1894

Texts designed for AS and A2 Level students

Russia 1815–81 by Russell Sherman (Hodder and Stoughton, Access to History series, 2002)

Alexander II, Emancipation and Reform in Russia, 1855–1881 by Maureen Perrie (Historical Association pamphlet, 1989)

Russia 1848–1917 by Jonathan Bromley (Heinemann Advanced History series, 2002)

More advanced reading

The Russian Empire, 1801–1917 by Hugh Seton-Watson (Oxford University Press, 1967)

Russia under the Old Regime by Richard Pipes (Weidenfeld and Nicolson, 1974)

Russia in the Age of Reaction and Reform, 1801–1881 by David Saunders (Longman, History of Russia series, 1992)

Imperial and Soviet Russia: Power, Privilege and the Challenge of Modernity by David Christian (Macmillan, 1997) provides a concise overview of recent work on modern Russian history.

The Industrialisation of Russia, 1700–1914 by M.E. Falkus (Macmillan, 1972) provides a good, concise guide to economic developments during this period.

The Russian Peasantry 1600–1930 by David Moon (Longman, 1999)

CHAPTER 3   Germany under Bismarck, 1871–1890

Texts designed for AS and A2 Level students

Bismarck and Germany, 1862–90 by D.G. Williamson (Longman, Seminar Studies series, 1986)

Bismarck and the German Empire, 1871–1918 by Lynn Abrams (Routledge, Lancaster Pamphlets, 1995)

More advanced reading

The most influential biographies of Bismarck are probably:

Bismarck, the Man and the Statesman by A.J.P. Taylor (Hamish Hamilton, 1955)

Bismarck and the German Empire by Erich Eyck (Allen and Unwin, 1968)

Bismarck, the White Revolutionary by Lothar Gall (Allen and Unwin, 1986)

Germany 1866–1945 by Gordon Craig (Oxford University Press, 1978)

The Fontana History of Germany: 1780–1918, the Long Nineteenth Century by David Blackbourn (Fontana, HarperCollins, 1997) provides an excellent introduction to recent work on German history in this period.

Imperial Germany 1850–1918 by Edgar Feuchtwanger (Routledge, 2001)

A more concise summary is provided in 'Bismarckian Germany' by Geoff Eley, in *Modern Germany Reconsidered, 1870–1945* G. Martel (ed.) (Routledge, 1992)

An Introduction to the Social and Economic History of Germany: Politics and Economic Change in the Nineteenth and Twentieth Centuries by Helmut Böhme (Blackwell, 1978) provides a concise introduction to the work of this important German historian.

CHAPTER 4   Wilhelmine Germany, 1888–1918

Texts designed for AS and A2 Level students

From Bismarck to Hitler: Germany 1890–1933 by Geoff Layton (Hodder and Stoughton, Access to History series, 1996)

Imperial Germany 1890–1918 by Ian Porter and Ian Armour (Longman, Seminar Studies series, 1991)

More advanced reading

Germany 1866–1945 by Gordon Craig (Oxford University Press, 1978)

The German Empire, 1871–1918 by Hans-Ulrich Wehler (Berg, 1985)

From Kaiserreich to Third Reich: Elements of Continuity in German History, 1871–1945 by Fritz Fischer (Unwin Hyman, 1986)

Society and Politics in Wilhelmine Germany by R.J. Evans (ed.) (Croom Helm, 1978)

Imperial Germany 1850–1918 by Edgar Feuchtwanger (Routledge, 2001)

The Fontana History of Germany 1780–1918: the Long Nineteenth Century by David Blackbourn (Fontana, HarperCollins, 1997) provides an excellent introduction to recent work on German history in this period.

'Wilhelmine Germany' by James Retallack, in *Modern Germany Reconsidered, 1870–1945* Gordon Martel (ed.) (Routledge, 1992) does the same in a more concise format.

CHAPTER 5   The crisis of Russian autocracy, 1894–1914

Texts designed for AS and A2 Level students

Reaction and Revolution: Russia 1881–1924 by Michael Lynch (Hodder and Stoughton, Access to History series, 1992)

The Origins of the Russian Revolution by Alan Wood (Routledge, Lancaster Pamphlets, 1993)

Russia 1848–1917 by Jonathan Bromley (Heinemann Advanced History series, 2002)

More advanced reading

The Russian Empire, 1801–1917 by Hugh Seton-Watson (Oxford University Press, 1967)

Russia under the Old Regime by Richard Pipes (Weidenfeld and Nicolson, 1974)

Russia in the Age of Modernisation and Revolution, 1881–1917 by Hans Rogger (Longman, History of Russia series, 1983)

The Industrialisation of Russia, 1700–1914 by M.E. Falkus (Macmillan, 1972)

The Tsarist Economy 1850–1917 by P. Gatrell (Batsford, 1986)

Imperial and Soviet Russia: Power, Privilege and the Challenge of Modernity by David Christian (Macmillan, 1997) provides a good, concise summary of recent developments in the study of this period.

The Russian Peasantry 1600–1930 by David Moon (Longman, 1999)

CHAPTER 6   The First World War: causes and course, 1900–1918

Texts designed for AS and A2 Level students

The Origins of the First World War by Gordon Martel (Longman, Seminar Studies series, 1987)

Rivalry and Accord: International Relations 1870–1914 by John Lowe (Hodder and Stoughton, Access to History series, 1996)

Origins of the First World War by Ruth Henig (Routledge, Lancaster Pamphlets, 1984)

More advanced reading

The historical literature on the First World War is enormous and is fed by a constant flow of new works. What follows is only a small sample of the works available.

On the causes of the war:

Origins of the First World War edited by H.W. Koch (Macmillan, 1972) deals in depth with the controversy launched by Fritz Fischer.

The origins of the First and Second World Wars by Frank McDonough (Cambridge University Press, Perspectives in History series, 1997) provides a concise guide to the historiographical arguments surrounding the causes of the war.

On the military detail of the war:

The First World War by John Keegan (Hutchinson, 1998)

The German High Command at War: Hindenburg and Ludendorff and the First World War by Robert Asprey (Warner Books, 1993)

The Eastern Front 1914–1917 by Norman Stone (Hodder and Stoughton, 1975)

A Naval History of World War I by Paul Halpern (UCL Press, 1994)

The First World War (Volume One: To Arms) by Hew Strachan (Oxford University Press, 2001)

The Pity of War by Niall Ferguson (Allen Lane, 1998) takes a broader view, addressing a series of questions concerning the mentalities that surrounded the declaration, the fighting and the organisation of the war.

Sites of Memory, Sites of Mourning: The Great War in European Cultural History by Jay Winter (Cambridge University Press, 1995) explores the emotional and cultural impact of the war.

CHAPTER 7   The Russian Revolutions, 1914–1924

Texts designed for AS and A2 Level students

The Russian Revolution by Anthony Wood (Longman, Seminar Studies series, 1979)

Reaction and Revolutions: Russia 1881–1924 by Michael Lynch (Hodder and Stoughton, Access to History series, 1992)

The Russian Revolution by Graham Darby (Longman, History in Depth series, 1998)

More advanced reading

A People's Tragedy: the Russian Revolution 1891–1924 by Orlando Figes (Jonathan Cape, 1996) is probably the most influential re-interpretation of the subject written since the collapse of the Soviet Union.

Imperial and Soviet Russia: Power, Privilege and the Challenge of Modernity by David Christian (Macmillan, 1997) provides a more concise guide to recent work.

The Russian Revolution 1917–1921: a Short History by James D. White (Edward Arnold, 1994)

The Soviet Union 1917–1991 by Martin McCauley (Longman, History of Russia series, 1993)

The Russian Revolution 1917–1921 by Ronald Kowalski (Routledge, Sources in History, 1997) provides a good range of documents on this period.

A History of Soviet Russia 1917–1929 by E.H. Carr (Penguin, 1966) remains a classic study of the subject, written from a viewpoint relatively favourable to the revolution.

CHAPTER 8   The USSR under Stalin, 1924–1941

Texts designed for AS and A2 Level students

Stalin and Stalinism by Martin McCauley (Longman, Seminar Studies series, 1995)

Stalin and Khrushchev: The USSR 1924–64 by Michael Lynch (Hodder and Stoughton, Access to History series, 1990)

Stalin and Stalinism by Alan Wood (Routledge, Lancaster Pamphlets, 1990)

More advanced reading

Stalin: a Political Biography by Isaac Deutscher (Penguin, 1966)

Hitler and Stalin: Parallel Lives by Alan Bullock (HarperCollins, 1991)

The Soviet Union 1917–1991 by Martin McCauley (Longman, History of Russia series, 1993)

The Great Terror: a Reassessment by Robert Conquest (Pimlico, 1992)

An Economic History of the USSR by Alec Nove (Penguin, 1969)

Stalin's Peasants by Sheila Fitzpatrick (Oxford University Press, 1994)

Imperial and Soviet Russia: Power, Privilege and the Challenge of Modernity by David Christian (Macmillan, 1997) provides a concise summary of recent writing on this period.

CHAPTER 9   Italy, 1870–1940

Texts designed for AS and A2 Level students

Italy: Liberalism and Fascism by Mark Robson (Hodder and Stoughton, Access to History series, 2000)

Mussolini and Fascist Italy by Martin Blinkhorn (Routledge, Lancaster Pamphlets, 1984)

Fascist Italy by John Hite and Chris Hinton (John Murray, Schools History Project, 1998)

More advanced reading

Mussolini by Denis Mack Smith (Weidenfeld and Nicolson, 1981)

Mussolini's Roman Empire by Denis Mack Smith (Penguin, 1977)

Modern Italy 1871–1982 by Martin Clark (Longman, History of Italy series, 1984)

Italian Foreign Policy 1870–1940 by C.J. Lowe and F. Marzari (Routledge and Kegan Paul, 1975)

Fascism in Italy: Society and Culture, 1922–1945 by E.R. Tannenbaum (Allen Lane, 1973)

Fascism in Italy: Its Development and Influence by Elizabeth Wiskemann (Macmillan, 1969)

CHAPTER 10   Germany, 1918–1945

Texts designed for AS and A2 Level students

The Weimar Republic by John Hiden (Longman, Seminar Studies series, 1974)

The Third Reich by David Williamson (Longman, Seminar Studies series, 1995)

From Bismarck to Hitler: Germany 1890–1933 by Geoff Layton (Hodder and Stoughton, Access to History series, 1996)

Germany: the Third Reich, 1933–45 by Geoff Layton (Hodder and Stoughton, Access to History series, 2000)

Hitler and Nazism by Jane Jenkins (Longman, History in Depth series, 1998)

More advanced reading

A vast literature exists on the history of Nazi Germany, and new works appear constantly. What follows can only be a selection of lasting, classic works.

The German Dictatorship by K.D. Bracher (Penguin, 1978)

The Hitler State by Martin Broszat (Longman, 1981)

A Social History of the Third Reich by R. Grunberger (Penguin, 1974)

The War against the Jews, 1933–45 by Lucy Dawidowicz (Pelican, 1975)

The Nazi Dictatorship: Problems and Perspectives of Interpretation by Ian Kershaw (Arnold, 1993) and

Modern Germany Reconsidered, 1870–1945 edited by Gordon Martel (Routledge, 1992) both provide good surveys of recent research and debate on Nazi Germany.

Weimar Germany by Paul Bookbinder (Manchester University Press, 1996)

The Rise of the Nazis by Conan Fischer (Manchester University Press, 1995)

Many biographies of Hitler have been published, of which the best are probably:

Hitler: A Study in Tyranny by Alan Bullock (Penguin, 1962)

Hitler and Stalin: Parallel Lives by Alan Bullock (HarperCollins, 1991)

Hitler by Joachim Fest (Penguin, 1973)

Hitler by Ian Kershaw (Arnold, 1991)

Himmler, Reichsführer SS by Peter Padfield (Macmillan, 1990) provides the same service for another prominent member of the Nazi leadership.

Nazism 1919–1945: a Documentary Reader edited by J. Noakes and G. Pridham (Exeter University, 1983) provides an excellent range of contemporary documents on Nazi Germany.

CHAPTER 11   The Twenty Years' Truce: international relations, 1919–1939

Texts designed for AS and A2 Level students

The Inter-War Crisis 1919–1939 by R.J. Overy (Longman, Seminar Studies series, 1994)

The Origins of the First and Second World Wars by Frank McDonough (Cambridge University Press, Perspectives in History series, 1997)

Versailles and After, 1919–1933 by Ruth Henig (Routledge, Lancaster Pamphlets, 1995)

Origins of the Second World War 1933–1939 by Ruth Henig (Routledge, Lancaster Pamphlets, 1985)

Hitler. Appeasement and the Road to War 1933–1941 by Graham Darby (Hodder and Stoughton, Access to History series, 1999)

More advanced reading

The Making of the Second World War by Anthony Adamthwaite (Allen and Unwin, 1977) includes a useful selection of documents.

The Foreign Policy of the Third Reich by Klaus Hildebrand (Batsford, 1973)

The Nazi Dictatorship: Problems and Perspectives in Interpretation by Ian Kershaw (Arnold, 1993)

Germany and Europe 1919–1939 by John Hiden (Longman, 1977)

France and the Coming of the Second World War by Anthony Adamthwaite (Cass, 1977)

Italian Foreign Policy, 1870–1940 by C.J. Lowe and F. Marzari (Routledge and Kegan Paul, 1975)

The Origins of the Second World War Reconsidered: The A.J.P. Taylor Debate after Twenty-Five Years Gordon Martel (ed.) (Routledge, 1986)

The Origins of the Second World War by A.J.P. Taylor (Penguin, 1964) and

Hitler: a Study in Tyranny by Alan Bullock (Penguin, 1962) remain classic studies of this subject.

CHAPTER 12   The Second World War

Texts designed for AS and A2 Level students

Many of the books on the national histories of the states that took part in the war contain details of the country's role in the Second World War. Little has been produced so far specifically for Sixth Form students that summarises the economic and social impacts of the war.

More advanced reading

Second World War by Sir Martin Gilbert (Fontana, 1990)

Total War: Causes and Courses of the Second World War by Peter Calvocoressi and Guy Wint (Pelican, 1974)

The Second World War by John Keegan (Pimlico, 1989)

The Road to Stalingrad by John Erickson (Weidenfeld and Nicolson, 1975) and

The Road to Berlin by John Erickson (Weidenfeld and Nicolson, 1983) form the definitive work on the war on the Eastern Front.

Hitler's War Aims: The Establishment of the New Order by Norman Rich (André Deutsch, 1974)

Resistance by M.R.D. Foot (Paladin, 1978)

Life with the Enemy by Werner Rings (Doubleday, 1982) deals with the balance between resistance and collaboration in the occupied territories.

War, Economy and Society 1939–1945 by Alan Milward (Allen Lane, 1977) is the classic work on the economics and the economic implications of the war.

The Battle for History: Re-Fighting the Second World War by John Keegan (Hutchinson, 1995) provides a concise summary of historical debates on this subject.

CHAPTER 13   Europe and the Cold War, 1945–1991

Texts designed for AS and A2 Level students

The Cold War 1945–1965 by Joseph Smith (Blackwell, Historical Association Studies, 1989)

The Origins of the Cold War 1941–1949 by Martin McCauley (Longman, Seminar Studies series, 2nd edition, 1995)

Russia, America and the Cold War 1949–1991 by Martin McCauley (Longman, Seminar Studies series, 1998)

The USA and the Cold War by Oliver Edwards (Hodder, Access to History series, 1997)

The Cold War 1945–1991 by John W. Mason (Routledge, Lancaster Pamphlets, 1996)

The Cold War by Hugh Higgins (Heinemann, 3rd edition, 1993)

More advanced reading

The Cold War 1947–1991 by Simon Ball (Hodder Headline, 1998)

Cold War Europe 1945–1989 by John W. Young (Edward Arnold, 1991)

Eastern Europe since 1945 by G. and N. Swain (Macmillan, 1993)

Western Europe since 1945 by D.W. Urwin (Longman, 4th edition, 1991)

Britain and the Cold War 1945–1991 by S. Greenwood (Macmillan, 2000)

The Cold War, the Great Powers and their Allies by J.P.D. Dunbabin (Longman, 1994)

CHAPTER 14   The development of western Europe, 1945–1991

Texts designed for AS and A2 Level students

Years of Division. Europe since 1945 by John Laver, Chris Rowe and David Williamson (Hodder and Stoughton, 1999)

More advanced reading

Europe in Our Time by Walter Laqueur (Penguin, 1992)

Western Europe: Economic and Social Change since 1945 edited by Max-Stephan Schulze (Longman, 1999)

Germany since 1945 by Lothar Kettenacker (Oxford University Press, 1997)

Reinventing Germany. German Political Development since 1945 by Anthony Glees (Berg, 1996)

France since 1945 by Robert Gildea (Oxford University Press, 2002)

Twentieth Century France: Politics and Society in France, 1898–1991 by James F. McMillan (Hodder Arnold, 1992)

Modern Italy, 1871–1982 by Martin Clark (Longman, History of Italy series, 1984)

The Reconstruction of Western Europe, 1945–1951 by Alan Milward (Routledge, 1984)

European Community: the Building of a Union by John Pindar (Oxford University Press, 1991)

The Government and Politics of the European Community by Neil Nugent (Palgrave Macmillan, 2002)

Index

Glossary terms

Profiles

MAIN INDEX